John Sherman
Ohio

JOHN SHERMAN'S

"RECOLLECTIONS

OF

FORTY YEARS

IN

THE HOUSE, SENATE AND CABINET.

AN AUTOBIOGRAPHY.))

VOLUME I.

ILLUSTRATED
WITH PORTRAITS, FAC-SIMILE LETTERS, SCENES, ETC.

GREENWOOD PRESS, PUBLISHERS
NEW YORK   1968

First Greenwood reprinting, 1968

LIBRARY OF CONGRESS catalogue card number: 68-28647

Printed in the United States of America

DEDHAM STREET, DEDHAM, ESSEX COUNTY, ENGLAND.—SHERMAN HALL ON THE RIGHT

PREFACE

THESE RECOLLECTIONS grew out of a long deferred purpose to publish a selection of my speeches on public questions, but in collecting them it became manifest that they should be accompanied or preceded by a statement of the circumstances that attended their delivery. The attempt to furnish such a statement led to a review of the chief events of my public life, which covers the period extending from 1854 to the present time. The sectional trouble that preceded the Civil War, the war itself with all its attendant horrors and sacrifices, the abolition of slavery, the reconstruction measures, and the vast and unexampled progress of the republic in growth and development since the war, presented a topic worthy of a better historian than I am. Still, as my life was interwoven with these events, I concluded that it was better that I state my recollection of what I saw or heard or did in those stirring times rather than what I said. Whether this conclusion was a wise one the reader must judge. Egotism is a natural trait of mankind. If it is exhibited in a moderate degree we pardon it with a smile; if it is excessive we condemn it as a weakness. The life of one man is but an atom, but if it is connected with great events it shares in their dignity and importance. Influenced by this reasoning I concluded to postpone the publication of my speeches except so far as they are quoted or described in these memoirs.

When I entered upon their preparation the question arose whether the book to be written was to be of my life, including ancestry and boyhood, or to be confined to the financial history of the United States with which I was mainly identified. This was settled by the publishers, who were more interested in the number of copies they could sell than in the finances of the United States.

Every man has a theory of finance of his own, and is indifferent to any other. At best the subject is a dry one. Still, the problem of providing money to carry on the expensive operations of a great war, and to provide for the payment of the vast debt created during the war, was next in importance to the conduct of armies, and those who were engaged in solving this problem were as much soldiers as the men who were carrying muskets or commanding armies. As one of these I feel it my duty to present the measures adopted and to claim for them such merit as they deserve.

These volumes do contain the true history of the chief financial measures of the United States government during the past forty years. My hope is that those who read them will be able to correct the wild delusions of many honest citizens who became infected with the "greenback craze," or the "free coinage of silver."

My chief regret is that the limit of these volumes did not permit me to extend my narrative to the memorable battles and marches of the Civil War, nor to a more general notice of my associates who distinguished themselves in civil life. The omission of military narrative is admirably compensated by the memoirs of the great commanders on either side, and better yet by the vast collection and publication, by the United States, of the "Records of the Rebellion." The attempt to include in these volumes my estimate of distinguished men still living who participated in the events narrated would greatly extend them and might lead to injustice.

One of the fortunate results of the Civil War has been to diminish the sectional prejudice that previously existed both in the north and in the south. I would not check this tendency, but will gladly contribute in every way possible to a hearty union of the people of all sections of our country, not only in matters of government, but also in ties of good will, mutual respect and fraternity. The existence of slavery in some of the states was the cause of the war, and its abolition was the most important result of the war. So great a change naturally led to disorder and violence where slavery had existed, but this condition, it is believed, is passing away.

Therefore I have not entered in detail into the measures adopted as the result of the abolition of slavery.

This preface is hardly necessary, but I comply with the general custom of adding at the beginning, instead of the end, an apology for writing a book. This seems to me to be the chief object of a preface, and I add to it an appeal for the kindly consideration of the readers of these volumes.

JOHN SHERMAN.

MANSFIELD, OHIO, August 30, 1895.

ILLUSTRATIONS

VOLUME I.

AUTOGRAPH LETTERS

VOLUME I.

TABLE OF CONTENTS.

VOLUME I.

CHAPTER I.

ANCESTRY OF THE SHERMAN FAMILY.

CHAPTER II.

MY BOYHOOD DAYS AND EARLY LIFE.

CHAPTER III.

OHIO; ITS HISTORY AND RESOURCES.

CHAPTER IV.

ADMISSION TO THE BAR AND EARLY POLITICAL LIFE.

CHAPTER V.

EARLY DAYS IN CONGRESS.

CHAPTER VI.

BIRTH OF THE REPUBLICAN PARTY.

CHAPTER VII.

RECOLLECTIONS OF THE FINANCIAL PANIC OF 1857.

CHAPTER VIII.

EXCITING SCENES IN CONGRESS.

CHAPTER IX.

LAST DAYS OF THE BUCHANAN ADMINISTRATION.

CHAPTER X.

THE BEGINNING OF LINCOLN'S FIRST ADMINISTRATION.

CHAPTER XI.

SPECIAL SESSION OF CONGRESS TO PROVIDE FOR THE WAR.

CHAPTER XII.

PASSAGE OF THE LEGAL TENDER ACT IN 1862.

TABLE OF CONTENTS.

CHAPTER XXIX.

I BEGIN MY DUTIES AS SECRETARY OF THE TREASURY.

CHAPTER XXX.

POLICY OF THE HAYES ADMINISTRATION.

CHAPTER I.

ANCESTRY OF THE SHERMAN FAMILY.

THE family name of Sherman is, no doubt, of Saxon origin. It is very common along the Rhine, and in different parts of the German Empire. It is there written Shearmann or Schurmann. I found it in Frankfort and Berlin. The English Shermans lived chiefly in Essex and Suffolk counties near the east coast, and in London. The name appears frequently in local records. One Sherman was executed for taking the unsuccessful side in a civil war. It was not until the beginning of the 16th century that any of the name assumed the arms, crest, and motto justified by their pride, property or standing. The motto taken, "Conquer Death by Virtue," is a rather meaningless phrase. It is modest enough, and indicates a religious turn of mind. Nearly every family of the name furnished a preacher. A few members of it attained the dignity of knighthood. A greater number became landed property-holders, and more were engaged in trade in London. Sir Henry Sherman was one of the executors of the will of Lord Stanley, Earl of Derby, May 23, 1521. William Sherman, Esq., purchased Knightston in the time of Henry VIII; and a monument to him is in Ottery St. Mary, dated 1542. As a rule the family belonged to the middle class and were engaged in active occupation, earning their own bread, with a strong sense of their rights and liberties as Englishmen.

The principal family of the name in the 16th century were the Shermans of Yaxley in the county of Suffolk, a full detail of which is given in Davy's Collections of that county. Edmond Sherman, my ancestor, was a member of this family. He was born in 1585 and was married to Judith Angier, May 26, 1611. He resided in Dedham, Essex county, England, then a place of some importance. He was a manufacturer of cloth, a man of means and high standing. He was a Puritan, with all the faults and virtues of a sectary. He resisted ship-money and the tax unlawfully imposed on tonnage and poundage. He had the misfortune to live at the time when Charles I undertook to dispense with Parliament, and to impose unlawful taxes and burdens upon the people of England, and when the privileges of the nobility were enforced with great severity by judges dependent upon the crown. He had three sons, John, baptized on the 4th of January, 1614; Edmond, baptized June 18, 1616, and Samuel, baptized July 12, 1618. He had a nephew, known as "Captain John," somewhat older than his sons, who was an active man in 1634.

At this time the migration to Boston, caused chiefly by the tyranny of Charles I, was in active operation. Hume, in his history, says:

"The Puritans, restrained in England, shipped themselves off for America, and laid there the foundations of a government which possessed all the liberty, both civil and religious, of which they found themselves bereaved in their native country. But their enemies, unwilling that they should anywhere enjoy ease and contentment, and dreading, perhaps, the dangerous consequences of so disaffected a colony, prevailed on the king to issue a proclamation, debarring these devotees access, even into those inhospitable deserts. Eight ships, lying in the Thames, and ready to sail, were detained by order of the council; and in these were embarked Sir Arthur Hazelrig, John Hampden, John Pym, and Oliver Cromwell, who had resolved, forever, to abandon their native country, and fly to the other extremity of the globe; where they might enjoy lectures and discourses, of any length or form, which pleased them. The king had afterwards full leisure to repent this exercise of his authority."

It appears that, influenced by the same motives, Edmond Sherman determined to remove his family, with his nephew,

"Captain John," to Boston. In one statement made in respect to them it is said that the father and his three sons and nephew embarked for Boston, but this is doubtful. It is certain, however, that his son, Rev. John Sherman and his son Samuel, and his nephew "Captain John," did go to Boston in 1634. It is quite as certain that if they were accompanied by their father and their brother Edmond, that the two latter returned again to Dedham in 1636. Edmond Sherman, senior, lived and died at Dedham. One of his descendants, Rev. Henry Beers Sherman, a few years ago visited Dedham and there found one of the church windows of stained glass bearing the initials of Edmond Sherman as having been his gift, and the record shows that one of the buttresses of the church was erected at his expense. Mr. Henry Beers Sherman there saw the pupils of a free school, endowed by Edmond Sherman and still in operation, attending the church in procession.

When in London, in the summer of 1889, I concluded to make a visit to "the graves of my ancestors." I examined Black's Universal Atlas to locate Dedham, but it was not to be found. I made inquiries, but could discover no one who knew anything about Dedham, and concluded there was no such place, although I had often read of it. I was compelled, therefore, to give up my visit.

Senator Hoar, a descendant, through his mother, of Roger Sherman of Revolutionary fame, was more fortunate or more persistent than I, for he subsequently found Dedham and verified the accounts we had of our common ancestor, and procured photographs, copies of which I have, of the monument of Edmond Sherman, of the church near which he was buried, and of the handsome school building, still called "the Sherman Library," that he had left by his will for the youth of Dedham, with a sufficient annuity to support it. Dedham is but two or three miles from Manningtree, a more modern town on the line of the railroad, which has substantially obscured the ancient and decayed village of Dedham.

The sexton of this church wrote General Sherman soon after he had become distinguished as a military leader, calling his attention to the neglected monument of his ancestor, Edmond Sherman, in the churchyard, and asking a contribution for its repair. The general sent a reply to the effect that, as his ancestor in England had reposed in peace under a monument for more than two centuries, while some of his more recent ancestors lay in unmarked graves, he thought it better to contribute to monuments for them here and leave to his English cousins the care of the monuments of their common ancestors in England. This letter is highly prized by the sexton and has been shown to visitors, among others to Senator Hoar, as a characteristic memento of General Sherman.

Captain John Sherman, "Captain John," soon after his arrival in Boston, settled in Watertown, Mass., where he married and had a large family of children. Among his descendants was Roger Sherman of the Revolution, by far the most distinguished man of the name. He had the good fortune to contribute to and sign the three most important papers of American history, the "Address to the King," the "Declaration of Independence" and the "Constitution of the United States." Among other descendants of Captain John Sherman were Hon. Roger Minot Sherman, of New Haven, a nephew of Roger Sherman, a distinguished lawyer and a leading participant in the Hartford Convention. William M. Evarts, George F. Hoar and Chauncey M. Depew are descendants of Roger Sherman or of his brother.

Rev. John Sherman, the eldest son of Edmond Sherman, was born on the 26th of December, 1613, at Dedham, England. He graduated at Immanuel College, Cambridge, left college a Puritan and came over to America in 1634, as above stated. He preached his first sermon at Watertown, Massachusetts, under a tree, soon after his arrival in this country. In a few weeks he went to New Haven, Connecticut, and preached in several places, but finally settled at Watertown, where he had a large family of children. His numerous descendants are well distributed throughout the United States, but most of them in the State of New York.

Samuel Sherman, the youngest son of Edmond Sherman,

is the ancestor of the family to which I belong. At the age of sixteen years he came with his brother, Rev. John and his cousin "Captain John," in April, 1634, in the ship "Elizabeth" from Ipswich, and arrived in Boston in June, and for a time settled in Watertown, Massachusetts. He afterwards moved to Weathersfield, Connecticut, thence to Stamford and thence to Stratford.

In Cothron's "History of Ancient Woodbury" there are found full details of the life of Samuel Sherman and his numerous descendants to the present generation. Of Samuel Sherman Mr. Cothron says:

"He was from Dedham, Essex county, England, came to this country in 1634, and previous to the date of the new plantation, at Woodbury, had been a leading man in the colony of Connecticut. He had assisted in the settlement of several other towns in the colony, and now undertook the same for Woodbury. He had been a member of the Court of Assistants, or Upper House of the General Court, and Supreme Judicial Tribunal, for five or six years from 1663, and held various offices and appointments of honor and trust. He is referred to in ancient deeds and documents as the 'Worshipful Mr. Sherman.' In 1676 he was one of the commission for Stratford and Woodbury."

The order of succession of the descendants of Samuel Sherman, the ancestor of the family to which I belong, is as follows:

1. JOHN SHERMAN, the fifth child of Samuel Sherman, was born at Stratford, Conn., February 8, 1650. He early moved to Woodbury. He died December 13, 1730.

2. JOHN SHERMAN 2nd, the fifth child of John, was baptized June, 1687. He married Hachaliah Preston, July 22, 1714. He died 1727.

3. DANIEL SHERMAN, the third child of John 2nd, was born August 14, 1721, and died July 2, 1799.

4. TAYLOR SHERMAN, the sixth child of Daniel, was born in 1758. He married Elizabeth Stoddard in 1787, and died in Connecticut May 15, 1815. His widow died at Mansfield, Ohio, August 1, 1848.

5. CHARLES ROBERT SHERMAN, the eldest child of Taylor, was born September 26, 1788, married Mary Hoyt, of Norwalk, Conn., May 8, 1810. He died on the 24th of June, 1829. His widow died at Mansfield, Ohio, September 23, 1852. They had eleven children, six sons and five daughters, all of whom lived to maturity. I am the eighth child of this family.

The names and dates of the birth of the children of my parents are as follows:

CHARLES TAYLOR SHERMAN, . . .	February 3, 1811.
MARY ELIZABETH SHERMAN, ...	April 21, 1812.
JAMES SHERMAN, ...	December 10, 1814.
AMELIA SHERMAN, ...	February 11, 1816.
JULIA ANN SHERMAN, ...	July 24, 1818.
WILLIAM TECUMSEH SHERMAN, . . .	February 8, 1820.
LAMPSON PARKER SHERMAN, . . .	October 31, 1821.
JOHN SHERMAN, ...	May 10, 1823.
SUSAN DENMAN SHERMAN, ...	October 10, 1825.
HOYT SHERMAN, ...	November 1, 1827.
FANNY BEECHER SHERMAN, . . .	May 3, 1829.

Mr. Cothron, in his "History of Ancient Woodbury," after referring to Samuel Sherman, makes this reference to his son John:

"The fame of his son John is particularly the property of the town. He was distinguished, not only at home, but also in the colony. He was Justice of the Quorum, or Associate County Judge, for forty-four years from 1684; a Representative of the town for seventeen sessions, and Speaker of the Lower House in May and October, 1711, and Captain in the Militia, a high honor in those days. He was the first Judge of Probate for the District of Woodbury, from its organization in 1719, for nine years. The District then comprised all of Litchfield county, and Woodbury in New Haven county. He was an assistant, or member of the Upper House, for ten years from 1713."

John Sherman 2nd, does not seem to have taken any active part in public affairs, and died before his father, at the age of forty. His son Daniel, who lived to the age of eighty, covering the period of the Indian wars, the French Canadian war, and the war of the Revolution, took an active part in all the great events of that period. Mr. Cothron says of him:

"Judge Daniel Sherman was perhaps the most distinguished man that had arisen in the town previous to his day. He was a descendant of Samuel Sherman, of Stratford, Connecticut, who emigrated to this country from England, in company with his brother, Rev. John Sherman, and his nephew, Captain John Sherman, ancestor of Hon. Roger Sherman. He was a Justice of the Quorum for twenty-five years, and Judge of the Litchfield County Court five years from 1786. For sixteen years he was Probate Clerk for the District of Woodbury, and Judge of that District thirty-seven years. He represented his native town in the General Assembly sixty-five semi-annual sessions, retaining the unbounded confidence of his fellow citizens. This was by far the longest period of time anyone has ever represented the town. He was a man of commanding powers of mind, of sterling integrity, and every way qualified for the various public trusts confided to his care. He died at a good old age, full of honor, and was followed by the affectionate recollections of the inhabitants of the town, among whom he had so long lived."

No portion of the people of the United States took a more decisive part in the Revolutionary contest of 1775 than those of Connecticut. The people of Woodbury caught the prevailing spirit, and, as early as September 20, 1774, had a public meeting and made patriotic resolves, and entered into associations for defense. Daniel Sherman, then fifty-four years old, presided at this meeting and was appointed president of the association of the delegates. Among other duties they were to perform, was to ascertain whether any persons within the limits of that town were hostile to the objects of the association, and in that case they, using the spelling of the time, were to

" Cause the truth of the case to be published in the Gazette, to the End that all such foes to ye Rights of British americai may be publikly known and universially Contemned as enemies to american Liberty and thensforth we Do bind ourselves to break off all Dealings With Such Persons and also with all Persons in other Towns and Citys who shall be found Guilty as above Expressed, and that it shall be ye Duty and Business of the sd Comtee to Receive and Communicate all Such intelligence as they shall judge to be conducive to ye Peace and Tranquility of this and the Neighbouring Colonies; this meeting presents their most thankfull acknowledgments to those truly Honourable and Worthy Gentlemen members of ye Congress who have Shewn themselves able advocates of the civil and Religious liberty of the american Colonys.

" Voated, that the doings of this meeting be Recorded by the Town Clerk, and a Copy thereof be forthwith sent to one of the printers of the Connecticut Journal to be published accordingly. The Whole of the above Written as voated in said Meeting."

He was a member of the "Committee of Inspection" of thirty, appointed at the beginning of the war. On the 12th of April, 1784, they resolved as follows:

" Voted, that those persons who joined the enemies of the United States in the course of the late Civil war of what description soever are denyed a residence in this Town from this date until the Genll Assembly shall grant them full liberty for that purpose."

At a meeting held on the 3rd of April, 1777, at which
Daniel Sherman was the Moderator, it was:

"Voated, that Each Able Bodied Effective man, who hath or shall
voluntarily Inlist into the Continental Army in such way and Manner
toward makeing the Quota of this Town for the space of Three years, or
during the war shall be Intitled to Receive out of the publick Treasury of
the Town the sum of Twenty Shillings Lawful money, as an Addition to
Each month's Wages he shall continue in the service, to be paid to him, or
to his order, at the End of Each six month's service."

This was kept up during the war. Provision was made for
a Council of Safety, appointed annually by the Assembly, of
from nine to fourteen of the most distinguished men in the
state, to aid the governor in the organization and conduct of
troops, of which Daniel Sherman, his cousin Roger Sherman,
Benjamin Huntington, and other distinguished men were members. This committee was frequently in session and the most
responsible, arduous and difficult details of the service were confided to its care. It was shown that during the war Daniel Sherman contributed provisions to soldier's families to the value of
2,718 pounds, 7 shillings and 8 pence. It would seem from the
following anecdote told of Daniel Sherman, that some of his
neighbors thought he had enjoyed his full share of honor:

"Mr. Sherman was a representative at the May session of the General
Assembly in 1791, and, it is related, desired to be elected to the October
session of the same year, in order to make the full number of thirty-three
years that he would then have represented the town. But at the time of
the election for the October session, the Moderator of the meeting happened
to think that he had his share of honors, and when he made proclamation
that the ballot-box was open for the reception of votes, remarked in a loud
tone of voice, 'Gentlemen, the box is now open; you will please to bring in
your ballots for him whom you *will have* for your first representative—
Honorable Daniel Sherman, of course!' This simple incident gave a change
to the popular current, and on counting the votes it was found that Honorable Nathaniel Smith was elected, instead of Mr. Sherman."

Taylor Sherman, my grandfather, the son of Judge Daniel
Sherman, was born in 1758. He was married in 1787 to
Elizabeth Stoddard and removed to Norwalk, Connecticut,
where he lived during the remainder of his life. He died on
the 15th of May, 1815.

My grandmother was born at Woodbury, Connecticut, on the 14th of June, 1767. She lived to a good old age and died at Mansfield, Ohio, on the 1st of August, 1848. She was a remarkable woman in many respects, a Puritan of the strictest faith, of large mold, being nearly six feet tall, and well proportioned. She was a granddaughter of Rev. Anthony Stoddard, a man whose history strikingly presents the peculiar characteristics of life in Connecticut during the 18th century. The contract between the church and town of Woodbury and Mr. Stoddard, for employment as pastor, commences as follows:

"At a lawfull Towns-meeting ye 13th of August, 1700, in ordr to ye settling of ye Reverend mr. Anthony Stoddard amongst us, in ye work of ye ministry. And for his encouragemt so to do;

" It was voted and agreed to allow him, as Mayntenance in ye Work of ye Ministry, seventy pounds per Annu, in provision pay, or to his Satisfaction, in Case of Faylure of provision pay. By provision pay, is intended, wheat, pease, indian corn & pork, proportionally : also fire wood :

" We do also promise, to build him an house here in Woodberry of known Demensions ; yt is to say, the Carpenters work & Masons work : hee providing nayles and glass ; by building ye sd house is intended, doors, floures, fitting up and playstering and partitions, finishing it, as also a well."

Then follow many other mutual stipulations, to which was added a supplemental agreement as follows:

" Since wch time at a Lawfull Towns-meeting ye 25th of Novembr, 1700, It was Voated and agreed yt ye abovesd specices for mr Stoddard's yearly mayntenance bee levyed at ye prices following : wheat at 4s 6d pr Bush : pork at 3c pr lb : Indian Corn 2s 6d pr Bush : pease three shillings pr Bushll : And these prices for this yeare ye Town will not vary from for ye future Exterordinary providences interposing being exceapted."

" Recorded from ye originalls pr Jon Minor, Recorder, March, 1700–1701."

Under this contract Mr. Stoddard served his congregation for sixty years, and died September 7, 1760, in his eighty-third year, and the sixty-first of his ministry. He was educated at Harvard College and graduated in 1679. Mr. Cothron, in 1872, says of him:

" He was at the same time, minister, lawyer and physician. Like many of the early ministers of the colony, he prepared himself for the practice of physic, that he might administer to the wants of the body, as well as those of the mind. In this capacity he was often called. The only person the author has found who ever saw him, was Deacon Amos Squire, of Roxbury, who died two or three years ago, aged ninety-nine, and who recollected having seen him when a lad about eight years of age, while on a visit in this capacity to his father, who had received a severe wound from an ax. He had also done what other ministers did not, and that was to perfect himself in legal knowledge."

It must be remembered that the pastor of a church in those days was in quite a different position than now, when the constitution guarantees to every one liberty to worship God according to the dictates of his conscience. The Congregational mode of worship was then adopted and established by law in Connecticut, but it was provided that all sober orthodox persons dissenting therefrom should, on representing it to the General Court, be allowed to worship in their own way. Such a privilege however, was regarded with distrust. Our fathers, who desired religious freedom and periled all for it in the wilderness, had not anticipated that they would speedily have an opportunity to extend that toleration to others which in the fatherland they had in vain sought for themselves. The town church was, therefore, in substance, the only church, and the preacher was the autocrat of the place.

Mr. Stoddard was not only preacher, lawyer and doctor, but he was also a fighter. In 1707 an expedition was made by the French and Indians against New England, which created general alarm throughout the country. Woodbury was exposed to the raids made by the Indians, and suspicions were entertained that the neighboring tribes would join the French and Indians in their foray. During the continuance of this war, on one Sabbath evening, after the conclusion of the services at church, while he was walking in his garden, he discovered an Indian skulking among the surrounding trees and bushes. Apparently without noticing the movements of the Indian, he contrived to re-enter his house, and obtained his gun. After playing the same game of skulking with his adversary for a while, Mr. Stoddard got a fair view of him, discharged his piece, and the Indian fell among the bushes. He dared not investigate farther that night, but having quietly given the alarm, the inhabitants sought their palisaded houses for the night. Early in the morning he discovered another red foe, in

the vicinity of his companion, and whom he also laid low with
his musket. By this time the people had assembled, and after
the country was scoured in all directions for several hours, and
no other savages were found, the alarm subsided.

Before leaving my Woodbury ancestors, who resided there
nearly one hundred and fifty years, I wish to relate my first
visit to Woodbury. I was at West Point, as one of the Board
of Visitors, one Saturday in June, 1873, when I concluded to
respond to an invitation I had received, and go to Woodbury
and spend the Sabbath there. I did so and found, as I had
anticipated, beautiful valleys with picturesque hills, a rural air
and a quiet, peaceful, Sunday outlook. I knew no one except
Hon. William Cothron, and him only by correspondence. I
believe he was superintendent of the Sunday school; but, at
all events, upon my presenting myself, and stating my desire
to explore Woodbury, he kindly consented, and went with me.
I located many of the most interesting objects in the town.
The large, well-built stone house of Daniel Sherman was still
standing, made after the usual pattern, two stories high with a
lean-to roof in the rear, and with low ceilings. He had lived
there during most of his active life, and had entertained Washington and Lafayette, when they at different times visited the
French vessels at Newport. The fortified house of Rev. Anthony
Stoddard was in a good state of preservation, with its project-
ing eaves and loop holes for defense. We visited the old church
and graveyard, and drove southward to what were called the
"Sherman settlements." Evidently the comparatively few
families in Woodbury were in a state of comfort as they were
found to be living in good houses and drawing, no doubt, an
income from investments in the great and growing West.

On that quiet Sabbath day the village of Woodbury recalled
to me Mr. John H. Bryant's description of his native village:

> "There lies a village in a peaceful vale,
>   With sloping hills and waving woods around,
>   Fenced from the blasts. There never ruder gale
>   Bows the tall grass that covers all the ground;
>   And planted shrubs are there, and cherish'd flowers,
>   And a bright verdure born of gentle showers."

Subsequently I again visited Woodbury with General Sherman. Mr. Cothron was still there and was very kind to us. It seemed to me that the old place had run down a little, that the walks were not so clean, the grass was not as fresh in the fields, and evidently the graveyards had lost some of their monuments, but a prominent one had been erected in the churchyard to Rev. Anthony Stoddard, to which General Sherman had contributed. We heard of no one of our name in Woodbury, but when General Sherman saw an old sign, "Sherman's Tannery," he said that he believed he had at last found some tangible evidence of the residence of our fathers in Woodbury; that Sherman had been a good honest tanner no doubt, and that was the most that could be said of anyone.

As I have said, my grandfather, Taylor Sherman, and his wife, Elizabeth Stoddard, moved from Woodbury to Norwalk, where he practiced his profession as a lawyer. He attained a good position as such, and for many years he was a Judge of Probate. He became early associated with the proprietors of the half million acres of land lying in the western part of the Western Reserve in Ohio, called "Sufferers' Land."

In the period immediately before and after the adoption of the constitution several of the states laid claim to western lands, founded upon grants by James I, the chief of which were the claims of Virginia to the region north and west of the Ohio River, and the claim of Connecticut to all the land lying west of Pennsylvania to the South Seas and north of the 41st parallel of latitude. These claims were finally compromised by Congress granting to Virginia all the land lying between the Scioto and the Miami Rivers in Ohio, and to Connecticut the land in Ohio north of the 41st parallel, extending westward of Pennsylvania one hundred and twenty miles.

During the Revolutionary War the coasts of Connecticut had been subjected to several raids by the British and Tories, and several towns, including Norwalk, Greenwich, Fairfield, Danbury, New Haven and New London, had been burned. Indemnity had been proposed, but the state was in no condition to pay such losses.

In the year 1800, the State of Connecticut granted to her

citizens, who were sufferers by fire during the Revolutionary
War, a half million acres of land, lying within the State of
Ohio, which was to be taken off the west part of what was
called the "Western Connecticut Reserve," now embraced in
the counties of Huron and Erie. By an act of the legislature
of the State of Ohio, passed in 1803, the sufferers were incorporated under the name of "The proprietors of the half million
acres of land, lying south of Lake Erie, called 'Sufferers' Land.'"
The affairs of this company, by that act, were to be managed
by a Board of Directors which, among other things, was authorized to locate and survey said half million acres of land, and
partition it among the different claimants.

On the first day of November, 1805, Taylor Sherman was
appointed by the Board of Directors an agent to survey the
above tract of land, and, on the 16th day of December, of the
same year, he entered into a contract with John McLane and
James Clarke, Jr., to survey, or have surveyed, said tract.
Taylor Sherman visited the fire lands, and fully performed the
duty imposed upon him. He also purchased a considerable
tract of this land in Sherman township, Huron county, which
was the foundation of the little fortune which he left to his
widow and children.

The whole of the Western Reserve, especially the western
part of it, was at that time in the possession of the Indians,
who soon afterwards engaged in open warfare with the white
settlers. Surveys, especially along the shores of Lake Erie,
were extremely difficult, owing to extensive bayous and swamps,
but the surveys were made where practicable, and where lines
could not be run, straight lines were drawn on the map, and
the contents estimated. This gave rise to long litigation, one
case being reported in the 13th Volume of Ohio Supreme Court
Reports.

The gift of Connecticut to the sufferers was a wise and liberal one, and after the War of 1812 it led to the migration to the
counties of Huron and Erie of a great number of persons from
the towns of Norwalk, Greenwich, Danbury, New Haven and
New London. The losses of the sufferers in these different towns
had been carefully examined and stated, and the sufferers were

allowed land in proportion to their losses. The formidable list of these sufferers is a striking proof of the savage and destructive manner in which the Revolutionary War was conducted by the British troops. The whole Western Reserve at the beginning of the 19th century was a wilderness, with not a single white inhabitant. The census of 1820, however, showed that it then contained a population of 58,608, while that of 1890 showed a population of 678,561. Of these a larger number and proportion were descendants of Connecticut parents than are now inhabitants of that state. The industries, commerce, wealth and intelligence of this region are not excelled by any community of the same size anywhere else in the country.

As an illustration of the condition of this region in 1812, it may be worth while to here record a truthful anecdote of Daniel Sherman, the son of Taylor Sherman, and whom we knew as "Uncle Dan." In the spring of 1812, when twenty-two years of age, he was sent by his father to make improvements on his land in Huron county, by building a log cabin and opening a clearing. He had with him a hired man of the name of John Chapman, who was sent to Milan, twelve miles away, to get a grist of corn ground, it being the nearest and only mill in the county. Either on the way there, or while returning, Chapman was killed by the Indians. Uncle Dan did not hear of this until the next day, when, with a knapsack on his back, he started for Mansfield, forty miles away. For thirty miles there was dense and unbroken forest without a settler. He arrived at a blockhouse, six miles from Mansfield, but concluded that was not strong enough to protect him. He then went to Mansfield, where they had a better blockhouse, but he heard so many stories of Indians that he did not feel safe there, and walked thence to his brother's house in Lancaster, about seventy-five miles away, through an almost continuous forest.

In November, 1813, Taylor Sherman was appointed, by President Madison, Collector of Internal Revenue for the Second District of Connecticut. He enjoyed the office but a short time and died, as already stated, on the 15th day of May, 1815.

A sketch of my father and mother will throw some light upon the lives of their children, but it is a delicate task to write of one's parents. As I was but six years old when my father died I have only a dim recollection of him, but materials for an interesting sketch of his brief but active career are abundant. I know of no citizen of Ohio of whom more anecdotes have been told, or whose general and social life has been more highly appreciated, or whose popularity has been more marked, than that of my father. During the early years of my life at the bar I met many of the older lawyers, contemporary with my father, and they all spoke of him in the highest praise, and generally had some incident to tell of him that happened in the days of the "Stirrup Court."

Charles Robert Sherman, my father, was born in Norwalk, Connecticut, September 26, 1788, the eldest son of Judge Taylor Sherman and Elizabeth Stoddard. He received the best educational advantages of his day, and, when fully prepared, commenced the study of law in the associated offices of his father and the Hon. Judge Chapman. He was admitted to the bar in 1810, and on May 8, of that year, married Mary Hoyt, also of Norwalk, who had grown up with him from childhood. In the same summer he went to Ohio to locate a home. He could not go into the northern part where his father's land lay, as it was then roamed over by hostile Indians, but followed the usual route to Ohio by Pittsburg and Wheeling to Zanesville. He located at Lancaster, but returned to Norwalk, Connecticut, in the fall of 1810. In 1811 he returned to Lancaster, accompanied by his wife. Ohio was then a frontier state, and in large portions of its territory an unbroken wilderness. The way to it from their New England home was far and weary, beset with many hardships and exposed to great dangers. My father and mother were obliged to journey the greater part of this distance on horseback, alternately carrying their infant child upon a pillow before them. I only advert to these incidents as they illustrate the self-reliant character of the man, and the brave, confiding trust of his wife. The little boy they carried upon the pillow, then their only son, was Charles Taylor Sherman.

Soon after their arrival in Lancaster my father took a leading part in the measures of defense against the British and the Indians. I find in an old and weather-beaten newspaper of

Lancaster, Ohio, called the "Independent Press," that on the 16th of April, 1812, at a meeting of the first regiment of the first brigade of the third division of the militia of Ohio, assembled at Lancaster for the purpose of raising a company of volunteers to march immediately to Detroit, my father, then major of that regiment, made a very effective address to the regiment, the result of which was the voluntary enlistment of the company required from Fairfield county. He was then twenty-four years of age, and, as this address is short, and is the best evidence of his mental qualities, and of the standing he had so early attained among the hardy settlers of that section, mostly from Pennsylvania, I here insert a portion of it:

"*Fellow Soldiers:*—The crisis has arrived in which your country calls upon you, her constitutional guardians, to rally round her standard and to defend her rights and liberties—you are this day assembled to declare whether you will voluntarily answer this call or not. Fellow soldiers, the general of brigade and at whose command and in whose name I now address you, cannot help but believe that in this regiment which he once had the honor, personally, to command, those choice spirits are to be found, that will not for a moment hesitate to come forward and give the answer to their country's call.

"You are not called upon to guard a tyrant's throne, or to enslave a nation of freemen, neither are your exertions required to redress a fancied wrong, or to revenge a supposed insult; but you are called upon to preserve your own dwellings from the flames—your families from destruction. Neither are you requested to go unprotected nor unprovided;—everything that the patriot soldier could possibly wish will be furnished you by the government—food complete and sufficient for the necessities or conveniences of life—compensation for your clothing,—arms of the best quality will be placed in your hands, which will be generously given you if you do, as I know you will, your duty.

"Should you chance to be disabled in the service, a pension will be given you that will enable you to live in comfort and in ease; or should the fortune of war number you with those brave and gallant patriots that fearlessly poured out their life's blood upon the heights of Bunker, the plains of Saratoga, or at the siege of Yorktown—your families shall not be left unprotected or unprovided; a generous and faithful government has promised that one hundred and sixty acres of land shall be given to your heirs, the more than means of existence, the means of every comfort that can render that existence desirable.

"These, then, fellow soldiers, are the terms upon which sixty-four of you are requested to draw your swords, shoulder your arms and march to

Detroit to defend the frontiers of your own territory. And from these columns are there not more than this small number that would rush upon even certain death at their country's call?

"The services required of you will not be arduous—'tis not that you should invade the territory of a distant enemy—'tis not that you should march far from your homes to fight battles in which you are not, and which you do not feel yourselves, interested; but it is to prevent the hostile foot of a foe from invading your territory—it is to guard the sacred altar of your liberties, cemented by the blood of your fathers, from the profanation of a tyrant's polluting touch—it is to guard your dwellings, your friends, your families, your all, from the desolating warfare of a fell savage foe—it is that the midnight and sleeping couch of our infants may not be awakened to death by the tremendous yell of an Indian warwhoop—it is that the gray hairs of our fathers may not become the bloody trophies of a cruel and insidious foe. Cruelty and a thirst for blood are the inmates of an Indian's bosom, and in the neighborhood of two contending powers they are never peaceful. If the strong hand of power does not bend them down they will raise the tomahawk and bare the scalping knife for deeds of blood and horror: the purity of female innocence, the decrepitude of age, the tenderness of infancy afford no security against the murderous steel of a hostile Indian: to guard against the probable incursions of bands of these murderers, I will not call them by the dignified name of warriors, are you called upon to arm: and who in such a cause would refuse to march or to bleed? And who would refuse to protect the scattered settlements on our frontiers—the humble cottage and its peaceful inhabitants?—Who would refuse to guard our fields from desolation, our villages from destruction, or our towns from ruin?—None, in whom there is a spark of patriot valor.

"But, fellow soldiers, you may be called upon to meet the legions of Great Britain; every appearance indicates a state of approaching hostilities—year after year has insult been added to insult—injury has followed injury with rapid strides, and every breeze comes laden with its tale of wrongs, and while we have borne their injuries and their insults our government has endeavored, but in vain, to reconcile our differences by amicable negotiation.

"The cup of our wrongs is full, and the voice of an indignant people demands redress and revenge by every means in our power; 'tis that voice that calls upon you to arm and meet the hosts of England.

"Do you fear the event of the contest? Call but to mind the period of '76, without a government, without friends, without armies, without men, without money, our fathers dared to resist her aggressions upon our liberties; she determined to enslave us, and a hardy band of freemen resolved on death rather than slavery, encountered and conquered her boasted legions, established our independence and left it as their richest legacy for us to maintain: and do we, their sons, possessing all the advantages that we could wish, all that they were deprived of, do we fear the contest when half the world is confederate against her? Where is the spirit of our fathers that urged them to battle and to victory? Is there no latent spark of patriot ardor that the wrongs and indignities of our country will kindle into a flame? Is there no thirst in our bosoms for glory? Is it nothing for your names to be enrolled on the list of fame? Does it rouse no generous and noble feelings in your breasts to be a guardian shield and avenging sword to your country? Are the grateful thanks of your countrymen and posterity no inducement to valorous acts?

"Go then, fellow soldiers, assist to shield your country from the desolation of an internal warfare, awake to honor and to glory, rouse the native courage of an American freeman and march to deeds of valor!

"Let the wings of fame come laden with the tale of your honors, and bring joy to your mothers' hearts, and the pride of valorous deeds to your fathers' bosoms; then shall your country reward and bless you — posterity shall venerate your names, the world shall own you as the constituent guardians of liberty and the bulwark of your nation's freedom!"

I presume the soldiers enlisted at Lancaster were a part of the army infamously surrendered by General Hull on the 16th of August, 1812. This event opened up the whole of the then western states and territories to the inroads of the British and Indians, but was brilliantly compensated by the splendid victory of Commodore Perry at the battle of Lake Erie, on the 10th of September, 1813, in which he destroyed the British fleet and announced his victory in the stirring words, "We have met the enemy, and they are ours!" This was followed by the complete triumph of General Harrison in the battle of the Thames, October 5, 1813, in which Tecumseh was killed, and the power of the British and Indians in that portion of the field of operations practically destroyed.

My father was appointed by Mr. Madison, on the 9th of November, 1813, as Collector of Internal Revenue for the Third District of Ohio. He was then engaged in the active practice of his profession. He was required to employ deputies in each of the counties of Fairfield, Pickaway, Madison, Franklin, Delaware, and Knox to collect internal revenue taxes, when assessed. He took great care in the selection of his deputies, and in all cases required bonds, with security, from each deputy. At this period the only money in Ohio was local bank paper money. No silver or gold coins could be had, and the purchasing power of notes varied with the success or defeat of our armies in the field. Internal taxes were imposed on distilled spirits, on the retailing of spirits, on salt, sugar, carriages, sales at auction, a stamp duty of one per cent. on bank notes, on all notes discounted by a bank, and on inland bills of exchange.

It is clearly shown by the papers on file in the treasury department that Mr. Sherman exercised the utmost care in the collection of these taxes through his deputies. No difficulty seems to have occurred until July, 1817, when the government, without previous notice, refused to take the paper then in circulation in Ohio, but demanded notes of the Bank of the United States, or its branches, one of which was located at Chillicothe. This left upon the hands of his deputies a large amount of money that soon became utterly worthless. The system of local banking failed and the loss fell upon the holders of notes, and, largely, upon the collectors of internal revenue and their deputies. Among my father's deputies the principal one seems to have been Peter Apple, of Pickaway county, who at the time of his appointment held a county office, was postmaster, and a justice of the peace. He was a leading man, of high character and standing, and supposed to be of considerable wealth. In 1817 he became embarrassed and insolvent, and was removed from his position as deputy. His bonds proved worthless, and the whole loss and liability fell upon my father. This, with other losses occurring through the failure of other deputies, was the most unfortunate event of his life. His correspondence with the Internal Revenue Bureau shows that he exercised the utmost care in keeping and reporting his accounts, and the difficulties and losses he sustained in converting local bills into such notes as the government would receive in payment of taxes. It is clearly shown that the loss was not caused by any failure or neglect on his part. In like circumstances, under the existing law, Congress has, in all cases where due diligence on the part of the collector has been proven, relieved the collector. My father declined to make any appeal for such relief, but applied the proceeds of all his property, and a large part of his earnings, to make good, as far as he could, the defalcations of his deputies. This loss was a great embarrassment for him and his family during his life. It did not affect his standing, either at home or with the government, but it deprived him of many comforts, and his family of advantages and opportunities for education which they otherwise would have had.

In the spring of 1815 my father was notified of the illness of his father in Norwalk, and immediately went to Connecticut, but, owing to the nature of the long journey, did not arrive until after his father's death. The will of Taylor Sherman gave to his wife, and daughter Elizabeth, all his real and personal estate in the State of Connecticut, subject to the payment of his debts, which were very small. He bequeathed to his two sons, Charles Sherman and Daniel Sherman, certain lands in the town of Sherman, county of Huron, Ohio, being part of the "Sufferers' Lands." The remainder of his property lying in the State of Ohio he gave equally to his wife and children. The estate was soon settled, and in the following year, 1816, my grandmother and her daughter, Elizabeth, moved to Ohio and became a part of the family of my father.

Under the old constitution of Ohio prior to 1850, the Supreme Court was composed of four judges. They met at Columbus in the winter to hold the court of last resort, but at other seasons they divided into circuit courts composed of two judges, and went from county to county attended by a bevy of the leading lawyers of the state, all mounted on horseback and always ready for fun or frolic. I gladly acknowledge that I have received many a kindness, and much aid in business as well as political and social life, from the kindly memory of my father. I shrink from writing of his personal traits and genial nature, but insert, instead, brief extracts from a sketch of him written, in 1872, as a part of a local history of Fairfield county, Ohio, by General William J. Reese, who knew him intimately. General Reese says:

"Established permanently at Lancaster in the prosecution of his profession, the subject of this sketch rapidly rose to eminence as a polished and eloquent advocate, and as a judicious, reliable counsellor at law — indeed, in the elements of mind necessary to build up and sustain such a reputation, few men were his equals, and fewer still his superiors, in the State of Ohio or out of it. But it was not only in the higher region of legal attainments that he gained superiority; his mind was enriched with choice classic cultivation also.

*   *   *   *   *   *   *   *

" Judge Sherman not only mastered the intricacies of Coke and Littleton, but, as I have stated, he made himself familiar with whatever was worthy of reading outside the books of law, and was therefore fitted to shine in the domain of general literature as well as in the realm of technical jurisprudence.

*   *   *   *   *   *   *   *

" During the pioneer years of Ohio its lawyers were obliged to perform extensive circuits to practice their profession ; they were accustomed to accompany the courts from county to county, and in this way to traverse an extent of country which, being uncalled for at present, would appear fabulous in statement and difficult to realize.

" Those early days also commemorated the warmest personal friendships in the profession, and, indeed, this could hardly have been otherwise, as they compelled its members into the closest habitual companionship. They rode together in the same primitive style, their saddle-bags stuffed with papers, documents, briefs, law-books, clothing, and, peradventure, some creature delectation also. They were exposed in common to the same inclemencies and impediments of travel, they lodged together at the same inns or taverns, messed at the same table, slept in the same rooms, and were not unfrequently coerced by twos into the same bed. Free, jovial, genial, manly, and happy times they were, when, after a hard-fought field-day of professional antagonisms in court, the evening hours were crowned with social amenities, and winged with wit and merriment, with pathos, sentiment and song.

*   *   *   *   *   *   *   *

" If the sayings and doings at the festive evenings of the early Ohio bar could be collected, there would be materials in rich abundance from which a sympathetic and facile pen could compile a volume of equal piquancy and sentimental refinement, of patriotic detail and humor, that alternate the pages of Sir Jonah Barrington, or any other winsome work of the kind. This will not be questioned for a moment when it is remembered that Henry Clay, Lewis Cass, Philip Doddridge, Willis Silliman, David K. Este, and Charles Hammond were frequent participants ; that Philoman Beecher, William W. Irvin, Thomas Ewing, William Stanberry, Benjamin Tappan, John M. Goodenow, Jacob Parker, Orris Parrish, and Charles Goddard habitually contributed to their entertainment, and that these were often signalized with the hilarious fun of Creighton and the quaint drolleries of Douglas. At these symposiums of recreation, and they were held whenever the courts used to meet, Charles R. Sherman was always the most welcome of companions, and contributed his full share even to the ambrosial feasts,

> ' When all such clustering portions had
> As made their frolic wild, not mad.'

" Thus endowed and so associated, he became a leading and a popular people's lawyer, from the Ohio River to our northern lake.

" In 1823 he was elected by the legislature to the bench of the Supreme Court of Ohio, and perhaps the only man in the state who doubted his ability for this high position was himself. He told the writer of these lines, when speaking on the subject of his appointment, that he assumed its duties with great personal diffidence and apprehension. He feared that he lacked the ripe experience of years necessary to hear and determine cases of magnitude in a court of the last resort. His official associates were Calvin Pease, Jacob Burnet, and Peter Hitchcock, and these are names of renown in the judicial history of Ohio.

" Judge Sherman upon the bench fully realized the large expectations of his professional friends and the public.

" His written opinions, published in 'Hammond's Reports of the Supreme Court,' demonstrate a mind of the choicest legal capabilities. They are clear, compact, yet comprehensive, intuitive, logical, complete, and conclusive, and are respected by the bar and courts in this and other states as judicial *dicta* of the highest authority. He won upon the bench, as he did at the bar, the affection and confidence of his associates. They esteemed him for his gentle and genial nature, for the brilliant flashes of his mind and the solid strength of his judgment; above all, for the stainless integrity of his character, as a judge and as a man.

" Under the provisions of our old constitution, the Supreme Court was required to hold an annual term or sitting in each county of the state, two of the judges officiating. In every court-room in Ohio where Judge Sherman presided he made friends. His official robes were worn by him as the customary habiliments of the man. He was never distant, haughty, morose, austere, or overbearing on the bench. It was not in his nature to be so anywhere, and it was therefore always a personal pleasure to practice in his courts. The younger members of the profession idolized him in every part of the state; for them and their early efforts he systematically sympathized, and he uniformly bestowed upon them the most gracious compliment that any judge upon the bench can render to the oldest practitioner at the bar — he gave them his interested and undivided attention.

" He had entered upon the sixth year of his official term, was in his manly meridian of life, in the full fruition of his matured intellectual powers, in the plenitude of his public usefulness, and in the enjoyment of apparent robust physical health, out upon his circuit, and about to hold a session of the Supreme Court at Lebanon, in Warren county, when suddenly, without

any premonition, he was struck down with a fatal malady, that was fright-
fully rapid in its termination. The best medical aid was summoned from
Cincinnati; it was vain. An express messenger was hurried to Lancaster
for Mrs. Sherman, but before she reached him her lamented husband was
dead.

"He died in Lebanon, June 24, 1829, in the 41st year of his age.

"I will not attempt to describe the outburst of public sorrow that prevailed over this event. It was general and sincere, touching and outspoken;
but it was in Lancaster, it was here in his happy home, which he made the
home always of genial and open-hearted hospitality — here among his neighbors and fellow-citizens of every class and description, all of whom knew
him and all of whom loved him — that the intelligence of his death came
with the most painful and startling abruptness. They could not comprehend it. But yesterday he was among them in perfect health, and now he
is dead. Men wept in our public streets. I do not believe he had a single
personal enemy on earth.

"Had Judge Sherman lived, higher and broader spheres of public usefulness would have opened before him. There is no doubt whatever that
the same spontaneity of opinion that placed him upon the supreme bench
would have again united, when the vacancy happened, to have sent him to
the Senate of the United States, and those who knew him knew full well
that his first prepared public utterance in that chamber upon any pending
matter of national importance would have secured to him a brilliant national
name. This is no fancy penciling. It was conviction with his contemporaries, and it would have been the record of history had he lived. As it is,
he has left to his children the heritage of his spotless public reputation — of
his loved and honored name.

"This fragmentary sketch would be more incomplete did I not mention
that Judge Sherman was a zealous and prominent member of the Masonic
fraternity, and that he filled its highest offices of honor in the several grand
bodies of Ohio."

General Reese, the author of this sketch, was born in Philadelphia, Pa., on the 5th of August, 1804. He was a graduate of
the University of Pennsylvania, studied law and was admitted
to practice in Philadelphia. He then came to Ohio and was admitted to the bar in Cincinnati and soon after settled in Lancaster. In 1829, soon after the death of my father, he married
my eldest sister, Mary Elizabeth. He did not long pursue his
profession but became a merchant. He was prominent as a
member of the board of public works. In old militia times he
was in command of the forces of the state as its only major-
general. He was grand master of the Grand Lodge of Masons

in Ohio for a series of years, and at the same time held high rank in the Grand Lodge of the United States. He was a handsome and accomplished gentleman, of pleasing manners, and liberal to a fault. He died on the 17th of December, 1883, at Lancaster, in his eightieth year.

Of my mother I can scarcely write without emotion, though she died more than forty years ago. Her maiden name was Mary Hoyt. She was a member of a family, mostly merchants and sailors, who had lived in Norwalk, Connecticut, since its first settlement. At the period of the American Revolution the Hoyt family, composed of several brothers, was divided in their allegiance, some as Tories, some as Whigs. My mother's grandfather was a Whig. It is a tradition in the family that one of the Tory brothers pointed out the house of his brother, at the capture of Norwalk by the British and Tories, as the nest of a rebel, and it was burned to the ground. In this it shared the fate of the greater part of the town. The Tories of the family went to St. Johns, but years after the war was over they and their descendants returned to Connecticut and New York, and many of them became prominent and respected citizens. Isaac Hoyt, my grandfather, was a prominent citizen of Norwalk, possessing considerable wealth for those days.

My mother was carefully educated at the then famous female seminary at Poughkeepsie, New York. I remember the many embroidered pictures, made with the needle and silk thread by the handicraft of my mother, as a school girl, carefully framed, that decorated the old house in Lancaster. The women of that day were trained more for the culture and ornament of the house, more to knit stockings and weave home spun than to make speeches on woman's rights. Soon after her graduation she married Charles Robert Sherman, as before stated, and their lives were blended. She sometimes rode with him when on the circuit, and always on horseback. It was an adage in the family, even to her grandchildren, that she was always ready for a visit. I never knew her to scold, much less to strike, her children. She was our sure refuge against grandmother, between whom and my mother there was, however, the warmest affection. When Aunt Elizabeth married Mr. Parker, grandmother followed her daughter to their home in Mansfield.

When my mother, by the death of her husband, was left a widow with eleven children and spare means of support, she received the sympathy of all her neighbors and the kindly encouragement of everyone in Lancaster. As her children scattered her resources increased, so that after one year of widowhood she was quite independent. Like Goldsmith's Vicar of Wakefield she was "passing rich" on four hundred dollars a year. Soon the houses of her children were open to her, but she clung to Lancaster until all her children had taken flight, when, in the summer of 1844, she accepted the invitation of her sons to make her home in Mansfield and removed there. She had there her house and home. Her two youngest daughters, and the writer of this, were her family, but in a very brief period all around her were married. She still continued to occupy her home, and always with some of her numerous grandchildren as her guests. She often visited her children, and her coming was always regarded by them as a favor conferred by her. And so her tranquil life flowed on until 1852, when she attended the state fair at Cleveland and contracted a bad cold. She returned to Mansfield only to die on the 23rd day of September, 1852, at the residence of her daughter, Mrs. Bartley.

Before closing this sketch of my ancestors, it seems proper that I refer to their religious beliefs and modes of worship. In England they were classed as Puritans, and were members of the Presbyterian church. In Connecticut they followed the doctrine and faith of the Congregational church of Anthony Stoddard. Daniel Sherman and his father were deacons of the congregation of Mr. Stoddard, and his granddaughter, the wife of Taylor Sherman, carried her faith and practice into her family, and maintained to her death the strict morals, and close observance of the Sabbath day, that was the established rule and practice of the Connecticut Congregationalist.

My mother's family, the Hoyts, were, with scarcely an exception, members of the Episcopal church. My mother was reared in that faith and practice from infancy, and was a member of that church at the time of her marriage. When she emigrated to Lancaster she found there no church of that denomination, and, therefore, joined the Presbyterian church under the pastorage of Rev. John Wright, who baptized all her children. At a later period, perhaps about 1840, when an Episcopal church was established in Lancaster, she resumed her attendance and worship in that church. When she removed to Mansfield she attended the Episcopal church at that place, partook of its sacraments and usages, and died in that faith and worship. All her living children and their families recognized and supported the Episcopal church as their church, except the children of General Sherman, who followed their mother and her maternal ancestors in the faith and worship of the Catholic church.

The writer of this has a firm belief in the Bible as the only creed of religious faith and duty, and willingly accords to every human being the right to choose his form of worship according to his judgment, but in case of doubt it is best to follow the teachings of his mother.

With this, the sketch of my ancestors closes. Many will think it is not part of my life, and that I have given too much space and importance to it. If so, I hope they will pass it over without reading. Each individual life is molded by one's ancestry, by the incidents of his childhood, the training he receives in the family and the school and the conditions and surroundings of his early days. The boy is father to the man. It is difficult for one in advanced age to recall or to measure the influence of each of these in forming his character, but a statement of them is a necessary preface to a history of his later life. My information as to my ancestry is chiefly derived from the admirable local histories of Connecticut, and, especially, from "Cothron's History of Ancient Woodbury," "Hutchinson's History of Connecticut," and the local records and traditions of Essex and Sussex counties in England.

I cannot claim for my ancestors superior rank, wealth or ability. They were not specially distinguished for any of these, but they were men of useful and honorable lives, of untarnished reputation, highly esteemed by their contemporaries, thorough republicans in the broad sense of that word, always for their country in any contest for the right, and willing to yield equal political and civil rights to all their countrymen of every creed and color.

ARMS OF THE SHERMAN FAMILY.

CHAPTER II.

MY BOYHOOD DAYS AND EARLY LIFE.

Born at Lancaster, Ohio, May 10, 1823 — Death of My Father and Its Effect on
Our Family — Early Days at School — A Dead Sheep in the Schoolroom —
Lesson in Sunday Sport — Some of My Characteristics — My Attack
on the Schoolmaster — Robbing an Orchard — A Rodman at
Fourteen, and My Experiences While Surveying — Debates
at Beverly — Early Use of Liquor — First Visit
to Mansfield in 1839 — The Famous Campaign of 1840 — I Begin the
Study of Law.

I WAS born at Lancaster, Ohio, on the 10th day of May, 1823, the eighth child of Charles and Mary Sherman. My first distinct recollection of events is connected with the scenes and incidents that followed the death of my father on the 24th day of June, 1829. I have a dim recollection before that time of being sent to school with my elder brothers to keep me out of mischief, and of my father praising me for learning the alphabet, but all other impressions of my infancy were absorbed in the great family tragedy. We were warned to keep quiet, and to remain out of doors, so as not to disturb mother, who was critically ill, and, as our grandmother was then supreme in the household, we knew that her will was law, and that punishment invariably followed an offense. During these enforced absences many were the wise resolves, or, rather, the conceits, that the boys discussed for "helping mother."

But time, which mellows every misfortune, brought us many changes. My sister, Elizabeth, was soon married to General William J. Reese. My brother, Charles, came home a full-fledged graduate, and, as we thought, very learned. Everybody was kind. The affairs of my father were settled. The homestead and garden were secured to my mother, and she had, in addition, a settled income from her father's estate of $400 a year, while grandmother had her "fire lands," and

BIRTHPLACE OF JOHN SHERMAN AT LANCASTER, OHIO

an assured but small income besides. In those days a little money went a great way; but there were eleven children of us to be cared for,—from Charles, aged eighteen, to Fanny, aged three months. The separation of this family was imperative, but the friends of my father were numerous, and their offerings were generous and urgent. Charles entered the family of our cousin, Mr. Stoddard, an old and leading lawyer in Dayton, Ohio, studied law, and in two years was admitted to the bar. James, the next eldest brother, accepted a clerkship in a store in Cincinnati, and from that time paid his own way, becoming a merchant, first in Lancaster, and later in Des Moines, Iowa. William Tecumseh was adopted into the family of Hon. Thomas Ewing, who lived in the same square with us in Lancaster. The two families were bound by ties and mutual aid which were highly creditable to both. My father, Judge Sherman, had been able to help Mr. Ewing in the beginning of his professional career, and Mr. Ewing gratefully and generously responded. They maintained the most intimate and cordial relations during their lives and their families have since continued them, the bond being strengthened by the marriage of William Tecumseh to Mr. Ewing's daughter, Ellen. Lampson P., the fourth son, was adopted into the family of Charles Hammond, of Cincinnati, a distinguished lawyer of marked ability, the reporter of the Supreme Court of Ohio, and editor and chief proprietor of the "Gazette," the leading newspaper published in his day in Cincinnati.

While the reduction of our family was thus taking place I was kept at school at Lancaster, where I made considerable advance in such studies as a lad from six to eight years of age can pursue. I have forgotten the names of my tutors. The present admirable system of common schools in Ohio had not then been adopted, but the private schools in Lancaster were considered very good, and most of the boys of school age were able at little cost to get the rudiments of an education.

In the spring of 1831, my father's cousin, John Sherman, a prosperous merchant of Mt. Vernon, Ohio, accompanied by his bride, visited my mother, and proposed to take me into his family and to keep me at school until I was prepared to enter

Kenyon College, five miles from Mt. Vernon. This was a kindly offer and was gratefully accepted. But I remember well the sadness I felt, and the tears I shed, over the departure from home into the midst of strangers. The old-fashioned stage coach was then the only medium of travel and the fifty miles between Lancaster and Mt. Vernon were to me a wearisome journey. For days after I arrived in Mt. Vernon I was moping either at the house or at the store, but ere long became accustomed to the change, and commenced my studies in the schools, which, as I remember them, were admirably conducted by teachers of marked ability, among whom were some who became distinguished in professional and business life. One of the families that I became intimate with was that of Mr. Norton, one of whose sons, J. Banning Norton, who lately died in Dallas, Texas, was my constant companion. We studied our lessons together, but frequently had quarrels and fights. It was a "fad" of his to wear his finger-nails very long. On one occasion I pummeled him well, but he scratched my face in the contest. When I went home, marked in this way, I was asked how I came to be so badly scratched and the best answer I could make was that I had fallen on a "splintery log," and this got to be a by-word in the school.

According to the usages of the time I was put early to the study of Latin, which then seemed to be regarded as the necessary foundation for an education. I must confess that during my stay in Mt. Vernon I was rather a troublesome boy, frequently involved in controversies with the teachers, and sometimes punished in the old-fashioned way with the ferule and the switch, which habit I then regarded as tyrannical and now regard as impolitic. I do not believe that the policy of punishment adopted in the schools of those times would be expedient to-day. It tended to foster a constant irritation between the teacher and the pupil.

Among my school adventures at Mt. Vernon was one I heartily regret. We had a teacher by the name of Lord. He was a small man, and not able to cope with several of the boys in the school. We called him "Bunty Lord." One evening after school four boys, of whom I was one, while playing on the commons, found a dead sheep. It was suggested that we carry the sheep into the schoolroom and place it on Lord's seat. This was promptly done and I wrote a Latin couplet, purporting that this was a very worthy sacrifice to a very poor Lord, and placed it on the head of the sheep. The next morning Lord found the sheep and made a great outcry against the indignity. Efforts were at once made to ascertain the actors in this farce, and proof was soon obtained. My handwriting disclosed my part in the case, and the result was a prompt discharge of the culprits from school; but poor Lord lost his place, because of his manifest inability to govern his unruly pupils.

Another teacher whom I remember was of a very different type. This was Matthew H. Mitchell. He was severe and dogmatic, allowing no foolishness in his school. He was strict and impartial in his treatment of the boys, and, though we did not like him, we respected his power.

I had one adventure during these early boyhood days which nearly cost me my life, and which Uncle John (as I called Mr. Sherman) converted into a religious warning. One Sunday there was a freshet in Owl Creek, on the south side of the town, and many people went to see it, I among the rest. I was reckless, and, against the advice of others, went out on a temporary foot-bridge which fell and I dropped into the raging waters. How I escaped I hardly know, but it was by the assistance of others. Uncle John said that I was punished by the Almighty for violating the Sabbath. Ever after that I was careful about Sunday sport.

I remember, while living at Uncle John's, witnessing the wedding of his niece, Miss Leavenworth, to Columbus Delano. I sat upon the stair steps during the ceremony, the first of the kind I ever saw. I mention this because of my long acquaintance with Mr. Delano and his family. He became a great lawyer and filled many offices of high public trust, and is now (1895) living in vigorous health, eighty-six years old. I also remember very well Henry B. Curtis and his family. He married a sister of Mrs. Sherman of Mt. Vernon, and had a number of children. He was a brother of Colonel Samuel R. Curtis, distinguished in the Civil War, was an accomplished lawyer, a careful business man and a gentleman in every sense of the word.

On the whole I regard my four years at Mount Vernon as well spent. I advanced in my studies so that I could translate Latin fairly well, I went through the primary studies, and obtained some comprehension of algebra, geometry and kindred studies. In the meantime the condition of our family had greatly changed and generally improved. My sister Amelia was happily married to Robert McComb, a merchant of Mansfield. My father's only sister was married to Judge Parker, of Mansfield, to which place my grandmother had followed her daughter, and my brother Charles had entered on his career as a lawyer in the same town.

Uncle John had a family of small children growing up and I felt I was in the way. My mother was anxious for me to return home as all her boys were away. I wanted to go. Uncle John, however, expressed his desire for me to stay and enter Kenyon College, but I knew that Mrs. Sherman preferred that I should leave as she had her young children to care for. The result was my return to Lancaster at the age of twelve. Mrs. Sherman is now living at Washington, D. C., at the age of eighty-seven, with her son John. I shall always remember with sincere gratitude her care and forbearance manifested toward a rather wild and reckless boy at the disagreeable age of from eight to twelve years. Affection may make a mother bear with the torment of her own child at that age, but will rarely induce an equal leniency toward that of another.

My return to Lancaster was a happy event in my life. I renewed my old acquaintance with boys of my age, and was on intimate terms with Philemon Ewing, Charles Garaghty, Frederick Reese, W. P. Rice, W. Winthrop Sifford and others. My brother, William Tecumseh, was three years my senior, and he and his associates of his own age rather looked down upon their juniors. Still, I had a good deal of intercourse with him, mainly in the way of advice on his part. At that time he was a steady student, quiet in his manners and easily moved by sympathy or affection. I was regarded as a wild, reckless, lad, eager in controversy and ready to fight. No one could then anticipate that he was to be a great warrior and I a plodding lawyer and politician. I fired my first gun over his shoulder. He took me with him to carry the game, mostly squirrels and pigeons. He was then destined to West Point, and was preparing for it. To me the future was all unknown.

I entered, with all the boys referred to and many others, the Academy of Mark and Matthew Howe, then well established, and of great reputation, — and deservedly so. The schoolrooms were large, and furnished with desks and chairs, an improvement upon the old benches with boards in front. The course of studies mapped out for me was much the same as I pursued at Mount Vernon, with a specialty of the first six books of Euclid, and of algebra. Latin was taught but little. From the first, arithmetic, algebra and surveying were my favorite studies, and in those I became proficient. We had an improvised theatre in which we acted plays and made speeches.

When I entered the school Matthew Howe was the regulator, teacher and dominie. He was the supreme autocrat, from whom there was no appeal. All the boys respected him, for he was certainly a good teacher, but they did not like his domineering way. I got along with him pretty well for some months, but one day after I had mastered my lessons I rested my head on my desk when I was sharply reproved by him. I said that I did not feel very well and had learned my lessons. He called me to the black-board and directed me to demonstrate some problem in my lesson of Euclid. I went, and, as I believed, had made the drawing and demonstrated the problem. He said I had not, that I had failed to refer to a corollary. I answered that he had not required this in previous lessons. Some discussion arose, when, with the ferule in his hand, he directed me to hold out mine. I did so, but as he struck my right hand, I hit him with all the force I could command with my left. This created great excitement in the school, all the students being present, my brother Tecumseh among them. It was said at the time that the boys were disposed to take sides with me, but I saw no signs of it. The result was that I was expelled from the school, but, by the intercession of my mother, and Mrs. Reese, after explanations, I was restored, and during my two years with Mr. Howe I had no other contention with him. He moved some years later to Iowa, where he established another academy, and lived a long and useful life. We had friendly correspondence with each other, but neither alluded to our skirmish over a corollary in Euclid.

The pupils had the usual disposition among boys to play tricks on each other. The academy was in a large square, the greater part of which was an orchard of apple trees. Mr. Howe lived on the corner of the square, some distance from the academy. The boys were forbidden to climb the trees to shake down the fruit, but were quite welcome to the fruit on the ground. One fall, when the apples were ripe, the boys conspired to play a trick upon some of the students and outsiders,—among them my brother Lampson, then on a visit home from Cincinnati,—who were easily persuaded to rob the orchard, none more willing than "Lamp." Those in the plot were to watch and prevent interference. When the time came we had detailed two or three boys in the academy to fire off muskets, well loaded with powder and nothing else, when the signal was given. Everything moved on according to programme. The boys detailed to shake down the apples were in the trees, when, all at once, the firing of musketry commenced. The boys dropped from the trees and scattered in every direction. Some were caught in the pea vines of Mr. Howe's garden, but most of them, with great labor, climbed over the high fence around the ground and dropped on the outside "with a thud," safe from powder! The dogs in the neighborhood lent their aid to the outcry, and everybody was convinced that ruffians had robbed Howe's orchard.

I suppose it will never occur that a generation of boys will not do these things. At seventy-two I know it was wrong. At thirteen I thought it was fun.

I now recall many pleasing memories of what occurred in the two years "at home" at that period when the life of a boy is beginning to open to the future. It is the period of greatest danger and highest hope. At that time, 1835 to 1837, every-body was prosperous. The development created by our system of canals had opened markets for our produce. The public national debt had been paid. The pet banks chartered after the destruction of the Bank of the United States started upon a wild scheme of inflation. A craze to purchase public land created an overflowing revenue. All causes combining created a deceptive prosperity that could end only in one way. All this was Greek to me. All I wanted, and the controlling wish of my life, was to help mother. She was always kind, loving and forbearing. No word of reproach ever fell from her lips to me. She was the same to all her children, but if there was any difference, or favor, it was for me. Even at that early age I had day dreams for the future, and mother was the central picture. If fortunes could be made by others why could I not make one? I wished I was a man. It began to appear to me that I could not wait to go through college. What were Latin and Greek to me, when they would delay me in making my fortune!

Near the close of 1836 I wrote to my brother Charles at Mansfield, asking him to get me employment. He discouraged me and said I should stick to my studies, but I insisted that I was strong and could make my own living. At this time Ohio had decided upon the improvement of the Muskingum River from Zanesville to Marietta, and the Board of Public Works had selected Colonel Samuel R. Curtis, a graduate of West Point, as chief engineer. He was a brother of Mr. Curtis, of Mount Vernon, and a friend of our family.

Charles had no difficulty in securing me employment as junior rodman if, at the age of fourteen, I could perform the duties required,—which Colonel Curtis doubted. The work was not to commence until the spring, when I was to be given a trial. I worked hard that winter, for hard work, I thought, was the way to fortune. I studied the mode of leveling. I saw a man on the Hocking canal operate his instrument, take the rear sight from the level of the water in the canal, then by a succession of levels backwards and forwards carry his level to the objective point. Then the man was kind enough to show me how, by simple addition and subtraction, the result wanted could be obtained. I was well advanced in arithmetic and in mathematics generally, and was confident, even if I was hardly fourteen years old, that I could do the work of a junior rodman.

About the first of May, 1837, the day of deliverance came. I was to be my own master and make my own living! A fortune gilded with hope was before me. I was to go in the stage thirty-six miles to Zanesville, and thence by stage-route down the Muskingum River, twenty-eight miles to McConnels-ville. When the stage arrived at my mother's house it was rather full, but there was still room enough for me. All the family, and my comrades, had gathered to see me off. My baggage, all new, was thrown into the boot, and I took my seat in the stage. My heart sank a little as the stage rolled over the hill and down the valley beyond, but the passengers wanted to know who I was, where I was going, and what I was going to do, and I think they got all the information they wanted, for why should I not tell them of my visions of hope, sometimes called plans? Oh! the golden dreams of childhood, the splendid anticipations of boyhood, the fields of conquest to be won, the fortunes to be made, all to vanish into thin air by the touch of reality.

I arrived at Zanesville long after dark, and very weary. I had never been in so large a town before. The hotel was full of people, but no one noticed me. I was hungry, but could only get the scraps left, as the supper hour was past. I was to leave in the morning at daylight without breakfast. I was shown into a small dark room, on the third floor, and was to be called in the morning. I did not like the place and was alone and in fear. I had more money than ever before. Might I not be robbed? I took the precaution to deposit my jack-knife on a chair within reach, to defend myself in case of attack! My fears were soon lost in sleep. In the morning I was aroused to take my place in the stage, but forgot my knife, my only weapon of defense, and it was lost to me for-ever. The bright morning revived my spirits. A hearty breakfast at Taylorsville revived all my hopes and plans.

I arrived at McConnelsville about noon and stopped at the only tavern in the place. I called at the headquarters of Colonel Curtis and introduced myself to him. He received me very kindly and introduced me to the office clerks, and to James M. Love, who, I was told, would take me within a week to the engineer corps, then running their levels at Beverly, sixteen miles away. I spent the week pleasantly with him, and was intimately associated with him during my service of two years. He subsequently studied law and practiced his profession at Coshocton. When the Mexican War was progressing he enlisted in one of the Ohio regiments, became a captain, and, I think, a major, and rendered good service. He subsequently migrated to Iowa and was appointed judge of the District Court of the United States for that state. This position he held for many years with distinction and honor. He died July 2, 1891.

When the time came for joining the corps Love proposed that we start in the morning for Beverly, but I insisted that, as it was only sixteen miles to Beverly, we could easily make the trip after dinner. I had never walked so far as sixteen miles in my life, but had walked or run three or four miles in an hour, and, by the rules of arithmetic, we could easily go sixteen miles in five or six hours. He yielded to my wishes, and, as our baggage had been sent by the stage, we started about one o'clock, light of heart and foot. When we had climbed the long hill south of McConnelsville, about a mile and a half, I was a little tired, and I asked how far we had gone; he said, 'a mile and a half!' I began then to appreciate my folly in not starting in the morning. He said nothing, but kept at my slower pace, giving me a rest occasionally. It was sun-down when we were six miles from Beverly, and I was completely tired out. Still neither of us proposed to stop, as we could have done at a farmer's house on the roadside. We reached the town of Beverly about ten o'clock, weary and hungry. This tramp taught me a lesson I never forgot,—not to insist upon anything I knew nothing about. We found the corps the next day in camp in one large tent on the east bank of the Muskingum River.

I had another experience, equally unpleasant, during our first evening in camp. The members of our corps, five or six in number, had been invited by Mr. Lindsley to attend a party at his house near by. They accepted, and, as Love and I had no invitations, we were left on guard in the tent containing the instruments and supplies. When we were alone there came up suddenly a storm of wind and rain,—not uncommon along the valley,—which flattened the tent and flooded the ground on which it stood. We were thoroughly soaked and utterly helpless, and, for a time, in real danger. I remember my utter collapse at this new misfortune, but all we could do was to wait and hope for the return of the corps. I must confess that I quietly mingled my tears with the rain, but I did not tell this to the boys when they returned after the storm was over. No great damage was done. The tent was soon raised and secured in place. The next morning I was given a rod and instructed how to use it. I noticed that my associates did not have much confidence in my ability to perform the duties, and, especially the senior rodman, John Burwell. I followed instructions, however, and reported my rod correctly. After a day or two they gave me a book in which I was to enter the levels. In a very short time they were satisfied that I could perform my duties, and I was soon trusted to make up the record of levels, and the necessary additions and subtractions in my book.

This little corps was composed of men, some of whom afterwards became proficient as engineers, lawyers or preachers. Among them were John R. Straughn, Wright Coffinberry, John Scott, John Burwell, and James M. Love. The line of surveys was soon completed to Marietta, the locks and dams were located, estimates of cost were carefully made, the materials to be used were purchased and the excavations and embankments to be made were computed. My associates soon found that I could do the work assigned me, and in this way I won their respect and forbearance.

After the surveys were completed, the members of the corps were located at different places to take charge of the work. Mr. Coffinberry was assigned to Lowell, and I was attached to him as an assistant. John Scott, who had been at West Point, and, I think, was a graduate, was assigned to Beverly, where a dam, lock and a short canal were to be constructed. In the fall of 1837 he was dismissed, I think, for intemperance. I was detailed, not exactly to take his place, for which I was unfitted, but to look after some details, and to keep the headquarters advised of the progress of the work. It was soon found that I was able to measure embankments, excavations, stone and other materials. The result was that I was continued, at my early age, practically in charge of the work I have mentioned. All plans came from headquarters and I was carefully instructed from there what to do and how to do it. This was a great and useful experience for me, and it continued until the summer of 1839.

During most of the time I lived in the family of Mr. Paul Fearing, an old and respected citizen of Beverly, who had long been engaged in what was called the river trade. He transported the produce of the country, chiefly pork, apples, wheat, and corn, from the neighboring region on flats and scows down the Muskingum, Ohio and Mississippi to New Orleans, stopping at the riverside towns, selling his commodities and buying others. The boats were sold at New Orleans for lumber. The captain and crew, generally consisting of two men, would return by steamer with the proceeds of their traffic in sugar, molasses and other productions of the south. This was the early mode of traffic, but it had been largely broken up by steamboats, so that at the time I refer to, Mr. Fearing's occupation was gone; but he had a comfortable little fortune, and, with his wife and only daughter, lived in a neat cottage on the banks of the river at Beverly, where I became practically a member of his family.

The community at Beverly was a very intelligent one, composed mainly of settlers from Massachusetts on the Ohio Company's purchase. The valley of the Muskingum is exceedingly fertile, but it is comparatively narrow and confined by picturesque hills and ridges, broken by water courses. The settlements were mostly in the valley, for the hill lands were rough, covered by poor soil, and were occupied chiefly for grazing.

The portion of the valley at Beverly, and south of it, was singularly fertile and pleasing, and very valuable. Its owners and occupants were mostly of New England birth and descent. Their productions had a ready market down the river, and in that age, before railroads, the valley had a great advantage in transportation and supplies over the interior parts of the state. The people were, as a rule, educated in good schools, and they had a college at Marietta and a female college at Zanesville. The proposed improvement of the Muskingum, they believed, would give them another advantage, by securing them water of a depth sufficient for boats in the dry seasons of the year, as well as during the "freshets," which they then had to depend upon, but which at best were not very reliable in their habits, as I found to my cost. This was to be corrected by the "improvement," which, in their delusive hope, was to give them cheap water transportation all the year around.

At that time railroads were in their infancy. They have since practically destroyed or crippled all internal navigation on inland rivers, reaching their iron arms over the United States, traversing north and south, east and west—a vast gridiron of roads, in value greater than the market value of all the land in the United States in 1837. Before the first railroad was built in Ohio the Muskingum improvement was completed, but it proved to be a bad investment. The canals of Ohio and this improvement were, perhaps, the necessary forerunner of the railroads to come, but the money expended on them was practically lost. And I believe that the experiment now being made by the United States in the improvement of the Ohio, Missouri and Mississippi Rivers will end in a like result on a grander scale. By the demolition of the forests which covered this great valley, the supply and distribution of the waters and rivers in this region will be so diminished at certain seasons as to render these water-ways worthless for navigation. Engineers may make dams that will hold water, and locks that may lift a steamboat, but if the clearing away of forests prevents the usual fall of rain and causes its absorption into the earth, and if the dispersion of water by its use and waste in cities, are to continue, the dam will not be filled,

JOHN SHERMAN AT THE AGE OF 19.

and the lock will be like a stranded vessel, fit only as a quarry for cut stone, or for a railway arch over a street of asphalt in a growing city. Captain Fearing railed against the steamboats as many now inveigh against the railroads, but these two great agencies will divide the commerce of the world between them. The railroads will possess the land, the steamboats the ocean and the great fresh waters of the world. Possibly steamboats may be utilized on short stretches of rivers, but even on these they will have to compete with railroads having wide-reaching connections which they do not possess. The money expended to levee the Mississippi may be lost by the United States, but the planters will receive some benefit from it in the protection given to their crops. The steamboats in interior waters will be exchanged for iron whalebacks, and new forces of a new nature, as yet only partly developed, such as electricity, will contest with steam as a motive power.

During the period of my stay on the Muskingum improvements I had very excellent opportunities for study, of which I regret to say I did not avail myself as well as I might have done. Still, I occupied my leisure in reading novels, histories, and such books as I could readily get. Many books were sent to me from Lancaster. I purchased a number, and found some in Beverly which were kindly lent to me. I read most of the British classics, as they are called, the Spectator, Shakespeare, Byron, and Scott. I read all I could find of the history of America. I tried to brush up my Latin, but without much success. I had the frequent company of my associates on the corps, all of whom were bright, able men, several years in advance of me in age. We were frequently called to headquarters at McConnelsville, a trip usually made on horseback, and where we always had not only a cheerful, but a very instructive time. Colonel Curtis was highly esteemed by us all, and his treatment of me was kind and fatherly. He frequently complimented me upon my work, and when he came through Beverly he visited me.

Among the diversions at Beverly we had occasional debates. One of these was upon the dangerous subject of temperance, a topic not then much discussed, for drinking of something stronger than water was almost as universal as eating, and considered equally necessary. However, there sprang up about that time a movement in favor of temperance. It was thought best to discuss the subject at a public meeting, a school teacher and I taking the side of temperance, and two other young men opposing us. The meeting was well attended, largely by the men employed on the public work who habitually received a certain number of "jiggers" of whisky a day, at regular hours. Whisky, not being taxed, was worth from fifteen to twenty-five cents a gallon. It was not an expensive luxury, and was regarded by all the workingmen on the improvement as a necessity. At the end of the debate, which I do not remember to have been a very notable one, the audience decided we had the best of the argument. The discussion created a great excitement. The workingmen took up the cry that the Cumberland Presbyterians, the prevailing sect there, and other Christians, were interfering with their habits and comfort, and when the young schoolmaster appeared the next day, they raised a shout and pursued him with sticks and stones. He escaped with difficulty across the river, thus getting out of the way. I heard of the trouble, but went up to the canal and made my usual measurements. Not a word was said to me and no unkindness shown. I understood afterwards that this was caused by a warning given them by the contractor, who, hearing of the assault upon the schoolmaster, told them that I was a part of the government and it would not do to attack me; that to disturb me would have a very bad effect upon them all. So, I was forgiven, and, indeed, I never had any controversy during my time there with anyone connected with the work, from John McCune, the contractor, to the humblest water carrier about the works.

Early in the winter of 1838, I think in November, I had made up my mind to go to Cincinnati on the usual leave after the close of the works. As an excuse, and to procure means of paying for the trip, I purchased, partly on credit, a barge and loaded it with barreled salt, apples and other commodities, intending before the freeze-up to avail myself of the usual rise in the river to float to the Ohio and thence to Cincinnati.

All went smoothly, the boat was loaded and floated as far as Luke Shute, when the river was found to be too low to proceed. Consequently the boat was tied up and placed under the care of a man who slept aboard. We waited for the river to rise, but it did not come. Both the Muskingum and Ohio Rivers were very low that season and finally froze up before the freshet came. This closing of navigation created a great demand for salt in Cincinnati, as that article could not be obtained from the up-river country, and it advanced to a price that would have yielded me a little fortune had my boat not been among those thus detained. I undertook to carry some of the salt by flatboats, but they were frozen up. The packing season in Cincinnati was going forward and salt bore a high price, but I knew it would fall the moment the river opened. It was apparent that I would lose on the salt, but I still clung to my purpose to go down the river. Finally the freshet came, some time in January, I think, and then, with three men on the barge, I floated down the river, tying up at nights for safety, and stopping occasionally to sell apples to the Kentucky farmers, I arrived at last in Cincinnati and soon found that salt had greatly fallen in value, so I sold the salt, boat and cargo upon the best terms I could get. The result was a loss of about one hundred dollars. However, I had a very pleasant visit in Cincinnati with my brother Lampson, who was connected with the "Cincinnati Gazette." He was a member of the family of Mr. Charles Hammond, his daughter, and son-in-law Mr. L'Hommedieu. Mr. Hammond had been a warm friend of my father's and was certainly one of the ablest writers of his day and generation, as well as an accomplished lawyer. He was much pleased at my adventure and especially with my rough shoes and warm Kentucky jeans. He told me not to be discouraged. and flattered me with the statement that a young fellow who could, at fifteen years of age, do what I had done would make his way in the world.

At that time I saw Judge Burnett at his residence. He had been a colleague of my father on the supreme bench, and during all his manhood had been distinguished as a lawyer and a man of marked ability. He wore a long queue, preserved the habits of the gentleman of the old school, and was proud of being a Federalist. His book called "Burnett's Notes" is perhaps the most valuable collection of historical data pertaining to the early history of Ohio now extant.

At this time I visited what was called Powers' "Hell." My brother Lampson and I took the boatmen with us, and "Lamp.," who was fond of playing practical jokes, and knew the place better than I did, took care to warn one of the roughest of my boatmen to seize hold of a bar which was before him, and which "Lamp." knew would be charged later with electricity, and to hold on to it for dear life. We heard a rumbling sound inside, and finally saw flashes resembling lightning, and we naturally seized on whatever was before us to await the opening of "Hell." After more sheet lightning the veil was drawn aside and there were before us representatives of human beings in every attitude of agony. At the same moment the electric current was passed through certain bars before us, on one of which the boatman held a firm grip, but no sooner was he charged with electricity than his hair flew on end, he looked the picture of terror, shouted in a loud voice, "O, hell!" and broke for the door. Soon after we followed also, and that, to us, was the end of a scene that ought never to have been exhibited.

I returned to Beverly in a steamboat and soon settled all the bills of the salt speculation, but had to call upon Mr. McComb and my brother, Charles, for a small sum to make up the deficit. I repaid this sum later on, but Mr. McComb never failed, whenever I made a business proposition that seemed hazardous, to say, with a great haw-haw: "Well, John, that is one of your salt speculations."

The election in the fall of 1838 resulted in the choice of a Democratic governor and state legislature, which, according to the politics of the time, involved an entire change of state officials and employes. Mr. Wall became a member of the Board of Public Works, and was assigned, among other works, to the charge of the Muskingum improvement. In the course of a few months, I think about the last of June, 1839, Col. Curtis was removed, and Mr. Macaboy was appointed superintendent in his place. At first it was uncertain whether changes would be made in the subordinates of the corps. Some of its members had become so much attached to Col. Curtis that they thought it right and proper to send him a letter expressing in substance their regret at his removal, their high estimate of his services, and thanks for his kindness to them. This was signed by Mr. Coffinberry, Mr. Burwell, Mr. Love and myself. I am not certain that others did not express the same friendly feelings, but, at all events, the four whose names I have mentioned were summarily dropped from the service.

Thus, after two years of faithful work with small pay, I was, at the age of sixteen, turned adrift on account of politics.

I find among my papers, dingy with age, the correspondence with Col. Curtis, and also the subsequent correspondence between Mr. Wall and myself, in respect to my removal. My letter to Mr. Wall was a disclaimer of any intention of disrespect to him in our letter to Col. Curtis, and his reply was that we alleged that Col. Curtis was removed without a cause, which he denied. I have no doubt, from a present reading of the papers, but that he would have retained me as a juvenile offender if I had made a suitable apology, but the instinct of a boy to stand up for his party was too strong. I was a Whig of sixteen, and it was glorious to be a victim of persecution.

I also find among my papers of that time, which I thought worthy of preservation, a multitude of essays on as many different subjects, and some efforts at poetry, all of which I consign to flames. Most boys have had the same experience. The only benefit I derived was the habit I formed of writing upon such subjects as attracted my attention by reading, a habit I continued when studying law, in preparing a case for trial, and in preparation for a debate in Congress.

I returned at once to Lancaster. The great financial depression, commencing in 1837, was now at its height. It was said that Ohio State six per cent. bonds had been sold at fifty cents on the dollar. Many banks were embarrassed and refused to discount notes, while several failed, and their circulating notes became worthless. I found that Lancaster had especially suffered, that many of its leading business firms had suspended or were on the brink of failure. I was then in excellent health, tall and slender and willing to work. I received temporary employment from Dr. Kreider, who was either Clerk of the Court or Recorder of Deeds, I do not remember which. He gave me a dollar and a half a day, which I regarded as a great favor, but the records were soon made up and I had nothing to do.

It was at this period of my life that I fell into very bad habits. Many of the boys about my age who were with me at Howe's school were still about Lancaster, and were out of employment like myself. We would meet on the street, or at the post office, or some place of resort, to talk over old times, and got into the habit of drinking poor wine, mostly made of diluted whisky and drugs. The general habit of drinking spirits was then more common than now, but I had not been subject to this temptation, as Col. Curtis was very strict in prohibiting all such drinking. With the jolly good fellows I met at Lancaster who had nothing to do, I could not refuse to join in drinking the health of each other, and thus I was conscious frequently of being more or less intoxicated. On one occasion, in the fall of 1839, I went home very sick from drinking. My mother received me with much surprise and sorrow, but neither complained nor scolded, and, with the utmost kindness, put me to bed and watched over and cared for me. I was not stupid enough to be unconscious of my degradation and her affection, and then and there resolved never to be in such a condition again, and from that time to this I am not conscious of having been under the influence of liquor. I have partaken of wine and spirits at weddings, feasts and dinners, I have used it as a medicine, and in response to toasts and compliments, but never to an extent to addle my brain or disturb my walk.

At that time intemperance was a common vice. Of the young men who were my contemporaries a very large proportion became habitual drunkards and died prematurely. No reform in my time has been so general and beneficial as that of the disuse of drinking intoxicating liquors, commencing in 1841. Formerly liquors were put on the sideboard or table, and the invitation "take a drink" was as common then as "take a seat" is now. This method of treating was shared in by preachers of the Gospel, and by all who observed the courtesies of social life. Now these conditions have greatly changed. Whisky is banished to the drug store, the grocery and the saloon, and even there it is under surveillance and so highly taxed as to furnish a large proportion of the national revenue.

Some time in the autumn of 1839 I visited Mansfield for the first time, on some business for General Reese, and it was then arranged that early in the next spring I should return to study law with my brother Charles. Mansfield was then a very unattractive village, badly located on parallel ridges and valleys, but precisely in the center of the very large county of Richland, then containing 900 square miles. The county covered a part of the high table-land that separated the waters of Lake Erie and the Ohio River. It was an almost unbroken forest during the War of 1812, with a few families living in log houses, protected by block houses of logs from the incursions of Indians, many of whom lived in the county. After the war it was rapidly settled, chiefly from Pennsylvania, and divided into farms of 160 acres or less, according to the new congressional plan of townships six miles square, sections one mile square, and subdivisions of forty, eighty, and one hundred and sixty acres. The topography of the county was high and rolling, from 900 to 1,350 feet above the sea, with innumerable springs of the purest water, and small streams and creeks, all rising in the county and flowing north or south into the Muskingum or Sandusky Rivers. The timber was oak, sugar, elm, hickory and other deciduous trees. This valuable timber was the chief obstruction to the farmers. It had to be deadened or cut away to open up a clearing for the cabin and the field. The labor of two or three generations was required to convert it into the picturesque, beautiful and healthy region it now is.

The village of Mansfield has been converted into a flourishing city of more than 15,000 inhabitants, with extensive manufacturing establishments and a network of railroads reaching out to Cleveland, Chicago, Pittsburg, Columbus, Cincinnati and Indianapolis. There was no sign of this development when I first visited the place.

On my return to Lancaster I applied myself closely to study and reading, mainly of history. I read Hume, Smollett and Miller's histories of England, Gibbon's "Decline and Fall of the Roman Empire," and such histories of the United States as I could procure. It was at this time that the memorable "Log Cabin and Hard Cider Campaign" of 1840 commenced. General Harrison had been nominated in December, 1839, at Harrisburg, by the Whig party. He was a distinguished general in the War of 1812, but had lived mainly a quiet, modest life on his farm at South Bend, near Cincinnati. The Democratic papers ridiculed him as a feeble old man, living in a cabin and drinking hard cider. The Whigs turned these sarcasms with great effect upon their adversaries. They compared the old soldier and his excellent war record, living in a cabin with the latch string out and eating corn bread, with "Matty Van, the used up man," living in a palace, with roast beef every day, eating from silver plate, with gold spoons, and drawing a salary of $25,000 a year. This was no doubt demagoguism, but there was back of it the great questions of protection to American industries, sound and stable currency, and the necessity of economy in public expenditures. A great meeting was held in Columbus in February, 1840. In the procession were log cabins, filled with farmers and hauled by a number of horses and oxen, and hard cider was on tap for all who chose to drink. Songs were improvised, especially by Greiner, the poet of the canvass. One of these songs, with the refrain, "The Log Cabin Candidate will March to Washington," became famous and prophetic.

Some time in March, 1840, taking the stage for Mansfield, I saw signs of political excitement all along the way, even at that early period of the canvass. My sister Susan, two years younger than I, was with me. We met with no adventure worthy of notice until we arrived at our destination, when, in ascending the hill to the public square, the coach slipped and fell over on its side. This we considered a bad omen. It was not, however, an unusual accident, as the roads were always bad in March, and the coaches of that day not worthy of the name. We were heartily welcomed into the family of Robert McComb, who had married my sister, Amelia.

I was to study law, but under the laws of Ohio I could not be admitted to practice until J arrived at the age of twenty-one years. Our liberal laws presumed that a man of ordinary capacity could master this profession in two years. What was I to do during the two spare years? This question was left to the decision of my uncle, Judge Parker, husband of my father's only sister. He was a peculiar character, and, as I will have occasion to refer to him again, I will give of him a brief biography. He was born in Nova Scotia. His father was a merchant of some wealth who early decided that his son should be educated in Ohio, and chose for him the college at Athens. There young Parker not only received his collegiate diploma, but became thoroughly attached to western habits and opinions. He studied law with my father at Lancaster, and, when admitted to the bar, went to Mansfield, where he practiced law. He was genial, social, and especially fond of the society of young people. I have often seen him stop on the streets of Mansfield to watch boys playing marbles. He was conceded to be an able lawyer, perhaps the best land lawyer and special pleader in that part of Ohio. But he was not an advocate, partly owing to occasional stuttering, but in jury cases employed my father until the latter became a judge of the Supreme Court.

Mr. Parker had for some years before 1840 retired from active practice, and was engaged with Robert McComb as a general merchant. During, or about 1842, he was elected by the legislature of Ohio presiding judge of the Court of Common Pleas, and became eminently popular, and deservedly so. He was to be my guide and counselor.

A few words in regard to my brother, Charles Taylor, will explain our relations, the confidence he reposed in me, and my deep obligations to him. He was then a bachelor thirty years old, with quite a lucrative practice, mainly in collecting debts due to New York and other eastern merchants. Our banking system was then as bad as it could be, exchange on New York was always at premium, and there was no confidence in our local banks. Charles was substantially the banker in Mansfield and surrounding counties for eastern merchants. He was a good speaker when he addressed a judge, and his briefs were clear statements of the law of the case, but when forced to speak to a jury he was exceedingly shy and sensitive. He avoided jury trials. He was a fair speaker on popular topics, and took great interest in current politics as a Whig. He was a member of the Harrisburg convention that nominated General Harrison for President, and made several creditable speeches in that canvass. He was married in the fall of 1840 to Miss Elizabeth Williams, of Dayton, Ohio, and I became a member of his family soon after.

The influence of the special traits and tendencies of Judge Parker and my brother Charles upon my life was soon manifest. My course of study, outlined by Judge Parker, commenced with Blackstone, followed soon after by Coke on Littleton. As a compromise I was allowed to read Kent's Commentaries, but Chitty's Pleadings had to go along with Kent. The disinclination of Charles to have anything to do with contested litigation became more marked, and I was compelled, long before my admission to the bar, to look after such cases as grew out of his practice. The pleadings then in vogue were the declarations, pleas and replications of the English common law. These I prepared after I had been a student for a year, and, in cases within the jurisdiction of a justice of the peace, I habitually appeared either in prosecution or defense.

As a matter of course, I was often outwitted and defeated, much to my chagrin. In one case submitted to arbitration, a pettifogger of bad repute by the name of Baldwin secured an award palpably unjust. I felt more keenly than my client the injustice done him, and never forgave Baldwin until he was indicted for perjury and driven out of the county in disgrace.

While pursuing my studies, I was able in various ways to make enough money to support myself. I wrote deeds and agreements, and drew the first map of Richland county, showing subdivisions in farms, the course of creeks and rivulets, and roads. I was also employed to collect small debts, and, towards the close of my probation, I was intrusted with large collections, one of which was in closing the business of an old firm with outstanding credits of more than $20,000.

In those days of primitive barter the merchant was the banker of all the farmers dealing with him. The farmer sold to the merchant most of his surplus products, including live stock and pork, and purchased all his supplies, mainly of clothing, tea, coffee, and the like, and the merchant made advances on the growing crop. At the close of a year the account was settled, generally with a balance in favor of the merchant. Little money was used. It was a traffic in commodities. It was not unusual for the merchant to drive horses and cattle to Pittsburg or further east, and send the proceeds to the eastern merchant.

In the fall of the year it was quite common for the farmer to load upon his wagon his surplus wheat and haul it fifty miles to Sandusky and Milan, receiving in return salt and farming implements, and the balance in money. Wheat was then the chief production of the farm, and was about the only article that would command cash. At this season the highway was often blocked with long trains of wagons that would not give way for other vehicles. At night the wagons would be parked on the roadside near a creek, and the farmers and their boys would have a regular joyous picnic on provisions brought from home. This was the life of a farmer before the days of railroads, and I am not sure but it was a more happy one than now. Then the village blacksmith or shoemaker, the tinker, the carpenter and the mechanic of every trade had his shop and was a far more important and independent citizen than now, when grouped into large manufacturing and machine works.

While a student, I was frequently sent by my brother to Wooster, the nearest bank, with large sums of money to purchase exchange on New York for his clients. These trips I always made on horseback. Once, as I was to start quite early in the morning, I received nearly $2,000 in bills the night before, in two packages, and placed them in my overcoat. In the morning I threw my overcoat over my arm and went for my horse. Before mounting I felt for the money and found it was gone. I started in alarm for the house and on my way found one package of $1,000 lying on the sidewalk at the

corner of the street where I had passed, but the other was
nowhere to be seen. I felt sure it was picked up by some one.
I at once gave notice to my brother, and he took immediate
measures to trace the finder. I cannot express the chagrin
and anxiety which I suffered on account of my carelessness,
but Charles uttered no reproach, but prepared to replace the
loss. Fortunately within a month the lost money was traced
to an "early drunkard," who found the package on the pave-
ment while going for his morning grog. He was watched and
at night was seen to take some money from his trunk. A
search warrant soon led to the restoration of the money, except
a small sum he had spent. This incident attached me the
more to my brother.

The social life in Mansfield, while I was a student, was very
pleasant and instructive. The freedom, and yet propriety of
intercourse among the young people, was notable. We had
social meetings, parties, dances, and an occasional ball during
the winter, but in summer, riding in carriages and on horseback
was the recreation of the day. Fleming's Ravine, about five
miles from Mansfield, was the general gathering place for young
and old. A small stream had cut a deep ravine with rocky
banks on either side. An old mill with its overshot wheel
spanned the ravine and filled it with noisy rattle. The adjacent
woods, where the fire was lit and the coffee made, and the farm
lands stretching beyond, made a picturesque scene often described and always admired. Here we had dances, frolics, speeches and fun, with healthy exercise in the open air. These frolics
were often made the subject of description in the newspapers.
On a notable occasion of one of these visits to Fleming's Ravine, Mr. Franklin Barker, a law student, wrote for one of the
local papers a pleasing description of the scene under the name
of "The Fairy's Tale." He paraphrased Byron as follows:

> "There was a sound of revelry by *day*
> And Richland's capital gathered then
> Her beauty and her chivalry and fair eyes
> Looked love to eyes that spoke again."

Many of the persons present were named, or so described as
to be recognized. There was a good deal of egotism and

assumption in the narrative which created much feeling among those who had not the good fortune to attend. Though I was present, and greatly enjoyed the picnic, I thought it was a good opportunity to prick the bubble of self esteem assumed by Barker, and wrote for the rival newspaper a counter description signed "A Looker On." This excited a good deal of interest at the time, but it has probably faded, after half a century, from the memory of the few who survive; it then created a rivalry and left its mark upon the future. The destruction of the mill by a flood, the cutting away of the wood and other causes, have changed this, so that the gathering place of the young of my day is a thing of the past.

During my study of law, the bar at Mansfield was considered a very able one, including among its members James Stewart, Thomas W. Bartley, Jacob Brinkerhoff, Charles Sherman and others. All of those named became judges, either of the courts of Ohio or of the United States. During the same period there were also many law students in the offices of these gentlemen, among them Samuel J. Kirkwood, George W. Geddes, Thomas H. Ford, Henry C. Hedges, Willard Slocum, Joseph Newman, Patrick Hull and others, who afterwards became distinguished in civil or military life. These students, myself among the number, organized a moot court, presided over by Joseph Newman, then in active practice as a partner of Mr. Stewart. We held famous moot courts in which cases were tried with all the earnestness, industry and skill that could have been evoked by real cases. In these trials Mr. Kirkwood and I were usually pitted against each other, although he studied late in life, and was then more than thirty years old. He was then a Democrat, but moved to Iowa in 1856, became a Republican war governor of that state and United States Senator. I have always regarded our contests in this moot court as the most important part of my legal training.

The course of study pursued under the direction of Judge Parker continued until my admission to the bar, though much interrupted by the variety and nature of my employment. I read, in addition to the routine works prescribed by Judge Parker, a great variety of literary and historical works, and had substantially practiced my profession a year or more in advance of my admission to the bar.

I arrived at the age of twenty-one on the 10th day of May, 1844, and promptly on time on that day I was presented to the Supreme Court "on the circuit," then sitting at Springfield, Ohio, for admission to the bar. Several other students were presented, and, according to the custom of that time, we were all referred to a committee composed of General Samson Mason, Hon. Charles Anthony and one other lawyer whose name I do not recall. All were leading lawyers of that place, and had been busily occupied in the court. We met that evening at the office of one of these gentlemen to pass the ordeal for which we had been preparing for years. A few questions were put to us which were answered, when some question was asked, the answer to which led to a decided difference of opinion among the examiners, and a practical suspension of our examination. It soon occurred to them that they were more interested in the cases coming on "to-morrow" than in our efficiency as incipient lawyers. I was asked under whom I studied. I answered Judge Parker, and they all agreed that anyone who was certified by him ought to be admitted.

My old and dearest friend, and boon companion, Dr. J. C. Buckingham, of Springfield, was then entering upon his profession. He was an admirable penman. He obtained leave of the clerk of the court, to write out my certificate of admission as a member of the bar, and this he did in beautiful form, handsomely illustrated. He attached to it an enormous seal, and it was duly signed by the clerk of the court. I have kept it as a memento of him, but have never had occasion to present it to anyone. He, poor fellow, died prematurely at Springfield, when in the full employment of his duties as a physician, and with the most hopeful prospects of success in his profession.

I must not forget that in my boyhood days I had a strong penchant for military parade. I remember well the respect always shown to the Revolutionary veterans, who survived to the period of my boyhood. At every meeting, political or otherwise, where these soldiers appeared to share in the assemblage of citizens, they were received with profound respect.

Hats came off. They were given the best seats, and every mark of honor was shown them. What boy did not feel the gushings of patriotic emotion when one of these old veterans appeared upon the stage. To a less degree, similar marks of respect were shown to the soldiers of the War of 1812; but, though this was as great and important an event in our history, it did not light the spark of patriotic fire like the Revolutionary War.

Before the war for the Union broke out, military spirit died away, especially in Ohio. Military organizations had fallen into disuse and popular contempt. We had, it is true, in times far apart, what were called militia musters, but Jack Falstaff's regiment was nothing to our militia. I had the honor to be a member of the staff of Colonel Urie, of Ashland, when the venerable General Wilson was the Commander-in-Chief of the militia of that part of Ohio. He was a hero of the War of 1812, and, as I remember, a gallant and fine-looking old gentleman. The regiment—so called—without guns, uniform, or anything proper for a soldier, was with some difficulty formed into line, but a wavering line, across the public square at Mansfield and along East and West Market streets, when, by some misunderstanding of orders, the right of the regiment marched to the right, and the left to the left. With some difficulty, and a good deal of swearing, they were brought back into line and dismissed. Militia day was a day of drunkenness and fighting. No wonder that years passed without muster. Such was the military condition of the United States when the War of the Rebellion sounded the tocsin of alarm, and our generation was called upon to meet the gravest struggle in American history.

CHAPTER III.

OHIO, ITS HISTORY AND RESOURCES.

Occupation by the Indians — Washington's Expedition to the Head of the Ohio
River — Commencement of the History of the State — Topography, Character-
istics, etc., in 1787 — Arrival of the First Pioneers — The Treaty of Green-
ville — Census of 1802 Showed a Population of 45,028 Persons —
Occupation of the "Connecticut Reserve" — Era of Internal
Improvement — Value of Manufactures in 1890 — Vast
Resources of the Buckeye State — Love of the
"Ohio Man" for His Native State.

THE life of a man is greatly influenced by the place of his birth, the surroundings of his boyhood, and the habits and customs of the community in which he lived. As I have been all my life a resident of Ohio, and for more than forty years have been one of its represen- tatives in Congress, or the Cabinet, I feel that a brief sketch of the history and resources of the state may not be out of place in this biography. No adequate history of the state has been written, though many works have given general outlines. The materials are copious, but I can only state a few events that mark the changes in its civilization. That it was once occu- pied by a race now entirely extinct is evidenced by numerous mounds, earthworks and lines of fortifications so extensive as to have required to construct them a dense population with a knowledge of mathematics far beyond that of any tribe or race existing on the American continent, when discovered by Colum- bus. The works of the mound builders can be seen, and have been described, but no ray of light has been cast upon, or plausible suggestion made to account for, the origin, existence or disappearance of this race.

Long after the settlement on the Atlantic Coast of the Thir- teen Colonies, the territory now included in the State of Ohio was a part of a vast unknown region north and west of the Ohio River. It was roamed over by numerous tribes of In- dians living in tents of bark or skins, whose residence was

(56)

generally as transitory as that of the wandering tribes of Arabia. Many of these Indian tribes were composed of a few families under the domination of a chief who went out from his kindred as Abraham did, and planted his tents where fancy led him, and moved at his whim or with his game. Every one of the Indian tribes that had been driven by the white man from the east and the south chose his camping and hunting grounds in the region of the O-hi-o, often driving away a weaker tribe. Their contests with white men had given them some knowledge of fire-arms, and some of them had been marshaled under arms in the wars between the English and the French, but, as a rule, the Indians encountered by our race since the landing at Jamestown were all of the same type of wandering savages. The difference between these tribes can be accounted for by their location, whether on the seashore or in the forest or plain, and by the strength of the tribe, from the powerful Six Nations to the feeble band in possession of some chosen valley.

Whatever may be said of the irrepressible conflicts between the white man and the Indians, waged often with savage and relentless cruelties on both sides, it may as truly be said that the same savage conflicts have been carried on between the different tribes of Indians, which often ended by the extermination of the weaker tribe, or the absorption of the feeble remnant with the stronger tribe. This was certainly the case with the Indian tribes of the northwest territory. Ohio was the battleground for destructive warfare between the Indian tribes long before the white man gained a foothold on its soil.

In 1755, when the war with France commenced, the English settlements covered the Atlantic Coast, but did not extend across the Alleghany Mountains, though a few hardy pioneers may have wandered into the wilderness beyond. But French missionaries, inspired with religious zeal, had penetrated all the northwest territory, including the great lakes. In 1673 Marquette and Joliet, two of these missionaries, after years spent with the Indians on the shores of the lakes, winning their confidence by humility and care, followed the lines of the Fox and Wisconsin Rivers from the shores of Lake Michigan, and discovered the great river "with a joy that could not be expressed," and floated upon its waters to the mouth of the Arkansas.

It is impossible to read the interesting narratives of these missionaries, of their life among the Indians of the northwest, and their enthusiastic description of the new and wonderful land they had discovered, without a feeling of admiration and reverence. The adventures and trials of these zealous priests read like romance; but their description of natural scenes, of great rivers, mountains and plains, now familiar to fifteen million of people, attest the accuracy of their statements and the courage and zeal with which they pursued their task.

The discovery of Marquette was diligently followed by Chevalier de la Salle, a knight of fortune, of wonderful endurance, who, after overcoming incredible difficulties, conducted an expedition by the way of the lakes and the Mississippi River to its mouth. Thus the King of France, by the piety and zeal of a priest and the courage of an adventurer, was able to base his claims to fully half the continent of North America upon grounds recognized as valid by European law, namely, the discovery of the St. Lawrence, the occupation of Canada, and the discovery of the Mississippi from its source to its mouth. The great body of the continent is drained by these two rivers. Their discovery and occupation was sufficient at that time to give to France the right of exclusive possession of that vast territory, for the title of the Indian tribes was not considered valid by Christian powers. While the priests of France were seeking to save the souls of the Indians, the Kings of France were seeking to rob them of their property.

The French, during this period, erected a line of posts from the mouth of the Mississippi, by way of the Wabash, Maumee and the lakes, to Montreal, and finally, in 1753, established a line of posts from Lake Erie to the junction of the Monongahela and Alleghany Rivers, where Pittsburg now stands, and claimed the whole country north of the Ohio from its source to its mouth.

And here, for the first time, comes into view the majestic form of George Washington, then a young man of twenty-two. He was sent by Governor Dinwiddie, of Virginia, to visit the several Indian tribes at the head of the Ohio River and the French forces at Venango. In the dead of winter he made his trip into the wilderness, and soon ascertained that it was the fixed purpose of the French authorities to occupy all the country to the sources of the Ohio, including a large section of what is now a part of Pennsylvania and New York. The commander, St. Pierre, declared his purpose of seizing every Englishman within the Ohio Valley. The result of the expedition of Washington left no choice to the English government, except to abandon their claim to the northwest territory, or to declare war. The English title was based upon their occupation of the shores of the Atlantic coast from Massachusetts to Georgia. It was claimed that this occupation carried the right to possession westward from sea to sea.

In the earliest grants to the colonies, especially to Virginia and Connecticut, their western boundaries extended to the South Sea. Where the South Sea lay, and what was the breadth of the continent, was not defined by these kingly grants. James I and his councilors then knew but little about America. There was no way to settle this disputed title between the two great powers but by war. A Virginia company had built a fort on the south side of the Ohio, below the site of the present city of Pittsburg. In 1754 the French troops occupied the point at the junction of the Monongahela and Alleghany, where the city of Pittsburg now is, and erected a fort.

Then followed the well-known war of the French and English, Braddock's defeat, the heroism of Washington, the capture of Quebec and the cession of Canada and the northwestern territory to Great Britain. It is impossible to overrate the importance of these events upon the future of America. The result was that the region east of the Mississippi River and north of the Ohio River was the property of Great Britain and the inheritance of the English race. The great northwest was theirs, and fairly won.

The extinction of the French title to the Ohio territory was at once followed by the claims of several colonies to parts of this territory under grants from the British crown; but the English government declared all the land west of the sources

of the Atlantic rivers as under the dominion of the king for
the use of the Indians, and all persons were forbidden to settle
or remain within it.   This dispute was postponed by the War
of the Revolution.   An event during the war, apparently of
small importance, had a controlling influence in securing to the
United States the northwestern territory.

The State of Virginia, claiming title under a grant from the
British crown to the regions west of the Alleghanies, in 1778,
organized an expedition, under Colonel George Rogers Clarke,
to punish and repel incursions of Indians, and capture the old
French posts then held by the English.   This he accomplished,
so that when negotiations for peace were entered upon in 1782
our plenipotentiaries could maintain the title of the United
States to the northwestern territory, not only by grants to the
English colonies, but by conquest in war, and actual possession
at the time of the negotiations.   The British insisted on making the Ohio River a boundary of the United States.   Mr.
Adams said that sooner than yield the western territory he
would exhort his countrymen to continue the war as long as
they could keep a soldier in the field.   Mr. Jay was equally
determined, and finally the line of the lakes was agreed to.

The treaty of peace recognized the St. Lawrence, the lakes
and the 49th parallel of latitude as the dividing line between
the United States and Canada.   But the question arose whether
the western territory was the property of the United States as
the result of their joint struggle for independence, or of the
several states under the grants of the English crown.   This
dangerous controversy delayed the formation of the federal
government; but it was happily settled by the cession of the
territory to the United States, with or without conditions and
reservations, by the several states claiming western lands.

As a part of this cession and settlement, and almost equal
in importance to the constitution of the United States, was the
celebrated ordinance organizing the northwestern territory.
This ordinance guaranteed the subdivision of the territory into
states, and secured to them, by a perpetual compact, the forms
and substance of a republican government, a proper disposition
of the public lands, and the formal prohibition of slavery in

the territories, and may be properly considered the commencement of the history of the State of Ohio.

We may here pause to consider the condition, topography and characteristics of the Territory, now the State, of Ohio in 1787, when the first territorial government was organized by Congress. It was bounded on the south and east by the Ohio River, touching on its northeast border the States of Pennsylvania and New York; on the north by Lake Erie, and on the west by an arbitrary line not then defined, and contained about 40,000 square miles. Its topography may be described as an elevated plain, its highest elevation being 1,540 feet above the sea, its lowest depression being 440 feet above the sea, and its mean altitude about 800 feet above the sea. It is traversed by the comb of a watershed between the river and the lakes, running from northeast to southwest across the state, much nearer the lake than the river, at an elevation above the sea of from 1,000 to 1,300 feet. The shed on either side is penetrated by rivers of clear, pure water, in valleys of great fertility, and usually with hillsides of a gentle slope and fertile soil.

In 1787 it was an unbroken wilderness covered with great forests and sparsely inhabited by savage tribes of Indians, only here and there tempered by the civilizing teachings of the missionary. One of the earliest descriptions I find of the famous Miami Valley is as follows:

" The land beyond the Scioto, except the first twenty miles, is rich and level, bearing walnut trees of huge size, the maple, the wild cherry and the ash; full of little streams and rivulets; variegated by beautiful natural prairies, covered with wild rye, blue grass and white clover. Turkeys abounded, and deer and elks, and most sorts of game; of buffaloes, thirty or forty were frequently seen feeding in one meadow. Nothing is wanting but cultivation to make this a most delightful country."

This favored land was thrown open for settlement at a time when the people of the states had been impoverished by the war, when there was neither money, credit nor commerce, when the government of the Continental Congress had fallen into contempt, and the new government was passing the ordeal of a vote in states jealous of each other. It was the only land subject to sale by the United States, for Kentucky was covered by Virginia grants, Western New York was the property of land companies, and all beyond was a *terra incognita.* There was a struggle for Ohio land among all the northern states, including Virginia and Maryland. Companies were formed, composed mostly of officers and soldiers of the Revolutionary War, to secure from Congress favorable land grants. Virginia and Connecticut had their ample reserves, New York had a large unoccupied region in her own territory, and the other northern states demanded their shares in the common property of the United States. The result was that all the states established settlements in Ohio, and, for the first time in our history, the descendants of the Puritans of New England, the Dutch of New York, the Germans and Scotch-Irish of Pennsylvania, the Jersey Blues, the Catholics of Maryland, the Cavaliers of Virginia and the loyal refugees of Canada united their blood and fortunes in establishing a purely American state on the soil of Ohio.

Among these early settlers were the foremost men of all the states, the Revolutionary stock that won independence, who carried their love of liberty and the principles and instincts of their localities to a soil more fertile than any of the old states, and with natural resources, climate and facilities for settlement and cultivation as favorable as any within their reach. The limits of this sketch will not permit details of the progress of this migration. The first difficulty it encountered was the toilsome way to the promised land. All roads, such as they were, crossed the Alleghany Mountains, or followed the longer route by the lakes. A voyage now easily made in a day then occupied sixty days on foot or on horseback, and every article of civilized life had to be transported with painful labor over rude paths and roads, relieved sometimes by barges and canoes on creeks and rivers.

When the first pioneers reached their destination, their land was already occupied. Every part of Ohio was then in the possession of Indians. The war they had maintained with the pioneers of Kentucky only prepared them for the desperate struggle with new invaders. The first settlement of the New England colony was made in Marietta, April, 1788. From that day to the close of the war with Great Britain in 1815 there were hostilities in some part of Ohio with the Indians. There is not a county in Ohio that was not at some time the scene of a battle with the Indians, or a skirmish, or a massacre.

The interesting "Historical Collections," recently published by Henry Howe, give many details of this local warfare. But, aside from the danger that lurked at all times over the cabin of the pioneer, there were more regular battles with the Indians fought on the soil of Ohio than in any other state of the Union. The defeat of General Harmer with 1,300 men, in 1790, in two battles in the Scioto valley, laid open to predatory warfare all the settlements in Ohio, and some in Kentucky. Every attempt at negotiation was defeated by British interference.

In the following year, 1791, a force of over 2,000 men was organized at Cincinnati under General St. Clair, and marched against the Indians at the head waters of the Maumee. While encamped they were attacked by the Indians and ignominiously defeated, losing a large number of officers and men. They retreated in disorder, abandoning their baggage and artillery, and throwing away their arms and accoutrements. The loss in this disastrous campaign was more than 900 men, of whom 600 were killed. This calamity spread terror throughout all the settlements as far as Pittsburg, and arrested for a time the migration to Ohio.

The successive defeats of Harmer and St. Clair greatly impressed General Washington with the necessity of marching an overwhelming force against the Indians, and he appealed to Congress for the necessary aid; but there was a manifest reluctance in Congress to vote supplies, even if the failure to do so involved the abandonment to the Indians of all the territory northwest of the Ohio. The supplies, however, were granted, and General Wayne, a Revolutionary hero, was placed in command.

In August, 1794, with a force of over 3,000 men, he advanced to the confluence of the Maumee and the Auglaize, and there destroyed the Indian villages and their abundant crops.

Following the Indians down the Maumee to a fort recently built by the British, the forces of General Wayne attacked the

Indians and inflicted upon them a disastrous defeat. This victory settled forever the occupancy of this territory by the white man, and the irreversible fate of the poor Indian, though, as it will appear hereafter, he struggled for this, his favorite region, for twenty years more.

In looking back over a period of one hundred years it is impossible to suppress a sense of injustice, and a feeling of sympathy for the Indian in his unequal struggle. After their defeat by General Wayne, a general conference of all the Indian tribes in the northwest was proposed, and agreed upon, to be held during the following year at Greenville. The full details of this conference are given by Judge Burnet, in his "Notes on the Northwestern Territory." General Wayne, in many "council fires," explained to the chiefs of the numerous tribes the terms of the treaties made at Forts McIntosh and Harmer, and demanded that they be ratified with additional concessions and grants. Many of the replies, in the figurative language of the Indians, are eloquent appeals to their "Great Father" and their "Elder Brothers" to allow them to possess in peace the land of their fathers; that they were not represented when these treaties were made, and that their terms had not been observed by their white brethren.

It was the same old story of injustice and wrong, of might against right. They were compelled to accept the terms offered them. The result was the cession by the Indians to the United States of 25,000 square miles of southern and eastern Ohio and many other tracts west of Ohio. The Indians were to receive in return $20,000 in presents, and an annuity of $9,500, to be distributed among the tribes. By this treaty confidence was restored to the settlements, and the tide of migration was renewed, and continued until the breaking out of the War of 1812. But the treaty of Greenville did not put an end to Indian hostilities. They still occupied northwestern Ohio, and that part of the reserve west of the Cuyahoga River. Occasional aggressions by both races led to outrages and murder, usually followed by encroachments on Indian territory. In 1805 the remainder of the Western Reserve was ceded by treaty. In 1818 the northwest part of Ohio was purchased by the United

MR. SHERMAN AT THE AGE OF TWENTY-THREE.

States by treaty, subject to certain reservations, all of which were subsequently ceded to the United States, the last by the Wyandots in 1842, when the remnant, about 700 souls, moved to Kansas.

The most important, and by far the most dangerous, conspiracy of Indians since the treaty of Greenville was organized by the "Prophet," a crazy enthusiast denounced as an impostor and accused of witchcraft, and his brother, Tecumseh, a warrior of approved courage, possessed of all the craft of the Indian, with remarkable intelligence and comprehensive views. They united most of the tribes who had participated in that treaty, and threatened with death all the chiefs who were concerned in the subsequent treaties. This excited the attention of General Harrison, then Governor of the Territory of Indiana, who, in 1811, after many ineffectual conferences with Tecumseh and the "Prophet," organized a force of 800 men and marched against the "Prophet's" town, in what is now Cass county, Indiana. The battle of Tippecanoe ensued, in which the Indians were totally defeated and the town burned. The loss of the troops was so great that General Harrison made a speedy retreat. The war with Great Britain soon followed, and Tecumseh entered the British service. He participated in most of the battles in Ohio and Michigan during that war, and was killed at the battle of the Thames on the 5th of October, 1813. With him ended all organized Indian hostilities in Ohio.

Prior to 1798 all the laws governing the northwestern territory were selected from the laws of the states by the territorial judges appointed by the President. In that year it was ascertained that the territory contained 5,000 white male inhabitants, when they were authorized, as a matter of right, to organize and elect representatives to a general assembly, who, with a legislative council, were authorized to pass laws, subject to the veto of the governor. The general assembly was duly organized on the 16th of September, 1799, and was remarkable for the ability and distinction of its members, most of whom had been soldiers in the Revolutionary War. This was the beginning of home rule in Ohio. The life of the territorial legislature was brief. Early in January, 1802, a census was taken

of the inhabitants in the eastern division of the Territory, now
the State of Ohio, by which it was found that it contained
45,028 persons. Congress promptly authorized the people to
form a constitution and state government. This authority was
speedily acted upon, a convention of thirty-five members was
elected, and a constitution adopted November, 1802, without
being submitted to the people.

This constitution remained unaltered in a single particular
for fifty years. It was regarded at the time, and ever since, as
a model framework of state government, clear and brief in its
provisions, but comprehensive enough to meet the necessities
of a people growing in population from 45,000 to 1,980,329 in
1850. The present constitution of Ohio was framed by a convention, which met at Columbus, on the 6th of May, 1850, and
adjourned on the 10th of March, 1851. This constitution was
ratified by a majority of the people, and is still in force.

The decennial growth of the population of Ohio is here
shown:

1802	45,028
1810	230,760
1820	381,295
1830	937,903
1840	1,519,467
1850	1,980,329
1860	2,339,511
1870	2,665,260
1880	3,198,062
1890	3,672,316

In 1802 Ohio was the eighteenth in rank among her sister
states; in 1810 the thirteenth; in 1820 the fifth; in 1830 the
fourth; in 1840 the third, and so continued until the recent
census, when the marvelous growth of Chicago placed Illinois
in advance of Ohio. This remarkable growth was accompanied
by rapid changes in the habits and conditions of the people.
Within a century they had their struggle with the Indians;
then their contest with nature in a new country covered by
forests—the "age of the pioneers;" then the period of internal
improvements, when roads and canals and means of transportation were the great objects of desire; then the marvelous

development of railroads, followed by manufactures. These
changes, following in succession, are the most striking features of the history of Ohio. I have already referred to the
pioneers who planted the first settlement, who bore the brunt
of Indian warfare, and firmly founded free institutions in
Ohio.

After this period, and the organization of the state government, the great migration to Ohio commenced which, within a
century, was destined to extend across the continent. The
settler was generally poor, bringing all his earthly possessions,
with wife and children, in a covered wagon, slowly traversing
difficult roads to the new and only land, then open to settlement. But the land was cheap, the title clear, the soil good,
and all were on the same footing, willing to help each other.
The task before him was discouraging. He found his quarter-
section in the unbroken forest, its boundary blazed on the
trees by the surveyor, and all around him a wilderness. His
first work was to erect a rough cabin of logs for a shelter ; his
next to clear an opening for a crop. Every new settler was a
welcome neighbor, though miles away. The mail, the newspaper, the doctor and the preacher were long in coming. In
this solitary contest with nature the settler had often to rely
upon his gun for food, upon simple remedies for new and
strange diseases, and upon the hope that his crop would be
spared from destruction by wild beasts.

This was the life of the early settler in every county in
Ohio, as each in its turn was organized and opened to settlement. A life so hard, was yet so attractive that many
pioneers, when a few neighbors gathered around them, preferred to sell their clearings and push further into the wilderness. In the meantime the older settlements attracted
newcomers. Mechanics and tradesmen came among them.
Then towns sprang up, and incipient cities, with corner lots
and hopeful speculations, tempted eastern capitalists to invest
their money in Ohio.

Ohio, in these early days, was the only outlet of the population of the northern and middle states. Emigrants from the
south, following lines of latitude, went into Kentucky and

Tennessee. The great west, with its vast prairies and plains, was not then accessible. Had it been so, the forests of Ohio might have been left in solitude for many years to come. During all this period, which we may properly call the pioneer stage, the settlers had no market for their produce, except to supply the demand of incoming immigrants. Grain and fruit would not bear the expense of transportation. The only way to obtain ready money was to convert corn and grain into hogs, horses and cattle, which were driven on the hoof to Pittsburg and eastern cities. But little money circulated, and that was chiefly irredeemable bank notes. The clothing of the people was mainly of linsey-woolsey, home-made. The spinning wheel, big and little, was to be found in every household. Settlers near the banks of the Ohio River, and its tributaries, had the advantage of floating their surplus products in rough barges down the Ohio to New Orleans for a market, so that the southern part of the state advanced rapidly, while the northern part was still in the possession of the Indians.

When the Indian title was extinguished settlers came from Pennsylvania into the counties immediately west of it, which are still, in the habits of the people, in the location of houses and barns and the cultivation of the soil, the precise counterpart of the region from which the settlers came. The "Connecticut Reserve" was slowly filled by the northern route of the lakes, almost exclusively from New England, and the habits and customs of that region were transported to their new homes, so that the "Western Reserve" to-day is a striking type of old Connecticut in habits, and with the same ideas. The lakes became the highway of commerce, and the inhabitants of the interior carried their surplus grain and produce in long lines of wagons to the new towns along the lake shore, where it was exchanged for the necessaries of life and enough money to pay taxes. All trade in the interior was by barter with merchants, who became the bankers of the people.

The construction of the Erie Canal, and the introduction of steamboats on the rivers and lakes, was the beginning of a great revolution. Then followed in Ohio the era of internal improvement by the construction of two lines of canal across the state, one from Cleveland, on Lake Erie, to Portsmouth, on the Ohio River, and the other from Toledo, on Maumee Bay, to the city of Cincinnati, with the lateral canal to Pittsburg, and the improvement of the Muskingum River by locks and canals.

Salmon P. Chase, then a young attorney at Cincinnati, in his introduction to his compilation of the laws of the state, published in 1833, thus describes the effect of these improvements upon the prosperity of Ohio:

"They have afforded to the farmer of the interior an easy access to market, and have enhanced the value of his farm and his productions. They have facilitated intercourse between different sections of the state, and have thus tended to make the people more united, as well as more prosperous. They have furnished to the people a common object of generous interest and satisfaction. They have attracted a large accession of population and capital. And they have made the name and character of Ohio well-known throughout the civilized world, as a name and character of which her sons may be justly proud."

This period of prosperity continued for twenty years, when, in 1846, a still greater revolution was introduced by the building of railroads. The first object of this was to furnish cheaper transportation of the produce of the farmer to the Ohio River and Lake Erie. The first railroads were from the interior, north and south. They were little better than tramways, supported by cross-ties with longitudinal stringpieces covered with thin strips of iron. The carriages were propelled by feeble engines, and it was thought a matter of great importance when, by this new motive power, a bushel of wheat could be transported from the interior to distances of from fifty to a hundred miles for from six to ten cents. While a young attorney, I thought it a grievous injustice that my client, one of the new railroad companies, was compelled by a jury to pay $2,000 for the right-of-way over twenty miles of farm land. It was soon discovered that railroads were to be so successful that they would supersede for the transportation of persons and passengers all kinds of water transportation, and that lines running long distances east and west would have the benefit of the through travel and traffic. In rapid succession several lines of railroad were built from the eastern cities across the state to the northwest, west and southwest. Within twenty years from the first construction of railways they had almost superseded all former modes of communication, and had reduced the rates of travel and transportation to less than one-half of the former rates.

After the close of the Civil War the construction of railroads rapidly increased, so that in 1890 the total miles of railway track in Ohio was 10,464, and the valuation for taxes was $102,950,642, a development in a single branch of industry far greater than in any other. This improvement led to the adoption of a system of free turnpikes in most of the counties in Ohio, constructed by local taxation, so that now Ohio is as well supplied with well-constructed turnpikes and railroads as any state in the Union, and perhaps, as well as many European states.

Another great change in the industry of the people of Ohio rapidly followed the construction of railroads. Manufacturing establishments of almost every kind were rapidly constructed, mostly since the war.

It appears by censuses, prior to 1890, that in 1850 the total value of manufactures of Ohio was $62,692,279; in 1860 it was $121,000,000; in 1870 it was $269,713,610; in 1880 it was $348,298,300. In 1890 it was over $500,000,000. During the single year 1889 there were incorporated over 400 new companies with a capital stock of $25,584,500. Almost every article needed for use by the people is thus produced at home, and great quantities of machinery, especially of farming machines of every variety, are exported to every state in the Union and to many foreign countries. The manufacturing industry has thus become second only to that of agriculture, and it is believed that, under the great impetus given by our protective laws, the time is not far distant when the value of manufactured products will be equal to, or greater than, the productions of the farm.

The most striking result of the change in the industries of Ohio is the rapid increase of city population, compared with

farming population. The following table will show the population of twenty cities, by the censuses of 1850 and 1890:

	1850.	1890.
Akron	3,266	27,601
Canton	2,603	26,189
Chillicothe	7,100	11,288
Cincinnati	115,435	296,908
Columbus	17,882	88,150
Cleveland	17,034	261,353
Dayton	10,977	61,220
Findlay	1,256	18,553
Hamilton	3,210	17,565
Ironton	.....	10,939
Lima	757	15,987
Mansfield	3,557	13,473
Newark	3,654	15,286
Portsmouth	4,011	12,394
Sandusky	5,087	18,471
Springfield	5,108	31,895
Steubenville	6,140	13,394
Tiffin	2,718	10,801
Toledo	3,829	81,434
Zanesville	7,929	21,009
	221,553	1,053,910

While the aggregate population of Ohio has increased 185
per cent. since 1850, that of the cities named has increased 475
per cent.

The growth of cities and manufactures has been accompanied by the discovery and development of a diversity of
mineral resources of great and increasing value.

The mining of coal was insignificant in 1850, while the
product of coal in 1890 is estimated at exceeding 12,000,000 tons.

Recently petroleum was discovered near Marietta and Lima,
places in Ohio remote from each other, thus supplying a new
element for commerce and a new agent for manufactures. Its
properties and innumerable uses have already been tested in
Pennsylvania. The annual supply by the census of 1890 was
12,471,466 barrels, second only to that of Pennsylvania, and has
not yet reached its maximum.

About the same period came the discovery of natural gas at Findlay, in Hancock and surrounding counties. This subtle and mysterious creation of nature has been applied locally as fuel for manufactures, and as light and heat in many cities and towns. The duration of its supply, however, cannot be determined.

The lakes on the north and the river on the south secure to the people of Ohio cheap water transportation for the importation and exportation of raw materials and finished products, while the physical features of the country north and south of Ohio, in a measure, compelled the construction of the great routes of railway over its soil.

From the beginning Ohio has taken a leading part in furnishing facilities for education to the rising generation. In early days, when the population was sparse and scattered, day schools were established, by voluntary effort, in counties, towns and neighborhoods where the population was sufficient to justify it. At an early period the State of Ohio established the common-school system, by which every child between the ages of seven and fourteen years is furnished with the rudiments of a good education. Some of these schools have been so far advanced that in them any child showing proficiency can secure, without cost, an education fully equal to that furnished by the colleges of the country forty years ago. The amount expended in 1890 for the support of public schools was $11,407,499. The number of teachers employed was 19,526. The number of persons enrolled between the ages of six and twenty-one was 1,123,985. The number of scholars who attended was 797,439. The average attendance was 549,269. The excellence of the system of common schools in Ohio is admitted on all hands to be equal to that of any other state or section.

The charitable institutions of the state, including children's homes, are equal to the best in any country in the world.

The building of churches and places of public worship commenced with the first settlement in Ohio, and has kept pace fully with the growth of population. In every community, great or small, churches are open for the worship of the Almighty God. The broadest toleration is not only permitted, but favored, by a universal public sentiment. Every denomination of Christians who number enough to make a congregation can readily secure a house of worship, not only by gifts from its members, but by contributions made by other professing Christians. The same charity is extended to Jews and Gentiles professing any creed or having any form of worship.

The standing, ability and influence of the men engaged in the professions in Ohio will compare favorably with any in the Union, and especially is this true of the lawyers of this state. Many of the lawyers who engaged in the fervent discussions which led to the Revolution and then participated in the war, thrown upon their own resources after the war, were among the early founders of the new settlements in Ohio. They chiefly framed the first laws of the state. Judge Burnet, one of them, had intrusted to him the preparation of most of the laws of the territorial government. The principal lawyers appeared in the constitutional convention and in the legislatures subsequent, and contributed more than their share in ingrafting upon our statutes the republican principles and ideas found in the first constitution and laws of the state. They shared with other settlers in all the hardships of pioneer life. Innumerable anecdotes of their voyages through the forests of southern and eastern Ohio, and the swamps of northwestern Ohio, are preserved among the traditions of the bar.

It was the habit in those early days for the principal lawyers of the state to follow the judges in their rounds from county to county, attending the courts and aiding local attorneys in the trial of important causes. They rode on horseback, with their clothing and books in their saddlebags, and, where a better lodging could not be found, camped in the woods by the roadside. The early judges of the Supreme Court, some of whom were transferred to the Supreme Court of the United States, rode in the same manner on their circuit, administering justice impartially, but firmly, for the salary of $1,000 a year, only raised to $100 a month about the year 1820. The doctors and preachers shared the general life and condition and the same homely fare as their patients and hearers.

A life like this developed individual character and produced many men of odd characteristics, strange manners and
peculiar dress and conversation. The almost universal use of
whisky during the pioneer period in the family circle and in
social life, and the habit of treating and drinking, led to
many wild scenes and fights, but, unlike their brethren of
the south, the contestants commonly were content with the
weapons nature gave them. It was not unusual, when a
quarrel arose, to gather around them, form a circle and give
them fair play and a free fight. There can be no doubt that
in those early days many rude scenes and fights and violence
of many kinds occurred, and such crimes were indulged with
more charity than now prevails. But it is equally true that
thefts and the meaner crimes were more rare than now,
and when disclosed were punished with greater severity than
acts of violence. The stealing of a horse was considered a
worse crime than manslaughter without malice or premedi-
tation.

But all these habits and ideas have been greatly changed
for at least fifty years. The habit of drinking spiritous liquor
at the homestead, in the family circle, or on the farm, has
almost entirely ceased. As a rule, it is confined to saloons
and bar-rooms, mostly in the cities and large towns, and a "free
fight" in the presence of spectators could not now occur in
any community in the state. The enforcement of the criminal
laws is as certain as in any other community. The discipline
of penitentiaries and reformatories and houses of correction is
founded upon the best examples of such institutions in the
older states, and the most civilized countries of Europe.

There is one other quality developed by the people of Ohio
which will be readily conceded by all. The people from the
earliest days were born politicians, vigorous in the defense of
their opinions and firm in the maintenance of all their rights.
The events in their history developed a military instinct
which led them to take an active part whenever their country
became involved in war. In the pioneer age nearly every
able-bodied man served either in Indian wars or in the War of
1812. In the Mexican War the State of Ohio furnished her

full quota of soldiers, and tendered thousands more. In the political contests that preceded the Civil War the lines between the two parties were sharply drawn, though when war was commenced by the firing upon Fort Sumter the people were practically united for its prosecution until the Union was restored by the unconditional surrender of the Confederate armies. Questions arose involving individual rights upon which the Democratic party was divided, but it is due to history to say that in the great struggle for national life the people of Ohio, without distinction of party, with few individual exceptions, were on the side of the Union.

The share taken by the several states in the Civil War is familiar to all. Invidious comparisons ought not to be made. It will be conceded that Ohio did its full part in this supreme contest. She furnished to the Union army 319,659 soldiers, or more than one-tenth of the national armies, out of a then population of 2,339,000, some of whom served in every considerable battle of the war. She furnished from among her sons the leading commanders of the Union army, and a long list of distinguished officers who were conspicuous in every battle of the war. The war Governors of Ohio were conspicuous in their zeal and ability in organizing recruits, and in care and attention to their comfort and wants. The people of Ohio, both men and women, contributed freely in many ways for the relief of the sick and wounded during the war, and after its close provided homes for needy soldiers, and for the children of those who fell.

I have carefully refrained from mentioning the names of the many illustrious citizens of Ohio who contributed most to the organization, growth and development of that state and of the United States, lest I omit others equally worthy of honorable mention. The Governors of Ohio have been selected for conspicuous service to the state, or to the United States, and, though the powers of that officer, under the constitution of Ohio, are not so great as in many of the states, they were distinguished for ability, integrity and high personal character. The roll of statesmen who have served Ohio in the Senate and House of Representatives of the United States

includes many of commanding influence in the national councils, two of whom have been Presidents of the United States,
two Chief Justices of the Supreme Court of the United States,
and many others have occupied seats as Justices of the
Supreme Court, as heads of departments of the executive
branch of the government, and Representatives of the highest
rank in our diplomatic service.

It is not intended to make a comparison of the merits of
individuals or parties, nor of Ohio with other states, old or
new. I concede that all the states, old or new, have contributed to the strength of the republic, the common hope and
pride of all American citizens. Local or state pride is entirely
consistent with the most devoted loyalty to the Union. All I
have sought is to present truthfully a mere outline of the
history and resources of a state carved within a century out of
a wilderness, having at the beginning no inhabitants but
savage men and wild beasts, no mark of civilization except
that made by an extinct race leaving no name or date or
history, and now converted into the peaceful home of four
millions of human beings, possessed of a full share of property
and wealth, a soil rich and fertile, well cultivated by independent farmers, yielding more than the entire production of all
the colonies that rebelled against Great Britain, and producing
by varied industries and developed resources more than all the
states produced when the constitution was adopted.

In intelligence, means of education, temperance, order and
religious observance, Ohio may fairly take its place among the
most favored communities in the world. It is a type of what
can be accomplished under favorable circumstances by a free
people under a free government, where each citizen enjoys the
full and undisputed possession of equal rights and opportunities. Ohio commenced its existence on the western border
line of civilization on the continent. The center of population
has already passed its borders, so that it now takes its place,
not in the west, but in the east. The new communities that
have been founded in the west are largely composed of the
sons and daughters of Ohio, who, following the example of
their ancestors, seek new fields for enterprise and industry.

I have observed that wherever I traveled in the west, however remote the place, I found the "Ohio man" well advanced among his fellow citizens, and actively contributing his full share to the growth and prosperity of the community in which he lived, but retaining his love for his native state, and always proud to say he was born in Ohio.

CHAPTER IV.

Admission to the Bar and Early Political Life.

Law Partnership with my Brother Charles — Changes in Methods of Court Practice —
Obtaining the Right-of-Way for a Railroad — Excitement of the Mexican War
and its Effect on the Country — My First Visit to Washington — At a
Banquet with Daniel Webster — New York Fifty Years ago — Mar-
riage with Margaret Cecilia Stewart — Beginning of My Political
Life — Belief in the Doctrine of Protection — Democratic
and Whig Conventions of 1852 — The Slavery
Question — My Election to Congress in 1854.

AFTER I was admitted to the bar I felt the natural ela-
tion of one who had reached the end of a long journey
after weary waiting. I spent two or three weeks in
visiting my relatives in Dayton and Cincinnati, attending the courts in those cities, where I observed closely the conduct of judges and lawyers in the trial of cases, and returned
to Mansfield full of confidence, and with a better opinion of
myself than I have entertained since.

The first object I sought to accomplish was the removal of
my mother and her two unmarried daughters, Susan and
Fannie, from Lancaster to Mansfield. At this time all her sons
were settled at homes distant from Lancaster, and her other
daughters were married and scattered. By an arrangement
between my brothers, Charles and Tecumseh, and myself, I was
to keep house with mother in charge, Susan and Fannie as
guests. This family arrangement was continued until Susan
and I were married and mother died.

To return to my admission to the bar. I felt that I was
now a man. I had heretofore banked mainly on the treasures
of hope. My brother, Charles Sherman, admitted me as an
equal partner in his lucrative practice, and thus I gained a
foot-hold in the profession. Fortunately for me, his timidity
required me to attend stoutly contested cases brought to us.
The old distinction between law and equity proceedings was
then preserved, and Charles was a very good equity counselor.

(78)

CHARLES T. SHERMAN,
ELDEST BROTHER OF SENATOR AND GENERAL SHERMAN.

With this line of distinction between us we never had any difficulty in arranging our business, or in dividing our labor. He was then agent and attorney for New York and eastern creditors, the confidential adviser of our leading business men, and the counselor of a very interesting sect, then quite numerous in Richland county, called Quakers, or Friends, who could not conscientiously take the usual oath, but in witnessing all necessary legal papers, and in contests, made their affirmations. There was, therefore, left to me the pleadings, oral or written, and the struggle of debate and trial. The practice of the bar in Ohio had greatly changed from that of the early decades of this century. As I have stated, the judges, in the earlier decades, accompanied by leading lawyers, mounted on horses, went from county to county and disposed of the docket. The local lawyers had but little to do. Now all this is changed. Each county has its bar and its leading lawyers, and only when the case is of great importance a "foreign" lawyer is called in. The change has been caused by the abnormal growth of population. In 1830 the total population of the state was only 938,000, that of many of the counties being very small. In 1850 the population had more than doubled, amounting to 1,980,000. In 1890 it was 3,672,000, well distributed among the counties according to their capacity for supporting this increase.

Other remarkable changes have also taken place during the same period. The entire mode of conducting business in early days has been abandoned. Cash payments and short accounts have taken the place of barter and credit. The Ohio banking law of 1846, followed and superseded by the national banking act of 1863, produced a radical change in the forms, credit and solvency of paper money, and, more than any other cause, has encouraged the holding of small savings of money in savings banks and like institutions. These favorable conditions tended to limit credits, to encourage savings, and to change the vocation and habits of lawyers.

Change in methods have also affected the legal profession. The adoption of a code of laws, and of new and simple pleadings, rendered useless half the learning of the old lawyers, driving some of them out of practice. I knew one in Mansfield who swore that the new code was made by fools, for fools, and that he never would resort to it. I believe he kept his word, except when in person he was plaintiff or defendant. Yet, the code and pleadings adopted in New York have been adopted in nearly all the states, and will not be changed except in the line of extension and improvement.

These reforms, and the many changes made in the organization of our state and federal courts, have to a considerable extent lessened the fees and restricted the occupation of lawyers. But it can be said that the leading members of the legal profession proposed and adopted these reforms, and always advocated any legislation that tended to simplify and cheapen litigation and at the same time protect life, property or reputation.

While these causes were operating against lawyers, agents of nature, hitherto unknown, undiscovered, and wonderful, were being developed, which were to completely revolutionize the methods of travel, the transportation of goods, and the modes of production, thus opening new fields for the employment of lawyers. Instead of assault and battery cases, suits for slander and the collection of debts, the attention of lawyers was directed to the development of railroads, banking institutions and other corporations.

The construction of railroads caused a most remarkable revolution in the habits and industries of our people. The first built in Ohio ran from Lake Erie or the Ohio River, north or south into the center of the state. Among them was the Sandusky & Mansfield road, originally a short line from Sandusky to Monroeville, intended to be run by horse power. It was soon changed to a steam road, the power being furnished by a feeble, wheezing engine, not to be compared with the locomotive of to-day. It was then extended to Mansfield, and subsequently to Newark, but was not completed until 1846. It was built of cross-ties three feet apart, connected by string pieces of timber about six by eight inches in dimensions, and a flat iron bar two and one-half inches wide and five-eighths of an inch thick. The worthlessness and danger of such a railroad was soon demonstrated by innumerable accidents caused by the spreading of rails, the "snaking" of the flat bars of iron through the cars, and the feebleness of the engines. Both road and engines soon had to be replaced. In every case which I recall the original investment in the early railroads was lost.

It was thought when the first railroad from Sandusky to Mansfield was completed that the road would save the farmer five or six cents a bushel on his wheat in its transit to the lake, and yield a handsome profit to the stockholders of the railroad. That was the great benefit anticipated. No one then thought of the movement by railroad, over vast distances, of grain, stock, and merchandise, but regarded the innovation as a substitute for the old wagon trains to the lake.

The construction of this railroad was considered at that time a great undertaking. It was accomplished mainly by the leading business men of Mansfield, but the road turned out to be a very bad investment, bankrupting some and crippling others. I was employed by the company to collect the stock and to secure by condemnation the right-of-way from Plymouth to Mansfield. Much of the right-of-way was freely granted without cost by the owners of the land. As the chief benefit was to inure to the farmers, it was thought to be very mean and stingy for one of them to demand money for the right-of-way through his farm. I went over the road from Mansfield to Plymouth with a company of five appraisers, all farmers, who carefully examined the line of the railroad, and much to my mortification, assessed in the aggregate for twenty miles of railway track, damages to the amount of $2,000. I honestly thought this an exorbitant award, but the same distance could not be traversed now at a cost for right-of-way for ten times that sum.

The present admirable roads in Ohio have been built mainly by the proceeds of bonds based upon a right-of-way.

In the meantime other railroads of much greater importance were being built, and the direction of the roads, instead of being north and south was from east to west, to reach a business rapidly developing west of Ohio of far greater importance than the local traffic of that state.

Among the most valuable of these railroads was the Pittsburg, Ft. Wayne & Chicago, now a part of the system of the Pennsylvania Railroad Company, by which it is leased. This road was built in sections by three different corporations, subsequently combined by authority of the legislatures of Pennsylvania, Ohio, Indiana, and Illinois. The first section was the Pittsburg & Ohio railroad from Pittsburg to Crestline, twelve miles west of Mansfield.

There is perhaps a no more remarkable material development in the history of mankind than that of railroads in the United States since 1845. The number of miles of such roads is now 171,804.72, the actual cost of which with equipment amounting to $9,293,052,143. The value of these railroads and their dependent warehouses and stations is probably greater to-day than was the value of the entire property of the United States in 1840.

Contemporaneous with railroads came the telegraph, the cable, and the telephone. The first telegraph wire was strung between Baltimore and Washington in 1844. The first telegraph line through the State of Ohio was from Cleveland via Mansfield to Columbus and Cincinnati, and was established in 1848. At the close of the session of the Supreme Court at Mansfield in that year, Judge Hitchcock, who presided, asked me the road to Mt. Gilead, in Morrow county, a county then recently created. I pointed to the telegraph wire stretched on poles, and told him to follow that. The old Judge, who had been on the supreme bench for over twenty years was quite amused at the direction given. He laughed and said he had been mislead by guideboards all his life, and now he was glad to be guided by a wire.

The development and changes, soon after my admission to the bar, turned somewhat the tide of my hopes and expectations. Our firm soon lost the business of collecting debts for eastern merchants by the establishment of numerous and safe banks under the state act of 1846. Several of the old banks, especially those at Wooster, Norwalk, and Massillon had utterly failed, and, I believe, paid no part of their outstanding notes. The new banks, founded upon a better system, one of

SUPREME COURT OF THE UNITED STATES OF AMERICA.

John Sherman, Esquire, of Mansfield,
State of Ohio

was, on motion first made to the Court in this behalf, by the Hon: Reverdy
Johnson,

duly admitted and qualified, as an Attorney and Counsellor of the Supreme Court of the United
States, on the 21st day of January in the year of our Lord one thousand eight hundred
and fifty-two , and of the Independence of the United States of America the 76th. -

In testimony whereof, I, William Thomas Carroll, Clerk of said Court, have hereunto set my hand and affixed the Seal of said Court, at the City of Washington, this 21st
day of January in the year of our Lord one thousand eight hundred and fifty=two. -

Wm Tho Carroll
Clk. Sup. Ct. U. S.

which was at Mansfield, rapidly absorbed the collection of eastern merchants from the part of Ohio in which we lived. This loss was, however, more than made good by our employment as attorneys for the several railroads through Richland county. My brother gradually withdrew from his business in Mansfield, and became the general attorney for the Pittsburg, Ft. Wayne & Chicago Railroad.

In the meantime I had taken a junior part in the trial of several cases in which I was greatly favored by Mr. Stewart, the most eminent member of his profession at Mansfield. He gave me several opportunities for testing my qualities before a jury, so that I gradually gained confidence in myself as a speaker.

My Uncle Parker was then judge of the Court of Common Pleas. So far from favoring me on account of my relation to him, he seemed to me to wish to demonstrate his impartiality by overruling my pleadings or instructing the jury against me. I am quite sure now that this was fanciful on my part, for he was universally regarded as being an excellent example of a just judge without favor or partiality.

During the early period of practice at the bar I studied my cases carefully and had fair success. I settled more cases by compromises, however, than I tried before a jury. I got the reputation of being successful by full preparation and a thorough knowledge of the facts and law of the case. In addressing a jury I rarely attempted flights of oratory, and when I did attempt them I failed. I soon learned that it was better to gain the confidence of a jury by plain talk than by rhetoric. Subsequently in public life I preserved a like course, and once, though I was advised by Governor Chase to add a peroration to my argument, I did not follow his advice. While I defended many persons for alleged crimes I never but once prosecuted a criminal. My old friend, Mr. Kirkwood, was the prosecuting attorney of the county, and I renewed with him my "moot court" experience in frequent contests between real parties.

During this period I became a member of the order of Odd Fellows in Mansfield. I took an active interest in the order, and was at one time Noble Grand of the lodge. I have continued ever since to pay my dues, but have not been able to attend the meetings regularly for some years. I have always thought, without any reference to its supposed secrecy, that it is an association of great value, especially in bringing young men under good social influences with men of respectable character and standing.

Among the political incidents of this period I recall the excitement that grew out of the Mexican War. The general feeling among all classes, and the universal feeling among the Whigs was, that the Mexican War was purposely and unjustly entered upon to extend the institution of slavery. There is, now, no doubt that such was the object of the war. After the battles at Palo Alto and Resaca de la Palma a call was made upon the people of Ohio for two regiments of volunteers. These were raised without much difficulty, one being placed under the command of Col. Thomas L. Hamer, the other under my old commander, Col. Samuel R. Curtis. I was somewhat tempted to enter the service, though I did not believe in the justice of the war. My old friend, Gen. McLaughlin, raised a company in Mansfield, and my comrade on the Muskingum Improvement, James M. Love, raised one in Coshocton, and Col. Curtis was to command the regiment. My brother, William Tecumseh, then captain in the regular army, was eager to go into the war. He had been stationed at Pittsburg, on recruiting service, but during the excitement visited us at Mansfield, and chafed over the delay of orders to join the troops, then under General Taylor. No doubt his impatience led him to be assigned to the expedition around Cape Horn to occupy California, this, greatly to his regret, keeping him out of the war with Mexico.

Whatever may have been the merits of this war in the beginning, its fruits were undoubtedly of immense value to this country. Without this war California might, like other provinces of Mexico, have remained undeveloped. In the possession of the United States its gold and silver have been discovered and mined, and, together with all the vast interior country west of the Mississippi, it has been developed with a rapidity unexampled in history.

In the winter of 1846–7, I for the first time visited the cities of Washington, New York and Boston. I rode in a stage coach from Mansfield to the national road south of Newark, and thence over that road by stages to Cumberland, the railroads not having yet crossed the mountains. From Cumberland I rode in cars to Baltimore, occupying nearly a day. From Baltimore I proceeded to Washington.

On my arrival I went to the National Hotel, then the most popular hotel in Washington, where many Senators and Members lodged. I found there, also, a number of charming young ladies whose company was much more agreeable to me than that of the most distinguished statesmen. We had hops, balls and receptions, but I recall very few public men I met at that time. Mr. Vinton, then the veteran Member from Ohio, invited me to join for a few days his mess; he was then boarding in a house nearly opposite the hotel, kept by an Italian whose name I cannot recall. He was a famous cook. The mess was composed entirely of Senators and Members, one of the former being Mr. Crittenden, of Kentucky. I was delighted and instructed by the free and easy talk that prevailed, a mixture of funny jokes, well-told stories and gay and grave discussions of politics and law.

My stay at the capital was brief as I wished to go to New York and Boston. In New York I received from a relative a letter of introduction to Benj. R. Curtis, then an eminent lawyer, and latterly a more eminent justice of the Supreme Court. When I presented my letter I was received very kindly and after a brief conversation he said he was able to do me a favor, that he had a ticket to a grand banquet to be attended by the leading men of Boston at Plymouth Rock, on the anniversary of the landing of the Pilgrim Fathers, and that Daniel Webster would preside. I heartily thanked him, and on the next day, prompt on time, I entered the train at Boston for Plymouth. When I arrived at the hotel, which is also a station-house of the railway, I did not know a single person in the great assemblage. In due time we were ushered into the dining hall where the banquet was spread. There was no mistaking Webster. He sat in the center of a cross table with

the British minister on his right and Jeremiah Mason on his
left. At the other end of the room sat Abbott Lawrence and
other distinguished men. The residue of the guests, merchants, poets, and orators of Massachusetts, filled every seat at
the tables. I sat some way down on the side and introduced
myself to my neighbors on the right and left, but my eye was
on Webster, from whom I expected such lofty eloquence as he
alone could utter.

Much to my surprise, when the time came for the oratory
to commence, Mr. Lawrence acted as toast master. We had
stories, songs, poetry and oratory, generally good and appropriate, but not from Webster. And so the evening waned.
Webster had been talking freely with those about him. He
displayed none of the loftiness associated with his name. He
drank freely. That was manifest to everyone. His favorite
bottle was one labeled "Brandy." We heard of it as being
"more than a hundred years old." It did not travel down to
us. Webster was plainly hilarious. At this time the conduc-
tor appeared at a side door and announced that in fifteen
minutes the cars would start for Boston. Then Webster arose
—with difficulty—he rested his hands firmly on the table and
with an effort assumed an erect position. Every voice was
hushed. He said that in fifteen minutes we would separate,
nevermore to meet again, and then, with glowing force and
eloquence, he contrasted the brevity and vanity of human life
with the immortality of the events they were celebrating,
which century after century would be celebrated by your
children and your children's children to the latest generation.

I cannot recall the words of his short but eloquent speech,
but it made an impress on my mind. If his body was affected
by the liquor, his head was clear and his utterance perfect.
I met Mr. Webster afterwards on the cars and in Washington.
I admired him for his great intellectual qualities, but I do not
wonder that the people of the United States did not choose
him for President.

Soon after the national Whig convention of 1852, of which
I was a member, I heard this story told by his secretary. In the
evening, when Mr. Webster was at his well-known residence

on Louisiana Avenue, near Sixth street, he was awaiting the ballots in the convention. When it came by the telegraph, "Scott 159, Fillmore 112, Webster 21," he repeated it in his deep tones and said: "How will this read in history?" He did not like either Scott or Fillmore, and was disappointed in the votes of southern members. To be third in such a contest wounded his pride. He died before the year closed. He was, perhaps, the greatest man of intellectual force of his time, but he had faults which the people could not overlook. Another incident about Mr. Webster, and the house in which he lived, may not be without interest. On New Year's day of 1860, Mr. Corwin, Mr. Colfax and myself made the usual calls together. Among the many visits we made, was one on a gentleman then living in that house. As we entered, Mr. Corwin met an old well-trained negro servant who had been a servant of Mr. Webster in this house. I noticed that Mr. Corwin lost his usual gayety, and as we left the house he turned to us, and, with deep emotion, asked that we leave him at his lodgings; that his long associations with Mr. Webster, especially his meetings with him in that house during their association as members of the cabinet of Fillmore, unfitted him to enjoy the usual greetings of the day. I felt that the emotion of such a man as Corwin was the highest possible compliment to the memory of Daniel Webster.

From Boston I returned to New York. There, in the families of two brothers of my mother, both then living, I had a glimpse of New York society. With Mr. Scott, the son-in-law of my uncle, James Hoyt, I made nearly one hundred of the usual New Year's visits, then customary in New York. This custom I am told has been abandoned, but the New York of to-day is quite different from the New York of 1847. It still retained some of the knickerbocker customs of the olden time. The site of the Fifth Avenue Hotel was then a stone-yard where grave stones were cut. All north of Twenty-third street, now the seat of plutocracy, was then sparsely occupied by poor houses and miserable shanties, and the site of Central Park was a rough, but picturesque body of woodland, glens and rocky hills, with a few clearings partly cultivated. Even

then the population of New York was about 400,000, or more
than three-fold that of any city in the United States,
and twenty-fold that of Chicago. Now New York contains
2,000,000 inhabitants, and Chicago, according to recent reports,
about 1,700,000. Many cities now exist containing over
100,000 inhabitants, the sites of which, in that year, were
within the limits of Indian reservations.

From New York I returned to Washington. Many incidents recur to me but they were of persons now dead and
gone, the memory of whom will not be recalled by the present
generation. Mr. Polk was then President. He was a plain
man, of ordinary ability and more distinguished for the great
events that happened during his presidency than for anything
he did himself. I attended one of his receptions. His wife
appeared to better advantage than he. I then saw Mr. Douglas
for the first time. I think he was still a Member of the
House of Representatives, but had attained a prominent
position and was regarded as a rising man. I wished very
much to see Henry Clay, the great favorite of the Whigs of
that day, but he was not then in public life.

There was nothing in Washington at that time to excite
interest, except the men and women in public or social life.
The city itself had no attractions except the broad Potomac
River and the rim of hills that surrounded the city. It then
contained about 30,000 inhabitants. Pennsylvania avenue was
a broad, badly paved, unattractive street, while all the other
streets were unpaved and unimproved. All that part of the
city lying north of K street and west of Fourteenth street,
now the most fashionable part of the city, was then a dreary
waste open, like all the rest of the city, as free pasturage for
cows, pigs, and goats. It was a city in name, but a village in
fact. The contrast between Washington then and now may
be referred to hereafter.

Upon my return from the east in February, 1847, I actively
resumed the practice of the law. I was engaged in several important trials, but notably one at Mount Vernon, Ohio, where
the contesting parties were brothers, the matter in dispute a
valuable farm, and the chief witness in the case the mother of

both the plaintiff and defendant. It was, as such trials are apt to be, vigorously contested with great bitterness between the parties. Columbus Delano was the chief counsel for the plaintiff, and I was his assistant. I remember the case more especially because during its progress I was attacked by typhoid fever. I returned home after the trial, completely exhausted, and on the Fourth of July, 1847, found myself in a raging fever, which continued more than two months before I was able to rise from the bed, and then I was as helpless as a child. I was unable to walk, and was lifted from the house into the carriage to get the fresh air, and continued under disability until October, when I was again able to renew my business.

During my practice thus far, I had been able to accumulate in property and money more than ten thousand dollars. I had, in addition to my practice, engaged in a profitable business with Jacob Emminger, a practical mechanic, in the manufacture of doors, blinds and other building materials. We acquired valuable pine-lands in Michigan and transported the lumber to our works at Mansfield. We continued this business until I was appointed Secretary of the Treasury, in March, 1877, when I sold out my interest and also abandoned the practice of the law.

I spent the winter of 1847-8 at Columbus, where I made many acquaintances who were of great service to me in after life, and had a happy time also with the young ladies I met there. Columbus was then the headquarters of social life for Ohio. It had a population then of about fifteen thousand, with few or no manufactures. It has now a population of more than one hundred thousand, the increase being largely caused by the great development of the numerous railroads centering there, and of the coal and iron mines of the Hocking Valley. It was also the natural headquarters of the legal profession, the Supreme Court of Ohio, then under the old constitution, and the District Court of the United States holding their sessions there.

On the first day of August, 1848, my grandmother, Elizabeth Stoddard Sherman, died at Mansfield at the residence of her daughter, Mrs. Parker. Her history and characteristics have already been referred to. She was to our family the connecting link between the Revolutionary period and our times. She had a vivid recollection of the burning of the principal towns of Connecticut by the British and Tories, of the trials and poverty that followed the War of the Revolution, of the early political contests between the Federalists and Republicans, of the events of the War of 1812, and of her journey to Ohio in 1816. She maintained a masterly care of her children and grandchildren. She was the best type I have known of the strong-willed, religious Puritan of the Connecticut school, and was respected, not only by her numerous grandchildren, but by all who knew her.

My brother-in-law, Thomas W. Bartley, was District Attorney of the United States during the administration of Mr. Polk, and, as he expected a change would be made by the incoming administration of Taylor, he advised me to become a candidate for his place, as that was in the line of my profession. I told him I doubted if my experience of the bar would justify me in making such an application, but he thought differently. I wrote to Mr. Ewing upon the subject and he answered as follows:

WASHINGTON, D. C., Dec. 31, 1848.

John Sherman, Esq., Mansfield, Ohio.

MY DEAR SIR :— I believe you would be able to perform the duties of District Attorney, but your youth would be an objection to your appointment, and in competition with one so long known, and so highly estimated, as Mr. Goddard is both professionally and politically, would probably make your prospects but little encouraging. If you conclude to withdraw your name, signify the fact and the reason by letter to Mr. Goddard and it may be of use to you hereafter. I am, with great regard,

Yours,   T. EWING.

I complied with his advice, though Mr. Goddard, I think, declined and Mr. Mason was appointed.

On the thirty-first of the same month I was married to Margaret Cecilia Stewart, the only child of Judge Stewart, whom I had known since my removal to Mansfield. She had been carefully educated at the Female College at Granville, Ohio, and at the Patapsco Institute, near Baltimore, Maryland. After the usual wedding tour to Niagara Falls, Montreal and Saratoga, we settled in Mansfield, and I returned to my profession, actively pursuing it until elected a member of Congress.

MR. SHERMAN'S FIRST HOME IN MANSFIELD, OHIO, ERECTED IN 1849.

Washington Dec 31st 1845

My dear Sir

I believe you would be exposed to
prepare the election of District Attorney, but
your firmth would be our objection to your ap
pointment, & in competition, with one so long
known & so highly estimated as Mr Goodland is
both professionally & politically would probably
render your prospect but little encouraging—
If you concluded to withdraw your name
simply the fact & the reason by letter to Mr
Goodland & it may be & use to you hereafter—
I am with great regard

Yours T. Ewing

John Zimmerman Esq
Brownfield Ohio

It is not worth while to follow my professional life into further detail. I shall not have occasion to mention that subject again. Sufficient to say that I was reasonably successful therein. During this period Henry C. Hedges studied law with my brother and myself, and when admitted to the bar became my partner. Mr. Stewart was elected by the legislature a judge of the Court of Common Pleas, and after the adoption of the new constitution of 1851, he was elected by the people to the same office.

I had determined in the fall of 1853 to abandon Mansfield and settle in Cleveland, then rapidly growing in importance as the leading city in the northern part of the state. I went so far as to establish an office there and place in it two young lawyers, nominally my partners, but the great political currents of that time soon diverted me from the practice of the law into the political contests that grew out of the repeal of the Missouri Compromise.

"The direful spring of woes unnumbered."

Before entering upon an account of my political life it seems appropriate for me to state my political bias and position. I was by inheritance and association a Whig boy, without much care for or knowledge of parties or political principles. No doubt my discharge from the engineer corps by a Democratic Board of Public Works strengthened this bias. I shouted for Harrison in the campaign of 1840. In 1842 I was enthusiastic for "Tom Corwin, the wagon-boy," the Whig candidate for Governor of Ohio. In that canvass Governor Corwin addressed a great meeting at Mansfield. I heard his speech, and was full of enthusiasm. Mr. Corwin was certainly the greatest popular orator of his time. His face was eloquent, changeable at his will. With a look he would cause a laugh or a tear. He would move his audience at his pleasure. I vividly remember the impression he made upon me, though I cannot recall anything he said. At the close of the meeting I was requested by the committee in charge to take Mr. Corwin in a buggy to Bucyrus. This I cheerfully did. I noticed that Mr. Corwin was very glum and silent, and to cheer him up I spoke of his speech and of the meeting. He turned upon me, and with some show of feeling, said that all the people who heard him would remember only his jokes, and warned me to keep out of politics and attend to my law. He told me that he knew my father, and was present at his death at Lebanon, where he, Mr. Corwin, lived. And then, brightening up, he gave me an interesting account of the early settlement of Ohio, and of the bar and bench, and of his early life as a wagon boy in Harrison's army. His sudden fit of gloom had passed away. I do not recall any circumstance that created a deeper impression on my mind than this interview with Mr. Corwin. His advice to keep out of politics was easy to follow, as no one could then dream of the possibility of a Whig being elected to office in Richland county, then called "the Berks of Ohio." Mr. Corwin was defeated at that election.

I took but little part in the campaign of 1844, when Mr. Clay was a candidate for President, but I then made my first political speech to a popular audience and cast my first vote. The meeting was held at Plymouth, and Honorable Joseph M. Root, the Whig candidate for Congress, was to be the orator. For some reason Mr. Root was delayed, and I was pressed into service. Of what I said I have not the remotest recollection, but my audience was satisfied, and I was doubly so, especially when Mr. Root came in sight. After that I made a few neighborhood speeches in support of the Whig candidate for governor, Mr. Mordecai Bartley, a gentleman who for several years had lived in Mansfield, but had long since retired from public office after eight years' service in the United States House of Representatives. Mr. Bartley received 147,738 votes, Mr. Tod, Democrat, 146,461 votes and Mr. King, Third Party, 8,411 votes; so close were parties divided in Ohio in 1844.

At this time I had but two definite ideas in respect to the public policy of the United States. One was a hearty belief in the doctrine of protection to American industries, as advocated by Mr. Clay, and, second, a strong prejudice against the Democratic party, which was more or less committed to the annexation of Texas, and the extension of slavery. I shared in the general regret at the defeat of Mr. Clay and the election of Mr. Polk. I took some part in the local canvasses in Ohio prior to

1848, but this did not in the least commit me to active political life. I was appointed a delegate to the national Whig convention, held in Philadelphia, in 1848, to nominate a presidential candidate. I accepted this the more readily as it gave me an opportunity to see my future wife at her school at Patapsco, and to fix our engagement for marriage upon her return home. The chief incident of the convention was the struggle between the friends of General Scott and General Taylor.

When the convention was being organized, Colonel Collyer, chairman of the Ohio delegation, said there was a young gentleman in that convention who could never hope to get an office unless that convention gave him one, and nominated me for secretary of the convention. Mr. Defrees said there was a delegate from Indiana in the same condition and moved that Schuyler Colfax be made assistant secretary. We then marched together to the platform and commenced our political life, in which we were to be closely associated for many years.

The nomination of General Taylor, cordially supported by me, was not acceptable to all the Whigs of Ohio. The hostility to slavery had grown chiefly out of the acquisition of Texas as a slave state. An anti-slavery party headed in Ohio by Salmon P. Chase cast 35,354 votes for Van Buren. General Taylor was defeated in Ohio mainly by this defection, receiving 138,360 votes. General Cass received 154,775 votes. General Cass received the vote of Ohio, but General Taylor was elected President, having received a majority of the electoral vote.

General Taylor proved a very conscientious and acceptable President. His death, on the ninth day of July, 1850, preceded the passage of the compromise measures of Henry Clay, commonly known by his name. They became laws with the approval of Millard Fillmore.

It was my habit during this period to attend the annual state conventions of the Whig party, not so much to influence nominations as to keep up an acquaintance with the principal members of my party. I had not the slightest desire for public office and never became a candidate until 1854. In the state convention of 1850 I heartily supported the nomination of General Scott for President, at the approaching election of

1852. In this convention an effort was made to nominate me for Attorney-General in opposition to Henry Stanbery. I promptly declined to be a candidate, but received a number of votes from personal friends, who, as they said, wanted to introduce some young blood into the Whig party.

I then began seriously to study the political topics of the day. I was classed as a conservative Whig, and heartily supported the compromise measures of 1850, not upon their merits, but as the best solution of dangerous sectional divisions. Prior to this time I do not remember to have given any study, except through the newspapers of the day, to the great national questions that divided the political parties.

In the spring of 1852 I was designated by the state convention as a delegate at large in association with Honorable Samuel F. Vinton to the national Whig convention of that year. I was an earnest advocate of General Scott, and rejoiced in his nomination. Here, again, the slavery question was obtruded into national politics. The clear and specific indorsement of the compromise measures, though supported by a great majority, divided the Whig party and led to the election of Franklin Pierce. In this canvass I took for the first time an active part. I was designated as an elector on the Scott ticket. I made speeches in several counties and cities, but was recalled at Wooster by a telegram stating that my mother was dangerously ill. Before I could reach home she was dead. This event was wholly unexpected, as she seemed, when I left home, to be in the best of health. She had accompanied her daughter, Mrs. Bartley, to Cleveland to attend the state fair, and there, no doubt, she was attacked with the disease of which she died. I took no further part in the canvass.

I wish here to call special attention to the attitude of the two great parties in respect to the compromise measures.

The Democratic national convention at Baltimore was held on the first of June, 1852. The resolutions of that convention in reference to slavery were as follows:

"12. *Resolved*, That Congress has no power under the constitution to interfere with, or control, the domestic institutions of the several states, and that such states are the sole and proper judges of everything appertaining to their own affairs, not prohibited by the constitution; that all efforts of the Abolitionists or others, made to induce Congress to interfere with questions of slavery, or to take incipient steps in relation thereto, are calculated to lead to the most alarming and dangerous consequences, and that all such efforts have an inevitable tendency to diminish the happiness of the people, and endanger the stability and permanency of the Union, and ought not to be countenanced by any friend of our political institutions.

"13. *Resolved*, That the foregoing proposition covers, and is intended to embrace, the whole subject of slavery agitation in Congress, and, therefore, *the Democratic party of the Union, standing on this national platform, will abide by, and adhere to, a faithful execution of the acts known as the compromise measures settled by the last Congress, 'the act for reclaiming fugitives from service labor,' included; which act, being designed to carry out an express provision of the constitution, cannot, with fidelity thereto, be repealed, nor so changed as to destroy or impair its efficiency.*

"14. *Resolved, That the Democratic party will resist all attempts at renewing in Congress, or out of it, the agitation of the slavery question, under whatever shape or color the attempt may be made.*"

The Whig convention, which met at Baltimore on the 16th of June, 1852, declared as follows:—

"8. *That the series of acts of the 32nd Congress, the act known as The Fugitive Slave Law included, are received and acquiesced in by the Whig party of the United States as a settlement in principle and substance of the dangerous and exciting questions which they embrace, and so far as they are concerned, we will maintain them, and insist upon their strict enforcement,* until time and experience shall demonstrate the necessity of further legislation to guard against the evasion of the laws on the one hand, and the abuse of their powers on the other—not impairing their present efficiency; and we *deprecate all further agitation of the question thus settled as dangerous to our peace, and will discountenance all efforts to continue or renew such agitation whenever, wherever or however the attempt may be made,* and we will maintain the system as essential to the nationality of the Whig party and the integrity of the Union."

It will be noticed that these platforms do not essentially differ from each other. Both declare in favor of acquiescence in the compromise measures of 1850. The Democratic party more emphatically denounces any renewal in Congress, or out of it, of the agitation of the slavery question under whatever name, shape or color, the attempt may be made. The Whig platform, equally positive in its acquiescence in the settlement made, known as the compromise measures, declared its purpose to: "Maintain them, and to insist upon their strict enforcement until time and experience shall demonstrate the necessity of further legislation to guard against the evasion of the laws."

It would seem that under these platforms both parties were committed to acquiescence in existing laws upon the subject of slavery, and to a resistance of all measures to change or modify them.

I took quite an active part in this canvass and wrote to Mr. Seward, then the great leader of the Whig party, inviting him to attend a mass meeting in Richland county, to which I received the following reply:

AUBURN, Sept. 20, 1852.

JOHN SHERMAN, ESQ., Mansfield, Ohio.

DEAR SIR:— I have the honor of receiving your letter urging me to accept the invitation of the Whig central committee to address a mass meeting in Richland county, Ohio, on the second of October. I appreciate fully the importance of the canvass in which we are engaged, and I have some conception of the responsibilities of the Whigs of Ohio. I wish, therefore, that it was in my power to comply with the wishes, expressed in several quarters, by going among them to attempt to encourage them in their noble and patriotic efforts, but it is impossible. Public and professional engagements have withdrawn me from my private affairs during the past two years, and the few weeks of interval between the last and the next session of Congress are equally insufficient for the attention my business requires and for the relaxation of public labors which impaired health demands. I am, dear sir, with great respect, your friend and humble servant,

WILLIAM H. SEWARD.

The election of 1852 resulted in the overwhelming defeat of General Scott, and the practical annihilation of the Whig party. Franklin Pierce received 244 electoral votes, and General Scott but 42.

The triumphant election of Mr. Pierce, on the platform stated, justified the expectation that during his term there would be no opening of the slavery controversy by the Democratic party. If that party had been content with the compromise of 1850, and had faithfully observed the pledges in its platform, there would have been no Civil War. Conservative Whigs, north and south, would have united with conservative Democrats in maintaining and enforcing existing laws. The

Auburn September 20th 1852.

Dear Sir

I have the honor of receiving your letter praying me to accept the invitation of the Whig Central Committee to address a Mass Meeting in Richland County, Ohio on the second of October.

I appreciate fully the importance of the cause in which we are engaged, and I have some conception of the responsibilities of the Whigs of Ohio. I wish therefore that it was in my power to comply with their wishes an expressed in several quarters by going among them to attempt to encourage them in their noble and patriotic efforts. But it is impossible Public and Professional engagements have withdrawn me from my private affairs during the past two years and the few weeks of interval between the last and the next session of Congress are equally insufficient for the attention my business requires and for the relaxation of public labors which impaired health demands.

I am, Dear Sir
With great respect
Your friend and servant.
William H Seward

John Sherman Esqr.
Mansfield
Ohio

efforts of the opponents of slavery and of aggressive pro-slavery propagandists would have been alike ineffective. The irrepressible conflict would have been indefinitely postponed. Yet, as will appear hereafter, the leaders of the 33rd Congress of both parties, and mainly on sectional lines, openly and flagrantly violated the pledges of their party, and renewed a contest that was only closed by the most destructive Civil War of modern times, and by the abolition of slavery. As this legislation brought me into public life, I wish to justify my statement by the public records, with all charity to the authors of the measures who no doubt did not anticipate the baleful events that would spring from them, nor the expanded and strengthened republic which was the final result. "Man proposes, but God disposes."

When the 33rd Congress met, on the 6th day of December, 1853, the tariff issue was practically in abeyance. The net ordinary receipts of the government for the fiscal year ending June 30, 1853, were $61,587,031.68. The net ordinary expenditures of the government for the same year, including interest on the public debt, were $47,743,989.09, leaving a surplus of revenue over expenditures of $13,843,042.59, of which $6,833,072.65 was applied to the payment of the public debt, leaving in the treasury, unexpended, about $7,000,000.00. The estimates for future years were equally favorable to the public credit. The financial and political condition of the United States was never more prosperous than when this Congress met. The disturbance of this condition can be attributed only to the passage of the act to organize the territories of Nebraska and Kansas approved by President Franklin Pierce, May 30, 1854. The 32nd section of that act contained this provision:—

"That the constitution and all laws of the United States which are locally inapplicable, shall have the same force and effect within the said Territory of Kansas as elsewhere within the United States, except the eighth section of the act preparatory to the admission of Missouri into the Union, approved March sixth, eighteen hundred and twenty, which, being inconsistent with the principle of non-intervention by Congress with slavery in the states and territories, as recognized by the legislation of eighteen hundred and fifty, commonly called the compromise measures, is hereby declared inoperative and void; it being the true intent and meaning of this act not to legislate slavery into any territory or state, nor to exclude it therefrom, but to leave the people thereof perfectly free to form and regulate their domestic institutions in their own way, subject only to the constitution of the United States: *Provided*, That nothing herein contained shall be construed to revive or put in force any law or regulation which may have existed prior to the act of sixth of March, eighteen hundred and twenty, either protecting, establishing, prohibiting or abolishing slavery."

This act contained a similar clause relating to Nebraska.

To understand the effect of this provision it is necessary to review the status of slavery in the United States under the constitution and existing laws.

The articles of Confederation make no mention of slavery or slaves. During and after the Revolution the general feeling was that slavery would be gradually abolished by the several states. In the Ordinance of 1787 for the government of the territories of the United States, northwest of the Ohio River, it was expressly provided that:

"There shall be no slavery nor involuntary servitude in the said territory, otherwise than in the punishment of crimes, whereof the parties shall have been duly convicted; provided, always, that any person escaping into the same, from whom labor or service is lawfully claimed in any of the original states, such fugitive may be lawfully reclaimed, and conveyed to the person claiming his or her labor or service as aforesaid."

This provision applied to all the territory of the United States that was subject to the jurisdiction of the Continental Congress.

The constitution of the United States did not mention either slaves or slavery. Its two provisions relating to the subject were the following:

"The migration or importation of such persons as any of the states now existing shall think proper to admit, shall not be prohibited by the Congress prior to the year one thousand, eight hundred and eight, but a tax or duty may be imposed on such importation, not exceeding ten dollars for each person." . . .

"No person held to service or labor in one state, under the laws thereof, escaping into another shall, in consequence of any law or regulation therein, be discharged from such service or labor, but shall be delivered up on claim of the party to whom such service or labor may be due."

The first clause quoted was intended to enable Congress to prohibit the introduction of slaves after the year 1808, and this was promptly done. The second provision was intended to authorize the recapture of slaves escaping from their owners to another state. It was the general expectation of the framers of the constitution that under its provisions slavery would be gradually abolished by the acts of the several states where it was recognized.

The first great controversy that grew out of slavery was whether Missouri should be admitted into the Union as a slave state, and whether slavery should exist in the western territories.

The following provision became part of the law of March 6, 1820, approved by President James Monroe, and known as the compromise measure of that year:

"That, in all that territory ceded by France to the United States under the name of 'Louisiana,' which lies north of 36 deg. 30 min. north latitude, not included within the limits of the state contemplated by this act, slavery and involuntary servitude, otherwise than in the punishment of crimes whereof the party shall have been duly convicted, shall be and is hereby, forever prohibited: *Provided, always,* That any person escaping into the same, from whom labor or service is lawfully claimed in any other state or territory of the United States, such fugitive may be lawfully reclaimed, and conveyed to the person claiming his or her labor or service, as aforesaid."

This compromise measure fixed the boundary line between free and slave states in all the territories then belonging to the United States. Slavery was thus forever prohibited within the Territories of Kansas and Nebraska. This happy solution was regarded as something more than a mere enactment of Congress. It was a territorial division between the two great sections of our country, acquiesced in by both without question or disturbance for thirty-four years. The memorable controversy that arose in the 31st Congress in 1850 in respect to the territory acquired from Mexico did not in the least affect or relate to the Territories of Nebraska and Kansas. The subject-matter of the several bills originally embraced in Mr. Clay's report of the committee of thirteen, defined the northern boundary of the State of Texas on the line of 36 deg. 30 min.

north latitude, provided for the addition of the State of California, for territorial governments for New Mexico and Utah, and for the surrender of fugitive slaves.

In the resolution annexing Texas to the United States there is this express recognition of the Missouri Compromise line:

"New states of convenient size, not exceeding four in number, in addition to said State of Texas, and having sufficient population, may hereafter, by the consent of said state, be formed out of the territory thereof, which shall be *entitled to admission* under the provisions of the Federal constitution; and such states as may be formed out of that portion of said territory lying *south of* 36 deg. 30 min. north latitude, commonly known as the Missouri Compromise line, *shall be* admitted into the Union with or without slavery, as the people of each state asking admission may desire."

The convention providing for the admission of California expressly stipulated by a unanimous vote that slavery should be forever prohibited in that state. The bill providing for a territorial government for New Mexico, the great body of the territory of which lay south of the parallel of latitude 36 deg. 30 min., provided, "That, when admitted as a state, the said territory, or any portion of the same, shall be received into the Union, with or without slavery, as their constitution may prescribe at the time of their admission."

The act organizing the Territory of Utah, lying entirely north of the 37th degree of latitude, contains no provision recognizing the right of the people of that territory to permit slavery within its borders. The situation of the state and its population precluded the possibility of establishing slavery within its borders.

It will be perceived that by the compromise measures of 1820 and 1850, the existence or prohibition of slavery was fixed by express laws, or by conditions which it was fondly believed defined the limits of slavery, and thus set at rest the only question that threatened the union of the states. This settlement was indorsed and ratified by the two great parties in their national platforms of 1852, with the solemn pledge of both parties that they would resist the re-opening of these questions.

The Senate of the 33rd Congress was composed of 36 Democrats, 20 Whigs and 2 Free Soilers. The House was composed of 159 Democrats, 71 Whigs, and 4 Free Soilers, with Franklin Pierce as President of the United States.

I need not narrate the long struggle in both Houses over the bill to organize the Territories of Nebraska and Kansas. It was a direct invitation for a physical struggle between the north and south for the control of these territories, but it finally passed on the 30th of May, 1854.

This act repealed in express terms the Missouri Compromise of 1820, and falsely stated the terms of the compromise measures of 1850, which, as I have shown, had no reference whatever to the Territories of Nebraska and Kansas. It re-opened, in the most dangerous form, the struggle between freedom and slavery in the western territories, and was the congressional beginning of the contest which culminated in the War of the Rebellion.

It is difficult, at this distance of time, to describe the effect of the act of 1854 upon popular opinion in the northern states. The repeal was met in Ohio by an overwhelming sentiment of opposition. All who voted for the bill were either refused a nomination or were defeated by the people at the polls. Party lines were obliterated. In every congressional district a fusion was formed of Democrats, Whigs and Free Soilers, and candidates for Congress were nominated solely upon the issues made by the Kansas and Nebraska bill.

I had carefully observed the progress of the bill, had read the arguments for and against it, and was strongly convinced that it was the duty of every patriotic citizen to oppose its provisions. The firm resolve was declared by the state convention of Ohio, composed of men of all parties, that the institution of slavery should gain no advantage by this act of perfidy. It was denounced as a violation of a plain specific pledge of the public faith made by acts of Congress in 1820 and in 1850. With this feeling there ran current a conviction that the measure adopted was forced by southern domination, and yielded to by ambitious northern dough-faces anxious to obtain southern support.

Unfortunately the drift of parties was on sectional lines. The whole south had become Democratic, so that a united south, acting in concert with a few members from the north, could control the action of Congress. I believe that a feeling did then prevail with many in the south, that they were superior to men of the north, that one southern man could whip four Yankees, that their institution of slavery naturally produced among the masters, men of superior courage, gentlemen who could command and make others obey. Whether such a feeling did exist or not, it was apparent that the political leaders in the south were, as a rule, men of greater experience, were longer retained in the service of their constituents, and held higher public positions than their associates from the north. Besides, they had in slavery a bond of union that did not tolerate any difference of opinion when its interests were involved. This compact power needed the assistance only of a few scattered members from the north to give it absolute control. But now the south was to meet a different class of opponents. There had been growing all over the north, especially in the minds of religious people, a conviction that slavery was wrong. The literature of the day promoted this tendency. The repeal of the Missouri Compromise aroused the combative feeling of the north until it became general among all parties and sects. Still, the north recognized the legal existence of slavery in the south, and did not propose to interfere with it, and was entirely content to faithfully observe the obligations of the constitution and the laws, including those for the return of fugitive slaves. A smaller, but very noisy body of men and women denounced the constitution as "a covenant with hell and a contract with the devil." A much larger number of conservative voters formed themselves into a party called the Free Soil party, who, professing to be restrained within constitutional limits, yet favored the abolition of slavery in the territories and District of Columbia. They invoked the moral influence and aid of the government for the gradual prohibition of slavery in the states. "Liberty is National, Slavery is Sectional," was their motto.

The strong controlling feeling of the great body of the Whigs and of the Democrats of the north, who opposed the Nebraska and Kansas law was that the law was a violation of existing compromises, designed to extend slavery over free territory, that it ought to be repealed, but, if repeal was impracticable, organized effort should be made to make both territories free states. "Slavery shall gain no advantage over freedom by violating compromises," was the cry of a new party, as yet without a name.

It was on this basis in the summer of 1854, I became a candidate for Congress. Jacob Brinkerhoff and Thomas H. Ford, both residents of Richland county, Ohio, and gentlemen of experience and ability, were also candidates, but we agreed to submit our pretensions to a convention in that county, and I was selected by a very large majority. A district convention was held at Shelby, in July. Mr. James M. Root, for several terms a Member of Congress, was my chief competitor, but I was nominated, chiefly because I had been less connected with old parties and would encounter less prejudice with the discordant element of a new party.

I made a thorough canvass through the district, composed of the counties of Huron, Erie, Richland and Morrow. I visited and spoke in every town and township in the district. William D. Lindsley, a Member of the 33rd Congress, was my competitor. He was a farmer, of popular manners, but defective education. When first a candidate a letter of his was published in which he spelled the word "corn" "korne." The Whig newspapers ridiculed him for his faulty spelling, but Democrats, who were offended at this criticism said they would show the Whigs how to plant corn, and the incident proved a benefit rather than an injury to Lindsley. He had been elected to Congress in 1852 against a popular Whig by a majority of 754. He had voted against the Nebraska bill, but had cast one vote that opened the way to the consideration of that bill, which action was made the subject of criticism. This did not enter as a national element in the canvass. The real issue was whether the Democrats and Free Soilers would vote for a Whig. Among the Free Soilers I was regarded as too conservative on the slavery question. They were not content with the repeal of the offensive provisions of the Nebraska act, but demanded the prohibition of slavery in all the territories and in the District of Columbia. This feeling was very strong in the important county of Huron.

When I spoke in North Fairfield I was interrupted by the distinct question put to me by the pastor of the church in which I spoke, and whose name I do not recall, whether I would vote for the abolition of slavery in the District of Columbia. I knew this was a turning point, but made up my mind to be frank and honest, whatever might be the result. I answered that I would not, that the great issue was the extension of slavery over the territories. I fortified myself by the opinions of John Q. Adams, but what I said fell like a wet blanket on the audience. I understood that afterwards, in a church meeting, the preacher commended my frankness and advised his people to vote for me.

This canvass, more than any other, assumed a religious tone, not on sectarian, but on moral grounds. Our meetings were frequently held in churches, and the speaker was invited to the pulpit, with the Bible and hymn-book before him, and frequently with an audience of men, women and children, arranged as for religious worship.

The probable course of Democrats opposed to the Nebraska bill was more a matter of doubt. They were in the main content with Mr. Lindsley and voted for him. But out of the general confusion of parties there arose what was known as the "Know-nothing" order, or American party, opposed to the Catholics, and to free immigration. It was a secret organization, with signs and grips. There were perhaps one thousand of them in my district, composed about equally of Democrats and Whigs. They were indifferent, or neutral, on the political issue of the day.

The result of the election in October was against the Democratic party in Ohio. Every Democratic candidate for Congress was defeated. Twenty-one Members, all opposed to the repeal of the Missouri Compromise, but differing in opinion upon other questions, were elected to Congress. The

United States of America:

THE STATE OF OHIO, EXECUTIVE OFFICE.

I, _William Medill_

GOVERNOR AND COMMANDER-IN-CHIEF OF THE STATE OF OHIO,

Do hereby Certify, that, at the Annual Election held on the Second Tuesday of October last, _John Sherman_ was duly elected a Representative in the _Thirty-fourth_ Congress of the United States, from the _Thirteenth_ Congressional District, within the State aforesaid.

In Testimony Whereof, I have hereunto subscribed my name, and caused the Great Seal of the State of Ohio to be hereunto affixed, at the City of Columbus, this _Ninth_ day of _December_ A. D. 1854.

THE GREAT SEAL OF THE STATE OF OHIO · 1802 ·

W. Medill

Wm Trevitt
Secretary of State.

composition of the delegation was somewhat peculiar, as the party had no name, and no defined principles except upon the one question of the extension of slavery. On the day of election everyone was in doubt. Mr. Kirkwood, who supported Mr. Lindsley, told me it was the strangest election he had ever seen, that everyone brought his ticket in his vest pocket, and there was no electioneering at the polls. He expressed his opinion, but not with much confidence, that Mr. Lindsley was elected. When the votes were counted, it was found that I had 2,823 majority, having carried every county in the district. Richland county, in which I lived, for the first time cast a majority adverse to the Democratic party, I receiving a majority of over 300 votes.

During the summer of 1855, the elements of opposition to the administration of President Pierce organized as the Republican party. County conventions were generally held and largely attended. The state convention met at Columbus on the 13th day of July, 1855. It was composed of heterogeneous elements, every shade of political opinion being represented. Such antipodes as Giddings, Leiter, Chase, Brinkerhoff, and Lew Campbell met in concert. The first question that troubled the convention was the selection of a president. It was thought impolitic to take one who had been offensively conspicuous in one of the old parties. The result was that I was selected, much to my surprise, and, for a time, much to my chagrin. Mr. Allison, since a distinguished Member of the United States Senate, was elected secretary of the convention. I had never presided over any assembly excepting an Odd Fellows' lodge. When I assumed the chair I no doubt soon exposed my inexperience. A declaration of principles was formulated as follows:

1. *Resolved*, That the people who constitute the supreme power in the United States, should guard with jealous care the rights of the several states, as independent governments. No encroachment upon their legislative or judicial prerogatives should be permitted from any quarter.

2. *Resolved*, That the people of the State of Ohio, mindful of the blessings conferred upon them by the "Ordinance of Freedom," whose anniversary our convention this day commemorates, should establish for their political guidance the following cardinal rules:

(1). We will resent the spread of slavery under whatever shape or color it may be attempted.

(2). To this end we will labor incessantly to render inoperative and void that portion of the Kansas and Nebraska bill which abolishes freedom in the territory withdrawn from the influence of slavery by the Missouri Compromise of 1820; and we will oppose by every lawful and constitutional means, the extension of slavery in any national territory, and the further increase of slavery territory or slave states in this republican confederacy.

3. *Resolved*, That the recent acts of violence and Civil War in Kansas, incited by the late Vice President of the United States, and tacitly encouraged by the Executive, command the emphatic condemnation of every citizen.

4. *Resolved*, That a proper retrenchment in all public expenditures, a thoroughly economical administration of our state government, a just and equal basis of taxation, and single districts for the election of members of the legislature, are reforms called for by a wise state policy and justly demanded by the people.

5. *Resolved*, That a state central committee, consisting of five, be appointed by this convention, and the said committee, in addition to its usual duties, be authorized to correspond with committees of other states for the purpose of agreeing upon a time and place for holding a national convention of the Republican party for the nomination of President and Vice President.

Joshua R. Giddings was the solitary member of the committee opposed to the resolutions, not, he said, because he objected to the resolutions themselves, but he thought they were a little too tender. They were not strong enough for the old guard and still they were better than none. If it offended his brother to eat meat he would eat no more while time lasted. He was opposed to this milk for babes. He disagreed with his colleagues, but had had the misfortune to disagree with people before. He was used to disagreement and hoped everybody would vote for the platform.

Lewis D. Campbell said his friend from Ashtabula wanted to make an issue with Frank Pierce. He did not wish to raise an issue with the dead. He hoped everybody would vote for the platform. He did not consider the resolutions milk for babes, but strong meat.

The platform was adopted by a unanimous vote.

The real contention was upon the nomination of governor. Salmon P. Chase was nominated, but there was difference of opinion concerning his somewhat varied political associations and some criticism of them. In 1845 he had projected what was called a liberty convention. In 1848 he had been a member of the Free Soil convention held at Buffalo and since 1849 had been a Senator of the United States. Thomas H. Ford, my townsman, was nominated as lieutenant governor, as the representative of the Whig party. Jacob Brinkerhoff, also of Mansfield, was nominated as judge of the Supreme Court. He had been a Member of Congress from 1843 to 1847 as a Democrat, but early took decided ground against the extension of slavery. He was the reputed author of what is known as the " Wilmot Proviso."

On the 8th day of August this famous proviso was offered as an amendment to a bill authorizing the President of the United States to employ $3,000,000 in negotiations for a peace with Mexico, by purchase of territory, by David Wilmot, of Pennsylvania, a Member of the House. "That, as an express fundamental condition to the acquisition of any territory from the Republic of Mexico by the United States, neither slavery nor involuntary servitude should ever exist in any part of said territory." This proviso was adopted by the House, but was rejected by the Senate. It was the basis of the organization known as the Free Soil party of 1848, and of the Republican party in 1856.

The other candidates on the ticket were fairly distributed. The canvass of 1855 was conducted mainly by Senator Chase and Colonel Ford. I participated in it to some extent, but was chiefly engaged in closing my business in preparation for the approaching session of Congress. The result of the election was as follows: Chase, 146,770 votes; Medill, 131,019; Allen Trimble, 24,276.

The election of Senator Chase, upon a distinctly Republican platform, established the fact that the majority of the voters of Ohio were Republicans as defined by the creed of that party.

In the summer of 1855 I made my first trip to Iowa, accompanied by Amos Townsend and James Cobean. At that time Iowa was a far-off state, thinly populated, but being rapidly settled. We passed through Chicago, which at that time contained a population of about 50,000. The line of railroad

extended to the Mississippi River.   From thence we traveled in
a stage to Des Moines, now the capital of Iowa, but then a
small village with about 1,000 inhabitants.   The northern and
western parts of the state were mostly unsold public lands, open
to entry.   My three brothers, James, Lampson and Hoyt, were
living in Des Moines.   James was a merchant in business.
Lampson was the editor and proprietor of a newspaper, and
Hoyt was actively engaged in the purchase and sale of land.
With Hoyt for guide we drove in a carriage as far north as
Fort Dodge, where a new land office had been recently established.   The whole country was an open plain with here and
there a cabin, with no fences and but little timber.   We
arrived at Fort Dodge on Saturday evening, intending to spend
some time there in locating land.   The tavern at which we
stopped was an unfinished frame building with no plastering,
and sash without glass in the windows.   On the next day, Sunday, Cobean invited us to join him in drinking some choice
whisky he had brought with him.   We did so in the dining-
room.   While thus engaged the landlady came to us and told
Cobean that she was not very well, and would be glad if he
would give her some whisky.   He handed her the bottle, and she
went to the other end of the room and there poured out nearly
a glass full and drank it.   Cobean was so much alarmed lest
the woman should become drunk that he insisted upon leaving
the town immediately, and we acquiesced and left.   Afterwards we learned that she became very drunk, and the landlord was very violent in denouncing us for giving her whisky,
but we got outside the county before the sun went down.   I
had frequent occasion to be in Fort Dodge afterwards, but
heard nothing more of the landlord or his wife.

The road to Council Bluffs from Des Moines was over a
high rolling prairie with scarcely any inhabitants.   The
village of Omaha, opposite Council Bluffs, contained but a few
frame houses of little value.   The settlement of Iowa and Nebraska after this period is almost marvelous.   Iowa now (1895),
contains over 2,000,000 and Nebraska over 1,200,000 people.
The twelve states composing the north central division of the
United States contained 5,403,595 inhabitants in 1850, and now

number over 24,000,000, or more than quadruple the number in 1850, and more than the entire population of the United States in that year. I have frequently visited these states since, and am not surprised at their wonderful growth. I believe there is no portion of the earth's surface of equal area which is susceptible of a larger population than that portion of the United States lying north of the Ohio River, and between the Allegheny Mountains and the Missouri River.

CHAPTER V.

Early Days in Congress.

My First Speech in the House — Struggle for the Possession of Kansas —
Appointed as a Member of the Kansas Investigating Committee — The
Invasion of March 30th, 1855 — Exciting Scenes in the Second
District of Kansas — Similar Violence in Other Territorial
Districts — Return and Report of the Committee — No
Relief Afforded the People of Kansas — Men of
Distinction in the 34th Congress — Long
Intimacy with Schuyler Colfax.

IN 1854 the Whig party had disappeared from the roll of
parties in the United States. It was a bad name for a
good party. English in its origin, it had no significance
in American politics. The word "Democratic," as applied
to the opposing party, was equally a misnomer. The word
"Democracy," from which it is derived, means a government
of the people, but the controlling power of the Democratic
party resided in the southern states, where a large portion of
the people were slaves, and the ruling class were slaveholders,
and the name was not applicable to such a people. The Republican party then represented the progressive tendency of the
age, the development of the country, the opposition to slavery
and the preservation of the Union. It was about to engage in
a political contest for the administration of the government.
It was in the minority in the Senate, and had but a bare plurality in the House. It had to contest with an adverse Executive and Supreme Court, with a well-organized party in possession of all the patronage of the government, in absolute control of the slaveholding states, and supported by strong minor-
ities in each of the free states.

This was the condition of parties when the 34th Congress
met in the old halls of the Senate and House of Representatives on the 3rd of December, 1855. The Senate was composed
of 43 Democrats and 17 Republicans. There were four vacancies. The House was composed of 97 Republicans, 82 Democrats, and 45 classed as Third Party men, mostly as Americans.

(110)

Eight Members were absent, and not yet classified. An unusual proportion of the Members were new in public life, the result of the revolution of parties caused by the Nebraska bill. The Senate was already organized with Mr. Bright, of Indiana, as president *pro tempore*.

The first duty of the House was to elect a speaker, a majority of the Members present being necessary to a choice. The balloting for speaker continued until February 2, 1856, when Nathaniel P. Banks was elected under the plurality rule. During these two months the House was without a speaker, and also without rules except the general principles of parliamentary law. The clerk of the last House of Representatives presided. Innumerable speeches were made, some of them very long, but many brief ones were made by the new Members who took the occasion to air their oratory. Timothy Day, one of my colleagues, a cynical bachelor and proprietor of the Cincinnati "Commercial," who sat by my side, was constantly employed in writing for his paper. When a new voice was heard he would put his hand to his ear, listen awhile and then, turning impatiently to his writing, would say to me: "Another dead cock in the pit." This cynical suppression of a new Member rather alarmed me, but on the 9th of January, as appears from the "Globe," I ventured to make a few remarks. When I sat down I turned to Mr. Day and said: "Another dead cock in the pit." He relieved me by saying: "Not quite so bad as that." The first speech I made in the House contained my political creed at the time. I here insert a paragraph or two:

"I desire to say a few words; and I would preface them with the remark, that I do not intend, while I have a seat in this House, to occupy much of its time in speaking. But I wish to state now why I have voted, and shall continue to vote, for Mr. Banks. I care not whether he is a member of the American party or not. I have been informed that he is, and I believe that he is. But I repeat I care not to what party he belongs. I understood him to take this position, — that the repeal of the Missouri Compromise was an act of great dishonor, and that under no circumstances whatever will he — if he have the power — allow the institution of human slavery to derive any benefit from that repeal. That is my position. I have been a Whig, but I will yield all party preferences, and will act in concert with men of all parties and opinions who will steadily aid in preserving our western territories for free labor; and I say now, that I never will vote for a man for speaker of this house, unless he convinces me, by his conduct and by his voice, that he never will, if he has the power to prevent it, allow the institution of slavery to derive any advantage from repealing the compromise of 1820.

"I believe Mr. Banks will be true to that principle, and, therefore, I vote for him without regard to his previous political associations, or to his adherence to the American party. I vote for him simply because he has had the manliness to say here, that, having the power, he will resist the encroachments of slavery, even by opposing the admission of any slave state that may be formed out of the territory north and west of Missouri."

Notwithstanding the promise I made not to occupy much of the time of the House in speaking, and the cynicism of my friend Day, I did partake frequently in the debate on the organization of the House. I became involved in a contest with Mr. Dunn, of Indiana, who had steadily refused to vote for Mr. Banks for speaker, to which I deemed proper to refer. He said he was not to be deterred from performing his duty, as he understood it, by the criticisms of the "neophyte" from Ohio. I replied at considerable length and with some feeling. In my reply I repeated my position in respect to the repeal of the Missouri Compromise, declaring: "If the repeal was wrong all northern and southern men alike ought to help to reinstate that restriction. Nothing less than that will satisfy the country; and if it is not done, as it probably will not be, we will maintain our position of resisting the admission of Kansas as a slave state, under all possible circumstances."

Later on in the debate I declared:

"I am no Abolitionist in the sense in which the term is used; I have always been a conservative Whig. I was willing to stand by the compromises of 1820 and 1850; but, when our Whig brethren of the south allow this administration to lead them off from their principles, when they abandon the position which Henry Clay would have taken, forget his name and achievements, and decline any longer to carry his banner — they lose all their claims on me. And I say now, that until this wrong is righted, until Kansas is admitted as a free state, I cannot act in party association with them. Whenever that question is settled rightly I will have no disposition to disturb the harmony which ought to exist between the north and south. I do not propose to continue agitation ; I only appear here to demand justice, — to demand compliance with compromises fully agreed upon and declared by law. I ask no more, and I will submit to no less."

This was a narrow platform, but it was the one supported by public opinion. I believed that a majority of the Members called Americans, especially those from the south, were quite willing that Kansas should be admitted as a free state, but local pride prevented such a declaration. It is easy to perceive now that if this had been promptly done the slavery question would have been settled for many years. But that opportunity was permitted to pass unused. The people, both north and south, were thoroughly aroused. No compromise was possible. The contest could only be settled by the force of superior numbers. That was the logic of the Nebraska bill, which was an appeal to the people of both sections, already greatly excited, to struggle for, and, if necessary, to fight for the possession of a large and beautiful territory. It forced the irrepressible conflict in the most dangerous form.

On the one side were the border ruffians of Missouri, hereafter described, backed by the general sentiment of the south, and actively supported by the administration and by leading Democrats who had held high positions in the public service. On the other side were a large number of free state men in the western states, who looked forward to the opening of Nebraska and Kansas as a new field of enterprise. They were quite ready to fight for their opinions against slavery. They were supported by a general feeling of resentment in the north, caused by the repeal of the Missouri Compromise.

Long before the meeting of Congress the actual struggle for the possession of Kansas commenced. After the passage of the Kansas bill we had reports in the newspapers of gross frauds at pretended elections of rival legislatures, of murder and other crimes, in short, of actual civil war in Kansas; but the accounts were contradictory. It was plainly the first duty of Congress to ascertain the exact condition of affairs in that territory. This could not be done until a speaker was elected.

On the 24th day of January, 1856, President Pierce sent to the House of Representatives, still unorganized, a message upon the condition of affairs in Kansas. A question was made whether a message from the President could be received before a speaker had been elected, but it was decided that the message should be read. The first paragraph is as follows:

"Circumstances have occurred to disturb the course of governmental organization in the Territory of Kansas, and produce there a condition of things which renders it incumbent on me to call your attention to the subject, and urgently to recommend the adoption by you of such measures of legislation as the grave exigencies of the case appear to require."

The President then gave his exposition of the condition of affairs in that territory. This exposition was regarded as a partisan one in favor of the so-called pro-slavery legislative assembly, which met the 2d day of July, 1855. He recommended "that a special appropriation be made to defray any expense which may become requisite in the execution of the laws or the maintenance of public order in the Territory of Kansas."

This was regarded as a threat of the employment of the army to enforce the enactments of a usurping legislature. Congress took no action upon the message until after the organization of the House. On the 14th of January, 1856, a motion was made by Mr. Houston that the message of the President, in reference to the Territory of Kansas, be referred to the committee of the whole on the state of the Union. This motion was agreed to. No further action was taken upon the message, but it remained in abeyance. Congress was not prepared to act without full information of the actual condition of affairs in that territory.

On the 19th of March, 1856, the House of Representatives adopted a series of resolutions offered by Mr. Dunn, of Indiana, as follows:

"*Resolved*, That a committee of three of the Members of this House, to be appointed by the speaker, shall proceed to inquire into and collect evidence in regard to the troubles in Kansas generally, and particularly in regard to any fraud or force attempted, or practiced, in reference to any of the elections which have taken place in said territory, either under the law organizing said territory, or under any pretended law which may be alleged to have taken effect therein since. That they shall fully investigate and take proof of all violent and tumultuous proceedings in said territory at any time since the passage of the Kansas-Nebraska act, whether engaged in by residents of said territory, or by any person or persons from elsewhere going into said territory and doing, or encouraging others to do, any act of violence or public disturbance against the laws of the United States, or the rights, peace, and safety of the residents of said territory ; and for that purpose said committee shall have full power to send for and examine and take copies of all such papers, public records, and proceedings, as in their judgment will be useful in the premises ; and also, to send for persons and examine them on oath, or affirmation, as to matters within their knowledge touching the matters of said investigation ; and said committee, by their chairman, shall have power to administer all necessary oaths or affirmations connected with their aforesaid duties.

"*Resolved, further*, That said committee may hold their investigations at such places and times as to them may seem advisable, and that they may have leave of absence from the duties of this House until they shall have completed such investigation. That they be authorized to employ one or more clerks, and one or more assistant sergeants-at-arms, to aid them in their investigation ; and may administer to them an oath or affirmation faithfully to perform the duties assigned to them respectively, and to keep secret all matters, which may come to their knowledge touching such investigation as said committee shall direct, until the report of the same shall be submitted to this House ; and said committee may discharge any such clerk or assistant sergeant-at-arms for neglect of duty or disregard of instructions in the premises, and employ others under like regulations.

"*Resolved, further*, That if any person shall in any manner obstruct or hinder said committee, or attempt so to do, in their investigation, or shall refuse to attend on said committee, and to give evidence when summoned for that purpose, or shall refuse to produce any papers, book, public record, or other proceeding in their possession or control, to said committee, when so required, or shall make any disturbance where said committee are holding their sittings, said committee may, if they see fit, cause any and every such person to be arrested by said assistant sergeant-at-arms, and brought before this House, to be dealt with as for a contempt.

"*Resolved, further*, That for the purpose of defraying the expenses of said commission, there be and hereby is appropriated the sum of ten thousand ($10,000) dollars, to be paid out of the contingent fund of this House.

"*Resolved, further*, That the President of the United States be and is hereby requested to furnish to said committee, should they be met with any serious opposition by bodies of lawless men in the discharge of their duties aforesaid, such aid from any military force as may, at the time, be convenient to them, as may be necessary to remove such opposition, and enable said committee, without molestation, to proceed with their labors.

"*Resolved, further*, That when said committee shall have completed said investigation, they report all the evidence so collected to this House."

On the 25th of March, 1856, the speaker appointed Lewis D. Campbell, of Ohio, William A. Howard, of Michigan, and

Mordecai Oliver, of Missouri, as the special committee of the House under the above resolution. On the same day Mr. Campbell requested to be excused from the committee referred to, and I was appointed by the speaker in his place, leaving Mr. Howard as chairman.

I accepted the position assigned me with much diffidence. I knew it was a laborious one, that it would take me away from my duties in the House, expose me to a great deal of fatigue and some danger, yet I felt that the appointment on so important a committee was a high compliment when given to a new Member, and at once made preparations for the task before me.

The committee organized at the city of Washington, on the 27th of March, 1856.

Mrs. Sherman expressed a strong desire to accompany me. I tried to frighten her from going, but this made her more resolute, and I consented. She remained with or near us during our stay in Kansas and Missouri, and for a time was accompanied by Mrs. Oliver, a charming lady, to whom we were much indebted for kindness and civility where most of her sex were unfriendly.

The investigation continued from our arrival at St. Louis, on the 12th day of April, 1856, until our arrival at Detroit, on the 17th day of June following, and was conducted in all respects like a judicial trial. The testimony taken filled an octavo volume of 1,188 pages.

Mr. Howard, during our stay in Kansas, was not in very good health, but he never relaxed in his labor until the testimony closed. He was a man of marked ability, a good lawyer, conservative in all his ideas and tendencies, and thoroughly fair and impartial. At his request I accompanied him, with our excellent corps of assistants, to his home in Detroit, where his health so failed that he was confined to his bed for a week. This threw upon me the preparation of the report. The resolutions, under which we were acting, did not require a report from the committee, but only required a report of all the evidence collected, to the House of Representatives, but we felt that such a report without a summary of the evidence

KANSAS INVESTIGATING COMMITTEE.

MORDECAI OLIVER,
COMMISSIONER.

W. BLAIR LORD,
STENOGRAPHER.

JOHN UPTON,
SERGEANT-AT-ARMS.

WM. A. HOWARD,
CHAIRMAN.

JOHN SHERMAN,
COMMISSIONER

and principal facts proven would not be satisfactory to the House.

The majority and minority reports contained 109 pages of printed matter and entered into full details as to the condition of affairs in that territory, and of every election held therein. When the act to organize the Territory of Kansas was passed, May 30, 1854, the greater portion of the eastern border of the territory was included in Indian reservations not open for settlements, and in no portion were there more than a few white settlers. The Indian population of the territory was rapidly decreasing, while many emigrants from different parts of the country, were anxiously waiting the extinction of the Indian title, and the establishment of a territorial government, to seek new homes on the fertile prairies which would be opened to settlement. It cannot be doubted that if the free condition of Kansas had been left undisturbed by Congress, that territory would have had a rapid, peaceful, and prosperous settlement. Its climate, its soil, and its easy access to the older settlements, would have made it the favored course for the tide of emigration constantly flowing to the west, and in a brief period it would have been admitted into the Union as a free state, without sectional excitement. If so organized, none but the kindest feelings would have existed between its citizens and those of the adjoining State of Missouri. Their mutual interests and intercourse, instead of endangering the harmony of the Union, would have strengthened the ties of national brotherhood.

The testimony taken by the committee clearly showed that before the proposition to repeal the Missouri Compromise was introduced into Congress, the people of western Missouri were indifferent to the prohibition of slavery in the territory, and neither asked nor desired its repeal.

When, however, the prohibition was removed by the action of Congress, the aspect of affairs entirely changed. The whole country was agitated by the reopening of a controversy which conservative men in different sections believed had been settled in every state and territory by some law beyond the danger of repeal. The excitement which always accompanied the discussion of the slavery question was greatly increased by the hope, on the one hand, of extending slavery into a region from which it had been excluded by law; and, on the other, by a sense of wrong done by what was regarded as a breach of public faith. This excitement was naturally transferred into the border counties of Missouri and the territory, as settlers favoring free or slave institutions moved into them.

Within a few days after the organic law passed, and as soon as its passage could be known on the border, leading citizens of Missouri crossed into the territory, held "squatter meetings," voted at elections, committed crimes of violence, and then returned to their homes. This unlawful interference was continued in every important stage in the history of the territory; *every election* was controlled, not by the actual settlers, but by the citizens of Missouri; and, as a consequence, every officer in the territory, from constable to legislator, except those appointed by the President, owed his position to non-resident voters. None were elected by the settlers, and no political power whatever, however important, was exercised by the people of the territory.

In October, 1854, the Governor of Kansas, A. H. Reeder, and other officers appointed by the President, arrived in the territory. Settlers from all parts of the country came in great numbers, entering their claims and building their cabins. The first election was for delegate to Congress and was held on the 29th of November, 1854. The governor divided the territory into seventeen election districts, appointed judges, and prescribed proper rules for the election. The report of the committee enters into full details as to this election and all subsequent thereto in each district. The conduct of the election in the second district, held at the village of Douglas, nearly fifty miles from the Missouri line, is a fair specimen of all the elections in Kansas. The report says:

"On the second day before the election large companies of men came into the district in wagons and on horseback, and declared that they were from the State of Missouri, and were going to Douglas to vote. On the morning of the election they gathered around the house where the election was to be held. Two of the judges appointed by the governor did not appear, and other judges were selected by the crowd ; all then voted. In order to make a pretense of right to vote, some persons of the company kept a pretended register of squatter claims, on which anyone could enter his name, and then assert he had a claim in the territory. A citizen of the district, who was himself a candidate for delegate to Congress was told by one of the strangers that he would be abused, and probably killed, if he challenged a vote. He was seized by the collar, called a damned Abolitionist, and was compelled to seek protection in the room with the judges. About the time the polls were closed these strangers mounted their horses and got into their wagons and cried out, 'All aboard for Westport.' A number were recognized as residents of Missouri, and among them was Samuel H. Woodson, a leading lawyer of Independence. Of those whose names are on the poll-books, 35 were resident settlers and 226 were non-residents."

In January and February, 1855, the governor, A. H. Reeder, caused a census to be taken of the inhabitants and qualified voters in Kansas. On the day the census was completed he issued his proclamation for an election to be held March 30, 1855, for members of the legislative assembly of the territory. The proclamation prescribed the boundaries of the districts, the places for polls, the names of judges, the apportionment of members, and the qualification of voters. Had it been observed, a just and fair election would have reflected the will of the people of Kansas. Before the election, however, false and inflammatory rumors were busily circulated among the people of western Missouri. They grossly exaggerated and misrepresented the number and character of the emigration then passing into the territory. By the active exertions of many of the leading citizens, the passions and prejudices of the people of that state were greatly excited. Several residents of Missouri testified to the character of the reports circulated among and credited by the people. These efforts were successful. By an organized movement, which extended from Andrew county, in the north, to Jasper county, in the south, and as far eastward as Boone and Cole counties (Missouri), companies of men were collected in irregular parties and sent into every council district in the territory, and into every representative district but one. The men were so distributed as to control the election in every district. They went to vote, and with the avowed design to make Kansas a slave state. They were generally armed and equipped, carrying with them their own provisions and tents, and so marched into the territory.

As this election was for a legislature, the validity of which was contested, the committee took great pains to procure testimony as to the election in each election district. The election in the second district is a fair specimen. In that district, on the morning of the election, the judges appointed by the governor appeared and opened the polls. Their names were Harrison Burson, Nathaniel Ramsay and Mr. Ellison. The Missourians began to arrive early in the morning, some 500 or 600 of them in wagons and carriages and on horseback, and under the lead of Samuel J. Jones, then postmaster of Westport, Missouri; Claiborne F. Jackson and a Mr. Steeley, of Independence, Missouri. They were armed with double-barreled guns, rifles, bowie-knives and pistols, and had flags hoisted. They held a sort of informal election off at one side, at first for governor of Kansas Territory, and shortly afterwards announced Thomas Johnson, of Shawnee Mission, elected governor. The polls had been opened but a short time when Mr. Jones marched with the crowd up to the window and demanded that they be allowed to vote, without swearing as to their residence. After some noisy and threatening talk, Claiborne F. Jackson addressed the crowd, saying they had come there to vote; that they had a right to vote if they had been there but five minutes, and he was not willing to go home without voting; this was received with cheers. Jackson then called upon them to form into little bands of fifteen or twenty, which they did, and went to an ox-wagon filled with guns, which were distributed among them, and proceeded to load some of them on the ground. In pursuance of Jackson's request, they tied white tape or ribbons in their button holes, so as to distinguish them from the "Abolitionists." They again demanded that the judges resign. Upon their refusing to do so they smashed in the window, sash and all, presented their pistols and guns, and at the same time threatened to shoot. Some one on the outside cried out not to shoot, as there were pro-slavery men in the house with the judges. They then put a pry under the corner of the house, which was built of logs, lifted it up a few inches, and let it fall again, but desisted upon being again told that there were pro-slavery men in the house. During this time the crowd repeatedly demanded to be allowed to vote without being sworn, and Mr. Ellison, one of the judges, expressed himself willing, but the other two judges refused; thereupon a body of men, headed by Sheriff Jones, rushed into the judges' room with cocked pistols and drawn bowie-knives in their hands, and approached Burson and Ramsay. Jones pulled out his watch and said he would give them five minutes to resign in, or die. When the five minutes had expired and the judges had not resigned, Jones now said he would give them another minute and no more. Ellison told his associates that if they did not resign there would be one hundred shots fired in the room in less than fifteen minutes, and then snatching up the ballot-box ran out into the crowd, holding up the ballot-box and hurrahing for Missouri. About that time Burson and Ramsay were called out by their friends, and not suffered to return. As Mr. Burson went out he put the ballot poll-books in his pocket and took them with him, and as he was going out Jones snatched some papers away from him, and shortly afterwards came out himself, holding them up, crying, "Hurrah for Missouri!" After he discovered they were not the poll-books he took a party of men with him and captured the books from a Mr. Umberger, to whom Burson had given them. They then chose two new judges and proceeded with the election. They also threatened to kill the judges if they did not receive their votes, or resign. They said no man should vote who would submit to be sworn; that they would kill any man who would offer to do so. Some of the citizens who were about the window, but had not voted when the crowd of Missourians marched up, upon attempting to vote were driven back by the mob, or driven off. One of them, Mr. I. M. Mace, was asked if he would take the oath, and upon his replying that he would if the judges required it, he was dragged through the crowd away from the polls, amid cries of "kill the damned nigger-thief," "cut his throat," "tear his heart out," etc. After they got into the outside of the crowd they stood around him with cocked revolvers and drawn bowie-knives, one man putting a knife to his breast so that it touched him, another holding a cocked pistol to his ear, while another struck at him with a club.

The Missourians declared they had a right to vote, if they had been in the territory but five minutes. Some said they had been hired to come there and vote, and got a dollar a day, "and by God they would vote or die there." They said the 30th day of March was an important day, as Kansas would be made a slave state on that day. They began to leave in the direction of Missouri in the afternoon, after they had voted, leaving some thirty or forty around the house where the election was held, to guard the polls till after the election was over. The citizens of the territory were not armed, except those who took part in the mob, and a large portion of them did not vote. Three hundred and forty-one votes were polled there that day, of which but some thirty were citizens. A protest against the election was prepared and sent to the governor.

A similarly organized and conducted election was held in each of the other districts of the territory, varying only in degrees of fraud and violence. In the fifteenth district it was proven that several hundred Missourians appeared and voted. Several speeches were made at the polls, and among those who spoke was Major Oliver, one of our committee. He urged all persons to use no harsh words and expressed a hope that nothing would be said or done to wound the feelings of the most sensitive on the other side, giving some reasons, based on the Missouri Compromise, why they should vote, but he himself did not vote. The whole number of votes cast in that district was 417. The number of legal voters was about 80. Of the names on the poll-book but 62 were on the census roll. But a small portion, estimated at one-fourth of the legal voters, voted.

The validity of the so called pro-slavery legislature rested upon this election. It is hardly necessary at this late day to say that such a legislative body could not rightly assume or lawfully exercise legislative functions over any law-abiding community. Their enactments were, by every principle of law and right, null and void. The existence of fraud at the election was admitted by every one, but it was defended on the ground that the New England Emigrant Aid Society had imported a great number of emigrants into Kansas for the sole purpose of making that territory a free state. This claim was thoroughly investigated and the organization and history of the society examined. The only persons who emigrated into the territory under the auspices of this company in 1855, prior to the election in March, was a party of 169 persons who came under the charge of Charles Robinson, and of whom sixty-seven were women and children. They came as actual settlers, intending to make their homes in the territory, and for no other purpose. Some of them returned, but most of them became settlers. A few voted at the election in Lawrence but the number was small. The names of these emigrants were ascertained and thirty-seven of them were found upon the poll-books. This company of peaceful emigrants, moving with their household goods, was distorted into an invading horde of pauper Abolitionists, who were, with others of a similar character, to control the domestic institutions of the territory, and then overturn those of a neighboring state.

The invasion of March 30 left both parties in a state of excitement, tending directly to produce violence. The successful party was lawless and reckless, while assuming the name of the "Law and Order" party. The Free State party, at first surprised and confounded, was greatly irritated, but soon resolved to prevent the success of the invasion. In some districts, protests were sent to the governor; in others such action was prevented by threats, in others by want of time, and in others by the belief that a new election would bring a new invasion. About the same time, all classes of men commenced carrying deadly weapons about their persons. Under these circumstances, a slight or accidental quarrel produced unusual violence. Lawless acts became frequent and passed unpunished. This unhappy condition of the public mind was further increased by acts of violence in western Missouri, where, in April, a newspaper, called the "Parkville Luminary," was destroyed by a mob, and numerous acts of violence and homicides committed. Some innocent persons were unlawfully arrested and others ordered to leave the territory. The first one notified to leave was William Phillips, a lawyer of Leavenworth, and upon his refusal the mob forcibly seized him, took him across the river, carried him several miles into Missouri, and then tarred and feathered him, shaving one side of his head and committing other gross indignities upon his person. Judge Lecompte, chief justice of the territory, Colonel L. N. Burns, of Weston, Missouri, and others, took part in and made speeches at a bitterly partisan meeting, the tendency of which was to produce violence and disorder.

After the most careful examination of the poll-books and the testimony taken, we were convinced beyond all doubt that the election of the 30th of March, 1855, was utterly void. It was the result of an organized invasion from the State of Missouri, a lawless seizure of the conduct of the election, and the open voting by thousands of persons who neither resided in nor pretended to be inhabitants of Kansas. Not content with voting they made false returns of votes never cast, and excluded legal voters because they were "Abolitionists."

A more wanton and shameless overthrow of popular rights cannot be found in history.

The so-called legislative assembly, thus elected, met at Pawnee, on the 2nd of July, 1855. It attempted to make laws for Kansas, and to that end adopted, in substance, the laws of the State of Missouri in gross as the laws for the territory, but, to retain its power, it provided that every officer of the territory, executive and judicial, was to be appointed by the legislature, or by some officer appointed by it.

The legality of this legislature was denied by the great majority of the people who never acquiesced in or obeyed its enactments, thus taking the only course open to them to secure a lawful government.

While the alleged legislative assembly was in session, a movement was instituted to form a state government, and apply for admission into the Union as a state. The first step taken by the people of the territory, in consequence of the invasion of March 30, 1855, was the circulation, for signature, of a graphic and truthful memorial to Congress. Every allegation in this memorial was sustained by the testimony. No further step was taken, as it was hoped that some action by the general government would protect them in their rights. When the alleged legislative assembly proceeded to construct the series of enactments referred to, the settlers were of opinion that submission to them would result in entirely depriving them of the rights secured to them by the organic law.

Their political condition was freely discussed in the territory during the summer of 1855. Several meetings were held in reference to holding a convention to form a state government, and to apply for admission into the Union as a state. Public opinion gradually settled in favor of such an application to the Congress to meet in December, 1855. The first general meeting was held in Lawrence, on the 15th of August, 1855. Other meetings were held in various parts of the territory, which indorsed the action of the Lawrence meeting, and delegates were selected in compliance with its recommendation. An election was called by a proclamation addressed to the legal voters of Kansas, requesting them to meet at their several precincts at the time and places named in the proclamation, then and there to cast their ballots for members of a constitutional convention, to meet at Topeka, on the fourth Tuesday of October.

Elections were held at the time and places designated, and the returns were sent to the executive committee.

The result of the election was proclaimed by the executive committee, and the members elect were required to meet on the 23rd of October, 1855, at Topeka. In pursuance of this proclamation and direction the constitutional convention met at the time and place appointed, and framed a state constitution. A memorial to Congress was also prepared, praying the admission of Kansas into the Union as a state under that constitution. The convention also provided that the question of the adoption of the constitution, and other questions, be submitted to the people, and required the executive committee to take the necessary steps for that purpose.

Accordingly, an election was held on the 15th day of December, 1855, in compliance with the proclamation issued by the executive committee who then issued a proclamation reciting the results of the election of the 15th of December, and at the same time provided for an election, to be held on the 15th day of January, 1856, for state officers and members of the general assembly of the State of Kansas. The election was accordingly held in several election precincts, the returns of which were sent to the executive committee who announced the result by a proclamation.

Thus, when we arrived in Kansas, two rival governments were in existence, one the result of fraud and force, the other confessedly incomplete, being without executive power or recognition. Congress alone could settle the controversy by recognizing one or the other. Its action and its failure to act will be stated further on.

A brief narrative of incidents while the committee was in Kansas may be of interest.

We arrived by steamer at a place called Westport Landing, near the mouth of the Kansas River. As I remember the place it was a mere hamlet, composed of three dwellings, a store, a tavern and a blacksmith shop. We passed over the high rolling prairie, where but a few and scattered cabins then existed, but which now is the site of Kansas City, a beautiful city of 90,000 inhabitants. About six miles from the landing we entered Westport, the headquarters of the Santa Fé trade. This important trade in 1854 was conducted with "prairie schooners," wagons of great dimensions rudely but strongly built, each hauled by four or six mules or Indian ponies, and all driven by as rough a set of men of mixed color, tribe and nativity as could be found anywhere in the world. Their usual dress was a broad brimmed felt hat, a flannel shirt, home-spun trousers, without suspenders, and heavy cowhide boots outside of their trousers, with a knife or pistols, or both, in their belts or boots. They were properly classed as border ruffians, and as a rule were whisky soaked.

The contrast of this region between then and now is a marked evidence of the wonderful change that has been made within a single generation. I have several times visited Kansas City and its environs since 1856. I have noted the change at each visit! The rolling prairie has been checkered with streets and avenues, and the squares and suburbs are dotted all over with residences, stores and workshops. The landing, once a single pier, now extends miles along the Missouri River. The border ruffians have disappeared with the Indians and "greasers," and have been replaced by an active, intelligent and prosperous community.

Mrs. Sherman and myself started in advance for Lawrence in an open buggy drawn by one horse, and were told to follow the trail, and this we had no difficulty in doing. We passed through one or more Indian reservations, over as beautiful a country as the sun shines upon, but without house or habitation, except Indian huts. We arrived at Lawrence, a town less than two years old, and were cordially received. The people there were fearing a raid by the "border ruffians," but this was fortunately postponed until our departure for Leavenworth.

The committee proceeded immediately to take testimony. Governor Reeder acted in behalf of the Free State side, and General Whitfield in behalf of the pro-slavery side, this being the conceded line of demarcation between the opposing factions. The town was in embryo, nothing finished, and my wife and I were glad to have a cot in a room in the unfinished and unoccupied "Free State Hotel," soon after burned to the ground by Jones, the marshal of Kansas, or his deputies. There was no difficulty in obtaining witnesses or testimony, but, as a rule, the witnesses on one side would only testify in Lawrence, and those on the other in Lecompton or Leavenworth. They were like soldiers in hostile armies, careful to keep outside of the enemy's camp.

Dr. Robinson, afterwards Governor Robinson, was then by far the ablest and bravest leader of the Free State cause. His history of the Kansas conflict is the most interesting yet published. When the committee visited Lecompton to take testimony, it was a surprise to us that he not only offered, but insisted upon going to that place, the headquarters and capital of the pro-slavery party. It was then scarcely a hamlet, and its existence depended entirely upon the success of that party.

Dr. Robinson and I rode together into the place. It was easy to see that he was not a welcome visitor. Everyone but the committee carried arms. Several murders and affrays had recently occurred, in regard to which we had taken evidence. Here we had access to the poll-books of the contested elections, and met on friendly terms with the officers of the territory, the chief of whom were Judge Lecompte, chief justice of the territory, after whom the town had been named, and Jones, the marshal of the United States. Governor Shannon was, I think, also there for a time. The quarters for lodging were even more limited here than in Lawrence. I slept in a cot side by side with the one occupied by Judge Lecompte, who, though a terror to the Free State men, seemed to me to be a good humored gentleman, more violent in his words than in his acts. We had no unpleasant incident while there, though such had been prophesied at Lawrence.

From Lecompton the committee went to Topeka, then quite a small village, now a city of 33,000 inhabitants. It was already ambitious to become the Free State capital of Kansas, by reason of its central position. There was then no settlement of any importance west of Topeka. Some testimony was taken, but we soon returned to Lawrence, and from thence went to Leavenworth. A large part of the distance between these places was an Indian reservation. Mrs. Sherman and I rode over it in a buggy, and found no white man's habitation on the way. Its great value and fertility was easily perceived, and it is now well settled by an active and prosperous population of white men. On the road we met an Indian seated near his wigwam, with a gun in his hand, and for a moment I feared that he might use it. He uttered some Indian gibberish, which we construed as an invitation to enter his hut. We tied our horse, entered, and found no one there but an old squaw. I gave the Indian some silver which he greedily took, but indicated by his motions that he wanted a drink of whisky, but this I was not able to give him.

Leavenworth was a new town near Fort Leavenworth, the then western military post of the army of the United States. We placed ourselves in communication with Colonel Sumner,

MR. SHERMAN AT THE AGE OF THIRTY-FIVE.

then in command, but we had no occasion to summon his official aid, though authorized by the resolutions under which we were acting to call for such assistance from any military force which was at the time convenient to us. However, our meetings there were more disturbed than at any other place. The trouble commenced at Lawrence shortly after our arrival at Leavenworth. A company of about 700 armed men, the great body of whom were not citizens of the territory, were marched into the town of Lawrence under Marshal Donaldson and Sheriff Jones, officers claiming to act under the law, and they then bombarded and burned to the ground a valuable hotel and one private house, and destroyed two printing presses and material. The posse, being released by the officers, proceeded to sack, pillage and rob houses, stores, trunks, even taking the clothing of women and children. The people of Leavenworth were much alarmed, as threats were made to clean out the "Black Republican Committee" at Leavenworth. No attempt of that kind was made. Later on, Dr. Robinson was arrested on a steamboat on the way with his wife to St. Louis. We had confided to him a copy of the testimony taken, to be delivered to Mr. Banks, speaker of the House. We believe that a knowledge of that fact caused the arrest, but, fortunately, Mrs. Robinson, who had the testimony safely secured in her clothing, was allowed to proceed to Washington. Dr. Robinson was taken back to Leavenworth and placed in prison, where I called upon him, but was rudely threatened, and was only allowed to speak to him in the presence of the jailor.

We were frequently threatened through anonymous letters. On one occasion, upon going in the morning to the committee room, I found tacked on the door a notice to the "Black Republican Committee" to leave Kansas "upon penalty of death." I cut it from the door and called upon a bystander to testify to the contents and the place from which it was taken.

On one Sunday morning, while sitting in my lodging, a very rough looking man entered, and I indicated to Mr. W. Blair Lord, our stenographer, to take down what he said. With many oaths and imprecations he told us that he had been robbed by ruffians of his horses and wagon a few miles from

Leavenworth; that he had offered to fight them, but they were cowards; that he was born in Richland county, Ohio, near Mansfield, and he wanted me to help him get his traps. I knew his family as famous fighters. I asked him if he would swear to his story. He said he would, and Mr. Lord read it to him, oaths and all, from his stenographic notes. He stared at Lord and demanded "Where in hell did you get that?" He was handed the stenographic notes and, after looking at them, he exclaimed: "Snakes, by God; but it is all true!" Whether he got his outfit and traps I never knew.

The evidence at Leavenworth being closed, the committee returned to Westport, Missouri. While we were there we saw an armed and organized body of residents of Missouri march across the line into Kansas to retaliate, as we were told, the murder of five pro-slavery men at Osawatamie. While they were marching into Westport from the east, Governor Shannon, in obedience to the summons of the committee, came into Westport from the territory, and in his presence they filed off in regular array into the territory. It was difficult to ascertain the precise causes of these murders, but it was shown that they were in retaliation for those of certain Free State men, one of whom was the son of John Brown, later the famous leader of the attack on the fort at Harper's Ferry, and who had acted for the committee in summoning witnesses to Lawrence. The testimony in respect to these murders was vague, and the murderers were not identified. Two years afterwards I met John Brown in Chicago, and asked him about the murder of the pro-slavery men at Osawatamie; he replied with spirit that they were not murdered, but that they had been arrested, tried by a jury, convicted and executed. The arrest, trial and execution must have been done during one night. He did not disclose the names of the executioners, but his cool statement was a striking picture of the scenes then enacted in Kansas by both sides; both appealed to the law of force and crime, and crime was justified by crime.

The evidence taken at Westport closed the investigation and Mr. Howard and I returned to Detroit, as already stated.

The report was approved by Mr. Howard, and presented by him to the House of Representatives, July 1, 1856, as a question of privilege. The reception of it gave rise to much debate, but in the end I was permitted on the same day to read it. The minority report of Mr. Oliver was presented July 11 cf that year. No action was taken on the reports, but they were widely published.

On July 31, 1856, I made a speech on the Kansas contested election between General Whitfield and Governor Reeder, during which I was drawn into a discussion with Alexander H. Stephens, of Georgia, and Mr. Oliver, of Missouri, in which the general questions involved in the Kansas controversy were fully debated. I closed with this language:

"The worst evil that could befall our country is civil war, but the outrages in Kansas cannot be continued much longer without producing it. To our southern brethren I especially appeal. In the name of southern rights, crimes have been committed, and are being committed, which I know you cannot and do not approve. These have excited a feeling in the northern states that is deepening and strengthening daily. It may produce acts of retaliation. You are in a minority and, from the nature of your institutions, your relative power is yearly decreasing. In excusing this invasion from Missouri — in attempting to hold on to an advantage obtained by force and fraud — you are setting an example which, in its ultimate consequences, may trample your rights under foot. Until these wrongs are righted, you must expect northern men to unite to redress them. It may not be this year, but, as sure as there is a God in heaven, such a union will be effected ; and you will gain nothing by sustaining northern agitators in violating the compromise of your fathers."

On July 28, 1856, I offered, as an amendment to the army appropriation bill, the following proviso:

"*Provided, nevertheless*, That no part of a military force of the United States herein provided for, shall be employed in aid of the enforcement of the enactments of the alleged legislative assembly of the Territory of Kansas, recently assembled at Shawnee Mission, until Congress shall have enacted either that it was or was not a valid legislative assembly, chosen in conformity with the organic law, by the people of said territory. And *Provided*, That until Congress shall have passed on the validity of the said legislative assembly of Kansas, it shall be the duty of the President to use the military force in said territory to preserve the peace, suppress insurrection, repel invasion, and protect persons and property therein, and upon the national highways in the State of Missouri, from unlawful seizures and searches. And *be it further provided*, That the President is required to disarm the present organized militia of the Territory of Kansas and recall all the United States arms therein distributed, and to prevent armed men from going into said territory to disturb the public peace, or aid in the enforcement or resistance of real or pretended laws."

After long debate, this was agreed to by a vote of 80 yeas to 47 nays. The deliberate purpose of a majority of the House was to prevent any further support of the Lecompton territorial legislature. This amendment, however, was disagreed to by the Senate and referred to a committee of conference. On the 18th of August, the last day of the session, the disagreement continued and the conference report was taken up for action. A motion was made that the House insist upon its amendments and agree to another committee of conference. This was defeated, but no definite action was taken, as a majority of the House was opposed to a further conference, and so the army bill failed.

On the same day the President, by proclamation, convened the two Houses in extra session to meet on the 21st day of August, three days later. The President, in his message, urged Congress to recede from the Kansas proviso to the army bill. The Republicans of the House were determined to insist upon that proviso, and, by repeated votes, refused to withdraw it or to reconsider it, but, after a session of nine days, the House finally yielded, but only after the Senate had agreed to an amendment, which contained the substance of the proviso offered by me, as follows:

"*Provided*, That no part of the military force of the United States, for the support of which appropriations are made by this act, shall be employed in aid of the enforcement of any enactment heretofore passed by the bodies claiming to be the territorial legislature of Kansas."

This amendment was agreed to and thus, in the final struggle, while no effective measures to relieve the people of Kansas from the tyranny imposed upon them were adopted, the declaration was made that the military force of the United States should not be used to aid in the enforcement of any enactment theretofore passed by bodies claiming to be the territorial legislature of Kansas.

Thus it appears that during this long and wearisome session (for in fact the two were but one), I was almost exclusively occupied in a futile effort to restore the prohibition of slavery in Kansas, according to the Missouri Compromise, but the struggle made was fruitful in good. It strengthened the Free State sentiment in Kansas, it aroused public sentiment in the north, and drove the south to adopt new and strange theories which led to divisions in the Democratic party and its disruption and overthrow in 1860. The compromise made was understood to be the work of Mr. Seward, and, though not satisfactory to the Republicans of the House, it was at least a drawn battle, and, like Bunker Hill to Yorktown, was the prelude to the Revolution that ended at Appomattox.

Among the many who attained distinction in the 34th Congress I can only refer to a few, the chief of whom was Nathaniel P. Banks, who, after a long struggle, was elected speaker. He was born in Waltham, Massachusetts, January 30, 1816. He had risen into prominence without any aid or advantage of early education or training. He was the son of an overseer in a cotton factory in Waltham, where he was for a time employed. He improved his leisure hours by the study of history, political economy and the science of government. He learned the trade of a machinist. He early acquired the habit of speaking well on various subjects, and was elected as a Democratic member of the legislature from his native town. In 1852 he was elected to Congress, running upon the ticket with General Pierce, the Democratic candidate for President. He took a decided stand against the repeal of the Missouri Compromise. He was a man of striking presence, with a fine voice and engaging manners. He filled the difficult position of speaker with great credit, and is still remembered by his associates as perhaps the best fitted for the special duties of speaker of the House of any Member since the time of Henry Clay. He was afterward elected Governor of Massachusetts and continued in that position for several years. When the war broke out he was appointed major-general of volunteers, but his service in the army was not marked. After the war was over he was re-elected to Congress, but seemed to have lost his power and influence. In later years his memory was impaired and he "lagged superfluous upon the stage." He died September 1, 1894.

Lewis D. Campbell, of Ohio, was elected to Congress in 1848 as a Whig, and re-elected to each successive Congress down to 1856, when his seat was contested and the House of Representatives decided against him. He and Banks were the leading candidates for the speakership of the 34th Congress, but the majority of the anti-Nebraska Members voted for Banks, and upon his election Campbell was made chairman of the committee of ways and means, and had substantial control of the business of that Congress. He never was in hearty sympathy with the Republican party. He was subsequently elected to the 42nd Congress in 1870 as a Democrat, but had lost, in a great measure, his influence. He served for a time as colonel of a regiment in the war. He was a man of marked ability but was too erratic to be a successful leader in any cause or party.

In 1850, at the early age of twenty-seven, Galusha A. Grow was elected a Representative in Congress from Pennsylvania. He was an active and very useful Member. He took strong ground against the repeal of the Missouri Compromise, and in 1859 was a competitor with me for the position of speaker, but withdrew in my favor after the first ballot. In the following Congress he was chosen speaker and rendered very valuable service as such. After a continuous service in Congress for fourteen years, he retired from active political life and engaged in important business enterprises, but always took an interest in political affairs. He was elected by an overwhelming majority as a Member of the 53rd Congress at large from his state.

Schuyler Colfax was a conspicuous Member of Congress from 1855 until he was nominated for the office of Vice President, in 1868, on the ticket with General Grant. During this long period he represented one district, and served for six years as speaker. He was a very industrious, active Member. As we were of about the same age, and our lives ran in parallel lines, we were often thrown together. We and our families in Washington messed together in a household for several years, and our intercourse was always friendly and intimate. When he became Vice President he remarked to me that I was first to enter the Senate, but he was first to become Vice President. After his service as Vice President, he retired from public life and delivered lectures upon many topics.

Many other Members of that Congress, equally worthy of note, have passed away from the scenes of life, and some few survive. I would gladly recall their memory if my space would allow.

CHAPTER VI.

Birth of the Republican Party.

D URING the first session of the 34th Congress, the opponents of slavery were without a party name or organization. They agreed only in the one demand,
that slavery should not be established in Kansas.
On other questions they voted on old party lines. The Members elected in 1854 in the northern states were Democrats,
Whigs or Free Soilers. Many of the Democrats still supported
the administration of President Pierce, and acquiesced in the
doctrine of popular sovereignty in the territories. A few of
the Whigs, of conservative leanings, acted with the Americans,
or "Know-Nothings," of the south. A strong popular movement was initiated in some of the western states as early as
1854 in favor of a new party. This was especially the case in
Wisconsin and Michigan. On the 6th of July, 1854, a popular
convention was held at Jackson, Michigan, composed of hundreds of men of all parties, who denounced slavery as a great
moral, social and political evil, and resolved that, postponing
and suspending all differences with regard to political economy
or administrative policy, they would act cordially and faithfully in unison to oppose the extension of slavery, and be
known as Republicans until the contest was terminated. This
name was assumed in other states of the north.

The state convention held in Ohio on July 13, 1855, formally declared itself a convention of the Republican party.

The long struggle in Kansas, the elections in 1855, and the contest for the speakership of the House, added strength to this movement, and the name "Republican" was formally given to the new party by the national convention held at Philadelphia, June 17, 1856, as the best expression of its views and principles.

It appeared for the time that the new party would carry the country in a blaze of enthusiasm. And, looking over the past, I am clearly of the opinion that this would have been the result but for the faulty nomination of Colonel John C. Fremont as the Republican candidate for President, and the sagacious nomination of James Buchanan as the Democratic candidate. The Republican party, still composed of uncertain elements, sought only for a candidate that was available. Seward or Chase was the natural candidate. They were fully identified with the principles and purposes of their party. They were men of marked ability, strong in their respective states, each elected governor of his state and sure of its support, but Chase was opposed on account of his advanced opinions on the slavery question, and Seward was actively opposed by the so-called American party, for his open hostility to its principles and policy. All these sought for a new man, and public opinion gradually, but strongly, turned to John C. Fremont. He had no experience in public life, but he attracted attention by his bold explorations in the west and, especially, by his marching to California, and occupation of this Mexican territory. A strong effort was made to secure the nomination of Justice McLean of the United States Supreme Court. He had been long in public life, had been a cabinet officer in two administrations, had been appointed to the supreme bench by Jackson, had held this position for twenty-six years, and was a man of spotless integrity. His nomination was strongly urged by conservative Republicans in all the northern states, and by the delegates from Pennsylvania especially by Thaddeus Stevens, who asserted that the nomination of Fremont would not only lose the State of Pennsylvania, to the Republicans, but that the party would be defeated at the presidential election. But the current of opinion in the west, in New

England and New York, was too strong in favor of Fremont, and he was nominated.

The Democratic national convention met at Cincinnati, June 2, 1856, for the nomination of candidates for President and Vice President. Popular feeling was then strongly aroused against that party by the assault of Brooks on Sumner, the removal of Reeder, the appointment of Shannon, the crimes in Kansas, and the recent sacking of Lawrence. A large proportion of northern Democrats, who still adhered to their party, were restless under the violence of their southern associates. It was this feeling, no doubt recognized by both northern and southern Democrats, that prevented the nomination of either Pierce or Douglas. Buchanan was regarded as a conservative man of great experience, who, being absent from the country during the entire period of the Kansas contest, would, it was believed, and as his supporters affirmed, pursue a quieting policy that would arrest and prevent further outrages and would secure fair elections in that territory. He was popular in Pennsylvania, had served for many years in each House of Congress, had creditably represented the United States as minister to Russia and Great Britain, had been Secretary of State and the head of the cabinet of President Polk. He was unanimously supported by the delegation from Pennsylvania, then a doubtful state, and, after many ballots and the defeat of Pierce, was nominated with the acquiescence of Douglas. This nomination greatly strengthened the Democratic party. It held in that party the protection Democrats, and a large proportion of those who in 1854 voted for anti-Nebraska Members of Congress. The appointment of Colonel Geary of Pennsylvania as Governor of Kansas, in the place of Governor Shannon, and his firm and impartial administration, greatly aided the Democratic party. It was regarded as evidence of a change of policy in Kansas, made at the request of Mr. Buchanan.

The American party met at the city of Philadelphia soon after the election of Banks as speaker, and nominated Millard Fillmore for President and Donelson for Vice President. This movement did not at first excite much attention, as it was known that in the north it would draw equally from the two great parties, and in the south could only affect injuriously the Democratic party. Its platform of principles was condemned by both the Republican and Democratic conventions.

Mr. Fillmore took strong ground against what he called a sectional ticket presenting both candidates from the free states, with the avowed purpose of one part of the Union ruling over the whole United States.

The nomination of Fremont, however, greatly strengthened the movement in favor of Fillmore. There was a large element of the old Whig party in the north, which, though friendly to Republican principles and willing to support Seward or McLean, yet would not vote for Fremont, who had none of the qualities that commanded their respect. Such men as Ewing, Everett, Winthrop and Hilliard, conspicuous leaders and eminent statesmen, announced their purpose to vote for Fillmore. Mr. Choate, the eminent lawyer and statesman of Massachusetts, declared his purpose to vote for Buchanan, upon the plausible ground that, as the choice was between Buchanan and Fremont, he was compelled, by a sense of duty, to vote for Buchanan.

At the same time leading Democrats in the south declared that if Fremont was elected the Union could not and ought not to be preserved. The Whigs of the south, with scarce an exception, were committed to the support of Fillmore and Donelson, and joined in an outcry of danger to the Union.

As the canvass progressed this feeling increased, and before its close it became apparent that some of the older and more populous Republican states would be lost by the Republican party. I shared in this feeling of distrust of Fremont, but gave him my support.

I was nominated without any opposition for re-election to Congress by a convention held at Shelby on 12th day of August, 1856, and was elected in October by a majority of 2,861.

I took an active part in the canvass, after the adjournment of Congress, mainly in southern Ohio, where it was apparent that the nomination of Buchanan was popular. In Pennsylvania, especially in Philadelphia, the cry was for "Buck, Breck and free Kansas." John G. Forney, the chairman of the Democratic state committee, promised that if Buchanan was elected there would be no interference with the efforts of the people of Kansas to make that territory a free state. The result of the canvass was that Buchanan carried the states of Pennsylvania, New Jersey, Indiana, Illinois and California at the November election and was elected.

In reviewing the past it is apparent that the election of Buchanan was necessary to convince the people of the north that no successful opposition to the extension of slavery could be made except by a party distinctly pledged to that policy. Mr. Buchanan encountered difficulties which no human wisdom could overcome. Whatever may have been his desire he was compelled, by the prevailing sentiment in his party, to adopt measures that made a conflict between the sections unavoidable. The election of Fremont would probably have precipitated this conflict before the north was ripe for it. His conduct during the early period of the war proves that he would have been unequal to such an emergency. His defeat was the postponement of the irrepressible conflict until it became apparent to all that our country must be all free or all slave territory. This was the lesson taught by the administration of Buchanan, and Lincoln was best fitted to carry it into execution.

Pierce was still President, but after his defeat for the nomination he changed his policy materially. Events were allowed to develop in Kansas with a growing tendency in favor of the Free State party. Judge Lecompte was removed from an office the duties of which he was totally unfit to perform. A large number of emigrants from many of the northern states were preparing to move in the spring to Kansas. Governor Geary of that territory, who had taken a decided stand in favor of equal and exact justice to all men, was met by opposition from the pro-slavery faction. His life was threatened and strong demands were made for his removal. He became satisfied that he would not be sustained by the administration, and on the 4th of March, 1857, resigned his position.

Immediately upon the assembling of Congress in December, 1856, and before the usual message had been sent to the President,

notifying him that the House of Representatives was prepared to enter upon the duties of the session, a contest sprang
up over the question of administering the oath of office to Mr.
Whitfield as a delegate from the Territory of Kansas, and a
struggle resulted which continued until the 9th of December,
when the oath of office was administered to him and he took
his seat.

President Pierce sent to the House of Representatives, December 2, 1856, his last message. He commenced it with a
careful review of the Kansas question and this led to a debate
which continued during the entire session. On the 8th of
December I undertook to answer as much of the message as
related to the slavery question. He had, in the message, defended the repeal of the restriction of slavery contained in the
Missouri Compromise, asserting that this compromise was un-
constitutional and abortive, but I showed that it had been
recognized as in full force by every administration since and including that of Monroe, that it did not extend to the territory
acquired from Mexico, and that it was consistent with the compromise acts of 1850. He asserted that the purpose was not
only to exclude slavery from Kansas, but also from places
where it then existed. I showed this to be inaccurate by the
express denial of such a purpose in every platform of the
Republican party. I then declared that "If I had my voice, I
would not have one single political Abolitionist in the northern states. I am opposed to any interference by the northern
people with slavery in the slave states; I act with the Republican party, with hundreds of thousands of others, simply
because the Republican party resists the extension, but does
not seek the abolition, of slavery."

My speech, as reported, expresses, as I believe, the limit and
extent of the aims of the Republican party at that time. The
only regret I feel is that the tone and temper of my remarks
were not such as should be addressed to the President of the
United States by a Member of Congress.

What I say of myself can be truthfully said of many other
Members. The feeling against the President was embittered
by the firm stand taken by him in support of a policy which

we regarded as unpatriotic, and dangerous in the highest degree
to the public peace and the national Union. In his last message he defended or excused the lawless efforts made by residents of Missouri to establish slavery in Kansas. He made no
effort to prevent the invasion of Kansas or the crimes committed against its citizens. He appointed many governors for
this territory, and in every instance where they sought to protect the rights of its people, he either removed them or denied
them his support. This was the case with Reeder and Shannon.
Even Governor Geary, whom he praised in his message, and
whom Buchanan had lauded during the canvass, was abandoned by both, and compelled to resign because he sought to
protect all citizens alike.

President Pierce was properly, according to usage, a candidate for re-election when the convention met to nominate his
successor, but he was defeated by Buchanan. Mr. Douglas,
the chief instrument in the passage of the Nebraska bill, met a
like fate. Buchanan was saved only by the popular cry of
"Buchanan, Breckenridge and Free Kansas," and the confident
belief, founded upon his declaration, that his election would
secure freedom to Kansas.

The political excitement existing during the whole of President Pierce's term entered into social life in Washington.
The President was not brought into contact with those who
differed with him in opinion. His family afflictions were, no
doubt, the partial cause of this. The sincere friendship that
often exists between political adversaries in public life were
not possible during this period. Social lines were drawn on
sectional lines, and in the north party lines became hostile
lines. Such causes, no doubt, led to unjust criticism of the
President, and, in turn, caused him to regard his political
adversaries as enemies to their country and disturbers of the
public peace. I scarcely remember seeing him during this
Congress, and was strongly prejudiced against him. A more
careful study of the motives and conduct of public men during
this period has changed my opinion of many of them, and,
especially, of President Pierce. That he was a genial, social
and agreeable companion is affirmed by all who were familiar

with him. That his opinions were honestly entertained, and firmly supported, is shown by his adherence to them without change or shadow of turning. In this respect he compares favorably with many leading men of his party, who stifled their opinions to meet the currents of the day. He had been a general of distinction in the Mexican War and a Member of both the Senate and House of Representatives. He was a leading lawyer in his state. His messages to Congress, considered in a literary view, were able state papers, clearly and strongly expressed. It was his great misfortune to have to deal with a controversy that he did not commence, but he did not shrink from the responsibility. He believed in the policy of non-intervention in the territories, and so did not prevent the "border ruffians" of Missouri crossing the line and voting at every election in Kansas, setting up a bogus legislature, adopting the laws of Missouri as the laws of Kansas, and establishing negro slavery in that territory. Fortunately a more numerous, courageous and intelligent population reversed all this, and led, not only to the exclusion of slavery in Kansas, but also to its abolition in the United States.

With the kindly biography of President Pierce, written by his friend, Nathaniel Hawthorne, before me, I can appreciate his ability, integrity and agreeable social qualities, and only regret that he was President of the United States at a time when the sagacity of a Jefferson, the determined courage of a Jackson, or the shrewdness and wisdom of a Lincoln, were needed to meet the difficulties and dangers which he had to encounter.

There is but one more personal incident of the 34th Congress I care to mention. Mr. Banks designated me as a member of the committee on foreign affairs. Mr. Alexander C. M. Pennington, as chairman of that committee, handed me the voluminous papers in reference to the French Spoliation Claims. They covered an interesting period of American history, embracing all that between 1793 and 1801, in which were involved important negotiations both in England and France, and outrages committed upon our, then, infant government by the governments of France and Great Britain. I had all the feeling of natural indignation against those great powers who sought to draw the United States into their controversies, and practice upon us enormities and outrages that we would not submit to for a moment in our day. Yet, after a full and careful examination of all the papers in the case, I became thoroughly satisfied that these claimants, whatever might be said as to their claims against the French government, had absolutely no foundation for a claim against the United States.

I wrote an adverse report, but it was suppressed in the committee. Bills for the payment of these claims were presented from time to time. In 1870 Senator Sumner reported favorably to the Senate a bill for the purpose from the committee on foreign relations. It was opposed by Senator Thurman and myself and again laid aside. On the 14th of December, 1882, the bill was again pressed, the debate which ensued clearly showing that the United States pressed these claims against France to the verge of war.

The whole case is this: certain depredations were committed by the French government and by the citizens of France, upon the citizens of the United States, previous to the beginning of the present century. The government of the United States did all it could to secure payment and compensation to its citizens for these depredations. The French government denied the validity of the claims, holding, on the other hand, that the government of the United States had violated the treaties made with it under circumstances of sacred obligation, that its citizens therefore were justified in doing what they had done in seizing upon American vessels, and taking from them goods called contraband of war, and in committing these depredations. It uniformly justified and maintained the action of its cruisers in doing these things. In other words, our claims were repudiated by France, their payment being refused, and, as we could not force their payment, we simply abandoned them. Recently they have been referred to the court of claims, without regard to lapse of time, and large sums of money are now being paid by the United States for the depredations committed by the French nearly one hundred years ago, to descendants, three generations removed, of merchants and ship owners, who, with all their losses, enjoyed the most profitable commerce in the history of our mercantile marine. Their payment is, perhaps, the most striking evidence of the improvidence of Congress in dealing with antiquated claims against the government.

The first year of Buchanan's administration, 1857, will always be noted as one of great political excitement, of sudden changes and unexpected results. At its beginning the Democratic party was in complete possession of all branches of the government. The House of Representatives, elected in the fall of 1856, had a strong Democratic majority. The Senate was composed of 37 Democrats, 20 Republicans and 4 Americans. The Supreme Court was composed of 5 Democrats from the slave states, and 2 Democrats and 2 Whigs from the free states. The cabinet of Buchanan had four members from the southern states and three from the northern. The south had full control of all departments of the government, with the President in hearty sympathy with the policy of that section. The condition of Kansas alone caused it trouble. The firm and impartial course of Governor Geary had imparted confidence and strength to the Free State citizens of that territory, who were now in an unquestioned majority through the large emigration from the north during the spring of 1857. The doctrine of popular sovereignty could not, therefore, be relied upon to establish slavery in Kansas, and it was abandoned. New theories had to be improvised and new agencies called into action.

I was present when the oath of office was administered to Mr. Buchanan, on the 4th of March, 1857. With my strong sympathy for the Free State people of Kansas, I hoped and believed that he would give some assurance that the pledges made for him in the canvass would be carried out, but the statement in his inaugural address, that the difference of opinion in respect to the power of the people of a territory to decide the question of slavery for themselves would be speedily and finally settled, as a judicial question, by the Supreme Court of the United States, in a case then pending before it, naturally, excited suspicion and distrust. It was regarded as a change of position, a new device in the interest of slavery. In two days after the inauguration, Chief Justice Taney delivered the opinion of the Supreme Court in the Dred Scott case, as to the status of negroes in the United States. He said:

" They had, for more than a century before, been regarded as beings of an inferior order, and altogether unfit to associate with the white race, either in social or political relations; and so far inferior that they had no rights which the white man was bound to respect, and that the negro might justly and lawfully be reduced to slavery for his benefit."

He said negroes "were not intended to be included in the word 'citizens' in the constitution, and therefore can claim none of the rights and privileges which that instrument provides for and secures to the citizens of the United States;" and announced as the opinion of the court that the Missouri Compromise act was not warranted by the constitution and was therefore void.

These declarations were in no sense necessary to the decision of the case before the court, as it was held that Dred Scott was a resident of Missouri and subject as a slave to the laws of that state.

Justices McLean and Curtis dissented from the decision of the court, and in elaborate opinions refuted, as I think, every position of the Chief Justice.

Thus the Kansas question became a political question in the Supreme Court. At once the south rejected the doctrine of popular sovereignty, and demanded, as a constitutional right, that slaves moved into a territory must be protected like other property, whether the people of the territory wish it or not. This was the first time in our history when this great tribunal entered into the political arena. Its action encouraged the south, but produced a strong feeling of resentment in the north, and widened the breach between the two great sections of the country.

Mr. Buchanan, early in his administration, found it necessary to appoint a Governor of Kansas. He selected Robert J. Walker, of Mississippi, who had held high positions in the national government, having been Secretary of the Treasury and Senator of the United States. He appointed Fred. P.

Stanton, of Tennessee, as secretary of the territory. Mr. Stanton had long been a Member of high standing of the House of Representatives. Both were southern men and both wished to see Kansas a slave state, but both were honorable men who would not seek to gain their ends by dishonest means. After a careful estimate, made by them, it was believed that there were, in the territory, 9,000 Free State Democrats, 8,000 Republicans, 6,000 pro-slavery Democrats, and 500 pro-slavery Americans. A strong effort was made by Governor Walker to induce these elements to join in a movement for a convention to frame a constitution, with a view to admit Kansas as a state in the Union. The Free State men, while anxious for such a result, were not willing to trust their adversaries with the conduct of such an election, without some safeguards against the repetition of the frauds and violence of previous elections. The result was that only 2,200 persons took part in choosing delegates to what became the notorious Lecompton convention.

Both before and after this so-called election Governor Walker promised that the constitution, when adopted, should be submitted to a vote of the people, and he added his assurance that the President of the United States would insist upon this condition. On the 12th of July Mr. Buchanan wrote to Governor Walker:

"On the question of submitting the constitution to the *bona fide* resident settlers of Kansas, I am willing to stand or fall. In sustaining such a principle we cannot fail. It is the principle of the Kansas-Nebraska bill, the principle of popular sovereignty, and the principle at the foundation of all popular government. The more it is discussed, the stronger it will become. Should the convention of Kansas adopt this principle, all will be settled harmoniously."

This promise was soon after violated, and the President declared in an open letter:

"At the time of the passage of the Kansas-Nebraska act slavery existed, and still exists, in Kansas, under the constitution of the United States. This point has at last been finally decided by the highest tribunal known to our laws. How it could ever have been seriously doubted is a mystery."

It was known that the delegates elected would adopt a proslavery constitution and ask for admission to the Union. It was equally well known that no such constitution would be adopted by the people of Kansas. Under these circumstances, the President, pressed by his cabinet, yielded to the demands of the south, violated his pledges, and supported the convention in the extreme measures adopted by it.

In the meantime the Free State party in Kansas, composed of nearly equal proportions of Republicans and Democrats, was persuaded by Governor Walker to take part in the regular election for the territorial legislature. The result was, the Free State party elected nine of the thirteen councilmen, and twenty-four of the thirty-nine representatives. This should have settled the Kansas controversy, and it would have done so on the principle of popular sovereignty, but a broader constituency in the south demanded that the doctrine of the Dred Scott case should be applied to and enforced, not only in Kansas, but in all the states. Henceforth the Lecompton constitution must be considered, not as a local question, but as a national one. The imperative issue, as pithily stated by Lincoln, was, all slave or all free states. The battle was to commence in Kansas, but was to become national in its scope.

The constitutional convention met on the 19th of October, 1857, within two weeks after the election of the legislature, but in its action little interest was taken, a quorum being preserved with difficulty. It adopted a pro-slavery constitution, which, it was well known, if submitted to the people, would be rejected by an overwhelming majority, and if not submitted would be resisted, if necessary, by open force. The President, Governor Walker, and all parties, had promised that the constitution, when framed, would be submitted to a popular vote. How not to do it, and yet appear to do it, was a problem worthy of a gang of swindlers, and yet the feeling was so strong in administration circles, that the plan devised as below given was cordially approved by the cabinet and acquiesced in by the President.

The constitution adopted by the convention provided: "The right of property is before and higher than any constitutional sanction, and the right of the owner of a slave to such slave and its increase is the same and as inviolable as the right of the owner of any property whatever." Another provision of the constitution was that it could not be amended until after the year 1864, and even then no alteration should "be made to affect the rights of property in the ownership of slaves."

The election was to be held on December 21, 1857. The people might vote for the "constitution with slavery" or the "constitution with no slavery." In either event, by the express terms of the constitution, slavery was established for a time in Kansas and the doctrine of the Dred Scott case was to be embodied in our laws. No opportunity was offered to the people to vote against the constitution.

It is difficult to characterize in proper terms the infamy of these proceedings. The Free State party would take no part in the proposed election on December 21, and it resulted, for the constitution with slavery, 6,226 votes, of which 2,720 were proven to be fraudulent; for the constitution without slavery, 589. Governor Walker promptly denounced the outrage. He said: "I consider such a submission of the question a vile fraud, a base counterfeit, and a wretched device to prevent the people voting even on the slavery question." "I will not support it," he continued, "but I will denounce it, no matter whether the administration sustains it or not."

Mr. Buchanan supported the scheme after the constitution had been adopted by the convention. The elections in the fall preceding were favorable to the Democrats, and Mr. Buchanan was naturally encouraged to hope that his party had regained popular ascendancy, but the Lecompton juggle created a profound impression in the north, and divided the Democratic party to a greater extent than did the Kansas-Nebraska bill, especially in the northwest and in Ohio, where the feeling of resentment was almost universal. Mr. Douglas, the great leader for the repeal of the Missouri Compromise, took immediate ground against the pro-slavery plan, and protested to the President against it. An open breach occurred between them.

When Congress assembled, the Lecompton scheme became the supreme subject for debate. Mr. Douglas assumed at once the leadership of the opposition to that measure. He said: "Up to the time of meeting of the convention, in October last, the pretense was kept up, the profession was openly made, and believed by me, and I thought believed by them, that the convention intended to submit a constitution to the people, and not to attempt to put a government into operation without such a submission." But instead of that, "All men must vote for the constitution, whether they like it or not, in order to be permitted to vote for or against slavery." Again he said: "I have asked a very large number of the gentlemen who framed the constitution, quite a number of delegates, and still a larger number of persons who are their friends, and I have received the same answer from every one of them. . . . They say if they allowed a negative vote the constitution would have been voted down by an overwhelming majority, and hence the fellows shall not be allowed to vote at all." He denounced it as "a trick, a fraud upon the rights of the people."

Governor Walker declared: "I state it as a fact, based on a long and intimate association with the people of Kansas, that an overwhelming majority of that people are opposed" to the Lecompton constitution, "and my letters state that but one out of twenty of the press of Kansas sustains it. . . . Any attempt by Congress to force this constitution upon the people of Kansas will be an effort to substitute the will of a small minority for that of an overwhelming majority of the people."

On the 28th of January, 1858, during the debate on the Lecompton constitution, I made an elaborate speech, entering fully into the history of that constitution and the events that preceded it, and closed as follows :

"In conclusion, allow me to impress the south with two important warnings she has received in her struggle for Kansas. One is, that though her able and disciplined leaders on this floor, aided by executive patronage, may give her the power to overthrow legislative compacts, yet, while the sturdy integrity of the northern masses stands in her way, she can gain no practical advantage by her well-laid schemes. The other is, that while she may indulge with impunity the spirit of fillibusterism, or lawless and violent adventure, upon a feeble and distracted people in Mexico and Central America, she must not come in contact with that cool, determined courage and resolution which forms the striking characteristic of the Anglo-Saxon race. In such a contest, her hasty and impetuous violence may succeed for a time, but the victory will be short-lived and transient, and leave nothing but bitterness behind. Let us not war with each other ; but, with the grasp of fellowship and friendship, regarding to the full each other's rights, and kind to each other's faults, let us go hand in hand in securing to every portion of our people their constitutional rights."

I may as well here briefly follow the progress and end of the Kansas controversy. Mr. Stanton, the acting governor in the absence of Governor Walker, convened an extra session of the territorial legislature, in which the Free State men had a majority. The legislature provided for an election to be held January 4, 1858, at which a fair vote might be taken on the constitution. At this election the vote stood: For the constitution with slavery, 138; for the constitution without slavery, 24; against the constitution, 10,226.

Notwithstanding this decisive evidence of the opposition to the Lecompton constitution by the people of Kansas, Mr. Buchanan sent a copy of it to Congress, and, recommending the admission of Kansas under that organic act, said :

" It has been solemnly adjudged, by the highest judicial tribunal known to our laws, that slavery exists in Kansas by virtue of the constitution of the United States. Kansas is therefore at this moment as much a slave state as Georgia or South Carolina."

During the controversy Gen. Denver, a conservative Democrat, a native of Virginia, long a resident of Ohio and a representative from California in the 34th Congress, was appointed Governor of Kansas. His predecessors, four of his own party, Reeder, Shannon, Walker and Stanton, had been either removed or compelled to resign, every one refusing to execute the extreme pro-slavery policy of the President. His efforts to secure justice to the citizens of Kansas would in all probability have led to his removal, but the march of events withdrew the question involved from the people of Kansas to the halls of Congress. The policy of the administration was driving a wedge into the Democratic party. The bill for the admission of Kansas under the Lecompton constitution passed the Senate by a vote of 33 yeas to 25 nays, four northern Democrats and two southern Americans voting with the Republicans against it.

In the House of Representatives, composed of 128 Democrats, 92 Republicans and 14 Americans, the bill was defeated by the adoption of an amendment which provided that the Lecompton constitution should be submitted to a vote of the people of Kansas, but this amendment was disagreed to by the Senate, and the disagreement was referred to a committee of conference. The result was the adoption of a substitute, known as the English bill. This bill, though faulty, and partisan, provided for the admission of Kansas under the Lecompton constitution, but provided also for a submission of the English bill to a vote of the people of Kansas. On the 2nd of August a vote was taken in Kansas, and 11,300, out of a total vote of 13,088, were cast against the English proposition. Thus the Lecompton constitution and the English bill were defeated, the exclusion of slavery made absolute, and the State of Kansas admitted into the Union as a free state, under a constitution approved by the people, but not until January 29, 1861.

This memorable result was the turning point of the slavery controversy. The people of the south hastened preparations for a dissolution of the Union and a civil war. The Confederate congress, meeting four days later, on February 9, elected Jefferson Davis as its president, he having resigned as United States Senator, January 21, 1861, eight days before Kansas was admitted to the Union.

I have given much space to this Kansas controversy, for I wish to impress upon the readers of this volume that the war was not caused by agitation for the abolition of slavery, but by aggressive measures for the extension of slavery over free territory. A large and influential class of southern men were born politicians, and were mainly slaveholders. They had, from the beginning of the government, a large influence, and held more public offices of chief importance than their northern associates. They were constantly complaining of opinions expressed by a comparatively few Abolitionists against slavery, while the great body of the north were either indifferent to or sympathized with them in their opposition to the Abolitionists.

CHAPTER VII.

RECOLLECTIONS OF THE FINANCIAL PANIC OF 1857.

Its Effect on the State Banks — My Maiden Speech in Congress on National Finances —
Appointed a Member of the Committee on Naval Affairs — Investigation of the
Navy Department and Its Results — Trip to Europe with Mrs. Sherman —
We Visit Bracklinn's Bridge, Made Famous by Sir Walter Scott —
Ireland and the Irish — I Pay a Visit to Parliament and
Obtain Ready Admission — Notable Places in Paris
Viewed with Senator Sumner — The Battle-
field of Magenta — Return Home.

IN the summer of 1857 there occurred one of those period-
ical revulsions which seem to come after a term of apparent prosperity. On the 24th of August the Ohio Life
Insurance & Trust Company failed. That single event, in
itself unimportant, indicated an unhealthy condition of trade,
caused by reckless speculation, high prices, the construction of
railroads in advance of their need, a great increase of imports,
and the excessive development of cities and towns. All credits
were expanded. The immediate results of the panic were the
suspension of credits, the diminution of imports, the failure of
banks, and the general or partial suspension or lessening of all
industries. The revenues of the government were greatly
diminished.

On the 1st of July, 1857, the balance in the treasury was
$17,710,000. On the 1st of July, 1858, the balance was reduced
to $6,398,000, and during the year preceding, the United States
borrowed $10,000,000. On the 1st of July, 1859, the surplus
was reduced to $4,320,000, and during the year preceding the
United States borrowed $20,774,000. This sudden change in
the financial condition of the treasury was an indication of a
like or greater change in the condition of every person engaged
in productive industries.

The panic especially affected the state banks. These banks
were authorized by the laws of the several states to issue notes

as money payable on demand, with no common system or methods of redemption, and varying in value according to the solvency of the banks issuing them. The banks in a few of the states maintained their notes at par, or at a small discount, but the great body of the notes could circulate only in the states where issued, and then only because their people could get no other money in exchange for their products. The necessities created by the Civil War compelled the United States to borrow large sums, and to aid in this a national currency was provided, concerning which a statement of the measures adopted will be made hereafter. It is sufficient here to state that the national currency adopted proved one of the most beneficial results of the war.

The financial stringency of 1857 led to a careful scrutiny of appropriations for the support of the government.

On the 27th of May, 1858, I expressed my views in respect to the expenditures of the United States. This speech was the first effort I made in Congress to deal with the finances of the national government. In the previous Congresses I had devoted my time to the struggle in Kansas. At the meeting of the 35th Congress, I naturally turned to the condition of our finances, then the paramount subject of interest in the country, and, especially in Ohio, devoting most of my time to a careful study thereof. The speech referred to on national finances was the result of much labor, and I believe it will bear favorable scrutiny even at this late day. It certainly attracted the attention of my colleagues, and no doubt led to my transfer, at the next Congress, to the committee of ways and means.

In this speech I stated fully the increase of expenditures and the diminution of the revenues, and the then condition of the treasury. I quote as follows:

"And yet, sir, for this alarming condition of the public finances, the administration has no measures of relief except loan bills and paper money in the form of treasury notes. No provision is made for their payment; no measure of retrenchment and reform; but these accumulated difficulties are thrust upon the future, with the improvidence of a young spendthrift. While the secretary is waiting to foresee contingencies, we are prevented by a party majority from instituting reform. If we indicate even the commencement of retrenchment, or point out abuses, on this side of the House, we are at once assailed by members of the committee of ways and means."

I cited the abuses and usurpations of the executive departments in diverting specific appropriations to purposes not authorized by law. I said: "The theory of our government is, that a specific sum shall be appropriated by a *law* originating in this House, for a specific purpose, and within a given fiscal year. It is the duty of the executive to use that sum, and no more, especially for that purpose, and no other, and within the time fixed."

I pointed out cases where the departments assumed the power to transfer appropriations made for one purpose, to other purposes in the same department. Another abuse by the executive departments was the habit of making contracts in advance of appropriations, thus, without law, compelling Congress to sanction them or violate the public faith. All these evils have since been remedied by restrictive legislation. The habit of the Senate to load down appropriation bills with amendments already refused by the House of Representatives, and then insist that, if not agreed to, the bill would fail, was more frequent then than now, but under the practice now established an amendment finally disagreed to by either House is abandoned.

An illustration of the former practice in the Senate occurred in the 36th Congress, when I was chairman of the committee on ways and means. An appropriation bill was loaded down with amendments, among them an appropriation of $500,000 each for the construction of public buildings in Charleston and New Orleans. The amendments were disagreed to and referred to a committee of conference, of which Senator Toombs was a member. His first expression in the committee was that the House must agree to the items for Charleston and New Orleans or the bill would fail. I promptly answered that I would report what he said to the House, and *the bill would fail*. He said nothing further, the conference agreed, and the bill passed without any mention of Charleston or New Orleans. Even now the abuse I refer to sometimes occurs, but the general rule and practice is to exclude any item of an appropriation bill not freely agreed to by both Houses.

It was generally agreed that the views expressed by me on the 27th of May were sound in principle, but the strong partisan feeling that ran through the speech weakened its effect. I insert the last two paragraphs:

"But, sir, I have no hope, while this House is constituted as it is now, of instituting any radical reform. I believe that the House of Representatives should be in opposition to the President. We know the intimate relations made by party ties and party feelings. We know that with a party House, a House a majority of whose Members are friends of the President, it is impossible to bring about a reform. It is only by a firm, able, and determined opposition — not yielding to every friendly request, not yielding to every urgent demand, not yielding to every appeal — that we can expect to reform the abuse in the administration of the government.

"At the beginning of this session, I did hope that a majority of this House would compose such an opposition; and while on the one hand it crushed the unholy attempt to impose an odious constitution — by force, or with threats or bribes — upon a free people, it would be prepared to check the reckless extravagance of the administration in the disbursement of the public funds. But the power of party ties and the executive influence were too potent. We can only look now to the virtue and intelligence of the people, whose potent will can overthrow Presidents, Senators, and majorities. I have an abiding hope that the next House of Representatives will do what this should have done, and become, like its great prototype, the guardian of the rights and liberties of the people."

At the beginning of the 35th Congress I was appointed by Speaker Orr a member of the committee on naval affairs, with Mr. Bocock as chairman. Among the subjects referred to that committee was the capture, by Commodore Paulding of the United States navy, of William Walker, engaged in an armed foray against Nicaragua. It was fully considered, and on the 3rd of February, 1858, the majority of the committee, through Mr. Bocock, made a full report, accompanied by the following resolutions:

"*Resolved*, That the act of Hiram Paulding, a captain of the United States navy, in arresting General William Walker, was not authorized by the instructions which had been given him from the navy department.

"*Resolved*, That while we have no reason to believe that the said Paulding acted from any improper motives or intention, yet we regard the act in question as a grave error, and deserving, for the reason already given, the disapproval of the American Congress."

By direction of the minority of the committee I submitted a minority report as a substitute, as follows:

"*Resolved*, That Commodore Hiram Paulding, in arresting William Walker and his associates, and returning them to the jurisdiction of the United States, acted within the spirit of his orders, and deserves the approbation of his country."

It appeared, from the documents submitted, that in September, 1857, Walker was fitting out, within the limits of the United States, a military expedition against the Republic of Nicaragua, that on the 18th of September, Lewis Cass, Secretary of State, issued a circular letter, warning all persons against setting on foot such expeditions, and urging all officers of the United States to enforce the provisions of law cited by him, to prevent such expeditions "so manifestly prejudicial to the national character and so injurious to the national interests."

A copy of this circular was transmitted to Commodore Paulding, for his guidance, by the Secretary of the Navy, and he was required to regard the instructions contained in it as addressed to himself. Commodore Chatard was suspended for failing to arrest Walker within the port of San Juan. Commodore Paulding arrived at San Juan on the 6th day of December. Walker and his men were in sight on shore, at Punta Arenas, opposite San Juan. This point, though within the limits of Nicaragua, has been successively claimed and occupied by Costa Rica, Nicaragua and the so-called Mosquito Kingdom, under British protection. It was an almost deserted point, to which a British subject had set up a doubtful title, founded upon a purchase from a pilot of the port of San Juan. Its occupants were engaged as a military force, and were then waging war against the existing government of Nicaragua—a government with which ours was at peace, and one so weak that it was inhuman to fight it. Although freshly landed from our shores, in violation of our laws, and controlling no spot except that they occupied—receiving, so far as we knew, no accessions or aid from the natives of the country, they issued orders and manifestoes headed:

"HEADQUARTERS ARMY OF NICARAGUA,
PUNTA ARENAS, December 2, 1857."

Their leader signed these orders:

"WILLIAM WALKER,
COMMANDER-IN-CHIEF, ARMY OF NICARAGUA."

There was no doubt that the expedition was the very one denounced by the Secretary of State in the circular, and by the Secretary of the Navy in his orders, for Walker and his men sought no disguise.

Under these circumstances, Commodore Paulding arrested Walker and his men, and returned them to the jurisdiction of the United States. This brief and imperfect sketch of the voluminous majority and minority reports of the committee will convey but a faint idea of the excitement created by this arrest. An attempt was made to censure Commodore Paulding, but it utterly failed. The purpose of Walker was to seize Nicaragua, adopt slavery and convert the Central American states into slaveholding communities, and thus strengthen slavery in the United States. It was the counterpart of the movements in Kansas, and was supported by powerful influence in the southern states.

Another investigation of great importance was ordered by the House of Representatives, upon the following resolutions introduced by me on the 18th of January, 1859:

"WHEREAS, D. B. Allen, a citizen of the State of New York, specifically charges that certain officers in the navy department, in awarding contracts for the construction of vessels of war of the United States, have been guilty of partiality, and of violation of law and their public duty: and whereas, grave charges have been made that money appropriated for navy yards and for the repair of vessels of the United States, has been expended for partisan purposes, and not for the purposes prescribed by law: Therefore,

"Resolved, That a committee of five members be appointed to examine, 1. Into the specifications and bids for, and the terms of, the contracts for the work and labor done, or materials furnished for the vessels of the United States, constructed, or in process of construction or repair, by the United

States, since the 4th day of March, 1857, and the mode and manner of award-ing said contracts, and the inducements and recommendations influencing said awards. 2. Into the mode and manner, and the purpose, in which the money appropriated for the navy and dock yards, and for the repair and increase of vessels, has been expended. That said committee have power to send for persons and papers, and have leave to report by bill or other-wise."

This investigation occupied most of the remaining session of that Congress. The committee of five was composed of Messrs. Sherman, Bocock, Ritchie, Groesbeck and Ready, three Democrats and two Republicans, of which I was chairman. The committee took a mass of testimony, disclosing abuses and frauds of a startling character, covering over 1,000 printed pages. The majority of the committee, Messrs. Bocock, Groes-beck and Ready, submitted a report condemning the glaring abuses proven, and, while reporting the inefficiency and incom-petency of subordinate officers and employes, yet declared that nothing had been proven which impeached the personal or official integrity of the Secretary of the Navy. They proposed the following resolutions:

"1. *Resolved*, That the testimony taken in this investigation proves the existence of glaring abuses in the Brooklyn navy yard, and such as require the interposition of legislative reform ; but it is due to justice to declare that these abuses have been slowly and gradually growing up during a long course of years, and that no particular administration should bear the entire blame therefor.

"2. *Resolved*, That it is disclosed, by the testimony in this case, that the agency for the purchase of anthracite coal for the use of the navy has been, for some time past, in the hands of a person wholly inefficient and grossly incompetent, and that reform is needed in the regulations which exist on that subject ; but there is no proof which traces any knowledge of such inefficiency and incompetency to the responsible authorities in Washington, nor any which shows that the need of reform grows especially out of any act of theirs ; but, on the contrary, it is expressly proven that the supply of coal for the naval service has been purchased during this administration upon terms relatively as favorable as ever heretofore.

"3. *Resolved*, That while we could never sanction or approve any arrangement, on the part of an officer of the government, which, under pre-tense of making contracts for supplies, was designed to confer especial and exclusive favor on individuals, yet, in the contract entered into in Septem-ber, 1858, between the navy department and W. C. N. Swift, for the supply of live oak to said department, it is clearly proven by the testimony that, if the Secretary of the Navy did contemplate any favor to said Swift, he did not design to bestow it to the detriment of the government, but that in all he did in this matter he kept always in view the good of the public and the interests of the service.

"4. *Resolved*, That in the letting of the contracts for the construction of the steam machinery for the vessels of the navy during the present administration, nothing has been shown which calls for the interposition of the Congress of the United States ; but it is manifest that the present head of the navy department has displayed a very laudable zeal to secure the greatest amount of speed and efficiency attainable for said vessels.

"5. *Resolved*, That nothing has been proven in this investigation which impeaches, in any way, the personal or official integrity of the Secretary of the Navy."

The minority report was made by Ritchie and myself on the 24th of February, 1859, in which we recommended the following resolutions :

"*Resolved*, That the Secretary of the Navy has, with the sanction of the President, abused his discretionary power in the selection of a coal agent and in the purchase of fuel for the government.

"*Resolved*, That the contract made by the Secretary of the Navy, under date of September 23, 1858, with W. C. N. Swift, for the delivery of live oak timber, was made in violation of law, and in a manner unusual, improper, and injurious to the public service.

"*Resolved*, That the distribution, by the Secretary of the Navy, of the patronage in the navy yard among Members of Congress was destructive of discipline, corrupting in its influence, and highly injurious to the public service.

"*Resolved*, That the President and Secretary of the Navy, by receiving and considering the party relations of bidders for contracts with the United States, and the effect of awarding contracts upon pending elections, have set an example dangerous to the public safety and deserving the reproof of this House.

"*Resolved*, That the appointment, by the Secretary of the Navy, of Daniel B. Martin, chief engineer, as a member of the board of engineers, to report upon proposals for constructing machinery for the United States, the said Martin at the same time being pecuniarily interested in some of said proposals, is hereby censured by this House."

No action was taken on these reports during that session, which terminated on the 4th of March ; but in the succeeding Congress the resolutions of the minority were reported favorably from the committee on the expenditures of the navy department, and, after debate, were adopted, a separate yea and nay vote being taken on each resolution, and the vote generally being 119 in favor of the resolution and 60 against, a large number of Democrats voting for each resolution.

This investigation, and the action of the House of Representatives upon it, led to radical reforms in the purchase of supplies in the navy department, and stamped with deserved censure the Secretary of the Navy, and his subordinates, who participated in his action.

In the spring of 1859, Mrs. Sherman and I started on my first trip to Europe, on the steamer "Vanderbilt," without any definite route or plan. Fortunately, we formed on shipboard some pleasant acquaintances, among others Judge Harris of the Supreme Court of New York, afterwards Senator of the United States, and his wife. Each had children by a former marriage, who had arrived at or near manhood or womanhood, and all were pleasant traveling companions. Mr. Platt and his wife, of New York, a young married couple, were of the party. We were fortunate in the weather and the sea. I had often encountered the waves of Lake Erie, but the ocean was to me the great unknown, and I imagined that from its magnitude, its waves would be in proportion to its size, but, instead, the waves of the Atlantic were a gentle cradle compared with the short and chopping movement of the lake. Since then I have crossed the ocean many times, but never was sea sick. We thought the voyage of eleven days a brief one, but now it is reduced to six or seven days, on vessels much greater and stronger. We landed safely at Southampton late in the evening. Many of the passengers left immediately for London, but our party, with others, went to the hotel. We seemed to overcrowd the capacity of the place. One of our passengers, a young gentleman from Baltimore, said to me he would drive out those Englishmen, who were quietly enjoying themselves in the waiting room. He had been a quiet gentlemanly passenger, but he changed his tone and manner, was boisterous in his talk and rather rude. One by one the Englishmen departed, slamming the door after them, casting a sour look at their persecutor, but he was not disturbed until "the coast was clear," and then quieting down in his usual manner he said he knew these Englishmen, and thought he would give them a chance to abuse the d——d Americans. After long waiting we had a good supper.

On the next day, or the day following, we visited the Isle of Wight, and what is misnamed the "New Forest"—which is very old instead of new, and is an open park instead of a forest—in the neighborhood. Like most travelers we soon went to London. This great city impressed me more by the association of great men and women who had lived and died in it than by the grandeur of its buildings and public works. Every street and many houses in it recalled the names of persons whose writings I had read, and of others whose deeds made them immortal. As Parliament was not in session we shortened our visit in London until our return. My trip to Scotland was especially interesting. Mrs. Sherman, a daughter of Judge Stewart, was in face and affinities a thorough Scotch woman, though her ancestors for several generations were born in America. She was familiar with Scottish history, and with the geography of Scotland. Our visit to Edinburgh and its environs was to her like a return to familiar scenes. In our slow progress towards the lakes we stopped at Callender over Sunday. After looking into the well-filled church we started for Bracklinn bridge, made famous in Scott's "Lady of the Lake." "Bracklinn's thundering wave" is a beautiful cascade made at a place called the Bridge of Bracklinn, by a mountain stream called the Keltie, about a mile from the village of Callender, in Menteith. Above a chasm where the brook precipitates itself from a height of at least 50 feet, there is thrown, for the convenience of the neighborhood, a rustic foot bridge, of about three feet in breadth, and without ledges, which is scarcely to be crossed by a stranger without awe and apprehension. We were told it was but a short walk, a mile or two, but we soon found that Scottish miles were very long. On the way we encountered an old woman, dressed in Scotch plaid, of whom we inquired the way to Bracklinn bridge. She pointed out the way, and in return asked us where we lived. We told her the United States. She replied, in language we could hardly understand, "Ah, ye maun come a lang way to spay it." She then told us where to leave the road and how to find the bridge. There was nothing remarkable at the bridge, nothing to justify "But wild as Bracklinn's thundering roar," but the genius of Sir Walter invested it with his glamour.

"It had much of glamour might
To make a lady seem a knight."

The lakes of Scotland we would call bays. The waters of the ocean fill the deep depressions between high hills. A boat ride over these interlocked waters was pleasing, but the views did not impress me like the lakes in Switzerland in the midst of high mountains, nor did they compare with the grandeur of the Yellowstone Lake, 6,000 feet above the sea, with surrounding mountains rising to the height of 12,000 feet, and covered with snow. We were much pleased with Scotland and its people until we arrived at Glasgow. Here we walked about the city. It seemed to be crowded with discontented, unhappy people, with sad faces and poorly clad. We were told not to go into certain portions of the city, as we might be insulted.

We soon left Glasgow for Belfast and visited different parts of Ireland, and especially the city of Cork, and Lake Killarney. The southern part of Ireland was very beautiful, the herbage was fresh and green, and the land productive. The great drawback was the crowds of beggars, who would surround us wherever we went, soliciting alms, but they were generally good humored. I saw little of the disposition to fight attributed to them. At a subsequent visit I saw much more of Ireland and the Irish people, but on this, my first visit, I left with a very kindly impression of the country and the people. We have more people of Irish descent in the United States than now live in Ireland, and they have done their full part in our development, not only as laborers, but in all the walks and professions of life. They are heartily welcomed in our midst. If all the discontented people of Ireland would migrate to the

United States, we would welcome them if they would leave their Irish vs. English politics behind them. We have enough possible points of controversy on this continent with Great Britain, without importing from that country old controversies that have been the occasion of wars and rumors of war for centuries.

We made but a short stay in Dublin and crossed the channel to Caernarvon. Here we took the old tally-ho coach. Despite all that is said about railroads and steamboats, I believe in the old-fashioned stage coach, and especially in the one in which we crossed the hills of Wales, in full view of Mount Snowdon. We remained over Sunday in a village on the way, inquired for the church, and were shown to a very pretty church building near by. When we entered we found perhaps ten or fifteen persons, mostly women. The pastor, with an assistant, soon entered, and services commenced. The pastor read his part, and the assistant led, and practically made, the responses. The singing was led by the assistant and shared in by the few women present. The sermon was short and lifeless, and the entire service—though read from the Book of Common Prayer, as fine a model of impressive English as exists—was spiritless. When we left the church we met lines of well-dressed, but plain, proper men, women and children in Sunday garb. I inquired where these people came from, and was informed they were Methodists on the way home from their meeting house. This settled the question with me. The church I attended was the "established church," supported by taxes on all the people, and the Methodist meeting was the church of the people, supported by their voluntary contributions. How such a policy could have been sustained so long was beyond my comprehension. Our policy of respect and toleration for all religious sects, but taxes for none, is a better one.

Our party, still consisting of Judge Harris and family, Mr. Platt and wife, and Mrs. Sherman and myself, visited several of the central counties and towns of England, chiefly the towns of Warwick, Stratford, Kenilworth and Leamington. This is well trodden ground for tourists, and I need not repeat the

many descriptions of interesting places and the historic names
and events attached to them.

When we returned to London, I visited the courts of law,
Westminster Abbey, and the new Parliament House. I had
no difficulty in gaining free access to the gallery of the House
of Commons by stating that I was a Member of the House of
Representatives. Though I had letters of introduction to members of Parliament I did not present them. Judge Harris was
greatly interested in the proceedings of the courts of London,
while I wandered through every part of the great city. We
attended, by invitation, a dinner given by the Goldsmith's
Guild, and accepted some invitations, among them that of Mr.
Morgan, the leading American banker in London.

Our congenial party then separated with mutual regret, Judge Harris going to the Rhine and Mrs. Sherman
and I to Paris. Here we remained some time. Senator
Sumner, not yet recovered from the blows of Brooks, had
been some time in Paris and accompanied us to many of the
noted places in that city—among them I remember the grave
of Lafayette.

Our visit was during the Franco-Italian-Austrian War. I
was anxious to reach the seat of war. On the way we made
hurried visits to Geneva, and Lake Leman. After traversing
this lake we took the coach over the Alps, on the road to Milan,
stopping several times on the way. We passed over the battle
field at Magenta but a few days after the battle was fought.
We saw there the signs of destructive war. The killed had
been buried and the wounded were in hospitals, but the
smell of dead horses poisoned the air, and the marks of the
battle were on almost every house. We pushed on to Milan
and were comfortably quartered. The city was full of soldiers on the way to the army to the eastward. It was then
known that a battle was about to be fought at Solferino. I
was very anxious to witness a battle. General Crittenden, of
the United States army, was attached as an aid to the
French army, and I sought the same facility, but the authorities would not permit it. I was assured that my horse would
be taken from me, especially as I could not speak French,

and that I would be treated as a spy unless I was formally attached to a particular command. I therefore gave up my contemplated trip and awaited the battle, which occurred in a day or two. I then returned to Switzerland by the Simplon Pass, and visited Berne, Luzerne, and Neuchâtel. From thence I returned to London and soon after embarked on the "Vanderbilt" for home.

CHAPTER VIII.

Exciting Scenes in Congress.

I am Elected for the Third Term — Invasion of Virginia by John Brown — His Trial
and Execution—Spirited Contest for the Speakership—Discussion Over Helper's
"Impending Crisis" — Angry Controversies and Threats of Violence in
the House — Within Three Votes of Election as Speaker—My Reply
to Clark's Attack — Withdrawal of my Name and Election of
Mr. Pennington — Made Chairman of the Committee of
Ways and Means — President Buchanan Objects
to Being " Investigated "—Adoption of the
Morrill Tariff Act — Views Upon the
Tariff Question—My Colleagues.

ON the 29th of July, 1858, I received the congressional
nomination for my third term without opposition,
and, in October following, was elected as a Member
of the 36th Congress, by a majority of 2,331 over S. J.
Patrick, Democrat.

The memorable campaign in Illinois in that year excited
profound interest throughout the United States, the debate between Douglas and Lincoln attracting universal attention. The
result was favorable to Douglas, and the legislature re-elected
him Senator, but Mr. Lincoln attained such distinction and
prominence as to place him at once in the position of a formidable candidate for the presidency in 1860. This debate made
it clear that the struggle between free and slave institutions
was to be continued and to become the controlling issue of the
future.

The murder of Broderick by Terry, in California, on the 13th
of September, 1859, under color of a duel, excited profound interest and made that state Republican. The election of a governor in Ohio, in the fall of that year, preceded by a debate of
much interest between William Dennison, the Republican candidate, and Judge Ranney, the Democratic candidate, added
greatly to the political excitement then existing, and ended in

the election of Mr. Dennison. A few days after this election—on the 17th of October—the invasion of the State of Virginia by John Brown startled the country, and, more than all other causes, aroused the southern people to a state of great excitement, amounting to frenzy. Brown, with a few followers of no distinction, captured the United States arsenal at Harper's Ferry, took possession of the bridge which crosses the Potomac, fortifying it with cannon, stopped trains, cut telegraph wires, killed several men, and seized many prominent citizens, holding them as hostages. Wild reports were circulated of a rise of the negroes in the neighborhood, the uprising accompanied by all the horrors of a servile war, and a general alarm prevailed throughout the State of Virginia and the south. The insurrection was, however, speedily suppressed, mainly by the state militia, and the few insurgents not killed were captured by United States marines under Colonel Robert E. Lee, soon afterwards to be commander-in-chief of the rebel forces in the Civil War.

Brown was tried for murder and executed. This foolish and criminal invasion was the work of a fanatic who all his lifetime had been a violent opposer of slavery, and who while in Kansas had participated more or less in the Osawatamie murders. His son was killed by the " border ruffians " near his home in Kansas, for which a fearful revenge was taken upon the murderers. Brown, having always been an Abolitionist, and being crazed by these events, believed it his duty to wage a relentless war against slavery, and, with the courage but shortsightedness of a fanatic, and with the hope of the assistance of the slaves of the south, undertook this wild scheme to secure their freedom.

Under such exciting conditions Congress convened on the 5th day of December, 1859, divided politically into 109 Republicans, 101 Democrats and 27 Americans. No party having a majority, it was feared by some that the scenes of 1855, when Banks was elected speaker only after a long struggle, would be repeated. That contest was ended by the adoption of the plurality rule, but in this case a majority could not agree upon such a rule, and the only possible way of electing a speaker

THE MIDDLE HOUSE SHOWS MR. SHERMAN'S FIRST RESIDENCE IN WASHINGTON, D. C., 1864, AND SITE OF HIS PRESENT HOME ON K ST
—SECRETARY STANTON'S HOUSE ON THE LEFT.

was by a fusing of Members until a majority voted for one person.

It was well understood that the Republican vote would be divided between Galusha A. Grow and myself, and it was agreed between us that whichever received a majority of the Republican vote should be considered as the nominee of that party. On the first vote for speaker, Thomas S. Bocock, of Virginia, the Democratic candidate, received 86 votes, I received 66, Galusha A. Grow 43, and 21 scattering. Mr. Grow then withdrew his name. On the same day John B. Clark, of Missouri, offered this resolution:

" WHEREAS certain Members of this House, now in nomination for speaker, did indorse and recommend the book hereinafter mentioned,

"*Resolved*, That the doctrine and sentiments of a certain book, called ' The Impending Crisis of the South — How to meet it,' purporting to have been written by one Hinton R. Helper, are insurrectionary and hostile to the domestic peace and tranquility of the country, and that no Member of this House who has indorsed and recommended it, or the compend from it, is fit to be speaker of this House."

In the absence of rules, Mr. Clark was allowed to speak without limit and he continued that day and the next, reading and speaking about the Helper book. John A. Gilmer, of North Carolina, offered as a substitute for the resolution of Mr. Clark a long preamble closing with this resolution:

"*Therefore resolved*, That, fully indorsing these national sentiments, it is the duty of every good citizen of this Union to resist all attempts at renewing, in Congress or out of it, the slavery agitation, under whatever shape and color the attempt may be made."

A motion was made to lay both resolutions on the table, and was lost by a tie vote of 116 yeas and 116 nays. In the absence of rules a general debate followed, in which southern Members threatened that their constituents would go out of the Union. The excitement over the proposition to compile a political pamphlet, by F. P. Blair, an eminent Democrat and slaveholder, from a book called "The Impending Crisis," written and printed by a southern man, seemed so ludicrous that we regarded it as manufactured frenzy. After John S. Millson, of Virginia, a conservative Democrat, who was opposed to the introduction of the Clark resolution, had exhibited unusual feeling, I said:

" I have until this moment regarded this debate with indifference, because I presumed it was indulged in for the purpose of preventing an organization. But the manner of the gentleman from Virginia, my respect for his long experience in this House, my respect for his character, and the serious impression which this matter seems to have made upon his mind, induce me to say a few words. I ask that the letter which I send up may be read."

The following letter was thereupon read from the clerk's desk:

WASHINGTON CITY, December 6, 1859.

DEAR SIR:—I perceive that a debate has arisen in Congress in which Mr. Helper's book, the 'Impending Crisis,' is brought up as an exponent of Republican principles. As the names of many leading Republicans are presented as recommending a compendium of the volume, it is proper that I should explain how those names were obtained in advance of the publication. Mr. Helper brought his book to me at Silver Spring to examine and recommend, if I thought well of it, as a work to be encouraged by Republicans. I had never seen it before. After its perusal, I either wrote to Mr. Helper, or told him that it was objectionable in many particulars, to which I adverted ; and he promised me, in writing, that he would obviate the objections by omitting entirely or altering the matter objected to. I understand that it was in consequence of his assurance to me that the obnoxious matter in the original publication would be expurgated, that Members of Congress and other influential men among the Republicans were induced to give their countenance to the circulation of the edition so to be expurgated

HON. JOHN SHERMAN.   F. P. BLAIR,
                                            Silver Spring.

I then continued:

" I do not recollect signing the paper referred to ; but I presume, from my name appearing in the printed list, that I did sign it. I therefore make no excuse of that kind. I never read Mr. Helper's book, or the compendium founded upon it. I have never seen a copy of either. And here, Mr. clerk, I might leave the matter ; but as many harsh things have been said about me, I desire to say that since I have been a Member of this House, I have always endeavored to cultivate the courtesies and kind relations that are due from one gentleman to another. I never addressed to any Member such language as I have heard to-day. I never desire such language to be addressed to me, if I can avoid it. I appeal to my public record, during a period of four years, in this body ; and I say now that there is not a single question agitating the public mind, not a single topic on which there can be sectional jealousy or sectional controversy, unless gentlemen on the other side of the House thrust such subjects upon us. I repeat, not a single question. We have pursued a course of studied silence. It is our intention to organize the House quietly, decently, in order, without vituperations; and we trust to show to Members on all sides of the House that the party with which I have the honor to act can administer this House and administer this government without trespassing on the rights of any."

Soon after, in answer to an inquiry from Shelton F. Leake, of Virginia, I said:

"Allow me to say, once for all, and I have said it five times on this floor, that I am opposed to any interference whatever of the people of the free states, with the relation of master and slave in the slave states."

This was followed by a heated debate, the manifest purpose of which was to excite sectional animosity, and to compel southern Americans to coöperate with the Democratic Members in the election of a Democrat for speaker. The second ballot, taken on the close of the session of December 8, exhibited no material change except that the Republican vote concentrated on me. I received 107 votes, Mr. Bocock 88, Mr. Gilmer 22, and 14 scattering.

The debate continued and was participated in by my colleague, S. S. Cox, who asked me about the fugitive slave law. I declined, as I had before, to answer any interrogatories and said: "I will state to him, and to gentlemen on the other side of the House, that I stand upon my public record. I do not expect the support of gentlemen on that side of the House, who have, for the last four years, been engaged in a series of measures—none of which I approve. I have no answers to give to them."

The third ballot produced no material change. I received 110, Bocock 88, Gilmer 20, and 13 scattering.

In the meantime, the invasion of Harper's Ferry was debated in the Senate at great length and with extreme violence, producing in both Houses intense irritation and excitement. Keitt, of South Carolina, charged upon the Republicans the responsibility of Helper's book and John Brown's foray, exclaiming: "The south here asks nothing but its rights. . . . I would have no more; but, as God is my judge, as one of its

Representatives, I would shatter this republic from turret to foundation-stone before I would take one tittle less." Lamar, of Mississippi, declared that the Republicans were not "guiltless of the blood of John Brown and his co-conspirators, and the innocent men, the victims of his ruthless vengeance." Pryor, of Virginia, said Helper's book riots "in rebellion, treason, and insurrection, and is precisely in the spirit of the act which startled us a few weeks since at Harper's Ferry." Crawford, of Georgia, declared: "We will never submit to the inauguration of a black Republican President."

The Republicans generally remained silent and demanded a vote.

Mr. Corwin, then a Representative from Ohio, elected after a long absence from public life, endeavored to quiet the storm. Frequent threats of violence were uttered. Angry controversies sprang up between Members, and personal collisions were repeatedly threatened by Members, armed and ready for conflict. No such scenes had ever before occurred in the Congress of the United States. It appeared many times that the threatened war would commence on the floor of the House of Representatives. The House remained in session the week between Christmas and New Year's Day. During this excitement my vote steadily increased until on the 4th day of January, 1860, on the 25th ballot, I came within three votes of election; the whole number of votes cast being 207; necessary to a choice 104, of which I received 101. John A. McClernand, of Illinois, received 33, Gilmer 14, Clement L. Vallandigham, of Ohio, 12, and the remainder were scattering.

At this time Henry Winter Davis, of Maryland, an American, said to me, and to others, that whenever his vote would elect me it should be cast for me. J. Morrison Harris, also an American from the same state, was understood to occupy the same position. Garnett B. Adrain, of New Jersey, an anti-Lecompton Democrat, who had been elected by Republicans, it was hoped would do the same. Horace F. Clark, of New York, also an anti-Lecompton Democrat who had been elected by Republicans, could at any moment have settled the controversy in my favor. It was well known that I stood ready to withdraw whenever the requisite number of votes could be concentrated upon any Republican Member. The deadlock continued.

On the 20th of January, 1860, Mr. Clark, who had introduced the Helper resolution, said:

"I wish to make a personal explanation with regard to my personal feelings in the matter of this resolution. I never read the letter of which the gentleman from Georgia speaks, and do not take to myself articles that appear in newspapers, unless they make imputations against my moral integrity. That resolution was introduced by me, as I have frequently remarked, with no personal ill-feeling towards Mr. Sherman, the Republican candidate for speaker, apart from what I considered to be an improper act of his — namely, the recommendation of that book. So far as that affects his political or social character, he must of course bear it."

I replied as follows:

"The gentleman from Missouri, for the first time, I believe, has announced that it was his purpose, in introducing this resolution, to give gentlemen an opportunity to explain their relations to the Helper book. I ask him now whether he is willing to withdraw the resolution for the purpose he has indicated, temporarily, or for any time?"

Mr. Clark said:

"I will endeavor to answer the gentleman. I avowed my purpose frankly at the time I introduced the resolution, in the remarks with which I accompanied its introduction. The gentleman from Ohio propounds the question more directly whether I am willing to withdraw the resolution for the purpose which I avow? Sir, at the very instant it was offered, I gave the gentleman that opportunity and I have given it to him since. I say to the gentleman that he has had two opportunities to make that explanation; but he has failed to relieve himself of the responsibility he took when he signed that book and recommended its circulation."

I replied:

"I will say that that opportunity has never been rendered to me. When the gentleman introduced his resolution, offensive in its character, at an improper time, in an improper manner, he cut off—what he says now he desires to give—an opportunity for explanation. It is true that three days afterwards, when the gentleman from Virginia (Mr. Millson) appealed to me, I stated to him frankly how my name became connected with that paper. I did not sign the paper; but it seems that the Hon. E. D. Morgan, a Member of the last Congress, and a friend of mine, came to me when I was in my place, and asked me to sign a recommendation for the circulation of a political pamphlet, to be compiled by a committee, of which Mr. Blair, a slaveholder of Missouri, was one, from a large book by Helper, a North Carolinian.   I said to him that I had not time to examine the book ; but if there was nothing offensive in it, he might use my name. Thereupon, this gentleman attached my name to that paper.   This information I did not have at the time the gentleman from Virginia addressed me; but I said to him I had no recollection of having signed the paper, but presumed I had, from my name appearing in the printed list.   I subsequently acquired it from Mr. Morgan, whose letter was published.   That I believe was sufficient under the circumstances.   I know there are Members on that side of the House who have considered it as satisfactory ; and my friends so regard it.   At the time I stated that I had not read the book, that I did not know what was in it.

"The gentleman alludes to another time.   The other day, when this subject was again brought before the House by him, in language which, although he claims to be courteous, I could not regard as such, when I was, by implication, but with a disclaimer of personal offense, charged with disseminating treason, with lighting the torch in the dwelling of my southern brethren, and of crimes of which, if I was guilty, I should not be entitled to a seat upon this floor, I then rose in my place, and told the gentleman from Missouri that if he would withdraw that resolution I would answer this book page by page, or those extracts one by one, and tell him whether I approved them or not.   The gentleman refused to withdraw the resolution.   Long ago he was notified by me, and my friend from Pennsylvania (Mr. Morris) announced on the floor, that this resolution was regarded by me as a menace, and, if withdrawn, would lead to a frank avowal, or disavowal.

"I say now that I do not believe it is the desire of the gentleman to give me that opportunity.   If he does desire it, I am willing to do now what I said I would have done then.   And I say, with equal emphasis, that never, so help me God, whether or not the speaker's chair is to be occupied by me, will I do so while that resolution is before this body, undisposed of.   I regard it as offensive in its tone, unprecedented, unparliamentary, and an invasion of the rights of representation.   Under the menace clearly contained in it, I never will explain a single word contained in those extracts.

"If the gentleman will withdraw his resolution, even for a moment, to relieve me from the menace — he may reinstate it afterwards if he chooses — I will then say what I have to say in regard to those extracts.   But while it stands before the House, intended as a stigma upon me, and sustained by an argument without precedent in parliamentary history, he cannot expect me to say more than I have done.   I believe not only my friends, but the gentlemen on the other side of the House, who have a sense of honor, believe that my position is correct.   I know that some of them regard my statement made on the third day of the session as full and satisfactory, and all that, under the circumstances, it was proper for me to indicate.

"For gentlemen now to press this matter; to agitate the country; to spread these extracts all over the south, and to charge the sentiments of this book upon me, and my associates here; to proclaim, day after day, that the Republicans entertain these sentiments and indorse them, is not that ingenuous, candid and manly course which a great party like the Democratic party ought to pursue. While we may conduct our political quarrels with heat, and discuss matters with zeal and determination, it ought to be done with fairness and frankness. The mode in which this resolution has been pressed before the country, and I, with my hands tied and my lips sealed as a candidate, have been arraigned day by day, is without a precedent, not only in history but in party caucuses, in state legislatures, in state conventions or anywhere else.

"I said when I rose the other day that my public opinions were on record. I say so now. Gentlemen upon the other side have said that they have examined that record to ascertain what my political opinions were. They will look in vain for anything to excite insurrection, to disturb the peace, to invade the rights of the states, to alienate the north and south from each other, or to loosen the ties of fraternal fellowship by which our people have been and should be bound together. I am for the Union and the constitution, with all the compromises under which it was formed, and all the obligations which it imposes. This has always been my position; and these opinions have been avowed by me on this floor and stand now upon your records. Who has brought anything from that record against me that is worthy of answer? . . .

"I have never sought to invade the rights of the southern states. I have never sought to trample upon the rights of citizens of the southern states. I have my idea about slavery in the territories, and at the proper time and in the proper way I am willing to discuss the question. I never made but one speech on the subject of slavery, and that was in reference to what I regarded as an improper remark made by President Pierce in 1856. I then spread upon the record my opinions on the subject; and I have found no man to call them into question. They are the opinions of the body of the Republicans. They are the opinions which I now entertain. Gentlemen are at liberty to discuss these questions as much as they choose, and I will bear my share of the responsibility for entertaining these opinions. But I now speak to my personal record. . . .

"Again these gentlemen, while publishing in their speeches all over the country that I am in effect a traitor, etc., by implication, it is true, disavowing, as I am glad to say each of them have done, any design to be personally offensive, but in a way that answers the same purpose; yet when called upon to show proofs or specifications, they fail to do so; and the only act for which I have been arraigned before the American people is that, in a moment when I was sitting here, busy at my desk, and one of my friends, and late a Member of this House, came to me and asked me to sign a paper recommending the publication of a political tract; that, when I authorized my name to be put to that recommendation, by that very act I became a traitor and would place the torch in the hands of the incendiary. I say this is not fair argument. And I again repeat that if the Member from Missouri (Mr. Clark) desires to know what my sentiments are in regard to the extracts read at the clerk's table, the only portion of the Helper book I have seen or read, I will give them if he will remove a menace from me. I never did do anything under menace. I never will. It is not in my blood and these gentlemen cannot put it there."

Mr. Clark rose to speak, but I continued:

"The gentleman will excuse me, I have, so far as I am concerned in this contest, been quiet and patient. I desire to see an organization of the House opposed to the administration. I think it is our highest duty to investigate, to examine and analyze the mode in which the executive powers of this government have been administered for a few years past. That is my desire. Yes sir, I said here, in the first remark I made, that I did not believe the slavery question would come up at all during this session. I came here with the expectation that we would have a business session, that we would examine into the business affairs of this government, and that we would analyze the causes of the increased expenditures of the government and the proper measures of redress and retrenchment. I did not believe that the slavery question would come up, and but for the unfortunate affair of Brown at Harper's Ferry, I did not believe there would be any feeling on the subject. Northern Members came here with kindly feelings, no man approving the foray of John Brown and every man willing to say so; every man willing to admit it as an act of lawless violence. We came here hoping that, at this time of peace and quiet, we might examine, inquire into, and pass upon, practical measures of legislation tending to harmonize the conflicting elements of the government and strengthen the bonds of Union. The interests of a great and growing people present practical questions enough to tax the ability and patriotism of us all.

"Such was our duty; but the moment we arrived here — before, sir, we had even a formal vote, — this question of slavery was raised by the introduction of the resolution of the gentleman from Missouri. It has had the effect of exciting the public mind with an irritating controversy. It has impaired the public credit and retarded the public business. The debate founded upon it has been unjust, offensive, wrong, not only to the Republicans here, not only to those with whom I act, but to all our common constituents, north and south. The gentlemen who have advocated that resolution have stirred up bad blood, and all because certain gentlemen have recommended that a compilation be made of a book. Even yet we may retrieve the loss of valuable time. We could now go to work, organize this House and administer the powers of this House with fairness and impartiality.

"In conclusion, let me say that by no act or effort have I sought the position I now occupy before the House. The honor was tendered me by the generous confidence and partiality of those with whom it has been my pride to act, politically. Their conduct in this irritating controversy has justified my attachment.

"If I shall ever reach the speaker's chair, it will be with untrammeled hands and with an honest purpose to discharge every duty in the spirit which the oath of office enjoins ; and to organize the House with reference to the rights and interests of every section, the peace and prosperity of the whole Union, and the efficient discharge of all the business of the government. And whenever friends who have so gallantly and liberally sustained me thus far believe that my name in any way presents an obstacle to success, it is my sincere wish that they should adopt some other. Whenever any one of my political friends can combine a greater number of votes than I have been honored with, or sufficient to elect him by a majority or plurality rule, I will not stand in this position one hour ; I will retire from the field, and yield to any other gentleman with whom I act, the barren honors of the speaker's chair ; and I promise my friends a grateful recognition of the unsolicited honor conferred upon me, and a zealous and earnest coöperation."

Pending the vote on the 39th ballot and before it was announced, Robert Mallory, of Kentucky, an American, appealed to the Democrats to vote for William N. H. Smith, of North Carolina, also an American, which would elect him. The Democrats thereupon changed their votes to Mr. Smith, making many speeches in explanation of their action. Perceiving that this would elect Mr. Smith I arose and for the first time cast my ballot for speaker, voting for Mr. Corwin. Three other Members who had voted for Mr. Smith changed their votes, which defeated the election on that ballot.

After this vote I conferred with Davis and George Briggs, of New York, Americans, and Adrain. I had the positive assurance of these three gentlemen that if I would withdraw they would vote for William Pennington, of New Jersey, and thus secure a Republican organization of the House. I referred this proposition to my Republican associates, and a majority of them were opposed to any change. Francis E. Spinner, of New York, said he never would change his vote from me, and Thaddeus Stevens said he never would do so until the crack of doom. When afterwards reminded of this Mr. Stevens said he thought he "heard it cracking."

I felt the responsibility, but on the 30th of January, 1860, I determined to withdraw. In doing so I made the following remarks, as printed in the "Congressional Globe:"

"Mr. clerk—[Loud cries of 'Down,' 'Down,' 'Order,' 'Order,' 'Let us have the question,' etc.] Eight weeks ago, I was honored by the votes of a large plurality of my fellow Members for the high office of speaker of this House. Since that time they have adhered to their choice with a fidelity that has won my devotion and respect; and, as I believe, the approbation of their constituents. They have stood undismayed amidst threats of disunion and disorganization; conscious of the rectitude of their purposes; warm in their attachment to the constitution and Union, and obedient to the rules of order and the laws. They have been silent, firm, manly. On the other hand, they have seen their ancient adversary and their only natural adversary, reviving anew the fires of sectional discord, and broken into fragments. They have seen some of them shielding themselves behind a written combination to prevent the majority of the House from prescribing rules for its organization. They have heard others openly pronounce threats of disunion; proclaim that if a Republican be duly elected President of the United States, they would tear down this fair fabric of our rights and liberties, and break up the union of these states. And now we have seen our ancient adversary, broken, dispersed and disorganized, unite in supporting a gentleman who was elected to Congress as an American, in open, avowed opposition to the Democratic organization.

"I should regret exceedingly, and believe it would be a national calamity, to have anyone who is a supporter, directly or indirectly, of this administration, or who owes it any allegiance, favor or affection, occupying a position of importance or prominence in this House. I would regard it as a public calamity to have the power of this House placed, directly or indirectly, under the control of this administration. It would be, it seems to me, a fatal policy to trust the power of this House to the control of gentlemen who have proclaimed that under any circumstances, or in any event, they would dissolve the union of these states. For this reason we would be wanting in our duty to our God and our country, if we did not avert such a result of this contest. I regard it as the highest duty of patriotism to submerge personal feelings, to sacrifice all personal preferences and all private interests, to the good of our common country. I said here a few days ago, and I always stood in the position, that when I became convinced that any of my political friends or associates could receive further support outside of the Republican organization, I would retire from the field and yield to him the honor of the position that the partiality of friends has assigned to me. I believe that time has now arrived. I believe that a greater concentration can now be made on another gentleman, who, from the beginning, has acted with me.

" Therefore, I respectfully withdraw my name as a candidate. And in doing so, allow me to return my heartfelt thanks for the generous and hearty support of all my political friends, and especially to those gentlemen with whom I have not the tie of a party name, but the higher one of a common purpose and sympathy. And if I can ask of them one more favor, it would be that in an unbroken column, with an unfaltering front and unwavering line, each of them will cast his vote in favor of any one of our number who can command the highest vote, or who can be elected speaker of this House."

A ballot was immediately taken, but, much to my chagrin, the gentlemen named did not change their votes, and Mr. Pennington still lacked three votes of an election. I again appealed to Davis and Briggs, and finally, on the 1st of February, Mr. Pennington received their votes. The result was announced; Pennington, 117 votes; McClernand, 85; Gilmer, 16; 15 scattering; giving Pennington a majority of one, and thus, after a long and violent contest, a Republican was elected speaker of the House of Representatives.

I was entirely satisfied with the result. I had received every Republican vote and the votes of a large number of anti-Nebraska Democrats and Americans. No cloud rested upon me, no allegation of misconduct or unfitness was made against me. I would have been easily and quickly elected but for the abnormal excitement created by Brown's invasion and the bitterness of political antagonism existing at that time. Many Members who felt it their duty to oppose my election, subsequently expressed their regret that I was not elected. I had voted for Mr. Pennington during the contest, had a high respect for him as a gentleman of character and influence, long a chancellor of his state, and a good Republican.

When the canvass was over, I felt a sense of relief. During its continuance, I had remained, with rare exceptions, silent, though strongly tempted, by political criticism, to engage in the debate. I had, during the struggle, full opportunity to estimate the capacity and qualifications of different Members for committee positions, and had the committees substantially framed, when Pennington was elected. I handed the list to him, for which he thanked me kindly, saying that he had but little knowledge of the personal qualifications of the Members.

With some modifications, made necessary by my defeat and his election as speaker, he adopted the list as his own. He designated me as chairman of the committee of ways and means, of which I had not previously been a member.

The organization of the House was not completed until the 9th day of February, 1860. The officers designated by the Republicans were generally elected. Congress seemed to appreciate the necessity of prompt and vigorous action on the business of the session. Still, whatever question was pending, political topics were the object of debate, but were rarely acted upon, as the condition of the House prevented anything like political action. Nearly all the measures adopted were of a non-political character. The chief work of the session was devoted to appropriations, and the preparation and enactment of a tariff bill. At that time, the great body of legislation was referred to the committee of ways and means, which then had charge of all appropriations and of all tax laws, and whose chairman was recognized as the leader of the House, practically controlling the order of its business.

By the 13th of March, I was able to say, in behalf of the committee, that all the annual appropriation bills were ready for the consideration of the House, and promised that if the House would sustain the committee, all these bills could be passed before the meeting of the Charleston convention. Notwithstanding the partisan bitterness which was exhibited against me while I was a candidate for speaker, I had no cause to complain of a want of support by the House, in the measures reported from that committee. Since then the work of that committee has been distributed among a number of committees.

The first political contest was caused by a message of President Buchanan, protesting against action under a resolution by the House of Representatives, passed on the 5th of March, providing for a committee of five members, to be appointed by the speaker, for the purpose of investigating "whether the President of the United States, or any other officer of the government, has, by money, patronage, or other improper means, sought to influence the action of Congress for or against the passage of any law pertaining to the rights of any state or territory." The committee appointed came to be commonly known as the covode committee.

This message was regarded as a plain interference with the unquestionable power of the House to investigate the conduct of any officer of the government, a process absolutely necessary to enable the House to exercise the power of impeachment. Upon the reception of the message I immediately replied to it, and a general debate arose upon a motion to refer it to the committee on the judiciary. That motion was adopted and the committee reported a resolution in the following words, which was finally adopted after debate, by a vote of 88 yeas and 40 nays:

"*Resolved*, That the House dissents from the doctrines of the special message of the President of the United States of March 28, 1860 ;

" That the extent of power contemplated in the adoption of the resolutions of inquiry of March 5, 1860, is necessary to the proper discharge of the constitutional duties devolved upon Congress ;

"That judicial determinations, the opinions of former Presidents and uniform usage, sanction its exercise ; and

" That to abandon it would leave the executive department of the government without supervision or responsibility, and would be likely to lead to a concentration of power in the hands of the President, dangerous to the rights of a free people."

This resolution was regarded as a severe reproach to the President, who was not content to let the matter rest there, but on the 25th of June sent to the House of Representatives, a message restating the position in his former message. He denounced the proceedings of that committee as a violation of the letter and spirit of the constitution. But for the lateness of the session the message would have been the subject of severe animadversion. Late as it was Benjamin Stanton, of Ohio, entered his protest and moved that the message be referred to a select committee of five, with power to report at the next session. This, after a brief debate, was adopted.

During the entire session, while the current business was progressing rapidly, the political questions involved in the pending presidential canvass, the topics of Kansas and slavery, were frequently obtruded into the debate. On the 23rd of April, William T. Avery, a Democratic Member from Tennessee charged that "an overwhelming majority of the Republican party in this House, headed by Mr. Sherman—in fact, every member of that party present when the vote was taken, excepting some fourteen or fifteen—indorsed the doctrine of the abolition of slavery everywhere."

In the course of a reply to this charge I said:

"I think there is not a Member on this side of the House who is not now willing to make the declaration broadly, openly, that he is opposed to any interference whatever with the relations of master and slave in the slave states. We do believe that Congress has the power to prohibit slavery in the territories; and whenever the occasion offers, whenever the proper time arrives, whenever the question arises, we are in favor of exercising that power, if necessary, to prevent the extension of slavery into free territory. We are frank and open upon this subject. But we never did propose, and do not now propose, to interfere with slavery in the slave states. I hope the gentleman will put these observations in his speech, so that the gentleman's constituents may see that we 'black Republicans' are not so very desirous of interfering with their interests or rights, but only desirous of preserving our own."

Mr. Ashmore inquired: "Are you not in favor of abolishing slavery in the District of Columbia?"

I replied:

"I have stated to my constituents, over and over again, that I am opposed to interference with slavery in the District of Columbia. That is my individual position. The Republican party never took a position on the subject. Some are for it, and some against it. I have declared to my constituents, over and over again, that I did not think it proper to agitate the question of the abolition of slavery in the District of Columbia; because I believe that this is the very paradise of the free negro. I believe that, practically, though not legally, he is better off in the District than in any portion of the United States. There are but few slaves here, and the number is decreasing daily. As an institution, slavery scarcely exists here, and I am willing to leave it to the effect of time."

On the 12th of March, 1860, Justin S. Morrill, of Vermont, by instruction of the committee of ways and means, reported a bill "to provide for the payment of outstanding treasury notes, to authorize a loan, to regulate and fix duties on imports, and for other purposes." This became the law commonly known as the Morrill tariff act, which, from the time of its introduction to this day, has been the subject of debate,

SENATOR JUSTIN S. MORRILL,
AUTHOR OF THE "MORRILL TARIFF," 1861.

amendment, criticism and praise. It was referred to the committee of the whole on the state of the Union, and its consideration occupied a large portion of the remainder of the session. Nearly one hundred Members entered into the debate and some of them made several speeches upon the subject. Being at the time much occupied with the appropriation bills, I did not give much attention to the debate, but had taken part in the preparation of the bill in the committee of ways and means, and concurred, with rare exceptions, in the principles and details of the measure.

Mr. Morrill was eminently fitted to prepare a tariff bill. He had been engaged in trade and commerce, was a man of sound judgment, perfectly impartial and honest. Representing a small agricultural state, he was not biased by sectional feeling or the interests of his constituents. He regarded the tariff as not only a method of taxation, but as a mode of protection to existing industries in the United States with a view to encourage and increase domestic production. He was moderate in his opinions, kind and fair in expressing them, and willing to listen with patience to any proposition of amendment. He still lives at the venerable age of eighty-five, and has been, during all the long period since the report of the bill named after him, to this time, in public life, and still retains the confidence and affection of his constituents and his colleagues.

I did not participate in the debate until the time came when, in the judgment of the committee of ways and means, it was necessary to dispose of the bill, either by its passage or defeat. On the 7th of May, 1860, the bill being before the House, I moved that all debate on it should cease at one o'clock the next day. Some opposition was evinced, but the motion was adopted. I then made my first speech upon the subject of the tariff. The introductory paragraphs state the then condition of the treasury as follows:

"The revenue act of March 3, 1857, which it is now proposed to repeal, has proved to be a crude, ill-advised, and ill-digested measure. It was never acted upon in detail in either branch of Congress, but was the result of a committee of conference in the last days of the session, and was finally passed by a combination of hostile interests and sentiments. It was adopted at a time of inflated prices, when the treasury was overflowing with revenue. When that condition of affairs ceased, it failed to furnish ordinary revenue, and by its incidental effects operated injuriously to nearly every branch of industry.

"It went into operation on the 1st of July, 1857. At that time there was in the treasury of the United States a balance of $17,710,114. The amount of the public debt then remaining unpaid, none of which was then due, was a little over $29,000,000. So that there was in the treasury of the United States, when the tariff act of 1857 went into operation, nearly enough to have paid two-thirds of the public debt. Within one year from that time, the public debt was increased to $44,910,777.

"On the 1st of July, 1859, the public debt had increased to $58,754,699. On the 1st of May, 1860, as nearly as I can ascertain, the public debt had risen to $65,681,099. The balance in the treasury on the first of July next, as estimated by me, will be $1,919,349.

＊　　＊　　＊　　＊　　＊　　＊　　＊　　＊　　＊

"Under the operation of the tariff of 1857, the deficit in the revenue is over $52,000,000. It may be stated thus:

Balance in the treasury, July 1, 1857.................... $17,710,114
Balance in the treasury, July 1, 1860, estimated..........   1,919,349
                                                           $15,790,765

Amount of public debt May 1, 1860..... $65,681,199
Amount of public debt July 1, 1857..... 29,060,386   36,620,813
                                                           $52,411,578

It was manifest from these statements that there was an imperative necessity for the passage of some measure to increase the revenues. We could hardly hope that, in the excited state of the public mind and the known position of the Senate, the bill could pass at that session. The government had been conducted for three years by borrowing money in time of peace. The appropriations had been reduced during that session by the committee of ways and means below the estimates of the treasury, as stated by me to the House. I then said:

"I desire now to say that the committee of ways and means, who have had charge of appropriation bills, have endeavored, faithfully and honestly, without regard to party divisions—and all parties in this House are represented in that committee—to cut down the appropriations to the lowest practicable point; and thus to reduce the expenses of the government. I have before me a table showing that, upon the estimates submitted to us, by the Secretary of the Treasury, for the ordinary expenses of the government, we have been able to reduce the amount about $1,230,000."

After a careful statement of the condition of the treasury and the necessity for further supplies, I expressed this opinion of the pending bill:

" In my judgment, Mr. Morrill's bill is a great improvement on the tariff of 1857." It is more certain. It is more definite. It gives specific duties. There is another reason why it is better than the tariff of 1857. That tariff is made up of complex and inconvenient tables. The number of tables is too great ; and in some cases the same article is in two tables. Thus, flaxseed comes in with a duty of ten per cent.; and yet linseed, the same thing, yielding the same product, the same oil, is admitted duty free. The bill of Mr. Morrill, on the other hand, fixes three *ad valorem* tables ; one at ten per cent., one at twenty, and the other at thirty. There is a number of specific duties, and then there is a free list. It conforms to our decimal currency, and the duties under it are easily calculated. There can be but little dispute about home and foreign valuation under it. It will yield a revenue sufficient to pay the expenses of the government. It is more simple and more certain. It substitutes specific for *ad valorem* duties whenever practicable. For these reasons, it is obvious Mr. Morrill's bill ought to receive the sanction of Congress."

The bill not only provided for a sufficient revenue, but was distinctively a bill for incidental protection to all American industries, impartially and fairly applied. I said I desired to have this bill passed,

" Because it is framed upon the idea that it is the duty of the government, in imposing taxes, to do as little injury to the industry of the country as possible; that they are to be levied so as to extend a reasonable protection to all branches of American industry. I think that is right. Every President of the United States, from Washington to this time, has recognized that principle, including Mr. Buchanan.

" We may make a tariff to raise the sum of $40,000,000, and injure every industrial interest of the country. The committee of ways and means report a tariff bill which will produce $65,000,000, and will do no injury to any industrial interest. I believe that it will give a reasonable fair protection for the great industries of agriculture, manufacture, and commerce, which lie at the basis of the prosperity of this country."

Mr. Morrill participated in this debate by brief but clear statements in respect to the details of the bill. On the 8th of May, 1860, he said, in the course of some remarks upon the bill:

" I think if the gentleman will examine this bill, he will find that the average rates of duties upon manufactured articles are not higher, but rather lower, than they are now; but being to a large extent specific, they will prove of great value to the country, in giving steadiness to our markets, as well as to the revenue; and because frauds will be to a very great extent obviated, which are now practiced under our *ad valorem* system, and which have made our government almost equal in infamy to that of Mexico and other countries, where their revenue laws are a mere farce."

The bill, despite its merits, was assailed with all forms of amendments from all parts of the House. Many of the amendments were adopted, until the bill became so mottled that Mr. Morrill, discouraged and strongly inclined against the bill as changed, was disposed to abandon it to its fate. He was not familiar with the rules, and, for this reason, labored under a disadvantage in the conduct of the bill. I believed not only in the merits of the measure, but that by a process strictly in accordance with the rules, it might be restored substantially as it was reported by the committee. To secure that effect Mr. Morrill offered an amendment in the nature of a substitute for the bill. To that I offered as an amendment a bill which embodied nearly all of the original bill as reported, with such modifications as were evidently favored by the House, without affecting the general principles of the measure.

The vote, upon my substitute being adopted in place of the substitute offered by Mr. Morrill, prevented any amendment to my amendment except by adding to it. The result of it was that the House, tired with the long struggle, and believing that the measure thus amended was in substance the same as the original bill reported, finally passed the bill on the 10th day of May, 1860, by the vote of 105 yeas to 64 nays.

As this was my birthday, I remember to have celebrated it, not only as my birthday, but as the day on which the Morrill tariff bill passed the House of Representatives.

We knew upon the passage of this bill that it could not pass the Senate during that session. It was taken up in that body, debated at considerable length, and finally, on the 20th of June, it was, in effect, postponed until the next session.

I might as well here follow the Morrill tariff bill to its final passage at the next session of this Congress.

On the 20th of December, 1860, Mr. Hunter, from the committee on finance, to whom was referred the tariff bill, reported it back with a recommendation that it be postponed until the 4th day of March following. This was, in effect, to reject the bill, as Congress terminated on that day. The committee on finance, and a majority of the Senate as then constituted, was opposed to the passage of the bill, but the secession movements, then openly threatened, soon changed the political complexion of the Senate, by the resignation of Senators on account of the secession of their states. On the 18th of January, 1861, Mr. Cameron, of Pennsylvania, moved to take up the bill, and, upon his motion, it was made a special order for the following Wednesday. On the 23rd of January it was referred to a committee of five members, consisting of Mr. Simmons, Mr. Hunter, Mr. Bigler, Mr. Fessenden, and Mr. Gwin. This was done on the same day when the committees of the Senate were reorganized on account of the withdrawal of Senators. The special committee appointed by the Vice President was friendly to the bill. Then for the first time it became possible to secure favorable action in the Senate. Many amendments were proposed and adopted by the Senate, but they did not materially affect the general principles upon which the bill was founded. It passed the Senate with these amendments by the decided vote of 25 yeas to 14 nays. All of the amendments of the Senate but one were promptly agreed to by the House, and an amendment was made to the Senate amendment, upon which a conference between the two Houses was ordered. Messrs. Simmons, Bigler and Hunter were the managers on the part of the Senate and Messrs. Sherman, Phelps and Moorhead on the part of the House.

On the 27th day of February, five days before the close of the session, the conferees reported to the Senate their agreement and the report of the committee was adopted without objection or division by that body, and also by the House of Representatives, and the bill was signed by President Buchanan.

This law, passed in the throes of a revolution, and only possible as the result of the withdrawal of Senators to engage in the war of secession, met all the expectations of its friends. It was fair, just and conservative, and would, in peaceful times, yield about $50,000,000 a year, the amount of national expenditures in 1860, and, at the same time, protect and strengthen all existing home industries, and lay the foundation for great increase in production. It was destined, however, to begin its existence at a period of revolution. The secession of eleven states precipitated the war, involving enormous expenditures, in the face of which all revenue laws were inadequate and powerless. The credit of the government, its resources and capacity for taxation, had to be appealed to. Resort was had to every possible mode of taxation that could be devised by the ingenuity of man, to supply the requirements of the war, and to maintain the public credit. The Morrill tariff act was, therefore, greatly modified by subsequent laws, the duties doubled and in some cases trebled. Internal taxes, yielding twofold the amount collected from customs, were levied, and cheerfully paid, and duties on imported goods were quickly increased. The details of this act became the victim of the war, but the general principles upon which it was founded, the application of specific duties where possible, and the careful protection extended to the products of the soil and the mine, as well as of the workshop, have been maintained to a greater or less extent until the present time.

I have participated in framing many tariff bills, but have never succeeded in securing one that I entirely approved. The Morrill tariff bill came nearer than any other to meeting the double requirement of providing ample revenue for the support of the government and of rendering the proper protection to home industries. No national taxes, except duties on imported goods, were imposed at the time of its passage. The Civil War changed all this, reducing importations and adding tenfold to the revenue required. The government was justified in increasing existing rates of duty, and in adding to the dutiable list all articles imported, thus including articles of prime necessity and of universal use. In addition to these duties, it was compelled to add taxes on all articles of home production, on incomes not required for the supply of actual wants, and, especially, on articles of doubtful necessity, such as spirits, tobacco and beer. These taxes were absolutely required to meet expenditures for the army and navy, for the interest on the war debts and just pensions to those who were disabled by the war, and to their widows and orphans.

These conditions have, in a measure, been fulfilled. The war is over; the public debt has been diminished to one-third of the amount due at the close of the war. The pension list is the chief and almost only outstanding obligation growing out of the war, but this is fully met by internal taxes on spirits, tobacco and beer. What is needed now is a tariff or tax on imported goods sufficient in amount to meet the current expenditures of the government, and which at the same time will tend to encourage the production in this country of all articles, whether of the farm, the mine or the workshop, that can be readily and at reasonable cost produced in this country.

And here we meet the difficulty that the mode, extent, manner and objects of tariff taxation are unhappily mixed up in our party politics. This should not be so. Whether the mode of taxation should be by a percentage on the *value* of goods imported, or by a duty imposed on the weight or quantity, depends upon the nature of the article. If the article is sold in the market by weight or quantity, the duty should be specific, *i. e.*, a certain rate on the unit of weight or quantity. If it is of such a nature that its value cannot be measured by weight or quantity the duty should be *ad valorem, i. e.*, a percentage of its value. This is matter of detail to be fixed by the custom of merchants. As a rule it is better to fix the duty upon weight or measure, rather than upon value, for by the former mode the amount is easily ascertained by the scale or yard stick, while to base the duty upon value, changing from day to day, is to invite fraud and litigation.

The extent or rate of duty to be imposed should depend entirely upon the pecuniary wants of the government, and the nature of the article imported. If the article is one of luxury, mainly consumed by the rich, the duty should be at a higher rate than upon an article in general use. This principle is sometimes disputed, but it would seem that in a republic a just discrimination ought to be made in favor of the many rather than

of the few. On this principle all political parties have acted.
The rates have been higher on silks, satins, furs and the like
than on goods made of cotton, wool, flax or hemp. To meet
the changing wants of the government all articles should be
classified in schedules, so that the rate of duty on a single
schedule, or on many schedules, could be advanced or lowered
without disturbing the general scheme of taxation.

As to the manner of taxation and the places where duties
should be collected, all will agree that they should be paid as
nearly as possible where the goods are to be consumed. The concentration of importations at any one port on the coast, or at
several ports, gives to the people residing at or near such favored
ports an advantage over the people living in the interior of the
country. The system of interior ports, or places of delivery to
which goods may be consigned, has been adopted and generally
approved. The object is that all parts of the country shall
have equal facilities and bear equally the burdens of taxation.

The method of importations should be so simplified that any
person, in any part of the United States, may order from any
commercial port or country any article desired and be able
to receive it and pay the prescribed duty, at any considerable
port or city in the United States that he may designate.

As to the objects of tariff taxation there is and always will
be an honest difference of opinion. The main purpose is to secure the revenue from foreigners seeking our market to dispose
of their products. The United States has the right, exercised
by every nation, to determine upon what terms the productions of foreign nations shall be admitted into its markets, and
those terms will be such as its interests may demand. Great
Britain may admit nearly all commodities free of duty, but
even that country is guided by her interests in all her commercial regulations. All other nations classified as civilized seek,
like the United States, by tariff laws, not only to secure revenue, but to protect and foster domestic industries. Japan
has won its entrance among civilized nations by securing treaties with European countries and the United States, by which
she has been relieved from restrictions as to her duties on

imports, and now has the right to regulate and fix her import duties as her interest dictates.

The United States has from the beginning of its government declared that one object of duties on imports is the encouragement of manufactures in the United States, and, whatever may be the dogma inserted in a political party platform, tariff legislation will continue to have a double object, *revenue and protection*. This was strikingly exemplified by the recent action of Congress in the passage of the tariff law now in force.

The real difficulty in our tariff laws is to avoid unequal and unjust discrimination in the objects of protection, made with a view to favor the productions of one state or section at the cost of another state or section. The dogma of some manufacturers, that raw materials should be admitted free of duty, is far more dangerous to the protective policy than the opposition of free traders. The latter contend that no duties should be levied to protect domestic industry, but for revenue only, while the former demand protection for their industries, but refuse to give to the farmer and miner the benefit of even revenue duties. A denial of protection on coal, iron, wool and other so-called raw materials, will lead to the denial of protection to machinery, to textiles, to pottery and other industries. The labor of one class must not be sacrificed to secure higher protection for another class. The earth and all that is within it is the work of God. The labor of man that tends to develop the resources buried in the earth is entitled to the same favor and protection as skilled labor in the highest branch of industry, and if this is not granted impartially the doctrine of protection proclaimed by the founders of our government, supported for more than a hundred years of wonderful progress, will be sacrificed by the hungry greed of selfish corporations, who ask protection for great establishments and refuse to grant it to the miner, the laborer and the farmer.

Another principle must be ingrafted into our tariff laws, growing out of new modes of production by corporations and combinations. Until recently each miner, each artisan, and each manufacturer, had to compete in the open market with everyone engaged in the same industry. The general public had the benefit of free competition. This tended to lower prices on many commodities, to increase the quantity produced, and to supply the home market, thus excluding importations. The tendency since the Civil War in every branch of industry has been to consolidate operations. To effect this, corporations have been created in most of the states and granted such liberal corporate powers, without respect to the nature of the business to be conducted, and with terms and privileges so favorable, that private enterprise without large capital cannot compete with them. Instead of small or moderate workshops, with a few hands, we now have great establishments with hundreds of employes, and all the capital of scores of stockholders under the control of a few men, and often of one man. This may be of benefit by reducing the cost of production, but it also involves two dangers, one the irrepressible conflict of labor with capital, and the other the combination of corporations engaged in the same business to advance prices and prevent competition, thus constituting a monopoly commanding business and controlling the market.

This power in the hands of a few is at this moment the disturbing element in many of our great industries. It is especially dangerous when it is promoted by rates of duty on imported goods higher than are necessary to cover the difference in the cost of labor here and abroad. When such conditions occur, the monopoly becomes offensive. Such combinations are denounced and punished by the laws of almost every civilized government and by the laws of many of our states. They should be denounced and punished by the laws of the United States whenever they affect any matter within the jurisdiction of the United States. Whenever the tendency of a monopoly is to prevent mutual competition, and to advance prices for any articles embraced in our tariff laws, the duty on the article should be at once reduced or repealed.

As Members of Congress, divided by party lines and crude platforms, must in the main, care for and protect local interests, I do not believe any fair, impartial and business tariff can be framed by them. It would be better for Congress, the law-making power, after determining the amount to be raised, to sanction and adopt a careful tariff bill, framed by an impartial commission, large enough to represent all sections and parties, all employers and employes. Hitherto, the tariffs framed by Congress have been rejected by the people. Each party, in its turn, has undertaken the task with like result. Let us try the experiment of a tariff framed, not by a party upon a party platform, but by the selected representatives of the commercial, industrial, farming and laboring classes. Let Congress place upon the statute book such a law, and the tariff question will cease to be the foot ball of partisan legislation.

The remainder of this session was occupied chiefly in the consideration of appropriation bills. These were carefully scrutinized; many estimates of the departments were reduced. As usual, appropriations were increased in the Senate, but most of the amendments were rejected in conference.

The bill authorizing a loan for the redemption of treasury notes was passed on the 22nd day of June. Congress adjourned at noon June 25, 1860.

This memorable Congress, commencing with a contest which threatened violence on the floor of the House of Representatives, was held unorganized for sixty days by a defeated party upon a flimsy pretext, and during all that time we had to listen to open threats of secession and disunion made by its members. No previous Congress had exhibited such violence of speech and action. When fully organized it quieted down, and, with occasional exceptions, proceeded rapidly to the discharge of its public duties. A greater number of contested bills were passed at this Congress than usual. Most of these measures came from the committee of ways and means. The members of that committee were Messrs. John Sherman, of Ohio, Henry Winter Davis, of Maryland, John S. Phelps, of Missouri, Thaddeus Stevens, of Pennsylvania, Israel Washburn, Jr., of Maine, John S. Millson, of Virginia, Justin S. Morrill, of Vermont, Martin J. Crawford, of Georgia, and Elbridge G. Spaulding, of New York. Of these but two, Mr. Morrill and myself, survive. A brief notice of those who are numbered with the dead may not be out of place.

Henry Winter Davis was the most accomplished orator in the House while he was a Member. Well educated in college, well trained as a lawyer, an accomplished writer and eloquent speaker, yet he was a poor parliamentarian, a careless member in committee, and utterly unfit to conduct an appropriation or tariff bill in the House. He was impatient of details, querulous when questioned or interrupted, but in social life and in intercourse with his fellow Members he was genial, kind and courteous. On one occasion, when I was called home, I requested him to take charge of an appropriation bill and secure its passage. He did as I requested, but he was soon embarrassed by questions he could not answer, and had the bill postponed until my return. I felt for Mr. Davis a personal attachment, and I believe this kindly feeling was reciprocated. He served in the House of Representatives during most of the war, and joined with Senator Wade in opposition to Mr. Lincoln's re-election in 1864. He died at Baltimore on the 20th of December, 1865, when in the full vigor of matured manhood.

John S. Phelps in 1860 was an old and experienced Member. Born in Connecticut he removed to Missouri as early as 1837. In 1844 he was elected to Congress as a Democrat, and continued as a Member sixteen years, being chairman of the committee of ways and means during the 35th Congress. He was a valuable Member, patient, careful, industrious, and had the confidence of the House. He was moderate in his political opinions, and, though a resident of Missouri, he took the Union side in the Civil War.

Thaddeus Stevens, one of the most remarkable men of the last generation, was born in Vermont near the close of the last century; and was well educated. He taught school and studied law. He removed to Pennsylvania and there engaged in turbulent politics; served several years as a member of the state legislature; was elected to Congress in 1848 and served four years. He was known to be an aggressive Whig and a dangerous opponent in debate; was re-elected in 1858 as a Republican and at once took the lead in the speakership contest. His sarcasm was keen and merciless. He was not a very useful member of the committee. He was better in the field of battle than in the seclusion of the committee. Still, when any contest arose in the House over bills reported by the committee, he was always ready to defend its action. Though a cynical old bachelor, with a deformed foot and with a bitter tongue for those he disliked, he was always charitable and kind to the poor. He was quiet and impartial in his charity, recognizing no distinction on account of color, but usually preferring to aid women rather than men. I was often the witness of his charities. He continued in active public life until his death on the 11th of August, 1868. For some time before his death he was unable to walk up the marble steps of the capitol and two stout negroes were detailed to carry him up in a chair. On one occasion when safely seated he grimly said to them, "Who will carry me when you die?" Mr. Stevens was a brave man. He always fought his fights to a finish and never asked or gave quarter.

Israel Washburn, Jr., of Maine, was one of three brothers, Members of this Congress. Israel was the eldest, and, perhaps, the most active, of the three. He received a classical education, studied law and was admitted to the bar in 1830. He was a good debater and a useful member of the committee. He had been in Congress ten years, including the 36th. He subsequently became governor of Maine, and collector of customs at Portland.

John S. Millson, of Virginia, had long been a Member of Congress, was fifty-two years old, and regarded as a safe, conservative man of fair abilities.

Martin J. Crawford, of Georgia, was a lawyer of good standing. He was elected a Member of Congress in 1854, and continued as such until the rebellion, in which he took an active part. When Georgia seceded, he, with his colleagues, formally withdrew from Congress. Crawford and I had been friendly, and somewhat intimate. He was a frank man, openly avowing his opinions, but with respectful toleration of those of others. After he withdrew we met in the lobby; he bade me good-bye, saying that his next appearance in Washington would be as

Envoy Extraordinary and Minister Plenipotentiary of the Confederate States. I told him that he was more likely to appear as a prisoner of war. I then warned him that the struggle would be to the death, and that the Union would triumph. Long afterwards, when I visited the fair at Atlanta, he recalled our conversation and admitted I was the best prophet. We spent the evening and far into the night talking about the past and the future. He evinced no regret for the result of the war, but quietly acquiesced, and was then a judge in one of the courts in that state.

Elbridge G. Spaulding, of New York, was an excellent Member. He had a taste for financial problems and contributed a good deal to the measures adopted, in this and the 37th Congress, to establish a national currency and to build up the public credit. These Members, with Mr. Morrill and myself, were charged with the most important legislation in the 36th Congress, and I believe that the general opinion of the House was that we did our duty well.

CHAPTER IX.

LAST DAYS OF THE BUCHANAN ADMINISTRATION.

My First Appearance Before a New York Audience — Lincoln's Nomination at the
Chicago Convention — I Engage Actively in the Presidential Canvass — Mak-
ing Speeches for Lincoln — My Letter to Philadelphia Citizens — Acts of
Secession by Southern States — How the South was Equipped by
the Secretary of the Navy — Buchanan's Strange Doctrine
Regarding State Control by the General Government —
Schemes "to Save the Country" — My Reply to
Mr. Pendleton on the Condition of the Im-
pending Revolution — The Ohio Dele-
gation in the 36th Congress —
Retrospection.

I HAVE followed this important session of Congress to its
close, but while the debate continued in Congress a
greater debate was being conducted by the people. Never
before was such interest felt in the political questions of
he day. In many of the cities of the country clubs were organized for political discussions, and persons in public life were
pressed to make speeches or lectures on the topics of the day.
The Young Men's Central Republican Union, of New York,
arranged a series of lectures, the first of which was delivered
by Frank P. Blair, the second by Cassius M. Clay, and the third
by Abraham Lincoln. The remarkable address of the last
named had great influence in securing his nomination for
President. It was the first time Mr. Lincoln had spoken in
New York, where he was then personally almost unknown. His
debate with Douglas had excited general attention. Using the
language of his biographers:

"When, on the evening of February 27, 1860, he stood before his
audience, he saw not only a well-filled house, but an assemblage of listen-
ers in which were many whom, by reason of his own modest estimate of
himself, he would have been rather inclined to ask advice from than to offer
instruction to. William Cullen Bryant presided over the meeting.

* * * * * * * * *

"The representative men of New York were naturally eager to see and
hear one who, by whatever force of eloquence or argument, had attracted

so large a share of the public attention. We may also fairly infer that, on his part, Lincoln was no less curious to test the effect of his words on an audience more learned and critical than those collected in the open air meetings of his western campaigns. This mutual interest was an evident advantage to both; it secured a close attention from the house, and insured deliberation and emphasis by the speaker, enabling him to develop his argument with perfect precision and unity, reaching perhaps the happiest general effect ever attained in any one of his long addresses."

His speech was printed by the leading papers of the city, and, in pamphlet form, was widely distributed and read.

I was invited by the Republican Union to make one of these addresses, and, though very much occupied and having little time for preparation, I accepted the invitation, and spoke at Cooper Institute in the city of New York on the 30th of April, 1860. It was my first appearance before a New York audience, and I confess that I was not satisfied with the address. I undertook, what I never attempted before, to read a political speech to a popular audience. While I was treated kindly I felt quite sure my speech was a disappointment. A recent reading of it confirms my opinion that it was not equal to the occasion or the audience.

I was also invited by the Republican Club of Philadelphia to make a speech ratifying the nomination of Lincoln and Hamlin and spoke at a meeting held May 28, 1860. My address was entirely impromptu, and was far better, both in manner and matter, than the speech in New York, and was received with great applause. Since that time, I have never attempted to make a popular address from manuscript. Every speaker should know the substance of what he intends to say, but ought to rely for his words upon the spirit and temper of his audience.

The summer of 1860 was ominous of domestic discord and civil war. The success of the Republicans in the House of Representatives, the violent scenes in the House, notably those between Potter, Pryor, Barksdale, and Lovejoy, were indications that the south was aggressive, and that the north would fight. The meeting of the Democratic convention at Charleston, on the 23rd of April, soon disclosed an almost equal division of its members as to slavery in the territories. The southern platform was adopted by a majority of one in its committee on resolutions, but rejected by a majority of the convention. This was the vital issue between the followers of Davis and Douglas, and Douglas won. A majority of the delegates from six of the southern states thereupon withdrew from the convention and adjourned to Richmond. Thus, the first secession was from a Democratic convention. The remainder of that convention adjourned to Baltimore, at which city Douglas was nominated for President. The seceding delegates nominated Breckenridge. Thus, the Democratic party, which, in every stage of the slavery controversy, had taken sides with the south, was itself broken on the rock of slavery, and condemned to certain defeat.

The Republican convention met at Chicago on the 16th of May, with a defined line of public policy which was adopted unanimously by the convention. The only question to be determined was, who should be the candidate for President, who would best represent the principles agreed upon. Seward, Chase and Bates were laid aside, and Abraham Lincoln, one stronger than any one of these, was unanimously nominated. The nomination of a candidate by a third party, ignoring the slavery question, did not change the issue. The conflict was now between freedom and slavery, an issue carefully avoided by the two great parties prior to the repeal of the Missouri Compromise.

Thus Douglas, as a consequence of his own act, was destined to defeat, and the irrepressible conflict was to be finally determined by the people in the choice between Lincoln and Breckenridge, with the distinct declaration, made by the delegates seceding from the Charleston convention, that if Lincoln was elected their states would secede from the Union, and establish an independent government founded upon slavery. This was the momentous issue involved in the election.

Congress adjourned on the 28th of June, 1860. On the 17th of July, I was unanimously renominated at Shelby. John Shauck, a venerable Quaker, 80 years of age, claimed the right to nominate me as he had done in previous conventions. He was absent at the moment, but the convention, in deference to his known wishes, awaited his coming. From that time until the election, I was actively engaged in the presidential canvass. I spent but little time in my district, as there was but a nominal opposition to my election. The Democratic candidate, Barnabus Burns, was a personal friend, and sympathized with me on many subjects. Scarcely a week day passed that I did not speak at least once.

Of the many speeches made by me in that canvass, I recall but very few. I have already referred to my debate with Cox, if it can properly be called a debate. It was friendly badinage. He charged me with pulling the Morrill tariff bill through by a trick. I answered that if it was a trick, it was a trick well played, as the bill passed by a vote of 105 to 64, many Democrats voting for it. He complained of the duties on wool, declaring that the farmers were sacrificed. I showed that the duties on wool had been advanced. He said I was president of a Know Nothing Lodge in Mansfield. I said this was simply a lie, and that there were plenty of Douglas Democrats before me who knew it. He said that I initiated therein, Sam Richey in a stable. I asked who told him that story, when the audience called out loudly for Burns. Mr. Burns rose and said he did not tell Mr. Cox so. I said I was glad to hear it, that it was a silly lie made out of whole cloth, and asked if Richey was present. Richey was in the crowd, and rose amid great laughter and applause and said: "Here I am." I said: "Well, friends, you see my friend, Richey, is a genuine Irishman, but he knows, as I know, that Cox's story is a falsification. Mr. Cox says I am a political thief; don't think he charges me with stealing sheep, he only means to say I stole squatter sovereignty. It is petty larceny at best. But I did not steal Douglas squatter sovereignty."

I then proceeded to define the difference between the only two parties with definite principles. The real contest was, not between Lincoln and Douglas, or between Cox and me, but between Breckenridge and Lincoln, between free institutions and slave institutions, between union and disunion. I refer to this debate with Cox to show how local prejudices obscured the problem then involved. The people of Ohio were divided on parallel lines, for Cox and I agreed on Kansas, but he was for Douglas and I for Lincoln, while the south was brooding over secession, if either Lincoln or Douglas should be elected.

I went into most of the congressional districts of Ohio and perceived a strong leaning in favor of Lincoln, but Douglas also had many supporters. The Democratic party of Ohio was satisfied with Douglas' popular sovereignty, especially as it, as they alleged, had secured freedom for Kansas. Breckenridge had no great following in Ohio, and Bell and Everett less.

I spent several days in the canvass in Pennsylvania, Indiana, New Jersey and Delaware, all warmly contested states, the votes of which would determine the election. It soon became apparent that Lincoln was the only candidate who could secure a majority of the electoral vote. This fact, and the known difficulty of securing an election by the House in case of failure of an election by the Electoral College, greatly aided Mr. Lincoln. I presented this argument with care and fullness in a speech delivered at Philadelphia on the 12th of September, 1860. It was printed at the time and largely circulated. I quote a paragraph, which contains the one fact upon which my argument rested:

"Owing to the division of the Democratic party, the Republican party is the only one that can hope to succeed by a direct vote of the people. This is a fact I need not discuss, for it was written at the threshold of the contest by the conventions of Charleston and Baltimore. If the election were to be determined by the rule of plurality — a rule now adopted in every state in the Union — intelligent men would consider it already decided; but the rule of the majority is fixed by the constitution, and if Pennsylvania does not vote for Lincoln, then the election devolves upon the House of Representatives. In that event the constitution requires the House to choose immediately, by ballot, a President from the persons, not exceeding three, having the highest number of electoral votes. The vote must be taken by states, and not by Representatives. The three millions of people of Pennsylvania will have only the same political power as the one hundred thousand people of Delaware."

I recently read this speech, and, in view of the events that followed, I can say that every prophecy made, and every argument stated, has been verified and sustained by the march

of events. My opening criticism of Mr. Buchanan's administration may seem to be partisan and unjust, but the general
opinion now is that his fault was feebleness of will, not inten-
tional wrong.   Mr. Buchanan was surrounded by men who had
already made up their minds to destroy the Union, one of
whom had already committed acts of treachery in the distribution of arms and military supplies, and all of whom avowed the
legality and rightfulness of secession.   I think what I said was
justified by the conditions existing when the speech was made.
The residue of my speech was certainly moderate enough to satisfy the most conservative mind.   I give the closing paragraphs:

" These are, so far as I know, the leading ideas of the Republican party.
I appeal to your candor if they do not commend themselves to the judgment
of reasonable men.   Is this the party which you would combine and con-
spire against, and to defeat which you would unite hostile elements?   Is it
to defeat these ideas that you would risk scenes of violence in the House, or
the subversion of the constitution by the Senate of the United States?   Is it
to defeat this noble policy that you would longer trust a broken-down, corrupt and demoralized administration?   Is it for this that you would continue
in power a party that, by a long enjoyment of the patronage of the government, has become reckless and corrupt?

" If you will take the responsibility of preventing the triumph of the
Republican party, you may do so, but it will require a close fusion of all the
elements to defeat it.   It is young and vigorous.   It has all the unity and
discipline of the old Democratic party.   It holds most of the opinions, modified by experience, of the old Whig party.   It has the conservative modera-
tion of the People's party, which has influenced its nominations.   It adheres
to every principle proclaimed by the old Republican party of Jefferson.
We have confidence in the integrity and patriotism, and wisdom of our
standard bearers—Lincoln and Hamlin.   If Mr. Lincoln cannot be recommended as a parlor President, like General Pierce, and is not familiar with
the etiquette of foreign courts, as is Mr. Buchanan, we know that he is honest, faithful, courageous and capable.   No man can read his celebrated debates with Mr. Douglas, without forming a high opinion of his capacity.
He is better for having lived but a short time in Washington, for that city
of politicians is not particularly celebrated for sound principles or rigid
morals.   Born in Kentucky, descended from a Pennsylvania stock, the son
and grandson of Virginians, raised in Indiana and Illinois, familiar by his
own experience with the wants and interests and aspirations of the people,
he possesses the same traits of character which made Jackson and Clay, in
their day and generation, leaders of parties and of men.   Let us, my friends,
unite in electing him President of the United States."

Lincoln was elected. He received 180 electoral votes; Breckenridge 72 ; Douglas 12 ; Bell 39. The question then was whether the people of the seceding states would try to carry into effect their declaration. I had no doubt they would try, but I was equally confident they would fail.

As events progressed in the south, citizens of the north held popular meetings in nearly all our cities and in many rural communities. I was invited by leading citizens of Philadelphia to attend a public dinner in that city in December, 1860. I could not attend in person, but wrote them a letter which defined clearly my convictions and my conception of the duties of our people in view of passing events. I insert it here :

WASHINGTON, December 22, 1860.

GENTLEMEN:—Your note of the 15th inst., inviting me to attend a public dinner in your city, on Friday evening next, was duly received.

I remember with pleasure the kindness shown me during the recent canvass by our political friends in Philadelphia, and would gladly avail myself of the proposed celebration, to mingle my personal thanks with your rejoicings, over the recent triumph of our political principles. Other engagements and duties, however, will not allow me that pleasure.

No state can dispute with Pennsylvania the honor of this triumph. Her own son was upon trial, and her voice of condemnation was emphatic and decisive. The election of Governor Curtin foreshadowed her decision, and strengthened our cause in every state where freedom of election is allowed to the people. Her verdict in November reconsidered and reaffirmed her verdict in October. And now, since the victory is won, let us not lose the fruits of it.

Fidelity to principle is demanded by the highest patriotism. The question is not whether this or that policy should prevail; but whether we shall allow the government to be broken into fragments, by disappointed partisans, condemned by four-fifths of the people. It is the same question answered by General Jackson in his proclamation of 1833. It is the same question answered by Henry Clay in the Senate in 1850. It is the same question answered by Madison and Jefferson, and recently by Wade and Johnson. It is a question which, I feel assured, every one of you will answer, in the patriotic language of General Jackson—' *The Union, it must be preserved.*'

Such would be the voice of the whole country, if the government was not now administered by those who not only threaten treason, but actually commit it, by turning the powers of the government against itself. They kill the government they have sworn to maintain and defend, because the people, whose agents they are, have condemned them. In this spirit we have seen a Secretary of the Treasury, charged with the financial credit of the government, offering for sale the bonds of the government, and at the same moment declaring that it will be overthrown, and that he would aid in overthrowing it. We see other high officers receiving *pay* for services to the government, and yet, at the same moment, plotting its destruction. We see the treasury robbed by subordinate officers amid the general ruin. Stranger still, we see the President of the United States acknowledging his duty to execute the laws, but refusing to execute them. He admits that the constitution is the supreme law; that neither a state nor the citizens of a state can disregard it; and yet, armed as he is with all the executive power, he refuses even to protect the property of the United States against armed violence. He will not heed General Cass, the head of his cabinet. He will not heed General Scott, the head of the army. He has transferred to southern states more than one hundred thousand arms, of the newest pattern and most effective calibre, to be turned against the government.

The American people are now trembling with apprehension lest the President allow our officers and soldiers to be slaughtered at their posts, for want of the aid which he has refused, or, what is far more disgraceful, shall order the flag of the Union to be lowered, without resistance to lawless force.

Treason sits in the councils, and timidity controls the executive power. The President listens to, and is controlled by, threats. He theorizes about coercing a state when he should be enforcing the laws against rebellious citizens. He admits that the states have surrendered the power to make treaties, coin money, and regulate commerce, and yet we will probably have the novel and ridiculous farce of a negotiation between the President and a state, for the surrender of forts, and arsenals, and sovereignty. Congress can do nothing, for the laws now are sufficient, if executed. Impeachment is too slow a remedy. The constitution provided against every probable vacancy in the office of President, but did not provide for utter imbecility.

The people, alarmed, excited, yet true to the Union and the constitution, are watching with eager fear, lest the noble government, baptized in the blood of the Revolution, shall be broken into fragments, before the President elect shall assume the functions of his office.

What pretext is given for this alarming condition of affairs?—for every treasonable act has its pretext. We are told that the people of the southern states *apprehend* that Mr. Lincoln will deprive them of their constitutional rights. It is not claimed that, as yet, their rights have been invaded, but upon an *apprehension* of evil, they will break up the most prosperous government the providence of God ever allowed to man.

We know very well how groundless are their apprehensions, but we are not even allowed to say so to our fellow-citizens of the south. So wild is their apprehension, that even such statesmen as Stephens, Johnson, Hill,

Botts and Pettigrew, when they say, 'wait, wait, till we see what this Republican party will attempt,' are denounced as Abolitionists—Submissionists. You know very well that we do not propose to interfere in the slightest degree with slavery in the states. We know that our leader, for whose election you rejoice, has, over and over again, affirmed his opposition to the abolition of slavery in the District of Columbia, except upon conditions that are not likely to occur; or to any interference with the inter-state slave trade, and that he will enforce the constitutional right of the citizens of the slave states to recapture their fugitive slaves when they escape from service into the free states. We know very well that the great objects which those who elected Mr. Lincoln expect him to accomplish will be to secure to free labor its just right to the territories of the United States; to protect, as far as practicable, by wise revenue laws, the labor of our people; to secure the public lands to actual settlers, instead of to non-resident speculators; to develop the internal resources of the country, by opening new means of communication between the Atlantic and the Pacific, and to purify the administration of the government from the pernicious influences of jobs, contracts, and unreasoning party warfare.

But some of you may say, all this is very well, but what will you do to save the Union? Why don't you compromise?

Gentlemen, remember that we are just recovering from the dishonor of breaking a legislative compromise. We have been struggling, against all the powers of the government, for six years, to secure practically what was expressly granted by a compromise. We have succeeded. Kansas is now free. The Missouri restriction is now practically restored by the incipient constitution of Kansas, and safer yet, by the will of her people. The baptism of strife through which she has passed has only strengthened the prohibition. There let it stand.

But our political opponents, who have dishonored the word compromise, who trampled, without a moment's hesitation, upon a compromise, when they expected to gain by it, now ask us to again compromise, by securing slavery south of a geographical line. To this we might fairly say: There is no occasion for compromise. We have done no wrong; we have no apologies to make, and no concessions to offer. You chose your ground, and we accepted your issue. We have beaten you, and you must submit, as we have done in the past, and as we would have done if the voice of the people had been against us. As good citizens, you must obey the laws, and respect the constituted authorities. But we will meet new questions of administration with a liberal spirit. Without surrendering our convictions in the least, we may now dispose of the whole territorial controversy by the exercise of unquestioned congressional power.

The only territory south of the line, except that which, by treaty with Indian tribes, cannot be included within the jurisdiction of a state, is New Mexico. She has now population enough for admission as a state. Let Congress admit her as a state, and then she has the acknowledged right to form, regulate, change, or modify her domestic institutions. She has now a nominal slave code, framed and urged upon her by territorial officers. Practically, slavery does not exist there. It never can be established there. In a region where the earth yields her increase only by the practice of irrigation, slave labor will not be employed. At any rate, it is better to settle all questions about slavery there, by admitting the territory as a state. While a territory, it is insisted that slavery shall be protected in it. We insist that Congress may prohibit it, and that the people have an undisputed right to exclude slaves. Why not, by terminating their territorial condition, determine this controversy? The same course might now properly be adopted with all the territories of the United States.

In each of the territories there are, now, small settlements scattered along the lines of transit. Within five years, the least populous will contain sufficient population for a Representative in Congress. Dakota, Washington, Nevada, and Jefferson are destined soon to be as familiar to us as Kansas and Nebraska. It is well worthy the consideration of the old states, whether it is not better to dispense with all territorial organizations — always expensive and turbulent — and, at once, to carve the whole into states of convenient size, for admission. This was the Jeffersonian plan, which did not contemplate territories, but states. It was also sanctioned by General Taylor, and, but for his death, would have been adopted.

This is an easy, effectual remedy, within the power of Congress, and in its nature an irrevocable act. There is no necessity of an amendment to the constitution. It is not at all probable that two-thirds of both Houses of Congress and three-fourths of the states can agree to any amendments. Why attempt it, unless to invite new contests, to again arouse sectional animosities? We know that if Mexico is acquired the south will demand it for slavery, and the north for free institutions. We must forego, for the present, new conquests, unless the love of acquisition is stronger than the love of domestic peace.

Suppose it to be conceded that the constitution should be amended, what amendment will satisfy the south? Nothing less than the protection of slavery in the territories. But our people have pronounced against it. All who voted for Mr. Lincoln or Mr. Douglas — over three million three hundred thousand citizens — voted against this claim. Less than a million voted for it. Should the great majority yield to a meagre minority, especially under threats of disunion? This minority demand that slavery be protected by the constitution. Our fathers would not allow the word 'slave' or 'slavery' in the constitution, when all the states but one were slaveholding. Shall we introduce these words when a majority of the states are free, and when the progress of civilization has arrayed the world against slavery? If the love of peace, and ease, and office, should tempt politicians and merchants to do it, the people will rebel. I assure you, whatever may be the consequence, they will not yield their moral convictions by strengthening the influence of slavery in this country. Recent events have only deepened this feeling.

The struggle to establish slavery in Kansas; the frequent murders and mobbings, in the south, of northern citizens; the present turbulence and violence of southern society; the manifest fear of the freedom of speech and of the press; the danger of insurrection; and now the attempt to subvert the government rather than submit to a constitutional election — these events, disguise it as you may, have aroused a counter irritation in the north that will not allow its representatives to yield merely for peace, more than is prescribed by the letter and spirit of the constitution. Every guarantee of this instrument ought to be faithfully and religiously observed. But when it is proposed to change it, to secure new guarantees to slavery, to extend and protect it, you invoke and arouse the anti-slavery feeling of the north to war against slavery everywhere.

I am, therefore, opposed to any change in the constitution, and to any compromise that will surrender any of the principles sanctioned by the people in the recent contest. If the personal-liberty bills of any state infringe upon the constitution, they should at once be repealed. Most of them have slumbered upon the statute book for years. They are now seized upon, by those who are plotting disunion, as a pretext. We should give them no pretext. It is always right and proper for each state to apply to state laws the test of the constitution.

It is a remarkable fact that neither of the border free states — New Jersey, Pennsylvania, Ohio, Indiana, Illinois, nor Iowa — have any such upon their statute books. The laws of these states, against kidnapping, are similar to those of Virginia and Kentucky. The laws of other states, so-called, have never operated to release a single fugitive slave, and may be regarded simply as a protest of those states against the harsh features of the fugitive slave law. So far as they infringe upon the constitution, or impair, in the least, a constitutional right, they are void and ought to be repealed.

I venture the assertion that there have been more cases of kidnapping of free negroes in Ohio, than of peaceable or unlawful rescue of fugitive slaves in the whole United States. It has been shown that the law of recapture and the penalties of rescue have been almost invariably executed. Count up all the cases of rescue of negroes in the north, and you can find in your newspapers more cases of unlawful lynching and murder of white men in the south. These cases have now become so frequent and atrocious, as to demand the attention of the general government. The same article of the constitution that secures the recapture of fugitives from service and justice, also secures the rights of citizens of Pennsylvania and Ohio to all the immunities and privileges of citizens of the several states. No law has been passed by Congress to secure this constitutional right. No executive authority interposes to protect our citizens, and yet we hear no threats of retaliation or rebellion from northern citizens or northern states. So, I trust, it may ever be.

The great danger that now overshadows us does not arise from real grievances. Plotters for disunion avail themselves of the weakness of the executive to precipitate revolution. South Carolina has taken the lead. The movement would be utterly insignificant if confined to that state. She is still in the Union, and neither the President nor Congress has the power to consent to her withdrawal. This can only be by a change in the constitution or the acquiescence of the people of the other states. The defense of the property of the United States and the collection of the revenues need not cause the shedding of blood, unless she commences a contest of physical force. The increase, in one year, of our population is greater than her entire population, white and black. Either one of several congressional districts in the west has more white inhabitants than she has. Her military power is crippled by the preponderance of her slaves. However brave, and gallant, and spirited her people may be, and no one disputes these traits, yet it is manifest she is weak in physical force. This great government might well treat with indulgence paper secession, or the resolves of her convention and legislature, without invoking physical force to enforce the laws among her citizens.

Without disrespect to South Carolina, it would be easy to show that Shay's rebellion and the whisky insurrection involved the government in greater danger than the solitary secession of South Carolina. But the movement becomes imposing when we are assured that several powerful states will very soon follow in the lead of South Carolina; and when we know that other states, still more powerful, sympathize with the seceding states, to the extent of opposing, and perhaps resisting, the execution of the laws in the seceding states.

In this view of the present condition of public affairs, it becomes the people of the United States seriously to consider whether the government shall be arrested, in the execution of its undisputed powers, by the citizens of one or more states, or whether we shall test the power of the government to defend itself against dissolution. Can a separation take place without war? If so, where will be the line? Who shall possess this magnificent capital, with all its evidences of progress and civilization? Shall the mouth of the Mississippi be separated from its sources? Who shall possess the territories? Suppose these difficulties to be overcome; suppose that in peace we should huckster and divide up our nationality, our flag, our history, all the recollections of the past; suppose all these difficulties overcome, how can two rival republics, of the same race of men, divided only by a line of a river for thousands of miles, and with all the present difficulties aggravated by separation, avoid forays, disputes, and war? How can we travel on our future march of progress in Mexico, or on the high seas, or on the Pacific slope, without collision? It is impossible. To peaceably accomplish such results we must change the nature of man. Disunion is war! God knows, I do not threaten it, for I will seek to prevent it in every way possible. I speak but the logic of facts, which we should not conceal from each other. It is either hostilities between the government and the seceding states; or, if separation is yielded peaceably, it is a war of factions — a rivalry of insignificant communities, hating each other, and contemned by the civilized world. If war results, what a war it will be! Contemplate the north and south, in hostile array against each other. If these sections do not know each other *now* they will *then.*

We are a nation of military men, naturally turbulent because we are free, accustomed to arms, ingenious, energetic, brave and strong. The same qualities that have enabled a single generation of men to develop the resources of a continent, would enable us to destroy more rapidly than we have constructed. It is idle for individuals of either section to suppose themselves superior in military power. The French and English tried that question for a thousand years. We ought to know it now. The result of the contest would not depend upon the first blow or the first year, but blood shed in civil war will yield its baleful fruit for generations.

How can we avert a calamity at which humanity and civilization shudder? I know no way but to cling to the government framed by our fathers, to administer it in a spirit of kindness, but in all cases, without partiality, to enforce the laws. No state can release us from the duty of obeying the laws. The ordinance or act of a state is no defense for treason, nor does it lessen the moral guilt of that crime. Let us cling to each other in the hope that our differences will pass away, as they often have in times past. For the sake of peace, for the love of civil liberty, for the honor of our name, our race, our religion, let us preserve the Union, loving it better as the clouds grow darker. I am willing to unite with any man, whatever may have been his party relations, whatever may be his views of the existing differences, who is willing to rely on the constitution, as it is, for his rights; and who is willing to maintain and defend the Union under all circumstances, against all enemies, at home or abroad.

Pardon me, gentlemen, for writing you so fully. I feel restrained, by the custom of the House of Representatives, from engaging there in political debate; and yet I feel it is the duty of every citizen to prepare his countrymen for grave events, that will test the strength and integrity of the government.

Believing that our only safety is in a firm enforcement of the laws, and that Mr. Lincoln will execute that duty without partiality, I join my hearty congratulations with yours that he is so soon to be the President of the United States. With great respect, I remain, very truly,

Your obedient servant,

JOHN SHERMAN.

Messrs. WM. READ, D. J. COCHRAN, L. S. FLETCHER, H. E. WALLACE, CHAS. O'NEILL, *Committee.*"

The leading events in the progressive secession may be briefly stated. The States of South Carolina, Georgia, Mississippi, Florida, Louisiana, Alabama, Arkansas, Texas, North Carolina, Tennessee, and Virginia, severally in the order named, adopted ordinances of secession. Each of them committed acts of war against the United States. They seized forts, navy yards, arsenals, customhouses, post offices and other public buildings of the United States. South Carolina, on the 27th of December, 1860, seized Fort Moultrie and Castle Pinckney, a lighthouse tender, and a schooner. On the 31st, she took possession of the United States arsenal, post office, and customhouse in Charleston, the arsenal containing seventy thousand stand of arms and other stores. On the 9th of January, 1861, she took possession of the steamer "Marion" at Charleston, and on that day the "Star of the West" was fired upon.

Georgia, on the second of January, 1861, took possession of Forts Pulaski and Jackson and the United States arsenal. On the 12th of January, she took possession of the arsenal at Augusta, containing howitzers, cannon, muskets and large stores of powder, ball and grape. On the same day she seized the United States steamer "Ida." On the 8th of February, she took possession of all the money received from customs. On the 21st, she seized three New York vessels at Savannah. Florida, on the 12th of January, 1861, took possession of the navy yards at Fort Barrancas and McRae; also the Chattahoochee arsenal, containing 800,000 cartridges of different patterns and 50,000 pounds of gunpowder.

Alabama took possession of Fort Morgan, the Mount Vernon arsenal, some pieces of cannon, and large amounts of munitions of war. She took possession also of the revenue cutter "Lewis Cass."

Mississippi, on the 20th of January, seized the fort at Ship Island and the United States hospital on the Mississippi River.

On the 11th of January, Louisiana took possession of Forts Jackson, St. Phillips and Pike, and the arsenal at Baton Rouge containing fifty thousand small arms, twenty heavy pieces of ordnance, three hundred barrels of powder and other military supplies. On the 28th, she took possession of all commissary and quartermaster stores in the possession of United States officials within her borders. On the first of February, she seized the mint and customhouse containing $599,303 in gold and silver.

Texas, on the 20th of February, took Forts Chadbourne and Belknap with all the property of the Overland Mail Company. On the 25th, General Twiggs, an officer of the army of the United States, traitorously surrendered all government stores in his command, estimated at $1,300,000 in value, including money and specie, thirty-five thousand stand of arms, twenty-six pieces of mountain artillery, and other military stores.

On the 2nd of March, she seized the revenue cutter "Dodge" and Fort Brown.

Arkansas seized the arsenal at Little Rock, containing nine thousand small arms, forty cannon, and a quantity of ammunition.

Virginia, according to the statement of Governor Letcher, would have seized Fortress Monroe, but that it was firmly held by national troops.

These were some of the acts of war committed by the seceding states before the inauguration of Abraham Lincoln.

What was done by the administration of James Buchanan to meet these acts of war? The answer to this question is a most painful confession of feebleness, vacillation and dishonor. It was shown conclusively that Floyd, the Secretary of War, during 1860 transferred from Springfield and other armories to southern arsenals 65,000 percussion muskets, 40,000 altered muskets and 10,000 rifles. On the 20th of October, he ordered 40 columbiads and four 32 pounders to be sent from the arsenal to the Fort, at Galveston in Texas, the building of which had hardly been commenced. It was shown by a report of a committee of the House that the vessels of the United States were dispersed by the Secretary of the Navy to distant ports, for the purpose of preventing their use in the defense of the property of the United States.

The Mobile "Advertiser" said:

"During the past year, 135,430 muskets have been quietly transferred from the northern arsenal at Springfield alone, to those in the southern states. We are much obliged to Secretary Floyd for the foresight he has thus displayed in disarming the north and *equipping the south for this emergency.*"

Jefferson Davis, on January 9, 1860, in introducing into the Senate a bill to authorize the sale of public arms to the several states and territories, significantly said: "There are a number of volunteer companies wanting to purchase arms, but the states have not a sufficient supply."

This bill was agreed to by the Senate by a party vote, yeas 28, nays 18. In the House the bill was never reported.

Mr. Buchanan, in his annual message at the beginning of the 2nd session of the 36th Congress, announced the startling doctrine that a state could not be coerced by the general government, and said:

"After much serious reflection, I have arrived at the conclusion that no such power has been delegated to Congress nor to any other department of the federal government. It is manifest, upon an inspection of the constitution, that this is not among the specific and enumerated powers granted to Congress; and it is equally apparent that its exercise is not 'necessary and proper for carrying into execution' any one of these powers."

Again he says:

"Without descending to particulars, it may be safely asserted that the power to make war against a state is at variance with the whole spirit and intent of the constitution. . . .

"The fact is, that our Union rests upon public opinion, and can never be cemented by the blood of its citizens shed in civil war. If it cannot live in the affections of the people it must one day perish. Congress possesses many means of preserving it by conciliation; but the sword was not placed in their hand to preserve it by force."

This doctrine, if acquiesced in, would leave the United States utterly powerless to preserve its own life, whatever might be the exigencies, even against the most insignificant state in the Union. It was manifest that while Buchanan remained President, and Commander-in-Chief of the army and navy, it was utterly futile to resist the secession of the least of these states, or even to protect the public property in them.

On the 4th of December, 1860, the House of Representatives organized what is known as the "committee of thirty-three," of which Mr. Corwin, of Ohio, was chairman. So much of the

President's message as related to the perilous condition of the country was referred to it. Propositions of all kinds were sent to the committee, but the final result was, as anticipated, a disagreement upon all the measures proposed.

On the 16th of January, 1861, Mr. Crittenden offered his celebrated resolutions, proposing certain amendments to the constitution of the United States, in relation to slavery, but they were rejected in the Senate and were not acted upon in the House.

A peace conference was held at Washington, at the request of the legislature of Virginia, composed of delegates from the several states appointed by the governors thereof. John Tyler was president and Thomas Ewing, of Ohio, was one of the most active and influential members of the conference. It sat during nearly all the month of February and recommended seven articles of amendment to the constitution. These propositions were adopted by the conference and reported to the Senate on the 2nd of March, and were rejected by a vote of 3 yeas and 34 nays. Subsequently they were again offered by Mr. Crittenden and rejected by a vote of 7 yeas and 28 nays. They were presented to the House on the 1st of March, 1861, and were there rejected.

A Senate committee of 13 was organized on the 18th of December, 1860, to consider the condition of the country, but its report was disagreed to by the Senate. Many other propositions of adjustment were made both in the Senate and House, but none of them were agreed to. Not only were no measures adopted to prevent secession, but it was proposed by Mr. Mason, that, to avoid the possibility of a conflict between the forces of the army and navy and of the seceding states, all the laws providing for the use of the army in aid of the civil authorities in executing the laws of the United States, should be suspended and made inoperative in those states. These were the laws passed during the term of President Jackson and, at his earnest request, to enable the government to enforce the laws of the United States against the opposition of the State of South Carolina. It was a striking presentation of the difference between General Jackson and James Buchanan.

Mr. Hunter, of Virginia, proposed to retrocede to the seceding states, the property of the United States. The last act of Jefferson Davis was to offer a joint resolution providing:

"That upon the application of a state, either through a convention or legislature thereof, asking that the federal forces of the army and navy may be withdrawn from its limits, the President of the United States shall order the withdrawal of the federal garrisons, and take the needful security for the safety of the public property which may remain in said state.

"That whenever a state convention, duly and lawfully assembled, shall enact that the safety of the state requires it to keep troops and ships of war, the President of the United States be, and he is hereby authorized and directed to recognize the exercise of that power by the state, and by proclamation to give notice of the fact for the information and government of all parties concerned."

On the 11th of February, 1861, Burton Craige, of North Carolina, offered a joint resolution:

"That the President of the United States be, and is hereby required to acknowledge the independence of said government (The Confederacy of the United States South) as soon as he is informed officially of its establishment; and that he receive such envoy, ambassador, or commissioner as may or shall be appointed by said government for the purpose of amicably adjusting the matters in dispute with said government."

Such was the hopeless condition of the United States in the last months of the administration of James Buchanan. It would appear from the resolute action of the seceding states, their union as Confederate States, the hopeless imbecility of the President of the United States, the presence of the seceded traitors in both houses of Congress, the weakness and feebleness of that body, left but little hope for the preservation of the Union. The future presaged a civil war, and opened up a dark prospect, a discouraging example for future republics, but the 4th of March came, and a new life was infused into the national councils.

The second session of the 36th Congress commenced on the 3rd day of December. The message of the President I have already commented upon. It was regarded as a feeble wail of despair, an absolute abnegation of the powers of the general government. No expectation or hope was indulged in that the President would do any act or say any word to arrest or delay the flagrant treason, then being committed in South Carolina. "After me the deluge" was written on every page of his message. Our only hope was in the good time coming, when, at the close of his term, he would retire to private life.

Having charge of the appropriation bills as chairman of the committee of ways and means, of the 36th Congress, I was only solicitous to secure the passage of these bills, so that the new administration would have money to meet the current wants of the government. Within a few days, all these bills were reported, and were pushed forward and passed at an early period of the session.

I purposely postpone consideration of the financial condition of the United States during this session so as to consider it in connection with the measures adopted at the called session in July, 1861.

The House of Representatives was almost constantly occupied in considering and rejecting the many schemes "to save the country," already referred to. The only political speech I made was in reply to an ingenious speech of my colleague, George H. Pendleton, made on the 18th day of January, 1861. I replied on the same day without preparation, but with a lively appreciation of the dangers before us. As I believe that it states fully and fairly the then condition of the impending revolution, I insert extracts from it here:

" I have listened with respect and attention to all that has fallen from my colleague. Much that he has said I approve ; but it seems to me that instead of appealing to this side of the House for conciliation, kindness and forbearance, he should appeal to those around him, who alone, provoke the excitement now prevailing in this country.

" He says the army should not be used to coerce a state. If by this he means that the army should not be used to conquer a state, to compel her to be represented, to maintain the courts or post offices within her limits, to burn her cities or desolate her fields, he is entirely correct. I do not believe that any administration will pursue such a policy. But, sir, we have a government, a great government, to maintain. It is supreme within the powers delegated to it ; and it is provided with ample authority to protect itself against foreign or domestic enemies. It has the exclusive right to collect duties on imports. It is the exclusive owner of forts, arsenals, navy yards, vessels, and munitions of war. It has a flag, the symbol of its nationality, the emblem of its power and determination, to protect all those who may of right gather under its folds. It is our duty, as the representatives of this government, to maintain and defend it in the exercise of its just powers. Has it trespassed upon the rights of a single individual ? Does any citizen of South Carolina allege that this government has done him wrong ? No man can say that. The government for years has been in the hands of the Democratic party, whose power and patronage have been controlled chiefly by southern citizens ; and now, when the Republican party is about to assume the reins, these citizens seek to subvert it. They organize revolution under the name of secession.

"What have they done ? The State of South Carolina has seized the customhouse in the city of Charleston, has closed that port, and prevented the United States from the exercise of their conceded exclusive power of collecting the revenue from imports. It has taken, by force, money from the treasury of the United States, and applied it to its own use. It has seized the arms and munitions of war of the United States deposited in arsenals within the conceded exclusive jurisdiction of the United States, and turned them against the army of the United States. It has seized a loyal citizen of the United States engaged in the discharge of his duty, imprisoned him, and threatened his life, for the exercise of a plain constitutional duty, charging him with treason against the State of South Carolina. It has taken citizens of different states rightfully and peacefully attending to their business, insulted them, inflicted the most degrading indignities upon them, and then forcibly expelled them. It has raised a military force of artillery, cavalry, and infantry, with the avowed purpose of expelling, or, to use their own chosen word, coercing, the United States from the forts, arsenals, and other property of the United States. When Major Anderson removed from Fort Moultrie to Fort Sumter, it seized Fort Moultrie, Fort Pinckney, and other property of the United States.

"More recently they fired upon a vessel in the employ of the United States, conveying reinforcements and provisions to our troops. In this act of war, they used the cannon and munitions of war paid for out of our treasury. Forts ceded by the State of South Carolina to the United States were used to expel a vessel of the United States in the pursuit of its lawful commerce. When the 'star-spangled banner' was hoisted to her masthead, as a sign of nationality, appealing to all the patriotic recollections which cluster around it—your flag, my flag, the flag of Virginia, of Ohio, of Kentucky, of Massachusetts, the flag of every state and of the whole Union, the rustle of whose folds has so often excited the pride and patriotic ardor of Americans in every part of the habitable globe—that flag, invoked for the protection of an unarmed vessel, carrying provisions to our own troops, was fired upon and dishonored. An act of war by citizens of the United States, and therefore an act of treason, was applauded by officers and citizens of that state, and perhaps by those of other states. It was not an act of war against you and me merely, but against every loyal and patriotic citizen of this great republic. Up to that moment we had done nothing.

This government had been more forbearing, more quiet, more complacent, under this series of offenses, than any government instituted since the foundation of governments.

" And now, Mr. chairman, the same lawless violence is breaking out in other parts of the country. Forts, arsenals, navy yards, and vessels of war, intrusted without defense to the patriotism of the people, have, upon one pretext or another, been seized, and are now held by lawless force. Upon the recommendation of Members of Congress, Fort Pulaski was seized by troops, under an order from the Governor of Georgia. I suppose there is not a Member upon the other side who will declare that it would be given up peacefully to the troops of the United States if it were demanded by our national authorities. More recently still, the navy yard at Pensacola was taken by an armed force, under the order of the Governor of Florida. I have here a telegraphic dispatch sent to this government :

January 12, 1861.—Commissioners appointed by the Governor of Florida, with a regiment of armed men at the gate, demanded the surrender of this navy yard, having previously taken possession of one of the magazines. I surrendered the place and struck my flag at half-past one o'clock, p. m., this day.

" Mr. chairman, suppose Great Britain, suppose France, suppose all the powers of the world combined, had thus outraged the flag of the United States ; would not every one of us have demanded men and money to wipe out the indignity, and to repel further like assaults, at whatever hazard ? Yet, sir, the Governor of Florida, before the State of Florida had seceded, goes with an armed force, seizes upon our property, and turns the guns of the people of the United States against the army and the navy of the United States. I am also told—with what truth I do not know—that cannon are planted upon the banks of the Mississippi River, at or near the city of Vicksburg, in the State of Mississippi, and that our steamboats are now compelled to land there and to give an account of themselves. We do not know at what moment they may be subject to tribute and seizure. To whom ? To the State of Mississippi ? I agree with all my colleagues from the State of Ohio, from both sides of this House, that there is one thing immutable—a law that is a higher law. It is, that the Mississippi River, gathering all the rivulets of the northwest into one current, must be permitted to float our commerce, uninterrupted and untrammeled, to the sea, or thousands of men will float down upon its waters and make it free.

" No one doubts, I suppose, that the forts at the mouth of the Mississippi are in the possession, not of the troops of the United States, but troops that will resist the troops of the United States. There is no doubt that Baton Rouge has been seized ; no doubt, sir, that act after act of war has been repeated.

" I ask you, as the representative of a brave people, what shall we do ? The question is not, shall we coerce a state ? but shall we not defend the property of the United States against all enemies, at home and abroad, here or wherever the flag of our country floats ? Must this government submit to insult and indignity ? Must it surrender its property, its flag, its nationality ? Do you, gentlemen from Virginia, whose great statesman had so large a share in laying the foundations of our government, desire to see it thus dishonored ? Are you ready to join excited men, who will not listen to reason ; who even spurn your patriotism as timidity ; who reject your counsels, and who would drag you as unwilling victims at the heel of their car of juggernaut, crushing under its weight all hope of civil liberty for ages to come ? Are you aroused into madness by political defeat ? . . .

"Sir, it was but the other day that I was told by a distinguished citizen of an absolute monarchy — and the remark made a deep impression on my mind — that he deplored the events now transacting around us ; that he deplored what he considered the inevitable fall of this republic, but, said he, one good will result from it ; it will stop forever the struggle for free institutions in Europe ; it will establish upon a secure basis the existing governments of the Old World. I felt that the remark was true. If this government cannot survive a constitutional election ; if it cannot defend its property and protect our flag ; if this government crumbles before the first sign of disaffection, what hope is there for free institutions in countries where kings and nobles and marshals and hereditary institutions and laws of primogeniture have existed for ages ? Sir, when the masses of any people, inspired by the love of country, have demanded in modern times the right of self-government, they have been pointed to France with its revolution of 1798, to South America, where changing republics rise and disappear so rapidly that not ten men in this House can tell me their names, and also to Mexico. God forbid that the despots of the Old World should ever adorn their infernal logic by pointing to a disrupted Union here ! It is said, with a poet's license, that —

'Freedom shrieked as Kosciusko fell.'

"But, sir, freedom will die with the fall of this republic, and the survivors of the calamity will find springing into existence military despotism north, south, east and west. Instead of two divisions, there will be many divisions. The condition of this country will be worse than that of Mexico, because we are a braver, a more powerful, people, who will fight each other with greater tenacity. If this republic is dissolved, the man now lives who will be the Napoleon of some section thereof. All history teaches us that whenever a free government is disrupted a military despotism of force is substituted for the will of the people ; and we have no right to suppose that our country will be an exception to the general rule.

"I appeal to the Representatives of the border states to arrest the progress of this storm for a little time, at least. Let us see whether there is any hope for peace and conciliation. If there is not, then, if we cannot agree, let us fight ; but if we can agree, let us do it like men, and not be hurried off by wild and insane feelings of rage and disappointment, by the weakest state in this confederacy. Sirs, if you do calm this storm, peace will again smile upon our country. If you do not, I see nothing but civil war before us. My colleague may paint in beautiful language the blessings of peace; and cry 'peace! peace!' when there is no peace; but, Mr. chairman, you and I see already rising in the west, where military feeling is so rife, a spirit which will not brook much longer the insults already cast upon the flag of our country. I do not threaten, for I dread — not for you or me, or the Members of this House, for I suppose we have the ordinary courage of our race, and we are but atoms in the storm — but thousands and millions of men, like us, will regret the day when this government was hurried into revolution, without opportunity for parley or delay.

"If your people will not aid the government in maintaining the public property in the seceding states, then we must do it in spite of you, or perish in the attempt. We must not allow the government to crumble at our feet. You can arrest this movement, and you alone can do it. I ask you, gentlemen from Virginia and the south, does not your blood boil with indignation when you read of the surrender of our forts and the dishonor of our flag? Are they not yours as well as mine? Has the feeling of sectionalism become stronger than the love of country? I ask if the same patriotism which brought your fathers and mine into common battlefields, amid all the storms of the Revolution, does not now rebel when you are forced into a civil war by the madness of a few men in the southern states? Sir, I do not believe it. For the moment, under the smart of imaginary wrongs, under the disappointment of political defeat, your people may be hurried into acts of madness; but when returning reason comes, woe be to those who have led them astray! Then a single wave of the star-spangled banner will silence the miserable party cries with which you have misled them.

"Let us not deceive ourselves with the idea that this government can be broken up on Mason and Dixon's line, or upon any other line, without involving us in all we dread. There is no man, with a head to reason and a heart to feel, who does not shudder at the idea of civil war. Do you suppose that this government can be divided in two, according to the plan of the gentleman from Virginia (Mr. Garnett), with this capitol, with the mouth of the Mississippi, with the territories, and a thousand things that unite us, without provoking civil war? Why, sir, we may do all we can to prevent it; we may throw ourselves into the breach; we may stand up and yield everything, or cringe down and yield everything; but I tell you that will not stop the surging waves. If this government is divided, though we may agree to separate in peace — though every man here may sign the bond — we know that events hurriedly running forward will bring these two sections in hostile array against each other; and then, what a war is there, my countrymen! I know that your southern people are brave, spirited, active, quick; no man doubts that; but if you have made any misapprehension about the northern people — if you suppose that, because they are cold, because they are not fired by your hot blood, they will not perform their duty everywhere, you are very much mistaken. We are the equals of each other; we are of the same blood, the same parentage, the same character; your warm sun has quickened your blood, but our cold climate has steadied our intellects and braced our energies.

"I again repeat, Mr. chairman, that we should not allow ourselves to be deceived by words. The question is not whether the United States will coerce a state, but whether a state shall coerce the government; whether this noble fabric, devised by our fathers, shall fall without a blow. I appeal to you again; I appeal to the Representatives of all the states, whether we shall allow Fort Sumter, the only place where our flag floats in the harbor of Charleston, to be surrendered at discretion.

"For one, I say, NEVER! NEVER! Even if to-morrow I should vote to give South Carolina license to leave the confederacy, if I had the power, yet, while that flag floats, it is the bounden and sacred duty of this government to protect it against all enemies, and at all hazards. I had fondly hoped, while we disagreed, and while I knew that our disagreement was marked and decided, that you, gentlemen of the south, would yourselves take the lead in the defense of our property and our honor; therefore I sat silent. I had hoped that, while we were discussing, you would insist upon the protection of the property of the United States, and that our flag should not be dishonored until we separated, in peace or in war.

"I was much struck by a remark made the other day by the honorable Senator from Mississippi (Mr. Davis), that if we could not agree with each other, we ought to separate in peace — that we should take this old flag, and fold it away, and keep it as a much-loved memento for us all. But, sir, we cannot do that now. It has been lowered and tarnished, and we all know and feel it.

"I was surprised that my colleague (Mr. Pendleton) did not vote for the resolution offered by the gentleman from New Jersey, in regard to Major Anderson. I hoped that the Ohio delegation would unite in favor of that resolution. I was still more surprised, allow me to say to the Representatives of Kentucky, that when their own gallant son had but performed his bounden duty they should have refused to vote to sustain him in his removal from Fort Moultrie to the strongest point in his command.

"The resolution simply expressed a desire to enforce the laws and to preserve the Union—no more. I am willing to stand on this platform. I can join heartily with all those who made that pledge, whatever else they may think or believe about the questions that divide our people. If we can stand by each other, if our constituents will stand by us in that emphatic declaration, I do believe the good ship that has borne us thus far on a prosperous voyage will outlive the storm. But, sir, if we yield too far to the fury of the waves; if we now surrender, without resistance, the forts, arsenals, dock-yards, and other property of the government, we only demonstrate that we are not fit for the duties assigned us; and, if our names survive our times, they will only be recorded as those of a degenerate race, who had not the manhood to preserve what their fathers won.

"Gentlemen cannot come here and say, 'We demand this; or, we demand that; stand and deliver.' That is the language of the highwayman. This is a great tribunal, where men reason and judge and weigh and doubt and hesitate and talk—and we have a good deal of that. No section and no state can, because the presidential election has gone against it, say, 'We will have this change in the constitution, or we will fire upon your flag; we will have that change in the constitution, or we will seize upon your forts.' That is not the principle upon which this government was founded. Mr. Jefferson, when elected President in 1801, declared the true principle. He said it was the duty of all good citizens to obey the constitution; to submit to a constitutional election; and he congratulated the country that the Federalists were willing to give the Democrats a fair trial. . . .

"Under the grave responsibility upon which we are acting, I feel it to be my duty to you, to my fellow-Members, and to my countrymen, north and south, to say frankly, that, in voting for this army bill, I vote with the expectation that the army will be used in protecting the acknowledged property of the United States, in recovering that which has been unlawfully taken, and in maintaining the Union.

"It may be said that the gravity of the events that surround us demands a greater force than is provided by this bill. The regular army is a mere skeleton. The present force will scarcely defend our frontier from Indian incursions; but it forms a nucleus capable of any re-enforcement demanded by the exigencies of the times. I do not contemplate, in any event, hostile invasions of the soil of any state, unless demanded for the defense of the acknowledged property of the United States. It is the duty of the government to suppress insurrection in a state; but in this event the military power can only be used in strict subordination to the civil authority. If the civil authority refuse to call for such aid, or suppress the courts, the military power cannot interfere. If the courts are closed, the duties of postmasters cannot be enforced, or the mails protected, and therefore the postal service must necessarily be suspended. No doubt this measure will soon be adopted. If the revenue is refused, or cannot be collected, then goods cannot be imported, and ports must be closed. If a state shall, in violation of the constitution, undertake to regulate commerce, then her commerce must be suspended.

"No doubt other measures can be devised that will preserve the peace of the country until the people of the states may confer in a constitutional way, unless one or more of the seceding states shall, by military force, shed the blood of their fellow-citizens, or refuse to surrender to the proper authorities the acknowledged property of the government. I know that all the gentlemen around me must deeply deplore a civil war, especially if that war shall involve the fate of this capital and the disruption of the government. No man can contemplate the inevitable results of such a war without the most serious desire to avert it. It is our duty as Members of this House, it is the duty of Congress, I am happy to say it is now the acknowledged duty of the President, as it is of the incoming administration, to use forbearance to the extremest point. Let not physical force be arrayed in civil war until the last hope of peace and conciliation has been exhausted; then let each branch of the government, acting in concert with each other, perform its respective duties, though the heavens fall!

"What can we do for peace and conciliation? I anticipate at once your reply; you say, 'Let us compromise; yield what we demand of you.' Let us compromise, and we will preserve the Union; civil war will be averted. This, I know, is the earnest appeal of patriotic men in the southern states, who would gladly give their lives to stop the march of treason in those states. How useless it is to talk about compromises, concessions, conciliation, adjustment, when, if everything was conceded, the integrity of the government may be broken up by a majority of a single state. If we hold this Union, and all the rights it secures to us, and all the hopes we base upon it, upon the whim or will of a single state, then, indeed, it is the weakest government ever devised by man. If a single state may destroy our nationality, then, indeed, is the wisdom of our fathers the wisdom of babes. We can no longer talk about the weakness of the old confederacy or anarchy of Mexico.

"Sir, we owe it as the most sacred of duties to put down this heresy. If it now fortifies itself by sectional animosities, if it rises from party rebellion to sectional and civil war, still it must, and will, be met with determined resistance. Upon this point, I am glad to say, the people of Ohio are united, if the unanimous voice of the legislature of that state is a true indication.

"Again, I say, what is the use of concession, conciliation, or compromise, when, if we yield everything you demand, you cannot say to us 'It will save us from disunion or war?' Are we not in danger of quarreling about terms of conciliation, when traitors are overthrowing the government we wish to preserve? Are we not dividing ourselves for their benefit? What will satisfy South Carolina and Florida and Mississippi and Alabama? They want disunion, and not compromise or conciliation. The Democratic party would not agree to their terms, and they seceded from the Charleston and Baltimore conventions. Is it likely that we will yield what our northern Democratic friends could not yield? Can you expect this 'black Republican party,' as you please to call it, will yield to you what your northern Democratic associates dare not? It is utterly idle to talk about any such terms of concession. I do not believe any terms which our people could yield, and preserve their own self-respect, would satisfy South Carolina, Florida, or some of the other southern states, because they are bent upon disunion.

"We know that gentlemen who represented South Carolina on this floor, if the newspapers correctly report them, declared in the Charleston convention, held recently, that they had brooded over this matter from long years, and that they only sought an opportunity, an occasion, or, if I may use the word, a pretext, for the secession of the State of South Carolina and the disruption of the Union. Some stated that they had brooded over disunion and prayed for its consummation since boyhood. We know, sir, that the seeds of this revolution were sowed in the time of Andrew Jackson and John C. Calhoun. We know that in 1832 the doctrines upon which this revolution is going forward were initiated, and from that time the young men of South Carolina have been educated in the school of disunion. They have cherished those doctrines in their innermost hearts. All the concessions we might make, all the compromises we could agree to, all the offerings of peace we could make for the salvation of this Union, would not be able to secure that desired end, if South Carolina could prevent it.

"Again, we might, on this side, properly say we have done nothing to impair any constitutional right. We propose to do nothing to infringe yours. We have succeeded in a constitutional way in electing a President of the United States. All we ask is that he may be inaugurated in peace, and may develop his policy in the usual manner. We can add that this is the demand of all our people, not only of those who voted for Mr. Lincoln, but of every loyal citizen. You tell us your people are excited and alarmed, that they apprehend that an overwhelming anti-slavery element is about to be inaugurated in power that will, directly or indirectly, affect the constitutional rights of your states.

"Perhaps you will confess, what you know to be true, that for political purposes, in the struggle of partisans for ascendancy, both parties in the south have united to fire the southern mind against the hated ' black Republicans ' of the north. Speeches have been distorted, single sentences have been torn from their context and made to deceive and mislead. Garrison, Wendell Phillips, Seward, Lincoln, and latterly Douglas, have been mixed in a hated conglomerate, and used to excite your people. A philosophic opinion of Mr. Seward has been construed as the statement of a settled purpose to overthrow slavery in the states, although in the very paragraph itself all idea of interference by the people of the free states with slavery in the slave states is expressly excluded. It is but a year since you inflamed your constituents because some of your fellow-Members recommended, without reading, a book written by one of your own citizens, containing obnoxious opinions about slavery. Nearly all of you gave birth, vitality, and victory to the Republican party, by adopting a policy you now join in condemning. Some of you broke down the only political organization that could compete with us, and thus gave us an easy victory. You have all contributed, more or less, in perverting the public mind as to our principles and purposes. And I tell you, gentlemen, that when you call the Republican party an abolition party, in the sense you use the word abolition ; when you quote from Garrison, Wendell Phillips, and from like extreme men, and circulate their opinions all over the south, telling the people of your states that the people of the north have been educated in these sentiments, profess them, and are going to put down slavery in the states, you do a great injustice to the intelligence and the safety of your people.

"I have heard here, over and over again, this course of agitation, pursued only the other day in the Senate of the United States. Mr. Douglas quoted from one of the speeches of Mr. Lincoln that passage so familiar to us all, that, in his opinion, the states would at some day be all slave or all free. Sir, in this time when the people of the southern states are in a storm of excitement, that speech of the Senator from Illinois is sent over those states as tending to show that Mr. Lincoln would in some way interfere with slavery in the states. Mr. Lincoln answered this inference with a solemn disclaimer over and over again on the same ' stump ' with that Senator. I ask whether it was just to quote the opinion without giving the disclaimer? It certainly was not. We might answer all you say by declaring that the Republican party does not propose to interfere with your constitutional rights. I have no doubt that the administration of Mr. Lincoln will carry out the doctrines of the Chicago platform ; but not the platform as you pervert it. Sir, it will convince the southern people that all the things said about us are unfounded. What, then, will be the fate of hundreds of politicians in the southern states who have stirred their people up to the present intense excitement ?

"Yet the baptism of misrepresentation, through which this Republican party has thus far advanced, does not excuse us from doing all in our power to produce conciliation, harmony, peace, quiet, a fair and honest adjustment of all the difficulties that surround us. . . .

"Now, Mr. chairman, I have gone over the whole field. I have given my views, speaking for no other man, frankly and fearlessly, and I will stand by them now and in the future. I have given you my opinion upon all these points. I tell you that this whole controversy was fought and won by us two years ago, and all you have to do now is to admit Kansas. That is the only act of power now needed. There let it stand. Let us live together like a band of brothers. If we cannot agree with you about slavery, why, you do not agree with us. I know there has been a great deal of intemperance of language on this subject ; but I ask, if it has been used upon our side, has it not been used upon yours ? If there has been harsh and violent words used, I have not uttered them that I know of. If I have, I beg every man's pardon ; because I think that violent language, calculated to stir up excitement and agitation, ought not to be used in a deliberative assembly. I ask you if you have not sins to repent of, if we have ? Let us be at peace. Let us go on with the administration of the government kindly, harmoniously, hopefully, trusting in that providence of Almighty God which has thus far guided and guarded us, until this nation has become a marvel to the world. Can we not go on in the same way in which we have gone on in the past ? Why not let the Republican administration be inaugurated in peace and quiet ? Try it in the name of God! Are you cowards, that you would flee from an apprehension ? I know you are not. Stand by the old ship of state ! Give the Republican administration a fair chance. If it does not do right, you will find thousands — ay, millions — in the northern states who will stand by you. I believe it will do right. Give it a trial. That is all we ask, and what we will demand at all hazards."

The delegation from Ohio, during this Congress, was regarded as a very strong one. I do not disparage any by a brief reference to a few.

Thomas Corwin was, by far, the most distinguished member of the delegation. I have already referred to his eminence as a popular orator. His speech against the Mexican War, though unfortunate as a political event, has always been regarded as one of the most eloquent ever made in either House of Congress. His speech in reply to Crary, of Michigan, is still remembered as the best specimen of humorous satire in our language. He had served in the legislature of Ohio, as a Member of Congress for ten years, as Governor of Ohio, as a Member of the Senate, and as Secretary of the Treasury. After an absence from public life for six years, he was elected a Member of the 36th Congress. Here he was regarded as the "peacemaker" of the House. In the contest for speaker, he made a long speech, in which he exhibited marked ability, humor, pathos and persuasive eloquence. As chairman of the committee of thirty, he did all that man could do to quiet the storm, to compromise and soothe the contending factions, but this was beyond human power. He was re-elected to the 37th Congress, but in 1861 was appointed minister to Mexico by Mr. Lincoln. In December, 1865, he attended a party of his Ohio friends, at which I was present. He was the center of attraction, and, apparently, in good health and spirits. He was telling amusing anecdotes of life in Ohio "in the olden times," to the many friends who gathered around him, when, without warning, he suffered a stroke of apoplexy and died within two or three days, leaving behind him none but friends. Tom Corwin, "the wagon-boy," had traveled through all the gradations of life, and in every stage was a kind friend, a loving father, a generous, noble and honest man.

The life of George H. Pendleton was a striking contrast to that of Corwin. He was a favorite of fortune. His father was a distinguished lawyer and Member of Congress. George had the advantage of a good education and high social position, a courtly manner, a handsome person and a good fortune. He served several terms in the House of Representatives and six years in the Senate. He was the candidate for Vice President on the Democratic ticket with McClellan, and a prominent candidate for nomination as President in 1868. He was minister to Germany during the first term of Cleveland as President. He died November 24, 1889. My relations with him were always pleasant.

Samuel S. Cox was an active, industrious and versatile Member of Congress for more than twenty years. He was born in Ohio, graduated at Brown University, was admitted to the bar, but, I believe, rarely practiced his profession. His natural bent was for editorial and political conflicts, in which most of his life was spent. He was a good debater, overflowing with humor without sarcasm. In the campaign of 1860, he and I had a running debate at long range. In a speech at Columbus, then his residence, I spoke of his erratic course on the Lecompton bill. He replied at Mansfield with shrewdness, humor and ability. I reviewed his speech at the same place, and we kept up a running fire during that canvass, but this did not disturb our friendly relations. Some years later, he removed to New York, where he was soon taken into favor, and was elected several times to Congress. He was the author of several books of merit, and was the champion of a measure establishing the life-saving service of the country upon its present footing. He may be classified as a leading Member of the House of Representatives, a bright and successful speaker and a copious author. He died September 10, 1889.

John A. Bingham was regarded, next to Mr. Corwin, as the most eloquent member of the Ohio delegation, and, perhaps with one or two exceptions, of the House of Representatives. He studied law and was admitted to the bar in 1840. He served for sixteen years in the House of Representatives on the judiciary and other important committees, and took an active and leading part in all the debates during this long period. He was a man of genial, pleasing address, rather too much given to flights of oratory, but always a favorite with his colleagues and associates. He was subsequently appointed United States minister to Japan, where he remained for many years. He still lives at a ripe old age at Cadiz, Ohio.

During the existence of the 36th Congress, I do not recall any political divisions in the committee of ways and means, unless the tariff is considered a political measure. It was not so treated by the committee. The common purpose was to secure sufficient revenue for the support of the government. The incidental effect of all duties was to encourage home manufactures, but, as the rule adopted was applied impartially to all productions, whether of the farm, mine, or the workshop, there was no controversy except as to the amount or rate of the duty. The recent dogma that raw materials should not have the benefit of protection did not enter the mind of anyone. The necessity of economy limited the amount of appropriations, but if the war had not changed all conditions, the revenues accruing would have been sufficient for an economical administration of the government.

In a retrospect of my six years as a Member of the House of Representatives, I can see, and will freely admit, that my chief fault was my intense partisanship. This grew out of a conscientious feeling that the repeal of the Missouri Compromise was an act of dishonor, committed by a dominating party controlled by slaveholders and yielded to by leading northern Democrats, headed by Douglas, with a view on his part to promote his intense ambition to be President of the United States. I felt that this insult to the north should be resented by the renewed exclusion, by act of Congress, of slavery north of the line of latitude 36 degrees 30 minutes. This feeling was intensified by my experience in Kansas during the investigation of its affairs. The recital by the Free State men of their story, and the appearance and conduct of the "border ruffians," led me to support extreme measures. The political feebleness of Mr. Buchanan, and the infamy of the Dred Scott decision, appeared to me conclusive evidence of the subserviency of the President

and the Supreme Court to the slave power. The gross injustice
to me personally, and the irritating language of southern Members in the speakership contest, aroused my resentment, so
that in the campaign of 1860 I was ready to meet the threats
of secession with those of open war.

It was unfortunate that the south at this time was largely
represented in Congress by men of the most violent opinions.
Such men as Keitt, Hindman, Barksdale, and Rust, were offensive in their conduct and language. They were of that class
in the south who believed that the people of the north were
tradesmen, hucksters, and the like, and therefore were cowards;
that one southern man was equal in a fight to four northern
men; that slavery was a patent of nobility, and that the owner
of slaves was a lord and master. It is true that among the
southern Members there were gentlemen of a character quite
different. Such men as Letcher, Aiken and Bocock entertained
no such opinions, but were courteous and friendly. But even
these shared in the opinions of their people that, as slavery
was recognized by the constitution, as an institution existing
in many of the states, it should not be excluded from the common territory of the Union, except by the vote of the people of
a territory when assuming the dignity and power of a state. It
would appear that as in 1860 the exclusion of slavery from
Kansas was definitely settled by the people of that state, and
that as the only region open to this controversy was New
Mexico, from which slavery was excluded by natural conditions, there was no reason or ground for an attempt to disrupt
the Union. In fact, this pretense for secession was abandoned
by South Carolina, and the only ground taken for attempting it
was the election of Mr. Lincoln as President of the United
States. If this was conceded to be a just cause for secession,
our government would become a rope of sand; it would be
worse than that of any South American republic, because our
country is more populous, and sections of it would have greater
strength of attack and defense. This pretense for secession
would not have been concurred in by any of the states north
of South Carolina, but for the previous agitation of slavery,
which had welded nearly all the slaveholding states into a

compact confederacy. This was done, not for fear of Lincoln, but to protect the institution of slavery, threatened by the growing sentiment of mankind. Upon this question I had been conservative, but I can see now that this contest was irrepressible, and that I would soon have been in favor of the gradual abolition of slavery in all the states. This could not have been effected under our constitution but for the Rebellion, so that, in truth, South Carolina, unwittingly, led to the only way by which slavery could be abolished in the present century.

The existence of slavery in a republic founded upon the declaration that all men are created equal, that they are endowed by their Creator with certain inalienable rights, and that among them are life, liberty and the pursuit of happiness, is an anomaly so pregnant with evil that it is not strange that while it existed it was the chief cause of all the serious contentions that threatened the life of the republic. The framers of the constitution, finding slavery in existence in nearly all the states, carefully avoided mention of it in that instrument, but they provided against the importation of slaves after a brief period, and evidently anticipated the eventual prohibition of slavery by the voluntary action of the several states. This process of prohibition occurred until one-half of the states became free, when causes unforeseen made slavery so profitable that it dominated in the states where it existed, and dictated the policy of the United States. The first controversy about slavery was happily settled by the Missouri Compromise of 1820. But a greater danger arose from the acquisition of territory from Mexico. This, too, was postponed by the compromise of 1850, but unhappily, within four years, the repeal of the Missouri Compromise re-opened the controversy that led to the struggle in Kansas. Douglas prescribed the doctrine of popular sovereignty. Davis contended that slaves were property and must be protected by law like other property. Lincoln declared that "a house divided against itself cannot stand," that slavery must be lawful or unlawful in all the states, alike north as well as south. Seward said that an irrepressible conflict existed between opposing and enduring forces, that the United States must and would become either entirely a slaveholding nation or entirely a free labor nation. Kansas became a free state in spite of Buchanan and then the conflict commenced. The southern states prepared for secession. Lincoln became President. The war came by the act of the south and ended with the destruction of slavery. This succession of events, following in due order, was the natural sequence of the existence of slavery in the United States.

> "God moves in a mysterious way,
> His wonders to perform."

CHAPTER X.

BEGINNING OF LINCOLN'S FIRST ADMINISTRATION.

Arrival of the President Elect at Washington — Impressiveness of His Inaugural
Address — I am Elected Senator from Ohio to Succeed Salmon P. Chase —
Letters Written to and Received from My Brother William Tecumseh — His
Arrival at Washington — A Dark Period in the History of the Country —
Letter to General Sherman on the Attack Upon Fort Sumter —
Departure for Mansfield to Encourage Enlistments — Ohio
Regiments Reviewed by the President — General McLaugh-
lin Complimented — My Visit to Ex-President
Buchanan — Meeting Between my Brother
and Colonel George H. Thomas.

ABRAHAM LINCOLN, the President elect, arrived in the city of Washington on the 23rd day of February, 1861, and, with Mrs. Lincoln, stopped at Willard's Hotel where I was then living. On the evening of his arrival I called upon him, and met him for the first time. When introduced to him, he took my hands in both of his, drew himself up to his full height, and, looking at me steadily, said: "You are John Sherman! Well I am taller than you; let's measure." Thereupon we stood back to back, and some one present announced that he was two inches taller than I. This was correct, for he was 6 feet $3\frac{1}{2}$ inches tall when he stood erect. This singular introduction was not unusual with him, but if it lacked in dignity, it was an expression of friendliness and so considered by him. Our brief conversation was cheerful, and my hearty congratulations for his escape from the Baltimore "roughs" were received with a laugh.

It was generally understood when Mr. Lincoln arrived that his cabinet was definitely formed, but rumors soon prevailed that dissensions existed among its members, that Seward and Chase were rivals, that neither could act in harmony with the other, and that both were discontented with their associates. I became satisfied that these rumors were true. I do not feel

at liberty, even at this late day, to repeat what was said to me
by some of the members selected, but I was convinced that
Lincoln had no purpose or desire to change the cabinet he had
selected in Springfield, and that he regarded their jealousies (if
I may use such a word in respect to gentlemen so distinguished) as a benefit and not an objection, as by that means he
would control his cabinet rather than be controlled by it.

Mr. Lincoln delivered his inaugural address from the east
steps of the capitol, on the 4th day of March, 1861. I sat near
him and heard every word. Douglas stood conspicuous behind
him and suggesting many thoughts. I have witnessed many in-
augurations, but never one so impressive as this. The condition of the south already organized for war, the presence of
United States troops with general Scott in command, the manifest preparation against threatened violence, the sober and
quiet attention to the address, all united to produce a profound
apprehension of evils yet to come. The eloquent peroration of
Mr. Lincoln cannot be too often repeated, and I insert it here:

"In *your* hands, my dissatisfied fellow-countrymen, and not in *mine*, is
the momentous issue of civil war. The government will not assail *you*.
You can have no conflict, without being yourselves the aggressors. *You*
have no oath registered in Heaven to destroy the government, while *I* shall
have the most solemn one to 'preserve, protect, and defend' it.

"I am loth to close. We are not enemies, but friends. We must not
be enemies. Though passion may have strained, it must not break, our
bonds of affection. The mystic chords of memory, stretching from every
battlefield and patriot grave, to every living heart and hearthstone, all
over this broad land, will yet swell the chorus of the Union, when again
touched, as surely they will be, by the better angels of our nature."

Salmon P. Chase, then Senator, was appointed Secretary of
the Treasury. I know with what doubt and reluctance he accepted this office. On the 7th of March his resignation as
Senator was communicated to the Senate. In anticipation of
it the legislature of Ohio was canvassing for his successor.
My name was mentioned with many others. I was in doubt
whether I ought to be a candidate, or even to accept the position if tendered. I had been elected as a Member of the next
Congress and was quite certain of election as speaker of the
House of Representatives. The Republicans had a decided

ABRAHAM LINCOLN.

FROM A PHOTOGRAPH TAKEN IN CHICAGO IN 1860.

Strafford Apl. 1, 1861

My dear Sir:

I congratulate you upon your election to the Senate of the U.S., but still I regret you have left the House where I think you might have rendered more important services to your country than you will find opportunity to do in the Senate. You could without doubt I think have been Speaker had you preferred any ambition for the post. That would have been for two years only, but it would be at a crisis that will figure in our history. There you are greatly needed on economical questions with our party — many of whom have no just idea of the responsibility of the Republican party, or a Republican Representative.

I see no material matter maturing for leaders in our House, and though I am glad to have you suited I do much regret your translation to the higher branch. I suppose we may be called back by Seward about the 1st of June.

Our Tariff Bill is unfortunate in being launched at this time as it will be made the Scape-goat of all difficulties. In fact the Southern Confederacy would have made a lower tariff had we left the old law in force and precisely the same troubles would have been presented. Yours very sincerely

Justin S. Morrill

Hon. John Sherman,
Mansfield. O.

majority in that body and a feeling was manifest that I should have, without opposition, the position of which I had been unjustly deprived by the previous House. This was to me a coveted honor. I, therefore, did not follow the advice of my friends and go to Columbus. A ballot was taken in the caucus of Republican members of the general assembly, and I received a plurality but not a majority, the votes being scattered among many other candidates of merit and ability. My name was then withdrawn. Several ballots were taken on a number of days without result. I was then telegraphed to come to Columbus. I went and was nominated on the first vote after my arrival, and promptly elected as Senator, to fill the vacancy occasioned by the resignation of Mr. Chase.

I received many letters of congratulation, among which were two which I insert:

DUBUQUE, March 23, 1861.

HON. JOHN SHERMAN:—Allow me to sincerely congratulate you upon your signal triumph at Columbus. I can assure you that no recent event has given me so much sincere gratification as your election, which I think a most worthy reward to a faithful public servant. Republics are not so ungrateful as I supposed when I was defeated for Dist. Atty.

Sincerely your friend, WM. B. ALLISON.

STRAFFORD, April 1, 1861.

HON. JOHN SHERMAN, Mansfield, Ohio.

MY DEAR SIR:— I congratulate you upon your election to the Senate of the U. S., but still I regret that you have left the House where I think you might have rendered more important services to your county than you will find opportunity to do in the Senate. You could without doubt, I think, have been Speaker, had you possessed any ambition for the position. That would have been for two years only, but it would be at a crisis that will figure in our history. Then you are greatly needed in economical questions with our party — many of whom have no just idea of the responsibility of the Republican party or a Republican Representative. I see no material worth mentioning for leaders in our House, and though I am glad to have you suited, I do much regret your translation to the higher branch. I suppose we may be called back by Seward about the 1st of June.

Our tariff bill is unfortunate in being launched at this time, as it will be made the scape-goat of all difficulties. In fact the southern Confederacy would have made a lower tariff had we left the old law in force and precisely the same troubles would have been presented.

Yours, very sincerely, JUSTIN S. MORRILL.

The Senate being then in special session, the oath prescribed by law was administered to me, and on the 23rd of
March, 1861, I took my seat in that body. I had, however,
before my election, witnessed, with deep humiliation, the Senate
debates, feeling that the Republican Senators were too timid in
the steps taken to purge that body of persons whom I regarded
as traitors. I cannot now read the debates without a feeling
of resentment. Breckenridge, Mason, Hunter and Powell still
retained their seats as Senators from Kentucky and Virginia,
and almost daily defended the secession of the southern states,
declaring that the states they represented would do likewise.
These and other declarations I thought should have been
promptly resented by the immediate expulsion of these Senators. Wigfall, of Texas, though his state had seceded, was permitted to linger in the Senate and to attend executive sessions,
where he was not only a traitor but a spy. His rude and
brutal language and conduct should have excluded him from
the Senate in the early days of the session, but he was permitted to retire without censure, after a long debate upon the
terms of his proposed expulsion. I took no part in the debate
of that session, which closed March 28, 1861, five days after my
becoming a Member. I remained in Washington until after
the fall of Sumter in April following.

During this period my brother, William Tecumseh, came to
Washington to tender his services in the army in any position
in which he could be useful. I had corresponded with him
freely in regard to his remaining in Louisiana, where he was
president of the Louisiana State Seminary of Learning and
Military Academy. He had been embarrassed in his position by
my attitude in Congress, and, especially, by the outcry against
me for signing the Helper book. He was very conservative in
his opinions in regard to slavery, and no doubt felt that I was
too aggressive on that subject. In the summer of 1860 he
made his usual visit to Lancaster, and, finding that I was engaged in the canvass and would on a certain day be at Coshocton, he determined to go and hear me "to see whether I was an
Abolitionist." He was greatly embarrassed by a memorable
speech made by Mr. Corwin, the principal speaker on that

Dubuque March 23rd 1861

Hon Jno Sherman,

Allow me. to sincerely congratulate you, upon your signal triumph at Columbus—
I can assure you, that no recent event, has given me, so much gratification as your election
I think a work worthy reward... to a faithful public test.— Republics are not so ungrateful
as I supposed when I was defeated for sixth dist;

Truly yours,
Wm B. Allison

occasion. We sat upon the stand together, and he very excit-
edly said: "John, you must not speak after Corwin." He was
evidently impressed with the eloquence of that orator and did
not wish me to speak, lest the contrast between our speeches
would be greatly to my disparagement. I told him that he
need not trouble himself, that I was to speak in the evening,
though I might say a few words at the close of Mr. Corwin's
address. He remained and heard me in the evening, and concluded on the whole that I was not an Abolitionist.

After the election of Mr. Lincoln I wrote him a letter,
which will speak for itself, as follows:

MANSFIELD, OHIO, November 26, 1860.

MY DEAR BROTHER:—Since I received your last letter, I have been so
constantly engaged, first with the election and afterwards in arranging my
business for the winter, that I could not write you.

The election resulted as I all along supposed. Indeed, the division of
the Democratic party on precisely the same question that separated the Republican party from the Democratic party made its defeat certain. The success of the Republicans has saved the country from a discreditable scramble
in the House. The disorders of the last winter, and the fear of their renewal, have, without doubt, induced many good citizens to vote for the
Republican ticket. With a pretty good knowledge of the material of our
House, I would far prefer that any one of the candidates be elected by the
people rather than allow the contest to be determined in Congress. Well,
Lincoln is elected. No doubt, a large portion of the citizens of Louisiana
think this a calamity. If they believe their own newspapers, or, what is far
worse, the lying organs of the Democratic party in the free states, they have
just cause to think so. But you were long enough in Ohio, and heard
enough of the ideas of the Republican leaders, to know that the Republican
party is not likely to interfere, directly or indirectly, with slavery in the
states or with the laws relating to slavery ; that, so far as the slavery question is concerned, the contest was for the possession of Kansas and perhaps
New Mexico, and that the chief virtue of the Republican success was in its
condemnation of the narrow sectionalism of Buchanan's administration and
the corruption by which his policy was attempted to be sustained. Who
doubts but that, if Buchanan had been true to his promises in submitting
the controversy in Kansas to its own people, and had closed it by admitting
Kansas as a free state, that the Democratic party would have retained its
power ? It was his infernal policy in that state (I can hardly think of the
mean and bad things he allowed there without swearing) that drove off
Douglas, led to the division of the Democratic party and the consequent
election of Lincoln.

As a matter of course, I rejoice in the result, for in my judgment the administration of Lincoln will do much to dissipate the feeling in the south against the north, by showing what are the real purposes of the Republican party. In the meantime, it is evident we have to meet in a serious way the movements of South Carolinian Disunionists. These men have for years desired this disunion ; they have plotted for it. They drove Buchanan into his Kansas policy; they got up this new dogma about slave protection ; they broke up the Charleston convention merely to advance secession ; they are now hurrying forward excited men into acts of treason, without giving time for passion to cool or reason to resume its sway. God knows what will be the result. If, by a successful revolution, they can go out of the Union, they establish a principle that will break the government into fragments. Some local disaffection or temporary excitement will lead one state after another out of the Union. We shall have the Mexican Republic over again, with a fiercer race of men to fight with each other. Secession is revolution. They seem bent upon attempting it. If so, shall the government resist ? If so, then comes civil war, a fearful subject for Americans to think of.

Since the election I have been looking over the field for the purpose of marking out a course to follow this winter, and I have, as well as I could, tested my political course in the past. There has been nothing done by the Republican party but what merits the cordial approval of my judgment. There have been many things said and done by Republican leaders that I utterly detest. Many of the dogmas of the Democratic party I like, but their conduct in administering the government, and especially in their treatment of the slavery question, I detest. I know we shall have trouble this winter, but I intend to be true to the moderate conservative course I think I have hitherto undertaken. Whatever may be the consequences, I will insist on preserving the unity of the states, and all the states, without exception and without regard to consequences. If any southern state has really suffered any injury or is deprived of any right, I will help redress the injury and secure the right. These states must not, merely because they are beaten in election, or have failed in establishing slavery where it was prohibited by compromise, attempt to break up the government. If they will hold on a little while, they will find no injury can come to them, unless, by their repeated misrepresentation of us, they stir up their slaves to insurrection. I still hope that no state will follow in the wake of South Carolina ; then the weakness of her position will soon bring her back again or subject her to ridicule and insignificance.

It may be supposed by some that the excitement in the south has produced a corresponding excitement in the north. This is true in financial matters, especially in the cities. In political circles it only strengthens the Republican party. Even Democrats of all shades say, 'The election is against us ; we will submit and all must submit.' Republicans say, 'The policy of the government has been controlled by the south for years, and we have submitted; now they must submit.' And why not? What can the Republicans do half as bad as Pierce and Buchanan have done?

But enough of this. You luckily are out of politics, and don't sympathize with my Republicanism, but as we are on the eve of important events, I write about politics instead of family matters, of which there is nothing new.   Affectionately yours,

JOHN SHERMAN.

In December I received this letter from him:

Louisiana State Seminary of Learning and Military Academy, ⎱
ALEXANDRIA, December 1, 1860. ⎰

DEAR BROTHER:— . . . The quiet which I thought the usual acquiescence of the people was merely the prelude to the storm of opinion that now seems irresistible. Politicians, by hearing the prejudices of the people and running with the current, have succeeded in destroying the government. It cannot be stopped now, I fear. I was in Alexandria all day yesterday, and had a full and unreserved conversation with Dr. S. A. Smith, state senator, who is a man of education, property, influence, and qualified to judge. He was, during the canvass, a Breckenridge man, but, though a southerner in opinion, is really opposed to a dissolution of our government. He has returned from New Orleans, where he says he was amazed to see evidences of public sentiment which could not be mistaken.

The legislature meets December 10, at Baton Rouge. The calling of a convention forthwith is to be unanimous, the bill for army and state ditto. The convention will meet in January, and only two questions will be agitated, — immediate dissolution, a declaration of state independence, and a general convention of southern states, with instructions to demand of the northern states to repeal all laws hostile to slavery and pledges of future good behavior. . . . When the convention meets in January, as they will assuredly do, and resolve to secede, or to elect members to a general convention with instructions inconsistent with the nature of things, I must quit this place, for it would be neither right for me to stay nor would the governor be justified in placing me in this position of trust; for the moment Louisiana assumes a position of hostility, then this becomes an arsenal and fort. . . .

Let me hear the moment you think dissolution is inevitable. What Mississippi and Georgia do, this state will do likewise.

Affectionately,   W. T. SHERMAN.

On the 15th of December I wrote him:

"I am clearly of the opinion that you ought not to remain much longer at your present post. You will, in all human probability, be involved in complications from which you cannot escape with honor. Separated from your family and all your kin, and an object of suspicion, you will find your position unendurable. A fatal infatuation seems to have seized the southern

mind, during which any act of madness may be committed. . . . If the
sectional dissensions only rested upon real or alleged grievances, they
could be readily settled, but I fear they are deeper and stronger. You can
now close your connection with the seminary with honor and credit to yourself, for all who know you speak well of your conduct, while by remaining
you not only involve yourself, but bring trouble upon those gentlemen who
recommended you.

"It is a sad state of affairs, but it is nevertheless true, that if the conventions of the southern states make anything more than a paper secession,
hostile collisions will occur, and probably a separation between the free and
the slave states. You can judge whether it is at all probable that the possession of this capital, the commerce of the Mississippi, the control of the
territories, and the natural rivalry of enraged sections, can be arranged without war. In that event, you cannot serve in Louisiana against your family
and kin in Ohio. The bare possibility of such a contingency, it seems to
me, renders your duty plain, to make a frank statement to all the gentlemen
connected with you, and with good feeling close your engagement. If the
storm shall blow over, your course will strengthen you with every man
whose good opinion you desire ; if not, you will escape humiliation.

"When you return to Ohio, I will write you freely about your return to
the army, not so difficult a task as you imagine."

General Sherman then wrote me as follows:

ALEXANDRIA, LA., December, 1861.
Events here seem hastening to a conclusion. Doubtless you know
more of the events in Louisiana than I do, as I am in an out-of-the-way
place. But the special session of the legislature was so unanimous in arming
the state and calling a convention that little doubt remains that Louisiana
will, on the 23rd of January, follow the other seceding states. Governor
Moore takes the plain stand that the state must not submit to a 'black Republican President.' Men here have ceased to reason ; they seem to concede that slavery is unsafe in a confederacy with northern states, and that
now is the time ; no use of longer delay. All concessions, all attempts to
remonstrate, seem at an end.

A rumor says that Major Anderson, my old captain (brother of Charles
Anderson, now of Texas, formerly of Dayton and Cincinnati, Larz, William
and John, all of Ohio), has spiked the guns of Fort Moultrie, destroyed it,
and taken refuge in Sumter. This is right. Sumter is in mid-channel,
approachable only in boats, whereas Moultrie is old, weak, and easily
approached under cover. If Major Anderson can hold out till relieved and
supported by steam frigates, South Carolina will find herself unable to control her commerce, and will feel, for the first time in her existence, that she
can't do as she pleases. . . .

A telegraph dispatch, addressed to me at Alexandria, could be mailed
at New Orleans, and reach me in three days from Washington.

I wrote him the following letter on the 6th of January, 1861:

DEAR BROTHER:— . . . I see some signs of hope, but it is probably a deceptive light. The very moment you feel uncomfortable in your position in Louisiana, come away. Don't for God's sake subject yourself to any slur, reproach, or indignity. I have spoken to General Scott, and he heartily seconds your desire to return to duty in the army. I am not at all sure but that, if you were here, you could get a position that would suit you. I see many of your friends of the army daily.

As for my views of the present crisis, I could not state them more fully than I have in the inclosed printed letter. It has been very generally published and approved in the north, but may not have reached you, and therefore I send it to you.   Affectionately your brother,
JOHN SHERMAN.

Later he wrote me:

ALEXANDRIA, January 16, 1861.

MY DEAR BROTHER : — I am so much in the woods here that I can't keep up with the times at all. Indeed, you in Washington hear from New Orleans two or three days sooner than I do. I was taken aback by the news that Governor Moore had ordered the forcible seizure of the Forts Jackson and St. Philip, at or near the mouth of the Mississippi ; also of Forts Pike and Wood, at the outlets of Lakes Bogue and Pontchartrain. All these are small forts, and have rarely been occupied by troops. They are designed to cut off approach by sea to New Orleans, and were taken doubtless to prevent their being occupied, by order of General Scott. But the taking the arsenal at Baton Rouge is a different matter. It is merely an assemblage of store-houses, barracks, and dwelling-houses, designed for the healthy residence of a garrison, to be thrown into one or the other of the forts in case of war. The arsenal is one of minor importance, yet the stores were kept there for the moral effect, and the garrison was there at the instance of the people of Louisiana. To surround with the military array, to demand surrender, and enforce the departure of the garrison, was an act of war. It amounted to a declaration of war and defiance, and was done by Governor Moore without the authority of the legislature or convention. Still, there is but little doubt but that each of these bodies, to assemble next week, will ratify and approve these violent acts, and it is idle to discuss the subject now. The people are mad on this question.

I had previously notified all that in the event of secession I should quit. As soon as a knowledge of these events reached me, I went to the vice president, Dr. Smith, in Alexandria, and told him that I regarded Louisiana as at war against the federal government, and that I must go. He begged me to wait until some one could be found to replace me. The supervisors feel the importance of system and discipline, and seem to think that my departure will endanger the success of this last effort to build up an educational establishment. . . . You may assert that in no event will I forego my allegiance to the United States as long as a single state is true to the old constitution. . . .

Yours,   W. T. SHERMAN.

And again:

Louisiana State Seminary of Learning and Military Academy,
ALEXANDRIA, January 18, 1861.

DEAR BROTHER: — Before receiving yours of the 6th, I had addressed a letter to Governor Moore at Baton Rouge, of which this is a copy:—

'*Sir:*—As I occupy a quasi military position under the laws of the state, I deem it proper to acquaint you that I accepted such position when Louisiana was a state in the union and when the motto of this seminary was inscribed in marble over the main door: "By the liberality of the General Government. The Union Esto perpetua." Recent events foreshadow a great change, and it becomes all men to choose. If Louisiana withdraw from the federal Union, I prefer to maintain my allegiance to the old constitution as long as a fragment of it survives, and my longer stay here would be wrong in every sense of the word. In that event, I beg that you will send or appoint some authorized agent to take charge of the arms and munitions of war here belonging to the state, or advise me what disposition to make of them. And furthermore, as president of the board of supervisors, I beg you to take immediate steps to relieve me as superintendent the moment the state determines to secede; for on no earthly account will I do any act or think any thought hostile to, or in defiance of, the United States.

With respect, etc.,   W. T. SHERMAN.'

I regard the seizure by Governor Moore of the United States arsenal as the worst act yet committed in the present revolution. I do think every allowance should be made to southern politicians for their nervous anxiety about their political powers and the safety of slaves. I think that the constitution should be liberally construed in their behalf, but I do regard this civil war as precipitated with undue rapidity. . . . It is inevitable. All legislation now would fall powerless on the south. You should not alienate such states as Virginia, Kentucky, Tennessee, and Missouri. My notion is that this war will ruin all politicians, and that military leaders will direct the events.   Yours   W. T. S.

On the first of February he wrote as follows:

"I have felt the very thoughts you have spoken. It is war to surround Anderson with batteries, and it is shilly-shally for the south to cry 'Hands off! No coercion!' It was war and insult to expel the garrison at Baton Rouge, and Uncle Sam had better cry 'Cave!' or assert his power. Fort Sumter is not material save for the principle; but Key West and the Tortugas should be held in force at once, by regulars if possible, if not, by militia. Quick! They are occupied now, but not in force. Whilst maintaining the high, strong ground you do, I would not advise you to interpose an objection to securing concessions to the middle and moderate states,— Virginia, Kentucky, Tennessee and Missouri. Slavery there is local, and even if the world were open to them, its extension would involve no principle. If these states feel the extreme south wrong, a seeming concession would make them committed. The cotton states are gone, I suppose. Of course, their commerce will be hampered. . . .

"But of myself. I sent you a copy of my letter to the Governor. Here is his answer:

"'Dear Sir:—It is with the deepest regret I acknowledge the receipt of your letter of the 18th instant. In the pressure of official business I can only request you to transfer to Professor Smith the arms, munitions, and funds in your hands, whenever you conclude to withdraw from the position you have filled with so much distinction. You cannot regret more than I do the necessity which deprives us of your services, and you will bear with you the respect, confidence, and admiration of all who have been associated with you. Very truly, your friend and servant,

THOS. D. MOORE.'

"This is very handsome, and I do regret this political imbroglio. I do think it was brought about by politicians. The people in the south are evidently unanimous in the opinion that slavery is endangered by the current of events, and it is useless to attempt to alter that opinion. As our government is founded on the will of the people, when that will is fixed, our government is powerless, and the only question is whether to let things slide into general anarchy, or the formation of two or more confederacies which will be hostile sooner or later. Still, I know that some of the best men of Louisiana think this change may be effected peacefully. But even if the southern states be allowed to depart in peace, the first question will be revenue.

"Now, if the south have free trade, how can you collect revenues in the eastern cities? Freight from New Orleans to St. Louis, Chicago, Louisville, Cincinnati, and even Pittsburg, would be about the same as by rail from New York, and importers at New Orleans, having no duties to pay, would undersell the east if they had to pay duties. Therefore, if the south make good their confederation and their plan, the northern confederacy must do likewise or blockade. Then comes the question of foreign nations. So, look on it in any view, I see no result but war and consequent changes in the form of government."

These letters, written at their dates, on the spur of the moment, present the condition of affairs as viewed by General Sherman and myself when they occurred.

With the convictions just stated General Sherman came to Washington about the time of my election to the Senate. He was deeply impressed with the certainty of war and of its magnitude, and was impelled by the patriotic sentiment that, as he had been educated at the expense of the government for military service, it was his duty, in the then condition of the country, to tender his services. I therefore escorted him to the White House. His statement of the interview given in his "Memoirs" is not very full, for, while Mr. Lincoln did say, in response to his tender, "I guess we will manage to keep house," he also expressed a hope, which General Sherman knew to be delusive, that the danger would pass by and that the Union would be restored by a peaceful compromise. This was, undoubtedly, the idea then uppermost in the minds of both the President and Mr. Seward. At this time the public mind in the north was decidedly in favor of concessions to the south. The Democrats of the north would have agreed to any proposition to secure peace and the Union, and the Republicans would have acquiesced in the Crittenden Compromise, or in any measure approved by Lincoln and Seward.

The period between the 4th of March and the 12th of April was the darkest one in the history of the United States. It was a time of humiliation, timidity and feebleness. Fortunately for the future of our country the rebels of the south were bent upon disunion; they were hopeful and confident, and all the signs of the times indicated their success. They had possession of all the forts of the south, except Fortress Monroe, Fort Sumter, and two remote forts in Florida. They had only to wait in patience, and Fort Sumter would necessarily be abandoned for want of supplies. Fortress Monroe could not be held much longer by the regular army, weakened as it was by the desertion of officers and men, and public sentiment would not justify a call for troops in advance of actual war. The people of South Carolina were frenzied by their success thus far, and, impatient of delay, forced an attack on Fort Sumter, then held by a small garrison under command of Major Robert Anderson. The first gun fired on the 12th of April, 1861, resounded throughout the United States and the civilized world, touching an electric chord in every family in the northern states and changing the whole current of feeling. From this time forth, among the patriotic people of the loyal states, there was no thought or talk of compromise. That this insult to our flag must be punished, "that the Union must and shall be preserved," were the resolves of millions of men, without respect to party, who but the day before were eager for compromise. The cold and cautious men of the north were at last awakened from their indifference.

The impression made upon my mind by the attack on Fort Sumter is expressed in a letter I wrote from Washington to my brother, General Sherman, as he was then called, at midnight of the 12th of April:

WASHINGTON, April 12, 1861.

DEAR BROTHER:—I was unexpectedly called here soon after receiving your letter of the 8th, and at midnight write you. The military excitement here is intense. Since my arrival I have seen several officers, many citizens, and all the heads of departments except Blair. There is a fixed determination now to preserve the Union and enforce the laws at all hazards. Civil war is actually upon us, and, strange to say, it brings a feeling of relief; the suspense is over. I have spent much of the day in talking about you. There is an earnest desire that you go into the war department, but I said this was impossible. Chase is especially desirous that you accept, saying that you would be virtually Secretary of War, and could easily step into any military position that offers.

It is well for you seriously to consider your conclusion, although my opinion is that you ought not to accept. You ought to hold yourself in reserve. If troops are called for, as they surely will be in a few days, organize a regiment or brigade, either in St. Louis or Ohio, and you will then get into the army in such a way as to secure promotion. By all means take advantage of the present disturbances to get into the army, where you will at once put yourself in a high position for life. I know that promotion and every facility for advancement will be cordially extended by the authorities. You are a favorite in the army and have great strength in political circles. I urge you to avail yourself of these favorable circumstances to secure your position for life; for, after all, your present employment is of uncertain tenure in these stirring times.

Let me now record a prediction. Whatever you may think of the signs of the times, the government will rise from this strife greater, stronger, and more prosperous than ever. It will display energy and military power. The men who have confidence in it, and do their full duty by it, may reap whatever there is of honor and profit in public life, while those who look on merely as spectators in the storm will fail to discharge the highest duty of a citizen, and suffer accordingly in public estimation. . . .

I write this in great hurry, with numbers around me, and exciting and important intelligence constantly repeated, even at this hour; but I am none the less in earnest. I hope to hear that you are on the high road to the 'General' within thirty days. Affectionately your brother,

JOHN SHERMAN.

Two days later I wrote him:

WASHINGTON, Sunday, April 14, 1861.

DEAR BROTHER :— . . . The war has really commenced. You will have full details of the fall of Sumter. We are on the eve of a terrible war. Every man will have to choose his position. You fortunately have the military education, prominence, and character, that will enable you to play a high part in the tragedy. You can't avoid taking such a part. Neutrality and indifference are impossible. If the government is to be maintained, it must be by military power, and that immediately. You can choose your own place. Some of your best friends here want you in the war department; Taylor, Shiras, and a number of others, talk to me so. If you want that place, with a sure prospect of promotion, you can have it, but you are not compelled to take it; but it seems to me you will be compelled to take some position, and that speedily. Can't you come to Ohio and at once raise a regiment? It will immediately be in service. The administration intends to stand or fall by the Union, the entire Union, and the enforcement of the laws. I look for preliminary defeats, for the rebels have arms, organization, unity; but this advantage will not last long. The government will maintain itself or our northern people are the veriest poltroons that ever disgraced humanity.

For me, I am for a war that will either establish or overthrow the government and will purify the atmosphere of political life. We need such a war, and we have it now. . . . Affectionately yours,

JOHN SHERMAN.

He wrote in reply:

"The time will come in this country when professional knowledge will be appreciated, when men that can be trusted will be wanted, and I will bide my time. I may miss the chance; if so, all right; but I cannot and will not mix myself in this present call. . . .

"The first movements of the government will fail and the leaders will be cast aside. A second or third set will rise, and among them I may be, but at present I will not volunteer as a soldier or anything else. If Congress meet, or if a national convention be called, and the regular army be put on a footing with the wants of the country, if I am offered a place that suits me, I may accept. But in the present call I will not volunteer."

He criticised the call for 75,000 militia for three months, saying that the best of men could only be made indifferent soldiers in three months, and that the best of soldiers could accomplish nothing in three months in such a country as ours. He therefore would not volunteer for such a service, but his mind was occupied with military plans. The correspondence between us shows that he had a better conception of the magnitude and necessities of the war than civilians like myself.

He wrote to Mr. Cameron, Secretary of War, from St. Louis, on May 8, 1861:

"I hold myself now, as always, prepared to serve my country in the capacity for which I was trained. I did not and will not volunteer for three months, because I cannot throw my family on the cold support of charity, but for the three years' call made by the President an officer could prepare his command and do good service. I will not volunteer, because, rightfully or wrongfully, I feel myself unwilling to take a mere private's place, and having for many years lived in California and Louisiana, the men are not well enough acquainted with me to elect me to my appropriate place. Should my services be needed, the record or the war department will enable you to designate the station in which I can render best service."

When Mr. Lincoln was elected President, there was no general feeling among the northern people that war would result from his election. It was not believed, although it had been threatened, that the southern states would take up arms to resist the accession of a President not of their choice. The love of Union and the orderly obedience to constituted authority had been so well established among our people that, while politicians might threaten, but few really believed that war, of which they knew nothing, was to come upon us. The result was that when the southern states, one by one, seceded, and Fort Sumter was fired upon, and the forts and arsenals of the south were captured, a new inspiration dawned upon the people of the north, a determination became general that, cost what it would, the Union should be preserved to our children and our children's children. That feeling was not confined to party lines. I am bound to say that the members of the Democratic party in the loyal States, in the main, evinced the same patriotic determination to maintain the cause of the Union, as those of the Republican party. Their sons and their kindred formed part of every regiment or force raised in the United States.

At this distance of time from the opening of the Civil War, I have endeavored to take an impartial retrospect of the causes that led the south to engage therein. Undoubtedly, the existence of negro slavery in the south was the governing incitement to war. The owners of slaves knew that the tenure of such property was feeble. Besides the danger of escape, there was the growing hostility to slavery in a preponderance of the people of the United States, restrained only by its recognition by the constitution. The slave owners believed that, by secession, they could establish a republic, founded on slavery, with an ample field in Mexico and Central America for conquest and expansion. They had cultivated a bitter sectional enmity, amounting to contempt, for the people of the north, growing partly out of the subserviency of large portions of the north to the dictation of the south, but chiefly out of the wordy violence and disregard of constitutional obligations by the Abolitionists of the north. They believed in the doctrine of an irrepressible conflict long before it was announced by Seward.

South Carolina, far in advance of other southern states, led in promulgating the legal rights of secession, until they came to be acquiesced in by all these states. They committed themselves to it in the Charleston convention. Their speakers declared, during the canvass, that if Lincoln was elected, their states would secede. When elected, the first gun was fired on Fort Sumter, in South Carolina, where all the people were determined on war. The struggle once commenced, the natural sympathy of the southern states was with South Carolina. The States of Virginia, North Carolina and Tennessee, where a strong Union sentiment prevailed, hesitated and delayed, but the young and active spirits were with the south, and these carried the states named into the general conflict. Once in the war, there was no way but to fight it out. I have no sympathy with secession, but I can appreciate the action of those who were born and reared under the influence of such teachings. Who of the north can say, that in like conditions, he would not have been a rebel?

Looking back from my standpoint now, when all the states are re-united in a stronger Union, when Union and Confederate soldiers are acting together in both Houses of Congress in legislating for the common good, when, since 1861, our country has more than doubled its population and quadrupled its resources, when its institutions have been harmonized by the abolition of slavery, when the seceding states are entering into a friendly and hopeful rivalry, in the development of their great resources, when they have doubled or trebled their production of cotton, when they are producing the greater part of their food, when they are developing their manufactures of iron and steel, and introducing the spindle and loom into their cities and villages, it seems to me that men of the south surely will appreciate, if they do not approve, what I said in the Senate early in the war:

"I would stake the last life, the last dollar, the last man, upon the prosecution of the war. Indeed, I cannot contemplate the condition of my country if it shall be dissevered and divided. Take the loyal states as they now stand and look at the map of the United States, and regard two hostile confederacies stretching along for thousands of miles across the continent. Do you not know that the normal condition of such a state of affairs would be eternal, everlasting war ? Two nations of the same blood, of the same lineage, of the same spirit, cannot occupy the same continent, much less standing side by side as rival nations, dividing rivers and mountains for their boundary. No, Mr. president, rather than allow this war to terminate except upon the restoration of the Union intact in all its breadth and length, I would sacrifice the last man and see the country itself submerged.

"Rather than yield to traitors or the intervention of foreign powers, rather than bequeath to the next generation a broken Union, and an interminable civil war, I would light the torch of fanaticism and destroy all that the labor of two generations has accumulated. Better a desert and universal poverty than disunion ; better the war of the French Revolution than an oligarchy founded upon the labor of slaves. But, sir, there is no need of this. The resources, wealth, and labor of twenty millions of freemen are amply sufficient to meet not only the physical, but financial, difficulties of the war. Thank God ! the test to which all nations in the course of their history are subjected, is applied to us when we have an insignificant national debt; when our resources were never more manifest; when the loyal states are so thoroughly united; when our people are filled with a generous enthusiasm that will make the loss of life and burden of taxation easy to bear. If we conquer a peace by preserving the Union, the constitution, our nationality, all our ample territories, the rebound of prosperity in this country will enable a single generation easily to pay the national debt, even if the war is protracted until desolation is written upon every rebel hearthstone."

This, I believe, expressed the spirit and determination of the loyal states of the north, at the beginning of the war.

With opinions so widely divergent in the two sections, and
with a fixed purpose of each to stand by them, there was no
way that poor frail human nature could devise to decide the
controversy except to fight.

From the graves of the dead, who fought on opposite sides
for their country or their state, there has been a resurrection,
honorable to both sections, a Union stronger, more united and
glorious than the Union established by our fathers, and with a
rebound of prosperity greater than we could conceive of in
1862. This war, though fearful in the sacrifice of property
and life, has resulted in a better understanding among the
people of both sections. Each has for the other a higher
respect and regard. I sincerely hope and believe in the good
time coming when sectional lines will not divide political parties, and common interests and a broader nationality will have
destroyed sectional feeling and jealousy.

As the result of the war we command the respect of all foreign nations. The United States, as a great republic, has become an example already followed by European nations. It
has at least secured the respect and forbearance of the ruling
class in Great Britain, who never forgot or forgave the rebellion of our ancestors against King George III and the parliament of Great Britain. It has stamped the language, the laws,
and the boasted freedom of Englishmen, upon a population
double that in the mother country, and they, in turn, are taking lessons from us in extending to their people equality of
rights and privileges.

I remained in Washington a few days and then started for
my home at Mansfield, to encourage enlistments, but found
that no help was needed; that companies were enlisted in a
day. One was recruited by William McLaughlin, a gallant
soldier in the war in Mexico, a major general of Ohio militia
who had arrived at the age of sixty years. He dropped his law
books and in twelve hours had a company of one hundred men
ready to move at the command of the governor. A like patriotism was aroused in all parts of the state, so that in a very
short time two full regiments, numbering 2,000 men, were organized under the command of Colonel A. McD. McCook, of the

United States army, and were on the way to Washington, then blockaded by the roughs of Baltimore. I met them at Harrisburg and went with them to Philadelphia. They were camped at Fairmont Park, and were drilled with other regiments by Colonel Fitz John Porter, the entire force being under the command of General Patterson.

When the blockade was opened, by the skill and audacity of General Benjamin F. Butler, the two Ohio regiments were ordered to Washington and were there reviewed by President Lincoln, at which time a pleasant incident occurred which may be worthy of mention. I accompanied the President to the parade, and passed with him down the line. He noticed a venerable man with long white hair and military bearing, standing in position at the head of his company with arms presented, and inquired his name. I said it was General McLaughlin and hurriedly told him his history, his politics and patriotism. The President, as he came opposite him, stopped, and leaving his party advanced to McLaughlin and extended his hand. McLaughlin, surprised, had some difficulty in putting his sword under his left arm. They shook hands and Lincoln thanked him, saying when men of his age and standing came to the rescue of their country there could be no doubt of our success. McLaughlin highly appreciated this compliment. He afterwards enlisted for the war and died in the service of his country.

These two regiments were subsequently ordered to Harrisburg, to which place they went, accompanied by me, and there they formed a part of the command of General Patterson, which was to advance on Martinsburg and Winchester to aid in a movement of General McDowell against the enemy at Bull Run. I was serving on the staff of General Patterson as a volunteer aid without pay. While at Harrisburg it was suggested to me that ex-President Buchanan, then at his country home near that city, had expressed a wish to see me. As our personal relations had always been pleasant, though our political opinions were widely different, I called upon him, I think with Colonel Porter, and we were cordially received. I was surprised at the frankness and apparent sincerity of the opinions expressed by him in relation to the war. He said he had done all he could to prevent the war, but now that it was upon us it was the duty of all patriotic people to make it a success, that he approved all that had been done by Mr. Lincoln, of whom he spoke in high terms of praise. I believe he was sincere in the opinions he then expressed, and know of nothing said or done by him since that time that could create a doubt of his sincerity.

About the middle of June the command of General Patterson moved slowly to Chambersburg, where it remained several days under constant drill, then to Hagerstown and to the village of Williamsport on the Potomac. While at the latter place General Sherman, who had been at Washington and received his commission as colonel of the 13th United States infantry, then being recruited, came to visit me at my lodgings in a country tavern. He then met for the first time in many years his old classmate, Colonel, afterwards Major-General, George H. Thomas, who then commanded a regular regiment of the United States army in the force under the command of General Patterson. The conversation of these two officers, who were to be so intimately associated in great events in the future, was very interesting. They got a big map of the United States, spread it on the floor, and on their hands and knees discussed the probable salient strategic places of the war. They singled out Richmond, Vicksburg, Nashville, Knoxville and Chattanooga. To me it has always appeared strange that they were able confidently and correctly to designate the lines of operations and strategic points of a war not yet commenced, and more strange still that they should be leading actors in great battles at the places designated by them at this country tavern.

The next day General Thomas crossed the river into Virginia, but the order was soon countermanded, it is said, by General Scott, and General Thomas returned to the north bank of the Potomac. General Sherman returned to Washington to drill his raw troops for the battle of Bull Run. I soon after returned by stage to Frederick, Maryland, to take my seat in the Senate, Congress having been convened to meet in special session on the 4th of July.

CHAPTER XI.

Special Session of Congress to Provide for the War.

Condition of the Treasury Immediately Preceding the War — Not Enough Money on Hand to Pay Members of Congress — Value of Fractional Silver of Earlier Coinage — Largely Increased Revenues an Urgent Necessity — Lincoln's Message and Appeal to the People — Issue of New Treasury Notes and Bonds — Union Troops on the Potomac — Battle of Bull Run — Organization of the "Sherman Brigade" — The President's Timely Aid — Personnel of the Brigade.

TO understand the measures to be submitted to Congress at its approaching session, it is necessary to have a clear conception of the condition of the treasury at that time, and of the established financial policy of the government immediately before the war.

On the meeting of Congress in December, 1860, the treasury was empty. There was not enough money even to pay Members of Congress. The revenues were not sufficient to meet the demands for ordinary expenditures in time of peace. Since 1857 money had been borrowed by the sale of bonds and the issue of treasury notes bearing interest, to meet deficiencies. The public debt had increased during the administration of Mr. Buchanan about $70,000,000. The Secretary of the Treasury, Howell Cobb, resigned on the 10th of December, 1860, declaring that his duty to Georgia required such action. He had aided in every possible way to cripple the department while in charge of it.

On the 16th of the same month Congress authorized the issue of $10,000,000 treasury notes, to bear interest at the lowest rate bid. On the 18th Secretary Philip F. Thomas, Mr. Cobb's successor, invited bids for $5,000,000 of treasury notes, part of the $10,000,000 authorized, at par, at the rate of interest offered by the lowest bidder. Offers at 12 per cent. or less were made for $1,831,000 (the bulk of the offers being at 12 per cent.), which were accepted and additional offers were received at interest varying from 15 to 36 per cent., but were refused. Immediately after the decision of the department on these offers was announced, the assistant treasurer at New York advised the secretary that certain parties would take the residue of the $5,000,000 offered, through the Bank of Commerce, at 12 per cent. This proposition was accepted, on condition that the amount required to make up the five millions should be deposited without delay. The whole amount was applied to the payment of overdue treasury notes and other pressing demands on the treasury.

Secretary Thomas resigned on the 11th of January, 1861, and John A. Dix became Secretary of the Treasury. In answer to my inquiry Secretary Dix, in an official letter, dated January 18, 1861, stated the terms of the sale of treasury notes and that: "The amount required to meet the outstanding current and accruing dues before the close of the present fiscal year, besides any additional charges on the treasury created by legislation during the present session of Congress, is $44,077,524.63." He recommended a further issue of $25,000,000 of bonds, and suggested that the states which had received deposits under the act for the distribution of surplus revenue in General Jackson's time might be called upon to return such deposits, and added: "If, instead of calling for these deposits, it should be deemed advisable to pledge them for the repayment of any money the government might find it necessary to borrow, a loan contracted on such a basis of security, superadding to the plighted faith of the United States that of the individual states, could hardly fail to be acceptable to capitalists."

In this connection I received the following note :

TREASURY DEPARTMENT, February 6, 1861.

HON. JOHN SHERMAN.

DEAR SIR :—I send a preamble and resolution, and a letter to your governor. Will you read and send them at once ? You, as a Member of Congress, can say what I cannot with propriety — that no states which

Geo: Loft
5. Feb. 1881.

Dear Sir:
I send a sample of
Legislation & a letter to the
Governor. Will you read &
send them at once? —

I am, of a number of Gov-
ern., can say that I cannot
with propriety — that to state,
while presenting Bonds of
the N.S. to the amount
of the further money in it
hand, will be likely to be

Called on to repay these
moneys — or all sums
owing to N.S. for the
Bonds of the N.S. will

Mm — I am truly yours
Office of DMK

Hon. John Alexander:

I cannot put all my notice
for down the Jan. Rate
act, if the time is they begin.

guarantee bonds of the United States to the amount of the public moneys in its hands, will be likely to be called on to repay those moneys—at all events during the twenty years the bonds of the United States will run.

I am truly yours,   JOHN A. DIX.

P. S.—I cannot put out my notice for a loan till your state acts, and the time is very short.

Subsequently I received the following letter:

TREASURY DEPARTMENT, February 11, 1861, 7 p. m.

DEAR SIR :—My plan for raising money to meet the outstanding liabilities of the government, and to enable the incoming administration to carry on its financial operations without embarrassment till it shall have time to mature a plan for itself, has met with an obstacle quite unexpected to me. The committee of ways and means in the House has declined to report a bill to authorize me to accept the guaranties voluntarily tendered by the states. Mr. Spaulding, of New York, and Mr. Morrill, of Vermont, I learn, have objections. Unless they withdraw their opposition the bill cannot be reported, and the plan must fail. In that case I shall not deem it proper to ask for a loan of more than two millions to meet the redemption of treasury notes, which fall due before the 4th of March. The state of the country is such that a larger amount thrown on the market would have a most disastrous influence on the public credit. I do not think I can borrow two millions at more than 90 per cent. With a guaranty such as the states have offered, I can get eight millions at par. The alternative is to authorize me to accept the guaranty, or leave the treasury with scarcely anything in it and with outstanding demands, some of them very pressing, of at least six millions of dollars, for you and your political friends to provide for. If anything is done it should be to-morrow, as I ought to publish the notice on Wednesday. Perhaps you can see the gentlemen referred to to-night and remove their objections. I am, very truly, your obedient servant,

JOHN A. DIX.

On the 8th of February, 1861, a bill became a law providing for the sale of $20,000,000 six per cent. bonds, and these were sold at the rate of $89.10 for $100, yielding $18,415,000.

Such was the humiliating financial condition of the government of the United States at the close of Mr. Buchanan's administration. The expenditures of the government for the fiscal year ending June 30, 1861, were $84,577,258.60, of which $42,064,082.95 was procured from loans and treasury notes, leaving a balance in the treasury, at the close of the fiscal year 1861, of $2,395,635.21. This condition still existed when Congress subsequently met in special session.

Under the sub-treasury laws then in force, the revenues of the government were received and held only in the treasury at Washington, and in sub-treasuries located in a few of the principal cities of the United States, and could be paid out only upon the draft of the treasurer of the United States, drawn agreeably to appropriations made by law. No money could be received into the treasury except gold and silver coin of the United States, and such treasury notes as were receivable for bonds. State bank notes were not received for government dues. This exclusion grew out of the general failure of banks after the War of 1812 and the panic of 1837, and had caused the outcry in 1840 of: "Gold for the office holders; rags for the people." But this policy of the government to receive only its own coin or notes was sustained by popular opinion.

Silver dollars were not in circulation in 1861. Their issue was provided for at the beginning of our government, but, as they were most of the time more valuable than gold coin of like face value, they were hoarded or exported. Their coinage was suspended by an order of President Jefferson in 1805, and after this order only 1,300 silver dollars were coined by the United States prior to 1836. From 1836 to 1861 silver dollars were coined in small quantities, the aggregate being less than one and one-half million, and they were generally exported. It is probable that when Mr. Chase became Secretary of the Treasury, there was not in the United States one thousand silver dollars. In 1853, and prior to that year, fractional silver coins were worth for bullion more than their face value, and, therefore, did not circulate. Small change was scarce, and fractional notes, called "shinplasters," were issued in many parts of the United States. Mexican coin, debased and worn, was in circulation. To remedy this evil Congress, by the act of February 21, 1853, during Pierce's administration, prescribed the weight of the silver half dollar as 192 grains instead of $206\frac{1}{4}$ grains, fixed by the coinage act of 1792, and the weight of the quarter, dime and half dime of silver was reduced in the same proportion. As these new coins were less valuable than gold at the rate coined, they were made a legal tender in payment of debts only for sums not exceeding five dollars. The silver bullion for these coins was purchased at market value, and the privilege theretofore granted to a depositor of silver bullion to have it coined for him was repealed. This law had the beneficial effect of driving out of circulation "shinplasters" and worn coins, and supplied in ample quantity new full weight silver coins of handsome device, the government receiving the profit of the difference between the market value of the silver and its coinage value. Under this law the coinage of silver rapidly increased, so that, within two years after the passage of the act of 1853, more silver was converted into fractional coins and was in active use among the people than was contained in all the silver dollars coined under "free coinage" from the beginning of the government to 1878.

While silver was thus made useful to the fullest extent possible, it was, from its weight and bulk, inadequate and inconvenient for the vast demands of the government during the the war. Silver and gold together could not meet this demand. There was known to be in the country at that time, of specie in circulation, $250,000,000, of state bank notes, $180,000,000, in all $430,000,000. This amount, experience had shown, was necessary to meet exchanges in ordinary times of peace. The disturbance of a civil war would likely stimulate production for a time and require even more circulation for current business. This circulation, if drawn from its ordinary channels, would bring no end of confusion and distress to the people, and the government, to meet the demand occasioned by carrying on a war, must look elsewhere for a circulating medium with which to meet its enormous disbursements which must necessarily be made almost wholly in actual cash—checks being, from the character of the payments, of little avail.

There was no escaping the issue of credit money in some form, and of whatever form adopted we knew that gold and silver would soon disappear under the shadow of war—that they would be hoarded or exported.

This is the universal result of great wars long protracted. It was our experience during our Revolution and the War of 1812, and of Great Britain and all European nations during the Napoleonic wars. What should take the place of gold and silver for currency? The only answer was to substitute for the time the notes of the United States, with all the sanction and credit which the republic could confer, in the place of coin. We could not, with safety, accept bank notes issued by state corporations, varying in terms and credit according to the laws of twenty-three separate states.

To establish a credit of our bonds and notes these measures at least were necessary : First, increase largely the revenues from customs duties to be paid in coin; second, impose all forms of internal taxes authorized by the constitution ; third, create a national currency redeemable in coin, with no fixed time for redemption, but made a legal tender for all debts, public and private, except customs duties ; fourth, borrow any moneys needed on the most favorable terms possible.

On the 4th of July, 1861, the Senate convened in compliance with the proclamation of the President, from whom it received a message containing a clear statement of the events that followed his inaugural address. He described the attack upon Fort Sumter and said :

"By the affair at Fort Sumter, with its surrounding circumstances, that point was reached. Then and thereby the assailants of the government began the conflict of arms, without a gun in sight or in expectancy to return their fire, save only the few in the fort, sent to that harbor years before for their own protection, and still ready to give that protection in whatever was lawful. In this act, discarding all else, they have forced upon the country the distinct issue, 'immediate dissolution or blood.'

"And this issue embraces more than the fate of these United States. It presents to the whole family of man the question, whether a constitutional republic, or democracy—a government of the people by the same people— can or cannot maintain its territorial integrity against its own domestic foes. It presents the question, whether discontented individuals, too few in numbers to control administration according to organic law in any case, can always, upon the pretenses made in this case, or on any other pretenses, or arbitrarily, without any pretense, break up their government, and thus practically put an end to free government upon the earth. It forces us to ask: 'Is there, in all republics, this inherent and fatal weakness?' 'Must a government, of necessity, be too *strong* for the liberties of its own people, or too *weak* to maintain its own existence?'

"So viewing the issue, no choice was left but to call out the war power of the government ; and so to resist force employed for its destruction, by force for its preservation."

He closed with this appeal to the people:

"It was with the deepest regret that the Executive found the duty of employing the war power in defense of the government forced upon him. He could but perform this duty, or surrender the existence of the government. No compromise by public servants could in this case be a cure ; not that compromises are not often proper, but that no popular government can long survive a marked precedent that those who carry an election can only save the government from immediate destruction by giving up the main point upon which the people gave the election. The people themselves, and not their servants, can safely reverse their own deliberate decisions.

"As a private citizen, the Executive could not have consented that these institutions shall perish ; much less could he, in betrayal of so vast and so sacred a trust as these free people have confided to him. He felt that he had no moral right to shrink, or even to count the chances of his own life, in what might follow. In full view of his great responsibility, he has, so far, done what he has deemed his duty. You will now, according to your own judgment, perform yours. He sincerely hopes that your views and your action may so accord with his as to assure all faithful citizens who have been disturbed in their rights of a certain and speedy restoration to them, under the constitution and the laws.

"And having thus chosen our course, without guile and with pure purpose, let us renew our trust in God, and go forward without fear and with manly hearts."

Secretary Chase also submitted to Congress, on the first day of the session, a clear statement of the financial condition of the United States. He estimated the sum needed for the fiscal year ending June 30, 1862, at $318,519,581. He recommended a large increase of duties on imports, especially upon such articles as were then free from duty; also a direct tax of $20,-000,000, to be apportioned among the states according to population; also a tax on distilled spirits, ale, beer, tobacco, bank notes, and other articles of domestic production. He also suggested that the property of those engaged in insurrection or in giving aid and comfort to insurgents should be made to contribute to the expenditures made necessary by their criminal misconduct. As the receipts from taxation would still be inadequate to meet the expenses of the war, he discussed the best mode and form of borrowing money, including bonds running for a long period with a fixed rate of interest, and treasury notes bearing interest, payable on demand.

Kansas having recently been admitted into the Union, twenty-three states were represented in the Senate by forty-six Senators. Eleven states being in open war against the United States, twenty-one of their Senators withdrew, but Andrew Johnson, of Tennessee, denying the validity of the secession of his state, remained in the Senate, making the total of Senators forty-seven. Some of these Senators were new in congressional life, and some had been transferred from the House of Representatives. This transfer of a Member, though eagerly sought, is not for a time agreeable. However conspicuous the Member may have been in the House, he must take his place in the Senate at the bottom of the ladder, and, according to Senatorial usage, must be reasonably modest in expressing his opinions. The withdrawal of so many Senators in 1861, however, gave the new Members better positions than usual. I was assigned to the committee on finance and on naval affairs.

At that time the committee on finance had charge of all bills appropriating money for the support of the government, all tax or revenue bills, all loan and coinage bills, and, generally, all bills relating to the treasury department, and to the finances of the government. It was soon manifest that, in view of the war, and the enormous sums required to conduct it, the task of the committee would be a Herculean one, and that the labor required would fall chiefly on Mr. Fessenden, the chairman of the committee, and, I may with due modesty add, myself. My former position in the House of Representatives, as chairman of the committee of ways and means, and my personal association with Secretary Chase, with whom I was intimate, led to my taking an active part in financial legislation, which was considered my specialty. Congress, in substantial conformity with the recommendations of Secretary Chase, passed the act to authorize a loan which was approved July 17, 1861, providing for the issue of $250,000,000 of bonds running twenty years, bearing not exceeding seven per cent. interest, or treasury notes for not less than fifty dollars each, bearing interest at not less than seven and three-tenths per cent. annually, and payable in three years, and treasury notes of less denomination than fifty dollars, not bearing interest and not exceeding $50,000,000, payable on demand, and commonly known as demand notes. We knew that this act was entirely inadequate for the great struggle before us. The problem was not whether we could muster men, but whether we could raise money. We had to create a system of finance that would secure an enlarged revenue, unquestioned credit, absolute certainty of payment of interest in coin, a national currency, and such economy as is possible during war.

The first feeble attempt to create a national currency was the issue of demand notes under the act of July 17, 1861, described as follows:

"And the Secretary of the Treasury may also issue, in exchange for coin, and as part of the above loan, or may pay for salaries or other dues from the United States, treasury notes of a less denomination than fifty dollars, not bearing interest, but payable on demand by the assistant treasurer of the United States, at Philadelphia, New York or Boston."

The fatal defect of these notes was the promise to pay on demand. How could they be paid? In what kind of money? They could not be paid out of the current revenue, for that was insufficient to meet current expenses. No reserve was provided for their payment, and, when paid, there was no authority for their re-issue. All other forms of securities bore interest, and these notes, not bearing interest, were convertible into bonds and that was the end of them. If that was the process why issue them at all? They did not prevent, but rather expedited, the disappearance of gold. Of American silver dollars there were none. Even the new fractional silver coins rose to a premium, and were hoarded or exported. Still, the necessity existed for some form of paper money that would be available for circulation. The solution of this problem was properly left to the next regular session of Congress.

Congress did not act upon the recommendations for internal taxes, but this subject was also left over until the next session. It did provide, however, for a large increase of revenue from imports, mainly upon articles that were then free from taxation and upon articles regarded as luxuries; also for a direct tax on the states of $20,000,000, and for a graded tax, from and after the first day of January, 1862, upon the annual income of every person residing in the United States, from whatever source the income should be derived; if such annual income should exceed the sum of $800 a tax of three per cent. on its excess above that limit. A provision was made reducing the tax on incomes from treasury notes and other securities of the United States one-half. The tax on incomes of citizens of the United States residing abroad was placed at five per cent., except on that portion derived from interest on treasury notes and other securities of the United States, which was taxed one and one-half per cent.

While Congress was engaged in legislative duties in Washington, the military forces of the Confederate States were gathering in Virginia, with the principal force at Manassas, about twenty-five miles southwest of Washington, under the command of General Beauregard. The Union troops, composed mainly of three months' volunteers, were in camp occupying the region about Washington on both banks of the Potomac River, under the immediate command of General McDowell, but with Lieutenant General Scott in full command. I frequently visited the Union camps where the soldiers, fresh from civil life and confident of easy success over the "rebels," were being drilled. The cry was, "On to Richmond!" They could not foresee the magnitude of the task they had undertaken. I will not attempt to narrate the incidents of the Battle of Bull Run. I knew it was to be fought on Sunday, the 21st of July. Soon after noon of that day I mounted my horse, and with James Rollins, a Member of Congress from Missouri, called on General Scott, and inquired for news of the battle then going on. He told us he was quite sure of a favorable result, but feared the loss of his gallant officers as, the troops being raw, it would be necessary for their officers to lead them. We crossed the pontoon bridge from Georgetown, and then, passing by Arlington, we went to a new fort on the main road from the Long Bridge. As we approached we could hear the distant firing of cannon. We asked a sentinel on duty if he had heard the sound all day. He said, "Yes, but not so loud as now." This was significant but not encouraging. We returned to my lodgings on Fifteenth street. Everywhere there was an uneasy feeling. At eight o'clock in the evening I started for the residence of the Secretary of War to get information of the battle. As I approached I was seized by the arm, and, turning, saw Secretary Cameron. I asked about the battle, but, without answering, he hurried me into his house and said: "Our army is defeated, and my brother is killed." He then gave way to passionate grief. His brother, Colonel Cameron, had been killed, and the Union army was in full retreat. I was enjoined to say nothing until morning. I obeyed his injunction. At eleven o'clock that night I heard the clatter of a horse's feet in full gallop. My nephew, Robert McComb, a boy about nineteen, a private soldier in an Ohio regiment, but detailed as an orderly, had been sent to the rear with a message. He saw the army in retreat, and, being well mounted and believing that discretion was the better part of valor, rode rapidly to my lodgings in Washington. It is uncertain whether he or "Bull-Run" Russell, an English reporter, made the best time to the Long Bridge. McComb gave me a doleful account of the battle and retreat. The official reports from both armies show that it was a drawn battle. General Sherman, in his "Memoirs," gives a graphic history of the battle and expresses the same opinion.

Still, the battle of Bull Run was an important event. It dispelled the illusion of the people of the north as to the duration and gravity of the war. It demonstrated the folly of ninety days' enlistments. It brought also, to every intelligent mind, the dangers that would inevitably result from disunion. On the 22nd of July, the day after the battle, the bill to authorize the employment of 500,000 volunteers became a law.

On the 29th of July two bills, one for the increase of the military establishment of the United States, and one to provide for the suppression of the rebellion, were passed. On the 5th of August an act passed for the better organization of the military establishment. Armed with the largest military power ever conferred upon a President, with the almost unlimited power of taxation, the administration of Mr. Lincoln entered upon the task before it.

Having passed these provisions in aid of the government, the special session of Congress closed on the 6th of August, 1861.

I immediately returned to my home at Mansfield. Regiments were being organized but it seemed to me that the mode of enlistment was too slow. The people, though still resolute, were somewhat troubled by the failure of military operations. I felt this so strongly that I determined at once to adopt some plan to raise a brigade to be composed of two regiments of infantry, one battery of artillery and one squadron of cavalry. When I made application to Governor Dennison for the requisite authority, he feared my plan might interfere with existing organizations then being enlisted in the different parts of the state, and I was persuaded to wait until after the 15th regiment was recruited and in the field, and the 42nd was well under way. I also made up my mind to delay actual recruiting until after the election in October of that year, so that no political bias might enter into it.

On the 24th of September I addressed a letter to the Hon. Simon Cameron, Secretary of War, as follows:

MANSFIELD, OHIO, September 24, 1861.
HON. SIMON CAMERON, Secretary of War:

. DEAR SIR:—I respectfully ask for an order granting me leave to recruit and organize, in this part of Ohio, a brigade of two regiments of infantry, one squadron of cavalry, and two companies of artillery. I know I can do it promptly. The squadron of cavalry authorized to Major McLaughlin may, if desired, be considered as part of the brigade.

For reasons that are probably unjust the governor and state military authorities are less successful than I hoped, and I know that I can get you recruits that they cannot. I wish no rank, pay, or expenses for myself, and will freely act without compensation. I care not who are the field officers, so I know they are men of honor, honesty and experience. I will only ask of the department the usual rations, pay and armament and equipage for the men ; I ask nothing for myself, will undertake upon my individual responsibility to purchase any of them desired, receiving in return government securities therefor.

I will so execute the order as not to interfere with the state authorities, and will act in subordination to them. I will freely confer with the government as to details, but would rather be left as free as practicable in the selection of officers.

I hope, my dear sir, this application will receive your sanction, and I will stake my reputation and property that what I offer shall be accomplished. Very truly yours,

JOHN SHERMAN.

On the same day, in order to secure the active coöperation of Secretary Chase, I wrote him as follows:

MANSFIELD, OHIO, September 24, 1861.

HON. S. P. CHASE, Secretary of the Treasury:

MY DEAR SIR:—I have to-day written to General Cameron, asking an order allowing me to recruit a brigade in this part of Ohio. I know I can do it. I ask no office, rank, pay, or expenses for myself, and will undertake to recruit this force in subordination to the state and general government, and within such limits as may be allowed. Whatever may be the reason, it is manifest that voluntary enlistment needs the spur of active exertion and solicitation. This I am willing to give, and, from offers freely made to me by personal acquaintances, know that I can enlist hundreds whom the state authorities cannot reach.

Can I ask your favorable influence and coöperation? I will pay my own expenses, and ask only rations, tents and armament for the men. Any of these I am willing to purchase upon my individual credit, receiving in payment government securities. I pledge you my reputation and all I am worth to accomplish what I offer.

If it is objected that my operation will interfere with state enlistments, I will agree to subordinate my movements to the orders of the governor, but for the good of the service I hope to be left as free as possible. In the selection of officers I should want to be especially consulted, so as to insure the honor, probity and personal habits of such officers. Further than this I have no choice.

If this meets your approbation promptly say so to General Cameron, and let him set me to work. Very truly yours,

JOHN SHERMAN.

About the same time I had arranged with Governor Dennison for a plan of enlistment which enabled the recruits to select their officers, by allowing persons securing a certain number of recruits to be captains, a less number first lieutenants, and a less number second lieutenants. The governor very kindly agreed that he would commission the persons selected in this way, leaving the regimental organization to be composed of the best material that could be found anywhere. On the 28th of September I issued and distributed, mainly in the region near the line of the Pittsburg, Fort Wayne & Chicago railroad, this circular:

"TO THE YOUNG MEN OF OHIO.

"I am authorized by the governor of Ohio to raise at once two regiments of infantry and a battery of artillery, and a squadron of cavalry.

"I am also authorized to recommend one lieutenant for each company, who shall at once receive their commission and be furnished with proper facilities for enlisting. I am now ready to receive applications for such appointments, accompanied with evidence of good habits and character, the age of applicant, and his fitness and ability to recruit a company.

"Major Wm. McLaughlin will command the squadron of cavalry.

"The company officers will be designated by the soldiers of each company, subject to the approval of the governor.

"The field officers are not yet designated, but shall be men of experience, and, if possible, of military education.

"The soldiers shall have, without diminution, all they are entitled to by law.

"Danger is imminent. Promptness is indispensable. Let the people of Ohio now repay the debt which their fathers incurred to the gallant people of Kentucky for the defense of Ohio against the British and Indians. They now appeal to us for help against an invasion more unjustifiable and barbarous.

"Letters can be addressed to me, marked "Free," at Mansfield, Ohio.

JOHN SHERMAN."

MANSFIELD, OHIO, September 28, 1861.

The matter thus rested until after the election on the 9th of October, when squads rapidly formed into companies, and within twenty days Camp Buckingham was opened near Mansfield.

In the performance of this self-imposed duty, I encountered but one difficulty, and at one time a very serious one, the selection of regimental officers, and especially of commanders of regiments. I knew that military warfare was an art, a trade, an occupation, where education, experience and preparation are absolutely essential to effective service. The materials for soldiers abound everywhere, but without discipline, order, obedience, and severe drilling men are not soldiers. It was my desire to secure for the commanders of regiments two graduates of West Point. I made application directly to Washington for various details of officers of the regular army, so that the soldiers in Camp Buckingham might have experienced drill masters from the beginning. I failed to receive an answer,

and went to Washington, earnestly impressed with the importance of my mission, and determined, if possible, that these
men enlisted by me should not be placed in the front of the
enemy until they had had all the benefit they could derive
from military discipline and drilling. When I arrived I found
that Secretary Cameron was indisposed to interfere with the
purely military details of the army, while General Scott, a
brave old soldier whom I always loved and admired, was firmly
of the opinion that the favorable result of the war depended
upon strengthening the regular army, maintaining its force
and discipline, and especially retaining its valuable officers.
The regular army, almost disbanded at the beginning of the war,
was gradually filling up upon the basis of a new organization
and long enlistments, but it was idle, it seemed to me, to expect
that the young men of the country would enlist in the regular
service. While ready to respond to the call of their country
in its actual peril, they had no purpose to become regular soldiers for life. It appeared to me, therefore, that the manifest
policy of the government should be to allow the regular army
to be gradually absorbed into the volunteer service, where the
young officers educated at the expense of the government
might impart instruction to regiments and brigades, instead of
to squads and companies. I spoke to General Scott about this,
and the result of my interview was very unpleasant. I fear we
both lost our temper, though I never ceased to respect the old
general for the great service he had rendered his country; but
his day was past.

After consulting Major Garesche, Assistant Adjutant General,
as to the names of officers, I then applied to the President, explained to him fully the situation of affairs, my promise, the
gathering of the soldiers in Camp Buckingham, their inexperience, and want of drill masters, their ardent patriotism, stated
my interview with General Scott, and appealed to him to help
me out of the dilemma.

I never shall forget the interview with Mr. Lincoln, for he
did not hesitate, but sent for Major Garesche, and gave me the
coveted order before I left him, directing the Secretary of War
to detail two second lieutenants, James William Forsyth, of

Ohio, and Charles Garrison Harker, of New Jersey, and Sergeants Bradley and Sweet, of the regular army, for service in the Ohio Volunteers, under my direction. This order was the key that unlocked the difficulty and gave to the force the elements of military discipline. At the same time the requisite orders were given for uniforms, arms of the best pattern, cannon, horses and various equipments.

I then procured the detail of Major Robert S. Granger, of the United States army, to command the camp and to organize the force. He had graduated as a cadet from Ohio, was one of the officers of the regular army surrendered by General Twiggs to the State of Texas before the beginning of the war, and had given his parole not to serve in the army until exchanged. Though this was not held to apply to the enlistment of volunteers he so construed his parole as to prevent him from serving in his regiment until duly exchanged. When this was done he entered the service and was rapidly promoted to Major General of Volunteers.

Within sixty days 2,340 young men of Ohio were formed into the 64th and 65th regiments, the 6th battery of artillery, and McLaughlin's squadron of cavalry, armed with the best arms then in the service, uniformed, equipped and partly drilled as soldiers, ready to march, and actually marching, to the seat of war. No better material for soldiers, and no better soldiers in fact, ever enlisted in any cause or any service.

I insert a letter from General Garfield written when he was in command of this brigade:

HEADQUARTERS, 20TH BRIGADE,
IN THE FIELD, 6 MILES FROM CORINTH, MISS., MAY 17, 1862.
HON. JOHN SHERMAN, Washington, D. C.

DEAR SIR : — I am now in command of the 20th Brigade, composed of the 64th and 65th Ohio (the regiments raised by yourself) and the 13th Michigan and 51st Indiana Regiments. I have sent forward to Washington the name of Lt. D. G. Swain (65th Ohio) of Salem, O., for appointment as A. A. Gen. on my staff. He is an excellent officer, and his nomination has been approved by Gen. Buell. I will be particularly obliged to you if you will aid in securing his appointment as soon as possible. The whole army advances toward Corinth this morning.

Very respectfully yours,   J. A. GARFIELD,
Brig. Gen. Vols., U. S. A.

Head Quarters 20th Brigade
In the Field. 6 miles from Corinth Miss
May 17 1862

Hon John Sherman
Washington D. C.
        Dear Sir,
                I am now in command
of the 20th Brigade. composed of the 64th
and 65th Ohio (the regiments raised by yourself) and the 13th Mich. & 51st Indiana
Regiments I have sent forward to
Washington the name of Lt. D. G. Swaim
(65th Ohio) of Salem. O. for appointment as
A. A. Gen on my staff. He is an excellent
officer, and his nomination has been approved
by Gen Buell. I will be particularly
obliged to you if you will aid in
securing his appointment as soon as
possible — The whole army advances
toward Corinth this morning —
        Very Respectfully Yours,
                J. A Garfield
                    Brig Gen Vol U.S.A.

War Department,
November 14, 1861.

Sir:

Your letter of the 10th inst.
is received.

Gen. Sherman was re-
called from the command in
Kentucky during my absence at
the north, on official business.
Since my return, on the 11th, I have
not had time to make any inquiries
concerning the causes of the change;
but I feel certain that it was not
from any want of confidence in
the patriotism or capacity of your
brother who has been ordered to
Missouri, under the immediate

command of Major General Halleck
of the regular army, and the fact
that he has been re-assigned is
evidence of the confidence reposed in
him.

Very respectfully,
Your obt svt
Simon Cameron,
Secretary of War.

Hon. John Sherman,
Camp Buckingham,
Near Mansfield,
Ohio.

When General Sherman was in Louisville in October, 1861, he was called upon by Secretary Cameron, and they engaged in a general discussion of the military situation. General Sherman said that for aggressive movements, the United States would require 200,000 men. This was so far beyond the ideas of the time that he was regarded as crazy, and was soon after relieved from his command by General Buell. Secretary Cameron was blamed for this, but his letter to me, here inserted, shows that he was absent from Washington when the order was made:

WAR DEPARTMENT, Nov. 14, 1861.

SIR:—Your letter of the 10th inst. is received. General Sherman was recalled from the command in Kentucky during my absence at the north on official business. Since my return on the 11th, I have not had time to make any inquiries concerning the cause of the change, but I feel certain it was not from any want of confidence in the patriotism or capacity of your brother. He has been ordered to Missouri, under the immediate command of Major General Halleck, of the regular army, and the fact that he has been so assigned is evidence of the confidence reposed in him.

Very respectfully, your obedient servant,

SIMON CAMERON, Secretary of War.

CHAPTER XII.

PASSAGE OF THE LEGAL TENDER ACT IN 1862.

My Interview with Lincoln About Ohio Appointments — Governmental Expenses
Now Aggregating Nearly $2,000,000 Daily — Secretary Chase's Annual Report
to Congress in December, 1861 — Treasury Notes a Legal Tender in Payment of Public and Private Debts — Beneficial Results from the Passage of the Bill — The War Not a Question of Men but of Money —
Proposed Organization of National Banks — Bank Bills Not
Taxed — Local Banks and Their Absorption by the Government — The 1862 Issue of $150,000,000 in "Green-
backs" — Legal Tender Act a Turning Point in
Our Financial History — Compensation
of Officers of the Government.

ABOUT this time I had an interview with Mr. Lincoln
which may be of interest. In making the local appointments in Ohio he was naturally governed largely
by his strong affinities for old Whig associates in Congress, of one of whom, General Schenck, he was especially fond.
I thought some of his appointments in Ohio were not judicious,
and concluded I would go to him and make a general complaint of the distribution of these offices. I felt that he failed to
consider the fact that the Republican party contained many men
who had not belonged to the Whig party. I requested an interview with him which was promptly granted, and called at his
office one evening. He was seated in an easy chair and seemed
to be in excellent humor. I proceeded to complain of some of
his appointments in Ohio and as I progressed the expression of
his face gradually changed to one of extreme sadness. He did
not say a word, but sank in his chair, placing his feet upon the
table, and looking, as I thought, the picture of despair. I proceeded with my complaint until I began mentally to reproach
myself for bothering the President of the United States with
so unimportant a matter as the choice of persons to fill local
offices in Ohio, when the country was in the throes of revolution.

(268)

Finally I told him I felt ashamed to disturb him with such matters and would not bother him again with them. His face brightened, he sat up in his chair and his whole manner changed, until finally he almost embraced me. He then told me many interesting stories of his short service in Congress and of the men with whom he was brought in contact. The close of the interview was very pleasant and I kept my promise to him about his appointments.

When Congress convened on the 2nd of December, 1861, the financial condition of the government was more alarming than at any other period during the war.

The Secretary of the Treasury had ample and complete authority, given him by the act of July, 1861, to borrow money on the credit of the government, but he could not deal with the system of state banks then existing in the several states. He was forbidden, by the sub-treasury act of 1846, to receive notes of state banks and was required to receive into and pay from the treasury only the coin of the United States ; but by the act of August 5, 1861, he was permitted to deposit to the credit of the Treasurer of the United States, in such solvent speciepaying banks, as he might select, any of the moneys obtained from loans, the moneys thus deposited to be withdrawn only for transfer to the regularly authorized depositaries, or for the payment of public dues, including certain notes payable on demand, as he might deem expedient. He had, however, no authority to receive from individuals or banks any money but coin.

The coin received from the Boston, New York, and Philadelphia banks, in payment of their subscriptions to the government loans, to the amount of nearly $150,000,000, had to be sent to every point in the United States to meet public obligations, and, when thus scattered, was not readily returned to the banks, thus exhausting their resources and their ability to loan again.

The demand notes, authorized by the act of July 17, 1861, were also paid out by the treasury; but from time to time were presented for redemption in coin or in payment of customs duties to the exclusion of coin, and thus both the banks and the government were greatly crippled, the banks suspending specie payments on the 30th day of December, 1861.

At this time an army of 500,000 Union soldiers was in the field, and a powerful navy, with vast stores of artillery and ammunition, had been created. In providing for their sustenance, comfort and equipment the government had been obliged to incur expenses far exceeding in magnitude any which had been hitherto known in its history, aggregating nearly $2,000,000 per day.

It was apparent that a radical change in existing laws relating to our currency must be made, or the government would practically be unable to make the current disbursements on account of the war, and the destruction of the Union would be unavoidable, notwithstanding the immense resources of the country which had then hardly been touched.

The annual report of Secretary Chase reached Congress on the 10th of December, having been delayed by the press of business. So much of it as related to the currency was the basis of the long debates that followed. The circulation of the banks of the United States on the 1st of January, 1861, was reported at $202,000,767. Of this $152,000,000, in round numbers, was in the loyal states, including West Virginia, and $50,000,000 in the rebel states, the whole constituting a loan without interest from the people to the banks, costing the latter only the expense of issue and redemption and the interest on the specie kept on hand for the latter purpose. The secretary called especial attention to the organization and nature of these banks, and questioned whether a currency of banks issued by local institutions under state laws was not in fact prohibited by the national constitution. He said:

"Such emissions certainly fall within the spirit, if not within the letter, of the constitutional prohibition of the emission of 'bills of credit' by the states, and of the making by them of anything except gold and silver coin a legal tender in payment of debts. However this may be, it is too clear to be reasonably disputed that Congress, under its constitutional powers to lay taxes, to regulate commerce, and to regulate the value of coin, possesses ample authority to control the credit circulation which enters so largely into the transaction of commerce, and affects in so many ways the value of coin. In the judgment of the secretary, the time has arrived when Congress should exercise this authority."

He described with great force the weakness of the state banking system, and the repeated losses by the people of the United States on account of the failure of such banks. He recommended two plans by either of which he held that these banks might be absorbed, and a national currency be substituted in the place of their issues. One plan proposed the gradual withdrawal from circulation of the notes of private corporations, and the issue in their stead of United States notes, payable in coin on demand, in amounts sufficient for the useful ends of a representative currency. The other proposed a system of national banks authorized to issue notes for circulation under national direction, to be secured as to prompt convertibility into coin by the pledge of the United States bonds and other needful regulations. He discussed these two plans at length, but concluded by recommending a system of national banks, the advantages of which would be uniformity in currency, uniformity in security, an effectual safeguard against depreciation, and protection from losses from discounts and exchanges. He expressed the opinion that such notes would give to the government the further advantage of a large demand for government securities, of increased facilities for obtaining the loans required for the war, a reduction of interest, and a participation by the government in the profit of circulation without risking the perils of a great money monopoly. It will be noticed that the secretary nowhere suggested the suspension of coin payments, or making the notes a legal tender in payment of public and private debts, or the redemption in coin of the bank notes to be issued.

These recommendations were referred to the committee of ways and means of the House, and by it to a sub-committee, of which Elbridge G. Spaulding, of New York, was chairman. Undoubtedly we owe to him, more than to any other individual Member, the important and radical changes made in our currency system by the act reported by him to the House and amended in the Senate. Mr. Spaulding perceived the objection to the recommendations of Secretary Chase that they did not provide for any payments but in coin, or call for a suitable provision that the notes when issued should be a legal tender for public and private debts, or for their reissue in case of payment, nor did they provide for the absorption of the demand notes outstanding, which were, on their face, payable on demand, an obligation that could not be ignored without severely impairing the public credit. It was also apparent that the system of national banks proposed by the secretary could not be organized and put in effective force for a year or more, and that in the meantime the state banks would be in a condition of suspension, without coin or the possibility of obtaining it, and, with no effective money which the people were bound to receive, or which the government could receive, it would have been difficult to carry on the operations of the war.

The first bill introduced by Mr. Spaulding, on the 30th of December, met some of these difficulties. It provided for the issue of $50,000,000 treasury notes, payable on demand, the notes to be receivable for all debts and demands due to or by the United States, to be a legal tender in payment of all debts, public or private, within the United States, and exchangeable at their face value, the same as coin, at the treasury of the United States, and the offices of the assistant treasurers in New York, Boston, Philadelphia, St. Louis, and Cincinnati, for any of the coupon or registered bonds which the secretary was authorized to issue. It also contained this provision: " Such treasury notes may be reissued from time to time as the exigencies of the public service may require," the first authority ever given for the reissue of treasury notes after redemption.

On the 7th of January, 1862, Mr. Spaulding reported the bill to the House with some important changes, and it soon became the subject of a long and interesting debate. On the 22nd of January, Secretary Chase returned Mr. Spaulding's bill to him and suggested some modifications, referring to the legal tender clause as follows, being his first reference to that clause:

"Regretting exceedingly that it is found necessary to resort to the measure of making fundable notes of the United States a legal tender, but heartily desiring to coöperate with the committee in all measures to meet existing necessities in the most useful and least hurtful to the general interest, I remain," etc.

In a letter to the committee of ways and means, on the 29th of January, the secretary said:

"The condition of the treasury certainly needs immediate action on the subject of affording provision for the expenditures of the government, both expedient and necessary. The general provisions of the bill submitted to me seem to me well adapted to the end proposed. There are, however, some points which may, perhaps, be usefully amended.

"The provision making United States notes a legal tender has doubtless been well considered by the committee, and their conclusion needs no support from any observation of mine. I think it my duty, however, to say, that in respect to this provision my reflections have conducted me to the same conclusions they have reached. It is not unknown to them that I have felt, nor do I wish to conceal that I now feel, a great aversion to making anything but coin a legal tender in payment of debts. It has been my anxious wish to avoid the necessity of such legislation. It is, however, at present impossible, in consequence of the large expenditures entailed by the war, and the suspension of the banks, to procure sufficient coin for disbursements ; and it has, therefore, become indispensably necessary that we should resort to the issue of United States notes. . . . Such discrimination should, if possible, be prevented ; and the provision making the notes a legal tender, in a great measure at least, prevents it, by putting all citizens, in this respect, on the same level, both of rights and duties."

On the 3rd of February the secretary wrote to Mr. Spaulding as follows:

"Mr. Seward said to me on yesterday that you observed to him that my hesitation in coming up to the legal tender proposition embarrassed you, and I am very sorry to observe it, for my anxious wish is to support you in all respects.

"It is true that I came with reluctance to the conclusion that the legal tender clause is a necessity, but I came to it decidedly, and I support it earnestly. I do not hesitate when I have made up my mind, however much regret I may feel over the necessity of the conclusion to which I come."

On the 5th of February the secretary became more urgent, and wrote to Mr. Spaulding the following brief note:

My Dear Sir:—I make the above extract from a letter received from the collector of New York this morning. It is very important the bill should go through to-day, and through the Senate this week. The public exigencies do not admit of delay.   Yours truly,

Hon. E. G. Spaulding.   S. P. Chase.

It will thus be perceived that, whatever may have been the constitutional scruples of Secretary Chase in respect to the legal tender clause, he yielded to it under the pressure of necessity, and expressed no dissent from it until, as chief justice, his opinion was delivered in the case of Hepburn vs. Griswold, in the Supreme Court of the United States.

The bill, much modified from the original, passed the House of Representatives by the decided vote of yeas 93, nays 59. As it passed the House it contained authority to issue, on the credit of the United States, United States notes to the amount of $150,000,000, not bearing interest, payable to bearer at the treasury of the United States, at Washington or New York. It provided that $50,000,000 of said notes should be in lieu of the demand treasury notes authorized by the act of July 17, 1861, and that said demand notes should be taken up as rapidly as practicable. It provided that the treasury notes should be receivable in payment of all taxes, duties, imports, excise, debts and demands of all kinds due to the United States, and all debts and demands owing by the United States to individuals, corporations and associations within the United States, and should be lawful money and a legal tender, in payment of all debts, public and private, within the United States.

This bill came to the Senate on the 7th of February. It was followed on the same day by a letter from Secretary Chase to Mr. Fessenden, as follows:

SIR:—The condition of the treasury requires immediate legislative provision. What you said this morning leads me to think that the bill which passed the House yesterday will hardly be acted upon by the Senate this week. Until that bill shall receive the final action of Congress, it seems advisable to extend the provisions of the former acts, so as to allow the issue of at least $10,000,000 in United States notes, in addition to the $50,000,000 heretofore authorized. I transmit a bill framed with that object, which will, I trust, meet your approval and that of Congress. Immediate action on it is exceedingly desirable.

The request for authority to issue $10,000,000 additional demand notes was immediately granted, and the bill was passed without opposition.

The currency bill was considered in the committee on finance of the Senate, and four important and radical amendments were reported by that committee. These amendments were as follows :

First—That the legal tender notes should be receivable for all claims and demands against the United States, of every kind whatsoever, " *except for interest on bonds and notes, which shall be paid in coin.*"

Second—That the secretary might dispose of United States bonds, " at the market value thereof, for coin or treasury notes."

Third—A new section authorizing deposits in the sub-treasuries at five per cent., for not less than thirty days, to the amount of $25,000,000, for which certificates of deposit might be issued.

Fourth—An additional section, No. 5, " that all duties on imported goods and proceeds of the sale of public lands," etc., should be set apart to pay coin interest on the debt of the United States ; and one per cent. for a sinking fund, etc.

It was felt that if no provision was made for the payment of the interest on the bonds in coin, they would depreciate more and more, while such payment would tend, as it did, to maintain them nearer to the specie standard. In order to obtain coin for the payment of interest, provision was made that all duties on imported goods, and the proceeds of the sale of public lands, should be payable in coin and be set apart to pay coin interest on the debt of the United States, and one per cent. for a sinking fund to provide for ultimate redemption of the bonds. These amendments were considered of prime importance. It was felt that the duty on imported goods should not be lessened by any depreciation of our local currency. Such importations were based upon coin values, and the tax levied upon them was properly required to be paid in coin. This security of coin payment enabled the government to sell the bonds at a far higher rate than they would have commanded without it, and tended also to limit the depreciation of United States notes. The bill and amendments were reported on the 12th, and became the subject of what was regarded as a very able debate.

There was decided opposition in the Senate to the legal tender clause, headed by Mr. Fessenden. Mr. Collamer, who also was opposed to it, made a motion to strike it out. Upon that subject I made my first lengthy speech in the Senate, a few extracts from which I insert:

"The motion of the Senator from Vermont now for the first time presents to the Senate the only question upon which the members of the committee of finance had any material difference of opinion, and that is, whether the notes provided for in this bill shall be made a legal tender in payment of public and private debts. Upon this point I will commence the argument where the Senator from Maine left it.

"In the first place, I will say, every organ of financial opinion—if that is a correct expression—in this country agrees that there is such a necessity, in case we authorize the issue of demand notes. You commence with the Secretary of the Treasury, who has given this subject the most ample consideration. He declares, not only in his official communications here, but in his private intercourses with the members of the committee, that this clause is indispensably necessary to the security and negotiability of these demand notes. We all know from his antecedents, from his peculiar opinions, that he would probably be the last man among the leading politicians of our country to yield to the necessity of substituting paper money for coin. He has examined this question in all its length and breadth. He is in a position where he feels the necessity. He is a statesman of admitted ability, and distinguished in his high position. He informs us that, without this clause, to attempt to circulate as money the proposed amount of demand notes of the United States, will prove a fatal experiment.

"In addition to his opinion, we have the concurring opinion of the Chamber of Commerce of the city of New York. With almost entire unanimity they have passed a resolution on the subject, after full debate and consideration. That resolution has been read by your secretary. You have also the opinion of the committee of public safety of the city of New York, composed of distinguished gentlemen, nearly all of whom are good financiers, who agree fully in the same opinion. I may say the same in regard to the Chambers of Commerce of the city of Boston, of the city of Philadelphia, and of almost every recognized organ of financial opinion in this country. They have said to us, in the most solemn form, that this measure was indispensably necessary to maintain the credit of the government, and to keep these notes anywhere near par. In addition, we have the deliberate judgment and vote of the House of Representatives. After a full debate, in which the constitutionality, expediency and necessity of this measure were discussed, in which all the objections that have been made here, and many more, were urged, the House of Representatives, by a large vote, declared that it was necessary to issue United States notes, and that this clause was indispensable to their negotiation and credit. . . .

"A hard necessity presses the government. $100,000,000 is now due the army, and $250,000,000 more up to July first. The banks of New York, Boston and Philadelphia, have exhausted their capitals in making loans to the government. They have already tied up their capital in your bonds. Among others, Mr. Vail, the cashier of the Bank of Commerce, the largest bank corporation in the United States, and one that has done much to sustain the government, appeared before the finance committee, and stated explicitly that the Bank of Commerce, as well as other banks of New York, could aid the government no further, unless your proposed currency was stamped by, and invested with, the attributes of lawful money, which they could pay to others as well as receive themselves.

"Bonds cannot be sold except at a great sacrifice, because there is no money to buy them. As soon as the banks suspended, gold and silver ceased to circulate as money. You cannot sell your bonds for gold and silver, which is the only money that can now be received under the sub-treasury law. This currency made a legal tender was necessary to aid in making further loans. I insisted that the bill was constitutional. The Senator from Vermont has read extracts from the debates in the national convention, and from Story's "Commentaries," tending to show that Congress cannot authorize the issue of bills of credit. But I submit to him that this question has been settled by the practice of the government. We issued such bills during the War of 1812, during the war with Mexico, and at the recent session of Congress. We receive them now for our services ; we pay them to our soldiers and our creditors. These notes are payable to bearer; they pass from hand to hand as currency; they bear no interest. If the argument of that Senator is true, then all these notes are unauthorized. The Senator admits that when we owe a debt and cannot pay it, we can issue a note. But where does he find the power to issue a note in the constitution? Where does he find the power to prescribe the terms of the note, to make it transferable, receivable for public dues? He draws all these powers as incidents to the power to borrow money. According to his argument, when we pay a soldier a ten dollar demand bill, we borrow ten dollars from the soldier ; when I apply to the secretary of the Senate for a month's pay, I loan the United States $250. This certainly is not the view we take of it when we receive the money, On the other hand, we recognize the fact that the government cannot pay us in gold. We receive notes as money. The government ought to give, and has the power to give, to that money, all the sanction, authority, value, necessary and proper, to enable it to borrow money. The power to fix the standard of money, to regulate the medium of exchanges, must necessarily go with, and be incident to, the power to regulate commerce, to borrow money, to coin money, to maintain armies and navies. All these high powers are expressly prohibited to the states and also the incidental power to omit bills of credit, and to make anything but gold and silver a legal tender. But Congress is expressly invested with all these high powers, and, to remove all doubt, is expressly authorized to use all necessary and proper means to carry these powers into effect.

"If you strike out the legal tender clause you do so with a knowledge that these notes will fall dead upon the money market of the world. When you issue demand notes, and announce to the world your purpose not to pay any more gold and silver, you then tender to those who have furnished you provisions and services this paper money. What can they do? They cannot pay their debts with it; they cannot support their families with it, without a depreciation. The whole then depends on the promise of the government to pay at some time not fixed on the note. Justice to our creditors demands that it should be a legal tender; it will then circulate all over this country, and it will be the lifeblood of the whole business of the country, and it will enable capitalists to buy your bonds. The only objection to the measure is that too much may be issued. He did not believe the issue of $150,000,000 would do any harm. It is only a mere temporary expedient. . . .

"I have thus, Mr. president, endeavored to reply to the constitutional argument of the Senator from Vermont. Our arguments must be submitted finally to the arbitration of the courts of the United States. When I feel so strongly the necessity of this measure, I am constrained to assume the power, and refer our authority to exercise it to the courts. I have shown, in reply to the argument of the Senator from Maine, that we must no longer hesitate as to the necessity of this measure. That necessity does exist, and now presses upon us. I rest my vote upon the proposition that this is a necessary and proper measure to furnish a currency — a medium of exchange — to enable the government to borrow money, to maintain an army and support a navy. Believing this, I find ample authority to authorize my vote. We have been taught by recent fearful experience that delay and doubt in this time of revolutionary activity are stagnation and death. I have sworn to raise and support your armies; to provide for and maintain your navy; to borrow money; to uphold your government against all enemies, at home and abroad. That oath is sacred. As a Member of this body, I am armed with high powers for a holy purpose, and I am authorized — nay, required — to vote for all laws necessary and proper for executing these high powers, and to accomplish that purpose. This is not the time when I would limit these powers. Rather than yield to revolutionary force, I would use revolutionary force. Here it is not necessary, for the framers of the constitution did not assume to foresee all the means that might be necessary to maintain the delegated powers of the national government. Regarding this great measure as a necessary and proper one, and within our power to enact, I see plain before me the path of duty, and one that is easy to tread."

The motion to strike out the legal tender clause in the bill was defeated by a vote of yeas 17, nays 22. The amendments proposed by the finance committee were agreed to substantially as reported by the committee. The bill finally passed by a vote of yeas 30, nays 7. The House agreed to the amendment providing for the payment of the interest on bonds and notes in coin, and disagreed to the remaining amendments, and these were referred to a committee of conference, composed of Messrs. Fessenden, Sherman and Carlisle, of West Virginia, of the Senate, and Messrs. Stevens, Horton, and Sedgwick, of the House. The conference met, and, after two or three days of full discussion, the material parts of the disagreements between the two Houses were settled. The provision that coin only be received for duties on imports, and that it be held as a fund to pay the interest on the bonded debt, was retained. The report of the conference was agreed to by both Houses, and on the same day the bill was approved by the President. Thus, the legal tender act, after a most able and determined opposition, became a law on the 25th of February, 1862.

It would be difficult to measure the beneficial results that rapidly followed the passage of this bill. The public credit was greatly strengthened by the provision for the payment of interest in coin furnished by duties on imported goods. The legal tender clause was acquiesced in by all classes, and we had, for the first time, in circulation national paper money as the actual standard of value. ' It was silent as to time of its payment, but each note contained a promise of the United States to pay a specific sum, and the implied obligation was to pay in coin as soon as practicable.

On the 11th of July, 1862, a further issue of $150,000,000 United States treasury notes (or "greenbacks," as they were commonly called from their color) of the same description was authorized, and subsequent issues increased the total amount to $450,000,000, the extreme limit. By the act of March 31, 1863, fractional currency was authorized to an amount not exceeding $50,000,000, to take the place of fractional silver coins, which had entirely disappeared from circulation, and this amount was issued.

The passage of the legal tender act was the turning point of our physical and financial history. Less than a year before the government was bankrupt ; our bonds bearing six per cent. interest were sold at a discount; our national expenditures exceeded our receipts; loans could only be made upon the basis of coin, and this coin was disappearing from circulation. We

had to appeal to the patriotism of bankers to accept the demand notes of the United States as money, with no prospect of
being able to pay them. Our regular army was practically disbanded by the disloyalty of many of its leading officers. Washington was then practically in a state of siege, forcing me, in
May, 1861, to go there at the heels of the 7th regiment of New
York militia, avoiding the regular channels of travel. The
city of Baltimore was decked under the flag of rebellion.
Through the State of Maryland, loyal citizens passed in disguise, except by a single route opened and defended by military
power. The great State of Kentucky, important as well from
its central position as from the known prowess and courage of
its people, hung suspended in doubt between loyalty and secession. In the State of Missouri, St. Louis was the only place of
unquestioned loyalty, and even there we regarded it a fortunate prize that we were able to take the public arms from a
government arsenal. The whole State of Virginia, with the
single exception of Fortress Monroe, was in the possession of
the revolutionary force.

But from the passage of the legal tender act, by which
means were provided for utilizing the wealth of the country in
the suppression of the rebellion, the tide of war turned in our
favor. Delaware, after a short hesitation, complied with the
proclamation of the President. Maryland had, by clear and
repeated votes and acts, arrayed herself on the side of the
Union. Her rebellious sons who fought against the old flag
could not tread in safety on a single foot of the soil of that
state. Western Virginia, the eastern peninsula, and many ports
on the eastern coast, were securely reclaimed. The State of
Kentucky had distinctly, by the vote of her people, and by the
action of all her constituted authorities, proclaimed her loyalty, and her sons were fighting side by side with the soldiers
of other states to expel traitors who, in her days of doubt,
had seized upon a small portion of her soil, which they still
occupied. In the State of Missouri the constituted authorities,
organized by a convention of the people duly elected, were sustained by physical power in nearly all the state, and the rebellion there was subsiding into bands of thieves, bridge burners.

and small parties of guerrillas, who could soon be readily controlled by local militia. In nearly every rebellious state, the government had secured a foothold, and an army of half a million men, armed, organized and disciplined, impatiently awaited the word of command to advance the old banner of our country against every foe that stood in its way. Where does the history of nations present an example of greater physical weakness followed so soon by greater physical strength? When have results more wonderful been accomplished in eight months?

At the beginning of the year 1862 we were physically strong but financially weak. Therefore, I repeat, the problem of this contest was not as to whether we could muster men, but whether we could raise money. There was great wealth in the country but how could it be promptly utilized? To that question the diligent attention of Congress was applied. The banks which had aided us with money were crippled and had suspended coin payments. The Secretary of the Treasury was begging at the doors of both Houses for means to meet the most pressing demands. On the 15th of January, 1862, the London "Post," the organ of Lord Palmerston, said:

" The monetary intelligence from America is of the most important kind. National bankruptcy is not an agreeable prospect, but it is the only one presented by the existing state of American finance. What a strange tale does not the history of the United States for the past twelve months unfold? What a striking moral does it not point? Never before was the world dazzled by a career of more reckless extravagance. Never before did a flourishing and prosperous state make such gigantic strides towards effecting its own ruin."

The legal tender act, with its provision for coin receipts to pay interest on bonds, whatever may be said to the contrary by theorists, was the only measure that could have enabled the government to carry on successfully the vast operations of the war. Our annual expenditures at that time were four times the amount of our currency; were three times the aggregate coin of the country; were greater than any ever borne by any nation in ancient or in modern times. The highest expenditure of Great Britain during her war with Napoleon, at a time when her currency was inflated, when she made the Bank of England notes a legal tender, was but £100,000,000.

Anticipating these enormous expenditures I introduced a bill which became a law on the 31st of July, 1861, which provided for a commission to examine and report as to the compensation of all offices for the government, the commission to be composed of two Members of the Senate, three Members of the House of Representatives, one officer of the navy, and one officer of the army, who were directed to examine and report, as soon as practicable, a fair and just compensation for each officer of the government, and such regulations as would secure a more economical collection of the revenue. When this bill was pending I stated its purpose and my hope to accomplish a reduction of the expenditures of the government, or, at least, an equalization of the salaries then paid to the different officers. We sought economy by the reduction of expenses. I was chairman of this commission, and Senator Clark, of New Hampshire, was my associate. The commission collected a mass of information, and upon it based several bills introduced in the second session of the 37th Congress. Some of these were made nugatory by the rise of prices, measured in most cases by the fall in the value of our currency, but many of their provisions were ingrafted into other bills that became laws.

The organization of national banks, authorized to issue circulating notes, is so intimately connected with legal tender United States notes that I think it proper to consider them in connection, though the banking law did not pass until 1863. The two forms of currency, one issued directly by the government as lawful money of the United States and a legal tender, and the other issued by private corporations, but secured by bonds of the United States, constitute a system of national currency which, organized in the midst of war, was an important aid to the government in its great struggle, and when placed at par with coin by the resumption act has proven to be the best paper money created by legislation in this or any other country.

The issue of circulating notes by state banks had been the fruitful cause of loss, contention and bankruptcy, not only of the banks issuing them, but of all business men depending upon them for financial aid. Inflation and apparent prosperity were often followed by the closing of one bank and distrust of all others. The notes of a broken bank were rarely paid, the assets of such bank being generally applied to the payment of other liabilities, leaving the loss to fall on the holders of the notes, mostly innocent persons of limited means. This led to the adoption in 1846 of the sub-treasury system, by which all payments to the treasury were required to be in coin, to be held until required for disbursements on government account. This protected the United States, but it did not save the people from loss, as, from necessity, they were compelled to use bank bills authorized by the several states, varying in value and security, and chiefly limited in circulation to the state in which issued. With a narrow view of the powers of the national government, Congress had repeatedly refused to authorize a national bank, a policy I heartily approve, not from a doubt of the power of Congress to grant such a charter, but from the danger of intrusting so vast a power in a single corporation, with or without security. This objection did not lie against the organization of a system of national banks extending over the country, which required every dollar of notes issued to be secured by a larger amount of bonds of the United States, to be deposited in the treasury of the United States, thus saving the note holder from all possibility of loss.

Secretary Chase, in his report of December 9, 1861, recommended that a tax be imposed upon notes issued by state banks and also that Congress should exercise its authority to establish a system of national banks, with proper safeguards and limitations. A bill was introduced for the latter purpose in the House of Representatives in 1861, but, owing to the urgency for legislation on war measures, it was not acted upon.

CHAPTER XIII.

Abolishment of the State Banks.

Measures Introduced to Tax Them out of Existence — Arguments That Induced
Congress to Deprive Them of the Power to Issue Their Bills as Money—Bill
to Provide a National Currency — Why Congress Authorized an Issue of
$400,000,000, of United States Notes — Issue of 5-20 and 10-40
Bonds to Help to Carry on the War—High Rates of Interest Paid—Secretary Chase's Able Management of the
Public Debt —Our Internal Revenue System — Repeal of the Income Tax Law — My Views
on the Taxability of Incomes.

L ONG before I became a Member of Congress I had
carefully studied the banking laws of the several
states. The State of Ohio adopted, in 1846, an improved system of banking. My study and experience
as a lawyer in Ohio convinced me that the whole system of
state banks, however carefully guarded, was both unconstitu-
tional and inexpedient and that it ought to be overthrown.
When I entered Congress I was entirely prepared, not only to
tax the circulation of state banks, but to tax such banks out of
existence. But, while this feeling prevailed in the west, the
opposite feeling prevailed in the New England and Middle
States, where their banking system had been so improved that
bank failures were rare, and bank bills were protected by mutual guaranties.

The Secretary of the Treasury had, in two annual messages,
proposed a tax on the circulation of bank bills. He believed
that the existing bank circulation prevented or embarrassed the
process of funding, by which alone the bonds of the United
States could be absorbed. He was forbidden by law to receive
bank bills in exchange for bonds or for any purpose, so that the
current money of the people was not available for the purchase of bonds. This was an additional argument for taxing
the state banks out of existence. I introduced a measure for

(284)

this purpose as an amendment to the revenue bill, but it was postponed to save it from defeat.

I introduced a bill in January, 1863, containing two sections, the first to levy a tax of two per cent. per annum on the circulation of all bank bills, and the second to provide for a tax of ten per cent. on all fractional currency under one dollar issued by corporations or individuals. Upon this bill I made a carefully prepared speech, not only defending the proposed tax, but declaring my purpose to urge a gradual increase of the tax until all state bank bills were excluded from circulation. As the reversal of this policy is threatened I feel justified in briefly restating the argument that induced Congress to deprive all state banks of the power to issue their bills as money.

I drew the distinction between the ordinary powers of banking and the issue of bank bills. I said that the business of banking proper consisted in loaning money, discounting bills, facilitating exchanges of productions by the agency of commercial paper, and in receiving and disbursing the deposits of individuals. The issue of bank bills was an exclusive privilege conferred only on a few corporations. It was a privilege that an individual could not enjoy. No person could issue his bills in the form of paper money without a corporate franchise granted him and his associates, either by a general banking law, or by an act of incorporation. All the business of banking might be exercised by private individuals except this franchise. There was no reason why any one individual or a partnership might not carry on all the business incident to banking except this one of issuing bills to circulate as money. The largest banking houses in the world did not exercise the privilege of issuing bills. The strongest banks in the United States, such as the Bank of Commerce of New York, had but little or no circulation, while the weakest banks supported themselves and made profit by issuing the largest quantity of bills authorized. The law then existing taxed heavily the business of banking proper. All commercial paper—checks, drafts, orders, bills of exchange, protests, bonds—every instrument that was used in the ordinary process of banking—was heavily taxed, while bank bills were not taxed at all. A private banker doing business had to pay a license of $100, but a bank of circulation was expressly exempted from the necessity of procuring a license. The tax law, as it stood, had this significant provision: "But not to include incorporated banks legally authorized to issue notes as circulation." Every commercial instrument was required to pay a stamp tax, but this did not attach to a bank bill. Bank notes issued for circulation were expressly excepted. The only tax levied upon banks of circulation was a tax of three per cent. on the net income. This tax could be deducted from the dividend of the stockholders. This discrimination in favor of the banks of circulation ran through all the tax laws, while other corporations, such as railroad companies, insurance companies and the like, were subject to heavy taxes.

The profits of banking were then very great. The average profits of the banks of New York were twelve and one-half per cent. per annum. The burdens imposed upon the banks by their charters were lessened by the suspension of specie payments. When the banks had to keep in their vaults coin to the amount of one-third of their circulation, and were liable to be called upon any day for the redemption of their notes in gold and silver, they might claim exemption from taxes on their circulating notes. But during the suspension of coin payment there was no such liability. Whether right or wrong the banks suspended specie payments, and increased their currency without paying either principal of it or interest, or tax on it, though in direct violation of law in some states.

I referred in my speech to an interview which was sought by the bankers of our chief commercial cities with the Secretary of the Treasury, to which they invited the financial committees of the two Houses to hear their propositions for carrying on the financial operations of the government. We all went to the office of the Secretary of the Treasury, and the proposition was there made that the United States should issue no paper money whatever, that the specie clause, as it is called, of the sub-treasury act should be repealed, and that we should carry on the war upon the basis of the paper money of the banks, legalizing the suspension of specie payments, and that the government should issue no paper except upon an interest of six per cent., or higher if the money markets of the world demanded more. That was their plan of finance, the plan substantially adopted in the War of 1812, and which had been condemned by every statesman since that time, a plan of carrying on the operations of our government by an association of banks over which Congress had no control, and which could issue money without limit so far as national laws affected it. That was the scheme presented to us by very intelligent gentlemen engaged in the banking business. They were honest and in earnest, but it appeared to me as pretentious and even ludicrous.

It was claimed that a tax on banks interfered with vested rights. I said that all taxes that were levied by the government were to maintain vested rights, liberty and life. All these corporate franchises were held subject to the power of taxation in Congress, which was sometimes necessary to be exercised in the most potent manner in order to maintain the government. The states could not, by an act of incorporation, place their property beyond the power of Congress. The only question was what rate of taxation ought to be adopted. The rate proposed—two per cent.—I insisted was not too high, because it was only one-third of the profit derived from the issue of paper money without interest, the principal of which was not paid in coin. I stated distinctly that the purpose of the bill was not merely to levy a reasonable tax on banks, but also to induce them to withdraw their paper, in order to substitute for it a national currency. I then reviewed in considerable detail the history of our currency legislation, from the act chartering the first bank of the United States to the beginning of our Civil War, showing the view taken by the most eminent statesmen of our country in favor of the establishment of uniform national currency as the highest object of legislation. Mr. Madison said in his message :

"It is, however, essential to every modification of the finances that the benefits of a uniform national currency should be restored to the community. The absence of the precious metals will, it is believed, be a temporary evil;

but, until they can again be rendered the general medium of exchange, it devolves on the wisdom of Congress to provide a substitute which shall equally engage the confidence and accommodate the wants of the citizens throughout the Union."

I said that when coin, the best of currency, was driven out of circulation, by the existence of war or extraneous circumstances, it was the duty of Congress to provide a substitute. In 1816 Congress did this by establishing the Bank of the United States. Most of the state banks shortly afterward exploded, and almost their entire issue outstanding at the time fell as a loss to the people of the United States. The Bank of the United States did furnish for a while a stable currency. After its charter expired in 1836, the controversy was between gold and silver, and paper money as a currency. Nearly all the statesmen of that time believed it was necessary to have a national currency in some form, but there was a party in the country that believed the only true national currency was gold and silver coin. After a controversy that I would not review, the sub-treasury system was finally adopted. The government had then no occasion to borrow money. Its debt was paid off and there was a large surplus in the treasury, which was distributed among the states. The agency of a United States bank was no longer necessary to sustain the public credit. The object then was to secure a safe deposit and custody of the public revenues. The state banks failed to furnish a safe redeemable currency. In 1837 their notes were in the hands of the people, depreciated and dishonored, if not entirely worthless. Therefore, I thought wisely, the sub-treasury system was adopted, by which gold and silver coin was the only money received or paid out by the government. I believed that such was a true policy in the absence of national banks. I also stated that if peace were restored to our country, we ought, as soon as possible, to go back to the basis of gold and silver coin, but, in the meantime, we must meet the exigencies of the hour. Paper money was then a necessity. Gold and silver were hoarded. War always had led, and always would lead, to the hoarding of the precious metals. Gold and silver flee from a state of war. All nations in the midst of great wars have been compelled to resort to paper money. It was resorted to by our fathers during the Revolution. It was only by the use of paper money that England maintained her wars with Napoleon. At several periods during these wars gold and silver were at a greater premium in England than they were in this country.

I then proceeded to discuss the power of Congress to issue paper money. I quoted an extract from the report of Mr. Dallas, in December, 1815, in which he said:

"By the constitution of the United States, Congress is expressly vested with the power to coin money, to regulate the value of domestic and foreign coin in circulation, and (as a necessary implication from positive provisions) to emit bills of credit; while it is declared by the same instrument that 'no state shall coin money, or emit bills of credit.' The constitutional authority to emit bills of credit has also been exercised in a qualified and limited manner. . . .

"The constitutional and legal foundation of the monetary system of the United States is thus distinctly seen; and the power of the federal government to institute and regulate it, whether the circulating medium consist of coin or of bills of credit, must, in its general policy, as well as in the terms of its investment, be deemed an exclusive power."

These extracts from a document of great ability, state the whole question in a few words. Congress has the power to regulate commerce; Congress has the power to borrow money, which involves the power to emit bills of credit; Congress has the power to regulate the value of coin. These powers are exclusive. When, by the force of circumstances beyond our control, the national coin disappears, either because of war or of other circumstances, Congress alone must furnish the substitute. No state has the power to interfere with this exclusive authority in Congress to regulate the national currency, or, in other words, to provide a substitute for the national coin.

I next stated the objections to local banks. The first was the great number and diversity of bank charters. There were 1,642 banks in the United States, established by the laws of twenty-eight different states, and these laws were as diverse, I might say, as the human countenance. We had the state bank system with its branches. We had the independent system, sometimes secured by local bonds, sometimes by state bonds, sometimes by real estate, sometimes by a mixture of these. We had every diversity of the bank system in this country that has been devised by the wit of man, and all these banks had the power to issue paper money. With this multiplicity of banks, depending upon different organizations, it was impossible to have a uniform national currency, for its value was constantly affected by their issues. There was no common regulator; they were dependent on different systems. The clearing house system adopted in the city of New York applied only to that city. There was no check or control over these banks. There was a want of harmony and concert among them. Whenever a failure occurred, such as that of the Ohio Life Insurance and Trust Company, it operated like a panic in a disorganized army; all of the banks closed their doors at once and suspended specie payments.

Another objection to these local banks was that of their unequal distribution among the states. In New England the circulation of the banks was about $50,000,000, while in Ohio, a state with three-fourths of the population of all New England, it was but $9,000,000. The contrast, if made with other states, was still more marked. I called attention to the fact that the circulation of banks in the eastern states had then reached about $130,000,000, and of that amount, $40,000,000 was circulating in the west. If these notes were driven out of circulation and the United States notes substituted, a contribution would be made to the treasury of the United States of $2,400,-000 a year, for the mere interest of a currency which the west did not prefer, but was compelled to use.

I called attention to the loss to the people by counterfeiting, which could not be avoided when we had such a multitude of banks. It then required experts to detect counterfeits. It was impossible to prevent counterfeiting. An expert could save the banks, but the loss fell upon the people. By the substitution of national currency we substantially could lose nothing by counterfeiting. The notes would be few in kind, only three or four of them, all issued by the United States, all of a uniform character, that could not be counterfeited. I described,

with some detail, the loss to the people of the United States by
bills of broken banks, computed then to be equivalent to five
per cent. per annum of all the bills issued. On an average, every
twenty years the entire bank circulation ceased to exist or
deteriorated.

The loss of exchange from the west to the east on local currency was one per cent. This loss was usually made a gain to
themselves by the bankers and "shavers." Under the most
favorable state of trade between the east and west an exchange of one per cent. was demanded for drafts and bills of
exchange. With a national currency, uniform and equal
throughout the country, this cost for exchange would not exist
or would be greatly reduced. I called attention to the then
increasing volume of local currency in the United States.
When the United States had issued $250,000,000 of notes, the
banks had largely increased their circulation. This tended to
depreciate both United States and bank notes.

I discussed at similar length the proposition that, as the
states were forbidden by the constitution to authorize the issue
of bills of credit, they were equally forbidden to authorize corporations to issue circulating notes, which were bills of credit.
Upon this point it seemed to me that the authorities were absolutely conclusive. That position was taken by the most eminent members of the constitutional convention, by Joseph
Story in his "Commentaries," by Daniel Webster, and other
great leaders of both parties since that time. It was in reference to these bills that Mr. Webster used the language often
quoted:

"A disordered currency is one of the greatest of political evils. It undermines the virtues necessary for the support of the social system, and
encourages propensities distructive of its happiness. It wars against industry, frugality, and economy ; and it fosters the evil spirits of extravagance
and speculation. Of all the contrivances for cheating the laboring classes of
mankind, none has been more effectual than that which deludes them with
paper money. This is the most effectual of inventions to fertilize the rich
man's field by the sweat of the poor man's brow. Ordinary tyranny, oppression, excessive taxation, these bear lightly on the happiness of the mass of
the community, compared with a fraudulent currency, and the robberies committed by depreciated paper."

In speaking of the bank circulation then afloat in the country, he further said:

"It is further to be observed that the states cannot issue bills of credit; not that they cannot make them a legal tender, but that they cannot issue them at all. Is not this a clear indication of the intent of the constitution to restrain the states, as well from establishing a paper circulation as from interfering with the metallic circulation? Banks have been created by states with no capital whatever, their notes being put into circulation simply on the credit of the state or the state law. What are the issues of such banks but bills of credit issued by the state? I confess, Mr. president, that the more I reflect on this subject, the more clearly does my mind approach the conclusion that the creation of state banks, for the purpose and with the power of circulating paper, is not consistent with the grants and prohibitions of the constitution."

I insisted that if there was no money in this country but United States notes, the process of funding would be going on day by day. Whenever there was too great an accumulation of these notes they would be converted into bonds; the operation would go on quietly and silently. I quoted the authority of Secretary Chase that it was his deliberate judgment, after watching this process with all his conceded ability, that but for the influence of this local bank paper he would be able to carry on the war without the issue of more paper money, that the currency then outstanding and that which by law he was authorized to issue would be sufficient to carry it on. Such a currency would lead to the conversion of the notes into bonds, and by this process the people would absorb the national loan and enable him to carry on the government without any sacrifice to them.

It was not strange that Mr. Jefferson, near the close of the War of 1812, stated more clearly than I could do the conflict between local bank paper and United States notes. He, who during his whole life was so mindful of the rights of the states, and so jealous of paper money, in brief and terse language designated the only way in which our country could carry on war. In his letter to Mr. Cooper, dated September 10, 1814, just at the close of the war, he said:

"The banks have discontinued themselves. We are now without any medium, and necessity, as well as patriotism and confidence, will make us all eager to receive treasury notes, if founded on specific taxes.

" Congress may now borrow of the public, and without interest, all the money they may want, to the amount of a competent circulation, by merely issuing their own promissory notes of proper denominations for the larger purposes of circulation, but not for the small. Leave that door open for the entrance of metallic money. . . . Providence seems, indeed, by a special dispensation, to have put down for us, without a struggle, that very paper enemy which the interest of our citizens long since required ourselves to put down, at whatever risk.

" The work is done. The moment is pregnant with futurity, and if not seized at once by Congress, I know not on what shoal our bark is next to be stranded. The state legislatures should be immediately urged to relinquish the right of establishing banks of discount. Most of them will comply, on patriotic principles, under the convictions of the moment, and the non-complying may be crowded into concurrence by legitimate devices."

I also quoted another extract to show that this matter filled the mind of Mr. Jefferson. He said:

" Put down the banks, and if this country could not be carried through the longest war, against her most powerful enemy, without ever knowing the want of a dollar, without dependence on the traitorous classes of her citizens, without bearing hard on the resources of the people, or loading the public with an indefinite burthen of debt, I know nothing of my countrymen. Not by any novel project, not by any charlatanry, but by ordinary and well-experienced means ; by the total prohibition of all paper at all times, by reasonable taxes in war, aided by the necessary emissions of public paper of circulating size, this bottomed on special taxes, redeemable annually as this special tax comes in, and finally within a moderate period—even with the flood of private paper by which we were deluged—would the treasury have ventured its credit in bills of circulating size, as of five or ten dollars, etc., they would have been greedily received by the people in preference to bank paper."

On the 26th of January, 1863, I introduced in the Senate a bill to "provide a national currency, secured by a pledge of United States stocks, and for the circulation and redemption thereof." This bill took the usual course, was referred to the committee on finance, was reported favorably with a number of amendments, and was fully debated in the Senate. On the 9th of February, 1863, a cursory debate occurred between Mr. Collamer, of Vermont, and myself, which indicated a very strong opposition to the passage of the banking bill. Various amendments were proposed and some adopted. I became satisfied that if a strong effort was not made the bill would either be defeated or postponed. I, then, without preparation, made a long, and, as I think, a comprehensive, speech covering the general subject and its principal details. It was the only speech of considerable length that was made in favor of the bill in the Senate. There seemed to be a hesitancy in passing a measure so radical in its character and so destructive to the existing system of state banks.

I said the importance of the subject under consideration demanded a fuller statement than had as yet been made of the principle and object of the bill. It was the misfortune of war that we were compelled to act upon matters of grave importance without that mature deliberation that would be secured in peaceful times. The measure affected the property of every citizen of the United States, and yet our action for good or evil must be concluded within a few days or weeks of that session. We were to choose between a permanent system designed to establish a uniform national currency based upon the public credit, limited in amount, and guarded by all the restraints which the experience of men had proved necessary, and a system of paper money without limit as to amount, except for the growing necessities of war.

I narrated the history of the bill, of its introduction in December, 1861, its urgent recommendation by the Secretary of the Treasury in two annual reports, and the conditions that then demanded immediate action upon it. I stated the then financial condition of the country. Gold was at a premium of between fifty and sixty per cent. and was substantially banished from circulation. We were in the midst of war, when the necessities of the government required us to have large sums of money. We could not choose as to the mode in which we should get that money. If we pursued the ordinary course, the course that had been sufficient in times of peace to raise money, of putting our bonds into the market and selling them for what they would bring, it would be at a great sacrifice. We knew this from the history of other nations and from our own experience. We therefore must look for some system of finance that would give us all the aid possible, either in the form of paper money or by the agencies of associated banks. We knew very well that after the war was over the government would still be largely in need of money.

I then reviewed the various financial measures since the commencement of the war. We were then in the peculiar condition of a nation involved in war without any currency whatever which by law could be used in the ordinary transactions of the public business. Gold was withdrawn by the suspension of specie payments. The money of the banks could not be used because the laws of the United States forbade it, and we were without any currency whatever. Under these circumstances, Congress had authorized the issue of $400,000,-000 of United States notes. That this measure was wise but few would controvert. We were compelled, by a necessity as urgent as could be imposed upon any legislature, to issue these notes. To the extent to which they were issued they were useful; they were a loan by the public and without interest; they were eagerly sought by our people; they were taken by our enemies in the south, by our friends in the north; they were taken in the east and the west. They furnished the best substitute for gold and silver that could then be devised, and if we could limit United States notes to the amount then authorized by law they would form a suitable and valuable currency.

We had but four expedients from which to choose. First, to repeal the sub-treasury act and use the paper of local banks as a currency; second, to increase largely the issue of United States notes; third, to organize a system of national banking, and fourth, to sell the bonds of the United States in the open market. I discussed each of these expedients in considerable detail. The practical objection to the further issue of United States notes was that there was no mode of redemption; they were safe; they were of uniform value, but there was no mode pointed out by which they were to be redeemed. No one was bound to redeem them. They were receivable but not convertible. They were debts of the United States but could not be presented anywhere for redemption. No man could present them except for the purpose of funding them into the bonds of the United States. They were not convertible into coin. They lacked that essential element in currency.

Another objection was that they were made the basis of state bank issues. Under the operation of the act declaring United States notes to be a legal tender, the state bank circulation had increased from $120,000,000 to $167,000,000. The banks sold their gold at a large premium, and placed in their vaults United States notes with which to redeem their own notes. While the government had been issuing its paper money some of the banks were inflating the currency, by issuing paper money on the basis of United States money. Illustrations of this inflation were given of existing banks, showing enormous issues based upon a comparatively small amount of legal tender notes. The issue of United States notes by the government, and the making them a legal tender, was made the basis of an inflated bank circulation in the country, and there was no way to check this except by uniting the interest of the government, the banks, and the people, together, by one uniform common system.

I said that during war local banks were the natural enemies of a national currency. They were in the War of 1812. Whenever specie payment was suspended, the power to issue a bank note was the same as the power to coin money. The power granted to the Bank of France and the Bank of England to issue circulating notes was greatly abused during the period of war. It was a power that ought never to be exercised except by the government, and only when the state was in danger. It was the power to coin money, because when a bank issued its bill without the restraint of specie payments, it substantially coined money and false money. This was a privilege that no nation could safely surrender to individuals or banks. Upon this point I cited a number of authorities, not only in our own country, but in Europe. While I believed that no system of paper money should depend upon banks, I was far from objecting to their agency. They were useful and necessary mediums of exchange, indispensable in all commercial countries. The only power they derived from corporation not granted to all citizens was to issue notes as money, and this power was not necessary to their business or essential to their profit. Their business connected them with the currency, and whether it should be gold or paper they were deeply interested in its credit and value. Was it not then possible to preserve to the government the exclusive right to issue paper money, and yet not injuriously affect the local banks? This was the object of that bill.

But, it was asked, why look at all to the interest of the banks, why not directly issue the notes of the government, and thus save to the people the interest on the debt represented by the notes in circulation? The only answer to this was that history taught us that the public faith of a nation alone is not sufficient to maintain a paper currency. There must be a combination between the interests of private individuals and the government. Our revolutionary currency, continental money, depreciated until it became worthless. The assignats of France, issued during her revolutionary period, shared the same fate. Other European countries which relied upon government money alone had a similar experience. An excessive issue of paper money by the government would produce bankruptcy and repudiation, not only of the notes issued, but of bonds also. The government of the United States had in circulation nearly $400,000,000 United States notes. We had a bank circulation of $160,000,000. If we increased our circulation, as was then proposed, it would create an inflation that would evidently lead to the derangement of all business affairs in the country. Whatever might be the hazards, we had to check this over expansion and over issue. If a further issue of United States notes were authorized, it would be at once followed by the issue of more bank paper, and then we would have the wildest speculation. Hitherto the inflation had not extended to many articles. Real estate had not been much affected by it.

The question then occurred whether the bank bill proposed by the Secretary of the Treasury, and introduced by me into the Senate, would tend to secure a national currency beyond the danger of inflation. This, the principal question involved, was discussed at length. I contended that the notes issued would be convertible into United States notes while the war lasted, and afterwards into coin; that the currency would be uniform, of universal credit in every part of the United States, while the bank bills, which it would supersede, were current only in the states in which they were issued. It would furnish a market for our bonds by requiring them to be held as the security for bank notes, and thus advance the value of the bonds. The state bank bills would be withdrawn, and the state banks would be converted into national banks with severe restrictions as to the amount of notes issued, and these only issued to them by the general government upon ample security. The similarity of notes all over the United States would give them a wider circulation. I insisted that the passage of the bill would promote a sentiment of nationality.

The policy of this country ought to be to make everything national as far as possible. If we were dependent on the United States for a currency and a medium of exchange, we would have a broader and more prosperous nationality. The want of such nationality, I then declared, was one of the great evils of the times; and it was that principle of state rights, that bad sentiment that had elevated state authority above the great national authority, that had been the main instrument by which our government was sought to be overthrown. Another important advantage the banks would derive from this system, I urged, would be that their notes would be guarded against all frauds and all alterations. There would be but five or six kinds of notes in the United States, instead of the great diversity there was then. In 1862 the number of banks existing was 1,500, and the number whose notes were not counterfeited was 253. The number of kinds of "imitations" was 1,861. The number of kinds of "alterations" was 3,039. The number of kinds of "spurious" was 1,685. This was the kind of currency that was proposed to be superseded. Under the new system, the banks would be relieved from all this difficulty.

Other advantages to the banks would be that they might become depositories of the public money, that their notes, being amply secured, would be received in all payments due to or from the United States, while the notes of the state banks could not be so received, as they were dishonored and disgraced from the beginning, being refused by the national government.

This is an imperfect view of the question as it was then presented to my mind. I knew the vote upon the passage of the bill would be doubtful. The New England Senators, as a rule, voted for the bill, but Senators Collamer and Foote had taken decided grounds against it, and it was believed that Mr. Anthony and his colleague would do likewise. I informed Secretary Chase of my doubt as to the passage of the bill, and especially whether Mr. Anthony would vote for it; without his vote I did not think it would pass. Mr. Chase called at the Senate and had an interview with Mr. Anthony, in my presence, in which he urged him strongly, on national grounds, to vote for the bill, without regard to local interests in his own state. His remarks made an impression upon Mr. Anthony who finally exclaimed that he believed it to be his duty to vote for the bill, although it would be the end of his political career. When the vote was taken his name was the first recorded in favor of the bill. It passed by a vote of 23 yeas and 21 nays, so that I was entirely correct that if he had voted against the bill it would have been defeated by a tie vote.

These two measures, the absorption of the state banks, and the establishment of the system of national banks, taken in connection with the legal tender act, were the most important financial measures of the war, and, tested by time, have fully realized the anticipations and confident assurance of their authors.

This system of national banks has furnished to the people of the United States a currency combining the national faith with the private stock and private credit of individuals. They have a currency that is safe, uniform, and convertible. Not one dollar of the notes issued by national banks has been lost by any person through the failure of a bank. We have a currency limited in amount, restrained and governed by law, checked by the power of visitation and by the limitation of liabilities, safe, uniform, and convertible in every part of the country. Every one of these conditions prophesied by me has been literally realized.

Next in importance to a national currency was the problem of the public debt. The issue of $50,000,000, demand notes, authorized in 1861, was a forced expedient to meet immediate demands. A prudent man, engaged in business, would not borrow money payable on call unless he had securities which he could immediately convert into money. Such liabilities are proper in a stock exchange or in a gambling operation, to be settled by the receipt or payment of balances on the rise or fall in the market of stocks or produce. These demand notes gave Secretary Chase more trouble than any other security, and they were finally absorbed in the payment of customs duties.

On the 17th of July, 1861, Congress authorized the Secretary of the Treasury to borrow, on the credit of the United States, within twelve months, $250,000,000, for which he was authorized to issue bonds, coupon or registered, or treasury notes, the bonds to bear interest not exceeding seven per cent., payable semi-annually, irredeemable for twenty years. The treasury notes were to be of any denominations fixed by the Secretary of the Treasury, not less than fifty dollars, and to be payable three years after date, with interest at the rate of seven and three-tenths per cent. per annum, payable semi-annually. He was also authorized to issue, in exchange for coin, as a part of the loan of $250,000,000, treasury notes payable on demand, already referred to, or treasury notes bearing interest at the rate of three and sixty-five hundredths per cent. per annum, and payable in one year from date and exchangeable at any time for treasury notes of fifty dollars and upwards. These forms of security were the most burdensome that were issued by the government during the war. The terms of these securities were somewhat altered by the act approved August 5, 1861.

These laws were superseded by the act of February 28, 1862, which may be regarded as the most important loan law passed during the war. It authorized the Secretary of the Treasury to issue, on the credit of the United States, $150,000,000 of United States notes, commonly called greenbacks, already described. Of these, $50,000,000 were to be in lieu of the demand treasury notes authorized to be issued by the act of July, 1861, above referred to. It also authorized the Secretary of the Treasury to issue $500,000,000 of coupon, or registered, bonds, redeemable at the pleasure of the United States after five years, and payable twenty years from date, bearing interest at the rate of six per cent. per annum, payable semi-annually. These are what were known as the 5-20 bonds. In reference to these securities, Secretary Chase, in his report of December 4, 1862, said:

"These measures have worked well. Their results more than fulfilled the anticipations of the secretary. The rapid sale of the bonds, aided by the issue of United States notes, furnished the means necessary for the conduct of the war during that year."

On the 3rd of March, 1863, the Secretary of the Treasury was authorized to borrow, from time to time, on the credit of the United States, a sum not exceeding $300,000,000 for the current fiscal year, and $600,000,000 for the next fiscal year, payable in coin, at the pleasure of the government, after such periods as may be fixed by the secretary, not less than ten, or more than forty, years from date. These bonds, known as the 10-40's, bearing five per cent. interest, were exempt from taxation by or under state or municipal authority. This act also provided for the issue of a large increase of non-interest bearing treasury notes, which were made lawful money and a legal tender in payment of all debts, public or private, within the United States, except for duties on imported goods and interest on the public debt. Additional 10-40 bonds were authorized by the act of June 30, 1864. But it may be said that the 5-20 and 10-40 bonds became the well-known, recognized securities of the United States, the sale of which at par, in connection with the treasury notes of different forms, furnished the United States the money to carry on the war. In the sale of these securities the secretary was actively assisted by the banks and bankers of the United States, and especially by Jay Cooke, who was the most effective agent of the government in the sale of 5-20 bonds.

Secretary Chase, in his report of December 10, 1863, discussed at length the objects to be kept studiously in view in the creation of debt by negotiations of loans or otherwise: First, moderate interest; second, general distribution; third, future controllability; and, fourth, incidental utility.

The first loans were made upon the extravagant rate of interest of seven and three-tenths per cent. The reason for this was the fact that there was no currency the secretary could receive in exchange for bonds. As already stated, specie payments were suspended by the banks December 31, 1861. He was forbidden by law to receive bank bills, and he knew that Congress would not and ought not to repeal this law. After such suspension coin was scarce and difficult to obtain. Afterwards, when the legal tender notes were authorized and issued, he sold his bonds bearing six per cent. interest at par for notes, but these notes had already largely depreciated compared with coin. Still, they were money, readily taken for all supplies, and enabled him to sell securities running a shorter period. A diversity of securities maturing at different times were exchanged for notes, and finally he was able to sell five per cent. bonds at par, so that, on the 30th of September, 1863, two months previous to his report, securities and notes then outstanding amounted to $1,222,113,559. The first bonds were irredeemable for twenty years. The second bonds were redeemable in five, but payable in twenty, years. The third bonds, bearing five per cent. interest, were redeemable after ten years. It will be perceived that under this arrangement the rate of interest on securities issued was constantly reduced. The notes received in payment of bonds depreciated or advanced in sympathy with the progress of our armies and the prospects of success. The general purpose was to secure as low a rate of interest as possible, to distribute the securities among the largest number of persons possible, to provide the best mode, time and terms for redemption, and to put the securities in such form as to be used as a currency. No one can question the wisdom of the management of the public debt by Secretary Chase.

The origin and development of the present system of internal taxes must be interesting to every student of finance. The policy of the government had been to confine, as far as possible, national taxes to duties on imports, and, in ordinary times, this source of revenue, exclusively vested in the United States, together with the proceeds of the sale of public lands, was ample to defray the current expenses of the government.

During and shortly after the War of 1812 resort was had to direct taxes apportioned among the states respectively, and to internal taxes authorized by the constitution under the name of excises, but the necessities of the treasury becoming more urgent, and the reliance on the public credit becoming more hazardous, Congress, at the special session which convened in May, 1813, determined to lay the foundation of a system of internal revenue, selecting in particular those subjects of taxation which would be least burdensome. These taxes were at first limited to one year, but were extended from time to time, so that they acquired the name of "war taxes." A direct tax of $3,500,000 was laid upon the United States, and apportioned among the states respectively for the year 1814. Taxes were imposed on sugar refined in the United States, on carriages, on licenses to distillers of spirituous liquors, and other forms of internal production. It was estimated that the internal taxes and the direct tax would yield $3,500,000. For the fiscal year ending June 30, 1815, internal taxes yielded $5,963,000. In 1816 they yielded $4,396,000. In 1817 they yielded $2,676,000, after which there was no revenue from internal taxes except from the collection of arrears, amounting in 1818 to $947,946, the law providing for such taxes having expired by limitation. A comparison between the receipts from this source then and the receipts subsequently derived from internal revenue, is a significant indication of the difference in population and wealth between 1812 and 1862.

When the Civil War commenced and the necessity of a large increase of revenue became apparent, Secretary Chase, in his report to Congress of the date of July 4, 1861, called attention to the necessity of provision for a gradual increase in the revenue to maintain the public credit, and to meet the current demands. His recommendation as to internal taxes has already been referred to. The act of August 5, 1861, previously mentioned, levied a direct tax of $20,000,000 and an income tax. This act proved to be a crude and imperfect measure, and it was modified or superseded by the act of July 1, 1862. This act, carefully framed, was the basis of the present system of internal revenue. It created a new office in the treasury department, to be called the office of commissioner of internal revenue. No less than thirteen acts of Congress were passed prior to August 1, 1866, enlarging and defining the duties of the office, and prescribing the taxes imposed by these several laws. When this act was first framed we anticipated much greater difficulties in the collection of the tax than actually occurred. We had doubts whether the taxation imposed by this law would be patiently submitted to by our constituents, but these misgivings soon disappeared and the taxes imposed by that act were cheerfully and promptly paid. I gave to the study and consideration of this act, and the various amendatory acts, a large portion of my time. At the end of the war internal taxes were cheerfully paid by the people, and yielded far more revenue to the government than the customs duties and all other sources of revenue combined.

The receipts from internal revenue for the first four years under this law were as follows:

For the year ending June 30, 1863........... $37,640,787
For the year ending June 30, 1864........... 117,145,748
For the year ending June 30, 1865........... 211,129,529
For the year ending June 30, 1866........... 310,906,984

These taxes were mainly upon spirits, tobacco and beer, but they also included stamp taxes of various kinds, special taxes on particular industries, and income taxes, so that practically nearly all forms of domestic manufactures were subject to a greater or less tax, according to the nature of the article. So sweeping were the provisions that it was frequently a matter of joke as well as comment.

Some one remarked to Senator Collamer that everything was taxed except coffins. He rejoined: "Don't say that to Sherman or he will have them on the tax list before night!"

The general prosperity that existed during the war under such a burden of taxation was frequently a matter of surprise. The truth is that all productive industries were active because of the enormous demand made by the army for supplies of all kinds, and everyone who was willing to work could find plenty of employment. The depreciation of the currency caused by the war did not embarrass anyone, as the interest on securities was promptly paid in coin, and greenbacks were the favorite currency of the people. The people did not stop to inquire the causes of the nominal advance in prices ; they only knew that the United States note was cheerfully received in every part of the United States as the current money of the country. At the beginning the tax on whisky was 20 cents per gallon, but it was gradually increased until it reached $2 a gallon, when frauds and illicit distilling became serious evils. The tax was then reduced to 90 cents a gallon.

When I became Secretary of the Treasury, I was impressed with the magnitude of illicit distilling, even after the rate was reduced. At that time several hundred men, mostly in the mountain regions of North Carolina and Tennessee, were under arrest for violation of the laws against illicit distilling. A delegation of them, accompanied by Senator Ransom, appeared before me, and I heard their apologies for distilling, and their complaints against the officers. We entered into a formal engagement by which they agreed to stop illicit distilling upon condition that they should be relieved of punishment for their past acts, and, so far as I could learn, they substantially observed their obligation. As a rule, they were rough mountaineers who regarded whisky as a prime necessity of life, and thought they ought to be allowed to convert their grain into something better.

As the necessity for excessive taxation diminished after the war was over, taxes on various articles were gradually repealed, until, in 1894, they consisted of practically four items, spirits, tobacco, fermented liquors, and oleomargarine. These are the figures for two years :

Objects of Taxation.	Receipts during fiscal years ended June 30—	
	1893.	1894.
Spirits	$94,720,260.55	$85,259,252.25
Tobacco......................	31,889,711.74	28,617,898.62
Fermented Liquors..............	32,548,983.07	31,414,788.04
Oleomargarine	1,670,643.50	1,723,479.90

In respect to these taxes, that on oleomargarine was not intended as, nor is it, a very material revenue tax. The purpose was especially to prevent the fraudulent imitation of butter by using an extract of beef. The tax on spirits, tobacco and beer ought to be retained as the best objects of taxation either of domestic or imported goods. Neither of these is an article of necessity, but all are used purely to gratify an appetite, in many cases indulged to excess.

All civilized nations have come to regard these articles as the best subjects of taxation. To the extent that whisky is used as a beverage it is hurtful in its influence upon the individual and upon society at large. It is the cause of innumerable crimes, of poverty and distress in the family and home. Still, it is an appetite that will be gratified, however severe may be the laws against its use, and while this habit exists the tax upon whisky, by limiting the quantity consumed, is beneficial to society at large. It is true that alcohol, the base of whisky, is useful in the arts and in the preparation of medicines and vinegar. If some feasible plan could be prescribed by which alcohol or spirits thus used could be freed from tax, it would be right to exempt it, but no such plan has been found that includes security against frauds being practiced to evade the tax on whisky. The tax on tobacco and cigars is a moderate one, but the consumption of them is far less dangerous than of spirits in their influence upon society. The tax on the cheaper form of tobacco and cigars is comparatively small and does not add materially to the cost of tobacco in any of its forms. No complaint is made of it. Its consumption is so general that the tax is fairly distributed and falls mainly upon the richer classes, as the tax is increased in proportion to the value of the tobacco. Beer, a beverage of almost universal use, yields the large sum of $30,000,000 a year, at the rate of one dollar a barrel. This does not cause a preceptible increase of the cost to the consumer, but rather tends to maintain the good quality of beer by the surveillance of the officers of internal revenue. No general complaint has been made of this tax. All internal taxes are collected at less cost than any other form of taxation devised, and should be maintained as long as the expenses growing out of the war shall remain unpaid.

The patience and even cheerfulness with which the people of the United States submitted to this severe taxation on their domestic productions, was a matter of surprise, not only among our own people, but in European countries. In 1867, accompanied by Mr. Adams, our minister to England, I had the pleasure of breakfasting with Mr. Gladstone at his official residence, and he referred to the ease with which we collected, without complaint, taxes so burdensome as ours then were. He asked me if it was true that we collected $1,600,000 annually from a tax on matches. I told him that we not only did so but that I had never heard a word of complaint, and the quality of matches was vastly improved while their price was actually reduced. He threw up his hands and said that the people of England would not submit to such tax and if any ministry would propose it, it would soon be out of power. Strange to say an administration of which Mr. Gladstone was at the head did subsequently propose such a tax, but it was so severely arraigned that it was at once abandoned.

The income tax, varied somewhat in terms from year to year, continued in force until 1870, when it was proposed to repeal it as no longer necessary. By the terms of the then existing law it expired in 1872. I urged as strongly as I could its retention at least until the time expired, but it was repealed. I then believed, and now believe, that a moderate income tax, levied on all incomes above the sum of $1,000, or above a sum that will supply the ordinary wants of an average family in the United States with the necessaries of life, should be levied, to be suspended, increased or diminished, from year to year, according to the exigencies of the public service. In the present condition of affairs, I doubt the expediency of such a tax, especially in view of the decision of the Supreme Court of the United States recently rendered.

The distinction made by that court between incomes from rent of land and other incomes seems narrow and technical. A tax upon the value of land is a direct tax, and must be apportioned among the states according to population, but it does not follow that a tax on income from land is a direct tax. An income means that gain which results from business, or property, of any kind, from the proceeds of a farm, the profits derived from trade and commerce, and from any occupation or investment. In common language the word income applies to money received from any source. It may be qualified as gross income and net income. It may be limited by words defining the source of the income, as, from land, merchandise or banking, but, in its general sense, it means gross savings from all sources. When received in money it is an income and not until then. An income tax was paid, and cheerfully paid, by American citizens during and since the war, in vast sums, and it did not occur to citizen, lawyer or judge that the constitution of the United States made a distinction between incomes from rents and income from notes or bonds. The states tax both land and bonds. Why may not the United States tax income from each alike? Many of the largest incomes in the United States are derived from rents. To except them by technical reasoning from a general tax on incomes will tend to disparage the Supreme Court among "plain people." If incomes from rents must be excepted, then no income tax ought to be assessed. This decision, if adhered to, may cripple the government in times of emergency. If made when the income tax was first imposed, it would have reduced the national revenue $347,000,000, for no income tax would have been enacted if rents were excluded from taxable incomes.

I do not propose to narrate the numerous internal revenue laws, which have been enacted and modified at every session of Congress since 1861, or the innumerable objects of taxation embraced in them, for such a narrative would fill too much space. The discussion of these laws occupied a large portion of the time of Congress. The articles or productions subject to taxation included for a time nearly everything for the use of man. I trust the time is far distant when such sweeping internal taxation will be required again, but if it should come, the Congress of that day can find in our experience resources more bountiful than Aladdin's lamp.

Direct taxes, to be apportioned among the states, are not likely to be again assessed after the experience we had as to the last direct tax. Besides the difficulty of collecting it, there is the palpable objection that it is an unequal, and therefore an unjust, tax. New states, and especially agricultural states, have not the same ability to pay direct taxes as older commercial and manufacturing states, having within them great cities with accumulated wealth, in the form of stocks, bonds and patents.

The office of commissioner of internal revenue has fortunately been filled, as a rule, by gentlemen of standing and character of a high order of intelligence, and their work has been of a great service to the United States. This important bureau ought to be, and no doubt will be, retained as a part of the organized machinery of the government, and the taxes collected by it will be necessary as long as our public debt remains, and until the list of pensioners will be obliterated by the hand of time.

CHAPTER XIV.

LINCOLN'S EMANCIPATION PROCLAMATION.

ANOTHER question of grave political significance was presented to the 37th Congress early in this session, that of the abolition of slavery in the District of Columbia. I had from the beginning declared my opposition to any interference with slavery in the District, but the changed condition of the country demanded a change of public policy in this respect. Slavery was made the pretext for, and, I believe, was, the real cause of the war. It had a foothold in the District of Columbia, but it existed there in its mildest form. By the census of 1860 there were, in the District of Columbia, 11,107 free negroes, 3,181 slaves, and 60,785 white people. It was considered the paradise of free negroes, where they were almost exclusively employed as laborers in household service.

When the war broke out a considerable number of slaves ran away from disloyal masters in Virginia and Maryland, seeking safety within our lines and finding employment in the District of Columbia. As the war approached, most of the slaves in the District were carried away by their owners into Virginia, and other southern states, so that in 1862 it was estimated there were not more than 1,500, and probably not 1,000, slaves in the District, while the number of free negroes increased to 15,000. As a matter of course, when Virginia seceded no attempt was made to recapture runaway slaves from that state, and they became practically free. It was known that there was at that time a strong disposition in Maryland to try the experiment of emancipation, and it was believed that after the war was over Virginia would adopt the same policy. Little doubt was felt as to the power of Congress to abolish slavery in the District, should such a course be deemed expedient. By the constitution Congress was invested with express "power to exercise exclusive legislation, in all cases whatsoever, over such district as may, by cession of particular states, and the acceptance of Congress, become the seat of government of the United States." This power had been recognized by the most eminent statesmen of our country, and also by the Supreme Court of the United States. Until Mr. Calhoun doubted or denied the power it was not questioned by any considerable number. The real question was whether that was the time for emancipation. I endeavored to give to the subject careful consideration, and came to the conclusion that it was expedient then to emancipate the very few slaves in the District, fewer than there had been at any time within forty years, and fewer than would likely be in case the war should end. I believed also that the social influence of Washington, and the wealth and property controlled and owned in a great measure by slaveholding residents there, had been always against the government of the United States and in favor of the Rebellion. While slavery existed it was a constant source of annoyance and irritation. The great mass of our constituents were opposed to slavery, morally, socially and politically. They felt that it was wrong and would not change their opinion. As long as slavery existed in the District, where Congress had the power to abolish it, agitation and excitement would be ceaseless. The great body of the people of the northern states were opposed to the institution theoretically, as were very many of the most intelligent people of the southern states. I felt that now was the time when this moral conviction should be heard and heeded by the national legislature. I felt that we were bound to consult the material interest of the people of the District, and that emancipation would add to the value of their property and also add to the population of the city. The abolition of slavery would bring to the city intelligent mechanics and laboring men who would never compete with the labor of slaves, and who, finding none there but freemen, would develop the great advantages of the city. In a speech I made upon the subject I enlarged upon this consideration and said:

"I see no reason why Washington, with a free population and as a free city, situated here at the head of the Potomac, with remarkable facilities of navigation, with great conveniences of communication, reaching to the west by the Baltimore and Ohio Railroad, the political capital of the country, might not be a great free city, illustrating by its progress the operation of free institutions. But it can only be done by the active, interested labor of free people. Simply as a municipal regulation it would be wise to abolish slavery in this District, because slavery is opposed to the moral convictions of the great mass of the people of this country, and the existence of slavery here keeps out of this District an active, loyal, true, manly, generous body of laborers, who will never compete in their labor with the labor of slaves."

There was another reason why the experiment of emancipation could be best tried in the District of Columbia. Emancipation was evidently the ultimate end of this question. We had the power to try the experiment. It would be an example likely to be followed at the close of the war by many of the border states. I therefore made up my mind in favor of the measure, made a long speech for the bill and voted for it. It became a law on April 10, 1862.

At that early day, I believed that it was the duty of Congress to confiscate the slaves in the seceding states as the natural result of the war. These states had placed themselves in a position by rebellion where they had no constitutional rights which we were bound to observe. The war being open and flagrant to break up the Union, they were not entitled to the benefit of any stipulation made in their favor as states in the Union. I also favored the granting of aid to any policy of emancipation that might be adopted in the border states of Maryland, Kentucky and Missouri, but Congress was indisposed to extend the provisions of the then pending measure beyond the District of Columbia.

The President of the United States, on September 22, 1862, issued his proclamation containing the following declaration:

" That on the first day of January, in the year of our Lord one thousand eight hundred and sixty-three, all persons held as slaves within any state or designated part of a state, the people whereof shall be in rebellion against the United States, shall be then, thenceforward, and forever, free ; and the executive government of the United States, including the military and naval authority thereof, will recognize and maintain the freedom of such persons, and will do no act or acts to repress such persons, or any of them, in any efforts they may make for their actual freedom."

This was carried out in a subsequent proclamation of January 1, 1863, in which the President declares:

" And by virtue of the power and for the purpose aforesaid, I do order and declare that all persons held as slaves, within said designated states and parts of states, are, and henceforward shall be, free ; and that the executive government of the United States, including the military and naval authorities thereof, will recognize and maintain the freedom of said persons."

This was the beginning of the end of slavery.

In following the important financial measures of the 37th Congress, I have purposely passed by, in their order of time, other measures of vital interest that were acted upon in that Congress. The military measures adopted were on the same grand scale as the financial measures I have referred to. In 1861 the United States contained a population of 32,000,000 people, of whom about 10,000,000 were in the seceding states, some of whom were opposed to secession, but a greater number living in states that did not secede were in hearty sympathy with the rebellion. No preparation for war had been made in any of the loyal states, while in the disloyal states preparations had been made by the distribution of arms through the treachery of Secretary Floyd. When the seceding states organized a confederate government, the executive branch of the general government was under the management and control of those who favored the rebellion, or were so feeble or indifferent that they offered no resistance whatever to such organization. The President of the United States declared, in an executive message, that the general government had no power to coerce a state. On the accession of President Lincoln, the confederate government was better organized for resistance than the Union

was for coercion. When war actually commenced, the capital
at Washington was practically blockaded, and in the power of
the Confederates.

The response of the loyal states to the call of Lincoln was
perhaps the most remarkable uprising of a great people in the
history of mankind. Within a few days the road to Washing-
ington was opened, but the men who answered the call were
not soldiers, but citizens, badly armed, and without drill or discipline. The history of their rapid conversion into real soldiers, and of the measures adopted by Congress to organize, arm
and equip them, does not fall within my province. The battles
fought, the victories won, and the defeats suffered, have been
recorded in the hundred or more volumes of "The Records of
the Rebellion," published by the United States. The principal
events of the war have been told in the history of Abraham
Lincoln by Nicolay and Hay, and perhaps more graphically by
General Grant, General Sherman, General Sheridan, Alexander
H. Stephens, Fitz Hugh Lee, and many others who actively
participated in the war, and told what they saw and knew of it.

The military committees of the two Houses, under the
advice of accomplished officers, formulated the laws passed by
Congress for the enlistment, equipment and organization of
the Union armies. Henry Wilson, of Massachusetts, was chairman of the committee on military affairs of the Senate, and he
is entitled to much of the praise due for the numerous laws required to fit the Union citizen soldiers for military duty. His
position was a difficult one, but he filled it with hearty sympathy for the Union soldiers, and with a just regard for both
officers and men.

Among the numerous bills relating to the war, that which
became the act to suppress insurrection, to punish treason and
rebellion, and to seize and confiscate the property of rebels, excited the greatest interest, giving rise to a long debate. It was
founded on the faulty idea that a territorial war, existing between two distinct parts of the country, could be treated as an
insurrection. The law of nations treats such a war as a contest between two separate powers, to be governed by the laws
of war. Confiscation in such a war is not a measure to be

GENERAL W. T. SHERMAN.

applied to individuals in a revolting section, but if the revolt is subdued, the property of revolting citizens is subject to the will of the conqueror and to the law of conquest. The apparent object of the law referred to was to cripple the power of the Confederate States, by emancipating slaves held in them, whenever such states fell within the power of the federal army. This object was accomplished in a better and more comprehensive way by the proclamation of the President. The confiscation act had but little influence upon the result of the war, except that it gathered at the wake of our armies in the south a multitude of negroes called "contrabands," who willingly performed manual labor, but were often an incumbrance and had to be fed and protected.

The freedom of these " contrabands " was the result of the war, and not of the confiscation act. In the later period of the war, they, in common with free negroes from the north, were organized into regiments commanded by white men, and rendered valuable service to the Union cause.

When the confiscation bill was pending, on the 23rd of April, 1862, I made a speech in support of an amendment offered by me and in substance adopted. A few extracts of my speech will show my opinions on this subject:

"Confiscation is not only justified by the laws of war, by the practice of many nations, but it is practiced by our enemies in the most obnoxious way. They seize all kinds of property of loyal citizens; they destroy contracts; confiscate debts. All the property of citizens of loyal states which is within a disloyal state is seized without exception, and that whether such citizen has aided the government or not. They also seize the property of all citizens in disloyal states who will not commit an act of treason by aiding them. Yet they profess to be governed by a constitution similar to the constitution of the United States, so far as it relates to the rights of person and property. They draw the distinction between the laws of war and the laws of peace. . . .

"Sir, it is time there was an end of this. We are at war. We must destroy our enemies or they will destroy us. We must subdue their armies and we must confiscate their property. The only question with me is as to the best measure of confiscation. That some one should be enacted, and that speedily, is not only my conviction of duty, but it will be demanded by those who will have to bear the burdens of this war. Now, it is the interest of every citizen in a seceding state to be a rebel. If a patriot, his property is destroyed. If a rebel, his property is protected alike by friend and foe.

Now, the burdens of the war will fall, by heavy taxation, upon loyal citizens, but rebels are beyond our reach. How long can we conduct such a war? Sir, we have been moderate to excess. War is a horrible remedy, but when we are compelled to resort to it, we should make our enemies feel its severity as well as ourselves. . . .

"If too much is attempted in the way of confiscation, nothing will be accomplished. If nothing is confiscated, you array against you all who wish in a civil war merely to preserve their property and to remain quiet. This is always a large class in every community. If rebellion will secure their property from rebels and not endanger it to the government, they are rebels. Those whose position or character have secured them offices among the rebels can only be conquered by force. Is it not, therefore, possible to frame a bill which will punish the prominent actors in the rebellion, proclaim amnesty to the great mass of the citizens in the seceding states, and separate them from their leader? This, in my judgment, can be done by confining confiscation to classes of persons. The amendment I propose embraces five classes of persons."

The confiscation act was more useful as a declaration of policy than as an act to be enforced. It was denounced by Confederates and by timid men in the north, but the beneficial results it aimed at were accomplished, not by law, but by the proclamation of the President and by the armed forces of the United States.

The several acts providing for enrolling and calling out the national forces gave rise to much debate, partly upon sectional lines. The policy of drafting from the militia of the several states, the employment of substitutes and the payment of bounties, were contested and defended. I insisted that if a special fund for hiring substitutes was raised, it ought to be by a tax upon all wealthy citizens, and not confined to the man who was drafted. These and numerous questions of a similar character occupied much time, and created much feeling. It is now hardly worth while, in view of the results of the war, to revive old controversies. It is sufficient to say that all the laws passed to organize the national forces and call out the militia of the several states in case of emergency contributed to the success of the Union armies. I do not recall any example in history where a peaceful nation, ignorant of military discipline, becoming divided into hostile sections, developed such military power, courage and endurance as did the United

States and Confederate States in our Civil War. Vast armies were raised by voluntary enlistments, great battles were fought with fearful losses on both sides, and neither yielded until the Confederates had exhausted all their resources and surrendered to the Union armies without conditions, except such as were dictated by General Grant—to go home and be at peace.

During the entire war Washington was a military camp. Almost every regiment from the north on the way to the army in Virginia stopped for a time in Washington. This was especially the case in 1861. It was usual for every new regiment to march along Pennsylvania avenue to the White House. Among the early arrivals in the spring of 1861 was a regiment from New Hampshire, much better equipped than our western regiments. My colleague, Ben Wade, and I went to the White House to see this noted regiment pass in review before Mr. Lincoln. As the head of the line turned around the north wing of the treasury department and came in sight, the eyes of Wade fell upon a tall soldier, wearing a gaudy uniform, a very high hat, and a still higher cockade. He carried a baton, which he swung right and left, up and down, with all the authority of a field marshal. Wade, much excited, asked me, pointing to the soldier: "Who is that?" I told him I thought that was the drum major. "Well," he said, "if the people could see him they would make him a general." So little was then known of military array by the wisest among our Senators.

It was quite a habit of Senators and Members, during the war, to call at the camps of soldiers from their respective states. Secretary Chase often did this and several times I accompanied him. The "boys," as they preferred to be called, would gather around their visitors, and very soon some one would cry out "a speech, a speech," and an address would usually be made. I heard very good speeches made in this way, and, in some cases, replied to by a private soldier in a manner fully as effective as that of the visitor.

In the early period of the war the private soldier did not forget that he was as good as any man. One evening Major, afterwards Major-General, Robert S. Granger and I were strolling through "Camp Buckingham," near Mansfield, Ohio, and came to a young soldier boiling beans. He was about to take them off the fire when Granger said: "My good fellow, don't take off those beans; they are not done." The young soldier squared himself and with some insolence said: "Do you think I don't know how to boil beans?" Granger, with great kindness of manner, said: "If you had eaten boiled beans in the army as many years as I have you would know it is better to leave them in the pot all night with a slow fire." The manner of Granger was so kindly that the soldier thanked him and followed his advice. General Granger died at Zanesville, Ohio, April 25, 1894, after having been on the retired list for over twenty-one years. He was a gallant, as well as a skillful, officer. Peace to his memory.

It was my habit, while Congress was in session during the war, to ride on horseback over a region within ten miles of Washington, generally accompanied by some army officer. I became familiar with every lane and road, and especially with camps and hospitals. At that time it could be truly said that Washington and its environs was a great camp and hospital. The roads were generally very muddy or exceedingly dusty. The great army teams cut up and blocked the roads which were of either clay or sand, but the air was generally refreshing and the scenery charming. I do not know of any city that has more beautiful environs, with the broad Potomac at the head of tide water, the picturesque hills and valleys, the woodland interspersed with deciduous and evergreen trees, the wide landscape, extending to the Blue Ridge on the west, the low lands and ridges of Maryland and the hills about Mt. Vernon. The city of Washington, however, was then far from attractive. It was an overgrown village, with wide unpaved avenues and streets, with 61,000 inhabitants badly housed, hotels and boarding houses badly kept, and all depending more or less upon low salaries, and employment by the government. All this has been changed. The streets and avenues have been paved and extended. The old site is now well filled with comfortable mansions and business blocks, and a large portion of the District outside of the city is being occupied with villas and market gardens. The mode of living has greatly changed.

Before and during the war, Senators and Members lived in boarding houses in messes, formed of families of similar tastes and opinions. Society, if it may be so called, was chiefly official, of which justices of the Supreme Court and cabinet officers were the head, and Senators and Members of Congress were the most numerous guests.

When I entered Congress my pay as a Member was $8 a day during the session, and it was said we had "roast beef;" but we paid for it if we had it. At the close of the 34th Congress the compensation was increased to $3,000 a year. During the latter part of the war and afterwards, prices of food, board and lodging were considerably advanced.

In 1864 I offered the proprietor of Willard's Hotel my monthly pay of $250 for board and lodgings, in very modest quarters, for my wife and myself, but he demanded $300 a month. This led me to purchase a house in which to live, a change which I have never regretted. It was quite the fashion then for the old families, who were in full sympathy with the Confederates, to underrate property (even their own) in Washington, on the ground that when the Confederacy was acknowledged the capital would be removed, and real estate could, therefore, be obtained upon very reasonable terms.

After the war the feverish revival of business growing out of our expanded currency led to such reckless extravagance in improvements by public officials in Washington that for a time it threatened the bankruptcy of the city, but, as this leads me in advance of events, I will recur hereafter to the Washington of to-day.

During 1870 Congress passed a law increasing the compensation of Senators and Members from $3,000 to $5,000 a year, and justified this increase by the inflated prices of everything measured by a depreciated currency. There would have been but little complaint of this by the people had not the law been made retroactive. It was made to take effect at the beginning of that Congress, though when the law was passed Congress was nearly ended. This "back pay," amounting to over $3,000, was very unpopular, and led to the defeat of many Members who voted for it. At home they were called "salary grabbers." Several Senators and Members, I among the number, declined to receive the back pay. But it was said that the Congressmen could apply for it at any time in the future when the excitement died away. This led me to write Francis E. Spinner, Treasurer of the United States, to ascertain how I could cover into the treasury my back pay. His answer was characteristic, and is here inserted. Spinner, long since dead, was a peculiar character. He was with me in the House of Representatives, was appointed Treasurer of the United States by President Lincoln, and continued as such until 1875. He was a typical officer, bold, firm and honest. He was also a true friend, a model of fidelity and courage.

TREASURY OF THE UNITED STATES,
WASHINGTON, July 3, 1873.

MY DEAR SIR : — Your letter of the 28th ultimo has been received.

I sympathize with you most fully. I too have had my share of lies told on me, by Dana and his 'Sun', and shall be disappointed if the libels are not continued, especially if I do right. Really you have a white elephant on your hands. You can neither take the back pay, nor leave it where it is, nor draw it and redeposit it, without subjecting yourself to the yelping of the damned curs, that bark at the heels of every honest man.

If you will turn to the proviso to Section 5, of the General Appropriation Bill, approved July 12, 1870, at page 251, volume 16, of the Statutes at Large, you will, I think, be satisfied that your back pay would never lapse to the treasury. Should you leave it, as it now is, I think it would at all times be subject to your order, and to the order of your heirs afterwards. The department has decided that the appropriations for the pay of Members of Congress is *permanent*. The papers say that the Comptroller has decided that the back pay would lapse in two years. I called on him to-day, and he furnished me with a copy of his opinion, which is herewith inclosed you, and wrote me a note, a copy of which is also inclosed, in which he says— 'it could not be carried back until after two years ; whether it can be carried back is another question, which I do not intend to decide.' There are two ways that the amount can be carried back into the treasury : First, by drawing out the amount, and redepositing it ; and second, by directing the secretary of the senate, by written order, to turn the amount into the treasury. I, of course, can't advise you what to do.

Very respectfully yours,
F. E. SPINNER, Tr., U. S.

HON. JOHN SHERMAN, Mansfield, Ohio.

In the spring of 1863, the financial operations of the government were eminently successful. In the fall of 1862, Secretary

War Department
Washington City, D.C.
Sep _____ 1862

Dear Sir

The Generals letter is returned herewith having been read with much interest and great admiration of his wisdom and patriotism. If our armies were commanded by such Generals we could not fail to have a speedy restoration of the authority of the Government and an end of the War.

I beg you to give him my warmest regards and no effort of mine will be spared to secure to the government the fullest exercise of his abilities. With thanks for the favor I am

Yours truly
Edwin M Stanton

Hon John Sherman

Chase endeavored to sell the $500,000,000 5–20 six per cent. bonds, authorized by the act of February 25, 1862, through experienced officers in New York, and could not get par for them. He then employed Jay Cooke, of Philadelphia, to take charge of this loan, and within a year it was sold by him, to parties all over the country, at par. The entire cost of placing the loan was less than three-eighths of one per cent. It furnished the greater part of the means necessary to conduct the war during 1863.

The early victories of Grant at Forts Henry and Donelson had rescued Kentucky, and opened up the Cumberland and Tennessee Rivers to the heart of the south. The battle of Shiloh, though won at a great sacrifice, inspired the western army with confidence, and gave General Sherman his first opportunity to prove his ability as a soldier. The timid handling of that army by Halleck and its subsequent dispersion by his orders, and the general operations of both the armies of the west and in Virginia, created a feeling of despondency in the loyal states which was manifested in the elections in the fall of 1862. The military operations in the early part of 1863 did not tend to restore confidence.

At this period I received the following letter from Secretary Stanton, which evidenced his appreciation of General Sherman:

WASHINGTON, D. C., December 7, 1862.

HON. JOHN SHERMAN.

DEAR SIR:—The general's letter is returned herewith, having been read with much interest and great admiration of his wisdom and patriotism. If our armies were commanded by such generals we could not fail to have a speedy restoration of the authority of the government, and an end of the war.

I beg you to give him my warmest regards, and no effort of mine will be spared to secure to the government the fullest exercise of his abilities. With thanks for the favor, I am, Yours truly,

EDWIN M. STANTON.

The attack by General Sherman upon the defenses of Vicksburg had been repulsed, but the effect of this had been counteracted by the capture of Arkansas post with over 5,000 prisoners. General Grant had failed in his operations in Mississippi. General Hooker had been defeated at Chancellorsville, and Lee

was preparing to make an advance into Maryland and Pennsylvania.

On May 1, 1863, Clement L. Vallandigham, for several years
a Member of Congress from Ohio, in a speech made at Mount
Vernon, denounced the government with great violence, and,
especially, an order issued by General Ambrose E. Burnside,
commanding the department of the Ohio, announcing that "all
persons, found within our lines, who commit acts for the benefit
of the enemies of our country, will be tried as spies or traitors,
and if convicted will suffer death." Burnside enumerated
among the things which came within his order, the writing or
carrying of secret letters, passing the lines for treasonable purposes, recruiting for the Confederate service. He said : "The
habit of declaring sympathy for the enemy will not be allowed
in this department ; persons committing such offenses will
be at once arrested, with a view to being tried or sent beyond
our lines into the lines of their friends."

Vallandigham denounced this order as a base usurpation of
arbitrary power; said that he despised it, and spat upon it, and
trampled it under his foot. He denounced the President, and
advised the people to come up together at the ballot box and
hurl the tyrant from his throne. Many of his hearers wore the
distinctive badges of "copperheads" and "butternuts," and, amid
cheers which Vallandigham's speech elicited, was heard a shout
that Jeff. Davis was a gentleman, which was more than Lincoln was.

This speech was reported to General Burnside. Early on
the 4th of May a company of soldiers was sent to arrest Vallandigham, and the arrest was made. Arriving at Cincinnati,
he was consigned to the military prison and kept in close confinement. This event caused great excitement, not only in
Cincinnati, but throughout the State of Ohio. On the evening
of that day a great crowd assembled at Dayton, and several
hundred men moved, hooting and yelling, to the office of the
Republican newspaper, and sacked and then destroyed it by
fire. Vallandigham was tried by a military commission, which
promptly sentenced him to be placed in close confinement in
some fortress of the United States, to be designated by the

commanding officer of the department, there to be kept during the continuance of the war. Such an order was made by General Burnside, but it was subsequently modified by Mr. Lincoln, who commuted the sentence of Vallandigham, and directed that he be sent within the Confederate lines. This was done within a fortnight after the court-martial. Vallandigham was sent to Tennessee, and, on the 25th of May, was escorted by a small cavalry force to the Confederate lines near Murfreesboro, and delivered to an Alabama regiment.

Vallandigham made a formal protest that he was within the Confederate lines by force, and against his will, and that he surrendered as a prisoner of war. His arrest for words spoken, and not for acts done, created great excitement throughout Ohio and the country. A public meeting was held in New York on May 16, which denounced this action as illegal—as a step towards revolution. The Democratic leaders of Ohio assumed the same attitude, and made a vigorous protest to the President. It is not necessary to state this incident more fully. Nicolay and Hay, in their history of Lincoln, narrate fully the incidents connected with this arrest, and the disposition of Vallandigham. The letters of the President in reply to Governor Seymour, and to the meeting in Ohio, are among the most interesting productions of Mr. Lincoln. He doubted the legality of the arrest. He quoted the provision of the constitution that the privilege of the writ of habeas corpus "should not be suspended unless, in cases of invasion or rebellion, the public safety may require it." He had suspended the privileges of that writ upon the happening of contingencies stated in the constitution and, therefore, the commanding officer was justified in making the arrest, and he did not deem it proper to interfere with the order of the commanding officer.

This incident was made more important when, on the 11th of June, the Democratic convention of the State of Ohio met at Columbus and there formally nominated Vallandigham as the candidate of that party for Governor of Ohio. This presented directly to the people of that state the question of the legality and propriety of the arrest of Vallandigham. The Republican party subsequently met and nominated for governor

John Brough, a life-long Democrat, but in thorough sympathy with the Union cause.

It is difficult, now, to describe the intense excitement in Ohio over the issue thus made—at times breaking into violence. Vallandigham was received with great favor in the different cities of the south, and finally, embarking on board of a vessel which ran the blockade at Wilmington, he arrived at Bermuda on the 22nd of June, from which place he took passage to Canada, arriving at Niagara Falls about the middle of July.

The feeling of anger and excitement among the loyal people of Ohio increased, so that it was manifest that if Vallandigham entered the state he would be in great danger, and a quasi civil war might have arisen. I heard men of character and influence say distinctly that if Vallandigham came into the state he would be killed, and they, if necessary, would kill him. It was then understood that Mr. Lincoln was disposed to allow him to enter the state. Senator Wade and I met at Washington and had a conversation with Mr. Lincoln. We told him the condition of feeling in Ohio, and of our confident belief that if his order of banishment was revoked, it would result in riots and violence, in which Vallandigham would be the first victim. He gave us no positive assurance, but turned the conversation by saying that he thought Vallandigham was safer under British dominion, where he would have plenty of friends.

In June, 1863, my health was somewhat impaired, and Mrs. Sherman and I concluded to visit New England for a change of scene, and for the benefit of the ocean air. We visited Newport in advance of the season and found it deserted. We went to Boston, and there heard of the advance of Lee in Pennsylvania, and the fierce contest going on in the rear of Vicksburg. I became uneasy and started for home with the intention of proceeding to Vicksburg, but at Cleveland we heard the glad tidings of great joy, the fall of Vicksburg and the defeat of Lee at Gettysburg.

These victories, occurring on the same day, aroused the enthusiasm and confidence of the loyal people of the United States, especially the people of Ohio. Instead of a trip to Vicksburg I was soon enlisted in the political canvass, and

WILLIAM DENNISON,
BORN AT CINCINNATI, OHIO, NOV. 23, 1815.
DIED AT COLUMBUS, OHIO, JUNE 15, 1882.

DAVID TOD,
BORN AT YOUNGSTOWN, OHIO, FEB. 21, 1805.
DIED THERE NOV. 13, 1868.

JOHN BROUGH,
BORN AT MARIETTA, OHIO, IN 1811.
DIED AT CLEVELAND, OHIO, AUG. 29, 1865.

THREE OHIO GOVERNORS.

this for nearly three months occupied my attention. Meetings were held in every county and in almost every township of the state. All on either side who were accustomed to speak were actively engaged. My opening speech was made at Delaware on the 29th of July. I was intensely interested in the canvass, and therefore insert a few paragraphs from that speech, as an indication of the state of feeling existing at that time :

" The political campaign in Ohio this season presents some singular features. We are in the midst of a great civil war, in which it is safe to say that one million of men are now arrayed in arms against each other. There are, perhaps, now, from Ohio, one hundred thousand of her best and bravest citizens in the field, in hospitals or camps, sharing the burdens of war. The immediate stake involved is nothing less than national existence, while the ultimate stake involves nothing less than civil liberty for generations yet to come. In the midst of this contest the Democratic party, through its most eloquent orators, endeavor to make a personal issue. They propose to withdraw our armies, to abandon the war, and to try the question whether their candidate for governor has been legally convicted as a traitor to his country.

" We are assured by Mr. Pugh, the Democratic candidate for lieutenant governor, who is one of the most eloquent and able young men in the state, that here in Ohio we have been subjected to a tyranny as intolerable as that of King Bomba of Naples. When we ask for evidence of this tyranny, we are told that Clement L. Vallandigham has been illegally convicted and illegally banished ; and that if we are fit to be free we must stop and examine the record in his case, and not be turned from it by clamors about prosecuting the war, or of concluding peace. And we are told that if we don't do all this we are helpless slaves and deserve no better fate. Now, as I do not desire to be a slave, and do not wish the people of my native state to be slaves, I will so far depart from my usual course in political discussion as to examine the personal issue thus made.

" I had supposed, fellow-citizens, that nowhere in the wide world did people live as free from oppression as in the State of Ohio. But the Democratic party has sounded the alarm that our liberties were jeopardized in that Mr. Vallandigham has been, as they assert, illegally convicted and banished. Before alluding to matters of more general interest I propose to consider that question.

" The candidate of the Democratic party was convicted by a military tribunal for aiding the enemy with whom we are at war. For this he was expelled beyond our lines, and was within the lines of the enemy when nominated for governor of Ohio. By the judgment of a military tribunal, composed mainly of his political friends, approved by General Burnside, the chief military officer within the state, sanctioned by Judge Leavitt—a judge selected by Vallandigham himself—of the United States court, he was convicted and sentenced to imprisonment during the war. By the mercy of the President he was released from imprisonment and sent beyond our lines. While thus banished as a convicted traitor, by military authority, the Democratic party of the State of Ohio nominated this man as a candidate for governor, and you are called upon to ratify and confirm that nomination, to intrust this man, convicted as a traitor, with the chief command of our militia, the appointment of all its officers, and the management of the executive authority of the state ; and that, too, in the midst of a war with the rebels he was convicted of aiding. . . .

"And here is the marked distinction between the two parties. The Union party strikes only at the rebels. The Democratic party strikes only at the administration. The Union party insists upon the use of every means to put down the rebels. The Democratic party uses every means to put down the administration. I read what is.called the Democratic Platform, and I find nothing against the rebels who are in arms against the best government in the world ; but I find numerous accusations against the authorities of the government, who are struggling to put down the rebels. I find no kindly mention of the progress of our arms, no mention of victories achieved and difficulties overcome ; no mention of financial measures without a parallel in their success ; no promise of support, no word of encouragement to the constituted authorities ; no allowance made for human error ; not a single patriotic hope. It is a long string of whining, scolding accusations. It is dictated by the spirit of rebellion, and, before God, I believe it originated in the same malignant hate of the constituted authorities as has armed the public enemies. I appeal to you if that is the proper way to support your government in time of war. Is this the example set by Webster and Clay, and the great leaders of the Whig party when General Jackson throttled nullification ; or is it the example of the tories of the Revolution?"

Brough visited, I think, every county in the state. Everywhere his meetings were large and enthusiastic, but it must be said also that the Democratic meetings, which were equally numerous, were very largely attended. The people were evidently anxious to hear both sides.

Towards the close of the campaign I accompanied Mr. Brough through the populous central counties of the state. We spoke, among other places, in Newark, Zanesville and Lancaster. The meetings were not merely mass meetings, but they were so large that no human voice could reach all those present, and speeches were made from several stands in the open air, each surrounded by as many as could hear. This indication of public feeling was somewhat weakened by the fact that the Democratic meetings were also very large, and the ablest members of that party were actively engaged in the canvass. The "martyr" in Canada was the hero of these meetings, and his compulsory arrest and absence from the state, but near its border, was the constant theme of complaint. It was observed that the rival meetings were attended by men of both parties in nearly equal numbers, so that it was difficult to form an opinion of the result. Mr. Brough kept a memorandum book containing the names of the counties in the state and the estimated majorities for or against him in each county. At night, when the crowds dispersed, he would take out his book, and, upon the information received that day, would change the estimate of his majorities. In view of the enormous attendance at, and interest in, the Democratic meetings, he was constantly lowering his estimated majority on the home vote, until finally it declined to 5,000, with the army vote known to be very largely in his favor. At Lancaster, where he had lived and published a strong Democratic paper for many years, and where I was born, he carefully analyzed his list, and, throwing his book upon the table, emphatically said that he would not reduce his majority of the home vote one vote below 5,000. The Democratic party, however, seemed confident of Vallandigham's election. The result was that Brough was elected by the unprecedented majority of 101,000, of which 62,000 was on the home vote and 39,000 on the vote of the soldiers in the field, they having the privilege of voting.

This settled once for all the position of Ohio, not only on the question of the war, but on the determination of its people to support Mr. Lincoln in the use of all the powers granted by the constitution as construed by him, and to prosecute the war to final success. Vallandigham remained in Canada until June, 1864, when he returned quietly to Ohio, where he was permitted to remain. His presence injured his party. His appearance in the national convention in Chicago in 1864, and active participation in its proceedings, and his support of General McClellan, greatly, I think, diminished the chances of the Democratic ticket. He died seven years later by an accidental wound inflicted by himself.

I have always regarded Brough's election in Ohio upon the issue distinctly made, not only as to the prosecution of the war, but in support of the most vigorous measures to conduct it, as having an important influence in favor of the Union cause equal to that of any battle of the war. The results of all the elections in the several states in 1863 were decidedly victories for the Union cause, and especially in New York, Pennsylvania, Ohio and Maryland.

CHAPTER XV.

A MEMORABLE SESSION OF CONGRESS.

Dark Period of the War — Effect of the President's Proclamation — Revenue Bill
Enacted Increasing Internal Taxes and Adding Many New Objects of Taxa-
tion — Additional Bonds Issued — General Prosperity in the North Following
the Passage of New Financial Measures — Aid for the Union Pacific
Railroad Company — Land Grants to the Northern Pacific — 13th
Amendment to the Constitution — Resignation of Secretary
Chase — Anecdote of Governor Tod of Ohio — Nomination of
William P. Fessenden to Succeed Chase — The Latter
Made Chief Justice — Lincoln's Second Nomination —
Effect of Vallandigham's Resolution — General
Sherman's March to the Sea — Second
Session of the 38th Congress.

THE 38th Congress met on the 7th of December, 1863. The Members of the House of Representatives were elected in the fall of 1862, perhaps the darkest period of the war for the Union cause. The utter failure of McClellan's campaign in Virginia, the defeat of Pope at the second battle of Bull Run, the jealousies then developed among the chief officers of the Union army, the restoration of McClellan to his command, the golden opportunity lost by him at Antietam, the second removal of McClellan from command, the slow movement of Halleck on Corinth, the escape of Beauregard, the scattering of Halleck's magnificent army, the practical exclusion of Grant and his command, and the chasing of Bragg and Buell through Kentucky — these, and other discouraging events, created a doubt in the public mind whether the Union could be restored. It became known during the happening of these events that Mr. Lincoln had determined upon the emancipation of slaves in states in rebellion by an executive act. He said to the artist, F. B. Carpenter:

"It had got to be midsummer, 1862; things had gone on from bad to worse, until I felt that we had reached the end of our rope on the plan of operations we had been pursuing ; that we had about played our last card,

(329)

and must change our tactics, or lose the game. I now determined upon the adoption of the emancipation policy; and without consultation with, or the knowledge of, the cabinet, I prepared the original draft of the proclamation."

Of the cabinet, Blair deprecated this policy on the ground that it would cost the administration the fall elections. Chase doubted the success of the measure and suggested another plan of emancipation, but said that he regarded this as so much better than inaction on the subject that he would give it his entire support. Seward questioned the expediency of the issue of the proclamation at that juncture. The depression of the public mind consequent upon repeated reverses was so great that he feared the effect of so important a step.

In consequence of this opposition, the proclamation was postponed. On the 22nd of September, the President, having fully made up his mind, announced to the cabinet his purpose to issue the proclamation already quoted. What he did, he said, was after full deliberation and under a heavy and solemn sense of responsibility.

The effect of this proclamation upon the pending elections in Ohio was very injurious. I was then actively engaged in the canvass and noticed that when I expressed my approbation of the proclamation, it was met with coldness and silence. This was especially so at Zanesville. The result was the election in Ohio of a majority of Democratic Members of Congress. This, following the overwhelming Republican victory in 1861, when Tod was elected governor by a majority of 55,203, was a revolution which could only be ascribed to the events of the war and to the issue of the proclamation. It may be also partially ascribed to the discontent growing out of the appointments, by Governor Tod, of officers in the volunteers. The same discontent defeated the renomination of Governor Dennison in 1861. Such is the usual result of the power of appointment, however prudently exercised.

The House of Representatives was promptly organized on the 7th of December, 1863, by the election of Schuyler Colfax as speaker. The session of Congress that followed was perhaps the busiest and most important one in the history of our government. The number of measures to be considered, the gravity of the subject-matter, and the condition of the country, demanded and received the most careful attention. The acts relating to the organization of the army and the one increasing the pay of soldiers, made imperative by the depreciation of our currency, as well as the draft and conscription laws, received prompt attention. The enrollment act, approved February 24, 1864, proved to be the most effective measure to increase and strengthen the army. The bounty laws were continued and the amount to be paid enlarged. The laws relating to loans, currency, customs duties and internal taxes required more time and occupied a great portion of the session. The revenue bill enacted at that session was far more comprehensive and the rates much higher than in any previous or subsequent law.. It provided for an increase of all internal taxes contained in previous laws, and added many new objects of taxation, so as to embrace nearly every source of revenue provided for by American or English laws, including stamp duties upon deeds, conveyances, legal documents of all kinds, certificates, receipts, medicines and preparations of perfumery, cosmetics, photographs, matches, cards, and indeed every instrument or article to which a stamp could be attached. It also provided for taxes on the succession to real estate, legacies, distributive shares of personal property, and a tax of from five to ten per cent. on all incomes above $600, upon all employments, upon all carriages, yachts, upon slaughtered cattle, swine and sheep, upon express companies, insurance companies, telegraph companies, theaters, operas, circuses, museums and lotteries, upon all banks and bankers, brokers, and upon almost every article of domestic production. It placed a heavy tax upon licenses, upon dealers in spirits, upon brokers, lottery-ticket dealers and almost every employment of life.

It largely increased the tax on spirits, ale, beer, porter, and tobacco in every form. Not content with this, on the last day of the session, Congress levied a special income tax of five per cent., to provide for the bounties promised to Union soldiers. This drastic bill occupied the attention of both Houses during a considerable portion of the session, and became a law only on the 30th of June, 1864, within four days of the close of the session. It was greatly feared that the law would create discontent, but it was received with favor by the people, few if any complaints being made of the heavy burden it imposed. The customs duties were carefully revised, not in the interest of protection but solely for revenue. Nearly all the articles formerly on the free list were made dutiable, and they proved to be copious sources of revenue, especially the duties on tea, coffee, spirits of all kinds, wines, cigars, and tobacco in every form.

During that session Congress passed two important loan bills, which practically confided to the Secretary of the Treasury the power to borrow money in almost any form that could be devised. The first act, approved March 3, 1864, authorized him to borrow, on the credit of the United States, $200,000,000 during the current fiscal year, redeemable after any period not less than five years, and payable at any period not more than forty years from date, in coin, and bearing interest at six per cent. per annum. It also provided for the issue of $11,000,000 5-20 bonds which had been sold in excess of the $500,000,000 authorized by law. By the act approved June 30, 1864, the Secretary of the Treasury was authorized to borrow, on the credit of the United States, $400,000,000, on bonds redeemable at the pleasure of the United States after a period of not less than five, nor more than forty, years from date, bearing an annual interest of not exceeding six per cent., payable semi-annually in coin. He was authorized to receive for such bonds lawful money of the United States, or, at his discretion, treasury notes, certificates of indebtedness or certificates of deposit, issued under any act of Congress. These bonds were similar in general description to the 5-20 bonds already provided for, but bore interest at five per cent. instead of six.

By these measures the people of the United States had placed in the power of the government almost unlimited sources of revenue, and all necessary expedients for borrowing. Strange as it may appear, under the operation of these laws the country was very prosperous. All forms of industry hitherto conducted, and many others, were in healthy operation.

Labor was in great demand and fully occupied. This will account for the passage of several laws that would not be justified except in an emergency like the one then existing. Among these was an act to encourage immigration, approved July 4, 1864. This act grew out of the great demand for labor caused by the absence of so many men in the army. A commission of immigration was provided. Immigrants were authorized to pledge their wages, for a term not exceeding twelve months, to repay the expense of their immigration. These contracts were declared to be valid in law and might be enforced in the courts of the United States or of the several states and territories. It provided that no immigrant should be compulsorily enrolled for military service during the existing insurrection, unless such immigrant voluntarily renounced, under oath, his allegiance to the country of his birth, and declared his intention to become a citizen of the United States. This law could only be justified by the condition of affairs then existing.

Another law, alike indefensible, but considered important at the time, regulating the sale of gold, was approved June 17, 1864. It declared unlawful a contract for the purchase or sale and delivery of any gold coin or bullion, to be delivered on any day subsequent to the making of the contract. It also forbade the purchase or sale and delivery of foreign exchange, to be delivered at any time beyond ten days subsequent to the making of such contract, or the making of any contract for the sale and delivery of any gold coin or bullion, of which the person making such contract was not at the time of making it in actual possession. It also declared it to be unlawful to make any loans of money or currency to be repaid in coin or bullion or to make any loan of coin or bullion to be repaid in currency. All these provisions were made to prevent what were regarded as bets on the price of gold. This law, however, proved to be ineffective, as all such laws interfering with trade and speculation must be, and was soon repealed.

The national banking act, which passed at the previous session, was carefully revised and enacted in a new form, and it still remains in force, substantially unchanged by subsequent laws. By this new act the office of comptroller of the currency was created. Under its provisions, aided by a heavy tax on the circulating notes of state banks, such banks were converted into national banks upon such conditions as secured the payment of their circulating notes.

The financial measures, to which I have referred, were the work of the committees of ways and means of the House and on finance in the Senate. They occupied the chief attention of both Houses, and may fairly be claimed by the members of those committees as successful measures of the highest importance. I was deeply interested in all of them, took a very active part in their preparation in committee, and their conduct in the Senate, and, with the other members of the committee, feel that the measures adopted contributed largely to the final triumph of the Union cause. Certainly, the full power of the United States, its credit and the property of its people were by these laws intrusted to the executive authorities to suppress the rebellion.

In addition to military and financial measures, that session was prolific in many other measures of primary importance. The Union Pacific Railroad Company, which had been chartered by the previous Congress, found itself unable to proceed, and appealed to Congress for additional aid. This was granted by the act of July 2, 1864. Under this act, the first lien of the United States for bonds advanced to the company, provided for by the act of 1862, was made subordinate to the lien of the bonds of the company sold in the market—a fatal error, which led to all the serious complications which followed. The proceeds of the sale of the first mortgage bonds of the company, with a portion of those issued by the United States in aid of the company, built both the Union and Central Pacific, so that the constructors of these roads, who were mainly directors and managers of the company, practically received as profit a large portion of the bonds of the United States issued in aid of the work, and almost the entire capital stock of the company. If the act had been delayed until after the war, when the securities of the United States rapidly advanced in value, it could not have passed in the form it did. The construction of the road was practically not commenced until the war was over. The constructors had the benefit of the advancing value of the bonds and of the increasing purchasing power of United States notes.

It was unfortunate that the bill for the construction of the Northern Pacific Railroad came up at the same time. It was a faulty measure, making excessive grants of public lands to aid in the construction of a railroad and telegraph line from Lake Superior to Puget Sound. It was an act of incorporation with broad and general powers, carelessly defined, and with scarcely any safeguards to protect the government and its lavish grants of land. Some few amendments were made, but mostly in the interest of the corporation, and the bill finally passed the Senate without any vote by yeas and nays.

These two bills prove that it is not wise during war to provide measures for a time of peace.

During the same session the Territories of Colorado, Nebraska and Nevada were authorized to form state governments for admission into the Union, and a government was provided for each of the Territories of Montana and Idaho. The great object of organizing all the Indian country of the west into states and territories was to secure the country from Indian raids and depredations.

By far the most beneficial action of Congress at this session was the passage of the 13th article of the constitution of the United States, viz., "Neither slavery nor involuntary servitude, except as a punishment for crime, whereof the party shall have been duly convicted, shall exist within the United States, or any place subject to their jurisdiction."

It was thoroughly debated, and passed the Senate by the large vote of 38 yeas and 6 nays. It subsequently received the sanction of the House and of the requisite number of states to make it a part of the constitution. This was the natural and logical result of the Civil War. In case the rebellion should fail, it put at an end all propositions for compensation for slaves in loyal states, and all question of the validity of the emancipation proclamation of Abraham Lincoln.

The following letter of Secretary Chase shows the extremity of the measures deemed to be necessary at this period of the war:

TREASURY DEPARTMENT, May 26, 1864.

MY DEAR SIR: — I inclose two drafts of a national bank taxation clause—one marked 'A,' providing for the appropriation of the whole tax to the payment of interest or principal of the public debt and repealing the real estate direct tax law, and another marked "B," dividing the proceeds of the tax between the national and the loyal states. In either form the clause will be vastly more beneficial to the country than in the form of the bill, whether original or amended.

I also inclose a draft of a section providing for a tax on banks not national in the internal revenue act. It substantially restates the House proposition limiting it to banks of the states. Some discrimination in favor of the national system which affords substantial support to the government as compared with the local system, which circulates notes in competition with those issued by the government, seems to me indispensably necessary. It is impossible to prevent the depreciation of the currency unless Congress will assume its constitutional function and control it; and it is idle to try to make loans unless Congress will give the necessary support to the public credit. I am now compelled to advertise for a loan of fifty millions, and, to avoid as far as practicable the evils of sales below par, must offer the long bonds of '81. Should the provisions I ask for be sanctioned, I shall anticipate a satisfactory premium. Should they be denied, I may still be able to negotiate one loan on pretty fair terms; but I dread the effects on future loans.

Hitherto I have been able to maintain the public credit at the best points possible with a surcharged circulation. My ability to do so is due mainly to the legislation of the session of 1862–63. I must have further legislation in the same direction if it is desired to maintain that ability.

Yours truly,   S. P. CHASE.

HON. JOHN SHERMAN.

A few days before the close of the session, on the 29th of June, 1864, Mr. Chase tendered his resignation as Secretary of the Treasury. This created quite a sensation in political circles. It was thought to be the culmination of the feeling created by the nomination of Lincoln and the alleged rivalry of Chase, but the statements made in the "History of Lincoln," by Nicolay and Hay, and the "Biography of Chase," by Schuckers, clearly show that the cause of the resignation arose long anterior to this event and gradually produced a condition of affairs when either Mr. Lincoln had to yield his power over appointments or Mr. Chase to retire from his office. No good would result from analyzing the events which led to this resignation. The cause was perhaps best stated by Mr. Lincoln in accepting it, as follows:

"Your resignation of the office of Secretary of the Treasury, sent me yesterday, is accepted. Of all I have said in commendation of your ability and fidelity I have nothing to unsay, and yet you and I have reached a point of mutual embarrassment in our official relation which it seems cannot be overcome or longer sustained consistently with the public service."

The nomination of David Tod, of Ohio, as Secretary of the Treasury to succeed Mr. Chase, was not well received in either House. If the Members had known Tod as well as I did, they would have known that he was not only a good story teller, but a sound, able, conservative business man, fully competent to deal with the great office for which he was nominated. His declination, however, prevented a controversy which would have been injurious, whatever might have been the result. An anecdote frequently told by him may, perhaps, explain his nomination.

When he was elected Governor of Ohio, he went to Washington to see Mr. Lincoln, to find out, as he said, what a Republican President wanted a Democratic Governor of Ohio to do in aid of the Union cause. He called at the White House, sent in his card, and was informed that the President was engaged, but desired very much to see Governor Tod, and invited him to call that evening at 7 o'clock. Promptly on time Governor Tod called and was ushered into the room where, for the first time, he saw Mr. Lincoln. Mutual salutations had scarcely been exchanged before the announcement was made that David K. Cartter was at the door. Mr. Lincoln asked the governor if he had any objection to Cartter hearing their talk. The governor said no, that Cartter was an old friend and law partner of his. Soon after Governor Nye of Nevada was announced. The same inquiry was made and answered, and Nye joined the party, and in the same way Sam. Galloway, of Ohio, and a famous joker from New York, whose name I do not recall, came in. Then grouped around the table, Nye led off with a humorous description of life in the mines in the early days of California,

and the others contributed anecdotes, humor and fun, in which
Lincoln took the lead, "and I" (as Tod told the story), "not to
be behindhand, told a story;" and so the hours flew on without any mention of the grave matters he expected to discuss
with the President. When the clock announced the hour of
eleven, Mr. Lincoln said he made it a habit to retire at eleven
o'clock, and, turning to Tod, said: "Well, Governor, we have
not had any chance to talk about the war, but we have had a
good time anyway; come and see me again." It then dawned
upon the governor that this little party of kindred spirits, all
friends of his, were invited by the President to relieve him
from an interview about the future that would be fruitless of
results. Neither could know what each ought to do until
events pointed out a duty to be done. Lincoln knew that Tod
was a famous story teller, as were all the others in the party,
and availed himself of the opportunity to relieve his mind
from anxious care.

Governor Tod told me this anecdote and related many of
the stories told at that symposium.

The nomination of William P. Fessenden as Secretary of
the Treasury was a natural one to be made, and received the
cordial support of the Members of the Senate, even of those
who did not like his occasional ill temper and bitterness.
And here I may properly pause to notice the traits of two men
with whom I was closely identified in public life, and for whom
I had the highest personal regard, although they widely differed from each other.

Mr. Fessenden was an able lawyer, a keen incisive speaker,
rarely attempting rhetoric, but always a master in clear, distinct statement and logical argument. He had been for a
number of years dyspeptic, and this, no doubt, clouded his
temper and caused many of the bitter things he said. When I
entered the Senate, I was, at his request, placed on the committee on finance, of which he was chairman. He was kind
enough to refer to my position in the House as chairman of
the committee of ways and means, and my action there, and to
express the hope that I would be able to aid him in dealing
with financial questions, in which he had had no training and

SCHUYLER COLFAX.   STEPHEN A. DOUGLAS.

WILLIAM PITT FESSENDEN.   THOMAS EWING.

but little interest. I accepted the position with pleasure, and in general coöperated with him, though on many important subjects we widely differed. His appointment as Secretary of the Treasury left me chairman of the committee on finance, but my intercourse with him continued while he was secretary. During the short period in which he held that office, I had many conferences with him in respect to pending questions. When he returned to the Senate, on the 4th of March, 1865, he resumed his old place as chairman of the committee on finance, and continued in that position nearly two years, when, his health becoming more feeble, he resigned his membership of that committee, and I again took his place as chairman and held it until appointed Secretary of the Treasury in 1877. His health continued to fail and he died at Portland, Maine, September 8, 1869.

With Mr. Chase I had but little acquaintance and no sympathy during his early political career. His edition of the "Statutes of Ohio" was his first work of any importance. He was at times supposed to be a Whig and then again classed as a Democrat. Later he became a member of the national convention of Free Soilers held at Buffalo, August 9, 1848, over which he presided. This convention was composed of delegates from eighteen states, and included in its active members many of the most eminent Whigs and Democrats of a former time. It nominated Martin Van Buren for the Presidency, and Charles Francis Adams for Vice President. General Taylor, the nominee of the Whig party, was elected President, but Mr. Van Buren received 291,342 votes, being nearly one-eighth of the whole number of votes cast.

It so happened that when the Ohio legislature met in December, 1848, it was composed of an equal number of Whigs and Democrats and of two members, Townsend and Morse, who classed themselves as Free Soilers. They practically dictated the election of Mr. Chase as United States Senator. They secured his election by an understanding, express or implied, with the Democratic members, that they would vote for Democrats for all the numerous offices, which, under the constitution of the state as it then stood, were appointed by the legislature. This bargain and sale—so-called—created among the Whigs a strong prejudice against Chase. But events in Congress, especially the act repealing the Missouri Compromise, practically dissolved existing parties, and left Mr. Chase in the vantage ground of having resisted this measure with firmness. He was universally regarded as a man of marked ability and honest in his convictions. In the election for Members of Congress in 1854, he supported what were known as the anti-Nebraska candidates, and, no doubt, contributed to their election. When he was nominated for governor, I was naturally brought into friendly relations with him, and these, as time advanced, were cordial and intimate. Our correspondence was frequent, mostly of a personal character, and our intimacy continued while he lived. When he was Secretary of the Treasury I was frequently consulted by him, and had, as I believe, his entire confidence. I have a great number of letters from him written during that period.

In September, 1864, Mr. Chase was my guest at Mansfield for a day or two. He was evidently restless and uneasy as to his future. I spoke to him about the position of chief justice, recently made vacant by the death of Taney. He said it was a position of eminence that ought to satisfy the ambition of anyone, but for which few men were fitted. Early in October I received a letter from him which shows he was actively engaged in the canvass, and that the common belief that he did not desire the election of Mr. Lincoln was without foundation. He wrote as follows:

LOUISVILLE, October 2, 1864.

MY DEAR SIR:—Some days since I informed the secretary of the state central committee that I would, as far as possible, fill the appointments which ill-health had obliged Gov. Tod to decline. Seeing afterwards, however, that he had determined to meet them himself, I acceded to requests from other quarters to give them what help I could. The first intimation I had that he would fail in any of them was your letter, put into my hands just as I was leaving Cincinnati for New Albany last Friday. It was then too late to recall my own appointments, and, of course, I cannot be at Mansfield. I should be glad to be there ; but regret the impossibility of it the less since I should not meet you. I am really glad you are going to Logansport. The election of Gov. Morton is of vast importance to our cause. And, then, Colfax, I feel most anxious for him. I hope you can go to his district. I wanted to go myself; but was urged to other parts of Indiana, and was left no chance to reach it till this week; which must be given to Ohio in aid of Stevenson and Bundy, except that I speak here to-morrow (Monday), and Tuesday night in Covington.

There has been a very large accumulation of troops here, for Sherman. Col. Hammond telegraphed the department at Washington yesterday that, communications being now re-established from Nashville to Atlanta, he could commence sending them forward immediately; and doubtless the movement will begin tomorrow. I congratulate *you* most heartily on his splendid success thus far and on the certainty that no effort will be spared to maintain his army at the highest possible point of efficiency.

There appears to be no truth in the report of a coöperative movement in aid of Sheridan for Tennessee. Burbridge's expedition is for a point beyond Abingdon where there are important salt works, and he intends returning thence through Knoxville. So I learn from one who ought to know; but don't understand it. *That game* seems hardly worth the candle.

We had a splendid meeting in Aurora yesterday and our friends are confident of Gov. Morton's re-election. Thousands of people stood in a pouring rain to hear me and Gov. Lane talk to them, and profounder or more earnest attention I never witnessed. It will gratify you, I am sure, to know that I receive, wherever I go, unequivocal manifestations of a popular confidence and appreciation, which I did not suppose I possessed.

There is not now the slightest uncertainty about the re-election of Mr. Lincoln. The only question is, by what popular and what electoral majority. God grant that both may be so decisive as to turn every hope of rebellion to despair!

You ask about Mr. Fessenden's remaining in the cabinet. He will be a candidate for re-election to the Senate; and if successful will leave his present post in March, or sooner if circumstances allow. He has been in communication with me since he took charge, and in every step, with perhaps one slight exception, his judgment has corresponded with mine. He sees several matters now in quite a different light from that in which they appeared to him when Senator. He would now, for example, *cordially support* your proposition for a heavy discriminating tax upon all unnational circulation. And he is more than just—he is very generous in his appreciation of the immense work of organization and effective activity to be found in the department.

How signally are events confirming my views as to the value of gold, compared with national currency. How clear it is now that if Congress had come boldly to the act of marked discriminative taxation on all non-national circulation and final prohibition after a few years, say two—or at most three— gold would now have been at not more than fifty per cent. premium and that resumption of specie payments might have been effected within a year. I trust the next session will witness bolder and better legislation. It will be one of your brightest honors that you so clearly saw and so boldly followed the path of reform ; for certainly no greater boon—except liberty itself— can be conferred upon a nation than a truly national and thoroughly sound currency.   Yours most truly,

S. P. CHASE.

HON. JOHN SHERMAN.

After the election he wrote me the following letter, in which he referred to the appointment of a chief justice, with an evident desire for the office :

CINCINNATI, November 12, 1864.

MY DEAR SIR :—The papers still state you are in Washington. I am glad of it, and hope you may be able to render good service to our friend, Fessenden. The task of preparing a report is no light one. At least it always made me sweat and keep late hours. May he find a safe deliverance from the labor.

All sorts of rumors are afloat about everything. Those which concern me most relate to the vacant seat on the bench ; but I give little heed to any of them. My experience in Washington taught me how unreliable they are. If what I hear is any index to the state of opinion, Mr. Lincoln must be satisfied that in acting on the purpose expressed in your letters, he will have the almost, if not quite, unanimous approval of the Union men throughout the country. So I "possess my soul in patience," and urge nothing.

If it did not seem to me a sort of indelicacy even to allow to anyone the slightest occasion to say that I solicit or even ask such an appointment as a favor or as a reward for political service, I should now be on my way to Washington ; but I think it due to myself as well as to the President to await his decision here ; though, if appointed, I hope the appointment will be considered as made from the country at large rather than from Ohio alone. My legal residence is here ; but my actual domicile is still in the District.

Please write me, if you can, when the President will act. Let me know too how the military and political aspects at Washington appear to you. We have achieved a glorious political victory, which must greatly help our military prospects and possibilities.

Mr. Miller has just come in and says he goes to Washington to-night. Had he come before I began, I should have spared you this letter ; only asking him to make verbally the inquiries I have just set down ; but I will send it with " answer respectfully solicited.

Yours very cordially,

S. P. CHASE.

HON. JOHN SHERMAN.

Early in December I received the following letter, which indicates very clearly that Mr. Chase was anxious for the position of chief justice, and wished his appointment made, if at all, before his arrival in Washington :

CLEVELAND, December 2, 1864.

MY DEAR SIR:—Yours of the 27th of November reached me here to-day. Yesterday I fulfilled my appointment to make an address on the dedication of the college edifice recently erected at Mount Union, under the patronage of the Pittsburg conference of the Methodist church. A number of leading men of the denomination were present and assured me of the profound wishes of themselves and the most influential men of the connection for my appointment. These indeed seem to be universal except with an inconsiderable number whom various circumstances have made unfriendly personally. So that I cannot doubt that the President's adherence to his declared intention is more important to our cause and to his administration than it is to me personally. Not to be appointed after such declarations and such expressions would, no doubt, be a mortification ; but it would not, I think, be any serious injury to me.

I expect to be in Washington, Tuesday or Wednesday. I should have been there long since had this appointment been determined either way ; but I must come now. My personal duties, unconnected with it, have required and now require my attention, and though I hated to come before I knew that there remains nothing to hope or fear concerning it, I must. I will be at the Continental, Philadelphia, Tuesday morning.

Our news from Tennessee is important and encouraging. Garfield's success against Forrest was brilliant. I hope Thomas will succeed as well against Hood.

General Sherman must now be near the coast. His enterprise is full of hazard, but a hazard wisely incurred as it seems to me. I ardently hope that ' out of the nettle, danger, he will pluck the flower, safety.'

Our majority on the presidential election in Ohio turns out much less than I anticipated. It will hardly, if at all, exceed fifty thousand.

Faithfully yours,

S. P. CHASE.

HON. JOHN SHERMAN.

When I returned to Washington at the beginning of the next session I called upon the President and recommended the appointment of Mr. Chase. We had a brief conversation upon the subject in which he asked me pointedly the question whether if Chase was appointed he would be satisfied, or whether he would immediately become a candidate for President. I told him I thought the appointment to that great office ought to and would satisfy his ambition. He then told me that he had determined to appoint him and intended to send the nomination to the Senate that day and he did so, December 6, 1864. After Mr. Chase had become chief justice he still had a lingering interest in the financial policy of the country. On March 1, 1865, I received from him the following letter. That portion which refers to the legal tender laws will naturally excite some interest in view of his decision against the power of Congress to make the notes of the United States a legal tender. He wrote:

AT HOME, March 1, 1865.

MY DEAR SIR : — More to fulfill a promise than with the hope of service I write this note.

Your speech on the finances is excellent. There are one or two points on which I shall express myself otherwise ; but, in the main, it commands the fullest assent of my judgment.

Your appreciation of the currency question exactly corresponds with my own ; only I would not give up the national currency even if we must endure for years depreciation through the issues of state banks before getting rid of them.

The clause in the bill, as it came from the House, imposing a tax of ten per cent. on all notes not authorized by Congress which may be paid out after this year by any bank, whether state or national, will do much towards making our currency sound.

I will briefly indicate what I should prefer and what I should most zealously labor to have sanctioned by Congress if I were at the head of the treasury department.

1. Let the monthly tax on state bank circulation be increased to one-half of one per cent.

2. Provide that any bank may pay into the national treasury the amount of its circulation in United States notes or national currency and that on such payment the bank making it shall be exempt from taxation on circulation.

3. Provide for the application to the redemption of the circulation represented by such payments, of the United States notes or national currency so paid in, and strictly prohibit the paying out of such notes for any other purpose.

This measure contemplates :

1. An exclusive national currency.

2. Relief of the state banks from taxation upon circulation which they cannot get in.

3. The assumption of the duty of redemption by the national treasury with means provided by the state banks.

4. Reduction in the amount in circulation while the payments into the treasury are being made and opportunity of some provision for redemption which will not again increase it.

The effect will be:

1. Healthful condition of currency and consequent activity in production and increase of resources.

2. Gradual restoration of national notes to equality with specie and the facilitating of resumption of specie payments.

3. Improvement of national credit.

4. Diminution of national expenditures and possible arrest of the increase of national debt.

Half measures are better than no measures; but thorough measures are best.

I will only add, that while I have never favored legal tender laws in principle, and never consented to them except under imperious necessity, I yet think it unwise to prohibit the making of any of the treasury notes authorized by the bill now before Congress legal tenders. The compound interest legal tender notes have then fulfilled all my expectations for their issue and use; and may be made most useful helps in gradual reduction of the volume of circulation by substituting them for legal tenders bearing no interest.

I cannot elaborate this now. You will see how the thing will work without any suggestion of mine. Faithfully your friend,

S. P. CHASE.

HON. JOHN SHERMAN.

From my long and intimate acquaintance with Chief Justice Chase I am quite sure that the duties of the great office he then held were not agreeable to him. His life had been a political one, and this gave him opportunity for travel and direct communion with the people. The seclusion and severe labor imposed upon the Supreme Court were contrary to his habits and injurious to his health. It took him some years to become accustomed to the quiet of judicial life. He presided over the Senate while acting as a court of impeachment during the trial of Andrew Johnson in 1868. While strongly opposed to the impeachment, he manifested no sign of partiality. He died in New York city on the 7th of May, 1873, at the age of sixty-five.

While Congress was in session, the Republican national convention met at Baltimore on the 7th day of June, 1864, to nominate candidates for President and Vice President of the United States, and to announce the principles and policy of the Republican party of the United States. The nomination of Mr. Lincoln had already been made by state legislatures and by the loyal people of the United States in every form in which popular opinion can be expressed. The feeble expressions of dissent were but a whisper compared with the loud proclamation coming from every loyal state in favor of Lincoln. The convention, with unanimous assent, ratified and confirmed the popular choice.

The nomination for Vice President was dictated by the desire to recognize the loyalty and patriotism of those who, living in states in rebellion, remained true and loyal to the Federal Union. Though Mr. Johnson disappointed the expectations of those who nominated him, yet at that time his courage and fidelity and his services and sacrifices for the cause of the Union fully justified his nomination.

More important, even, than the choice of candidates, was the declaration by the convention of the policy of the Republican party. The key-note of that policy was the third resolution, as follows:

"*Resolved*, that as slavery was the cause, and now constitutes the strength of this rebellion, and as it must be always and everywhere hostile to the principles of republican government, justice and the national safety demand its utter and complete extirpation from the soil of the republic; and that we uphold and maintain the acts and proclamations by which the government, in its own defense, has aimed a deathblow at the gigantic evil. We are in favor, furthermore, of such an amendment to the constitution, to be made by the people in conformity with its provisions, as shall terminate and forever prohibit the existence of slavery within the limits or the jurisdiction of the United States."

This was the logical result of the war. If it was carried into full execution, it would settle on a just and sure foundation the only danger that ever threatened the prosperity of the Union. This was happily carried into full effect by the constitutional amendment to which I have already referred.

The Democratic convention met at Chicago on the 29th of August, 1864, and nominated George B. McClellan as the candidate for President and George H. Pendleton as Vice President; but far more important and dangerous was the second, and the only material resolution of the platform which was drawn by Vallandigham and was as follows:

"*Resolved*, that this convention does explicitly declare, as the sense of the American people, that after four years of failure to restore the Union by the experiment of war, during which, under the pretense of a military

necessity of a war power higher than the constitution, the constitution itself
has been disregarded in every part, and public liberty and private right alike
trodden down, and the material prosperity of the country essentially impaired, justice, humanity, liberty and the public welfare demand that immediate efforts be made for a cessation of hostilities with a view to an ultimate convention of all the states, or other peaceable means, to the end that,
at the earliest practicable moment, peace may be restored on the basis of the
federal union of all the states."

This was a false declaration, and was also a cowardly surrender to enemies in open war. These two resolutions made
the momentous issue submitted to the American people. From
the moment it was made the popular mind grew stronger and
firmer in favor of the prosecution of the war and the abolition
of slavery, and more resolute to resist the surrender proposed
to rebels in arms. Prior to the adoption of this resolution,
there was apparent languor and indifference among the people
as to who should be President, but after its adoption there
could be no doubt as to the trend of popular opinion. Every
sentiment of patriotism, the love of flag and country, the pride
of our people in the success of our soldiers, and the resentment
of the soldiers themselves at this slur on their achievements—
all contributed to the rejection of the candidates and the platform of the Democratic party, and the overwhelming victory
of the Republican party.

I had already entered into the canvass when this resolution
of Vallandigham was adopted. It was only necessary to read
it to the people of Ohio to arouse resentment and opposition.
The scattered opposition to Mr. Lincoln, much of it growing
out of his conservatism, at once disappeared. The discontented
Republicans who met in convention at Cleveland again became
active in the Republican ranks. The two parties that grew out
of factional politics in New York, the Blair party and its
opponents in Missouri, and the army of disaffected office-
seekers, waived their dissensions and griefs. Horace Greeley
and the extreme opponents of slavery, represented by Wendell Phillips, not satisfied with the slow, but constitutional,
process of emancipation proposed by Lincoln, when compelled
to choose between that plan of abolition and unconditional

surrender to slavery, naturally voted for Lincoln. The great body of patriotic Democrats in all the states, who supported the war, but were still attached to their party, quietly voted for Lincoln. In Ohio, especially, where a year before they voted against Vallandigham for his disloyalty, they naturally voted against his resolution for surrender to the rebels.

During the campaign I accompanied Johnson to Indiana where he made patriotic speeches to great audiences. His arraignment of the autocracy of slaveholders in the south was very effective. The current of opinion was all in favor of Lincoln. The result of the election for Members of Congress in the states voting in October was a decisive indication of the result in November. All the central states elected a large majority of Republican Members of Congress. In Ohio the Union party had a majority of over 50,000 and elected 17 Republican and 2 Democratic Members of the House of Representatives. In 1862 Ohio elected 14 Democratic and 5 Republican Members. The presidential election that followed on the 8th of November, 1864, resulted in an overwhelming victory for Lincoln. He received 212 and McClellan 21 electoral votes, the latter from the States of New Jersey, Delaware and Kentucky. This political victory had a more decisive effect in defeating the rebellion than many battles. I returned to Washington soon after the election.

I was naturally deeply interested in the movements of General Sherman's march to the sea. Towards the close of November we had all sorts of rumors from the south, that General Sherman was surrounded by Confederate troops, that his supplies were cut off, that successful attacks had been made upon his scattered forces. I naturally became uneasy, and went to President Lincoln for consolation and such news as he could properly give me. He said: "Oh no, we have no news from General Sherman. We know what hole he went in at, but we do not know what hole he will come out of," but he expressed his opinion that General Sherman was all right. Soon after, authentic information came that General Sherman had arrived at Savannah, that Fort McAllister was taken, and the army was in communication with the naval forces. The capture of Savannah and the northward march of General Sherman's army is part of the familiar military history of the country.

The second session of the 38th Congress convened on the 5th of December, 1864. It was a busy and active session confined mainly to appropriation, loan and currency bills. The necessary expenditures had been so greatly increased by the war that the aggregate amounts appropriated naturally created some opposition and alarm, but there was no help for it. As chairman of the committee on finance I did all I could to reduce the appropriations for civil expenses, but in respect to military expenditures there could be scarcely any limit, the amount necessary being dependent upon military success. The hopeful progress of the war gave encouragement that in a brief period the power of the Confederate States would be exhausted and peace would follow. We had, however, to legislate upon the basis of the continued prosecution of the war, and it therefore became necessary to increase the revenues in every possible way, and to provide for new loans. The act approved March 3, 1865, authorized the Secretary of the Treasury to borrow not exceeding $600,000,000, and to issue therefore bonds or treasury notes of the United States in such form as he might provide. This was the last great loan authorized during the war. An act to provide internal revenue to support the government was approved on the same day, which modified many of the provisions of the previous act, but added subjects of taxation not embraced in previous laws. It especially increased the taxes on tobacco in its various forms. The 6th section provided:

"That every national banking association, state bank, or state banking association, shall pay a tax of ten per centum on the amount of notes of any state bank or state banking association, paid out by them after the first day of July, eighteen hundred and sixty-six."

This tax on state bank circulation was a practical prohibition of all state bank paper, and before the time fixed for the commencement of the tax, this circulation entirely disappeared.

Additional duties were placed upon certain foreign importations. Provisions were also made for the collection in the insurrectionary district within the United States of the direct
taxes levied under the act of 1862. During the entire session
my labor was excessive, and when it closed my health and
strength were greatly impaired.

CHAPTER XVI.

Assassination of Abraham Lincoln.

ON the 4th of March, 1865, at the inauguration of the President and Vice President elect, a scene occurred in the Senate chamber, which made a serious impression, and was indicative of what was to occur in the future. About eleven o'clock of that day Andrew Johnson, Vice President, was shown into the room in the capitol assigned to the Vice President. He complained of feeling unwell and sent for either whisky or brandy, and must have drank excessively of it. A few minutes before twelve o'clock he was ushered into the Senate to take the oath of office and to make the usual brief address. He was plainly intoxicated and delivered a stump speech unworthy of the occasion. Before him were assembled all the principal officers of the government and the diplomatic corps. He went on in a maudlin and rambling way for twenty minutes or more, until finally he was suppressed by the suggestion of the secretary that the time for the inauguration had arrived, and he must close.

The procession was formed for the inauguration at the east front of the capitol, where a great multitude was gathered. There Mr. Lincoln delivered his memorable inaugural address.

Referring to the condition of the controversy at the time of his former inaugural, he said:

" Both parties deprecated war; but one of them would *make* war rather than let the Union survive; and the other would *accept* war rather than let it perish. And the war came."

He hopefully predicted the result of the war, but he said:

" Yet, if God wills that it continue until all the wealth piled by the bondman's two hundred and fifty years of unrequited toil shall be sunk, and until every drop of blood drawn with the lash shall be paid by another drawn with the sword, as was said three thousand years ago, so still it must be said, ' The judgments of the Lord are true and righteous altogether.' "

His peroration will always be remembered for its impressive eloquence:

" With malice towards none, with charity for all, with firmness in the right, as God gives us to see the right, let us strive on to finish the work we are in; to bind up the nation's wounds; to care for him who shall have borne the battle, and for his widow, and his orphan; to do all which may achieve and cherish a just and lasting peace among ourselves and with all nations."

Soon after the adjournment I was invited by Secretary Stanton, with many other Senators and our families, to take a trip to the south in the steamer " Baltic." Among those on board were Senators Simon Cameron, Wade, Zach. Chandler, and Foster, of Connecticut, then president *pro tempore* of the Senate. The sea was exceedingly boisterous. Nearly all on board were sea sick, but none so badly as Wade and Chandler, both of whom, I fear, violated the third commandment, and nearly all the party were in hearty sympathy with them. I was a good sailor and about the only one who escaped the common fate. We visited the leading places of interest along the coast, but especially Charleston, Beaufort and Savannah. Charleston had but recently been evacuated. General Sherman was then on his march through North Carolina. In Charleston everything looked gloomy and sad. I rode on horseback alone through different parts of the city, and was warned by officers not to repeat the ride, as, if my name was known, I would be in danger of being shot.

We arrived in Beaufort on Sunday morning. The town was then full of contrabands. We remained there that day and received an invitation from a negro preacher to attend religious services at his new meeting-house. About fifteen or twenty of the party went to the "meeting-house," a new unfinished skeleton-frame house of considerable size without any plastering—a mere shell. We were shown to seats that had been reserved for us. The rest of the congregation were negroes in every kind of dress and of every shade of color. The scene was very interesting, but the sermon of the preacher was little better than gibberish. He was a quaint old man, wearing goggles and speaking a dialect we could hardly understand. At the close of his sermon he narrated how the meeting-house had been built; that John had hauled the logs, Tom, Dick and Harry, naming them, had contributed their labor, but they were in debt something over $200, and, with a significant glance at our little party, he thought this was a good time to take up a collection. No sooner was this said than Cameron, whispering to us, said: "Lets pay it; I'll give twenty dollars," and when the hat came around, instead of the usual dimes and quarters in ragged currency, it received greenbacks of good denominations. In the meantime the old preacher, highly elated, called upon the audience to sing "John Brown's Body." A feeble, piping voice from an old negro woman started the singing and the rest of the negroes, with loud melodious voices, joined in, and, before it was through, the rest of us joined in. The hat, when returned to the preacher, was found to contain more than fifty dollars in excess of the amount necessary to pay off the debt. Then, with many thanks to us by the preacher, the audience was requested to remain standing until their visitors left.

Our visit at Savannah was very interesting. We there found many leading citizens of the town who were social and kind, treating us in a friendly way by rides around the city.

In the latter part of March, I was invited by General Sherman, then on a visit to Grant near Petersburg, Virginia, to go with him to Goldsboro, North Carolina, where his army was then encamped. Secretary Stanton was my next door neighbor, and our families were intimately associated. I invited his eldest son, Edwin, then a young man studying law, to accompany me, an invitation which he gladly accepted. We joined General Sherman at Fortress Monroe and accompanied him on the steamer "Bat" to Newbern and thence by rail to Goldsboro. There was a sense of danger in traveling by rail through a country mostly unoccupied, but we reached the army at Goldsboro safely. There I had my first view of a great army in marching garb. Most of the troops had received their new uniforms and equipments, but outlying regiments were constantly coming in, ragged, with tattered hats, shoes and boots of every description, almost black from exposure and the smoke of the pine woods, and as hardy a looking set of men as one could conceive of. They had picked up all kinds of paraphernalia, "stove pipe" hats being the favorite, and had all sorts of wagons gathered in their march. Their appearance was rapidly changed by new uniforms. After a brief visit I returned to Washington, and thence to my home at Mansfield.

I was invited soon after, on the 14th of April, to attend a mass meeting at Columbus to celebrate the success of the Union army. I accepted the invitation and attended an immense meeting in the open air on the capitol grounds, and there Samuel Galloway and myself made addresses. Meetings were held, congratulations uttered in the evening of that day. The whole city was in holiday attire, ornamented with flags, and everywhere and with everybody, there was an expression of joy. I retired late at night to my room in the hotel, and after my fatigue slept soundly.

Early the next morning Rush Sloane, a personal friend, rapped at my door and announced to me the news of the assassination of Lincoln, and, as then reported, that of Seward. The change from joy to mourning that day in Columbus was marked and impressive. No event of my life created a more painful impression than this news following the rejoicings of the day before. I returned to Washington and attended the funeral services over the body of Mr. Lincoln, then about to be carried on the long journey to his old home in Springfield, Illinois.

On the 6th of May, in response to the invitation of my neighbors in Mansfield, I made an address upon the life and character of the dead President. It expressed the opinion and respect I then entertained for him, and now I could add nothing to it. As time moves on his name and fame become brighter, while most of his contemporaries are one by one forgotten.

Soon after the death of Mr. Lincoln, the terms of the surrender of General Johnston to General Sherman became the subject of a violent controversy. On the 21st of April, Secretary Stanton issued an order to General Grant to proceed immediately to the headquarters of General Sherman and direct operations against the enemy. He issued a bulletin in which he intimated that Davis and his partisans were on their way to escape to Mexico or Europe with a large amount of gold plundered from the Richmond banks and from other sources, and that they hoped to make terms with General Sherman by which they would be permitted with their effects, including their gold plunder, to go to Mexico or Europe. The most violent and insulting paragraphs were published in the newspapers, substantially arraigning General Sherman as a traitor and imputing to him corrupt motives. I felt myself bound at once, not to defend the terms of surrender, but to repel the innuendoes aimed at General Sherman. This led me into a controversy with Mr. Stanton, not worth while to recall.

I believed then and still believe that he was under the influence of perhaps a well-grounded fear that his life was in danger. The atmosphere of Washington seemed to be charged with terror, caused by the assassination of Lincoln, the wounding of Seward and the threats against all who were conspicuous in political or military life in the Union cause. Now, since we are fully informed of all the surrounding circumstances connected with the surrender, and the belief of General Sherman that he was strictly carrying out the policy of President Lincoln, it is plain that he acted in what he supposed was the line of duty. He did not comprehend that the fatal crime in Washington changed the whole aspect of affairs. His agreement with Johnston was on its face declared to be inoperative until approved by the authorities at Washington, and, while the political features of the surrender could not be approved, a simple notification of disapproval would have been cheerfully acted upon and the orders of the President would have been faithfully carried out.

General Sherman, when he received notice of the disapproval of his action, at once notified Johnston, and new terms were arranged in exact accordance with those conceded by General Grant to General Lee.

I remained in Washington until the arrival, on the 19th of May, of General Sherman's army, which encamped by the roadside about half way between Alexandria and the Long Bridge. I visited the general there and found that he was still smarting under what he called the disgrace put upon him by Stanton. I advised him to keep entirely quiet, said the feeling had passed away and that his position was perfectly well understood. I persuaded him to call on the President and such members of the cabinet as he knew, and accompanied him. He was dressed in full uniform, well worn, was bronzed and looked the picture of health and strength. As a matter of course he refused to call on Stanton and denounced him in unmeasured terms, declaring that he would insult him whenever the opportunity occurred. When he came in contact with his fellow officers and found that they sympathized with him his anger abated, and by the time the great review took place, he seemed to have recovered his usual manner.

The review of General Meade's army was to occur on Tuesday, May 23, and that of General Sherman's, as it was called, on the 24th. General Sherman, with his wife and her father, Hon. Thomas Ewing, and myself, were present on the reviewing stand on the first day of the review. He received on the stand the congratulations of hundreds of people and seemed to enjoy every moment of time. He was constantly pointing out to Mr. Ewing and myself the difference between the eastern and western armies, in which he evidently preferred the Army of the West. On the next day, prompt to the time stated, attended by a brilliant staff, he rode slowly up Pennsylvania avenue at the head of his column, and was followed by a magnificent

EDWIN M. STANTON,

SECRETARY OF WAR,

BORN AT STEUBENVILLE, OHIO, DEC. 19, 1814.
DIED AT WASHINGTON, D. C., DEC. 24, 1869.

army of 65,000 men, organized into four army corps, and marching with that precision only possible with experienced troops. His description of the scene in his "Memoirs" proves his deep interest in the appearance of his army and his evident pride in it. When he arrived at the grand stand, where the President reviewed the troops, he dismounted, left the line, came upon the stand and took his place by the side of the President. Everyone knew his relations to Stanton, and was curious to see the result of their meeting. I stood very near the general, and as he approached he shook hands with the President and the members of the cabinet, but when Stanton partially reached out his hand, General Sherman passed him without remark, but everyone within sight could perceive the intended insult, which satisfied his honor at the expense of his prudence. However, it is proper to say that these two men, both eminent in their way, became entirely reconciled before the death of Mr. Stanton. General Sherman always stopped with me when he was temporarily in Washington, and I know that in a very brief period they met and conversed in a friendly way. When Mr. Stanton lay upon his death bed, General Sherman not only called upon him, but tendered his services, and exhibited every mark of respect for him.

The great body of the volunteer forces was disbanded, the officers and soldiers were returning to their homes. To most of them the war was a valuable lesson. It gave them a start in life and a knowledge and experience that opened the door to all employment, especially to official positions in state and nation. In all popular elections the soldier was generally preferred. This was a just recognition for his sacrifices and services. I hope and trust that while a single survivor of the War of the Rebellion is left among us, he will everywhere be received with honor and share all the respect which the boys of my generation were so eager to grant and extend to the heroes of the Revolutionary War. The service of one was as valuable as the other, rendered on a broader field, in greater numbers, with greater sacrifices, and with the same glorious results of securing the continuance of an experiment of free government, the most successful in the history of mankind and which is now, I profoundly trust, so well secured by the heroism and valor of our soldiers, that for generations and centuries yet to come no enemy will dare to aim a blow at the life of the republic. For the wounded and disabled soldiers and the widows and orphans of those who fell, a larger provision of pensions was freely granted than ever before by any nation in ancient or modern times. Provision was made by the general government, and by most of the loyal states, for hospitals and homes for the wounded. The bodies of those who died in the service have been carefully collected into cemeteries in all parts of the United States. If there has been any neglect or delay in granting pensions, it has been caused by the vast number of applications—more than a million—and the difficulty as time passes in securing the necessary proof. The pension list now, thirty years after the war, requires annually the sum of more than $150,000,000, or three times the amount of all the expenses of the national government before the war. No complaint is made of this, but Congress readily grants any increase demanded by the feebleness of age or the decay of strength. I trust, and believe, that this policy will be continued until the last surviving soldier of the war meets the common fate of all.

I participated in the canvass of 1865, when General Jacob D. Cox, the Republican candidate for governor in Ohio, and a Republican legislature were elected with but little opposition. The first duty of this legislature was to elect a Senator. There was a friendly contest between General Robert C. Schenck, Hon. John A. Bingham and myself, but I was nominated on the first ballot and duly elected.

I received many letters from Horace Greeley, in the following one of which he showed a great interest in my re-election to the Senate:

NEW YORK, February 7, 1865.

HON. JOHN SHERMAN:

MY DEAR SIR:— Yours of the 5th inst. at hand. I can assure you that the combination to supplant you in the Senate is quite strong and confident of success. I did not mean to allude to the controversy, but was compelled to by the dispatch which got into our columns. I observe J. W. wrote

My dear Sir:

Yours of the 5th is just at hand. I can assure you that the commotion to supplant you on the Senate is quite strong, and certain of success. I did not mean to allude to the contro-versy, but was compelled to by the dispatch so beetroot into our columns. I because J. W. wrote "Loeoble" "as he says, out the change to "Loyal." "was a very awkward one in these days; so I felt com-pelled to correct it.

I fear move the soills of Thad. Stevens in the Treasury than those of Mosby in our tree

Yours,
Horace Greeley

Hon. John Freeman.

'locality' as he says, but the change to 'loyalty' was a very awkward one in these days; so I felt compelled to correct it.

I fear more the raids of Thad. Stevens on the treasury than those of Mosby on our lines.   Yours,

HORACE GREELEY.

When Congress met on the 4th of December, 1865, it had before it two important problems which demanded immediate attention. One was a measure for the reconstruction of the states lately in rebellion and the other was a plan for refunding and paying the public debt. It was unfortunate that no measure had been provided before the close of the war defining the condition of the states lately in rebellion, securing the freedmen in their new-born rights, and restoring these states to their place in the Union. Therefore, during the long vacation, from April to December, the whole matter was left to executive authority. If Lincoln had lived, his action would have been acquiesced in. It would have been liberal, based upon universal emancipation of negroes, and pardon to rebels. It was supposed that President Johnson would err, if at all, in imposing too harsh terms upon these states. His violent speeches in the canvass of 1864, and his fierce denunciation of the leaders in the Rebellion, led us all to suppose that he would insist upon a reconstruction by the loyal people of the south and that reasonable protection would be extended to the emancipated negroes. The necessity of legislation for the reconstruction of the Confederate states was foreseen and provision had been made by Congress, during the war, by what was known as the Wade-Davis bill, to provide for the reorganization of these states. During the 37th Congress, Henry Winter Davis, though not then a Member of the House of Representatives, prepared a bill to meet this exigency. It was a bill to guarantee to each state a republican form of government. It embodied a plan by which these states, then declared by Congress to be in a state of insurrection, might, when that insurrection was subdued or abandoned, come back freely and voluntarily into the Union. It provided for representation, for the election of a convention and a legislature, and of Senators and Members of Congress. It was a complete guarantee to the people of the insurrectionary states that upon certain conditions these states might resume their place in the Union when the insurrection had ceased. This bill he handed to me. I introduced it at his request. It was referred to the judiciary committee, but was not acted upon by it.

Afterwards Mr. Davis came into the 38th Congress as a Member of the House of Representatives. Among the first acts performed by him after taking his seat was the introduction of this same bill. On the 15th of December, 1863, it was debated in the House of Representatives and passed by a very decided vote, and was sent to the Senate. It was reported to the Senate favorably, but in place of it was substituted a proposition offered by B. Gratz Brown, of Missouri. This substitute provided a mode by which the eleven Confederate states might, when the Rebellion was suppressed within their limits, be restored to their old place in the Union. The bill was sent back to the House with the proposed substitute. A committee of conference was appointed, and the House preferring the original bill, the Senate receded from its amendment, and what was known as the Wade-Davis bill passed. It went to President Lincoln, who did not approve it, and it did not become a law, but on the 8th of July, 1864, after the close of the session, he issued the following proclamation :

"WHEREAS, at the late session Congress passed a bill to guaranty to certain states, whose governments have been usurped or overthrown, a republican form of government, a copy of which is hereunto annexed ; and whereas the said bill was presented to the President of the United States for his approval less than one hour before the *sine die* adjournment of said session, and was not signed by him ; and whereas the said bill contains, among other things, a plan for restoring the states in rebellion to their proper practical relation in the Union, which plan expresses the sense of Congress upon that subject, and which plan it is now thought fit to lay before the people for their consideration :

"Now, therefore, I, Abraham Lincoln, President of the United States, do proclaim, declare, and make known, that while I am (as I was in December last, when by proclamation I propounded a plan for restoration) unprepared, by a formal approval of this bill, to be inflexibly committed to any single plan of restoration ; and while I am also unprepared to declare that the free state constitutions and governments already adopted and installed in Arkansas and Louisiana shall be set aside and held for naught, thereby repelling and discouraging the loyal citizens who have set up the same as to further effort, or to declare a constitutional competency in Congress to abolish slavery in states, I am at the same time sincerely hoping and expecting that a constitutional amendment abolishing slavery throughout the nation may be adopted."

He added his reasons for not approving the Wade-Davis bill. He did not entirely disapprove of it, but said it was one of numerous plans which might be adopted. Mr. Sumner stated, on the floor of the Senate, that he had had an interview with President Lincoln immediately after the publication of that proclamation, and it was the subject of very minute and protracted conversation, in the course of which, after discussing the details, Mr. Lincoln expressed his regret that he had not approved the bill. I have always thought that Mr. Lincoln made a serious mistake in defeating a measure, which, if adopted, would have averted many if not all the difficulties that subsequently arose in the reconstruction of the rebel states.

The next and closing session of that Congress neglected to provide for the reorganization of these states, and, thus, when Mr. Johnson became President, there was no provision of law to guide him in the necessary process of reconstruction. Thus, by the disagreement between Congress and President Lincoln, which commenced two years before the close of the war, there was no law upon the statute book to guide either the President or the people of the southern states in their effort to get back into the Union. It became imperative during the long period before the meeting of Congress that President Johnson should, in the absence of legislation, formulate some plan for the reconstruction of these states. He did adopt substantially the plan proposed and acted upon by Mr. Lincoln. After this long lapse of time I am convinced that Mr. Johnson's scheme of reorganization was wise and judicious. It was unfortunate that it had not the sanction of Congress and that events soon brought the President and Congress into hostility. Who doubts that if there had been a law upon the statute book by which the people of the southern states could have been guided in their effort to come back into the Union, they would have cheerfully followed it, although the conditions had been hard? In the absence of law both Lincoln and Johnson did substantially right when they adopted a plan of their own and endeavored to carry it into execution. Johnson, before he was elected and while acting as military governor of Tennessee, executed the plan of Lincoln in that state and subsequently adopted the same plan for the reorganization of the rebel states. In all these plans the central idea was that the states in insurrection were still states, entitled to be treated as such. They were described as "The eleven states which have been declared to be in insurrection." There was an express provision that:

"No Senator or Representative shall be admitted into either branch of Congress from *any of said states* until Congress shall have declared *such state* entitled to such representation."

In all the plans proposed in Congress, as well as in the plan of Johnson, it was declared that states had no right while in insurrection to elect electors to the electoral college; they had no right to elect Senators and Representatives. In other words they could not resume the powers, rights and privileges conferred upon states by the Constitution of the United States, except by the consent of Congress. Having taken up arms against the United States, they by that act lost their constitutional powers within the United States to govern and control our councils. They could not engage in the election of a President, or of Senators or Members of Congress; but they were still states. The supreme power of Congress to change, alter or modify the acts of the President and to admit or reject these states and their Senators and Representatives at its will and pleasure, and the constitutional right of the respective Houses to judge of the election, returns and qualifications of its own Members were recognized. When Mr. Johnson came into power he found the Rebellion substantially subdued. His first act was to retain in his confidence, and in his councils, every member of the cabinet of Abraham Lincoln, and, so far as we know, every measure adopted by him had the approval and sanction of that cabinet. Every act passed by Congress, with or without his assent, upon every subject whatever, connected with reconstruction, was fairly and fully executed. He adopted all the main features of the Wade-Davis bill—the only one passed by Congress. In his proclamation of May 9, 1865, he provided:

"First, That all acts and proceedings of the political, military, and civil organizations which have been in a state of insurrection and rebellion within the State of Virginia against the authority and laws of the United States, and of which Jefferson Davis, John Letcher, and William Smith were late the respective chiefs, are declared null and void."

Thus, with a single stroke, he swept away the whole superstructure of the Rebellion. He extended the tax laws of the United States over the rebel territory. In his proclamation of May 29, he says;

"To the end, therefore, that the authority of the government of the United States may be restored, and that peace, order, and freedom may be established, I, Andrew Johnson, President of the United States, do proclaim and declare that I hereby grant to all persons who have directly or indirectly participated in the existing Rebellion, *except as hereinafter excepted,* amnesty and pardon, with restoration of all rights of property, *except as to slaves,* and except in cases where legal proceedings, under the laws of the United States providing for the confiscation of property of persons engaged in rebellion, have been instituted, &c."

He enforced in every case full and ample protection to the freedmen of the southern states. No complaint from them was ever brought to his knowledge in which he did not do full and substantial justice. The principal objection to his policy was that he did not extend his proclamation to all the loyal men of the southern states, including the colored as well as the white people. It must be remembered in his justification that in every one of the eleven states before the Rebellion the negro was, by its laws, excluded from the right to vote. In Ohio, Pennsylvania and New York that right was limited. In a large majority of the states, including the most populous, negro suffrage was then prohibited. It would seem to be a great stretch of power on his part, by a simple mandatory proclamation or military order, to confer the franchise on a class of people, who were then prohibited from voting not only in the eleven southern states, but in a majority of the northern states. Such a provision, if it had been inserted, could not have been enforced, and, in the condition in which slavery left the negro race, it could hardly be defended. I cannot see any reason why, because a man is black, he should not vote, and yet, in making laws, as the President was then doing, for the government of the community, he had to regard the prejudices, not only of the people among whom the laws were to be executed, but also of the army and the people who were to execute those laws, and no man can doubt but what at that time there was a strong and powerful prejudice in the army and among all classes of citizens against extending the right of suffrage to negroes, especially down in the far south, where the great body of the slaves were in abject ignorance.

It must be also noted that in the Wade-Davis bill Congress did not and would not make negro suffrage a part of its plan. Even so radical an anti-slavery man as my colleague, Senator Wade, did not propose such a measure. The effort was made to give emancipated negroes the right to vote, and it was abandoned. By that bill the suffrage was conferred only upon *white* male loyal citizens. And in the plan of the President, he adopted in this respect the very same conditions for suffrage as those proposed by Congress. I believe that all the acts and proclamations of President Johnson before the meeting of Congress were wise and expedient, and that there would have been no difficulty between Congress and the President but for his personal conduct, and, especially, his treatment of Congress and leading Congressmen. The unfortunate occurrence, already narrated, at his inauguration, was followed by violent and disrespectful language, unbecoming the President, especially, his foolish speech made on the 22nd of February, 1866, in which he selected particular persons as the objects of denunciation. He said:

"I fought traitors and treason in the south. I opposed the Davises, the Toombses, the Slidells, and a long list of others, which you can readily fill without my repeating the names. Now, when I turn round, and at the other end of the line find men, I care not by what name you call them, who still stand opposed to the restoration of the Union of these states, I am free to say to you that I am still in the field."

And again he said:

"I am called upon to name three at the other end of the line; I am talking to my friends and fellow-citizens, who are interested with me in this government, and I presume I am free to mention to you the names of those whom I look upon as being opposed to the fundamental principles of this government, and who are laboring to pervert and destroy it."

VOICES: "Name them!" "Who are they?"

He replied:

"You ask me who they are. I say Thaddeus Stevens, of Pennsylvania, is one; I say Mr. Sumner, of the Senate, is another; and Wendell Phillips is another."

The violence of language, so unlike that of Abraham Lincoln, added to the hostility to Mr. Johnson in Congress, and, I think, more than any other cause, led to his impeachment by the House of Representatives.

In the beginning of the controversy between Congress and the President, I tried to act as a peacemaker. I knew Mr. Johnson personally, his good and his bad qualities. I sat by his side in the Senate chamber during the first two years of the war. I was with him in his canvass in 1864. I sympathized with him in his struggles with the leaders of the Rebellion and admired his courage during the war, when, as Governor of Tennessee, he reorganized that state upon a loyal basis. The defect of his character was his unreasoning pugnacity. He early became involved in wordy warfare with Sumner, Wade, Stevens and others. In his high position he could have disregarded criticism, but this was not the habit of Johnson. When assailed he fought, and could be as violent and insulting in language or acts as anyone.

Under these circumstances I made a long and carefully considered speech in the Senate on the 26th of February, 1866, in which I stated the position of Congress on the reconstruction measures, and the policy adopted by Johnson from Lincoln. Either of the plans would have accomplished the provisional restoration of these states to the Union, while all agreed that, when admitted, they would be armed with all the powers of states, subject only to the constitution of the United States. I believed then, and believe now, that the quarrel with Johnson did much to weaken the Republican party. In consequence of it several Republican Senators and Members severed their connection with that party and joined the Democratic party. Johnson, irritated by this antagonism, drifted away from the measures he had himself advocated and soon after was in open opposition to the party that elected him. I here insert passages from my speech, which expressed my views at the time, and which I now feel were justified by the then existing opinions and conditions of political life:

"Sir, I can imagine no calamity more disgraceful than for us by our divisions to surrender, to men who to their country were enemies in war, any or all of the powers of this government. He, who contributes in any way to this result, deserves the execrations of his countrymen. This may be done by thrusting upon the President new issues on which the well-known principles of his life do not agree with the judgment of his political associates. It may be done by irritating controversies of a personal character. It may be done by the President turning his back upon those who trusted him with high power, and thus linking his name with one of the most disgraceful in American history, that of John Tyler. I feel an abiding confidence that Andrew Johnson will not and cannot do this ; and, sir, who will deny that the overbearing and intolerant will of Henry Clay contributed very much to the defection of John Tyler? But the division of the Whig party was an event utterly insignificant in comparison with the evil results of a division in the Union party.

"Where will be the four million slaves whom by your policy you have emancipated? What would be their miserable fate if now surrendered to the custody of the rebels of the south? Will you, by your demand of universal suffrage, destroy the power of the Union party to protect them in their dearly purchased liberty? Will you, by new issues upon which you know you have not the voice of the people, jeopard these rights which you can by the aid of the Union party secure to these freedmen? We know that the President can not and will not unite with us upon the issues of universal suffrage and dead states, and he never agreed to. No such dogmas were contemplated, when, for his heroic services in the cause of the Union, we placed him, side by side, with Mr. Lincoln as our standard-bearer. Why, then, present these issues? Why decide upon them? Why not complete the work so gloriously done by our soldiers by securing union and liberty to all men without distinction of color, leaving to the states, as before, the question of suffrage.

"Sir, the curse of God, the maledictions of millions of our people, and the tears and blood of new-made freemen will, in my judgment, rest upon those who now for any cause destroy the unity of the great party that has led us through the wilderness of war. We want now peace and repose. We must now look to our public credit. We have duties to perform to the business interests of the country, in which we need the assistance of the President. We have every motive for harmony with him and with each other, and for a generous and manly trust in his patriotism. If ever the time shall come when I can no longer confide in his devotion to the principles upon which he was elected, I will bid farewell to Andrew Johnson with unaffected sorrow. I will remember when he stood in this very spot, five years ago, repelling with unexampled courage the assaults of traitors. He left in their hands wife, children, property, and home, and staked them all on the result. I will remember that when a retreating general would have left Nashville to its fate, that again, with heroic courage, he maintained his post. I will remember the fierce conflicts and trials through which he and his fellow-compatriots in east Tennessee maintained our cause in the heart of the Confederacy. I will remember the struggles he had with the aristocratic element of Tennessee, never ashamed of his origin and never far from the hearts of the people.

"Sir, you must not sever the great Union party from this loyal element of the southern states. No new theories of possible utopian good can compensate for the loss of such patriotism and devotion. Time, as he tells you in his message, is a great element of reform, and time is on your side. I remember the homely and encouraging words of a pioneer in the anti-slavery cause, an expelled Methodist preacher from the south, who told those who were behind him in his strong anti-slavery opinions: 'Well friends, I'll block up awhile; we must all travel together.' So I say to all who doubt Andrew Johnson, or who wish to move more rapidly than he can, to block up awhile, to consolidate their great victory with the certainty that reason and the Almighty will continue their work. All wisdom will not die with us. The highest human wisdom is to do all the good you can, but not to sacrifice a possible good to attempt the impracticable. God knows that I do not urge harmony and conciliation from any personal motive. The people of my native state have intrusted me with a position here extending four years beyond the termination of the President's term of office. He can grant me no favor.

"If I believed for a moment that he would seek an alliance with those who, by either arms or counsel or even apathy, were against their country in the recent war, and will turn over to them the high powers intrusted to him by the Union party, then, sir, he is dishonored, and will receive no assistance from me; but I will not force him into that attitude. If he shall prove false to the declaration made by him in his veto message, that his strongest desire was to secure to the freedmen the full enjoyment of their freedom and property, then I will not quarrel with him as to the means used. And while, as he tells us in this same message, he only asks for states to be represented which are presented in an attitude of loyalty and harmony and in the persons of representatives whose loyalty cannot be questioned under any constitutional or legal test, surely we ought not to separate from him until, at least, we prescribe a test of their loyalty, upon which we are willing to stand. We have not done it yet. I will not try him by new creeds. I will not denounce him for hasty words uttered in repelling personal affronts.

"I see him yet surrounded by the cabinet of Abraham Lincoln, pursuing Lincoln's policy. No word from me shall drive him into political fellowship with those who, when he was one of the moral heroes of this war, denounced him, spit upon him, and despitefully used him. The association must be self-sought, and even then I will part with him in sorrow, but with the abiding hope that the same Almighty power that has guided us through the recent war will be with us still in our new difficulties until every state is restored to its full communion and fellowship, and until our nation, purified by war, will assume among the nations of the earth the grand position hoped for by Washington, Clay, Webster, Lincoln, and hundreds of thousands of unnamed heroes who gave up their lives for its glory."

I received many letters in commendation of this speech, among others the following from Thurlow Weed, who was in full sympathy with Secretary Seward:

ALBANY, N. Y., February 28, 1866.

DEAR SHERMAN:—You have spoken words of wisdom and patriotism —spoken them boldly at the right time. They will help save the Union —and they will save the Union particularly if fanatics and despots will allow it to be saved. Just such a speech at the moment it was made is worth more than all that has been said in Congress since the session commenced. I thank you gratefully for it. Yours truly,

THURLOW WEED.

I still hoped that the pending civil rights bill would be approved by the President, and that then the controversy would end. On the 17th of March, 1866, I made a speech at Bridgeport, Conn., in which I said:

"Now, I say, that upon all these various propositions, upon the necessity of a change in the basis of representation, upon the necessity for protecting the negroes, upon this question of suffrage — upon all these questions that have arisen in our politics of late, the differences between Andrew Johnson and Congress are not such as need excite the alarm of any patriotic citizen. No, my friends, we have a great duty to perform to our country. Every man in public life now has a heavy responsibility resting upon him, in the discharge of which he is bound to follow the dictates of his own conscience, given to him by Almighty God. There are, there must be, differences of opinion ; God has so made us that we must differ ; it is the established nature of the human mind to disagree. It is only by discussion and comparison of views that the highest human wisdom is elicited. Therefore, I say again, that no Union man need feel anxious or uneasy because of the differences

Alby, Feb 2 8.

Dear Sherman

You have spoken
works of wisdom and patriotism
- spoken them boldly at the right
time. They will help save the
Union — and they will save the
Union if Fanatics and Despots will allow it to be saved.
Just such a speech at the moment
it was made is worth the
more than all that has been said
in Congress since the Session commenced. I thank you gratefully for
it.

Truly Yours
Thurlow Weed

Hon John Sherman.

between the President and Congress. Let me tell you, as the solemn conviction with which I address you to-night, that Andrew Johnson never will throw the power we have given him into the hands of the Copperhead party of the United States.

" I have many reasons for this faith. One is that no nomination has ever been sent by Andrew Johnson to the Senate of the United States of any man of that stripe of politics. No flattery, no cajolery can draw him from that line. He is a man who fights his own battles, and whether they are old friends or foes that assail him he fights them with equal freedom and boldness, and sometimes, perhaps indiscreetly; but that is a fault of his character, which need excite no uneasiness in the minds of the people.

" On Thursday, the day that I left Washington, we sent to him a bill which secures to all the colored population of the southern states equal rights before the law, the civil rights bill. It declares that no state shall exclude any man on account of his color from any of the natural rights which, by the Declaration of Independence, are declared to be inalienable ; it provides that every man may sue and be sued, may plead and be impleaded, may acquire and hold property, may purchase, contract, sell and convey ; all those rights are secured to the negro population. That bill is now in the hands of the President. If he sign it, it will be a solemn pledge of the law-making power of the nation that the negroes shall have secured to them all these natural and inalienable rights. I believe the President will sign it."

Unfortunately at the end of ten days the President sent to the Senate the civil rights bill, referred to, with his message vetoing it. It passed both Houses with the requisite two-thirds majority, and thus became a law. This veto was followed by other vetoes, and, practically, the President abandoned his party. From this time forth, I heartily joined with my political associates in the measures adopted to secure a loyal reorganization of the southern states. I was largely influenced by the harsh treatment of the freedmen in the south under acts adopted by the reconstructed legislatures. The outrages of the Ku-Klux Klans seemed to me to be so atrocious and wicked that the men who committed them were not only unworthy to govern, but unfit to live. The weakness of the position of Congress in the controversy with Mr. Johnson, was, that it had furnished no plan of reconstruction and he was compelled to act upon the urgency of events. Many efforts were made to provide legislation to take the place of the proclamations and acts of the President, but a wide divergence of opinion in the Republican party manifested itself, and no substantial progress was made until near the close of the second session of the 39th Congress. Several bills were then pending in each House to provide governments for the insurrectionary states. On the 13th of February, 1867, during the short session, a bill with that title came from the House of Representatives. It was manifest unless this bill could be acted upon, that, in the then condition of Congress, all legislation would fail. It was kept before the Senate and thoroughly debated. On the 16th of February, after consultation with my political colleagues, I moved a substitute for the House bill. The fifth section of this substitute embodied a comprehensive plan for the organization of the rebel states with provision for elections in said states, and the conditions required for their admission and restoration to the Union and the exercise by them of all the powers of states, and provided for the election of Senators and Members of Congress. In presenting this substitute, I briefly stated my reasons for it, as follows:

"The principle of this bill is contained in the first two lines of the preamble. It is founded upon the proclamation of the President and Secretary of State made just after the assassination of President Lincoln, in which they declared specifically that the Rebellion had overthrown all civil governments in the insurrectionary states, and they proceeded by an executive mandate to create governments. They were provisional in their character, and dependent for their validity solely upon the action of Congress. These are propositions which it is not now necessary for me to demonstrate. Those governments have never been sanctioned by Congress, nor by the people of the states where they exist. Taking that proclamation and the acknowledged fact that the people of the southern states, the loyal people, whites and blacks, are not protected in their rights, but that an unusual and extraordinary number of cases occur of violence, and murder, and wrong, I do think it is the duty of the United States to protect those people in the enjoyment of substantial rights.

"Now, the first four sections of this substitute contain nothing but what is in the present law. There is not a single thing in the first four sections that does not now exist by law.

"The first section authorizes the division of the rebel states into military districts. That is being done daily.

"The second section acknowledges that the President is the commanding officer of the army, and it is made his duty to assign certain officers to those districts. That is clearly admitted to be right.

"The third section does no more than what the Supreme Court in their recent decision have decided could be done in a state in insurrection. The Supreme Court in their recent decision, while denying that a military tribunal could be organized in Indiana because it never had been in a state of insurrection, expressly declared that these tribunals might have been, and might now be, organized in insurrectionary states. There is nothing in this third section, in my judgment, that is not now and has not been done every month within the last twelve months by the President of the United States. The orders of General Sickles, and many other orders that I might quote, have gone further in punishment of crime than this section proposes.

"Now, in regard to the fourth section, that is a limitation upon the present law. Under the present law many executions of military tribunals are summarily carried out. This section requires all sentences of military tribunals which affect the liberty of the citizen to be sent to the commanding officer of the district. They must be approved by the commanding officer of the district; and so far as life is concerned the President may issue his order at any moment now, or after this bill passes, directing that the military commander of the district shall not enforce a sentence of death until it is submitted to him, because the military officer is a mere subordinate of the President, remaining there at the pleasure of the President.

"There is nothing, therefore, in these sections, that ought to alarm the nerves of my friend from Pennsylvania, or anybody else. I cannot think that these gentlemen are alarmed about the state of despotism that President Johnson is to establish in the southern states. I do not feel alarmed; nor do I see anything in these sections as they now stand that need endanger the rights of the most timid citizen of the United States. They are intended to protect a race of people who are now without protection.

"Now, in regard to the fifth section, which is the main and material feature of this bill, I think it is right that the Congress of the United States, before its adjournment, should designate some way by which the southern states may reorganize loyal state governments in harmony with the constitution and laws of the United States, and the sentiment of the people, and find their way back to these halls. My own judgment is that the fifth section will point out a clear, easy, and right way for these states to be restored to their full power in the government. All that it demands of the people of the southern states is to extend to all their male citizens, without distinction of race or color, the elective franchise. It is now too late in the day to be frightened by this simple proposition. Senators can make the most of it as a political proposition. Upon that we are prepared to meet them. But it does point out a way by which the twenty absent Senators, and the fifty absent Representatives can get back to these halls, and there is no other way by which they can justly do it.

"It seems to me that this is the whole substance of the bill. All there is material in the bill is in the first two lines of the preamble and the fifth section, in my judgment. The first two lines may lay the foundation by adopting the proclamation issued first to North Carolina, that the Rebellion had swept away all the civil governments in the southern states ; and the fifth section points out the mode by which the people of those states in their own manner, without any limitations or restrictions by Congress, may get back full representation in Congress. That is the view I take of this amended bill ; and taking that view of it I see no reason in the world why we should not all vote for it."

The substitute was adopted on the same day and the bill, thus amended, was passed by a vote of yeas 29, nays 10. In the House it was agreed to with slight amendments, which were finally concurred in by the Senate, on February 20, 1867. It was sent to the President and was not approved by him, but was, on the 2nd of March, passed over his veto by a vote of two-thirds of both Houses.

Upon this law, long deferred, the several states mentioned in it were organized and restored to their place in the Union. The preamble and fifth and sixth sections of this law are as follows:

"AN ACT TO PROVIDE FOR THE MORE EFFICIENT GOVERNMENT OF THE REBEL STATES.

" WHEREAS, no legal state governments or adequate protection for life or property now exists in the rebel states of Virginia, North Carolina, South Carolina, Georgia, Mississippi, Alabama, Louisiana, Florida, Texas, and Arkansas ; and whereas it is necessary that peace and good order should be enforced in said states until loyal and republican state governments can be legally established : Therefore,

" *Be it enacted by the Senate and House of Representatives of the United States of America in Congress assembled :* . . .

" SEC. 5. *And be it further enacted,* That when the people of any one of said rebel states shall have formed a constitution of government in conformity with the constitution of the United States in all respects, framed by a convention of delegates elected by the male citizens of said state, twenty-one years old and upward, of whatever race, color, or previous condition, who have been resident in said state for one year previous to the day of such election, except such as may be disfranchised for participation in the Rebellion, or for felony at common law, and when such constitution shall provide that the elective franchise shall be enjoyed by all such persons as have the qualifications herein stated for electors of delegates, and when such constitution shall be ratified by a majority of the persons voting on the question of ratification who are qualified as electors for delegates, and when such constitution shall have been submitted to Congress for examination and approval, and Congress shall have approved the same, and when said state, by a vote of its legislature, elected under such constitution, shall have adopted the amendment to the constitution of the United States, proposed by the 39th Congress, and known as article fourteen, and when said article shall have become a part of the constitution of the United States, said state shall be declared entitled to representation in Congress, and Senators and Representatives shall be admitted therefrom on their taking the oath prescribed by law, and then and thereafter the preceding sections of this act shall be inoperative in said state : *Provided,* That no person excluded from the privilege of holding office by said proposed amendment to the constitution of the United States shall be eligible to election as a member of the convention to frame a constitution for any of said rebel states, nor shall any such person vote for members of such convention.

"SEC. 6. *And be it further enacted,* That, until the people of said rebel states shall be by law admitted to representation in the Congress of the United States, any civil governments which may exist therein shall be deemed provisional only, and in all respects subject to the paramount authority of the United States at any time to abolish, modify, control, or supersede the same ; and in all elections to any office under such provisional governments all persons shall be entitled to vote, and none others, who are entitled to vote, under the provisions of the fifth section of this act ; and no person shall be elegible to any office under any such provisional governments who would be disqualified from holding office under the provisions of the third article of said constitutional amendment."

At the same time, the financial question, embracing the currency, the public debt and the national revenue were of the highest importance and demanded immediate consideration. Hugh McCulloch, the Secretary of the Treasury, had been during most of his life a banker in the State of Indiana, of acknowledged ability as such, but with little or no experience as a financier dealing with public questions. He was the first comptroller of the currency under the banking act, and rendered valuable service in organizing the system of national banks, though he had not originally favored the system, but was, at the time of its adoption, a strong supporter of sound state banks. In his first report to Congress on the 4th of December, 1865, he, as Secretary of the Treasury, took strong ground against United States notes as a circulating medium and their being made a legal tender as money. He regarded the legal tender acts as war measures, and, while he did not recommend their repeal, he expressed his opinion that they ought not to remain in force one day longer than would be necessary to enable the people to prepare for a return to the constitutional currency. He denied the authority of Congress to issue these notes except in the nature of a loan, and affirmed that the statute making them a legal tender for all debts, public and private, was not within the scope of the duties or the constitutional power of Congress; that their issue as lawful money was a measure necessary in a great emergency, but, as this emergency did not then exist, the government should, as speedily as possible, withdraw them, and he recommended that the work of retiring the notes should be commenced without delay and carefully and persistently continued until all were retired. He proposed to do this by the sale of bonds for United States notes outstanding and their withdrawal and cancellation. He recommended as a substitute the notes of national banks, but even these notes he thought redundant, and said:

"There is no fact more manifest than that the plethora of paper money is not only undermining the morals of the people by encouraging waste and extravagance, but is striking at the root of our material prosperity by diminishing labor . . . and if not speedily checked, will, at no distant day, culminate in widespread disaster. The remedy, and the only remedy within the control of Congress, is, in the opinion of the secretary, to be found in the reduction of the currency."

The chief part of his report was devoted to the danger of inflation and the necessity of contraction. He said the longer contraction was delayed the greater must the fall eventually be, and the more serious its consequences.

In accordance with the recommendations of Secretary McCulloch, a bill was introduced in the House by Justin S. Morrill, which authorized the Secretary of the Treasury, at his discretion, to sell any of the description of bonds authorized by the act of March 3, 1865, the proceeds to be used only to retire treasury notes or other obligations issued under any act of Congress. This bill as reported would have placed in the power of the secretary the retirement of all United States notes at his discretion. An amendment was made in the House which provided:

"That of United States notes not more than ten millions of dollars may be retired and canceled within six months from the passage of this act, and thereafter not more than four millions of dollars in any one month."

The bill as it came to the Senate was as follows:

"An act to amend an act entitled 'An act to provide ways and means to support the government,' approved March third, eighteen hundred and sixty-five.

"*Be it enacted by the Senate and House of Representatives of the United States of America in Congress assembled,* That the act entitled 'An act to provide ways and means to support the government,' approved March third, eighteen hundred and sixty-five, shall be extended and construed to authorize the Secretary of the Treasury, at his discretion, to receive any treasury notes or other obligations issued under any act of Congress, whether bearing interest or not, in exchange for any description of bonds authorized by the act to which this is an amendment; and also to dispose of any description of bonds authorized by said act, either in the United States or elsewhere, to such an amount, in such manner, and at such rates, as he may think advisable, for lawful money of the United States, or for any treasury notes, certificates of indebtedness, or certificates of deposit, or other representatives of value, which have been or which may be issued under any act of Congress, the proceeds thereof to be used only for retiring treasury notes or other obligations issued under any act of Congress ; but nothing herein contained shall be construed to authorize any increase of the public debt : *Provided*, That of United States notes not more than ten millions of dollars may be retired and canceled within six months from the passage of this act, and thereafter not more than four millions of dollars in any one month : *And provided further*, That the act to which this is an amendment shall continue in full force in all its provisions, except as modified by this act.

"Sec. 2. *And be it further enacted*, That the Secretary of the Treasury shall report to Congress at the commencement of the next session the amount of exchanges made or money borrowed under this act, and of whom and on what terms ; and also the amount and character of indebtedness retired under this act, and the act to which this is an amendment, with a detailed statement of the expense of making such loans and exchanges."

This bill, without change, became a law April 12, 1866. I believed then, and now know, that the passage of this law was a great misfortune. It enabled the Secretary of the Treasury to retire at a rapid rate United States notes and to largely increase the bonded indebtedness of the United States. It would no doubt have brought us abruptly to the specie standard and made us dependent for circulating notes upon the issues of national banks.

At this time there was a wide difference of opinion between Secretary McCulloch and myself as to the financial policy of the government in respect to the public debt and the currency. He was in favor of a rapid contraction of the currency by funding it into interest bearing bonds. I was in favor of maintaining in circulation the then existing volume of currency as an aid to the funding of all forms of interest-bearing securities into bonds redeemable within a brief period at the pleasure of the United States, and bearing as low a rate of interest as possible. Both of us were in favor of specie payments, he by contraction and I by the gradual advancement of the credit and value of our currency to the specie standard. With him specie payments was the primary object, with me it was a secondary object, to follow the advancing credit of the government. Each of us was in favor of the payment of the interest of bonds in coin, and the principal, when due, in coin. A large proportion of national securities were payable in lawful money, or United States notes. He, by contraction, would have made this payment more difficult, while I, by retaining the notes in existence, would induce the holders of currency certificates to convert them into coin obligations bearing a lower rate of interest.

CHAPTER XVII.

INDEBTEDNESS OF THE UNITED STATES IN 1865.

Organization of the Greenback Party — Total Debt on October 31, amounts to $2,808,549,437.55 — Secretary McCulloch's Desire to Convert All United States Notes Into Interest Bearing Bonds — My Discussion with Senator Fessenden Over the Finance Committee's Bill — Too Great Powers Conferred on the Secretary of the Treasury — His Desire to Retire $10,000,000 of United States Notes Each Month — Growth of the Greenback Party — The Secretary's Powers to Reduce the Currency by Retiring or Canceling United States Notes Is Suspended — Bill to Reduce Taxes and Provide Internal Revenue — My Trip to Laramie and Other Western Forts with General Sherman — Beginning of the Department of Agriculture.

DURING this period a party sprang up composed of men of all parties called the Greenback party, who favored an increase of United States notes, and the payment of all United States bonds and securities in such notes. This difference of opinion continued until the resumption of specie payments, in January, 1879.

I propose to state here the measures adopted in respect to the national currency and debt during the rest of the administration of President Johnson.

The total debt of the United States on the 31st of October, 1865, was $2,808,549,437.55 in twenty-five different forms of indebtedness of which, $1,200,000,000 was payable at the option of the Secretary of the Treasury, or within a brief period. The amount of United States notes outstanding was then $428,160,569, and of fractional currency $26,057,469, in all $454,218,038. All of this money was in active circulation, in great favor among the people, worth in use as much as national bank notes, and rapidly rising in value compared with coin. It was the least burdensome form of indebtedness then existing. The treasury notes and compound interest notes were in express terms payable in this lawful money, and, therefore, bore a higher rate of interest than the bonds, which, by their express terms or necessary implication, were payable in coin only.

It was insisted that the amount of United States notes was in excess of what was needed for currency in time of peace and might safely be gradually reduced. This effort to contract the currency was firmly resisted by several Senators, myself among them. The Supreme Court decided that Congress had full power to make these notes a legal tender. They were far better than any form of currency previously existing in the United States. During the war, when the expenditures of the government reached nearly $1,000,000,-000 a year they were indispensable. Those most opposed to irredeemable paper money acknowledged this necessity. The only objection to them was that they were not equivalent to coin in purchasing power. After the war was over, the general desire of all was to advance these notes nearer to par with coin, but not to withdraw them. The rising credit and financial strength of the United States would, it was believed, bring them to par without injustice to the debtor, but the rapid withdrawal of the notes would add to the burden of debts and cripple all forms of industry. It would convert the compound interest notes and treasury notes bearing seven and three tenths per cent. interest, amounting to over $1,000,-000,000 expressly payable in United States notes, into coin liabilities. The bill prepared at the treasury department contemplated the conversion of all United States notes into bonds. In that form the bill was defeated in the House of Representatives, but it was reconsidered and an amendment was then made limiting the retirement of notes to $4,000,000 a month. This gained for the bill enough votes to secure its passage. Even the withdrawal of $48,000,000 a year was soon found to be oppressive and was subsequently repealed.

When this bill came before the committee on finance, I found myself alone in opposition to it. I could not impress my colleagues of the committee with the grave importance of the measure, and its wide-reaching influence upon our currency, debt and credit. They regarded it simply as a bill to change the form of our securities. I felt confident that without the use of United States notes we could not make this exchange. When the bill was brought before the Senate by Mr. Fessenden, chairman of the committee, he made no statement of its terms, but only said:

"I have merely to say that this bill is reported by the committee on finance without amendment as it came from the House of Representatives. The committee on finance, on careful examination of it, came to the conclusion that the bill was well enough as it stood, and did not deem it advisable to make any amendment. It has been before the Senate a considerable time, and I presume every Senator understands it. I ask, therefore, for the question."

I replied:

"I regret very much that I differ from the committee on finance in regard to this bill. This is the only bill on the subject of the public debt on which I have not been able to concur with that committee. . . .

"If Senators will read this bill they will find that it confers on the Secretary of the Treasury greater powers than have ever been conferred, since the foundation of this government, upon any Secretary of the Treasury. Our loan laws, heretofore, have generally been confined to the negotiation of a single loan, limited in amount. As the war progressed, the difficulties of the country became greater, and we were more in the habit of removing the limitations on the power of the Secretary of the Treasury; but generally the power conferred was confined to a particular loan then in the market. This bill, however, is more general in its terms. This bill authorizes the Secretary of the Treasury to sell any character of bonds without limit, except as to the rate of interest. The authority conferred does not limit him to any form of security. It may run for any period of time within forty years. He may sell the securities at less than par, without limitation as to rate. He may sell them in any form he chooses. He may put them in the form of treasury notes or bonds, the interest payable in gold or in paper money. He may undertake, under the provisions of this bill, to fund the whole debt of the United States. The only limit as to amount is the public debt, now $2,700,000,000. The power conferred on the Secretary of the Treasury is absolute. It is not only for this year, or during the current fiscal year, or for the next year, but it is for all time, until the act shall be repealed. It gives him absolute power to negotiate bonds of the United States to the amount of $2,700,000,000, without limiting the rate at which they shall be sold, and only limiting the rate of interest inferentially. The description of the bonds in the act of March 3, 1865, referred to here, would probably limit the rate of interest to six per cent. in coin, and seven and three-tenths per cent. in currency; but with this exception there is no limitation.

" It seems to me that in the present condition of our finances there is no necessity for conferring these large powers on the Secretary of the Treasury. The people are not generally aware of the favorable condition of our finances. The statement of the public debt laid on our tables the other day does not show fully the condition of the finances. It is accurate in amounts, but does not give dates of the maturity of our debts. But a small portion of the debt of the United States will be due prior to August, 1867, that will give the secretary any trouble. But little of the debt which he will be required to fund under the provisions of this bill matures before August, 1867. The temporary or call loan, now over one hundred millions, may readily be kept at this sum even at a reduced rate of interest. The certificates of indebtedness, amounting to sixty-two millions, may easily be paid from accruing receipts, or, if necessary, may be renewed or funded at the pleasure of the secretary. None of the compound interest notes or the seven-thirty notes mature until August, 1867.   .   .   .

" There is, therefore, no immediate necessity for these vast powers. The question then naturally occurs, why grant them ? I have carefully considered this question, and I do not think there is now any immediate necessity for granting these powers. No debt is maturing that is likely to give the government any trouble ; and yet we are now about to confer, upon the Secretary of the Treasury, powers that we cannot, in the nature of things, recall. It is true we may repeal this law next year, but we know very well that when these large powers are granted they are very seldom recalled; they are made the precedents of further grants of power and are very rarely recalled. It seems to me that the whole object of the passage of this bill is to place it within the power of the Secretary of the Treasury to contract the currency of the country, and thus, as I think, to produce an unnecessary strain upon the people. This power I do not think ought to be given to him. The House of Representatives did not intend to give him this power. They debated the bill a long time, and it was defeated on the ground that they would not confer on the secretary this power to reduce the currency, and finally it was only passed with a proviso contained in the bill which I will now read :

" ' *Provided*, That of United States notes not more than $10,000,000 may be retired and canceled within six months from the passage of this act, and thereafter not more than $4,000,000 in any one month.'

" The purpose of the House of Representatives was, while giving the secretary power to fund the debt as it matured or even before maturity, giving him the most ample power over the debt of the United States, to limit his power over the currency, lest he might carry to an extreme the view presented by him in his annual report. If this proviso would accomplish the purpose designed by the House of Representatives, I would cease all opposition to this bill ; but I know it will not, and for this very obvious reason, that there is no restraint upon the power of the Secretary of the Treasury to accumulate legal tender notes in the treasury. He may retire

$200,000,000 of legal tender notes by retaining them in his possession without cancellation, and thus accomplish the very purpose the House of Representatives did not intend to allow him to accomplish. He may sell the bonds of the United States, at any rate he chooses, for legal tenders, and he may hold those legal tenders in his vaults, thus retiring them from the business of the country, and thus produce the very contraction which the House of Representatives meant to deny him power to do. Therefore, this proviso, which only limits the power of canceling securities or notes, does not limit his power over the currency, and he may, without violating this bill, in pursuance of the very terms of the bill, contract the currency according to his own good will and pleasure.

" My own impression is, that the Secretary of the Treasury, in carrying out his own policy, will do so. He says he will not contract it unreasonably or too rapidly, but I believe he will contract the currency in this way. He has now in the vaults of the treasury $60,000,000 in currency and $62,000,-000 in gold—a larger balance, I believe, than was ever before kept in the treasury until within the last two or three months ; a larger balance than was ever found in the treasury during the war. What is the object of accumulating these vast balances in the treasury ? Simply to carry out his policy of contraction. With this power of retaining in the treasury the money that comes in, what does he care for the limitation put upon this bill by the House of Representatives ? That says that he shall not retire and cancel more than $10,000,000 of United States notes within six months, and not more than $4,000,000 in any one month thereafter ; but why need he retire and cancel them when he can retain them in the vaults of the treasury, and thus contract the currency ? . . .

" I do not doubt in the least either the integrity or the capacity of the present incumbent of the treasury department. I have as much confidence in him as anyone ; but this question of the currency is one that affects so intimately all the business relations of life, the property of every man in this country, his ability to pay taxes, his ability to earn food and acquire a living, that no man ought to have the power to vary the volume of currency. It ought to be regulated by law, and the law ought to be so fixed and so defined that every business man may transact his business with full knowledge of the amount of the currency, with all its limits and qualifications. I ask you, sir, how any prudent or judicious man can now engage in any important business, in which he is compelled to go in debt, with this large power hanging over him. It would be unsafe for him to do so. The amount of the currency ought to be fixed by law, whether much or little. There ought to be a limit, and no man ought to have the power at pleasure to enlarge or contract that limit. . . .

" Then there is the further power to reduce the currency, a power that has not heretofore been granted to any Secretary of the Treasury. The amount heretofore has been fixed and limited by law. By the first clause of this bill the secretary is authorized to receive treasury notes, or United States notes of any form or description, and there is no limitation to this power, except the clause which I have read to you. That limits his power to retire and cancel the United States notes, but not to accumulate the enormous balances on hand. My own impression has been, and when this bill was before the committee on finance I believed, it would be better for that committee to report to the Senate a financial project to fund the debt of the United States. I believe that now is the favorable time to do it. If a five per cent. bond, a long bond of proper description and proper guarantee, was now placed upon the market, with such ample powers to negotiate it as ought to be given to the Secretary of the Treasury, such a loan as was authorized two years ago, at a reduced rate of interest, to be exempt from taxation, I have no doubt whatever, the Secretary of the Treasury could fund every portion of the debt of the United States as it matured. . . .

"I do not like to embarrass a bill of this kind with amendments, because I know it is difficult to consider amendments of this sort, requiring an examination of figures and tables. I have prepared a bill very carefully, with a view to meet my idea, but I will not present it now in antagonism to this bill passed by the House of Representatives and the view taken by the finance committee, because I know, in the present condition of the Senate, it would not probably be fully considered. My only purpose now is to point out the fact that is perfectly clear to the mind of every sensible man who has examined this bill, that the bill as it stands does not carry out the manifest intention of the House of Representatives when they passed it, and that the proviso, limiting the power of the secretary over the legal tender currency, does not accomplish the purpose which they designed, and without which I know the bill never could have passed the House of Representatives."

MR. FESSENDEN: "If the House of Representatives did not understand what they were doing when they passed this bill, it arises from the fact that they did not give the rein to their imagination, as the honorable Senator from Ohio seems to have done to his, and take it for granted that the Secretary of the Treasury had a purpose to accomplish, and that he would not hesitate to take any means in his power to accomplish it, improperly against the manifest will of Congress, against the interests of the country, and against his own interests as Secretary of the Treasury."

I replied:

"I appeal to the Senator whether that is a fair statement of my argument?"

MR. FESSENDEN: "That is the way precisely that I understand it."

I said:

"That is precisely as no gentleman could have understood me. I never said that the secretary improperly would do so and so by any means. It is one of the honorable Senator's modes of stating propositions."

MR. FESSENDEN: "I certainly did not mean to say that the honorable Senator supposed he designed to do so, but such seems to be the result of his argument — that the Secretary of the Treasury having the power, as he says, there is danger that he might abuse it in that precise way : else his argument amounts to nothing at all as against the bill. I certainly acquit my friend of any sort of desire or intention to throw any imputation on the Secretary of the Treasury. That he did not mean to do." . . .

I said:

" I do not think it wise to confer on the Secretary of the Treasury the power to meet the indebtedness not accruing for a year, or two, or three years. I do not think it is necessary, in our present financial condition, to authorize him to go into market now and sell bonds at current market rates with a view to pay debts that do not mature for a year or two. I have no doubt before the five-twenty loans are due we shall retire every dollar of them at four or five per cent. interest. No one who heeds the rapid developments of new sources of wealth in this country, the enormous yield of gold now, the renewal of industry in the south, the enormous yield of cotton, the growing wealth of this country, and all the favorable prospects that are before us, doubts the ability of this government before this debt matures to reduce it to four or five per cent. interest. . . .

" The Secretary of the Treasury may sell bonds at any rate to meet debts as they accrue, but that is not the purpose of this bill."

MR. FESSENDEN : " That is all the purpose there is in it."

I said :

" Then there is no necessity for it."

MR. FESSENDEN: " Yes, there is. I differ from you."

I continued :

" We have here the tables before us. The honorable Senator and I know when this debt matures. . . .

" That is the power now given, and he will use the power. He may think it to his interest to retire the whole of the seven-thirties or the ten-forties ; but is it wise for us to give him that power now, at the heel of the war and before things have settled down? I do not think it is.

" I repeat, I do not wish to call in question the integrity of the Secretary of the Treasury. The Senator interjects by saying we must look ahead. I have done so. The difference between us is that I anticipate that the future of this country will be hopeful, buoyant, joyous. We shall not have to beg money of foreign nations, or even of our own people, within two or three years. Our national debt will be eagerly sought for, I have no doubt. I take a hopeful view of the future. I do not wish now to cripple the industry of the country by adopting the policy of the Secretary of the Treasury, as he calls it, by reducing the currency, by crippling the operations of the government, when I think that under any probability of affairs in the future, all this debt will take care of itself. I believe that if the Secretary of the Treasury would do nothing in the world except simply sit in his chair, meet the accruing indebtedness, and issue his treasury warrants, this debt will take care of itself, and will fund itself at four or five per cent. before very long. All that I object to in this bill is the power it gives the Secretary of the Treasury over the currency, to affect the currency of the country now and to anticipate debts that are not yet due. . . .

"That is what I am afraid of, his interference to contract the currency. The honorable Senator from Maine, however, would seem to think that I impute to him a wrong motive, and therefore I corrected him when he made the remark that I seemed to suppose the secretary was doing this improperly. I think not. The Secretary of the Treasury informed us that he desired to reduce the currency, and he has been doing it as far as he could. He has been accumulating large balances. He was opposed to the proviso which has been inserted in this bill, and yielded to it only with reluctance. That is admitted on all hands, and he is not precluded either in honor or propriety from carrying out his policy if you gave him the power to do it."

This bill became a law on the 12th of April, 1866. President Johnson relied entirely upon McCulloch, and had no opinions upon financial topics.

Now, nearly thirty years after the passage of this act, it is manifest that it was by far the most injurious and expensive financial measure ever enacted by Congress. It not only compelled the United States to pay the large war rates of interest for many years, but postponed specie payments until 1879. It added fully $300,000,000 of interest that might have been saved by the earlier refunding of outstanding bonds into bonds bearing four to five per cent. interest. Mr. Fessenden, then chairman of the committee on finance, committed a grave error in hastily supporting the bill, an error which I believe he deeply regretted and which, in connection with his failing health, no doubt led him to resign his position as chairman of that committee. Although our debate was rather sharp, it did not disturb our friendly relations. With McCulloch in the treasury department, nothing could be done.

If the funding clauses of this act had been limited to the conversion of compound interest notes, treasury notes bearing interest, certificates of indebtedness, and temporary loans into bonds redeemable at the pleasure of the United States after a brief time, bearing not exceeding five per cent. interest, retaining in circulation during this process of refunding all the then outstanding United States notes, the result would have been greatly beneficial to the United States, but this was not the chief object of the Secretary of the Treasury. His primary object was to convert United States notes into interest-bearing bonds, and thus force the immediate resumption of specie payments or the substitution of national bank notes for United States notes. The result of his refunding was largely to increase the amount of six per cent. bonds, the most burdensome form of security then outstanding. In October, 1865, the amount of six per cent. bonds was $920,000,000; on the 1st of July, 1868, the six per cent. bonds outstanding were $1,557,844,-600. The increase of these bonds under the operation of this law was thus over $637,000,000.

The result of this policy of contraction was not only to increase the burden of the public debt, but it created serious derangement of the business of the country. It excited a strong popular opposition to the measures adopted.

The Greenback party, as it was called, grew out of this policy of contraction, and for a time threatened to carry the election of a majority of the Members of Congress. It contended practically for an unlimited issue of legal tender United States notes, and the payment of all bonds and securities in United States notes. This, however, did not disturb Secretary McCulloch. In his annual report of December 3, 1866, he again urged the policy of a further reduction of United States notes. He was not satisfied with the reduction already provided for, and recommended that the reduction should be increased from $4,000,000 a month, as contemplated by the act of April 12, 1866, to $6,000,000 a month for the fiscal year, and to $10,000,000 per month thereafter. He said:

" The *policy* of contracting the circulation of the government notes should be definitely and unchangeably established, and the *process* should go on just as rapidly as possible without producing a financial crisis or seriously embarrassing those branches of industry and trade upon which our revenues are dependent. That the policy indicated is the true and safe one, the secretary is thoroughly convinced. If it shall not be speedily adopted and rigidly, but judiciously, enforced, severe financial troubles are in store for us."

He insisted that the circulation of the country should be further reduced, not by compelling the national banks to retire

their notes, but by the withdrawal of United States notes.
When reminded of the great saving of interest in the issue of
$400,000,000 United States notes, he answered:

"Considerations of this nature are more than counterbalanced by the
discredit which attaches to the government by failing to pay its notes according to their tenor, by the bad influence of this involuntary discredit upon the
public morals, and the wide departure, which a continued issue of legal tender notes involves, from past usages, if not from the teachings of the constitution itself."

He said:

"The government cannot exercise powers not conferred by its organic
law or necessary for its own preservation, nor dishonor its own engagements
when able to meet them, without either shocking or demoralizing the sentiment of the people ; and the fact that the indefinite continuance of the circulation of an inconvertible but still legal tender currency is so generally
advocated indicates how far we have wandered from old landmarks both in
finance and ethics."

The growing opposition of the people at large to the contraction of the currency seemed to have no effect upon his
mind.

He again recurs to the same subject in his annual report to
Congress, in December, 1867. After stating that the United
States notes, including fractional currency, had been reduced
from $459,000,000 to $387,000,000, and the funded debt had
been increased $684,548,800, he urged as a measure regarded by
him as important, if not indispensable for national prosperity,
the funding or payment of the balance of interest-bearing
notes, and a continued contraction of the paper currency. He
urged that the acts authorizing legal tender notes be repealed,
and that the work of retiring the notes which had been issued
under them should be commenced without delay, and carefully
and persistently continued until all were retired.

This policy of contraction, honestly entertained and persistently urged by Secretary McCulloch in spite of growing
stringency, led Congress, by the act of February 4, 1868, to suspend indefinitely the authority of the Secretary of the Treasury
to make any reduction of the currency by retiring or canceling
United States notes.

Who can doubt that if he had availed himself of the power given him to refund the interest-bearing notes and certificates of the United States into bonds bearing a low rate of interest, leaving the United States notes bearing no interest to circulate as money, he would have saved the government hundreds of millions of dollars? If irredeemable notes were a national dishonor, why did he not urge their redemption in coin at some fixed period and then reissue them, and maintain their redemption by a reserve in coin?

The act of February 25, 1862, under which the original United States notes were issued, provided that:

"Such United States notes shall be received the same as coin, at their par value, in payment for any loans that may be hereafter sold or negotiated by the Secretary of the Treasury, and may be reissued from time to time as the exigencies of the public interest shall require."

This provision would have maintained the parity of United States notes at par with bonds, but under the pressure of war it was deemed best by Congress, upon the recommendation of Secretary Chase, to take from the holder of United States notes the right to present them in payment for bonds after the first day of July, 1863. If this privilege, conferred originally upon United States notes, had been renewed in 1866, with the right of reissue, bonds and notes would together have advanced to par in coin. But this is what the contractionists especially opposed. They demanded the cancellation of the notes when presented, a contraction of the currency when offering our bonds. It is easy now to perceive that a conservative use of United States notes, convertible into four per cent. bonds, would have steadily advanced both notes and bonds to par in coin. But the equally erroneous opposing opinions of contractionists and expansionists delayed for many years the coming of coin resumption upon a fixed quantity of United States notes.

Among the acts of this Congress of chief importance is the act approved July 13, 1866, to reduce taxes and provide internal revenue. The passage of such an act required much labor in both Houses, but especially so in the House of Representatives, where tax bills must originate. It was a compromise measure, and, unlike previous acts, did not reach out for new objects of taxation, but selected such articles as could bear it best, and on some of these the tax was increased. A great number of articles that enter into the common consumption of the people and are classed as necessaries of life were relieved from taxation. The general purpose of the bill was in time to concentrate internal taxes on such articles as spirits, tobacco and beer. The tax on incomes was continued but limited to the 30th of June, 1870. I have already stated the marked development of internal taxation, and this measure was one of the most important in the series to produce great revenue at the least cost, and of the lightest burden to the taxpayer.

Soon after the passage of the act, approved April 12, 1866, to contract the currency, I introduced a bill, "To reduce the rate of interest on the national debt and for funding the same." In view of the passage of that act I did not expect that a funding bill would meet with success, but considered it my duty to present one, and on the 22nd of May, 1866, made a speech in support of it. The bill provided for the voluntary exchange of any of the outstanding obligations of the United States for a bond running thirty years, but redeemable at the pleasure of the United States after ten years from date, bearing interest at the rate of five per cent., payable annually. On reading that speech now I find that, though I was much more confident than others of converting our maturing securities into five per cent. bonds, the general opinion then prevailing, and acted upon by the Secretary of the Treasury, was to issue six per cent. bonds as already stated. I soon found that it was idle to press the funding bill upon Congress, when it was so much occupied with reconstruction and with Andrew Johnson. The refunding and many other measures had to be postponed until a new administration came into power. Congress had unfortunately authorized the issue of six per cent. bonds for accruing liabilities, and thus postponed refunding at a lower rate of interest.

The long and exciting session of Congress that ended on the 28th day of July, 1866, left me in feeble strength and much discouraged with the state of affairs. I had arranged with

General Sherman to accompany him in an official inspection of army posts on the western plains, but did not feel at liberty to leave Washington until Congress adjourned. The letter I wrote him on the 8th of July expresses my feelings as to the political situation at that time:

UNITED STATES SENATE CHAMBER, }
WASHINGTON, July 8, 1866. }

DEAR BROTHER : — It is now wise for you to avoid all expressions of political opinion. Congress and the President are now drifting from each other into open warfare. Congress is not weak in what it has done, but in *what it has failed to do*. It has adopted no unwise or extreme measures. The civil rights bill and constitutional amendments can be defended as reasonable, moderate, and in harmony with Johnson's old position and yours. As Congress has thus far failed to provide measures to allow legal Senators and Representatives to take their seats, it has failed in a plain duty. This is its weakness, but even in this it will have the sympathy of the most of the soldiers, and the people who are not too eager to secure rebel political power. As to the President, he is becoming Tylerized. He was elected by the Union party for his openly expressed radical sentiments, and now he seeks to rend to pieces this party. There is a sentiment among the people that this is dishonor. It looks so to me. What Johnson is, is from and by the Union party. He now deserts it and betrays it. He may varnish it up, but, after all, he must admit that he disappoints the reasonable expectations of those who intrusted him with power. He may, by a coalition with copperheads and rebels, succeed, but the simple fact that nine-tenths of them who voted for him do not agree with him, and that he only controls the other tenth by power intrusted to him by the Union party, will damn him forever. Besides, he is insincere ; he has deceived and misled his best friends. I know he led many to believe he would agree to the civil rights bill, and nearly all who conversed with him until within a few days believed he would acquiesce in the amendments, and even aid in securing their adoption. I almost fear he contemplates civil war. Under these circumstances you, Grant, and Thomas ought to be clear of political complications. As for myself, I intend to stick to finance, but wherever I can I will moderate the actions of the Union party, and favor conciliation and restoration. Affectionately yours,

JOHN SHERMAN.

After the adjournment I proceeded to St. Louis, and with General Sherman and two staff officers, went by rail to Omaha. This handsome city had made great progress since my former visit. We then went by the Central Pacific railroad to Fort Kearney, as far as the rails were then laid. There our little party started through the Indian Territory, riding in light wagons with canvas covers, each drawn by two good army mules, escorted by a squad of mounted soldiers. We traveled about thirty miles a day, camping at night, sleeping in our wagons, turned into ambulances, the soldiers under shelter tents on blankets and the horses parked near by. The camp was guarded by sentinels at night, and the troopers lay with their guns close at hand. Almost every day we met Indians, but none that appeared to be hostile. In this way we traveled to Fort Laramie. The country traversed was an unbroken wilderness, in a state of nature, but singularly beautiful as a landscape. It was an open prairie, traversed by what was called the North Platte River, with scarcely water enough in it to be called a creek, with rolling hills on either side, and above, a clear sky, and air pure and bracing. It was the first time I had been so far out on the plains, and I enjoyed it beyond expression. I was soon able to eat my full share of the plain fare of bread and meat, and wanted more.

After many days we reached Fort Laramie, then an important post far out beyond the frontier. We remained but a few days, and then, following south along the foot hills, we crossed into the Laramie plains to Fort Sanders. This was the last post to the west in General Sherman's command. From thence we followed the course of the Cache la Poudre. On the way we camped near a station of the Overland Stage Company, for change of horses and for meals, in a charming and picturesque region. The keeper of the station soon called and inquired for me, and I found that he was a former resident of Mansfield, who married the daughter of an old friend. He invited our party to his house, and there I met his wife, who, in this region without any neighbors or habitations near, seemed to be perfectly happy and fearless, though often disturbed by threatened Indian outbreaks. We were handsomely entertained. It was a great relief to sleep one night in a comfortable bed, after sleeping for many nights with two in a narrow wagon. We then proceeded to Greeley, where we found a small settlement of farmers. From thence to Denver, we found a few cabins scattered over a vast open plain stretching as far as the eye could reach to the east, with the mountains on the west rising in grandeur and apparently presenting an insurmountable barrier. I have seen many landscapes since that were more bold and striking, but this combination of great mountains and vast plains, side by side, made an impression on my mind as lasting as any natural landscape I have seen.

At Denver, General Sherman and I were handsomely entertained by the citizens, many of whom General Sherman knew as soldiers under his command during the war, and some of whom I knew as former residents of Ohio. They were enthusiastic in their praise of Colorado. It seemed to me the air was charged with a superabundance of ozone, for everyone was so hopeful of the future of Denver, that even the want of rain did not discourage them and some of them tried to convince me that irrigation from the mountains was better than showers from the sky. Denver was then a town of less than 5,000 inhabitants and now contains more than 110,000. Colorado had less than 50,000 inhabitants in 1870, and in 1890 it had 412,198, an increase of nearly ten fold in twenty years. But this marvelous growth does not spring from the invigorating air and flowing springs of Colorado, but from the precious metals stored in untold quantities in her mountains. From Denver General Sherman had to continue his inspection to the southern posts, and I was called home to take part in the pending canvass. I started in a coach peculiar to the country, with three or four passengers, over a distance of about four hundred miles to Fort Riley, in Kansas. We had heard of many Indian forays on the line we were to travel over and there was some danger, but it was the only way to get home. Each of the passengers, I among the number, had a good Winchester rifle, with plenty of ammunition. The coach was a crude rattle-trap, noisy and rough, but strong and well adapted to the journey. It was drawn by four horses of the country, small but wiry. We had long reaches between changes. The stations for meals had means of defense, and the food set before us was substantial, mainly buffalo beef, chickens and bread. A good appetite (always a sure thing on the plains) was the best sauce for a substantial meal, and all the meals were dinners with no change of courses. We saw on the way many evidences of Indian depredations, one of which was quite recent, and two or three settlers had been killed. We met no Indians on the way, but we did meet myriads of buffaloes, scattered in vast herds to the north and south of us as far as the eye could reach. It is sad to reflect that all these animals have been exterminated, mainly in wanton sport by hunters who did not need their flesh for food or their hides for leather or robes. This destruction of buffaloes opened the way for herds of domestic cattle, which perhaps in equal numbers now feed upon the native grass of the prairies.

In a recent visit to western Nebraska and South Dakota, I saw these cattle in great numbers in good condition, cheaply cared for and sold for four cents a pound on the hoof. The owners of these cattle purchased land from settlers who had acquired title under the homestead or pre-emption laws, as suitable sites for ranches, including a permanent lake or pond for each, an indispensable requisite for a ranch. This being secured, they built houses to live in and sheds for the protection of their cattle in winter, and thus obtained practical possession, without cost or taxes, of all the government land needed for their ranges. Sad experience has convinced settlers in all the vast rainless region of the west, that they cannot produce grain with any certainty of harvesting a crop, and thousands who have made the experiment in western Kansas and Nebraska and in eastern Colorado and Wyoming have recently abandoned their improvements and their claims. It seems now that this part of our country must be given up to the herders of cattle. The Indians and buffaloes have disappeared and the "cowboys" and domestic cattle and horses have taken their place, to give way, no doubt, in time, to the farmer, when the water will be drawn from the earth by artesian wells, and life and vitality will thus be given to a soil as rich as the Kansas valley.

We reached the end of our stage ride at Fort Riley, and were glad to enter into the cars of the Kansas Pacific railroad, though they were as dirty and filthy as cars could well be. All this has been changed. Now the ride over the plains from

Kansas City to Denver can be made, in a comparatively few hours, in comfort and safety.

I returned to Ohio to take my usual part in the canvass in the fall of 1866, and returned to Washington in time for the meeting of Congress on the first Monday in December.

Prior to 1862 but little attention was given by Congress to the greatest and most important industry of mankind, that of agriculture. This is especially true of the United States, where the majority of its inhabitants are engaged in farming. Agriculture has furnished the great body of our exports, yet this employment had no representative in any of the departments except a clerk in the Patent Office. The privileges granted by that bureau to inventors had no relation to work on the farm, though farming was greatly aided by invention of farm implements during the period of the war, when a million of men were drawn from their occupations into the army. This anomaly led to the passage, on the 15th of May, 1862, of the act to establish the department of agriculture. Though called a department its chief officer was a commissioner of agriculture, who was not for many years a member of the cabinet. The first commissioner, Isaac Newton, appointed by Lincoln, was a peculiar character, a Quaker of Philadelphia, a gardener rather than a farmer, but he was an earnest and active officer. The appropriations for his department were very small, but enabled him to distribute valuable seeds and cuttings, which were in great demand and of real service to farmers. I early took an active part in promoting his efforts and especially in procuring him appropriations and land where he could test his experiments. He applied for authority to use that portion of Reservation No. 2 between 12th and 14th streets of the mall in Washington, then an unsightly waste without tree or shrub, but he was notified that the use of it was essentially necessary to the war department as a cattle yard. When the war was over Congress appropriated it for the use of his department. He took possession of it about the middle of April, 1865, and, though the ground was an unbroken soil of tenacious clay, he fertilized and pulverized a part of it and planted a great variety of seeds for propagation, and covered the remaining portions of it with grass and cereals. His reports increased in interest and were in great demand. His office work was done in inconvenient parts of the Patent Office, and the necessity of better accommodations was constantly pressed upon Members of Congress. I took an active interest in the subject, and offered an amendment to the civil appropriation bill to appropriate $100,000 for a suitable building for the department of agriculture on the reservation mentioned. There was a disposition in the Senate to ridicule Newton and his seeds, and Mr. Fessenden opposed the appropriation as one for an object not within the constitutional power of Congress. The amendment, however, was adopted on the 28th day of February, 1867. Newton died on the 19th of June of that year, but on the 22nd of August, John W. Stokes, as acting commissioner, entered into a contract for the erection of the building, and Horace Capron, as commissioner, completed the work within the limits of the appropriation, a rare result in the construction of a public building. The building is admirably adapted for the purposes designed. The unsightly reservation has been converted by Mr. Capron and his successors in office into one of the most beautiful parks in Washington. The department of agriculture is now represented in the cabinet, and in practical usefulness to the country is equal to any of the departments.

CHAPTER XVIII.

THREE MONTHS IN EUROPE.

DURING the last session of the 39th Congress the relations between President Johnson and Congress became such that it was deemed advisable to provide by law for a session of the new Congress on the 4th of March, 1867, that being the commencement of the term for which the Members were elected.

The law, in my opinion, ought to be a permanent one, so that the will of the people, as evidenced by the elections, may be promptly responded to. But such was not the purpose of this act. The reason was that, under the claim of authority made by the President, there was a fear that he might recognize the states in insurrection before they had complied with the conditions prescribed by law for reconstruction.

In pursuance of this law the 40th Congress met on the day named.

I took the oath as Senator, my colleague, Benjamin F. Wade, president *pro tem.* of the Senate, administering it. I became chairman of the committee on finance by the voluntary retirement of Mr. Fessenden. I knew this had been his purpose during the session just closed. He complained of his health, and that the confinement and labor of the position he held

added to his infirmity. At the same time it was agreed that
the duties of the committee should be divided by referring all
appropriations to a committee on appropriations, and I was to
choose between the two committees. The House of Representatives had already divided the labors of the committee of ways
and means, a corresponding committee to that on finance,
among several committees, and the experiment had proved a
success. I preferred the committee on finance, and remained
its chairman until I became Secretary of the Treasury. Mr.
Fessenden took the easy and pleasant position of chairman of
the committee on public buildings and grounds, and held that
position until he died in September, 1869. I have already expressed my opinion of his remarkable ability as a debater and
as a statesman of broad and conservative views. His only
fault was a hasty temper too often displayed, but as often
regretted by him.

Congress adjourned on the 30th of March, to meet again on
the 3rd of July. The Senate was called to a special session
by proclamation of the President on the 1st day of April,
1867. It remained in session until the 20th of April and then
adjourned *sine die.*

I did not remain until the close of the session, but about
the 10th of April sailed from New York for Europe in the
steamer "City of Antwerp." I went for needed rest, a change
of air and scene, and had in view, as one of the attractions of
the voyage, a visit to the exposition at Paris in that year. My
associates on the ocean were Colonel Morrow, United States
Army, and John A. Kasson, Member of Congress from Iowa,
and we remained together until I left London.

I had no plan, route or business, except to go where I drifted
with such companions as I met. The only limitation as to time
was the duty of returning to meet the adjourned session of the
Senate in July. I have no memoranda in respect to the voyage
and preserved no letters about it. Still, the principal scenes
and events are impressed on my mind and I will narrate them
as I now recall them.

The passage on the ocean was a favorable one. We had
some rain but no winds that disturbed my digestion. But few

on the vessel were seasick, and these mainly so from imagination. The captain, whose name I do not recall, was a jolly Englishman, but a careful, prudent and intelligent officer. I sat by his side at his table. After leaving port we soon took our places at table for our first meal on board. He inquired of me if I was a good sailor. I told him I would be as regular in my attendance at meals as he. He laughed and said he would like to wager some wine on that. I cheerfully accepted his bet, and, true to my promise, I did not miss a meal during the voyage, while he three or four times remained at his post on deck when the air was filled with fog or the waves were high. He paid the bet near the end of the voyage, and a number of his passengers, including Morrow and Kasson, shared in the treat.

I can imagine no life more pleasing than a tranquil, but not too tranquil, sea, with a good ship well manned, with companions you like, but not too many. The quiet and rest, the view of the ocean, the sense of solitude, the possibility of danger, all these broken a little by a quiet game of whist or an interesting book—this I call happiness. All these I remember to have enjoyed on this, my fifth trip on the ocean.

In due time we arrived at Queenstown in Ireland. It was about the time a party of Irishmen, in some town in England, rescued some of their countrymen from a van in charge of English constables, one or more of whom were killed or wounded. Morrow, Kasson and I concluded we would spend a few days in "Ould Ireland." Morrow and Kasson believed they were of Irish descent, though remotely so as their ancestors "fought in the Revolution." We remained in and about Cork for two or three days. We visited and kissed the Blarney Stone, saw the Lakes of Killarney, and drove or walked about the interesting environs of Cork and Queenstown. We sought no acquaintance with anyone.

We were all about the age of forty, physically sound, and both Morrow and Kasson had the military air and step of soldiers. We soon became conscious that we were under surveillance. One day an officer called at our lodgings and frankly told us that there was so much excitement about Fenian disturbances in England, and such political ferment in Ireland, that an examination of the baggage of passengers was required and he wished to examine ours. I told him who we were, and introduced him to Morrow and Kasson, and offered my trunk for inspection. They did the same, Kasson producing also a small pistol from his valise. The officer had heard of that pistol. Kasson had fired it at birds hovering about the vessel. This had been reported to the police. The officer took the pistol and it was returned to Kasson some days after at Dublin. Morrow ridiculed the pistol and told the officer that Kasson could not hit or hurt him at ten paces away, but the officer was only half satisfied. We soon after went to Dublin, but we felt that we were under suspicion. All Americans were then suspected of sympathizing with the Irish. We told our consul at Dublin of our adventures at Cork, and he said we were lucky in not being arrested. We went to a steeple chase a few miles from Dublin, where gentlemen rode their own horses over a long and difficult route, leaping barriers and crossing streams. We enjoyed the scene very much and mingled freely in the great crowd, but always feeling that we were watched. The next day we started to cross the channel to Holyhead.

We took the steamer at Dublin Bay and found aboard a large company of well-dressed passengers, such as we would find on a summer excursion from New York. Morrow, who was a handsome man of pleasing manners and address, said he could pick out Americans from the crowd. I doubted it. He said: "There is an American," pointing out a large, well-built man, who seemed to be known by the passengers around him. I said he was an Englishman. Morrow stepped up to him and politely said that he had a wager with a friend that he was an American. "Not by a d—d sight," replied the Englishman. Morrow apologized for the intrusion, but the gentleman changed his tone and said that his abrupt answer was caused by a letter he had lately received from a nephew of his whom he had sent to America to make his fortune. His nephew had written him that now that the rebels were put down, the next thing to do would be to put down "old England." Morrow said there was too much of that kind of gasconade in America, and that after our desperate struggle at home we would not be likely to engage in one with England.

We arrived safely in London. In my first visit in 1859, with my wife, we were sight-seers. Now I sought to form acquaintance with men whose names were household words in all parts of the United States. By the courtesy of our consul general at Liverpool, Thomas H. Dudley, I met John Bright, Disraeli, and many others less conspicuous in public life. I have already mentioned my breakfast with Gladstone during this visit. Mr. Dudley, then in London, invited Mr. Bright to a dinner as his principal guest. Of all the men I met in London, Mr. Bright impressed me most favorably. Finely formed physically, he was also mentally strong. He was frank and free in his talk and had none of the hesitation or reserve common with Englishmen. He was familiar with our war and had no timidity in the expression of his sympathy for the Union cause. If we ever erect a monument to an Englishman, it should be to John Bright. I heard Disraeli speak in the House of Commons and was introduced to him at a reception at Lord Stanley's. In the ten days spent in London I saw as much of social life as could be crowded into that time. Charles Francis Adams was then United States minister at London, and I am indebted to him for many acts of kindness. When we were Members of the House of Representatives together he had the reputation of being cold and reserved and he was not popular with his fellow Members, but in London he was distinguished for his hospitality to Americans. He certainly was very kind to me, entertaining me at dinner and taking pains to introduce me to many peers and members whose names were familiar to me. While receptions are very common in London during the session, the Englishman prefers dinners as a mode of entertainment. It is then he really enjoys himself and gives pleasure to his guests. The sessions of parliament, however, interfere greatly with dinners. The great debates occur during dining hours, so that, as Mr. Adams informed me, it was difficult to arrange a dinner that would not be broken up somewhat by an unexpected debate, or a division in the House of Commons. The precedence of rank had to be carefully observed. The unsocial habit of not introducing guests to each other tended to restrain conversation and to make the dinner dull and heavy. Still the forms and usages in social life in London are much like those in Washington. But here the ordinary sessions of each House of Congress terminate before six o'clock, leaving the evening hours for recreation.

The presidential mansion is the natural resort of all who visit Washington. The doors are always open to visitors at stated hours, and the President is easy of access to all who call at such hours. Formerly presidential receptions were open to all comers, and the result was a motley crowd, who formed in line and shook hands with the President, bowed to the attending ladies, passed into the great east room and gradually dispersed. In late years these receptions have become less frequent, and in their place we have had diplomatic, military and navy, and congressional receptions, for which invitations are issued. During the usual period before Lent card receptions are given by the cabinet, by many Senators and Members, and by citizens, for which invitations are issued. I know of no place where the entrance into society is so open and free as in Washington.

From London I went, by way of Dieppe and Rouen, to Paris, where my first call was on General Dix and his family. Next I visited the exposition, and wandered through and about and around it. I have attended many exhibitions, but never one before or since that combined such magnitude and completeness in size, form and location, and such simplicity in arrangement and details, as the Paris Exposition of 1867. I spent ten days in this inspection, and in walking and driving around Paris and its environs. Through the kindness of General Dix, then envoy extraordinary and minister plenipotentiary, I received invitations to the many meetings and receptions given by Mayor Haussman and other officers of the French government to visitors from abroad connected with the exposition. I accepted some of them, but purposely postponed this social part of my visit until I returned from Berlin.

From Paris I went to Antwerp via Brussels. At this latter place I met Doctor John Wilson, then United States consul at

Antwerp. He was an old friend at Washington, where he served during the greater part of the war as an army surgeon. He was a man of remarkable intelligence, familiar with nearly every part of Europe, and especially with France, Belgium and Prussia. He readily acquiesced in my invitation to accompany me to Berlin. On the invitation of Henry S. Sanford, our minister to Brussels, I returned to that city, and met at dinner the principal officers of Belgium, such as we designate cabinet ministers. I drove with Mr. Sanford to Waterloo and other famous historic places in and about that beautiful city.

From Brussels we went to the Hague, where General Hugh Ewing, a brother-in-law of General Sherman, was United States minister. After a brief stay in Holland, General Ewing, Doctor Wilson and myself went to Berlin. Prussia was then a kingdom of rising power, and Berlin was a growing city, but not at all the Berlin of to-day. Bismarck was recognized as a great statesman and, although far less prominent than he afterwards became, he was the one man in Germany whom I desired to see or know. Mr. Joseph A. Wright, late United States minister at Berlin, had recently died, and his son, John C. Wright, who was in charge of the legation, had no difficulty in securing me an audience with Bismarck, accompanying me to the official residence, where I was introduced to him. Bismarck spoke English with a German accent, but was easily understood. When I spoke of recent events in Europe he would turn the conversation to the United States, asking me many questions about the war and the principal generals in the opposing armies. He was in thorough sympathy with the Union cause, and emphatically said that every man in Prussia, from the king to his humblest subject, was on the side of the Union, and opposed to the Rebellion. What a pity, he said, it would have been if so great a country as the United States had been disrupted on account of slavery. I mentioned my visit to the international fair at Paris and my intention to return, and he said he would be there.

This interview, which lasted, perhaps, forty minutes, was as informal and frank as the usual conversation of friends. Bismarck was then in full health and strength, about fifty years old, more than six feet high, and a fine specimen of vigorous manhood in its prime.

I found the same feeling for the United States expressed by a popular meeting in the great exposition hall in Berlin. Our little party was escorted to this place on Sunday afternoon by Mr. Kreismann, our consul at Berlin. As we entered the hall, Mr. Kreismann advanced to the orchestra, composed of several military bands, and said something to the leader. When we took our seats at one of the numerous tables he told me to pay attention after the first item of the second part of the programme before me, and I would hear something that would please me. At the time stated, a young man advanced to the front of the stage, with a violin in his hand, and played exquisitely the air *"Yankee Doodle Is the Tune,"* and soon after the entire band joined in, filling the great hall with American music. The intelligent German audience, many of whom knew the national airs of all countries, realized at once that this addition to the programme was a compliment to Americans. They soon located our little party and then rose, and fully two thousand persons, men, women and children, waved their handkerchiefs and shouted for America.

The feeling in favor of the United States was then strong in all parts of Europe, except in France and England. In these countries it was somewhat divided—in France by the failure of Maximilian, and in England by the rivalry of trade, and sympathy with the south. Generally, in referring in Europe to the people of the United States, the people speak of us as Americans, while those of other parts of America are Canadians, Mexicans, etc.

After a pleasant week in Berlin I went by way of Frankfort, Wiesbaden and Cologne to Paris. The exposition was then in full operation. It may be that greater numbers attended the recent exposition at Chicago, but, great as was its success, I think, for symmetry, for plans of buildings, and arrangement of exhibits, the fair at Paris was better than that at Chicago. The French people are well adapted for such exhibits. The city of Paris is itself a good show. Its people almost live out of doors six months of the year. They are quick, mercurial, tasteful and economical. A Frenchman will live well on one-half of what is consumed or wasted by an American. I do not propose to describe the wonderful collection of the productions of nature or the works of men, but I wish to convey some idea of life in Paris during the thirty days I spent in it.

Louis Napoleon Bonaparte was then Emperor of the French, and Haussman was mayor of the city of Paris. General Dix, as before stated, was United States minister plenipotentiary and envoy extraordinary at the court of France. Upon my arrival, I hired what in Paris is called an apartment, but which includes several rooms, comprising together a comfortable residence. Many similar apartments may be in the same building, but with them you need have no communication, and you are detached from them as fully as if each apartment was a separate house. The concierge, generally a woman, takes charge of your room, orders your breakfast if you require one, and keeps the key of your apartment when you are absent. It is a charming mode of living. You can dine or lunch when you will, and are master of your time and your apartment. I employed a neat, light carriage and one horse, with a driver who knew a smattering of several languages, and found him trusty and faithful—all this at a cost that would disgust the ordinary hotel proprietor in the United States, and especially the hack driver of any of our cities. This, in Paris, was the usual outfit of a gentleman.

General Dix advised me on whom and when and how I should make my calls. My card in the usual form announced that I was "Sénateur des États Unis d'Amérique." A Parisian could not pronounce my name. The best he could do was to call me "Monsieur le Sénateur." With a few words of French I acquired, and the imperfect knowledge of English possessed by most French people, I had no difficulty in making my way in any company. I received many invitations I could not accept. I attended a reception at the Palais Royal, the residence of the mayor, dressed in the ordinary garb for evening parties, a dress coat and trousers extending to the knees, and below black silk stockings and pumps. I felt very uncomfortable in this dress when I entered the reception room, but, as I found every gentleman in the same dress, soon became reconciled to it. Subsequently I attended a reception at the Tuileries, at which I was presented by General Dix to the emperor and empress.

One feature of this presentation I shall always remember. The general company had been gathered in the great hall. The diplomatic representatives of many countries were formed in line according to their rank, attended by the persons to be presented. Soon a door was opened from an adjoining room and the Emperor of the French, escorting, I think, the Empress of Russia, passed along the line and saluted the ambassadors and ministers in their order, and the ladies and gentlemen to be presented were introduced by name to the emperor. General Dix presented Fernando Wood, of New York, and myself. Following the French emperor came the Emperor of Russia escorting the Empress Eugenie of France, and the same mention of our names was made to her. Following them came kings, the Prince of Wales and others of like rank, each accompanied by distinguished peers of his country. Third or fourth in this order came the King of Prussia, Prince Bismarck, and General Von Moltke. When Bismarck passed he shook hands with Dix and recognized me with a bow and a few words. If the leaders in this pageant could have foreseen what happened three years later—that King William would be an emperor, that Bonaparte would be his prisoner and Eugenie a refugee from republican France—the order of this march would have been reversed.

Soon after this reception, I was invited by the emperor to attend, with General Dix and his daughter, a dinner at the Tuileries. Such an invitation is held to be in the nature of a command. I accompanied them, and was agreeably surprised to find that the dinner was quite informal, though more than forty sat at the table. When I entered the room one of the ladies in waiting came to me and introduced me to a lady whom I was to escort to the table. Presently she returned and said: "Oh, I understand monsieur does not speak French, and marquise does not speak English. Will monsieur allow me to be a substitute?" I agreed with great pleasure. Both the

guests and the hosts were promptly on time. I was introduced
to the emperor and empress. She was very gracious to her
guests, passing from one to another with a kindly word to all.
I noticed her greeting to Miss Dix was very cordial. The
emperor engaged in a conversation with me that continued
until the dinner was announced,—fully ten minutes. He
asked many questions about the war, and especially about
General Sherman. I answered his questions as I would to any
gentleman, but felt uneasy lest I was occupying time that he

Par Ordre de l'Empereur,

Le Chambellan de Service a l'honneur
de prévenir Monsieur

Scherman

qu' ile est invité a Diner au Palais des
Tuileries le Mardi 27 Juin a 7 heures ½

Vte du Mauseny

INVITATION FROM NAPOLEON III.

should bestow on others. General Dix was by my side, and
encouraged the conversation. When the dinner was announced each guest knew his place from the card furnished
him, and the party was seated without confusion.

I need not say that the young lady I escorted was a charming woman. I did not learn whether she was married or not,
but have always regarded her action in relieving me from a
silent dinner as the highest mark of politeness. She was
bright and attractive, and I certainly did and said all I could

to amuse her, so what I expected to be a dull dinner turned out to be a very joyful one.

It is impossible for an American to visit Paris without enjoyment and instruction. The people of Paris are always polite, especially to Americans. The debt of gratitude for the assistance of France in our War of the Revolution is never forgotten by a true American, and Frenchmen are always proud of their share in establishing the independence of America. The two Bonapartes alone did not share in this feeling. The Americans are liberal visitors in Paris. They spend their money freely, join heartily in festivities, and sympathize in the success and prosperity of the French republic. If I was not an American I certainly would be a Frenchman. I have visited Paris three times, remaining in it more than a month at each visit, and always have been received with civility and kindness. Though it is a great manufacturing city, chiefly in articles of luxury requiring the highest skill, yet it is also a most beautiful city in its location, its buildings, public and private, its museums and opera houses, its parks and squares, its wide streets and avenues, and especially the intelligence of its people. Science and art have here reached their highest development. We may copy all these, but it will require a century to develop like progress in America.

I returned to England for a few days and then took the steamer "City of Paris" for New York, where I arrived on the 13th of July. I took the cars for Washington and arrived ten days after the session had commenced.

While I was in Paris a special international commission, composed of delegates from seventeen nations, was sitting to consider, and, if possible, agree on a common unit of money for the use of the civilized world. Mr. Samuel B. Ruggles, a gentleman of the highest standing and character, was the representative of the United States on this commission. It should be remembered that at this time the only currency in circulation in the United States was the legal tender notes of the United States and the notes of national banks. Neither gold nor silver coin was in circulation, both being at a premium in currency. At this time silver bullion was at a premium over gold bullion, the legal ratio being sixteen to one. In other words, sixteen ounces of silver were worth, in the open market, three to five cents more than one ounce of gold. All parties in the United States were then looking forward to the time when United States notes would advance in value to par with gold, the cheaper metal.

The question before the commission was how to secure a common coin that would be the measure of value between all nations, and thus avoid the loss by exchange of the coins of one nation for those of another. Mr. Ruggles knew that I had studied this question, and therefore wrote this letter:

PARIS, May 17, 1867.

My DEAR SIR :—You are, of course, aware that there is a special committee now in session, organized by the Imperial Commission of France, in connection with the ' Paris Exposition,' composed of delegates from many of the nations therein represented. Its object, among others, is to agree, if possible, on a common unit of money, for the use of the civilized world.

I perceive that the opinions of the committee are running strongly in favor of adopting, as the unit, the existing French five-franc piece of gold.

May I ask what, in your opinion, is the probability that the Congress of the United States, at an early period, would agree to reduce the weight and value of our gold dollar, to correspond with the present weight and value of the gold five-franc piece of France ; and how far back such a change would commend itself to your own judgment ?

I would also ask the privilege of submitting your answer to the consideration of the committee.

With high respect, faithfully your friend,

SAMUEL B. RUGGLES,

U. S. Commissioner to the Paris Exposition and Member of the Committee.

HON. JOHN SHERMAN,

Chairman of the Finance Committee of the Senate of the United States, etc., etc., etc., now in Paris.

To this letter I made the following reply :

HOTEL JARDIN DES TUILERIES, May 18, 1867.

My DEAR SIR :—Your note of yesterday, inquiring whether Congress would probably, in future coinage, make our gold dollar conform in value to the gold five-franc piece, has been received.

There has been so little discussion in Congress upon the subject that I cannot base my opinion upon anything said or done there.

The subject has, however, excited the attention of several important commercial bodies in the United States, and the time is now so favorable that I feel quite sure that Congress will adopt any practical measure that will secure to the commercial world a uniform standard of value and exchange.

The only question will be, how can this be accomplished?

The treaty of December 23, 1865, between France, Italy, Belgium, and Switzerland, and the probable acquiescence in that treaty by Prussia, has laid the foundation for such a standard. If Great Britain will reduce the value of her sovereign two pence, and the United States will reduce the value of her dollar something over three cents, we then have a coinage in the franc, dollar and sovereign easily computed, and which will readily pass in all countries; the dollar as five francs and the sovereign as 25 francs.

This will put an end to the loss and intricacies of exchange and discount.

Our gold dollar is certainly as good a unit of value as the franc; and so the English think of their pound sterling. These coins are now exchangeable only at a considerable loss, and this exchange is a profit only to brokers and bankers. Surely each commercial nation should be willing to yield a little to secure a gold coin of equal value, weight, and diameter, from whatever mint it may have been issued.

As the gold five-franc piece is now in use by over 60,000,000 of people of several different nationalities, and is of convenient form and size, it may well be adopted by other nations as the common standard of value, leaving to each nation to regulate the divisions of this unit in silver coin or tokens.

If this is done France will surely abandon the impossible effort of making two standards of value. Gold coins will answer all the purpose of European commerce. A common gold standard will regulate silver coinage, of which the United States will furnish the greater part, especially for the Chinese trade.

I have thought a good deal of how the object you propose may be most readily accomplished. It is clear that the United States cannot become a party to the treaty referred to. They could not agree upon the silver standard; nor could we limit the amount of our coinage, as proposed by the treaty. The United States is so large in extent, is so sparsely populated, and the price of labor is so much higher than in Europe, that we require more currency per capita. We now produce the larger part of the gold and silver of the world, and cannot limit our coinage except by the wants of our people and the demands of commerce.

Congress alone can change the value of our coin. I see no object in negotiating with other powers on the subject. As coin is not now in general circulation with us, we can readily fix by law the size, weight, and measure of future issues. It is not worth while to negotiate about that which we can do without negotiation, and we do not wish to limit ourselves by treaty restrictions.

In England many persons of influence and different chambers of commerce are earnestly in favor of the proposed change in their coinage. The change is so slight with them that an enlightened self-interest will soon induce them to make it, especially if we make the greater change in our coinage. We have some difficulty in adjusting existing contracts with the new dollar ; but as contracts are now based upon the fluctuating value of paper money, even the reduced dollar in coin will be of more purchasable value than our currency.

We can easily adjust the reduction with the public creditors in the payment or conversion of their securities, while private creditors might be authorized to recover upon the old standard. All these are matters of detail to which I hope the commission will direct their attention.

And now, my dear sir, allow me to say in conclusion that I heartily sympathize with you and others in your efforts to secure the adoption of the metrical system of weights and measures.

The tendency of the age is to break down all needless restrictions upon social and commercial intercourse. Nations are now as much akin to each other as provinces were of old. Prejudices disappear by contact. People of different nations learn to respect each other as they find that their differences are the effect of social and local custom, not founded upon good reasons. I trust that the industrial commission will enable the world to compute the value of all productions by the same standard, to measure by the same yard or meter, and weigh by the same scales.

Such a result would be of greater value than the usual employments of diplomatists and statesmen. I am very truly yours,

JOHN SHERMAN.

As the result of its investigation the commission agreed, with entire unanimity, that the gold five-franc piece should be adopted as the unit of value, and that the coins of all nations represented should be based upon that unit or multiples thereof. This would require a slight change in the quantity of gold in the dollar of the United States, amounting to a reduction of about three cents, a reduction in the pound sterling of England of about one penny, and a slight reduction or increase in the gold coins of other countries.

Mr. Ruggles reported the proceedings and recommendation of the commission to the President, and his report was referred to Congress.

A private letter to me from Mr. Ruggles, dated December 30, 1867, shows the nature of the opposition to the measure proposed, being entirely from British opposition to a change in the pound sterling. He wrote:

NEW YORK, December 30, 1867.

MY DEAR MR. SHERMAN :—You may have perceived, within the last week, articles in the 'New York Evening Post,' the 'New York Times' and the 'World,' on the subject of the proposed monetary unification; the first denying its *propriety*, the second its *practicability*, and the third underrating its *importance*.

The articles are hastily and ignorantly and, in some respects, bitterly written. My first impulse was to briefly answer each of them in its respective newspaper. On further reflection, it seemed more decorous that, as a member of the 'conference,' I should first appear before the Senate committee now in possession of all the papers, and there render any proper explanations, and not obtrude myself as a combatant in the newspapers, prematurely and only partially defending my official action. If, however, you should think that the articles should be answered without delay, I could readily cause it to be done, by other persons.

I cannot but think that the dignity of the subject, formally presented as it now is, to our national authorities, by a diplomatic assemblage representing nearly all the civilized nations of the Christian world, entitles it to a full discussion before the Senate committee, to be followed by a maturely considered report, fairly weighing and presenting to the country all the merits and demerits, facilities and difficulties of the measure.

I am just at the moment confined to my house by an 'influenza,' but if I can be of any service, either before the committee or elsewhere, I shall hold myself subject to your official call, for any duty, after the 7th or 8th of January, which you may indicate.

You must have perceived that my report to the department of state, having in view the possibility of European readers, abstained from some considerations which might properly be brought to the notice of the committee of the American Senate.

It is strange, indeed, to see American newspapers eagerly maintaining the inviolability of the 'pound sterling,' when it has become entirely evident that the great monetary struggle of the future must lie between the British pound and the American dollar. In truth, this was virtually admitted in the 'conference' by Mr. Graham, one of the British delegates, and master of the royal mint. With high regard, faithfully yours,

SAMUEL B. RUGGLES.

HON. JOHN SHERMAN,
    Chairman Senate Finance Committee, etc., etc., etc.

We were called upon to legislate upon the subject. The French government promptly acquiesced in the coin proposed. Mr. Ruggles' report said that several governments had already assented to it. The report was referred to the committee on finance of the Senate, who submitted a favorable report with a bill to carry out the recommendations, and that report was published. There was no dissent from the plan except that

Senator Morgan, of New York, thought it would interfere with the profit of New York brokers in changing dollars into pounds. As a matter of course, it would have interfered with the exchanges of New York and London, the great money centers of the world. It would have interfered with bullion dealers who make profit in exchanging coins; but the whole of it was for the benefit of each country.

No man can estimate the benefit it would have conferred upon our own people. It was only defeated by the refusal of Great Britain to assent to the change of her pound sterling by the reduction of its value about one penny. But pride in its existing coins, so strong in that country, defeated the measure, although it had been assented to by her representatives in that monetary congress; and so the thing ended.

It is easy now to perceive that if this international coin had been agreed to it would have passed current everywhere, as it could rapidly be exchanged at sight without going through the hands of brokers. I do not believe that Mr. Morgan would have insisted on his opposition, as the only ground of his objection was, it would have destroyed the business of the money changers of New York. Even his resistance would have been ineffectual, as the committee and the Senate were decidedly in favor of the bill and the opposition of New York brokers would have added strength to the measure.

The greatest statesmen of Europe and America have sought for many years to unify the coinage of nations, and to adopt common standards of weights and measures, so that commerce may be freed from the restrictions now imposed upon it, but Great Britain has steadily opposed all these enlightened measures, and thus far has been able to defeat them.

My report from the committee on finance, made to the Senate June 7, 1868, contains a full statement of the acts of the monetary conference at Paris, and of the approval of its action by many of the countries there represented, and of the support given to the plan in Great Britain by many of her ablest statesmen and the great body of her commercial classes, but the party then in power in parliament refused its sanction, and thus, as already stated, the measure failed.

It has been quite common, during recent discussions about silver, to attribute the alleged demonetization of that metal to the action of the Paris monetary conference. In 1867, when this conference was in session, as already stated, sixteen ounces of silver were worth more than one ounce of gold. Fifteen and one-half ounces of silver were the legal equivalent of one ounce of gold in all European countries. No suggestion was made or entertained to disturb the circulation of silver. The only object sought was to secure some common coin by which other coins could be easily measured. As gold was the most valuable metal in smallest space, and the five-franc gold piece of France was the best *unit* by which other coins could be measured, other gold coins were to be of multiples of the unit, so that five francs would be a dollar and five dollars would be a pound. The coins of other nations would be made to conform to multiples of this unit.

It was perfectly understood that, while silver was the chief coin in domestic exchanges in every country, it was not convenient for foreign commerce, owing to its bulk. The ratio between gold and silver was purely a domestic matter, to be determined by each country for itself. It is apparent that the chief cause of the fall of the market value of silver is its increased production. This affects the price of every commodity, cotton, corn, or wheat as well as silver. The law of supply and demand regulates value. It is the "higher law" more potent than acts of Congress. If the supply is in excess of demand the price will fall, in spite of legislation. The most striking evidence of this was furnished by our recent legislation by which we purchased over 400,000,000 ounces of silver at its market value and hoarded it, and yet the price of it steadily declined. We can coin it into silver dollars, but we can keep these dollars at par with gold only by receiving them as the equal of gold when offered.

CHAPTER XIX.

IMPEACHMENT OF ANDREW JOHNSON.

Judiciary Committee's Resolution Fails of Adoption by a Vote of 57 Yeas to 108
Nays—Johnson's Attempt to Remove Secretary Stanton and Create a New
Office for General Sherman—Correspondence on the Subject—Report of
the Committee on Impeachment, and Other Matters Pertaining to
the Appointment of Lorenzo Thomas—Impeachment Resolu-
tion Passed by the House by a Vote of 126 Yeas to 47
Nays—Johnson's Trial by the Senate—Acquittal of
the President by a Vote of 35 Guilty to 19 Not
Guilty — Why I Favored Conviction —
General Schofield Becomes Secretary of
War—"Tenure of Office Act."

D URING the spring and summer of 1867 the question
of impeaching Andrew Johnson, President of the
United States, was frequently discussed in the House
of Representatives. The resolutions relating to his
impeachment were introduced by James M. Ashley, of Ohio, on
the 7th of March, 1867, and they were adopted on the same day.
These resolutions instructed the judiciary committee, when
appointed, to continue the inquiry, previously ordered, into
certain charges preferred against the President of the United
States, with authority to sit during the sessions of the House,
and during any recess the Congress might take.

On the 25th of November, 1867, a majority of the committee
on the judiciary reported a resolution of impeachment, as
follows :

"*Resolved*, That Andrew Johnson, President of the United States, be
impeached of high crimes and misdemeanors."

This resolution was accompanied by a long report and the
testimony, all of which was ordered to be printed, and made the
special order for Wednesday, December 4, 1867. James F. Wilson, of Iowa, made a minority report against the resolution of impeachment, signed by himself and Frederick E. Woodbridge, of
Vermont. Samuel S. Marshall, of Illinois, also made a minority
report in behalf of himself and Charles A. Eldridge, of Wisconsin.

On the 7th of December, the resolution of impeachment reported by the committee on the judiciary at the previous session was disagreed to by a vote of 57 yeas and 108 nays. This decision of the House of Representatives against an impeachment on the charges then made was entirely justified. This imposing process was not authorized for misconduct, immorality, intoxication or neglect of duties, such as were alleged in the report of the committee, but only for high crimes or misdemeanors. The House properly made this distinction, and here the accusations against the President would have ended, but for his attempt, in violation of the constitution and law, to place General Lorenzo Thomas in an important office without the advice and consent of the Senate, then in session.

In the latter part of 1867, and the early part of 1868, I became involved in a controversy, between President Johnson, General Grant and General Sherman, which caused the last-named serious embarrassment. As much of the correspondence between these parties has been published in the "Sherman Letters," I at first thought it best not to make any reference to the matter, but upon reflection, and to explain subsequent events, I insert the letters in their order.

General Sherman was summoned to Washington, by the President, and upon his arrival there wrote me the following letter:

WASHINGTON, October 11, 1867.

DEAR BROTHER :—I have no doubt that you have been duly concerned about my being summoned to Washington.

It was imprudently done by the President without going through Grant. But I think I have smoothed it over so that Grant does not feel hurt. I cannot place myself in a situation even partially antagonistic with Grant. We must work together. Mr. Johnson has not offered me anything, only has talked over every subject, and because I listen to him patiently, and make short and decisive answers, he says he would like to have me here. Still he does not oppose my going back home. . . .

On Monday I will start for St. Louis by the Atlantic and G. W. road, and pass Mansfield Tuesday. Can't you meet me and ride some miles ? I have been away from home so much, and must go right along to Fort Laramie, that I cannot well stop at Cleveland or Mansfield, and would like to see you for an hour or so to hear your views of the coming events. . . .

Yours affectionately,

W. T. SHERMAN.

And on his return to St. Louis he continues :

. . . I have always talked kindly to the President, and have advised Grant to do so. I do think that it is best for all hands that his administration be allowed to run out its course without threatened or attempted violence. Whoever begins violent proceedings will lose in the long run. Johnson is not a man of action but of theory, and so long as your party is in doubt as to the true mode of procedure, it would be at great risk that an attempt be made to displease the President by a simple law of Congress. This is as much as I have ever said to anybody. I have never, by word or inference, given anybody the right to class me in opposition to, or in support of, Congress. On the contrary, I told Mr. Johnson that from the nature of things he could not dispense with a Congress to make laws and appropriate money, and suggested to him to receive and make overtures to such men as Fessenden, Trumbull, Sherman, Morgan, and Morton, who, though differing with him in abstract views of constitutional law and practice, were not destructive. That if the congressional plan of reconstruction succeeded, he could do nothing, and if it failed or led to confusion, the future developed results in his favor, etc.; and that is pretty much all I have ever said or done. At the meeting of the society of the army of the Tennessee on the 13th inst., I will be forced to speak, if here, and though I can confine myself purely to the military events of the past, I can make the opportunity of stating that in no event will I be drawn into the complications of the civil politics of this country.

If Congress could meet and confine itself to current and committee business, I feel certain that everything will work along quietly till the nominations are made, and a new presidential election will likely settle the principle if negroes are to be voters in the states without the consent of the whites. This is more a question of prejudice than principle, but a voter has as much right to his prejudices as to his vote. . . .

I answered :

MANSFIELD, OHIO, November 1, 1867.

DEAR BROTHER :— . . . I see no real occasion for trouble with Johnson. The great error of his life was in not acquiescing in and supporting the 14th amendment of the constitution in the 39th Congress. This he could easily have carried. It referred the suffrage question to each state, and if adopted long ago the whole controversy would have culminated ; or, if further opposed by the extreme radicals, they would have been easily beaten. Now I see nothing short of universal suffrage and universal amnesty as the basis. When you come on, I suggest that you give out that you go on to make your annual report and settle Indian affairs. Give us notice when you will be on, and come directly to my house, where we will make you one of the family.

Grant, I think, is inevitably the candidate. He allows himself to drift into a position where he can't decline if he would, and I feel sure he don't want to decline. My judgment is that Chase is better for the country and for Grant himself, but I will not quarrel with what I cannot control.

JOHN SHERMAN.

And later I wrote:—

If you can keep free from committals to Johnson, you will surely as you live be called upon to act as President. The danger now is that the mistakes of the Republicans may drift the Democratic party into power. If so, the Rebellion is triumphant, and no man active in suppressing it will be trusted or honored. Grant is not injured by his correspondence with Johnson, but no doubt feels annoyed. . . .

At this time President Johnson had come to open disagreement with Mr. Stanton, his Secretary of War, and wished to force him from the cabinet. Mr. Stanton had refused to resign and had been upheld by Congress. The President then turned for help in his difficulties to General Grant, commanding the army; but the latter found that any interference on his part would be illegal and impossible.

Mr. Johnson then planned to create a new office for General Sherman, that of brevet general of the army, in order to bring him to Washington.

The following letters and telegrams refer to this difficulty:

(Confidential.) LIBRARY ROOM, WAR DEPARTMENT, ⎱
WASHINGTON, D. C., January 31, 1868. ⎰

TO THE PRESIDENT:—Since our interview of yesterday I have given the subject of our conversation all my thoughts, and I beg you will pardon my reducing the result to writing.

My personal preferences, if expressed, were to be allowed to return to St. Louis to resume my present command, because my command was important, large, suited to my rank and inclination, and because my family was well provided for there, in house facilities, schools, living, and agreeable society.

Whilst, on the other hand, Washington was for many (to me) good reasons highly objectionable. Especially because it is the political capital of the country and focus of intrigue, gossip, and slander. Your personal preferences were, as expressed, to make a new department east adequate to my rank, with headquarters at Washington, and to assign me to its command —to remove my family here, and to avail myself of its schools, etc.; to remove Mr. Stanton from his office as Secretary of War, and have me to discharge the duties.

To effect this removal two modes were indicated: To simply cause him to quit the war office building and notify the treasury department and the army staff departments no longer to respect him as Secretary of War; or to remove him, and submit my name to the Senate for confirmation. Permit me to discuss these points a little, and I will premise by saying that I have spoken to no one on the subject, and have not even seen Mr. Ewing, Mr. Stanbery, or General Grant since I was with you.

It has been the rule and custom of our army, since the organization of the government, that the officer of the army second in rank should be in command at the second place in importance, and remote from general headquarters. To bring me to Washington would put three heads to an army, —yourself, General Grant, and myself,—and we would be more than human if we were not to differ. In my judgment it would ruin the army, and would be fatal to one or two of us.

Generals Scott and Taylor proved themselves soldiers and patriots in the field, but Washington was fatal to both. This city and the influences that centered here defeated every army that had its head here from 1861 to 1865, and would have overwhelmed General Grant at Spottsylvania and Petersburg, had he not been fortified by a strong reputation already hard earned, and because no one then living coveted the place. Whereas in the west we made progress from the start, because there was no political capital near enough to poison our minds and kindle into light that craving itching for fame which has killed more good men than bullets. I have been with General Grant in the midst of death and slaughter—when the howls of people reached him after Shiloh; when messengers were speeding to and fro, between his army and Washington, bearing slanders to induce his removal before he took Vicksburg; in Chattanooga, when the soldiers were stealing the corn of the starving mules to satisfy their own hunger; at Nashville, when he was ordered to the 'forlorn hope' to command the army of the Potomac, so often defeated—and yet I never saw him more troubled than since he has been in Washington, and has been compelled to read himself a 'sneak and deceiver,' based on reports of four of the cabinet, and apparently with your knowledge. If this political atmosphere can disturb the equanimity of one so guarded and so prudent as he is, what will be the result with one so careless, so outspoken, as I am? Therefore, with my consent, Washington never.

As to the Secretary of War, his office is twofold. As cabinet officer he should not be there without your hearty, cheerful consent, and I believe that is the judgment and opinion of every fair-minded man. As the holder of a civil office, having the supervision of moneys appropriated by Congress, and of contracts for army supplies, I do think Congress, or the Senate by delegation from Congress, has a lawful right to be consulted. At all events, I would not risk a suit or contest on that phase of the question. The law of Congress of March 2, 1867, prescribing the manner in which orders and instructions relating to 'military movements' shall reach the army, gives you, as constitutional commander in chief, the very power you want to exercise, and enables you to prevent the secretary from making any such orders and instructions, and consequently he cannot control the army, but is limited and restricted to a duty that an auditor of the treasury could perform. You certainly can afford to await the result. The executive power is not weakened, but, rather, strengthened. Surely he is not such an obstruction as would warrant violence or even a show of force which could produce the very reaction and clamor that he hopes for, to save him from the absurdity of holding an empty office 'for the safety of the country.'

With great respect, yours truly,
W. T. SHERMAN.

HEADQUARTERS MILITARY DIVISION OF THE MISSOURI, ⎞
ST. LOUIS, Mo., February 14, 1868. ⎠

To THE PRESIDENT :

DEAR SIR :—It is hard for me to conceive you would purposely do me an unkindness, unless under the pressure of a sense of public duty, or because you do not believe me sincere.

I was in hopes, since my letter to you of the 31st of January, that you had concluded to pass over that purpose of yours, expressed more than once in conversation, to organize a new command for me in the east, with headquarters in Washington ; but a telegram, from General Grant, of yesterday says that 'the order was issued ordering you' (me) 'to Atlantic division;' and the newspapers of this morning contain the same information, with the addition that I have been nominated as 'brevet general.' I have telegraphed to my own brother in the Senate to oppose my confirmation, on the ground that the two higher grades in the army ought not to be complicated with brevets, and I trust you will conceive my motives aright. If I could see my way clear to maintain my family, I should not hesitate a moment to resign my present commission and seek some business wherein I would be free from those unhappy complications that seem to be closing about me, in spite of my earnest efforts to avoid them ; but necessity ties my hands, and I submit with the best grace I can, till I make other arrangements.

In Washington are already the headquarters of a department, and of the army itself, and it is hard for me to see wherein I can render military service there. Any staff officer with the rank of major could surely fill any gap left between those two military offices ; and by being placed at Washington I shall be universally construed as a rival to the general in chief, a position damaging to me in the highest degree. Our relations have always been most confidential and friendly, and if, unhappily, any cloud of difficulty should arise between us, my sense of personal dignity and duty would leave me no alternative but resignation. For this I am not yet prepared, but I shall proceed to arrange for it as rapidly as possible, that when the time does come (as it surely will if this plan is carried into effect), I may act promptly.

Inasmuch as the order is now issued, I cannot expect a full revocation of it, but I beg the privilege of taking post at New York, or at any point you may name, within the new military division, other than Washington.

This privilege is generally granted to all military commanders, and I can see no good reasons why I, too, may not ask for it ; and this simple concession, involving no public interest, will much soften the blow which, right or wrong, I construe as one of the hardest I have sustained in a life somewhat checkered with adversity.

With great respect, yours truly,
(Signed)   W. T. Sherman, Lieutenant General.

Headquarters Military Division of Missouri, }
St. Louis, February 14, 1868. }

Dear Brother : — . . . I am again in the midst of trouble, occasioned by a telegram from Grant saying that the order is out for me to come to the command of the military division of the Atlantic, headquarters at Washington. The President repeatedly asked me to accept of some such position, but I thought I had fought it off successfully, though he again and again reverted to it.

Now, it seems, he has ordered it, and it is full of trouble for me. I wrote him one or two letters in Washington, which I thought positive enough, but have now written another, and if it fails in its object I might as well cast about for new employment. The result would be certain conflict, resulting in Grant's violent deposition, mine, or the President's.

There is not room on board of one ship for more than one captain.

If Grant intends to run for President I should be willing to come on, because my duties would then be so clearly defined that I think I could steer clear of the breakers—but now it would be impossible. The President would make use of me to beget violence, a condition of things that ought not to exist now.

He has no right to use us for such purposes, though he is commander in chief. I did suppose his passage with Grant would end there, but now it seems he will fight him as he has been doing Congress. I don't object if he does so himself and don't rope me in. . . .

If the President forces me into a false position out of seeming favor, I must defend myself. It is mortifying, but none the less inevitable.

Affectionately,   W. T. Sherman.

(Telegram.)   Washington, February 14, 1868.
From St. Louis, February 14, 1868.

To General U. S. Grant, Commander U. S. Army :

Your dispatch informing me that the order for the Atlantic division was issued, and that I was assigned to its command, is received.

I was in hopes I had escaped the danger, and now, were I prepared, should resign on the spot, as it requires no foresight to predict such must be the inevitable result in the end.

I will make one more desperate effort by mail, which please await.

(Signed)   W. T. Sherman, Lieutenant General.

(Telegram.)   Dated St. Louis, February 14, 1868.

Received at House of Representatives, February 14.

To Hon. John Sherman :

Oppose confirmation of myself as brevet general on ground that it is unprecedented, and that it is better not to extend the system of brevets above major general. If I can't avoid coming to Washington I may have to resign.   W. T. Sherman, Lieutenant General.

This correspondence, some of which was published, excited a great deal of attention, and I received many letters in regard to it, one of which I insert :

Washington, D. C., February 17, 1868.

Dear Sherman :—How nobly and magnanimously your gallant brother has acted. If A. J. was not callous to all that would affect gentlemen generally, he would feel this rebuke stingingly. But since he has betrayed the men who elected him he is proof against such things.

Yours very truly,   Schuyler Colfax.

Upon the receipt of General Sherman's telegram I requested the committee on military affairs to take no action upon his nomination, as he did not desire, and would not accept, the proposed compliment. This correspondence then followed :

Headquarters Military Division of the Missouri,   }
St. Louis, Mo., February 17, 1868.   }

Dear Brother :— . . . I have not yet got the order for the Atlantic division, but it is coming by mail, and when received I must act. I have asked the President to let me make my headquarters in New York, instead of Washington, making my application on the ground that my simply being in Washington will be universally construed as rivalry to General Grant, a position which would be damaging to me in the extreme.

If I must come to Washington, it will be with a degree of reluctance never before experienced. I would leave my family here on the supposition that the change was temporary. I do not question the President's right to make the new division, and I think Congress would make a mistake to qualify his right. It would suffice for them to nonconfirm the brevet of general. I will notify you by telegraph when the matter is concluded.

Affectionately, _____   W. T. Sherman.

(Telegram.)   Received Washington, February 20, 1868.

From St. Louis, Mo., February 20, 1868.

To General U. S. Grant :

The President telegraphs that I may remain in my present command. I write him a letter of thanks through you to-day. Congress should not have for publication my letters to the President, unless the President himself chooses to give them. (Signed)   W. T. Sherman, Lieut. General.

Fortieth Congress, U.S.

HOUSE OF REPRESENTATIVES.

Washington, D.C. Feb 17 1868.

Dear Sherman

How nobly & magnan
-imously your gallant brother
has acted. If A.J. was
not callous to all that
would affect gentlemen
generally, he would feel
this rebuke stingingly. But,
since he has betrayed the men who
elected him he is proof agst. such things

Yrs truly

Schuyler Colfax

HEADQUARTERS ARMY OF THE UNITED STATES, ⎱
WASHINGTON, February 21, 1868. ⎰

DEAR SIR :—By General Grant's direction I inclose a copy of a dispatch from General Sherman, seeming to indicate his preference that the correspondence in question should not now be made public.

Respectfully yours,   C. B. COMSTOCK, B. B. S.

HON. JOHN SHERMAN, United States Senate.

A few days after this, General Sherman went to Washington in response to the President's order, and while there had several interviews with the President relating to the change of his command. He objected very strongly, as has been seen, to any such change, because he felt that he could not hold a command in Washington without interfering with Grant's interests, and because he had a rooted objection to living in Washington in the midst of the turmoil of politics. These objections were embodied in three letters which General Sherman wrote and showed to Grant before he sent them to the President. One of them found its way into the public press, and created a disturbance which called forth the following letters:

HEADQUARTERS ARMY OF THE UNITED STATES, ⎱
WASHINGTON, D. C., February 22, 1868. ⎰

HON. J. SHERMAN, United States Senate.

DEAR SIR :—The 'National Intelligencer' of this morning contains a private note which General Sherman sent to the President whilst he was in Washington, dictated by the purest kindness and a disposition to preserve harmony, and not intended for publication. It seems to me the publication of that letter is calculated to place the general in a wrong light before the public, taken in connection with what correspondents have said before, evidently getting their inspiration from the White House.

As General Sherman afterwards wrote a semi-official note to the President, furnishing me a copy, and still later a purely official one sent through me, which placed him in his true position, and which have not been published, though called for by the 'House,' I take the liberty of sending you these letters to give you the opportunity of consulting General Sherman as to what action to take upon them. In all matters where I am not personally interested, I would not hesitate to advise General Sherman how I would act in his place. But in this instance, after the correspondence I have had with Mr. Johnson, I may not see General Sherman's interest in the same light that others see it, or that I would see it in if no such correspondence had occurred. I am clear in this, however, the correspondence here inclosed to you should not be made public except by the President, or with the full sanction of General Sherman. Probably the letter of the 31st of January, marked 'confidential,' should not be given out at all.   Yours truly,   U. S. GRANT.

The following letter was addressed to the "National Intelligencer," a Washington newspaper:

UNITED STATES SENATE CHAMBER, }
WASHINGTON, February 22, 1868. }

GENTLEMEN : — The publication in your paper yesterday of General Sherman's note to the President, and its simultaneous transmission by telegraph, unaccompanied by subsequent letters withheld by the President because they were 'private,' is so unfair as to justify severe censure upon the person who furnished you this letter, whoever he may be. Upon its face it is an informal private note dictated by the purest motives—a desire to preserve harmony—and not intended for publication. How any gentleman receiving such a note could first allow vague but false suggestions of its contents to be given out, and then print it, and withhold other letters because they were 'private,' with a view to create the impression that General Sherman, in referring to ulterior measures, suggested the violent expulsion of a high officer from his office, passes my comprehension. Still I know that General Sherman is so sensitive upon questions of official propriety in publishing papers, that he would rather suffer from this false inference than correct it by publishing another private note, and as I knew that this letter was not the only one written by General Sherman to the President about Mr. Stanton, I applied to the President for his consent to publish subsequent letters. This consent was freely given by the President, and I therefore send copies to you and ask their publication.

These copies are furnished me from official sources ; for while I know General Sherman's opinions, yet he did not show me either of the letters to the President, during his stay here, nervously anxious to promote harmony, to avoid strife, and certainly never suggested or countenanced resistance to law—or violence in any form. He no doubt left Washington with his old repugnance to politics, politicians, and newspapers very much increased by his visit here.   JOHN SHERMAN.

UNITED STATES SENATE CHAMBER, February 23, 1868.

DEAR BROTHER:—I received your letters and telegrams, and did not answer because events were moving so rapidly that I could say nothing but might be upset before you got the letter.

Now you can congratulate yourself upon being clear of the worst complications we have ever had. Impeachment seems to be a foregone conclusion so far as the House of Representatives is concerned, based upon the alleged *forcible* expulsion of Stanton. No one disputes the right of the President to raise a question of law upon his right to remove Stanton, but the forcible removal of a man in office, claiming to be in lawfully, is like the forcible ejectment of a tenant when his right of possession is in dispute. It is a trespass, an assault, a riot, or a crime, according to the result of the force. It is strange the President can contemplate such a thing, when Stanton is already stripped of power, and the courts are open to the President to try his right of removal. The President is acting very badly with respect to you. He creates the impression that you acted disingenuously with him. He has published your short private note before you went to Annapolis, and yet refuses to publish your formal one subsequently sent to him, because it was 'private.' The truth is, he is a slave to his passions and resentments. No man can confide in him, and you ought to feel happy at your extrication from all near connection with him. . . . Grant is anxious to have your letters published, since the note referred to was published. I will see Grant and the President this evening, and if the latter freely consents, I will do it informally ; but if he doubts or hesitates, I will not without your expressed directions. In these times of loose confidence, it is better to submit for a time to a wrong construction, than to betray confidential communications. Grant will, unquestionably, be nominated. Chase acquiesces, and I see no reason to doubt his election. . . .   Affectionately,

JOHN SHERMAN.

HEADQUARTERS MILITARY DIVISION OF THE MISSOURI, }
ST. LOUIS, Mo., February 25, 1868. }

DEAR BROTHER:— . . . I am in possession of all the news up to date—the passage of the impeachment resolution, etc.—but I yet don't know if the nomination of T. Ewing, Senior, was a real thing or meant to compromise a difficulty.

The publication of my short note of January 18, is nothing to me. I have the original draft which I sent through Grant's hands, with his indorsement back to me. At the time this note must have been given to the reporter, the President had an elaborate letter from me, in which I discussed the whole case, and advised against the very course he has pursued, but I don't want that letter or any other to be drawn out to complicate a case already bad enough.

You may always safely represent me by saying that I will not make up a final opinion till called on to act, and I want nothing to do with these controversies until the time comes for the actual fight, which I hope to God may be avoided. If the Democratic party intend to fight on this impeachment, which I believe they do not, you may count 200,000 men against you in the south. The negroes are no match for them. On this question, the whites there will be more united than on the old issue of union and secession. I do not think the President should be suspended during trial, and, if possible, the Republican party should not vote on all side questions as a unit. They should act as judges, and not as partisans. The vote in the House, being a strictly party vote, looks bad, for it augurs a prejudiced jury. Those who adhere closest to the law in this crisis are the best patriots. Whilst the floating politicians here share the excitement at Washington, the people generally manifest little interest in the game going on at Washington. . . .

Affectionately yours,

W. T. SHERMAN.

UNITED STATES SENATE CHAMBER, ⎰
WASHINGTON, March 1, 1868. ⎱

DEAR BROTHER: — Your letter of the 25th is received. I need not say to you that the new events transpiring here are narrowly watched by me. So far as I am concerned, I mean to give Johnson a fair and impartial trial, and to decide nothing until required to do so, and after full argument. I regard him as a foolish and stubborn man, doing even right things in a wrong way, and in a position where the evil that he does is immensely increased by his manner of doing it. He clearly designed to have first Grant, and then you, involved in Lorenzo Thomas' position, and in this he is actuated by his recent revolt against Stanton. How easy it would have been, if he had followed your advice, to have made Stanton anxious to resign, or what is worse, to have made his position ridiculous. By his infernal folly we are drifting into turbulent waters. The only way is to keep cool and act conscientiously. I congratulate you on your lucky extrication. I do not anticipate civil war, for our proceeding is unquestionably lawful, and if the judgment is against the President, his term is just as clearly *out* as if the 4th of March, 1869, was come. The result, if he is convicted, would cast the undivided responsibility of reconstruction upon the Republican party, and would unquestionably secure the full admission of all the states by July next, and avoid the dangerous questions that may otherwise arise out of the southern vote in the Presidential election. It is now clear that Grant will be a candidate, and his election seems quite as clear. The action of North Carolina removed the last doubt of his nomination.   Affectionately yours,

JOHN SHERMAN.

_____

HEADQUARTERS MILITARY DIVISION OF THE MISSOURI, ⎰
ST. LOUIS, March 14, 1868. ⎱

DEAR BROTHER : — I don't know what Grant means by his silence in the midst of the very great indications of his receiving the nomination in May. Doubtless he intends to hold aloof from the expression of any opinion, till the actual nomination is made, when, if he accepts with a strong radical platform, I shall be surprised. My notion is that he thinks that the Democrats ought not to succeed to power, and that he would be willing to stand a sacrifice rather than see that result. . . . I notice that you Republicans have divided on some of the side questions on impeachment, and am glad you concede to the President the largest limits in his defense that are offered. I don't see what the Republicans can gain by shoving matters to an extent that looks like a foregone conclusion.

No matter what men may think of Mr. Johnson, his office is one that ought to have a pretty wide latitude of opinion. Nevertheless, the trial is one that will be closely and sternly criticised by all the civilized world. . . .   Your brother,

W. T. SHERMAN.

At this time I wrote from Washington:

You notice the impeachment proceedings have commenced. As a matter of course, I have nothing to say about them. It is strange that they have so little effect on prices and business. The struggle has been so long that the effect has been discounted. . . .

The President was very anxious to send you to Louisiana, and only gave it up by reason of your Indian command. He might think that your visit to Europe now was not consistent with the reason given for your remaining at St. Louis. Still, on this point you could readily ask his opinion, and if that agrees with Grant's you need feel no delicacy in going. No more favorable opportunity or time to visit Europe will likely occur. . . .

General Sherman responded:

I hardly know what to think of the impeachment. Was in hopes Mr. Johnson would be allowed to live out his term, and doubt if any good will result by a change for the few months still remaining of his term. A new cabinet, and the changes foreshadowed by Wade's friends, though natural enough, would have insufficient time to do any good. I have a private letter from Grant as late as March 18, but he says not a word of his political intentions. So far as I know, he would yet be glad of a change that would enable him to remain as now. . . .

On the 27th of February, 1868, Mr. Stevens made the following report:

"The committee on reconstruction, to whom was referred, on the 27th of January last, the following resolution :

"'Resolved, That the committee on reconstruction be authorized to inquire what combinations have been made or attempted to be made to obstruct the due execution of the laws ; and to that end the committee have power to send for persons and papers, and to examine witnesses on oath, and report to this House what action, if any, they may deem necessary ; and that said committee have leave to report at any time.'

"And to whom was also referred, on the 21st day of February, instant, a communication from Hon. Edwin M. Stanton, Secretary of War, dated on said 21st day of February, together with a copy of a letter from Andrew Johnson, President of the United States, to the said Edwin M. Stanton, as follows :

EXECUTIVE MANSION, }
WASHINGTON, D. C., February 21, 1868. }

SIR : — By virtue of the power and authority vested in me, as President, by the constitution and laws of the United States, you are hereby removed from office as secretary for the department of war, and your functions as such will terminate upon the receipt of this communication.

You will transfer to Brevet Major General Lorenzo Thomas, Adjutant General of the Army, who has this day been authorized and empowered to act as Secretary of War *ad interim*, all records, books, papers, and other public property now in your custody and charge.

Respectfully yours,

ANDREW JOHNSON.

HON. EDWIN M. STANTON, Washington, D. C.

"And to whom was also referred by the House of Representatives the following resolution, namely :

" ' *Resolved*, That Andrew Johnson, President of the United States, be impeached of high crimes and misdemeanors :'

" Have considered the several subjects referred to them, and submit the following report :

" ' That in addition to the papers referred to the committee, the committee find that the President, on the 21st day of February, 1868, signed and issued a commission or letter of authority to one Lorenzo Thomas, directing and authorizing said Thomas to act as Secretary of War *ad interim*, and to take possession of the books, records, and papers, and other public property in the war department, of which the following is a copy :

EXECUTIVE MANSION,
WASHINGTON, February 21, 1868.

SIR:—Hon. Edwin M. Stanton having been this day removed from office as secretary for the department of war, you are hereby authorized and empowered to act as Secretary of War *ad interim*, and will immediately enter upon the discharge of the duties pertaining to that office. Mr. Stanton has been instructed to transfer to you all the records, books, papers, and other public property now in his custody and charge.   Respectfully yours,   ANDREW JOHNSON.

To BREVET MAJOR GENERAL LORENZO THOMAS, Adjutant General of the United States Army, Washington, District of Columbia.

Official copy respectfully furnished to Hon. Edwin M. Stanton.

L. THOMAS,
Secretary of War *ad interim*.'

"Upon the evidence collected by the committee, which is herewith presented, and in virtue of the powers with which they have been invested by the House, they are of the opinion that Andrew Johnson, President of the United States, be impeached of high crimes and misdemeanors. They therefore recommend to the House the adoption of the accompanying resolution :

THADDEUS STEVENS,
GEORGE S. BOUTWELL,
JOHN A. BINGHAM,
C. T. HULBURD,
JOHN F. FARNSWORTH,
F. C. BEAMAN,
H. E. PAINE."

"Resolution providing for the impeachment of Andrew Johnson, President of the United States :

" ' *Resolved*, That Andrew Johnson, President of the United States, be impeached of high crimes and misdemeanors in office.' "

On the 24th of February the resolution providing for impeachment was adopted by a vote of 126 yeas and 47 nays.

On the same day Mr. Stevens introduced the following resolution, which was agreed to:

" *Resolved*, That a committee of two be appointed to go to the Senate
and, at the bar thereof, in the name of the House of Representatives and of
all the people of the United States, to impeach Andrew Johnson, President
of the United States, of high crimes and misdemeanors in office, and
acquaint the Senate that the House of Representatives will, in due time,
exhibit particular articles of impeachment against him and make good the
same ; and that the committee do demand that the Senate take order for the
appearance of said Andrew Johnson to answer to said impeachment.

" 2. *Resolved*, That a committee of seven be appointed to prepare and
report articles of impeachment against Andrew Johnson, President of the
United States, with power to send for persons, papers, and records, and to
take testimony under oath."

The speaker then announced the following committees
under these resolutions:

Committee to communicate to the Senate the action of the House ordering an impeachment of the President of the United States :—Thaddeus
Stevens, of Pennsylvania, and John A. Bingham, of Ohio.

Committee to declare articles of impeachment against the President of
the United States : — George S. Boutwell, of Massachusetts ; Thaddeus
Stevens, of Pennsylvania ; John A. Bingham, of Ohio ; James F. Wilson, of
Iowa ; John A. Logan, of Illinois ; George W. Julian, of Indiana ; and
Hamilton Ward, of New York.

The trial of this impeachment by the Senate was an imposing spectacle, which excited profound interest during its continuance. It was soon developed that the gravamen of the
charges was not the removal of Stanton, but was the attempt
of the President to force General Lorenzo Thomas into a high
office without the advice and consent of the Senate.

In the trial of this impeachment I wished to be, and I think
I was, absolutely impartial. I liked the President personally
and harbored against him none of the prejudice and animosity
of some others. I knew he was bold and rash, better fitted for
the storms of political life than the grave responsibilities of
the chief magistrate of a great country. His education, such
as it was, was acquired late in life, when his character was
formed and his habits fixed. Still, his mind was vigorous and
his body strong, and when thoroughly aroused he was an able

speaker; his language was forcible and apt and his influence over a popular audience was effective. I disliked above all things to be a judge in his case. I knew some of my associates were already against the President, and others were as decided in his favor. I resolutely made up my mind, so far as human nature would admit, to fairly hear and impartially consider all the evidence produced and all the arguments made.

The counsel for the President were Henry Stanbery, B. R. Curtis, Jeremiah S. Black, William M. Evarts, William S. Groesbeck, and Thomas A. R. Nelson. The managers on the part of the House of Representatives were John A. Bingham, George S. Boutwell, James F. Wilson, John A. Logan, Thomas Williams, Benjamin F. Butler and Thaddeus Stevens. The trial lasted nearly two months, was ably conducted on both sides, and ended by the acquittal of the President, on the eleventh article of impeachment, by a vote of 35 guilty and 19 not guilty. Two-thirds of those voting not having pronounced "guilty," as required by the constitution, the President was acquitted upon this article. Two other articles were voted on with the same result. Thereupon, on the 26th day of May, 1868, the Senate sitting as a court of impeachment adjourned without day. Mr. Stanton resigned and General Schofield became Secretary of War.

I voted for conviction for the reasons stated in the opinion given by me. I have carefully reviewed this opinion and am entirely content with it. I stated in the beginning my desire to consider the case without bias or feeling. I quote in full the opening paragraphs:

"This cause must be decided upon the reasons and presumptions which by law apply to all other criminal accusations. Justice is blind to the official station of the respondent, and to the attitude of the accusers speaking in the name of all the people of the United States. It only demands of the Senate the application to this cause of the principles and safeguards provided for every human being accused of crime. For the proper application of these principles we ourselves are on trial before the bar of public opinion. The novelty of this proceeding, the historical character of the trial, and the grave interests involved, only deepen the obligation of the special oath we have taken to do impartial justice according to the constitution and laws.

FORTIETH CONGRESS U.S. SECOND SESSION

SENATE CHAMBER.

MAY 16TH AND 26TH 1868.

The vote of the Senate, sitting as a High Court of Impeachment for the trial of ANDREW JOHNSON, President of the United States, upon the 11th, 2nd and 3rd Articles.

S. P. Chase, Chief Justice.   _J. W. Forney_, Secretary.

Guilty.

1. B. F. Wade
2. H. W. Corbett
3. Cornelius Cole
4. L. M. Morrill
5. Wm M Stewart
6. J W Patterson
7. Justin S. Morrill
8. James W. Nye
9. Tim. O. Howe
10. Henry Wilson
11. A. H. Cragin
12. W. Sprague
13. Jas Harlan
14. O S Ferry
15. Aly. Ramsey
16. John Conness
17. Geo. F. Edmunds
18. Fred T. Frelinghuysen
19. H R Anthony
20. Jn. Howard
21. S. C. Pomeroy
22. W. J. Willey
23. Rich. Yates
24. Charles Sumner
25. Alex. G. Cattell
26. Geo. H. Williams
27. Jas. Chandler
28. E. D. Morgan
29. John Sherman
30. John M. Thayer
31. Roscoe Conkling
32. C. A. Drake
33. Simon Cameron
34. T. W. Tipton
35. O. P. Morton

Not Guilty.

1. T. A. Hendricks
2. J. A. Buckalew
3. D. Drenton
4. J. R. Doolittle
5. Thos. C. McCreery
6. George Vickers
7. J. B. Henderson
8. Lyman Trumbull
9. E. G. Ross
10. W. P. Fessenden
11. Garrett Davis
12. J. A. Bayard
13. Jos. S. Fowler
14. Jno Grimes
15. Daniel S. Norton
16. Willard Saulsbury
17. Reverdy Johnson
18. P. G. Van Winkle
19. James Dixon

Entered according to Act of Congress in the year 1868 by JAMES T. B. McGUIRE, in the Clerk's Office of the District Court for the District of Columbia.

"And this case must be tried upon the charges now made by the House of Representatives. We cannot consider other offenses. An appeal is made to the conscience of each Senator of guilty or not guilty by the President of eleven specific offenses. In answering this appeal a Senator cannot justify himself by public opinion, or by political, personal, or partisan demands, or even grave considerations of public policy. His conscientious conviction of the truth of these charges is the only test that will justify a verdict of guilty. God forbid that any other should prevail here. In forming this conviction we are not limited merely to the rules of evidence, which, by the experience of ages, have been found best adapted to the trial of offenses in the double tribunal of court and jury, but we may seek light from history, from personal knowledge, and from all sources that will tend to form a conscientious conviction of the truth. And we are not bound to technical definitions of crimes and misdemeanors.

"A willful violation of the law, a gross and palpable breach of moral obligations tending to unfit an officer for the proper discharge of his office, or to bring the office into public contempt and derision, is, when charged and proven, an impeachable offense. And the nature and criminality of the offense may depend on the official character of the accused. A judge would be held to higher official purity, and an executive officer to a stricter observance of the letter of the law. The President, bound as a citizen to obey the law, and specially sworn to execute the law, may properly, in his high office as chief magistrate, be held to a stricter responsibility than if his example was less dangerous to the public safety. Still, to justify the conviction of the President there must be specific allegations of some crime or misdemeanor involving moral turpitude, gross misconduct, or a willful violation of law, and the proof must be such as to satisfy the conscience of the truth of the charge.

" The principal charges against the President are that he willfully and purposely violated the constitution and the laws, in the order for the removal of Mr. Stanton, and in the order for the appointment of General Thomas as Secretary of War *ad interim*. These two orders were contemporaneous — part of the same transaction — but are distinct acts, and are made the basis of separate articles of impeachment."

I stated the grounds of my conviction that the action of the President, in placing Lorenzo Thomas in charge of the office of Secretary of War, without the advice and consent of the Senate, was a clearly illegal act, committed for the purpose of obtaining control of that office. I held that the President had the power to remove Secretary Stanton, but that he had not the power to put anyone in his place unless the person appointed was confirmed by the Senate.

Did the act of March 2, 1867, commonly known as the "tenure of office act," confer this authority? On the contrary, it plainly prohibits all temporary appointments except as specially provided for. The third section repeats the constitutional authority of the President to fill all vacancies happening during the recess of the Senate by death or resignation, and provides that if no appointment is made during the following session to fill such vacancy, the office shall remain in abeyance until an appointment is duly made and confirmed, and provision is made for the discharge of the duties of the office in the meantime. The second section provides for the suspension of an officer during the recess, and for a temporary appointment *during the recess.* This power was exercised and fully exhausted by the suspension of Mr. Stanton until restored by the Senate, in compliance with the law. No authority whatever is conferred by this act for any temporary appointment during the session of the Senate, but, on the contrary, such an appointment is plainly inconsistent with the act, and could not be inferred or implied from it. The sixth section further provides:

"That every removal, appointment, or employment, made, had, or exercised, contrary to the provisions of this act, and the making, signing, sealing, countersigning, or issuing of any commission or letter of authority for, or in respect to, any such appointment or employment, shall be deemed, and are hereby declared to be, high misdemeanors, and, upon trial and conviction thereof, every person guilty thereof shall be punished by a fine not exceeding $10,000, or by imprisonment not exceeding five years, or both said punishments, in the discretion of the court."

This language is plain, explicit, and was inserted not only to prohibit all temporary appointments except during the recess, and in the mode provided for in the second section, but the unusual course was taken of affixing a penalty to a law defining the official duty of the President. The original bill did not contain penal clauses; but it was objected in the Senate that the President had already disregarded mandatory provisions of law, and would this; and therefore, after debate, these penal sections were added to secure obedience to the law, and to give to it the highest sanction.

I quote my view of the action of the President:

"Was not this act willfully violated by the President during the session of the Senate?

"It appears, from the letter of the President to General Grant, from his conversation with General Sherman, and from his answer, that he had formed a fixed resolve to get rid of Mr. Stanton, and fill the vacancy without the advice of the Senate. He might have secured a new Secretary of War by sending a proper nomination to the Senate. This he neglected and refused to do. He cannot allege that the Senate refused to relieve him from an obnoxious minister. He could not say that the Senate refused to confirm a proper appointee, for he would make no appointment to them. The Senate had declared that the reasons assigned for suspending Mr. Stanton did not make the case required by the tenure of office act, but I affirm as my conviction that the Senate would have confirmed any one of a great number of patriotic citizens if nominated to the Senate. I cannot resist the conclusion, from the evidence before us, that he was resolved to obtain a vacancy in the department of war in such a way that he might fill the vacancy by an appointment without the consent of the Senate, and in violation of the constitution and the law. This was the purpose of the offer to General Sherman. This was the purpose of the appointment of General Thomas. If he had succeeded as he hoped, he could have changed his temporary appointment at pleasure, and thus have defied the authority of the Senate and the mandatory provisions of the constitution and the law. I cannot in any other way account for his refusal to send a nomination to the Senate until after the appointment of General Thomas. The removal of Mr. Stanton by a new appointment, confirmed by the Senate, would have complied with the constitution. The absolute removal of Mr. Stanton would have created a temporary vacancy, but the Senate was in session to share in the appointment of another. An *ad interim* appointment, without authority of law, during the session of the Senate, would place the department of war at his control in defiance of the Senate and the law, and would have set an evil example, dangerous to the public safety — one which, if allowed to pass unchallenged, would place the President above and beyond the law.

"The claim now made, that it was the sole desire of the President to test the constitutionality of the tenure of office act, is not supported by reason or by proof. He might, in August last, or at any time since, without an *ad interim* appointment, have tested this law by a writ of *quo warranto*. He might have done so by an order of removal, and a refusal of Mr. Stanton's requisitions. He might have done so by assigning a head of a department to the place made vacant by the order of removal. Such was not his purpose or expectation. He expected by the appointment of General Sherman at once to get possession of the war department, so when General Thomas was appointed there was no suggestion of a suit at law, until the unexpected resistance of Mr. Stanton, supported by the action of the Senate, indicated that as the only way left."

It is difficult to convey, by extracts, a correct idea of a carefully prepared opinion, but this statement shows my view of the case, and, entertaining it, I felt bound, with much regret, to vote "guilty" in response to my name, but I was entirely satisfied with the result of the vote, brought about by the action of several Republican Senators. There was some disposition to arraign these Senators and to attribute their action to corrupt motives, but there was not the slightest ground for these imputations. Johnson was allowed to serve out his term, but there was a sense of relief when General Grant was sworn into office as President of the United States.

CHAPTER XX.

The Fortieth Congress.

Legislation During the Two Years — Further Reduction of the Currency by the Secretary Prohibited — Report of the Committee of Conference — Bill for Refunding the National Debt — Amounted to $2,639,382,572.68 on December 1, 1867 — Resumption of Specie Payments Recommended — Refunding Bill in the Senate — Change in My Views — Debate Participated in by Nearly Every Senator — Why the Bill Failed to Become a Law — Breach Between Congress and the President Paralyzes Legislation — Nomination and Election of Grant for President — His Correspondence with General Sherman.

DURING the 40th Congress, extending from the 4th of March, 1867, to the 4th of March, 1869, the chief subjects of debate were the contraction of the currency, the refunding of the public debt, the payment of United States notes in coin, and a revision of the laws imposing internal taxation and duties on imported goods.

Early in the first session of this Congress, the opposition of the people to the policy of contraction, constantly pressed by Secretary McCulloch, became so imperative that both Houses determined to take from him all power to diminish the volume of currency then in circulation. On the 5th of December, 1867, Robert C. Schenck, chairman of the committee of ways and means, reported a bill in the following words:

"*Be it enacted,* etc., That so much of an act entitled "An act to amend an act to provide ways and means to support the government," approved April 12, 1866, as authorizes the Secretary of the Treasury to retire United States notes to an amount not exceeding $4,000,000 in any one month, is hereby repealed.

"Sec. 2. *And be it further enacted,* That from and after the passage of this act the further reduction of the currency by retiring or canceling United States notes shall be, and hereby is, prohibited."

This bill was taken up for consideration on the 7th of December, and, after a brief debate, with little opposition, passed the House by the vote of 127 yeas and 32 nays. It was sent to the Senate, referred to the committee on finance, and was carefully considered. That committee, with but two dissenting voices, directed me to report the bill to the Senate with a single amendment. On the 9th of January, 1868, I called up the bill for consideration, and made a brief explanation, in which I said the committee, after full reflection, had thought proper to recommend the passage of the bill of the House of Representatives, in substance as it was sent to us, only changing the phraseology. I said that the bill contemplated further legislation during that session. It was understood by all that some more comprehensive measures must be adopted during that session, but until further legislation there should be no more contraction of the currency. I thus stated the reasons which, in my opinion, justified the passage of the bill :

" *First.* It will satisfy the public mind that no further contraction will be made when industry is in a measure paralyzed. We hear the complaint from all parts of the country, from all branches of industry, from every state in the Union, that industry for some reason is paralyzed, and that trade and enterprise are not so well rewarded as they were. Many, perhaps erroneously, attribute all this to the contraction of the currency—a contraction that I believe is unexampled in the history of any nation. $140,000-000 have been withdrawn out of $737,000,000 in less than two years. There is no example, that I know of, of such rapid contraction. It may be wise, it may be beneficial, but still it has been so rapid as to excite a stringency that is causing complaint, and I think the people have a right to be relieved from that.

" *Second.* This bill will restore to the legislature their power over the currency, a power too important to be delegated to any single officer of the government. I do not wish to renew the discussion that occurred here two years ago on the passage of the law of April 12, 1866 ; but it is still my opinion, as it has been always, that the question of the amount of currency ought to be fixed by Congress. We have the power to coin money, and to regulate the value thereof. We have coined money in the form of paper money, and certainly the power of Congress in this respect ought not to be delegated to any single officer. If contraction ought to be established as the policy it should be by Congress, not by the Secretary of the Treasury, and it is not wise to confer upon any officer of the government a power of this kind, which can be and may be properly controlled and limited by Congress.

" *Third.* This will strongly impress upon Congress the imperative duty of acting wisely upon financial measures, for the responsibility will then rest entirely upon Congress, and will not be shared with them by the Secretary of the Treasury.

" *Fourth.* It will encourage business men to continue old, and embark in new, enterprises, when they are assured that no change will be made in the measure of value without the open and deliberate consent of their representatives.

" These considerations are amply sufficient to justify this measure, but it is only preliminary to others of far greater importance that must command our attention. These involve —

" 1. The existence of the banking system of the United States.

" 2. The time and manner of resuming specie payments.

" 3. The mode of redeeming the debt of the United States and the kind of money in which it may be redeemed; and, in this connection, the taxes, if any, that may be levied upon the public creditors.

" 4. Such a reduction of our expenditures and taxes as will relieve our constituents, as far as practicable, from the burdens resulting from the recent war."

This led to a long debate, which continued until the 15th of January, when the bill, as amended, passed by a vote of 33 yeas and 4 nays.

These decisive votes against contraction definitely settled the policy of the government to retain in circulation the then existing volume of United States notes. The disagreement between the two Houses was referred to a committee of conference, and the conferees reported the bill in the following form:

" *Be it enacted by the Senate and House of Representatives of the United States of America in Congress assembled,*

" That, from and after the passage of this act, the authority of the Secretary of the Treasury to make any reduction of the currency, by retiring or canceling United States notes, shall be, and is hereby, suspended; but nothing herein contained shall prevent the cancellation and destruction of mutilated United States notes, and the replacing of the same with notes of the same character and amount."

This bill was sent to the President, and, not having been returned by him within ten days, it became a law without his approval, under the constitution of the United States.

On the 17th of December, 1867, I reported from the committee on finance a bill for refunding the national debt and for a conversion of the notes of the United States. This bill was accompanied by an elaborate report. This report was carefully prepared by me, and met, I believe, the general approval of the committee on finance. In that Congress there were but five Democratic Senators, and it so happened that all the members of the committee on finance were Republicans, but these represented widely different opinions on financial subjects. I undertook, in this report, to deal in a general way with these topics. Upon a careful reading of it now I find but little that I do not approve. The general policy set out in this report was subsequently embodied into laws, but the measures relating to refunding the debt and the resumption of specie payments were not adopted until several years after the date of the report.

The ascertained debt on the first day of December, 1867, as stated by the Secretary of the Treasury, was $2,639,382,572.68, divided as follows:

DEBT BEARING COIN INTEREST.

5 per cent. bonds, 10-40's and old fives	$205,532,850 00	
6 per cent. bonds of 1867 and 1868...	14,690,941 80	
6 per cent. bonds, 1881.............	282,731,550 00	
6 per cent. 5-20 bonds..............	1,324,412,550 00	
Navy pension fund................	13,000,000 00	
		$1,840,367,891 80

DEBT BEARING CURRENCY INTEREST.

6 per cent. bonds..................	18,601,000 00	
3-year compound interest notes......	62,249,360 00	
3-year 7-30 notes..................	285,587,100 00	
3 per cent. certificates.............	12,855,000 00	
		$379,292,460 00

MATURED DEBT NOT PRESENTED FOR PAYMENT.

3-year 7-30 notes, due August 15, 1867	$2,855,400 00	
Compound interest notes, matured June 10, July 15, August 15, and October 15, 1867.................	7,065,750 00	
Bonds, Texas indemnity............	260,000 00	
Treasury notes, acts July 17, 1861 and prior thereto.................	163,011 64	
Bonds, April 15, 1842..............	54,061 64	
Treasury notes, March 3, 1863.......	868,240 00	
Temporary loan...................	2,880,900 55	
Certificates of indebtedness.........	31,000 00	
		$14,178,363 83

DEBT BEARING NO INTEREST.

United States notes................ $356,212,473 00
Fractional currency................ 30,929,984 05
Gold certificates of deposit.......... 18,401,400 00
                                        ————————— $405,543,857 05

Total debt................................ $2,639,382,572 68
Amount in treasury, coin........... $100,690,645 69
Amount in treasury, currency........ 37,486,175 24
                                        ————————— 138,176,820 93

Amount of debt less cash in treasury........... $2,501,205,751 75

Besides the amounts thus stated there were large balances
due to loyal states, upon accounts not then rendered or ascertained, and to individuals for losses sustained during the war.

The ascertained debt consisted of twenty different forms of
liability, some payable in coin and some in lawful money.
Much of this debt was due on demand, but the great body of
it was payable in from one to twenty years, while the unascer-
tained debt was being stated from time to time and had to be
met from accruing revenues. Nearly $300,000,000 of debt had
been paid out of current revenue since the close of the war.
The first recommendation of the committee was that the debt
should be refunded as rapidly as practicable into bonds bearing
as low a rate of interest as possible, payable in twenty or thirty
years, but redeemable at the pleasure of the United States in
five or ten years. This recommendation was based on the fixed
policy of the government to limit the duration of a bond within a lifetime, and thus leave it to the option of the government
to pay its indebtedness and to reduce the rate of interest after
a brief period, if the condition of the public revenues and of
the money market should enable it to do so.

Here the question arose whether the bonds known as the
5-20 bonds could be paid in lawful money after the period of
five years, when, by their terms, they were redeemable. These
bonds promised to pay so many dollars. Other bonds were specifically payable in coin, and still other bonds were payable in
lawful money; that is, in United States notes. These notes
were then at a discount, being worth in the market about 88
cents in coin. But the notes were obligations of the United

States, and it was the duty, and then within the power of the United States, to advance these notes to par in coin.

The majority of the committee, I among them, believed that the United States should not take advantage of its own wrong, in not redeeming its notes in coin, but should either advance these notes to par in coin, or pay its bonds in coin. The committee, therefore, recommended that both the notes and bonds should be received in exchange for the funding bonds, and that the notes should be reissued and maintained at par with coin, and be supported by a reserve of coin ample to maintain the notes at par with coin. In other words, the United States would resume specie payments. The committee expressed the opinion that, with the system of taxation then in existence, this policy of refunding and resumption could be maintained, and that the rate of interest then paid could be reduced to four or five per cent., and the money then in circulation would be kept at par with coin at the cost only of the interest on the bullion and coin held to meet any notes presented for redemption. The committee also recommended that the internal and tariff taxes be revised to correct irregularities or defects, and to repeal such as were oppressive.

While the committee opposed any contraction of the currency it also opposed any increase of it. The general theory of the report was to advance both bonds and notes to par in coin, and to issue bonds in such form and terms that the government could redeem them, or renew them at lower rates of interest.

The report states:

"Your committee are therefore of opinion that no legal tender notes, beyond the amount now limited by law, should be issued under any pressure of financial or political necessity until they are convertible into gold and silver. Our duty is to elevate the 'greenback,' the standard of national credit, to the standard of gold, the money of the world. Until then we are not on a substantial foundation. Let us make the dollar of our promise in the pocket of a laboring man equal to the dollar of our mint. The rapidity of the process is a question of public policy. It may be by gradually diminishing the volume of currency, or be left at its present amount until increased business or improved credit bring it up to the specie standard."

The refunding bill was taken up by the Senate on the 27th of February, 1868, and was fully discussed by me. After stating its general objects I said:

"It is with this view, and actuated by this principle, that the committee on finance have endeavored to make this bill a bill of relief, reducing, if possible, consistent with the public faith, the interest of the public debt, and giving increased value to United States notes. We have endeavored in this bill to accomplish three results: First, to reduce the rate of interest with the voluntary consent of the holders of our securities; second, to make a distinct provision for the payment of the public debt; and third, to give increased value to United States notes, and to provide for a gradual resumption of specie payments. All these are objects admitted to be of the highest importance. The only question is, whether the measure proposed tends to accomplish them."

I then quoted the example of the United States and Great Britain in reducing the rate of interest on public securities. I do not approve all I said in that speech. It has been frequently quoted as being inconsistent with my opinions and action at a later period. It is more important to be right than to be consistent. I then proposed to use the doubt expressed by many people as to the right of the government to redeem the 5–20 bonds in the legal tender money in circulation when the bonds were sold, as an inducement to the holders of bonds to convert them into securities bearing a less rate of interest but specifically payable in coin. Upon this policy I changed my opinion. I became convinced that it was neither right nor expedient to pay these bonds in money less valuable than coin, that the government ought not to take advantage of its neglect to resume specie payments after the war was over, by refusing the payment of the bonds with coin. I acted on this conviction when years afterwards the resumption act was adopted, and the beneficial results from this action fully justified my change of opinion.

The debate on this bill was participated in by nearly every Senator, and was conceded to be the most comprehensive and instructive debate on financial questions for many years.

The bill, as it then stood, authorized the Secretary of the Treasury to issue registered or coupon bonds of the United States, in such form and of such denominations as he might prescribe, payable, principal and interest, in coin, and bearing interest at the rate of five per cent. per annum, payable semi-annually, such bonds to be payable forty years from date and to be redeemable in coin after ten years.

It authorized the exchange of the bonds commonly known as the 5–20 bonds for the bonds authorized by that bill. It also authorized the holders of United States notes to the amount of $1,000, or any multiple of that sum, to convert them into the five per cent. bonds provided for by the bill. This bill passed the Senate on the 14th of July, 1868. It passed the House of Representatives soon after, with amendments that were disagreed to by the Senate. The bill and amendments were referred to a conference committee which reported a modified bill which passed both Houses and was sent to President Johnson, but at so late a period of the session that it was not approved by him and thus failed to become a law.

The committee on finance at the next and closing session of that Congress deemed it useless to report another funding bill, and on the 16th of December, 1868, I reported, by direction of that committee, the following resolution:

"*Resolved by the Senate*, That neither public policy nor the good faith of the nation will allow the redemption of the 5–20 bonds until the United States shall perform its primary duty of paying its notes in coin or making them equivalent thereto ; and measures shall be adopted by Congress to secure the resumption of specie payments at as early a period as practicable."

This resolution was the foundation of the act "to strengthen the public credit," the first act subsequently adopted in General Grant's administration. Neither this nor any other financial measure was pressed to a conclusion, as we knew that any measure that would be sanctioned by Congress would probably be vetoed by the President. This, however, did not stop the almost continous financial debate which extended to currency, banking, funding and taxation. The drift of opinion was in favor of resumption without contraction, and funding at low rates of interest on a coin basis. The wide breach between Congress and the President paralyzed legislation. But one vital question had been settled, that no further contraction of the currency should occur; and it was well settled, though not embodied in law, that no question would be made as to the payment of bonds in coin.

While Congress was drifting to a sound financial policy, the President and his Secretary of the Treasury were widely divergent, the former in favor of repudiation, and the latter in favor of paying and canceling all United States notes.

President Johnson, in his last annual message to Congress, on the 9th of December, 1868, substantially recommended a repudiation of the bonds of the United States, as follows:

"Upon this statement of facts it would seem but just and equitable that the six per cent. interest now paid by the government should be applied to the reduction of the principal in semi-annual installments, which in sixteen years and eight months would liquidate the entire national debt. Six per cent. in gold would, at present rates, be equal to nine per cent. in currency, and equivalent to the payment of the debt one and a half times in a fraction less than seventeen years. This, in connection with the other advantages derived from their investment, would afford to the public creditors a fair and liberal compensation for the use of their capital, and with this they should be satisfied. The lessons of the past admonish the lender that it is not well to be over anxious in exacting from the borrower rigid compliance with the letter of the bond."

While the President wished to apply the interest on the United States bonds to the redemption of the principal, the Secretary of the Treasury was pressing for the restoration of the specie standard. I quote from his report to Congress, made on the same day the message of the President was sent us:

"The first and most important of these measures are those which shall bring about, without unnecessary delay, the restoration of the specie standard. The financial difficulties under which the country is laboring may be traced directly to the issue, and continuance in circulation, of irredeemable promises as lawful money. The country will not be really and reliably prosperous until there is a return to specie payments. The question of a solvent, convertible currency, underlies all other financial and economical questions. It is, in fact, a fundamental question; and until it is settled, and settled in accordance with the teachings of experience, all attempts at other financial and economical reforms will either fail absolutely, or be but partially successful. A sound currency is the lifeblood of a commercial nation. If this is debased the whole current of its commercial life must be disordered and irregular. The starting point in reformatory legislation must be here. Our debased currency must be retired or raised to the par of specie, or cease to be lawful money, before substantial progress can be made with other reforms."

Under these circumstances, it was manifest that no wise financial legislation could be secured until General Grant should become President of the United States.

The Republican national convention met at the city of Chicago, on the 20th of May, 1868. It declared its approval of the reconstruction policy of Congress, denounced all forms of repudiation as a national crime, and pledged the national good faith to all creditors at home and abroad, to pay all public indebtedness, not only according to the letter, but the spirit, of the law. It favored the extension of the national debt over a fair period for redemption, and the reduction of the rate of interest whenever it could be honestly made. It arraigned, with severity, the treachery of Andrew Johnson, and deplored the tragic death of Abraham Lincoln. The entire resolutions were temperate in tone; they embodied the recognized policy of the Republican party, and made no issue on which Republicans were divided.

The real issue was not one of measures, but of men. The nomination of General Grant for President, and of Schuyler Colfax for Vice President, upon the basis of reconstruction by loyal men, was antagonized by the nomination, by the Democratic convention, of Horatio Seymour for President and Francis P. Blair for Vice President, upon the basis of universal amnesty, and immediate restoration to power, in the states lately in rebellion, of the men who had waged war against the government.

In this contest, Grant was the representative Union soldier of the war, and Seymour was the special representative of the opponents in the north to the war. Grant received 197 electoral votes, and Seymour 72.

A few hours in advance of the meeting of the national convention, there was a great mass meeting of soldiers and sailors of the war, a delegation from whom, headed by General Lucius Fairchild, of Wisconsin, entered the convention after its organization and presented this resolution:

"*Resolved*, That as the soldiers and sailors, steadfast now as ever to the Union and the flag, fully recognize the claims of Gen. Ulysses S. Grant to the confidence of the American people, and believing that the victories won under his guidance in war will be illustrated by him in peace by such measures as will secure the fruits of our exertions and restore the Union upon a loyal basis, we declare our deliberate conviction that he is the choice of the soldiers and sailors of the Union for the office of President of the United States."

This resolution was received with great applause. Henry S. Lane, of Indiana, leaped upon a chair, and moved to nominate Grant by acclamation. This was done without rules and amid great excitement.

I need not say that I gave to General Grant my cordial and active support. From the beginning of the canvass to the end, there was no doubt about the result. I spoke in his behalf in several states and had frequent letters from him. Assuming that his election was already foreordained, I invited him to stop with me at Mansfield, on his way to Washington, and received from him the following autograph letter, which, though dated at the Headquarters, Army of the United States, was written at Galena, Illinois:

HEADQUARTERS ARMY OF THE UNITED STATES, }
WASHINGTON, D. C., October 26, 1868. }

DEAR SENATOR : — Your invitation to Mrs. Grant and myself to break our journey east and spend a day or two with you was duly received, and should have been sooner acknowledged. I thank you for the invitation and would gladly accept it, but my party will be large and having a special car it will inconvenience so many people to stop over. Mrs. Grant too and her father are anxious, when they start, to get through to Washington before they unpack.   Yours truly,   U. S. GRANT.
HON. J. SHERMAN, U. S. S.

On the same day he wrote a letter to General Sherman, which was referred to me by the latter. I regard this letter, which exhibits clearly the cordial relations existing, at the time, between these two men, as of sufficient interest to justify its publication:

HEADQUARTERS ARMY OF THE UNITED STATES,
WASHINGTON, D. C., October 26, 1868.

DEAR GENERAL :—Your letter inclosing one from your brother was duly received. As I did not want to change your determination in regard to the publication of the correspondence between us, and am getting to be a little lazy, I have been slow in answering. I had forgotten what my letter to you said but did remember that you spoke of the probable course the Ewings would take, or something about them which you would not probably want published with the letters. The fact is, general, I never wanted the letters published half so much on my own account as yours. There are a great many people who do not understand as I do your friendship for me. I do not believe it will make any difference to you in the end, but I do fear that, in case I am elected, there will be men to advocate the 'abolition of the general' bill who will charge, in support of their motion, lack of evidence that you supported the Union cause in the canvass. I would do all I could to prevent any such legislation, and believe that without my doing anything the confidence in you is too genuine with the great majority of Congress for any such legislation to succeed. If anything more should be necessary to prove the falsity of such an assumption the correspondence between us heretofore could then be produced.

I agree with you that Sheridan should be let alone to prosecute the Indian War to its end. If no treaty is made with the Indians until they can hold out no longer we can dictate terms, and they will then keep them. This is the course that has been pursued in the northwest, where Crook has prosecuted war in his own way, and now a white man can travel through all that country with as much security as if there was not an Indian in it.

I have concluded not to return to Washington until after the election. I shall go very soon after that event, however. My family are all well and join me in respects to Mrs. Sherman and the children.

Yours truly,
U. S. GRANT.

LT. GEN. W. T. SHERMAN, U. S. Army.

In the spring of 1871 there was a good deal of feeling against Grant, and some opposition indicated to his renomination for the presidency. Several influential papers had recommended the nomination of General Sherman, who then, as always afterwards, had resolutely announced his purpose not to allow his name to be used in connection with the office of President. This suggestion arose out of the feeling that injustice had been done to General Sherman by the Secretary of War, Mr. Belknap, who practically ignored him, and issued

Long Branch, N. J.
June 14th 1871.

Dear Senator:

Being absent
at West Point until last
evening, for the last
week, your letter of the
5th inst. inclosing one to
you from Gen. Sherman
is only just received. Under
no circumstances would I

publish it, and now
that the New York Herald
has published like state-
ments from him, it
is particularly unneces-
sary. — I think his
determination never
to give up his present
position be wise one,
for his own comfort,
and the public knowing
it will relieve him
from the suspicion
of acting and speaking
with reference to the

effect his acts and sayings
may have upon his chances
for political preferment.
If he should ever change
his mind however no one
has a better right than
he has to aspire to any
thing within the gift of
the American people.
Very Truly Yours
U. S. Grant

Hon. J. Sherman,
U. S. S.

orders in the name of the President, greatly interfering with the personnel of the army. This led to the transfer of General Sherman from Washington to St. Louis. General Sherman made no complaint of Grant, who had the power to control the action of the Secretary of War, but the general impression prevailed that the friendly relations that had always subsisted between the President and General Sherman had been disturbed, but this was not true. I have no doubt that Grant, in the following letter, stated truthfully his perfect willingness that General Sherman should, if he wished, be made his successor as President:

LONG BRANCH, N. J., June 14, 1871.

DEAR SENATOR:—Being absent at West Point until last evening, for the last week, your letter of the 5th inst., inclosing one to you from General Sherman, is only just received. Under no circumstances would I publish it; and now that the 'New York Herald' has published like statements from him it is particularly unnecessary. I think his determination never to give up his present position a wise one, for his own comfort, and the public, knowing it, will relieve him from the suspicion of acting and speaking with reference to the effect his acts and sayings may have upon his claims for political preferment. If he should ever change his mind, however, no one has a better right than he has to aspire to anything within the gift of the American people.   Very truly yours,

HON. J. SHERMAN, U. S. S.   U. S. GRANT.

CHAPTER XXI.

BEGINNING OF GRANT'S ADMINISTRATION.

His Arrival at Washington in 1864 to Take Command of the Armies of the United States — Inaugural Address as President — "An Act to Strengthen the Public Credit" Becomes a Law on March 19, 1869 — Formation of the President's Cabinet — Fifteenth Amendment to the Constitution — Bill to Fund the Public Debt and to Aid in the Resumption of Specie Payment — Bill Finally Agreed to by the House and Senate — A Redemption Stipulation Omitted — Reduction of the Public Debt — Problem of Advancing United States Notes to Par with Coin.

PRESIDENT Grant entered into his high office without any experience in civil life. In his training he was a soldier. His education at West Point, his services as a subordinate officer in the Mexican War, and as the principal officer in the Civil War of the Rebellion, had demonstrated his capacity as a soldier, but he was yet to be tested in civil life, where his duties required him to deal with problems widely differing from those he had successfully performed in military life. I do not recall when I first met him, but am confident it was before his coming to Washington, in March, 1864, to take command of the armies of the United States. His arrival in Washington then was not generally known until he entered the dining hall at Willard's hotel. He came in alone, and was modestly looking for a vacant seat when I recognized him and went to him and invited him to a seat at my table. He quietly accepted, and then the word soon passed among the many guests at the tables, that General Grant was there, and something like an ovation was given him. His face was unknown, but his name and praise had been sounded for two years throughout the civilized world. His coming to take full command of the Union forces was an augury of success to every loyal citizen of the United States. His personal memoirs, written in the face of death, tell the story of his life in

(446)

a modest way, without pretension or guile. I am not sure that he added to his fame by his eight years of service as President of the United States, but what he did in subduing the Rebellion will always keep his name among those of the greatest benefactors of his country. He was elected because of his military services, and would have been elected in 1868 by any party that put him in nomination, without respect to platform or creed.

He opened his inaugural address with these words:

"Your suffrages having elected me to the office of President of the United States, I have, in conformity with the constitution of our country, taken the oath of office prescribed therein. I have taken this oath without mental reservation and with the determination to do to the best of my ability all that it requires of me. The responsibilities of the position I feel but accept them without fear. The office has come to me unsought. I commence its duties untrammeled. I bring to it a conscientious desire and determination to fill it to the best of my ability to the satisfaction of the people.

"On all leading questions agitating the public mind I will always express my views to Congress, and urge them according to my judgment; and when I think it advisable will exercise the constitutional privilege of interposing a veto to defeat measures which I oppose. But all laws will be faithfully executed whether they meet my approval or not.

"I shall on all subjects have a policy to recommend, but none to enforce against the will of the people. Laws are to govern all alike, those opposed as well as those who favor them. I know no method to secure the repeal of bad or obnoxious laws so effective as their stringent execution."

And closed with these words:

"In conclusion I ask patient forbearance one toward another throughout the land, and a determined effort on the part of every citizen to do his share toward cementing a happy Union ; and I ask the prayers of the nation to Almighty God in behalf of this consummation."

I believe he strictly performed what he thought was his duty, and if he erred, it was from a want of experience in the complicated problems of our form of government. The executive department of a republic like ours should be subordinate to the legislative department. The President should obey and enforce the laws, leaving to the people the duty of correcting any errors committed by their representatives in Congress.

The first act of the 41st Congress, entitled "An act to strengthen the public credit," was introduced in the House of Representatives by General Schenck, on the 12th of March, 1869, and was passed the same day. It came to the Senate on the 15th of March, and, on my motion, was substituted for a similar bill, reported from the committee on finance, and, after a brief debate, was passed by the decisive vote of 42 yeas and 13 nays, as follows:

"That in order to remove any doubt as to the purpose of the government to discharge all just obligations to the public creditors, and to settle conflicting questions and interpretations of the laws by virtue of which said obligations have been contracted, it is hereby provided and declared that the faith of the United States is solemnly pledged to the payment in coin, or its equivalent, of all obligations of the United States not bearing interest, known as United States notes, and of all interest-bearing obligations of the United States, except in cases where the law authorizing the issue of any such obligations has expressly provided that the same may be paid in lawful money or other currency than gold and silver. But none of said interest-bearing obligations not already due shall be redeemed or paid before maturity, unless at such time United States notes shall be convertible into coin at the option of the holder, or unless at such time bonds of the United States bearing a lower rate of interest than the bonds to be redeemed can be sold at par in coin. And the United States also solemnly pledges its faith to make provision, at the earliest practicable period, for the redemption of the United States notes in coin."

It was approved by the President and became a law on the 19th of March. Thus the controversy as to the payment of bonds in coin was definitely decided.

But little else of importance was done by Congress during this session. The usual general appropriation bill for the Indian department having failed in the previous Congress, a bill for that purpose was introduced in the House of Representatives and became a law on the 10th of April. The bill to provide for deficiencies was passed on the same day. A change was made in the tax on distilled spirits and tobacco, and provision was made for submitting the constitutions of Virginia, Mississippi and Texas to a vote of the people. A number of measures of local importance were passed, and, on the 10th of April, the Congress adjourned without day.

U. S. GRANT.

The Senate convened in pursuance of a proclamation of the President immediately on the adjournment of Congress, and after a few days, confined mainly to executive business, adjourned.

The early movements of Grant as President were very discouraging. His attempt to form a cabinet without consultation with anyone, and with very little knowledge, except social intercourse with the persons appointed, created a doubt that he would not be as successful as a President as he had been as a general, a doubt that increased and became a conviction in the minds of many of his best friends. The appointments of Stewart and Borie were especially objectionable. George S. Boutwell was well fitted for the office of Secretary of the Treasury, to which he was appointed after Stewart was excluded by the law. Washburne was a man of ability and experience, but he was appointed Secretary of State only for a brief time, and was succeeded by Hamilton Fish. Mr. Fish was eminently qualified for that office, and during both of the terms of Grant discharged the duties of it with great ability and success. Jacob D. Cox, of Ohio, was an educated gentleman, a soldier of great merit, and an industrious and competent Secretary of the Interior.

The impression prevailed that the President regarded these heads of departments, invested by law with specific and independent duties, as mere subordinates, whose functions he might assume. This is not the true theory of our government. The President is intrusted by the constitution and laws with important powers, and so by law are the heads of departments. The President has no more right to control or exercise the powers conferred by law upon them than they have to control him in the discharge of his duties. It is especially the custom of Congress to intrust to the Secretary of the Treasury specific powers over the currency, the public debt and the collection of the revenue. If he violates or neglects his duty he is subject to removal by the President, or impeachment by the House of Representatives, but the President cannot exercise or control the discretion reposed by law in the Secretary of the Treasury, or in any head or subordinate of any department of the government. This limitation of the power of the President, and the distribution of power among the departments, is an essential requisite of a republican government, and it is one that an army officer, accustomed to give or receive orders, finds it difficult to understand and to observe when elected President.

Congress convened on the 6th of December, 1869. The chief recommendations submitted to Congress by the President related to the gradual reconstruction of the states lately in rebellion, to the resumption of specie payments and the reduction of taxation. The relations of Great Britain and the United States growing out of the war were treated as a grave question, and a hope was expressed that both governments would give immediate attention to a solution of the just claims of the United States growing out of the Civil War. The message was brief, modest, conservative and clear. He closed by saying that on his part he promised a rigid adherence to the laws and their strict enforcement.

The most important measure consummated during this Congress was the adoption of the 15th amendment of the constitution of the United States, declared, in a proclamation of the Secretary of State, dated March 30, 1870, to have been ratified by the legislatures of twenty-nine of the thirty-seven states, as follows :

" The right of citizens of the United States to vote shall not be denied or abridged by the United States, or by any state, on account of race, color, or previous condition of servitude."

It is a question of grave doubt whether this amendment, though right in principle, was wise or expedient. The declared object was to secure impartial suffrage to the negro race. The practical result has been that the wise provisions of the 14th amendment have been modified by the 15th amendment. The latter amendment has been practically nullified by the action of most of the states where the great body of this race live and will probably always remain. This is done, not by an express denial to them of the right of suffrage, but by ingenious provisions, which exclude them on the alleged ground of ignorance, while permitting all of the white race, however ignorant, to vote at all elections. No way is pointed out by which Congress can enforce this amendment. If the principle of the 14th amendment had remained in full force, Congress could have reduced the representation of any state, in the proportion which the number of the male inhabitants of such state, denied the right of suffrage, might bear to the whole number of male citizens twenty-one years of age, in such state. This simple remedy, easily enforced by Congress, would have secured the right of all persons, without distinction of race or color, to vote at all elections. The reduction of representation would have deterred every state from excluding the vote of any portion of the male population above twenty-one years of age. As the result of the 15th amendment, the political power of the states lately in rebellion has been increased, while the population, conferring this increase, is practically denied all political power. I see no remedy for this wrong except the growing intelligence of the negro race, which, in time, I trust, will enable them to demand and to receive the right of suffrage.

The most important financial measure of that Congress was the act to refund the national debt. The bonds known as the 5-20's, bearing interest at six per cent., became redeemable, and the public credit had so advanced that a bond bearing a less rate of interest could be sold at par. The committee on finance of the Senate, on the 3rd day of February, 1870, after more care and deliberation than, so far as I know, it has ever bestowed on any other bill, finally reported a bill to fund the public debt, to aid in the resumption of specie payments, and to advance the public credit.

The first section authorized the issue of $400,000,000 of bonds, redeemable in coin at the pleasure of the United States, at any time after ten years, bearing interest at five per cent.

The second section authorized the issue of bonds to the amount of $400,000,000, redeemable at the pleasure of the government, at any time after fifteen years, and bearing interest at four and a half per cent.

The third section authorized the issue of $400,000,000 of bonds, redeemable at any time after twenty years, and bearing interest at the rate of four per cent.

The proceeds of all these bonds were to be applied to the redemption of 5–20 and 10–40 bonds, and other obligations of the United States then outstanding.

It will be perceived that this bill provided for the issue of securities, all of which were redeemable within twenty years, and two-thirds of which were redeemable within fifteen years; so that if the bill, as reported by the committee on finance, had become the law, no such difficulty as we labored under eighteen years later, when we had a large surplus revenue, would have existed.

The bill passed the Senate, in substantially the form reported from the committee on finance, by the large vote of 33 to 10, and was, perhaps, the most carefully prepared of any of the financial measures of the government.

In opening the debate, I called the attention of the Senate to the great advantage the government had derived from making its bonds redeemable at brief periods, like the 5–20 bonds, the 10–40 bonds, and the treasury notes. I also called attention to the fact that the same principle of maintaining the right to redeem had been ingrafted in the bill then before the Senate, that the duration of the bonds was divided into three periods of ten, fifteen, and twenty years, during which time, by the gradual application of the surplus revenue, the whole debt might be paid. This was the bill sent by the Senate to the House of Representatives, and if it had been adopted by the House, there would have been no trouble about the application of the surplus revenue, but by common consent it would have been used in the speedy extinction of the public debt.

The bill was sent to the House of Representatives on the 11th of March, and there seems to have slept for nearly three months without any action on the part of the House.

On the 6th of June the committee on ways and means reported House bill 2167, covering the same subject-matters as were contained in the Senate bill. The consideration of this bill was commenced, by sections, on the 30th of June. The material part of the first section of this bill is as follows:

"That the Secretary of the Treasury is hereby authorized to issue, in a sum or sums not exceeding in the aggregate $1,000,000,000, coupon or registered bonds of the United States, in such form as he may prescribe, and of denomination of $50, or some multiple of that sum, redeemable in coin of the present standard value at the pleasure of the United States after thirty years from the date of their issue, and bearing interest payable semi-annually in such coin at the rate of four per cent. per annum."

Thus it will be perceived that instead of the three series of bonds provided by the Senate, the House proposed to authorize the issue of $1,000,000,000, redeemable in coin after thirty years from the date of their issue, with interest at four per cent. This difference in the description of the bonds was the chief difference between the propositions of the House and the Senate. To emphasize this difference I quote what was said by the chairman of the House committee, Mr. Schenck, in reporting the bill:

"It is a proposition to refund a portion of the public debt of the country at a very much lower rate of interest. It is a proposition that $1,000,000,000 of that debt shall take the form of bonds, upon which the United States will agree to pay only four per cent. per annum. But, in order to make those bonds acceptable to capitalists at home and abroad, further provision is made that the bonds themselves shall have a longer time to run, not merely for thirty years, but that they shall only be redeemable after thirty years; thus giving them, without the objections, the advantages which in a great degree attach to a perpetual loan."

This bill, with a very limited debate, passed the House on the 1st of July, and then immediately was offered as a substitute for the Senate bill, and was adopted.

Those two rival propositions, differing mainly upon the question of the character of the bonds to be issued, were sent to a committee of conference, composed on the part of the Senate of Messrs. Sherman, Sumner and Davis. The chief controversy in the conference was as to the description of funding bonds to be provided for. After many meetings it was finally agreed that the bonds authorized should be $200,000,000 five per cent. bonds, $300,000,000 four and a half per cent. bonds, of the character described in the Senate bill, and $1,000,000,000 of four per cent. bonds, as described in the House bill. In other words, it was a compromise which, like many other compromises, was in its results an injury of great magnitude, but it was an honest difference of opinion between the Senate and the House, in which, tested by the march of time, the Senate was right and the House was wrong. But it was perfectly manifest that without this concession by the Senate to the House, the bill could not have passed, and even with this concession the first report of the committee of conference was disagreed to by the House, because of certain provisions requiring the national banks to substitute the new bonds as the basis of banking circulation.

This disagreement by the House compelled a second committee of conference, in which the contested banking section was stricken out, and the bill agreed to as it now stands on the statute books.

And thus thirty-year securities, subsequently at a premium of more than twenty-five per cent., were forced into the law by the determined action of the House.

This proved to be an error. No bonds should have been authorized that did not contain a stipulation that the government might pay them at pleasure, after a brief period and before they became due. This stipulation during the war was inserted in the 5–20 and the 10–40 bonds. Its wisdom and importance were demonstrated by the early substitution of bonds bearing a lower rate of interest for the 5–20 six per cent. bonds. When this precedent was cited, and its saving to the government shown, it was strongly urged by the House conferees that such a provision would prevent the sale of bonds, and that there was no probability that bonds bearing less than four per cent. could be sold at any time at par. This was proven to be an error within a short period, for securities of the United States bearing three per cent. interest have been sold at par.

Some years later, Senator Beck, of Kentucky, arraigned me for consenting to the issue of bonds running thirty years, but I was able to show by the public records that I resisted this long duration of the four per ·cent. bonds, that the House insisted upon it, and that Mr. Beck, then a Member of the House, voted for it. The same objection was made by the Senate conferees to the bonds bearing four and a half and five per cent., that no stipulation was made authorizing the government to anticipate the payment of these bonds. Under the Senate bill the bonds would have been redeemable in a brief period, and would, no doubt, have been redeemed by bonds bearing four, three and a half, or three per cent. interest.

The bill, as it passed, authorized the conversion of all forms of securities, then outstanding, into the bonds provided for by the refunding act at par one with the other. The Secretary of the Treasury could sell the bonds provided for by the refunding act at par, and with the proceeds pay off the then existing securities as they became redeemable. In the discussion of this bill in the Senate, on the 28th of February, 1870, I made a carefully prepared speech, giving a detailed history of the various securities outstanding, and expressed the confident opinion that the existing coin bonds bearing six per cent. interest, and other securities bearing interest in lawful money, could be refunded into bonds running for a short period, bearing a reduced rate of interest. I said :

"After a long and memorable debate of over two months in both Houses of Congress, the act of February 25, 1862, was adopted. That was a revolutionary act. It was a departure from every principle of the financial policy of this government from its foundation. It overthrew, not only the mode and manner of borrowing money, but the character of our public securities, and was the beginning of a new financial system, unlike anything that had been ventured upon by any people in the world before. This new policy was adopted under the pressure of the severest necessities, and only because of those necessities, and was intended to meet a state of affairs never foreseen by the framers of the constitution.

"Now, sir, it is important to understand the principles of this act; for this act was the foundation of all the financial measures during the war. It was upon the basis of this act, enlarged and modified from time to time, that we were enabled to borrow $3,000,000,000 in three years and to put down the most formidable rebellion in modern history. This act was based upon certain fundamental conditions.

"Extraordinary power was conferred upon the Secretary of the Treasury to borrow money in almost any form, at home or abroad, practically without limitation as to amount, or with limits repeatedly enlarged. Every form of security which the ingenuity of man could devise was provided for by this act or the acts amending it. Under these acts bonds were issued, payable in twenty years, treasury notes were issued, certificates of indebtedness, compound-interest notes, and other forms of indebtedness, with varying rates of interest. There were, however, distinct limitations upon the nature and character of these loans. It was stipulated first, that more than six per cent. interest in gold should not be paid on the bonds issued, nor more than seven and three-tenths interest in currency should be paid on the notes issued ; and *second, all the loans provided by this act were short loans,* re-deemable within a short period of time at the pleasure of the United States. Thus the gold bonds were redeemable after five years, the treasury notes were redeemable after three years, and all forms of security were within the power of the United States at the end of five years at furthest. And third, no securities were to be sold less than par. Their unavoidable depreciation was measured, not by the rate of their discount, but by the depreciation of the currency. We held our bonds at par in paper money, though at times they were worth only forty per cent. of gold. . . .

"Now, Mr. president, it may be proper to state the reasons for this policy. Short loans were adopted that we might not bind the future to the payment of usurious rates of interest. We recognized the existence of a great pressing necessity that would tend to depreciate the public credit ; and we took care, therefore, not to make those loans for a long period, so as to bind the future to the payment of the rates which we were then compelled to pay.

"We provided for gold interest and gold revenue, to avoid the extreme inflations of an irredeemable currency. We wished to rest our paper fabric on a coin basis, and to keep constantly in view ultimate specie payments. I believe but for that provision in the loan act of February 25, 1862, that in 1864 our financial system would have been utterly overthrown. There was nothing to anchor it to the earth except the collection of duties in coin and the payment of the interest on our bonds in coin.

"But, sir, the most important and the most revolutionary principle of the act of February 25, 1862, was the legal tender clause. This was a measure of imperious and pressing necessity. I can recall very well the debates in the Senate and in the House of Representatives upon the legal tender clause. We were then standing in the face of a deficit of some $70,000,000 of unpaid requisitions to our soldiers. Creditors in all parts of the country, among them the most powerful corporations of this country, had refused our demand notes, then very slightly depreciated. We were under the necessity of raising two or three million dollars per day. We were then organizing armies unheard of before. We stood also in the presence of defeat, constant and imminent, which fell upon our armies in all parts of the country. It was before daylight was shed upon any part of our military operations. We adopted the legal tender clause then as an absolute expedient. Remembering the debate, I know with what slow steps the majority of the Senate came to the necessity of adopting legal tenders."

The debt of the United States on the 31st of August, 1866, when it reached its maximum, amounted to $2,844,649,627. On the 1st of March, 1870, the debt had been reduced to less than $2,500,000,000, of which about $400,000,000 was in United States notes, for the redemption of which no provision was made. It was the confident expectation of Congress, which proved to be correct, that before the refunding operations were complete, the debt would be gradually reduced, so that the sum of $1,500,000,000, provided for in the law, would be sufficient to refund all existing debts, except United States notes, into the new securities.

The process of refunding progressed slowly, was confined to the five per cent. bonds, and was somewhat interrupted by the financial stringency of 1873.

By the act approved January 20, 1871, the amount of five per cent. bonds authorized by the act approved July 14, 1870, was increased to $500,000,000, but the act was not to be construed to authorize any increase of bonds provided for by the refunding act.

Prior to the 24th of August, 1876, there had been sold, for refunding purposes, the whole of the $500,000,000 five per cents. authorized by that act, and on that day Lot M. Morrill, Secretary of the Treasury, entered into a contract for the sale of $40,000,000 of the four and a half per cent. bonds authorized by the refunding act. By this process of refunding an annual saving had been made of $5,400,000 a year, by the reduction of interest in the sale of $540,000,000 bonds. On the 9th day of June, 1877, I, as Secretary of the Treasury, terminated the contract made by Mr. Morrill, my predecessor, and placed on the market the four per cent. bonds provided for by the refunding act. The subsequent proceedings under this act will be more appropriately referred to hereafter.

The more difficult problem remained of advancing United States notes to par in coin. This could be accomplished by reducing the amount of these notes outstanding, and, thus, by their scarcity, add to their value. They were a legal tender in payment for all debts, public and private, except for duties on imported goods and interest on the public debt. As long as these notes were at a discount for coin they could circulate only in the United States, and until they were at par with coin, coin would not circulate as money in the United States, except to pay coin liabilities. The notes were a dishonored, depreciated promise, the purchasing power of which varied day

by day, the football of "bulls and bears." In many respects
these notes were better than any other form of depreciated
paper money, for the people of the United States had full confidence in their ultimate redemption. They were much better
and in higher favor with the people than the state bank notes
which they replaced and which were not only depreciated like
United States notes but had been often proven worthless in
the hands of innocent holders. They were as good as national
bank notes, however well secured, for these notes were not payable in coin, but could be redeemed by United States notes.
Still, with all their defects the United States notes were the
favorite money of the people, and any attempt to contract
their volume was met by a strong popular opposition.

As already stated, the gradual reduction of the volume of
United States notes, urged so strongly by Secretary McCulloch
and provided for by the resumption act, met with popular opposition and was repealed by Congress. Under these conditions it became necessary to approach the specie standard of
value without a contraction of the currency. The act to
strengthen the public credit, already referred to, was the beginning of this struggle. The government was, by this act,
committed to the payment of the United States notes in coin
or its equivalent. But when and how was not stated or even
considered. The extent to which Congress would then go, and
to which popular opinion would then consent, was the declaration that the "United States solemnly pledges its faith to
make provision at the earliest practicable period for the redemption of the United States notes, in coin." Many events
must occur before the fulfillment of this promise could be
attempted.

CHAPTER XXII.

Our Coinage Before and After the War.

But Little Coin in Circulation in 1869 — General Use of Spanish Pieces — No Mention
of the Dollar Piece in the Act of 1853 — Free Circulation of Gold After the
1853 Act — No Truth in the " Demonetization " Charge — Account of the Bill
Revising the Laws Relative to the Mint, Assay Offices and Coinage of the
United States — Why the Dollar was Dropped from the Coins — Then
Known Only as a Coin for the Foreign Market — Establishment
of the " Trade Dollar " — A Legal Tender for Only Five Dol-
lars — Repeated Attempts to Have Congress Pass a Free-
Coinage Act — How it Would Affect Us — Controversy
Between Senator Sumner and Secretary Fish.

AT the date of the passage of the act "to strengthen
the public credit," on March 19, 1869, there was but
little coin in circulation in the United States except
gold coin, and that was chiefly confined to the Pacific
coast, or to the large ports of entry, to be used in payment of
duties on imported goods.   Silver coins were not in circulation.
The amount of silver coined in 1869 was less than one million
dollars and that mainly for exportation.   Fractional notes of
different denominations, from ten to fifty cents, were issued by
the treasury to the amount of $160,000,000, of which $120,000,-
000 had been redeemed, and $40,000,000 were outstanding in
circulation or had been destroyed.   These fractional notes
superseded silver coin as United States notes superseded gold
coin.   The coinage laws as they then existed were scattered
through the laws of the United States from 1793 to 1853, and
were in many respects imperfect and conflicting.

The ratio fixed by Alexander Hamilton, of fifteen ounces of
silver as the equivalent of one ounce of gold, was, at the time it
was adopted, substantially the market ratio, but the constant
tendency of silver to decline in relative value to gold had been
going on for years and it continued to decline, almost impercep-
tibly perhaps, and the legal ratio in France having been fixed

at fifteen and a half to one, there was an advantage in shipping gold to that country from this, and consequently very little if any of our gold, even if coined, came into circulation. By the act of 1793 foreign coins were made a legal tender for circulation in this country, and the Spanish silver dollar, on which ours was founded, with its 8ths or "real" pieces, found great favor. Singularly enough, in Mexico and the West Indies, the Spanish population would exchange their dollars for ours, dollar for dollar, although their pieces, if not worn, were each three grains heavier. This led to an exchange of our dollars for the Spanish ones, which were promptly recoined at the mint at a fair profit to the depositor.

This put upon the government the expense of manufacturing coins with no advantage. The evil grew so great that in 1806 the further coinage of our silver dollars was prohibited by President Jefferson, in an order issued through the state department, as follows:

DEPARTMENT OF STATE, May 1, 1806.

SIR:—In consequence of a representation from the director of the Bank of the United States, that considerable purchases have been made of dollars coined at the mint for the purpose of exporting them, and as it is probable further purchases and exportations will be made, the President directs that all the silver to be coined at the mint shall be of small denominations, so that the value of the largest pieces shall not exceed half a dollar.

I am, etc.,   JAMES MADISON.

ROBERT PATTERSON, ESQ., Director of the Mint.

The coinage of the silver dollar at our mint was not resumed until 1836. The small and worn Spanish pieces, being legal tender, also drove from circulation our fractional coins coming bright and plump from the mint. Bank notes and these worn pieces furnished the circulation of the country.

The condition of the currency became so objectionable that in 1830 the subject was taken up by a special committee of the House of Representatives, appointed for that purpose. Three reports were submitted, in one of which the committee stated that of $37,000,000 coined at our mints only $5,000,000 remained in circulation. A bill was submitted to the House fixing the ratio at 15.625 to one, and was strongly urged. There appeared no special opposition to the measure for a time, but the feeling of opposition to the circulation of bank bills had become very strong among the people and was reflected by the administration.

In the Senate the opposition to bank bills was headed by Thomas H. Benton, who openly advocated so changing the coinage ratio that gold would circulate to the exclusion of the notes, and perhaps incidentally of silver also. The matter of providing for silver, however, received little attention. The ratio was changed to sixteen to one, John Quincy Adams and Daniel Webster joining with Calhoun and Benton in bringing it about. It was well understood at the time that the operation of this act would banish silver. The object of the change was distinctly stated, especially by Mr. Benton, who said:

"To enable the friends of gold to go to work at the right place to effect the recovery of that precious metal, which their fathers once possessed; which the subjects of European kings now possess; which the citizens of the young republics to the south all possess; which even the free negroes of San Domingo possess; but of which the yeomanry of this America have been deprived for more than twenty years, and will be deprived forever, unless they discover the cause of the evil and apply the remedy to its root."

By the act of 1834, superadded to by the act of 1837, the ratio of sixteen to one instead of fifteen to one was adopted. The result was that gold coins were largely introduced and circulated; but as sixteen ounces of silver were worth more than one ounce of gold, the silver coins disappeared, except the depreciated silver coin of other countries, then a legal tender. To correct this evil, Congress, on the 21st of February, 1853, provided for the purchase of silver bullion by the government, to be coined by it and not for the owners of the bullion. That was the first time the government had ever undertaken to buy bullion for coinage purposes. It provided for the purchase of silver bullion and the coinage of subsidiary silver coins at the ratio of less than fifteen to one. No mention was made of the dollar in the act of 1853. It had fallen into disuse and when coined was exported, being more valuable as bullion than as coin.

As the value of the minor coins was less than gold at the coinage ratio, they were limited as a legal tender to five dollars in any one payment. They were, in fact, a subsidiary coin made on government account, and, from their convenience and necessity, were maintained in circulation. They were similar to the coins now in use, revived and reënacted by the resumption act of 1875.

It was not the intention of the framers of this law to demonetize silver, because they were openly avowed bimetallists, but it limited coinage to silver bought by the government at market price. They saw, in this expedient, a way in which silver could be more generally utilized than in any other. Mr. R. M. T. Hunter, an avowed bimetallist, in a report to the United States Senate, said:

"The mischief would be great indeed if all the world were to adopt but one of the precious metals as the standard of value. To adopt gold alone would diminish the specie currency more than one-half; and the reduction the other way, should silver be taken as the only standard, would be large enough to prove highly disastrous to the human race."

He evidently did not consider the purchase of silver bullion at its coinage value by the government, instead of the free coinage of silver, as monometallism.

After the passage of the act of 1853, gold in great quantities, the product of the mines in California, was freely coined at the ratio of sixteen to one, and was in general circulation. If, then, the purchase of silver, instead of the free coinage of silver, is the demonetization of silver, it was demonetized practically in 1834, and certainly in 1853, when the purchase of silver and its use as money increased enormously. In 1852 the coinage of silver was less than $1,000,000. In the next year the coinage of silver rose to over $9,000,000, and reached the aggregate of nearly $50,000,000 before the beginning of the Civil War. Then, as now, the purchase of silver bullion led to a greater coinage than free coinage.

This was the condition of our coinage until the war, like all other great wars in history, drove all coins into hoarding or exportation, and paper promises, great and small, from five cents to a thousand dollars, supplanted both silver and gold.

When, therefore, it became necessary to prepare for the coinage of gold and silver to meet the requirements of the act of 1869, "to strengthen the public credit," it was deemed by the treasury department advisable to revise and codify the coinage laws of the United States. Mr. Boutwell, then Secretary of the Treasury, with the assistance of John Jay Knox, deputy comptroller, afterwards comptroller, of the currency, and the officers of the mints of the United States, prepared a complete code of the coinage laws. It was submitted to experts, not only to those in the treasury but also to all persons familiar with the subject. The bill was entitled, "An act revising and amending the laws relative to the mint, assay offices, and coinage of the United States."

The law, tested by experience, is conceded to be an excellent measure. A single provision of this bill has been the subject of charges and imputations that the silver dollar was, in a fraudulent and surreptitious way, "demonetized" by this act. There is not the slightest foundation for this imputation. The bill was sent to me as chairman of the committee on finance, and submitted to the Senate with this letter :

TREASURY DEPARTMENT, April 25, 1870.

SIR: —I have the honor to transmit herewith a bill revising the laws relative to the mint, assay offices, and coinage of the United States, and accompanying report. The bill has been prepared under the supervision of John Jay Knox, deputy comptroller of the currency, and its passage is recommended in the form presented. It includes, in a condensed form, all the important legislation upon the coinage, not now obsolete, since the first mint was established, in 1792; and the report gives a concise statement of the various amendments proposed to existing laws and the necessity for the change recommended. There has been no revision of the laws pertaining to the mint and coinage since 1837, and it is believed that the passage of the inclosed bill will conduce greatly to the efficiency and economy of this important branch of the government service.

I am, very respectfully, your obedient servant,

GEO. S. BOUTWELL, Secretary of the Treasury.

HON. JOHN SHERMAN,
Chairman Finance Committee, United States Senate.

Section 15 of the original bill omitted the silver dollar. It was as follows :

"SEC. 15. *And be it further enacted*, That of the silver coin, the weight of the half dollar, or piece of 50 cents, shall be 192 grains; and that of the quarter dollar and dime shall be, respectively, one-half and one-fifth of the weight of said half dollar. That the silver coin issued in conformity with the above section shall be a legal tender in any one payment of debts for all sums less than one dollar."

Section 18 prohibited all coins except those named, as follows:

"SEC. 18. *And be it further enacted*, That no coins, either gold, silver, or minor coinage, shall hereafter be issued from the mint other than those of the denominations, standards, and weights herein set forth."

Special attention was called to the dropping out of the silver dollar, both by Secretary Boutwell and Mr. Knox, and the opinion of experts was invited and given on this special matter and communicated to Congress. These sections, in the three years that the bill was pending in Congress, were changed either in the House or Senate in only one or two unimportant particulars.

Accompanying the report of Mr. Knox were the statements of Robert Patterson, of Philadelphia, confessedly one of the ablest scientists and metallists in the United States, in favor of dropping from our coinage the silver dollar. Dr. Linderman, the director of the mint, made the same recommendation. In the report accompanying the introduction of the bill, under date of April 25, 1870, Comptroller Knox gives the history of the silver dollar and the reasons for its discontinuance as follows:

"The dollar unit, as money of account, was established by the act of Congress April 2, 1792, and the same act provides for the coinage of a silver dollar, 'of the value of a Spanish milled or pillar dollar, as the same is now current.' The silver dollar was first coined in 1794, weighing 416 grains, of which $371\frac{1}{4}$ grains were pure silver, the fineness being 892.4. The act of January 18, 1837, reduces the standard weight to $412\frac{1}{2}$ grains, but increases the fineness to 900, the quantity of pure silver remaining $371\frac{1}{4}$ grains as before, and at these rates it is still coined in limited amount."

He then says:

"The coinage of the silver dollar piece, the history of which is here given, is discontinued in the proposed bill. It is, by existing law, the dollar unit, and assuming the value of gold to be fifteen and one-half times that of silver, being about the mean ratio for the past six years, is worth in gold a premium of about three per cent. (its value being 103.12) and intrinsically more than seven per cent. premium in our other silver coin, its value thus being

107.42. The present laws consequently authorize both a gold dollar unit and a silver dollar unit, differing from each other in intrinsic value. The present gold dollar piece is made the dollar unit in the proposed bill, and the silver dollar piece is discontinued. If, however, such a coin is authorized, it should be issued only as a commercial dollar, not as a standard unit of account, and of the exact value of the Mexican dollar, which is the favorite for circulation in China and Japan and other oriental countries.

"NOTE.—Assuming the value of gold to be fifteen and one-half times that of silver, the French 5-franc piece is worth about $96\frac{1}{2}$ cents (96.4784); the standard Mexican dollar 104.90, our silver dollar piece 103.12, and two of our half-dollar pieces 96 cents."

The finance committee carefully examined the bill. We were not in any hurry about it. It was sent to us in April, 1870, and was printed and sent, by the order of the Senate, to everyone who desired to read it or look over it.

That committee was composed of Messrs. Sherman, Williams, Cattell, Morrill, Warner, Fenton and Bayard.

The bill was reported unanimously to the Senate December 19, 1870, after lying in the committee room for eight months.

The dollar was dropped from the coins in the bill framed in the treasury department. It was then an unknown coin. Although I was quite active in business which brought under my eye different forms of money, I do not remember at that time ever to have seen a silver dollar. Probably if it had been mentioned to the committee and discussed it would have been thought, as a matter of course, scarcely worthy of inquiry. If it was known at all, it was known as a coin for the foreign market.

No one proposed to reissue it. The Pacific coast had six intelligent, able, and competent Senators on the floor of the Senate. They would have carefully looked out for the interest of silver, if the bill affected them injuriously. The authority given in the bill as it finally passed for coining the so-called trade dollar, met all the demands of the silver producing states. But the silver dollar at that time was worth more than the gold dollar. California and Nevada were on the gold standard.

The bill was printed over and over again, finally reported, and brought before the Senate. It was debated there for three days. Every Senator from the Pacific coast spoke upon the measure. Representing the committee, I presented the questions as they occurred from time to time, until finally we differed quite seriously upon the question of a charge for the coinage of gold. The only yea and nay vote in the Senate on the passage of that bill, after two days debate, occurred on the 10th of January, 1871. Those who voted in favor of the bill were Messrs. Bayard, Boreman, Brownlow, Casserly, Cole, Conkling, Corbett, Davis, Gilbert, Hamlin, Harlan, Jewett, Johnston, Kellogg, McCreary, Morton, Nye, Patterson, Pomeroy, Pool, Ramsey, Rice, Saulsbury, Spencer, Stewart, Stockton, Sumner, Thurman, Tipton, Trumbull, Vickers, Warner, Willey, Williams, Wilson and Yates—36.

Every one of the six Members of the Pacific coast voted for the bill after full debate.

Against this bill were Messrs. Abbott, Ames, Anthony, Buckingham, Carpenter, Chandler, Fenton, Hamilton, of Texas, Harris, Howell, Morrill, of Vermont, Pratt, Scott and Sherman —14.

So that on the only yea and nay vote which was ever taken upon the bill I voted against it. It was not on account of demonetizing the silver dollar. I did not do it because of that, but I did it because gold was then only coined for the benefit of private depositors; we were not using gold except for limited purposes. Gold was the standard in California, and we thought the people of that state ought to continue to pay the old and reasonable rate for coinage of one-fifth of one cent to the dollar. No action was taken on the bill in the House of Representatives, and it failed to pass during that Congress. At the beginning of the next Congress the bill was introduced by Wm. D. Kelley, and reported by him favorably to the House of Representatives. It gave rise to considerable debate, especially the section defining the silver coins. No one proposed to restore the old silver dollar, but the House inserted a coin precisely the equivalent of five francs, or two half dollars of our subsidiary coin, and this franc dollar, as it was called, was made, like other subsidiary coins, a legal tender for only five dollars. On the 9th of April, 1872, Mr.

Hooper, having charge of the bill, called especial attention to the dropping of the old dollar and the substitution of the French dollar. He said, on April 9, 1872:

"Section 16 reënacts the provisions of existing laws defining the silver coins and their weights, respectively, except in relation to the silver dollar, which is reduced in weight from 412½ to 384 grains ; thus making it a subsidiary coin in harmony with the silver coins of less denomination, to secure its concurrent circulation with them. The silver dollar of 412½ grains, by reason of its bullion and intrinsic value being greater than its nominal value, long since ceased to be a coin of circulation, and is melted by manufacturers of silverware. It does not circulate now in commercial transactions with any country, and the convenience of those manufacturers, in this respect, can better be met by supplying small stamped bars of the same standard, avoiding the useless expense of coining the dollar for that purpose. The coinage of the half dime is discontinued for the reason that its place is supplied by the copper nickel five-cent piece, of which a large issue has been made, and which, by the provisions of the act authorizing its issue, is redeemable in United States currency."

When the bill was sent to the Senate it, in compliance with the memorial of the legislature of the State of California, inserted in place of the French dollar, of 384 grains of standard silver, a dollar containing 420 grains of standard silver, called the "trade dollar." This was urged upon the ground that, as the Mexican dollar contained 416 grains, or 3½ grains more than the old silver dollar, it had an advantage in trade with China and Japan over our dollar, and that a coin containing a few grains more than the Mexican dollar would give our people the benefit of this use for silver. This dollar was, in conference, agreed to by the House, but was a legal tender for only five dollars. On. final action on that bill, the conferees on the part of the Senate were Messrs. Sherman, Scott and Bayard. The amendment of the Senate adopting the trade dollar was agreed to by the House, and the bill passed in both Houses without a division.

There never was a bill proposed in the Congress of the United States which was so publicly and openly presented and agitated. I know of no bill in my experience which was printed, as this was, thirteen times, in order to invite attention to it. I know no bill which was freer from any immoral or wrong influence than this act of 1873.

During the pendency of this bill, the Senators and Representatives from the Pacific coast were in favor of the single standard of gold alone. This was repeatedly shown during the debates, but now they complain that the silver dollar was demonetized, and that, though present, taking the most active interest in the consideration of the bill, they did not observe that the silver dollar was dropped from the coinage. The public records are conclusive against this pretense. Mr. Stewart, Senator from Nevada, and all the Senators from the Pacific coast, who took an active part in the debate on the bill, must have known of the dropping of the silver dollar from the coinage. It appears from the "Congressional Record" that, on the 11th of February, 1874, Mr. Stewart said :

"I want the standard gold, and no paper money not redeemable in gold ; no paper money the value of which is not ascertained ; no paper money that will organize a gold board to speculate in it."

Again, only a few days after this, on the 20th of February, when he was speaking in favor of the resolution, instructing the committee on finance to report a bill providing for the convertibility of treasury notes into gold coin or five per cent. bonds, he said :

" By this process we shall come to a specie basis, and when the laboring man receives a dollar it will have the purchasing power of a dollar, and he will not be called upon to do what is impossible for him or the producing classes to do, figure upon the exchanges, figure upon the fluctuations, figure upon the gambling in New York ; but he will know what his money is worth. Gold is the universal standard of the world. Everybody knows what a dollar in gold is worth."

To review the history of the act of 1873 : It was framed in the treasury department after a thorough examination by experts, transmitted to both Houses of Congress, thoroughly examined and debated during four consecutive sessions, with information called for by the House of Representatives, printed thirteen times by order and broadly circulated, and many amendments were proposed, but no material changes were made in the coinage clause from the beginning to the end of the controversy. It added the French dollar for a time, but that was superseded by the trade dollar, and neither was made a legal tender but for five dollars. It passed the Senate on the 10th of January, 1871—36 yeas and 14 nays—every Senator from the Pacific coast voting for it.

It was introduced in the House of Representatives by Mr. Kelley, at the next session. It was debated, scrutinized, and passed unanimously, dropping the silver dollar, as directly stated by Mr. Hooper. It was reported, debated, amended, and passed by the Senate unanimously. In every stage of the bill, and every print, the dollar of 412½ grains was prohibited, and the single gold standard recognized, proclaimed, and understood. It was not until silver was a cheaper dollar that any-one demanded it, and then it was to take advantage of a creditor.

It has always been within the power of Congress to correct this error, if error was made; but Congress has refused over and over again to do it. When the controversy arose, in 1878, on the Bland bill, and the House of Representatives pro-posed the free coinage of silver, the Senate rejected it after a deliberate contest, and substituted in place of it what is called the Bland-Allison act, which required the purchase, by the government, of silver bullion at its market value, and its coinage to a limited amount. Every effort has been made, from that time to this, to have the Congress of the United States pass a free coinage act.

If this is done, it will be to secure a cheaper dollar of less purchasing power, with the view to enable debtors to pay debts, contracted on the basis of gold coin, with silver coins, worth, with free coinage, less than one-half of gold coin.

In reviewing, at this distance of time, the legislation of 1873, in respect to the coinage of silver, I am of the opinion that it was fortunate that the United States then dropped the coinage of the old silver dollar. No one then contemplated the enormous yield of silver from the mines, and the resulting fall in the market value of silver, but, acting upon the experience of the past, that a parity between silver and gold could not be maintained at any fixed ratio, Congress adopted gold as the standard of value, and coined silver as a subsidiary coin, to be received and maintained at a parity with gold, but only a legal tender for small sums. This was the principle adopted in the act of 1853, when silver was more valuable than gold at the legal ratio. Silver was not then coined into dollars, because it was then worth more as bullion than as coin. It was needed for change, and, under the law of 1853, it was furnished in abundance. Similar laws are now in force in all countries where gold is the sole standard. Under these laws, a larger amount of silver is employed as subsidiary coins than when the coinage of silver was free.

The same condition of coinage now exists in the United States. While silver is reduced in market value nearly one-half, silver coins are maintained at par, with gold at the old ratio, by the fiat of the government. It is true that the purchase of silver, under recent laws, involved a heavy loss to the government, but the free coinage of silver, under the ratio of sixteen to one, would exclude gold from our currency, detach the United States from the monetary standard of all the chief commercial nations of the world, and change all existing contracts between individuals and with the government. In view of these results, certain to come from the free coinage of silver, I am convinced that until some international arrangement can be made, the present system of coinage should continue in force. This has now become a political, or, rather, a monetary question, to be decided sooner or later, by popular opinion, at the polls. This subject will be further discussed at a later period, when efforts were made to adopt the free coinage of silver at the old ratio.

Prior to the meeting of Congress in December, 1870, a controversy had arisen between Senator Sumner and Secretary Fish, which created serious embarrassment, and I think had a very injurious influence during that and succeeding sessions of Congress. Mr. Sumner had long been chairman of the committee on foreign relations, and no doubt exercised a domineering power in this branch of the public service. Mr. Fish and Mr. Sumner had differed widely in respect to the annexation of San Domingo and certain diplomatic appointments and former treaties, among them the highly important English negotiation for the settlement of claims growing out of the war. On these topics the President and Mr. Sumner could not agree. Mr. Sumner insisted that the hasty proclamation by Great Britain of neutrality between the United States and the Southern Confederacy was the gravamen of the Alabama claims. The President and Mr. Fish contended that this proclamation was an act of which we could not complain, except as an indication of an unfriendly spirit by Great Britain, and that the true basis of the Alabama claims was that Great Britain, after proclaiming neutrality, did not enforce it, but allowed her subjects to build cruisers, and man, arm and use them, under cover of the rebel flag, to the destruction of our commercial navy.

This difference of opinion between the President and Mr. Sumner led to the removal of John L. Motley, our minister to England, who sided with Sumner, and unquestionably intensified the feeling that had arisen from the San Domingo treaty.

As to that treaty it was a conceded fact that before the President had become publicly committed to it he had, waiving his official rank, sought the advice and counsel of Mr. Sumner, and was evidently misled as to Mr. Sumner's views on this subject. The subsequent debating, in both open and executive session, led to Mr. Sumner's taking the most extreme and active opposition to the treaty, in which he arrayed with great severity the conduct of the naval officers, the Secretary of the Navy, Mr. Fish and the President. This was aggravated by alleged public conversations with Mr. Sumner by "interviewers," in which the motives of the President and others were impugned.

In the meantime, social relations between the Secretary of State and Mr. Sumner had become impossible; and—considering human passion, prejudice and feeling—anything like frank and confidential communication between the President and Mr. Sumner was out of the question.

A majority of the Republican Senators sided with the President. We generally agreed that it was a false-pretended neutrality, and not a too hasty proclamation of neutrality, that gave us an unquestionable right to demand indemnity from Great Britain for the depredations of the Alabama and other English cruisers. And as for the San Domingo treaty, a large majority of Republican Senators had voted for it—though

I did not; and nearly all of us had voted for the commission of inquiry of which Mr. Wade was the chief member.

When we met in March, it was known that both these important subjects would necessarily be referred to the committee on foreign relations, and that, aside from the hostile personal relations of Mr. Sumner and the Secretary of State, he did not, and could not, and would not, represent the views of a majority of his Republican colleagues in the Senate, and that a majority of his committee agreed with him. Committees are and ought to be organized to represent the body, giving a majority of the members to the prevailing opinion, but fairly representing the views of the minority. It has been the custom in the Senate to allow each party to choose its own representatives in each committee, and in proportion to its numbers.

In the Republican conference the first question that arose was as to Mr. Sumner. He was the oldest Senator in consecutive service. He was eminent not only as a faithful representative of Republican principles, but as especially qualified to be chairman of our foreign relations. He had long held that position, and it was not usual in the Senate to change the committees, but to follow the rule of seniority, placing Senators of the majority party in the order of their coming into the Senate and those of the minority at the foot of the list.

In deciding Mr. Sumner's case, in view of the facts I have stated, two plans were urged:

First—To place him at the head of the new and important committee of privileges and elections, leaving the rest of the committee on foreign relations to stand in the precise order it had been, with one vacancy to be filled in harmony with the majority.

Second—To leave Mr. Sumner to stand in his old place as chairman, and to make a change in the body of the committee by transferring one of its members to another committee, and fill the vacancy by a Senator in harmony with the majority.

My own opinion was that the latter course was the most polite and just; but the majority decided, after full consideration and debate, upon the first alternative.

Simon Cameron was next to Mr. Sumner on the list of Republican members of the committee, and, by uniform usage, became its chairman.

This affair created feeling in the Senate which it is difficult now to realize, but it was decided in a Republican caucus, in which there was an honest difference of opinion. We foresaw, whichever way it should be decided, that it would create —and it did create—bad feeling among Senators, which existed as long as Mr. Sumner lived. I think it proper to make this statement of my own views at the time, though by the happening of great events this incident has almost passed out of memory.

Mr. Sumner died in Washington, March 11, 1874. He was distinguished for his literary attainments, and his strong opposition to the institution of slavery and his severe arraignment of it. The brutal attack made upon him by Preston S. Brooks created profound sympathy for him.

CHAPTER XXIII.

Some Events in My Private Life.

Feuds and Jealousies During Grant's Administration — Attack on Me by the Cincinnati "Enquirer" — Reply and Statement Regarding My Worldly Possessions — I Am Elected to the Senate for the Third Term — Trip to the Pacific with Colonel Scott and Party — Visit to the Yosemite Valley — San Diego in 1872 — Return Via Carson City and Salt Lake — We Call on Brigham Young — Arrival Home to Enter Into the Greeley-Grant Canvass — Election of General Grant for the Second Term.

I HAVE purposely followed the legislation of Congress on financial questions until the passage of the act of 1873, passing over other events in my personal history and that of President Grant.

It can hardly be said that we had a strictly Republican administration, during his two terms. While Republicans were selected to fill the leading offices, the policy adopted and the controlling influence around him were purely personal. He consulted but few of the Senators or Members, and they were known as his personal friends. Mr. Conkling, by his imperious will, soon gained a strong influence over the President, and from this came feuds, jealousies and enmities, that greatly weakened the Republican party and threatened its ascendency. This was a period of bitter accusations, extending from the President to almost everyone in public life. During the entire period of Grant's administration, I was chairman of the committee on finance of the Senate, and had to act upon all questions of taxation, debt, banking or finance, and had occasion to talk with the President upon such measures, but he rarely expressed any opinion or took any interest in them. His veto of the bill to increase the amount of United States notes, on the 22nd of April, 1874, was an exception, but on this he changed his mind, as he had expressed his approval of the bill when pending. He was charged with being in a whisky ring and with other offensive imputations, all of which were without the slightest foundation.   General Grant was, in every sense of the word, an honest man.   He was so honest that he did not suspect others, and no doubt confided in, and was friendly with, those who abused his confidence.   It was a period of slander and scandal.

I did not escape the general crimination.   I usually met accusations with silence, as my accusers were answered by others.   In March, 1871, the Cincinnati "Enquirer" contained the following imputation:

"We are informed that a gentleman who lately filled a responsible office in this city, who has recently returned from Washington, says that the Southern Railroad bill would have passed the United States Senate if it had not, unfortunately, happened that Senator Sherman had no direct pecuniary interest in it.   In these days, and with such Congresses, it takes grease to oil the wheels of legislation."

On the 12th of March I wrote to the editors of the "Enquirer" the following note, after quoting the editorial:

UNITED STATES SENATE CHAMBER, }
WASHINGTON, March 12, 1871. }

To THE EDITORS OF THE 'ENQUIRER:'

GENTLEMEN:—Some one, perhaps in your office, sends me the following editorial, cut from your paper:

   *   *   *   *   *   *   *   *   *

All I can say in reply is that it contains a falsehood and a calumny. I introduced the bill for the Southern Railroad; am strongly in favor of it, and pressed it at every stage as rapidly as the rules of the Senate and the strong opposition to it would allow.   This is known by every Senator, and I am quite sure Judge Thurman and Mr. Davis would say so. I alone took an active interest in the bill, and at the very moment your editorial was received I was pressing a Republican caucus to make it an exception to a resolution not to take up general legislation at this session.   Everyone familiar with our rules knew that it was the sheerest folly to try to pass the bill on the last day of the session, especially as against our appropriation bills.   When it does pass it will take days of debate, and will not receive support from any of your political associates, who think Kentucky can block up all intercourse between the north and south.   Still I yielded to the earnest desire of the trustees to try to get a vote, but failed to get the floor at 3 o'clock in the morning, the only moment it was possible to submit even the motion to take it up.   The bill to abolish the duty on coal was taken up and was not acted on, nor would the railroad bill, or any other contested bill, have passed at that stage of the session.

As to the base imputation you attribute to 'a gentleman who lately filled a responsible office in this city,' I can only say that, whether it originates with you or anyone else, it is utterly false. Neither in this nor in any measure that has passed Congress, or is pending, have I had any direct pecuniary interest. I respectfully ask that you print this, and also the name of the 'gentleman' you refer to.

I intend, in the interests of the city of Cincinnati and of the whole country, to press the Southern Railroad bill, and to secure its passage as soon as possible, but it is rather poor encouragement to read such libels in a prominent paper in your city.   Yours etc.,   JOHN SHERMAN.

This was followed by an article in the "Enquirer" embodied in my reply, as follows :

WASHINGTON, March 20, 1871.

GENTLEMEN :—In your editorial in the 'Enquirer' of March 17, in commenting on my card to you as to my action on the Cincinnati Southern Railroad bill, you repeat my statement that 'neither in this nor in any measure that has passed Congress, or is pending, have I had any pecuniary interest,' and you say :

'If this is true, he has certainly been a very badly slandered gentleman. Somehow or other there is a popular impression that Mr. Sherman has contrived to make his connection with politics a highly lucrative business, and that he has exhibited, since he has been in Congress, a worldly thrift that is remarkable. There is a further impression that he is now a very rich man, whereas, a few years ago, before he was in public affairs, his circumstances were decidedly moderate. Perhaps our senatorial friend may not be aware of the existence of these derogatory reports, and will thank us for giving him an opportunity, now that he knows of their existence, to disprove them.'

I have not been ignorant that there has been a studied effort—ascribed by me to the common tactics of political warfare—to create the impression, by vague innuendo, that I have used my official position to make money for myself. I know that this charge or imputation is without the slightest foundation, and I now repeat that I never was pecuniarily interested in any question, bill or matter before Congress ; that I never received anything in money, or property, or promise, directly or indirectly, for my vote or influence in Congress or in the departments ; that I have studiously avoided engaging in any business depending upon legislation in Congress. The only enterprise in which I ever engaged, which rests upon an act of Congress, is that in 1862, after the bill passed authorizing the construction of a street railroad in this city, I, with others, openly subscribed stock, and undertook to build it in pursuance of the act of Congress.

From the position assigned me here, I have had to deal with great questions involving our financial system of currency, taxes and debt, and I can appeal to all my associates in Congress, to each of the eminent men with whom, as Secretaries of the Treasury, I have been intimate, and to every man of the multitude with whom I have been brought into contact, to say whether I have ever been influenced in my course by pecuniary interest.

But you say that the impression is that I am a very rich man, whereas, before I was in public affairs, my circumstances were decidedly moderate. This allegation contains two gross exaggerations. When I entered public life, I was largely engaged in my profession and other lucrative business. If I had not engaged in politics, I might have been the rich man you suppose. I am not this day relatively richer, considering the changed value of property, than I was when I entered the Senate. Some time ago it was stated in your paper that I was worth millions. A very small fraction, indeed, of one million dollars will cover all I am worth. My property consists mainly of real estate, palpable to the eye, and the rest of it is chiefly in a railroad with which I was connected before I entered public life.

I have managed my business affairs with reasonable care, prudence, economy and success. What I have is the result of this.

You kindly offer me an opportunity to disprove to you these reports. Well, how can I? What charge is made against me? How can I fight shadows? How can a man prove himself innocent against an innuendo?

But as you offer me the opportunity, I now invite Mr. Faran to come to my home at Mansfield, and I will show him all I possess there, and render him a full account of all I have elsewhere, and if I can't fairly account for it without being suspected of receiving bribes, or gifts, or stealing, then he can repeat these baseless accusations with an easy conscience.

You may ask why I have not met these derogatory reports before. Perhaps I ought, but I feel the humiliation of such a controversy, and thought it time enough when a specific charge was made. And I am told by Mr. Hedges, my former law partner, that in my absence, last summer, he corrected some gross misstatements in your paper about me, and that you refused or neglected to publish it — even to notice it. As, however, you now, in a courteous way, invite this letter, I take great pleasure in accepting your offer. Very truly yours, JOHN SHERMAN.

MESSRS. FARAN & McLEAN, editors of the 'Enquirer.'

I doubted the policy of my publishing such a letter, or of taking any notice of so indefinite a charge, but the response from the press was fair, especially from the "Shield and Banner," a Democratic paper printed in Mansfield, as follows:

"We publish a letter of Hon. John Sherman to the editors of the Cincinnati 'Enquirer.' It is hardly necessary that we should say that we have no sympathy with the political creed of John Sherman. Between him and us there is a vast and wide difference; but we are not, we trust, so much of the partisan that we cannot do justice to a neighbor, if that neighbor differs with us. We have known John Sherman, not only during all his public life, but from the time we became a resident of Mansfield, now covering a period of thirty years, and we have always known him as industrious, prudent and careful in his profession, and economical and thrifty in his business. We placed very little credence in the rumors that he was a man of immense wealth. His property is mostly in real estate. He was fortunate in getting hold of very desirable property in and around our city, and the advance in that has doubtless given him a competence ; but it is folly to charge him with being a millionaire. We have, in common with our neighbors, enjoyed his hospitality, and his style of living is neither extravagant nor ostentatious.

"Mr. Sherman is one of our townsmen, and although all wrong as a politician and statesman, and holding to a creed we utterly disapprove, he is a highminded and honorable man, and we are bound to accept his statement about his pecuniary affairs as true."

I have often since been accused of the crime of "being rich," but as nearly all my possessions are visible to the naked eye, and their history and acquisition are known to so many, I think I am not required to prove that I have not made them as the result of legislation or my holding public trusts.

My second term in the Senate expired on the 4th of March, 1873. The election of my successor devolved upon the legislature that convened on the first Monday of January, 1872.

The canvass in Ohio, in the summer and fall of 1871, was an active and exciting one and attracted great interest in other states. The result would indicate the strength or weakness of Grant's administration. I felt it was necessary, not only for my re-election, but for the success of the Republican party, that every effort should be made to elect a Republican majority in the legislature, and I, therefore, at the state convention and in most of the congressional districts of Ohio, made earnest speeches in behalf of the state ticket and members of the legislature. I received many letters of encouragement, one of which, from Senator Carpenter in reference to my speech in the convention, I insert:

WASHINGTON, D. C., July 20, 1871.

HON. JOHN SHERMAN.

DEAR SIR :—I have just read your speech to the state convention of Ohio. *It is splendid.* The only fault I have to find with it is, that you have covered the whole ground and reduced us "lesser lights" to the necessity of repeating and elaborating. This is *very mean of you;* you might have left some topic of the next campaign untouched, for us to dwell upon. But you have pre-empted everthing and we must follow after.

Very truly yours, MATT H. CARPENTER.

Hon John Sherman

Dear Sir;

I have just read your speech to the State Convention of Ohio. It is splendid.

The only fault I have to find with it, is, that you have covered the whole ground, and reduced us "Upper lights" to the necessity of repeating & elaborating.

This is very mean of you; you might have left some topic of the next campaign untouched, for us to dwell upon.

But you have pre-empted everything and we must follow after.

Truly yours

Matt H Carpenter

Utica N.Y. Oct. 13. 1871.

My dear Sir

Pardon me for
certainties touching your
Election and the Legislature,
and having watched the
canvass with sincere interest
I congratulate you most
heartily on the result.

Your own speeches
have been among the best
you ever made, and your
Courage has been full of
the pluck without which
no canvass and no political
contest

Faithfully
John ...man
...field Ohio.

Critics is strong & truthful.

This state is ours, unless
our people are discouraged
from voting in the County
by the belief that with
Tammany to count, it
matters not what majorities
roll up above the Highlands.

Notwithstanding the gross
statement of the Tribune are
inspired by the Tribune, we
have done nothing here
to the contrary. ...
minority, but the best men
in the...Millard they voted small
prevent a split in our majority
with regard to the...letter, and
probably altered delegation in the
next National Convention. Very sincerely
...

The legislature was elected in October, 1871, but the majority for the Republicans was so small that the election of a Republican Senator was in doubt.

I received many hearty letters of congratulation on our success in Ohio from my colleagues in the Senate, among them one from Senator Conkling as follows:

UTICA, N. Y., October 13, 1871.

HON. JOHN SHERMAN, MANSFIELD, OHIO.

MY DEAR SIR:—Having waited for certainties touching your election and the legislature, and having watched the canvass with sincere solicitude, I congratulate you most heartily upon the result.

Your own speeches have been among the best you ever made, and your canvass has been full of the pluck without which no canvass and no political contest is thorough or truthful.

This state is ours unless the people are discouraged from voting in the country by the belief that with Tammany to count, it matters not what majority roll up above the Highlands.

Notwithstanding the grievous statement of the 'Tribune' and inspired by the 'Tribune,' we have done nothing harsh to the anti-administration minority, but the least and mildest thing which would prevent a split in our organization with trouble for the future, and probably a double delegation in the next national convention. Yours sincerely, ROSCOE CONKLING.

It was conceded that a decided majority of the Republican members of the legislature were in favor of my re-election, but it was believed that an effort would be made by five Republican members to combine with the Democratic members and thus secure the election of ex-Governor Jacob D. Cox.

A Republican legislative caucus was convened on the evening of January 4th, to nominate a candidate. The first and informal ballot gave me 61 votes to 14 scattering and the second ballot 71 votes to 4 scattering. This settled the matter unless the few dissenting votes could combine with the solid Democratic vote upon some other candidate. It was soon found that this attempt would be abortive, as several Democrats, and especially those from Richland and Fairfield counties, would vote for me if the choice came between Cox and myself. Every effort was made by General Ashley and the few others who were opposed to my nomination to combine upon anyone who could defeat me. They offered their support to Governor Hayes, but this was promptly refused by him. The same effort was made with Governor Dennison, General Garfield and General Schenck, and failed.

The joint convention for the election of a Senator was held on the second Tuesday of January. It was an open meeting. The voting was soon over on roll call, and the result was as follows: Sherman 73; Morgan 64; Cox 1; Schenck 1; Perry 1. Thus I was elected by six majority over all. When this result was known five Democrats changed from Morgan to Cox, and others were preparing to do so when Lieutenant Governor Mueller announced the result of the vote. He was an educated German of high standing, but his English was very imperfect. His decision that I, having received a majority of the votes cast, was duly elected, was clearly right, and this was conceded, but his imperfect English created great noise and merriment. It was printed in the "Ohio Statesman," on the same day, as follows:

"John Sherman, having received seventy-three votes for President in Congress [laughter], I mean for Senator in Congress, which being a majority over all them others, I declares John Sherman duly elected Senator in Congress from Ohio."

If the changing of the minority vote had proceeded, some of the Democratic votes would have been cast for me, and my majority would have been increased, but I preferred the election as it occurred. My election for the third term was after a hot political contest, but it left no wounds unhealed. Most of the gentlemen opposed to me became afterwards my warm friends.

In July, 1872, two months after the close of the session of Congress, I received the following letter from Thomas A. Scott, President of the Texas and Pacific Railroad Company:

PHILADELPHIA, July 19, 1872.

HON. JOHN SHERMAN, Mansfield, Ohio.

MY DEAR SIR:—A few gentlemen connected with the Texas and Pacific road, and myself, propose to go to the Pacific coast, leaving Philadelphia about the 12th to the 15th of August.

If your engagements will permit, I shall be very glad indeed to have you go with us.

I am going from San Francisco to San Diego, and shall return by way of San Francisco; the trip will occupy about thirty days.

Please let me hear from you, and, if possible, let me have the pleasure of your company.   Very truly yours,

THOMAS A. SCOTT, President.

I accepted the invitation, and with a very agreeable party of ladies and gentlemen, among whom were Mr. W. T. Walters, of Baltimore, and his daughter, made my first voyage to the Pacific coast. Mr. Scott, as president of the Pennsylvania Railroad Company, had command, by courtesy, of every convenience of travel. We had a dining car which we could attach to any train, with ample room for beds, and a full supply of provisions. The journey to San Francisco was broken by several stops on the way at places that we thought interesting.

Great changes had occurred in the brief period since my trip in an ambulance with General Sherman. The Indians and buffaloes had disappeared from the plains, the former placed on reservations distant from the railroad, and the latter by gradual extinction. When we crossed the Laramie plains I was in, to me, a "terra incognita." The great basin of Salt Lake, with the varied and picturesque scenery to the east and west of it, attracted our attention, but the want of water, the dry air, the dust and the absence of trees and vegetation of any kind, condemn all that country to waste and desolation, except in a few places where irrigation can be had. The Nevada range of mountains was crossed at night, but we were to explore them on our return. When the broad valley of the Sacramento opened to our view, we could hardly express our delight. Here, indeed, was the land of gold, with its clear air, its grand mountains, its rich plains.

Aside from the wonderful variety of its scenery, the history of California has always excited poetic interest—its long settlement by mixed races living in quiet peaceful harmony, mainly as herdsmen and shepherds, suddenly disturbed and conquered without firing a gun, by an aggressive race who soon revolutionized the habits of the natives, and planted a new civilization, with all the bad as well as the good elements of our race. Then the discovery of gold, immediately following the conquest of California, drew to it, from all parts of the United States, the most restless and adventurous of our population, some of the worst and many of the best. The rapid admixture of these diverse elements threatened for a time hostile conflicts, in which criminals, under cover of law, committed murder and other crimes, and peaceful, law-abiding citizens were compelled to appeal to force and mob law to preserve civilization.

The railway soon brought us through Sacramento to San Francisco, where we remained several days. We were kindly received and entertained. The enterprise of Scott was not then favored in San Francisco, but this did not prevent our hearty welcome. Here I met Mr. Hollister, whom I had known in Ohio. He was the great shepherd of California. I was informed that he owned 100,000 sheep, divided into flocks of about 3,000 each. These flocks were wintered at a large ranch near the Pacific coast belonging to him. The climate was mild, and the sheep could live without shelter during the winter. The flocks would start eastwardly over the great valley, each flock cared for by a shepherd, a boy and a dog, feeding in the open country, some of the flocks reaching the Mariposa valley, one hundred miles away. When the grass failed they were turned to the west to their home. Whether this tale is an exaggeration I cannot say, but certain it is that at that time sheep raising and the production of wool was one of the chief industries of California. Hollister was also interested in woolen manufacture, especially of blankets, equal to any in the world. When I knew him in Ohio, he and his brother were the owners, by inheritance, of a large and valuable farm in Licking county. When gold was discovered in California, Hollister sold to his brother one-half of the farm, and with the proceeds purchased a large flock of the best Ohio sheep, and drove them to California, taking two years for the journey. He was fond of telling his adventures, and proud of his success. He died a few years since in California, but whether his good fortune followed him to the close of his life I do not know. He was very kind to our party and accompanied us to San Diego.

From San Francisco we made a trip to the Mariposa Grove, and the Yosemite valley. We traveled by rail to a small station nearest the grove. Then by stage we rode to the terminus of the line. From there we went but a short distance to the grove. This majestic survivor of the forest has been so often described that details are not necessary. We measured the trees, and rode on horseback nearly one hundred feet through one of the fallen monsters. We also attempted to form a ring with hands and arms extended around one of these trees, but our party was not numerous enough to encircle it. I felt a sense of insignificance when I realized the long life of some of these trees, estimated to span forty generations of men, and still in health and strength. We returned to the stage station and again mounted our horses and mules for the perilous adventure of a descent into the Yosemite valley. It so happened that Mr. Bell, the keeper of the station, was a former resident of Bellville, in Richland county, Ohio, in which I live. He knew me well, and his wife I knew as the daughter of a leading farmer of that county. I thought I might utilize this acquaintance by asking him to see that I was well mounted to descend to the valley. Much to my surprise a spirited horse, well accoutred, was brought out for Colonel Scott, and a shaggy short-legged mule, with a California saddle and a common but stout bridle, was brought out for me. I felt that Bell had disregarded the obligation of "auld acquaintance," but said nothing.

My mount started at the heels of the cavalcade in a steady walk, but I noticed he was sure-footed, and that, at the end of two or three weary hours, he had passed most of the party and soon after was close in the wake of Colonel Scott. In the meantime, I had noticed that I was the subject of merriment. My feet were in close proximity to the ground. The length of my legs was out of proportion to that of the legs of the mule. When we came to descend the mountain, however, at an angle of nearly forty-five degrees, on a very narrow path, I found that my mule could turn the bends of the track, and, by a peculiar gathering of his feet, could slide down difficult places, while Colonel Scott, on his already jaded horse, was troubled and worried. He dismounted when the path widened and asked me to go ahead. He then followed me, leading his horse. After that, I made up my mind that my Richland county friend had not failed me in my hour of need.

As for the scenery through which we were passing, no language can describe it. We saw, four thousand feet below, a beautiful little valley about half a mile wide at the widest part, with what appeared to be a very small stream dancing along from side to side of the valley, and surrounded by precipitous mountains in every direction. The eye and mind can now vividly recall the picture of the scenes then around me. My mule had my confidence, but I feared lest some fatal mishap might befall some of my companions, and especially I feared for a lady who ventured the journey, but she fortunately displayed pluck and coolness, and at the end of the day we all arrived at the hut in the valley safe and sound, but very weary. Since that time, I understand that a good road has been made up the valley, by which tourists can enjoy the grandest scenery in nature, without the risk we took.

We enjoyed a hearty supper of plain food, and a sound sleep on corn-husk mattresses. The next day we explored the valley, and enjoyed the changing views of near and distant mountains. These have often been described, but they can only be appreciated by a personal visit. We left the valley by another route to the north, and reached the railroad by a different line of stages.

Returning to San Francisco, we took the boat for San Diego, stopping, on the way, at Santa Barbara and San Pedro. From this place we drove to Los Angeles, then a typical Mexican town of great interest. The good people hoped for the railroad, but Colonel Scott expected the road of which he was president would be able to reach San Diego.

Our arrival at San Diego was an event of interest to the few people of that town. We inspected the remarkable harbor and the surrounding country. It was apparently a good site for a great city. Fresh water was the great want and rain-falls were rare, but it was claimed that an ample supply of water could be had from the hills. The real obstacle to that site, as a terminus for the railroad, was the mountains east of San Diego, which, upon a survey, were found to be extremely difficult, and this turned the route to Los Angeles, over natural passes and through the beautiful region of San Bernardino.

We returned, by boat, to San Francisco, and soon after turned our way eastward. We stopped at Reno, and went by rail to Carson City, the capital of Nevada. It was then an embryo town. From there we went to Lake Tahoe, one of the finest bodies of water on the earth. Its clear, cold waters filled a natural basin in the midst of the Nevada range of mountains, which was supplied by the melting snows. We then returned to Carson City, ascended, by rail, an inclined plain of high grade, to Virginia City. Most of the party descended into the mines, but I was prevented from doing so by an attack of neuralgia, a complaint from which I never suffered before or since, caused, as it was said, by the high altitude and thin air. Here I met several natives of Ohio, who had sought their fortunes in the far west. They were very kind to the party and to myself. It got to be a common remark, that Ohio had everything good in the west. I could answer that they all seemed to deserve what they had. I was disposed to be proud of them and of my native state, but soon after, on the way east, we heard of an atrocious murder committed by two Ohio men. This turned the tables on my native state, and I was compelled to confess that bad men came from Ohio as well as from other states; but, if so, Ohio people excelled in the atrocity of their crimes as well as in the excellence of their merits!

Our next stopping place was at Salt Lake City. Whatever opinion we may have of the religious creed and dogmas of the Mormons, we cannot deny the industry and courage of that sect in building up a city in a wilderness where natural conditions seemed to forbid all hope of success in such an enterprise. And yet there it was, a well-ordered city laid out with squares, avenues, streets, and reservations for schools, churches and other public uses, with water introduced in great abundance. All the needs of city life were provided, such as stores, markets and shops. We were invited by the delegate in Congress, from Utah, to call on Brigham Young, and we did so. He was a large, well-built man, then about sixty years old. He took great interest in the enterprise of Colonel Scott and seemed familiar with all the railways built or projected in the western country. There was nothing in his conversation or manner that indicated the "crank," nor did he exhibit any of the signs of a zealot or fanatic. He made no allusions to his creed or the habits of his followers and betrayed no egotism or pride. He has died since but the organization he left behind him is still in existence, and the Mormon faith is still the creed and guide of the great body of those who followed Brigham Young into the wilderness, and of their numerous descendants. It is to be hoped that the government and people of the United States will let the Mormons severely alone, allowing them to believe what they will, and to do in the way of worship what they choose. In this way only can their confidence in alleged revelations be shaken, and Mormonism will disappear among the many vain attempts of humanity to explore the mysteries of life and death. Persecution never weakens delusions, nor disturbs faith, however ignorant and groundless.

From Salt Lake our party went to Cheyenne and thence to Denver. This city was growing rapidly and was plainly destined to be the principal center of the mineral development of several states. I had, on a previous trip, visited the interesting region of the "Garden of the Gods," Colorado Springs and Pike's Peak. Our party left Denver for home. On the long stretch via Kansas City, St. Louis and Indianapolis we saw nothing new, as we were traveling over familiar ground. It was early in September, when corn, the great western staple, was approaching maturity, and the earth was giving forth its increase. We were crossing the largest and perhaps most fertile valley of the world. All of it had been redeemed from nature and the Indians, within one hundred years. During our trip we had passed through great cities, prosperous towns and amidst wonderful scenery. All of the route except through the Yosemite valley was passed over in a palace car. The ocean voyage was in a steamboat even more luxurious than the palace car. All this rapid development did not satisfy the desire of Colonel Scott and Mr. Walters. Their minds were occupied with vast railroad projects, some of which were accomplished before their death. I also had my dreams but they related to public policies rather than internal improvements and some of these have been realized.

I was awakened one bright morning in September and told that the car was in Ohio. This was enough to drive sleep from my eyelids. I looked out upon the rich lands of the Miami valley, the comfortable homesteads on every farm, the fat cattle and herds of sheep, the broad fields of yellow corn, and every sign of fertility. All these, and perhaps a little admixture of state pride, led me to say that, after all, the people of Ohio need not go beyond the bounds of that state with any hope to improve their condition or to secure a better opportunity for a happy life. I soon parted with my friends with sincere regrets, for in our journeyings we were in truth a happy family.

The canvass in Ohio was then progressing for the election of a President and Members of Congress, in which I was expected, as usual, to take a part. The strange anomaly of Horace Greeley running on a Democratic ticket was enough in itself to excite opposition, especially in the southern states. The result was that General Grant, in November, 1872, was elected President by 31 states with 286 electoral votes. Greeley died after the election, and before the electors voted, so that no electoral vote was counted for him. If he had lived he would probably have received 60 electoral votes.

CHAPTER XXIV.

The Panic of 1873 and Its Results.

Failure of Jay Cooke and Co. — Wild Schemes "for the Relief of the People" —
Congress Called Upon for Help — Finance Committee's Report for the Redemption of United States Notes in Coin — Extracts from my Speech in Favor
of the Report — Bill to fix the Amount of United States Notes —
Finally Passed by the Senate and House — Vetoed by President Grant and Failure to Pass Over His Objections —
General Effect Throughout the Country of the
Struggle for Resumption — Imperative Necessity of Providing Some Measure of Relief.

DURING the first four years of General Grant's administration the financial condition of the United States
was eminently prosperous. The total reduction of
the national debt, from the 1st of March, 1869, to the
1st of November, 1873, was $383,629,783, the annual saving of
interest resulting therefrom being $27,432,932. During this
period the value of United States notes compared with coin
steadily increased. The funding of the six per cent. bonds into
five per cent. bonds, under the refunding act, continued at the
rate of about $85,000,000 a year. The credit of the United
States steadily advanced during this period, so that the Secretary of the Treasury, in his report of 1873, stated that it had not
stood higher since the close of the Rebellion than it did at that
time. This improvement of the public credit was accompanied
with a large reduction of internal taxes and duties on imported
goods. The business of the country was prosperous, the increase and extension of railroads and the development of new
industries was marked, indicating great prosperity.

All this was subsequently changed by the happening of a
panic in September, 1873. The cause of this was attributed to
over-trading, to the expansion of credits, and to rash investments made in advance of public needs. This panic commenced by the failure of Jay Cooke & Co., of Philadelphia, an

enterprising firm of high standing, then engaged in selling the bonds of the Northern Pacific Railroad Company. I was engaged at that time, with a committee of the Senate, of which William Windom was chairman, in examining many plans of public improvements, especially in the increase of facilities for water transportation at the mouth of the Mississippi river, and at the great lakes on our northern boundary, improvements since then made with great benefit to the commerce of the United States. Roscoe Conkling, of New York, was a member of that committee. We were at Buffalo when the failure of Cooke & Co. was announced. We all felt that for the present, at least, our duties as a committee were at an end. The panic spread so that in a month all industries were in a measure suspended. The wildest schemes for relief were proposed, in and out of Congress. The panic spread to the banks, which were compelled in self-defense to call in their loans, to withhold their circulating notes, and contract their business. As usual on the happening of such a panic, an appeal was made to the treasury for relief, a demand was made for an increase of the volume of the United States notes, and that the Secretary of the Treasury should use the money of the government to buy exchange.

The New York Produce Exchange applied to the Secretary of the Treasury on the 29th of September, 1873, in resolutions, as follows:

" WHEREAS, The critical condition of the commercial interests of the country requires immediate relief by the removal of the block in negotiating foreign exchange; therefore be it

" *Resolved*, That we respectfully suggest to the Secretary of the Treasury the following plans for relief in this extraordinary emergency:

" First, That currency be immediately issued to banks or bankers, upon satisfactory evidence that gold has been placed upon special deposit in the Bank of England, by their correspondents in London, to the credit of the United States, to be used solely in purchasing commercial bills of exchange.

" Second, That the President of the United States and the Secretary of the Treasury are respectfully requested to order the immediate prepayment of the outstanding loan of the United States due January 1, 1874."

This request had, as a matter of course, to be denied. But the secretary did purchase $13,000,000 of bonds for the sinking fund, to the full extent the condition of the treasury allowed.

It is difficult to realize or to convey by description the wild ideas developed by such a panic. The government for the time being is expected to provide a remedy for a condition it did not create, but, instead of aiding, the government is most likely to need aid. The revenues from importations fell off and the value of United States notes declined.

When Congress convened in December, 1873, the wildest schemes for relief to the people were proposed. A large increase of United States notes was demanded. More than sixty bills, resolutions and propositions were introduced in the Senate in respect to the currency, the public debt and national banks, all bearing upon the financial condition of the country, expressing every variety of opinion, from immediate coin payments to the wildest inflation of irredeemable paper money. All these were referred to the committee on finance, then composed as follows: Messrs. Sherman (chairman), Morrill, of Vermont, Scott, Wright, Ferry, of Michigan, Fenton and Bayard.

The several measures referred to the committee were taken up and considered, but the same wide divergence of opinion was developed in the committee as existed outside of Congress among the people.

The majority of the committee reported to the Senate the following resolution:

"*Resolved*, That it is the duty of Congress during its present session to adopt definite measures to redeem the pledge made in the act approved March 18, 1869, entitled 'An act to strengthen the public credit,' as follows: 'And the United States also pledges its faith to make provision, at the earliest practicable period, for the redemption of the United States notes in coin;' and the committee on finance is directed to report to the Senate, at as early a day as practicable, such measures as will not only redeem this pledge of the public faith, but will also furnish a currency of uniform value, always redeemable in gold or its equivalent, and so adjusted as to meet the changing wants of trade and commerce."

Mr. Ferry, of Michigan, a member of the committee, offered the following substitute for the pending resolution:

"That the committee on finance is directed to report to the Senate, at as early a day as practicable, such measures as will restore commercial confidence and give stability and elasticity to the circulating medium through a moderate increase of currency."

Upon these adverse propositions a long debate followed without practical results. I made a long speech on the 16th day of January, 1874, in favor of the resolution of the committee. I then said :

"At the outset of my remarks I wish to state some general propositions established by experience, and the concurring opinions of all writers on political economy. They may not be disputed, but are constantly overlooked. They ought to be ever present in this discussion as axioms, the truth of which has been so often proven that proof is no longer requisite.

" The most obvious of these axioms, which lies at the foundation of the argument I wish to make to-day, is that a specie standard is the best and the only true standard of all values, recognized as such by all civilized nations of our generation, and established as such by the experience of all commercial nations that have existed from the earliest period of recorded time. While the United States, as well as all other nations, have for a time, under the pressure of war or other calamity, been driven to establish other standards of value, yet they have all been impelled to return to the true standard ; and even while other standards of value have been legalized for the time, specie has measured their value as it now measures the value of our legal tender notes.

" This axiom is as immutable as the law of gravitation or the laws of the planetary system, and every device to evade it or avoid it has, by its failure, only demonstrated the universal law that specie measures all values as certainly as the surface of the ocean measures the level of the earth.

" It is idle for us to try to discuss with intelligence the currency question until we are impressed with the truth, the universality, and the immutability, of this axiom. Many of the crude ideas now advanced spring from ignoring it. The most ingenious sophistries are answered by it. It is the governing principle of finance. It is proved by experience, is stated clearly by every leading writer on political economy, and is now here, in our own country, proving its truth by measuring daily the value of our currency and of all we have or produce. I might, to establish this axiom, repeat the history of finance, from the shekels of silver, 'current money with the merchant,' paid by Abraham, to the last sale of stock in New York. I might quote Aristotle and Pliny, as well as all the writers on political economy of our own time, and trace the failure of the innumerable efforts to establish some other standard of value, from the oxen that measured the value of the armor of Homeric heroes to the beautifully engraved promise of our day ; but this would only be the hundred-times-told tale which every student may find recorded, not only in schoolbooks, but in the writings of Humboldt, Chevalier, Adam Smith, and others of the most advanced scientific authorities. They all recognize the precious metals as the universal standard of value. Neither governments, nor parliaments, nor congresses can change this law. It defies every form of authority, but silently and surely asserts itself as a law of necessity, beyond the jurisdiction of municipal law.

* * * * * * * * *

"Of late years much difficulty has grown out of the slightly varying value of silver and gold, as compared with each other, and the tendency of opinion has been to adopt gold alone as the standard of value. The United States has twice changed the relative value of these metals, and other modern nations have been driven to similar expedients. At the Paris monetary conference, held in 1867, which I had the honor to attend, the delegates of twenty nations represented agreed to recommend gold alone as the standard of value. The United States, and nearly all the commercial nations, have adopted this standard, and reduced the use of silver to a mere token coinage of less intrinsic value than gold, but maintained at par with gold by the right to be converted into gold at the will of the holder. So that for all practical purposes we may regard gold as the only true standard, the true money of the world, by which the value of all property, of all productions, of all credits, and of every medium of exchange, and especially of all paper money, is tested.

"Specie, in former times, was not only the universal standard of value, but it was the general medium of all exchanges. In modern times this is greatly changed. Specie is still the universal standard of value, but it has ceased to be even the usual medium of exchange. The failure to distinguish between the standard of value and the medium of exchanges occasions many of the errors into which so many fall, and nearly every Senator who has spoken on one side of the question has fallen into this error. Specie has lost a portion of its sovereign power, for with the enormous increase of exchanges it was found that, valuable as it is, it is too heavy to transport from place to place as a medium of exchange. The perils of the sea, the dangers of theft and robbery, led to devices to substitute promises to pay gold in place of the actual gold.

* * * * * * * * *

"Mr. president, thus far my remarks are founded upon the experience of ages, applicable to all countries and to all commercial nations of our time. I present them now as axioms of universal recognition. And yet I have heard these axioms denounced in this debate as 'platitudes,' useless for this discussion in the Senate of the United States. The wisdom of ages, the experience of three thousand years, the writings of political economists, are whistled down the wind as if we in the Senate were wiser than all who have reasoned and thought and legislated upon financial problems— that all this accumulated wisdom consists of 'platitudes' unworthy to influence an American Senate in the consideration of the affairs of our day and generation.

"Sir, I do not think so. If we disregard these 'platitudes,' we only demonstrate our own ignorance and punish our constituents with evils that we ought to avoid. I purpose now to pursue the argument further, and to prove that we are bound, both by public faith and good policy, to bring our currency to the gold standard ; that such a result was provided for by the financial policy adopted when the currency was authorized ; that a departure from this policy was adopted after the war was over, and after the necessity for a depreciated currency ceased ; and that we have only to restore the old policy to bring us safely, surely, and easily to a specie standard.

"First, I present to you the pledge of the United States to pay these notes in coin 'at the earliest practicable period.' In the 'act to strengthen the public credit,' passed on the 18th day of March, 1869, I find this obligation :

" 'And the United States also solemnly pledges its public faith to make provision, at the earliest practicable period, for the redemption of the United States notes in coin.'

   *   *   *   *   *   *   *   *   *

" The Congress of the United States, in order to put into form its sense of this obligation, passed the act ' to strengthen the public credit,' and the last and most important clause of this act is the promise which I have just read, that these notes should be paid, 'at the earliest practicable period,' in coin.

   *   *   *   *   *   *   *   *   *

" On the day we made that promise, the 18th of March, 1869, the greenbacks, the notes of the United States, were worth $75\frac{3}{4}$ cents in gold ; or in other words, gold was at a premium of thirty-two per cent. . . .   What was the result ? After you enacted that law—the faith of the people of the United States that you would redeem this pledge—the value of your greenbacks advanced, not rapidly, but gradually, and in one year, to within twelve per cent. of par in gold.

   *   *   *   *   *   *   *   *   *

" Mr. president, we see, then, the effect of this promise. And I here come to what I regard as a painful feature to discuss—how have we redeemed our promise ? It was Congress that made it, in obedience to the public voice ; and no act of Congress ever met with a more hearty and generous approbation. But I say to you, with sorrow, that Congress has done no single act the tendency of which has been to advance the value of these notes to a gold standard ; and I shall make that clearer before I get through. Congress made this promise five years ago. The people believed it and business men believed it. Four years have passed away since then, and your dollar in greenbacks is worth no more to-day than it was on the 18th of March, 1870 ; and no act of yours has even tended to advance the value of that greenback to par in gold, while every affirmative act of yours since that time has tended to depreciate its value and to violate your promise.

   *   *   *   *   *   *   *   *   *

" Every bond that was issued was issued only upon the sacred pledge contained in this act, that the interest of that bond should be paid in coin ;

and the principal should be paid, when due, in coin. The fifth section of the act provides that all duties on imported goods shall be paid in coin ; and that this money shall be set aside as a special fund to pay the interest on the bonded debt in coin. Then, in order to secure the greenbacks, it authorized any holder of greenbacks to pay any government debt with them ; it authorized the holder of greenbacks to pay any debt, public or private, with them ; and every citizen of the United States was bound to take them. Then it authorized them to be converted into six per cent. bonds of the United States — those bonds payable, principal and interest, in gold. If the policy provided for by this act had been maintained, we would long since have been at specie payments, without any serious disturbance of our monetary affairs.

* * * * * * * * *

" Now, Mr. president, I come to show the Senate how this provision, the convertible clause of the act of February 25, 1862, was repealed. On the 3rd of March, 1863, Congress passed 'An act to provide ways and means for the support of the government.' This act was passed during the dark hours of the war. The currency of the country did not flow into the treasury rapidly enough to pay our army. I remember that at about the time this act was passed there were very large unpaid requisitions. The Secretary of the Treasury, instead of issuing any more six per cent. bonds, desired to float a 10–40 five per cent. bond ; in other words, to reduce the burden of interest upon the public debt. At this time there were three hundred millions of circulation outstanding, and with all the rights, and all the privileges, conferred upon the greenbacks, they did not flow into the treasury fast enough to furnish means to carry on the operations of the war.

* * * * * * * * *

" In other words, the suspension of this convertibility clause was passed with a view to promote conversion ; to encourage conversion ; to induce conversion ; and, if possible, to induce a conversion into a five per cent. gold bond instead of into a six per cent. bond. When the Secretary of the Treasury presented this view to Congress he was at once met with the pledge of the public faith ; with the promise printed upon the back of the greenbacks that they could be converted into six per cent. bonds at the pleasure of the holder ; and that we could not take away that right. This difficulty was met by the ingenuity of the then Senator from Vermont (Mr. Collamer). He said that no man ever exercised a right which could not properly be barred by a statute of limitations ; and if this right was injurious to the people of the United States, and prevented the conversion of these notes into bonds, we might require the holder of these notes to convert them within a given time ; that we could give them a reasonable time within which they could convert them into six per cent. bonds, and after that take away the right.

"The act of March 3, 1863, was amended by inserting this clause :

"'And the holders of United States notes, issued under or by virtue of said acts, shall present the same for the purpose of exchanging the
same for bonds, as therein provided, on or before the 1st day of July, 1863 ;
and thereafter the right so to exchange the same shall cease and determine.'

*   *   *   *   *   *   *   *   *

"Now, Mr. president, I have shown you that the greenbacks were
based upon coin bonds ; that they had the right to be converted into coin
bonds ; that that right was taken away as to the 5–20 bonds ; but that, in
practice and in effect, the greenback was convertible into an interest-bearing bond of the United States up to 1866, and until the passage of the law
to which I will now refer.

*   *   *   *   *   *   *   *   *

"If this act had contained a simple provision restoring to the holder of
the greenback the right to convert his note into bonds there would have
been no trouble. Why should it not have been done ? Simply because the
then Secretary of the Treasury believed that the only way to advance the
greenbacks was by reducing the amount of them ; that the only way to get
back to specie payments was by the system of contraction. If the legal
tender notes could have been wedded to any form of gold bond by being
made convertible into it, they would have been lifted, by the gradual advance of our public credit, to par in gold, leaving the question of contraction to depend upon the amount of notes needed for currency. Sir, it was
the separation of our greenbacks from the funding system that created the
difficulty we have upon our hands to-day ; and I say now that, in my judgment, the only true way to approach specie payments is to restore this principle, and give to the holder of the greenback, who is your creditor, the
same right that you give to any other creditor. If he has a note which you
promised to pay and cannot, and he desires interest on that note by surrendering it, why should you not give it to him ? No man can answer that. It
is just as much a debt as any other portion of the debt of the United
States."

Finally, after more than three months study and debate, a
majority of the committee agreed upon a measure and directed
me to report it to the Senate. It fixed the maximum limit of
the United States notes at $382,000,000. It provided for a
gradual payment of these notes in coin or in five per cent.
bonds, at the option of the Secretary of the Treasury, from the
1st of January, 1876. It was entitled "An act to provide for
the redemption and reissue of United States notes and for free
banking."

In obedience to the instructions of the committee, on the 23rd of March, 1874, I reported the bill as an original measure, and said:

"It is due to the members of the committee on finance that I should say that the bill which I have just reported, as it appears on its face, is in the nature of a compromise measure, which is more or less acceptable all around, but at the same time there are certain features of the bill which members of the committee on finance will feel at liberty to express their opposition to, and also to propose amendments to. It is due to them that I should make this statement. The bill itself, as appears on its face, is the result of great labor, long consideration, and the consequence of compromise. In many cases we were not able, however, to reconcile conflicting opinions; and on those points, of course, members of the committee will feel themselves at liberty to oppose certain features of the bill."

Mr. Thurman said:

"I should like to inquire of my colleague whether he proposes to-day or to-morrow, when he makes the motion that he indicated, to state what, in the opinion of the committee reporting this bill, will be its practical effect, so that we may have the views of the committee as to the workings of the bill should it become a law. I am sure I, for one, should like very much to know what the committee, who have devoted so much time to this subject, think will be the practical working of the measure, at any time that it suits the convenience of the chairman of the committee to make such statement."

I replied:

"When the subject is introduced, if it be convenient, to-morrow, I propose to make a very brief statement of the effect of each section, as we understand it; but I do not intend, by any long speeches or any remarks, to prolong this matter unnecessarily. I have expressed my own individual views, and each member of the committee, I suppose, stands to the opinions expressed by him in the speeches he has made in the Senate—speeches that were carefully considered, and by which the position of each Senator was stated; but undoubtedly I shall feel it my duty, when the bill is called up, to state what I regard as the actual practical effect of these different propositions; and some of them, I will now say, I assented to with great reluctance."

On the next day the bill was taken up in the Senate, and I then stated the general provisions of the bill. I insert extracts from my speech, which indicate the difficulties we encountered:

"Mr. president, some complaint has been made in the Senate and in the country at the delay in the presentation, by the committee on finance, of some bill covering the financial question; but a moment's reflection will, I am sure, convince every Senator that there has been no fault on the part of that committee. From the beginning of the session to this hour that committee, under the direction of the Senate, has been studying and discussing the various plans and propositions which were referred to the committee ; and I may say that over sixty different propositions, either coming in the form of petitions or in the form of bills, have been sent to the committee, all of them suggesting different plans and ideas. It was impossible to consider all these and to agree upon any comprehensive measure until within a day or two.

" There was another consideration. The committee found itself divided in opinion, precisely as the country is, and precisely as the Senate is, into as many as three different classes of opinion. There were, first, those who desired to take a definite and positive step toward the resumption of specie payments. There were, second, those who desired an enlargement of the currency, or what we commonly call an inflation of the currency. There were, third, those who, while willing to see the amount of bank notes increased and the question of the legal tenders settled in some form, were also desirous that some definite step should be taken toward a specie standard. There were these differences of opinion.

" For the purpose of ascertaining the views of the Senate, and not involving ourselves in reporting a bill that would be defeated as the bill of the last session was, we presented, early in the session, resolutions of a general character which stated these three ideas : First, the resolution of the majority of the committee that some definite step should be taken toward specie payments. Then there was the amendment offered by the gentleman who now occupies the chair [Mr. Ferry, of Michigan], that there ought to be an increase of the currency without reference to any plan of redemption. Third, there was the proposition made by the Senator from Delaware [Mr. Bayard], that measures should be taken at once looking to the resumption of specie payments.

" These propositions were discussed, and the committee were enlightened by that discussion ; at least they obtained the opinions of Members of the Senate. Subsequently, in the course of our investigation, a question about the $25,000,000 section (section 6 of the act of July 12, 1870) came up, and the committee deemed it right, by a unanimous vote, to ascertain the sense of the Senate as to whether they wished this section carried into execution. As it stood upon the statute book it was a law without force. It was a law so expressed that the comptroller said he could not execute it. Therefore the committee reported a bill which would have provided the necessary details to carry into execution that section of the existing law. But in the present temper of the public mind, in the Senate and in the country, that bill was discussed, and has been discussed day after day, without approaching the question at all. During all this time the committee have been pursuing their inquiries, and finally they have reported the bill which is now before us.

" The measure that is reported is not a satisfactory one to any of us in all its details. Probably it is not such as the mind of any single Member of the Senate would propose. It is in the nature of a compromise bill, and therefore, while it has the strength of a compromise bill, it has also the weakness of a compromise bill. There are ideas in it which, while meeting the views of a majority, taken separately will be opposed by others. I am quite sure that I say nothing new to the Senate when I say it does not in all respects meet my own views. But there is a necessity for us to yield some of our opinions. We cannot reconcile or pass any measure that will be satisfactory to the country unless we do so. Any positive victory by either extreme of this controversy will be an absolute injury to the business of the country. Therefore, any measure that is adopted ought to be so moderate, pursuing such a middle course, such a middle ground, that it will give satisfaction to the country. It must be taken as a whole; and therefore the effect of amending this proposition will be simply to destroy it. If an amendment in the direction of expansion is inserted, it will drive away some who would be willing to support it as it is. If an amendment in the way of contraction is proposed and carried by a majority of the Senate, it will drive away those who might be willing to take this measure as a compromise. The only question before the Senate now is, whether this is a fair compromise between the ideas that have divided the people of this country and the Members of the Senate; whether it will surely improve our currency while giving the relief that is hoped for by a moderate increase of the currency. Now I ask the secretary to read the first section of the bill."

The chief clerk read section 1, as follows:

Be it enacted by the Senate and House of Representatives of the United States of America in Congress assembled, That the maximum limit of United States notes is hereby fixed at $382,000,000, at which amount it shall remain until reduced as hereinafter provided.

I then continued:

"It is manifest to every Senator that the initial step in this controversy is to fix the aggregate limit of United States notes. The United States notes, although they are very popular, and justly so, in this country, are at this moment inconvertible; they are irredeemable, and they are depreciated. These are facts admitted on all hands. In making that statement I do not intend at all to deny that the United States notes have served a great and useful purpose; and though I was here at the birth of them and advocated them in all stages of their history, yet I am compelled to say at this moment, twelve years after their issue, that they are inconvertible; they are irredeemable; and they are depreciated this day at the rate of twelve per cent. They have been legally inconvertible since July 1, 1863, and practically inconvertible since the close of the war; that is, the government refuses to receive them, either in payment of customs or in payment at par of any bond of the United States offered by it. They are irredeemable on their very face. They have depreciated almost from the date of their issue, at one time being worth only forty cents in gold, and to-day only worth ninety cents. That is the condition of the United States notes.

"Now, there is another thing admitted by all Senators. I do not trespass on any disputed ground when I say that every addition to the volume of these notes, while they thus stand depreciated, irredeemable, and inconvertible, is as certain to further depreciate them, as it is that to pour water into an overflowing bucket will cause it still more to overflow; as certain as the law of gravitation; as certain as anything human or divine. It is equally true that any contraction of this currency, any withdrawal of the amount of it, is undoubtedly an appreciation of its value, making it nearer and nearer to the standard of gold.

"This is so plain a proposition that it is not necessary to discuss it; and the whole people of the country understand it; the plainest and simplest people understand it as well as the wisest. Those who desire to increase prices, to start and put in operation new enterprises, desire an increase of the currency without any plan of redemption. Those, on the other hand, who want to get back to the specie standard, to appreciate the value of these notes, desire to withdraw them, get them out of the way, or give new uses and new values to them so as to advance them nearer and nearer to the standard of gold. Therefore it is that I say the very first step at the outset of this controversy is to settle what is the legal limit of these notes; how many are there now authorized by law; how many are there outstanding. And here it is a strange thing that on this very point, a purely legal question, the most important one in our financial discussion, there is a great difference of opinion. There ought not to be uncertainty or room for a difference of opinion upon a question of this kind. It ought to be settled. On the one hand it is insisted by Senators who compose the majority of the committee on finance that the legal limit of United States notes is $356,-000,000; that the amount which has been already issued, of what is known as the $44,000,000 reserve, was unlawfully issued, although under great press of circumstances and without any intention on the part of the secretary to do more than he thought he had a lawful right to do. On the other hand it is insisted by other Senators that the legal limit of United States notes is $400,000,000; and here is a margin of $44,000,000 upon which there is a dispute of law as to the power of the secretary to issue it. That dispute ought to be settled at once. It is a question that ought not to be in doubt a moment, because the power to issue that $44,000,000 places it in the discretion of the Secretary of the Treasury either to advance or to lower the value of all property in the United States, of all debts in the United States, of everything that is measured by United States notes.

"Should we undertake to say that the secretary did wrong in exceeding the limit at $356,000,000? A majority of the committee believe that that is now the legal limit, and believe it conscientiously. But should we undertake to fix that as the legal limit? Twenty-six million dollars of the

$44,000,000 are outstanding. They are now issued; they are now a part of the currency of the country. They are just as much the currency as that which was issued before. You cannot distinguish between them. You cannot say which of the $382,000,000 now outstanding is legal and which is illegal. So far as the United States are concerned, they are all debts of the United States which we are bound to pay, whether they have been issued legally or illegally. I do not understand even my friend from Delaware to dispute the duty and obligation of the United States to pay these notes, even if they have been illegally issued. There can be no question about it. It is impossible to distinguish between them. The only question is whether our agent exceeded his authority or not. Therefore, without raising the question as to the legality of this issue, reserving to each Senator his own opinion on the subject, we have adopted as the *status quo* $382,000,000, the amount now outstanding; and we recognize that amount as the maximum legal obligation of the United States in the form of notes, and we propose upon that basis to erect our superstructure. We therefore say that we will raise no question as to the mode of retiring the $26,000,000; we will simply say that the amount now outstanding shall never be exceeded. That is a recognition, at least, that they are outstanding lawfully and properly; at any rate, so far as the obligation of the United States to pay them is concerned.

"Mr. president, a limit ought to be fixed. But there is a difference of opinion as to what should be the limit. If I had the power to fix this limit I should say that the limit which was fixed by the old law should remain at $356,000,000; and I would provide a mode and manner of issuing United States bonds to retire the $26,000,000 slowly and gradually, without disturbing the ordinary business of the country. I would thereby seek to recover the ground we have lost by what has occurred since the panic, and go back to the standard prior to that time. But I know that would be very difficult; that would involve an increase of the bonded debt. Our revenues are not sufficient to call in this $26,000,000. We have no surplus revenue now as we had a year or two ago. We could only do it by the issue of bonds, and the process itself would be a very hard one. Besides, it is probable that public opinion and the judgment of Congress would not sustain such a proposition; and therefore it is hardly worth while to recommend it. We assume, therefore, that the $382,000,000 is the present limit, and we say that shall be the maximum limit.

     *   *   *   *   *   *   *   *   *

"I said it was a compromise by the committee. I speak of a majority of the committee. As a matter of course my friend is at liberty to dissent from any of its propositions. On questions of this kind committees are very rarely unanimous; but I will say that on this point a very decided majority of the committee concurred in the section.

"To the second section I wish to invite the careful and earnest attention of the Senate. This section is an honest effort to deal with the great problem of redemption. Every Senator who has spoken contemplates that a time must come when all the United States notes must be redeemed in coin. The public faith of the United States is so pledged. The notes were issued with the understanding that they should be paid in coin. No man could survive politically in this country who would declare that it was his purpose never to pay these notes in coin. My friend who now presides [Mr. Ferry, of Michigan], speaks always of his measure of inflation as a means of bringing about at some time specie payments ; and I will say that in the Senate I have not heard any Senator deny that it is the duty of the United States at some time to pay these notes in coin. In all this discussion there is at least that one point agreed upon. If I state this too strongly I hope I will be here corrected.

"Now, Mr. president, how shall it be done, and when shall it be done ? I say that now, nine years after the close of our Civil War, twelve years after these notes have been authorized and issued, five years after the dominant party has declared its purpose to pay them at the earliest day practicable, there should be no longer delay. The United States ought to do something toward the fulfillment of that pledge and the performance of that duty. There must be something very peculiar in the condition of our country that will justify a longer delay, a longer procrastination in the performance of this solemn pledge, this public policy—our own political obligation.

"Mr. president, this section is the result of the patient consideration of the committee on finance as to how this result is to be brought about ; and upon this very section there is most likely to be a contrariety and difference of opinion among Senators, because the mode and manner of redemption is the thing which has excited the public mind and upon which men all over the country differ. I wish, therefore, to deal with this question. We have got to pay these notes in coin. The time when is not defined by the law. Are we prepared now to fix a day when we will pay these notes in coin ? If the condition of our country was such as to justify it, I would greatly prefer fixing the time when these notes should be paid in coin ; but I am disposed to agree with what has been stated by the Senator from Indiana, and by other Senators, that in the present condition of our coinage, the present condition of our foreign trade, we are not prepared to fix a definite day when we will pay in coin. Why ? I find, by reference to official documents, that we now have in gold and silver coin in this country about $140,000,000. This statement of Dr. Linderman does not include the bullion on hand. How much that is I am not prepared to state. The whole amount of gold and silver coin in the country, however, is about $140,000,000. Some of that is in circulation in the Pacific states, but the bulk of it is in the treasury of the United States, the property of individuals and the property of the United States. The total annual production of gold and silver in this country cannot be estimated at over $70,000,000 ; and heretofore, at least $50,000,000 of this has been exported over and above the amount that has been imported. The balance of trade has been against us ; and although I do not regard that as entering much into the calculation, yet it is a fact that until recently, perhaps, the balance of trade has been against us. The annual coinage of the United States for the last year or two has been largely increasing, and last year the coinage of the United States was $38,689,183, besides a stamping into fine bars, which operates as a kind of coinage, of $27,517,000. So that there has been in fact converted, of gold and silver, into coin, or bars stamped by the United States, $66,000,000 during the last year, showing a use and employment of gold in this country that is now rapidly increasing.

"But still this state of affairs would not justify us in saying that we are prepared to declare a resumption of specie payments absolutely upon the basis of $800,000,000 of paper money, including our fractional currency. I am, therefore, not prepared to say that the United States can, on a fixed day, within a reasonable time—within such a time as would give confidence in our ability to perform it—say that we will absolutely redeem our notes in coin.

"I know that Senators here, for whose opinion I have the highest respect, who are probably more sanguine of our ability and capacity to do this than I am—many of those who have agreed with me and coöperated with me—think we are able and strong enough to fix the time for the absolute resumption of specie payments; but I have always doubted it. Indeed I have thought there was a better way to reach the great result. But if we cannot fix the time when we will redeem in coin, can we not give additional value to our United States notes, so as to gradually appreciate them to the coin standard, and thus advance toward specie payments if we cannot reach the goal? Because we cannot accomplish all that we have agreed to do in a given time, does that relieve us from the necessity of progressing in that direction? When we have before us a long journey that will take months to pass, perhaps years, shall we delay starting on that journey because we cannot reach the end of it in a year or two? Not at all. I therefore say that the time has arrived this moment when the United States ought to do something to advance its notes to the specie standard.

"Now what is that something? There are two propositions, and only two propositions, that have been made, aside from absolute coin redemption, that have had any strength whatever. One is to allow the United States notes to be received in payment of customs duties, the other is to allow United States notes to be converted into bonds. In regard to the first, I agree entirely that if the matter was open now to our choice and selection, one of the best methods we could adopt to advance our notes to par in gold would be by repealing that restriction which prevents the receiving of them for customs duties; but we are met there by the sacred pledge of the United States; we are met there by the fact that customs duties are, by the law of 1862, agreed to be collected in coin."

Mr. Bayard inquired:

"Does not the law provide that the customs duties shall be paid in coin or in notes of the United States? Is not the alternative given by the law?"

I replied:

"O, no. If the Senator will look at section 5 of the act of February 25, 1862—my friend from Vermont can turn to it in a moment—he will find that there is an express stipulation that the customs duties shall be collected in coin, and that this coin shall be set aside as a pledge— legal language is used—and shall only be applied, first, to the payment of the interest on the public debt, and, secondly, to the establishment of a sinking fund of one per cent. That was the basis of the obligation of the United States to pay in coin, and but for the fact that we collected our customs duties in coin during the war we could not have paid the interest on our public debt in coin, and therefore our bonds would have sunk out of sight. That pledge we cannot now violate ; and I never have yet been able to bring my mind to the consideration of any proposition whatever which would even shock or excite the fear of the public creditors in that respect. The safety of the public creditors consists in having a specific fund for the payment of their interest ; the principal will take care of itself ; and that fund has always been maintained in the darkest hours of the war. Except the propositions that have been made here and there to impair that fund by allowing a portion of the customs duties to be paid in currency, it has never been either invaded or threatened ; but all such propositions have been voted down. I, therefore, while I see the policy and the expediency of allowing these notes to be used in payment of customs duties, simply say we are precluded from that remedy because we have mortgaged that fund, and we have no power to take them for any purpose except that which the mortgage stipulates.

*　　*　　*　　*　　*　　*　　*　　*　　*

"We then come to the redemption in bonds. There is the moral obligation, on the part of the United States, which has issued its notes payable in coin, but for reasons of public policy does not pay in coin, to give to its creditors its notes bearing interest in place of coin. The United States cannot plead inability to pay interest on its notes if it will not or cannot pay the principal. Why should not the United States give its obligation bearing interest just as any individual would have to do? There is a moral obligation which rests upon the United States every day of the year to every holder of these notes, because, although the United States has not said when it will redeem these notes in coin, yet it is bound to do what it can to give them additional value. Although it may not receive these notes for customs duties, why can it not receive these notes in payment of bonds? Why discriminate against these notes in the sale of bonds? The answer is, that during the war we were compelled to do it ; and so we were. I very reluctantly yielded to that necessity. We were compelled to do it ; but, sir, it was only expected that that would continue to the close of the war ; and, practically, during the whole of the war these notes were received at par for bonds at par.

"If, therefore, we are to take any step toward specie payments, why not give to the holder of United States notes who demands it, a bond of the United States bearing a reasonable rate of interest in exchange for his notes? This should only be done after a reasonable time, so as to prevent any injury to the private contracts between debtor and creditor. When we cannot pay the coin, we are honorably and sacredly bound to pay in a bond of the United States, which in ordinary times would approximate to par in gold. In other words, this is a qualified redemption. The Senator from Indiana calls it a 'half-way measure.' It is a half-way measure in the right direction, and indeed it is practical specie payment."

The bill led to a long continuous debate which extended to the 6th of April, 1874. Several amendments were offered and adopted which enlarged the maximum of notes to $400,000,000, and greatly weakened the bill as a measure of resumption of specie payments. By reason of these amendments many of those who would have supported the bill as introduced voted against it on its passage, I among the number. The bill, however, passed the Senate by a vote of yeas 29 and nays 24. The title of the bill was changed to "A bill to fix the amount of United States notes and the circulation of national banks, and for other purposes." This change of title indicates the radical change in the provisions of the bill. Instead of a return to specie payments, it provided for an expansion of an irredeemable currency.

The bill, as it passed the Senate, was as follows:

"*Be it enacted*, etc., That the maximum amount of United States notes is hereby fixed at $400,000,000.

"Sec. 2. That forty-six millions in notes for circulation, in addition to such circulation now allowed by law, shall be issued to national banking associations now organized and which may be organized hereafter, and such increased circulation shall be distributed among the several states as provided in section 1 of the act entitled 'An act to provide for the redemption of the three per cent. temporary loan certificates and for an increase of national bank notes,' approved July 12, 1870. And each national banking association, now organized or hereafter to be organized, shall keep and maintain, as a part of its reserve required by law, one-fourth part of the coin received by it as interest on bonds of the United States deposited as security for circulating notes or government deposits; and that hereafter only one-fourth of the reserve now prescribed by law for national banking associations shall

Hiram, O. Sept 25, 1874

Dear Senator—

In accordance with the arrangement made with you and with the Central Committee, we have fixed you for a mass meeting at Warren on Saturday afternoon Oct 10th. I hope I shall not embarrass you by suggesting that in your speech you take occasion to say a few words in reference to my standing and public service as a Representative— It will do much to counteract the prejudice that a knewledge of Andersint acerie unto have created against one— I write about figures if you will be willing to speak at an other place the same evening— Let us me no very anxious to have you do so. Please telegraph me at Garrettsville Ohio tomorrow here— and oblige— Very truly Yours

J.A. Garfield

consist of balances due to an association available for the redemption of its circulating notes from associations in cities of redemption, and upon which balances no interest shall be paid."

The bill was taken up in the House of Representatives on the 14th of April, 1874, and, without any debate on its merits, was passed by the vote of 140 yeas and 102 nays.

On the 22nd of April, President Grant returned the bill to the Senate with his veto, and the Senate, upon the question, "Shall the bill pass notwithstanding the objections of the President of the United States," voted 34 yeas and 30 nays. I voted nay. The president of the Senate declared "that two-thirds of the Senators present not having voted in the affirmative the Senate refuses to pass the bill."

Thus, for that session, the struggle for resumption ended; but the debate in both Houses attracted popular discussion, and tended in the right direction. The evil effects of the stringency in monetary affairs, the want of confidence, the reduction of the national revenue, the decline of domestic productions, all these contributed to impress Congress with the imperative necessity of providing some measure of relief. Instead of inflation, of large issues of paper money by the United States and the national banks, there grew up a conviction that the better policy was to limit and reduce the volume of such money to an amount that could be maintained at par with coin.

During the canvass that followed I spoke in many parts of Ohio, confining myself chiefly to financial questions. The stringency of the money market which occurred the preceding year still continued, and great interest was manifested in the measures proposed during the preceding session, especially in the defeat of the bill to prevent the contraction of the currency. At the request of General Garfield I spoke in Warren in his Congressional district, where he met, for the first time, a decided opposition. I insert his autograph letter, the original being in his familiar hand writing:

HIRAM, OHIO, September 25, 1874.

DEAR SENATOR:—In accordance with the arrangement which I made with you and with the central committee, we have posted you for a mass meeting at Warren, on Saturday afternoon, October 10. I hope I shall not embarrass you by suggesting that in your speech you take occasion to say a few words in reference to my standing and public service as a representative. It will do much to counteract the prejudice that a small knob of persistent assailants have created against me. I write also to inquire if you will be willing to speak at another place the same evening. If so, we are very anxious to have you do so. Please telegraph me to Garrettsville, Ohio, and oblige,   Very truly yours,

J. A. GARFIELD.

CHAPTER XXV.

Bill for the Resumption of Specie Payments.

Decline in Value of Paper Money — Meeting of Congress in December, 1874 — Senate
Committee of Eleven to Formulate a Bill to Advance United States Notes to
Par in Coin — Widely Differing Views of the Members — Redemption of Frac-
tional Currency Readily Agreed to — Other Sections Finally Adopted —
Means to Prepare for and Maintain Resumption — Report of the Bill
by the Committee on Finance — Its Passage by the Senate by a
Vote of 32 to 14 — Full Text of the Measure and an Ex-
planation of What It Was Expected to Accomplish —
Approval by the House and the President.

WHEN Congress met in December, 1874, the amount
of United States notes outstanding was $382,000,-
000. The fractional notes outstanding convertible
into legal tenders amounted to $44,000,000, and the
amount of national bank notes redeemable in lawful money was
$354,000,000, in all $780,000,000. Each dollar was worth a fraction less than 89 cents in coin. While these notes were at a
discount coin did not and could not circulate as money. The
government exacted coin for customs duties and paid coin for
interest on its bonds. If there was an excess of coin received
from customs to pay interest then the excess was sold at a premium. If the receipts from customs were insufficient to pay
the interest on bonds, the government had to buy the coin and
pay the premium. The people who were demanding more
money to relieve the stringency did not see that the best way to
get more money into circulation was to adopt measures that
would make United States notes and bank notes equal to coin,
when all three forms of money would enter into circulation
and thus give them more money and all kinds of equal value.

While our paper money was depreciated the gold and silver
bullion from our mines went abroad and was converted into
foreign coin, while a large portion and perhaps a majority of
our people demanded more paper money, which declined in

value in exact proportion to its increase. During the war vast expenditures compelled us to use paper money; the return of peace and the excess of revenue over expenditures should have been promptly followed by coin payments or notes payable in coin. We delayed this process so long that the popular mind rested content with depreciated money, but the panic of 1873, and the feverish speculation which preceded it, convinced the great body of our business men that there was no remedy for existing evils but a return to specie payments.

Another bill concerning currency and free banking was reported by Horace Maynard, of Tennessee, on the 29th of January, 1874, from the committee on banking and currency of the House of Representatives, which provided for free banking and a gradual reduction and cancellation of United States notes by the issue of notes payable in gold in two years from the passage of the bill. This was fully debated in the House of Representatives and amended and passed. In the Senate it was reported by me from the committee on finance, with a substitute which provided for free banking and that on and after the 1st of January, 1877, any holder of United States notes might present them for payment either in coin or five per cent. bonds of the United States, at the suggestion of the Secretary of the Treasury. This substitute was amended in the Senate by striking out all provisions for the redemption of United States notes, leaving the measure one for free banking alone. The House disagreed to the amendments and a committee of conference was appointed which resulted in a measure fixing the amount of United States notes outstanding at $382,000,000, and making no provision for their redemption. It was a crude and imperfect measure. I voted for it because it provided for a redistribution of national banks among the states. I said: "Because I cannot get a majority of both Houses of Congress to agree to specie resumption I ought not therefore to refuse to vote for a bill on the subject of banking and currency." The bill was approved by the President on the 20th of June, 1874. This long struggle prepared the way for the result accomplished at the next session.

When Congress met in December, 1874, the feeling that the remedy for existing evils was the return to specie payments, was general among Republican Senators and Members. The abortive efforts of the previous session and the veto of President Grant of one of the bills referred to contributed to it. At the first Republican conference I called attention to the necessity of our uniting, if possible, on some measure that would advance United States notes to par in coin and moved that a committee of eleven Senators be created to formulate a bill for that purpose. It was agreed to, and, as the names of the Senators composing the committee have already been published, I feel justified in repeating them: The committee consisted of Senators John Sherman (chairman), William B. Allison, George S. Boutwell, Roscoe Conkling, George F. Edmunds, Thomas W. Ferry, F. T. Frelinghuysen, Timothy O. Howe, John A. Logan, Oliver P. Morton, and Aaron A. Sargent.

When the committee met it was agreed that each member should state how far he would go in the direction of specie resumption. When these statements were made it was manifest that the divergence of opinion was so great that an agreement was almost impossible. Yet, the necessity of an agreement was so absolute that a failure to agree was a disruption of the Republican party.

The first section of the act to provide for the resumption of specie payments, which related to the coinage and issue of fractional silver under the act of February 21, 1853, and the redemption of an equal amount of fractional currency until the whole amount of such fractional currency outstanding should be redeemed, was readily agreed to. This fractional currency was so worn and filthy, and it cost so much to reissue, that by general consent its destruction was agreed to, and its replacement by bright new silver coin, which followed, was heartily welcomed.

The second section was an unjust concession to the miners of gold. It repealed the coinage charge for converting standard gold bullion into coin. This charge had been maintained, not only to cover the cost of coining, but to prevent the exportation of American coins. If the coins were of less value than the bullion of which they were made, however small the difference, they would not be exported while bullion could be had for exportation. The concession was made and the charge for coinage of gold was prohibited.

The free banking provisions in the third section were not seriously contested. The contraction of the volume of United States notes as national bank notes increased, was one of the chief subjects of disagreement. It was finally agreed that this contraction should extend only to the retirement of United States notes in excess of $300,000,000.

The most serious dispute was upon the question whether United States notes presented for redemption and redeemed could be reissued. On the one side it was urged that, being redeemed, they could not be reissued without an express provision of law. The inflationists, as all those who favored United States notes as part of our permanent currency were called, refused to vote for the bill if any such provison was inserted, while those who favored coin payments were equally positive that they would vote for no bill that permitted notes once redeemed to be reissued. This appeared to be the rock upon which the party in power was to split. I had no doubt under existing law, without any further provision, but that United States notes could be reissued. It was finally agreed that no mention should be made by me for or against the reissue of notes, and that I must not commit either side in presenting the bill.

The date for general resumption of specie payments on all United States notes was fixed on the first of January, 1879, four years from the framing of this bill. The important and closing clause of the bill was referred to Mr. Edmunds and myself. It provided the means to prepare for and to maintain resumption. It placed under the control of the Secretary of the Treasury all the surplus revenue in the treasury, and gave him full power to issue, sell and dispose of, at not less than par in coin, any of the bonds described in the refunding act. We were careful to select phraseology so comprehensive that all the resources and credit of the government were pledged to redeem the notes of the United States, as fully and completely as our Revolutionary fathers pledged to each other their lives, their fortunes, and their sacred honor, in support of the declaration of American independence.

After every sentence and word of this bill had been carefully scrutinized, I was authorized by every member of the committee to submit it to the committee on finance, and to report it from that committee as the unanimous act of the Republican Senators. We naturally expected some support from Mr. Bayard and other Democratic Senators, who, no doubt, were in favor of specie payments, but they perhaps thought it best not to share the risk of the measure.

I reported the bill from the committee on finance on the 21st of December, 1874, and gave notice that on the next day I would call it up with a view to immediate action. On the 22nd, after the morning business, I moved to proceed to the consideration of the bill, and gave notice that I intended to press it to its passage, from that hour forward, at the earliest moment practicable. It was well understood that the bill was the result of a Republican conference. It was taken up by the decisive vote of 39 yeas to 18 nays.

It was not my purpose to do more than to present the provisions of the bill. My brief statement led to a desultory debate, participated in almost exclusively by Democratic Senators, the Republican Senators remaining silent. Several votes were taken, each showing a majority of more than two-thirds in favor of the bill and against all amendments. It passed the Senate without change by the vote of 32 yeas to 14 nays.

I here insert the bill as introduced and passed, with my statement in support of its provisions:

AN ACT TO PROVIDE FOR THE RESUMPTION OF SPECIE PAYMENTS.

"*Be it enacted by the Senate and House of Representatives of the United States of America in Congress assembled,* That the Secretary of the Treasury is hereby authorized and required, as rapidly as practicable, to cause to be coined, at the mints of the United States, silver coins of the denominations of ten, twenty-five, and fifty cents, of standard value, and to issue them in redemption of an equal number and amount of fractional currency of similar denominations, or, at his discretion, he may issue such silver coins through the mints, the sub-treasuries, public depositaries, and post offices of the United States ; and, upon such issue, he is hereby authorized and required to redeem an equal amount of such fractional currency, until the whole amount of such fractional currency outstanding shall be redeemed.

"Sec. 2. That so much of section three thousand five hundred and twenty-four of the Revised Statutes of the United States as provides for a charge of one-fifth of one per centum for converting standard gold bullion into coin is hereby repealed ; and hereafter no charge shall be made for that service.

"Sec. 3. That section five thousand one hundred and seventy-seven of the Revised Statutes, limiting the aggregate amount of circulating notes of national banking associations, be, and is hereby, repealed ; and each existing banking association may increase its circulating notes in accordance with existing law, without respect to said aggregate limit ; and new banking associations may be organized in accordance with existing law, without respect to said aggregate limit ; and the provisions of law for the withdrawal and redistribution of national bank currency among the several states and territories are hereby repealed. And whenever, and so often, as circulating notes shall be issued to any such banking association, so increasing its capital or circulating notes, or so newly organized as aforesaid, it shall be the duty of the Secretary of the Treasury to redeem the legal tender United States notes in excess only of three hundred millions of dollars, to the amount of eighty per centum of the sum of national bank notes so issued to any such banking association as aforesaid, and to continue such redemption as such circulating notes are issued until there shall be outstanding the sum of three hundred million dollars of such legal tender United States notes, and no more. And on and after the first day of January, anno Domini eighteen hundred and seventy-nine, the Secretary of the Treasury shall redeem in coin the United States legal tender notes then outstanding, on their presentation for redemption at the office of the assistant treasurer of the United States in the city of New York, in sums of not less than fifty dollars. And to enable the Secretary of the Treasury to prepare and provide for the redemption in this act authorized or required, he is authorized to use any surplus revenues from time to time in the treasury not otherwise appropriated, and to issue, sell, and dispose of, at not less than par in coin, either of the descriptions of bonds of the United States described in the act of Congress approved July fourteenth, eighteen hundred and seventy, entitled 'An act to authorize the refunding of the national debt,' with like qualities, privileges, and exemptions, to the extent necessary to carry this act into full effect, and to use the proceeds thereof for the purposes aforesaid. And all provisions of law inconsistent with the provisions of this act are hereby repealed."

I said :

" Mr. president, I do not intend to reopen the debate on financial topics of the last session. That debate was carried to such great length that it was not only exhaustive, but it was exhausting, not only mentally but physically.

The Senate is composed of the same persons who shared in that debate, and it is utterly idle for us, in this short session, to reopen it and to invite the discussion of the various topics presented in that debate. The Senate is now within less than three months, a little more than two months, of its adjournment, and there is a general feeling throughout the country, shared by all classes of people, that this Congress ought to give some definite notice to the people of this country as to their purpose in the important topics embraced in this bill ; and I say to Senators on all sides of the House that this bill contains enough to accomplish the important object declared by the title of the bill, and this without reviving all the troublesome and difficult questions which were discussed at the last session. It contains a few simple propositions which may be separated from the mass of financial topics discussed at the last session. Its purpose is declared upon the title of the bill, 'An act to provide for the resumption of specie payments.' Every word, every line, and every provision, of this bill is in harmony with that title. It will tend to promote the resumption of specie payments. It may fall short in many particulars of the desire of some Senators ; and it does go further in that direction than some Senators were willing to support at the last session. It is a bill which demands reasonable concession from every Member of the Senate. If we undertake now to seek to carry out the individual views of any Senator, we cannot accomplish the passage of any bill to promote this object, and therefore this bill has demanded of everyone who has consented to it thus far a surrender of some portions of his opinions as to measures and means to accomplish the great purpose. I will consider my duty done, so far as this bill is concerned, by simply stating its provisions and calling attention to the character of these provisions, without entering into a single topic that gave rise to the long discussion at the last session.

" The bill is intended to provide for the resumption of specie payments. The first section of the bill provides for the resumption of specie payments on the fractional currency. It is confined to that subject alone. It so happens that at this particular period of time the state of the money market, the state of the demand for silver bullion, and more especially the recent action of the German Empire, which has demonetized silver and thus cheapened that product, enables us now, without any loss of revenue, without any sacrifice, to enter the market for the purchase of bullion and resume specie payments on our fractional currency. The market price of bullion to-day will justify the government of the United States, without any sacrifice, at a price about equivalent to, or perhaps a trifle above, our fractional currency— scarcely a shadow above our fractional currency — to purchase silver bullion in the money markets of the world, mostly of our own production, perhaps entirely of our own production. This bill simply directs that the Secretary of the Treasury shall purchase this bullion and shall coin silver coin and substitute that in the place of fractional currency. To that extent it is a resumption of specie payments upon the silver standard for the fractional currency. This section is recommended not only by the Secretary of the

Treasury and the President of the United States, but I believe will meet the general concurrence of every Member of the Senate, and we fortunately are enabled to embrace the present time to commence this operation without any loss to the government, except perhaps the cost of the coinage of this silver may have to be paid out of the treasury of the United States. That coinage may be done in the ordinary course of business without any increase of expenditures. The mints of the United States are now prepared, immediately upon the passage of this bill, to resume the coinage of silver coins of all the legal denominations. Therefore the committee has provided that the Secretary of the Treasury shall proceed to coin the silver coins, and in one of several ways to issue them in the place of fractional currency.

" I need not dwell further upon this section, because I believe it will meet with the general assent of the Senate. It provides for the immediate resumption of specie payments upon the fractional currency, or at least as immediate as possible ; that is, as soon as the government of the United States can, in the mints of the United States, coin the silver coin. That process may continue one, two, or three years, how long we cannot tell, depending entirely upon the force that may be employed in that direction. It takes a much longer time to coin these small coins than gold coins, and the operation will probably take more time than it would to coin any considerable amount of gold coin."

Mr. Hamilton, of Maryland, inquired:

" I would ask the Senator if there is authority to reissue that fractional currency ? "

I said:

" I will come to that in a moment. The second section of this bill simply removes an inducement that now exists to export our gold bullion from the United States to Great Britain, where, by the long established laws of that country, they coin money free of charge. This section involved the surrender of about $85,000 a year of revenue ; that is, the government of the United States received last year for coining gold coin, $85,000, or one-fifth of one per cent. on forty-five millions of gold coined. The only sacrifice of revenue, therefore, by the second section of the bill, is the sacrifice or surrender of $85,000, which heretofore has been levied upon those who produce gold bullion in order to convert it into coin. In the opinion of many men, among them the Secretary of the Treasury, the director of the mint, and perhaps a large number of Senators heretofore, this will tend, in a slight degree at any rate, to prevent the exportation of the gold of our own country into foreign parts, because when the government of the United States undertakes to put gold bullion in the form of gold coin without additional charge the tendency will inevitably be for the gold bullion to flow into the mints for coinage, and being put into the form of American coin, it is thought by a great many people that this will tend to prevent its exportation. To the extent it does so it prepares us for specie payments. That is the whole of the second section.

"The third section of the bill contains only two or three affirmative propositions. The first is that after the passage of this act banking shall be free. Perhaps there is no idea stronger in the minds of the American people than a feeling of hostility against a monopoly — a privilege that one man or set of men can enjoy which is denied to another man or set of men. Under the law as it now stands banking is substantially free in the southern and some of the western states; but banking is not free in the great commercial states, in the older states, where wealth has accumulated for ages. This may be a mere sentimental point, but it is well enough to meet it; and by the operation of this bill banking is made free, so that there will be no difficulty hereafter for any corporation organized as a national bank either to increase its circulation or for banks, to be organized under the provisions of existing law, to issue circulating notes to any extent within the limits and upon the terms and provisions of the banking law. This section, therefore, by making banking free, provides for an enlargement of the currency in case the business of the community demands it, and in case any bank in the United States may think it advisable or profitable to issue circulating medium in the form of bank notes, under the conditions and limitations of the banking law. Coupled with that is a provision, an undertaking, on the part of the United States, that as banks are organized or as circulating notes are issued, either by old or new banks, the government of the United States undertakes to retire eighty per cent. of that amount of United States notes. In other words, it proposes to redeem the United States notes to the extent of eighty per cent. on the amount of bank notes that may be issued; and here is the first controverted question that arises on this bill and the first that is settled.

"It may be asked if we provide for the issue of circulating notes to banks, why not provide for the retirement of an equal amount of United States notes. The answer is that under the provisions of the banking act, by the law as it now stands, a bank cannot be organized and maintained in existence unless the reserve which is in that bank, or required for that bank in the ordinary course of business, either on its deposits or circulation, is at least equal to twenty per cent. of the amount of its circulating notes, so that it was believed, according to the judgment of the best business men of the country, and I may say with the comptroller of the currency, that the retirement of eighty per cent. of the amount of bank notes is fully equivalent to keeping the amount of circulating medium in actual circulation on the same footing, so that this provision of the bill neither provides for a contraction nor expansion of the currency, but leaves the amount to be regulated by the business wants of the community, so that when notes are issued to a bank eighty per cent. of the amount in United States notes is redeemed, and this process continues until United States notes are reduced to three hundred millions."

Mr. Schurz asked:

" Will the Senator permit me to ask him a question in reference to this section ? When the eighty per cent. of greenbacks are retired will they be destroyed and never issued again ? "

I replied:

" I will speak of that in a moment in connection with other sections. Now, Mr. president, that is all there is in regard to banking in this bill and also in regard to the retirement of the United States notes until the time for the resumption of specie payments comes, when this bill provides for actual redemption in coin of all notes presented. It has always been a question in the minds of many people as to whether it is wise to fix a day for specie payments. That matter was discussed at the last session of Congress by many Senators, and the general opinion seemed to be that if we would provide the means by which specie payments would be resumed it might not be necessary to fix the day ; but, on the other hand, it is important to have our laws in regard to the currency fix a probable time, or a certain time, when everybody may know that his contracts will be measured by the coin standard. We also know, by the example of other nations which have found themselves in the condition in which we are now placed, and by some of the states when specie payments were suspended, that they have adopted a specific day for the resumption of specie payments. In England, by the bank act of 1819, they provided for the resumption of specie payments in 1823, making four years. In our own state—in New York, in Ohio, in nearly all the states—when there has been a temporary suspension of specie payments a time has been fixed when the banks were compelled to resume, and this bill simply follows the example that has been set by the states, by England, and by other nations, when they have been involved in a like condition.

" This bill also provides ample means to prepare for and to maintain resumption. I may say the whole credit and money of the United States is placed by this bill under the direction of the proper executive officers, not only to prepare for but to maintain resumption, and no man can doubt that if this bill stands the law of the land from this time until the 1st day of January, 1879, specie payments will be resumed, and that our United States notes will be converted at the will of the holder into gold and silver coin.

" These are all the provisions contained in this bill. They are simple and easily understood, and every Senator can pass his judgment upon them readily.

" Now I desire to approach a class of questions that are not embraced in this bill. Many such, and I could name fifty, are not included in this bill ; and I may say this : that if there should be a successful effort, by the Senate of the United States, to ingraft any of this multitude of doubtful or contested questions upon the face of this bill it would inevitably tend to its defeat. I am free to say that if I were called upon to frame a bill to accomplish the purpose declared in the title of this bill, I would have provided some means of gradual redemption between this and the time fixed for final specie payments. All these means are open to objection.

"There have been three different plans proposed to prepare for specie payments, and only three. They are all grouped in three classes. One is what is called the contraction plan. The simplest and most direct way to specie payments is, undoubtedly, the gradual withdrawal of United States notes or the contraction of the currency. Now, we know very well the feeling with which that idea is regarded, not only in this Senate, but all through the country. It is believed to operate as a disturbing element in all the business relations of life ; to add to the burden of the debtor by making scarce that article in which he is bound to pay his debts ; and there has been an honest, sincere opposition to this theory of contraction. Therefore, although it may be the simplest and the best way to reach specie payments, it is entirely omitted from this bill.

"The second plan, that I have favored myself often, and would favor now, if I had my own way, and had no opinion to consult but my own, is the plan of converting United States notes into a bond that would gradually appreciate our notes to par in gold. That has always been a favorite idea of mine. There is nothing of that kind in this bill, except those provisions which authorize the Secretary of the Treasury to issue bonds to retire the greenbacks as bank notes are issued ; and it also authorizes the Secretary of the Treasury to issue bonds to provide for and to maintain resumption. I therefore have been compelled to surrender my ideas on this bill in order to accomplish a good object without using these means that have been held objectionable by many Senators.

"The third plan of resumption has been favored very extensively in this country, which is the plan of a graduated scale for resumption in coin or bullion ; what I call the English plan. That is, that we provide now for the redemption, at a fixed rate or scale of rates, of so much gold for a specific sum of United States notes. At present rates we would give about $90 of gold for $100 of greenbacks, and then provide for a graduated scale by which we would approach specie payments constantly, and reach it at a fixed day. This may be called a gradual redemption. This, also, is objectionable to many persons, from the idea that it compels us to enter the money markets of the world to discount our own paper. It is an ideal objection, but a very strong objection ; an objection that has force with a great many people. We have undertaken to redeem these notes in coin, and it is at least a question of doubtful ethics whether we ought to enter into the markets of the world and buy our own notes at a discount. Although that plan has been adopted in England and successfully carried into execution, yet there is a strong objection to it in this country, and therefore that mode is abandoned.

"Either of these plans I could readily support ; but they have met and will meet with such opposition that we cannot hope to carry them or ingraft them in this bill without defeating it. We have then fallen back on these gradual steps: First, to retire the fractional currency; second, to reduce United States notes as bank notes are increased; and then to rest our plan of redemption upon the declaration, made on the faith of the United States, that at the time fixed by the bill we will resume the payment of the United States notes in coin at par. That is the whole of this bill."

On the 7th of January, 1875, the bill was considered in the House of Representatives and, after a very brief conversational debate, passed by the vote of yeas 136, nays 98.

On the 14th of January, 1875, the President sent a message to the Senate approving the bill but also containing recommendations of further legislation upon matters that had been carefully excluded from the bill. He added at the close of the message this paragraph:

"I have ventured upon this subject with great diffidence, because it is so unusual to approve a measure—as I most heartily do this, even if no further legislation is attainable at this time—and to announce the fact by message. But I do so, because I feel that it is a subject of such vital importance to the whole country, that it should receive the attention of, and be discussed by, Congress and the people, through the press and in every way, to the end that the best and most satisfactory course may be reached of executing what I deem most beneficial legislation on a most vital question to the interests and prosperity of the nation."

Thus, after a memorable debate, extending through two sessions of Congress, a measure of vital importance became a law, and when executed completely accomplished the great object proposed by its authors. The narrative of the steps leading to resumption under this act will be more appropriate hereafter.

CHAPTER XXVI.

RESUMPTION ACT RECEIVED WITH DISFAVOR.

It Is Not Well Received by Those Who Wished Immediate Resumption of Specie Payments — Letter to "The Financier" in Reply to a Charge That It Was a "Political Trick," etc. — The Ohio Canvass of 1875 — Finance Resolutions in the Democratic and Republican Platforms — R. B. Hayes and Myself Talk in Favor of Resumption — My Recommendation of Him for President — A Democrat Elected as Speaker of the House — The Senate Still Republican — My Speech in Support of Specie Payments, Made March 6, 1876 — What the Financial Policy of the Government Should Be.

THE resumption act was generally received with disfavor by those who wished the immediate resumption of specie payments. It was the subject of much criticism in the financial journals, among others "The Financier," which described it as a political trick, an evasion of a public duty, and as totally inadequate for the purpose sought to be accomplished. I took occasion to reply to this article in the following letter:

UNITED STATES SENATE CHAMBER,
WASHINGTON, January 10, 1875.

DEAR SIR: — As I am a subscriber to 'The Financier' you will probably allow me to express my surprise at the course you have pursued in respect to the finance bill recently passed by Congress. Claiming as you do to be a 'monetary and business' journal, you might be expected to treat fairly a measure affecting so greatly the interests you represent; but you have not done so. You have treated it as a political trick, an evasion, a disgrace to Congress. You complained that it was passed without debate and that its inception and passage were shameful. But as you say in your last number 'that it is well to examine it hopefully, to find *what good may have been done, if any,* although from a *bad motive,*' I take the liberty to correct errors even in your 'hopeful' view of the law, so that you may be more hopeful still. You assume that the Secretary of the Treasury is not authorized to issue five per cent. gold bonds to prepare for and to maintain resumption, because the amount of five per cent. bonds authorized in the act of 1870 is nearly exhausted. This is an error. The secretary can issue either four and a half or five per cent. gold bonds to an amount sufficient to execute the law. The act of 1870 is only referred to for the 'description' of the bonds to be issued, and the only limit to the amount is the sum necessary, and the only limit to their sale is that they must not be sold at less than par in coin.

You say that *one trick* of the bill is 'that there is no provision for carrying on the withdrawal of legal tenders after their maximum reaches $300,000,000.' Now this 'trick' was advocated by you one year ago; it was voted for by every specie paying Member of Congress at the last session, and nearly every writer on the subject has contended that if the legal tenders were reduced to $300,000,000, and the treasury was supported by a reasonable reserve, specie payments could be resumed and maintained. Besides, no one believes that $100,000,000 of bank notes will be issued under this act, and this provision only relieves some people from an idle fear of an improbable event. You must have noticed that when banks retire their notes, as they have done and will do rapidly, this is a reduction of the currency, while every issue of notes to new or old banks involves a retirement of a ratable amount of United States notes. What you say about playing with a movable 'reserve' is equally wrong. Neither the fractional currency nor the 'eighty-two million' redeemed can be reissued, and I stated so when the bill was pending under debate, and no lawyer could put a different construction upon the bill. As to United States notes, a part of the $300,000,000 redeemed after resumption of specie payments, we did refuse to provide whether they could be reissued or not, and we acted wisely. When the question is hereafter determined by Congress, the controversy will be whether the notes *when reissued* shall have the *legal tender* quality, or be simple treasury notes receivable for public dues.

Last session the public press scolded at our long and fruitless debate on finances, and I agreed with the press. This session the same Senators, enlightened by the long debate and heeding the call of the press, gave to the subject the most careful and deliberate consideration, and agreed upon this bill without much debate, and yet the press is not happy. The act does not go so far as I wished, but everything in it is right in itself, and is in the right direction. Its chief merit is that it establishes a public policy which no political party or faction will be strong enough to overthrow, and which, if it had not been adopted now, the Democratic party in the next Congress would have defeated. The pretense that the Democratic party, as represented in the next House, would have favored any bill for specie payments is utterly false. Therefore the measure grants to the Secretary of the Treasury powers enough to execute it, but if we can secure the aid of a Democratic House we can make it more certain and effective.

Very truly yours,   JOHN SHERMAN.

EDITOR OF 'FINANCIER.'

In the Ohio canvass of 1875 the resumption act became the chief subject of controversy. R. B. Hayes, after having previously served for four years as governor of the state, was again nominated for that office. William Allen, then governor, was renominated upon the Democratic ticket, in opposition to the resumption act and in favor of fiat money, upon which issue the election mainly turned.

The eighth resolution of the Democratic platform was as follows:

"That the contraction of the currency heretofore made by the Republican party, and the further contraction proposed by it, with a view to the forced resumption of specie payment, have already brought disaster to the business of the country, and threaten it with general bankruptcy and ruin. We demand that this policy be abandoned, and that the volume of currency be made and kept equal to the wants of trade, leaving the restoration of legal tenders to par with gold, to be brought about by promoting the industries of the people and not by destroying them."

The Republican convention in their second resolution declared:

"That a policy of finance be steadily pursued, which, without unnecessary shock to business or trade, will ultimately equalize the purchasing capacity of the coin and paper dollar."

Ex-Governor Hayes and I opened the state canvass in the county of Lawrence on July 31, 1875, and took strong ground in favor of the resumption act. At the beginning it appeared that the people were not quite prepared for any measure looking to resumption, but as the contest progressed and the subject was fully and boldly presented by Mr. Hayes and myself, the tide of opinion ran in our favor and Hayes was elected by a small majority. The ex-governor did not evade the issue, but in every speech supported and urged the policy of resumption as a matter of the highest interest.

In the approaching nomination for President, Governor Hayes was frequently spoken of as a candidate to succeed General Grant, and I also was mentioned in the same connection, but, feeling confident that Mr. Hayes would be a stronger candidate than myself, and fully determined not to stand in his way, on the 21st of January, 1876, I wrote a letter to a personal friend, and the Member of the Senate from the district in which I live, in which I urged the nomination of Governor Hayes as the most available candidate in the approaching presidential canvass. This letter no doubt contributed to his strength and prevented any possibility of the division of the vote of Ohio in the convention. The letter I give in full :

WASHINGTON, D. C., January 21, 1876.

DEAR SIR :—Your letters of the 2nd and 19th inst. were duly received, and I delayed answering the first sooner partly from personal reasons, but mainly that I might fully consider the questions raised by you as to the approaching presidential contest, the importance of which cannot be over-stated. The election of a Democratic President means a restoration to full power in the government of the worst elements of the rebel Confederacy.

The southern states are to be organized, by violence and intimidation, into a compact political power only needing a small fragment of the northern states to give it absolute control where, by a majority rule of the party, it will govern the country as it did in the time of Pierce and Buchanan.

If it should elect a President and both Houses of Congress, the con-stitutional amendments would be disregarded, the freedmen would be nominally citizens but really slaves ; innumerable claims, swollen by perjury, would be saddled upon the treasury, the power of the general government would be crippled, and the honors won by our people in subduing rebellion would be a subject of reproach rather than of pride. The only safeguard from these evils is the election of a Republican President, and the adoption of a liberal Republican policy which should be fair and even generous to the south, but firm in the maintenance of all the rights won by the war. Our election in Ohio last fall shows that even under the most adverse circumstances we can win on this basis.

Every movement made by this Democratic House of Representatives is an appeal to every man who ever voted with the Republican party to rally to its support again, and' to every man who fought in the Union army to vote with us to preserve the results of his victory.

All we need is such a presidential ticket as will give assurance that we mean to stand by our principles, and that will administer the government honestly and economically.

As to candidates, the drift of public opinion is rapidly reducing the list and has already settled adversely the chances of many of them. Above all, it has positively closed the question of a third term. The conviction that it is not safe to continue in one man for too long a period the vast powers of a President, is based upon the strongest reasons, and this conviction is sup-ported by so many precedents set by the voluntary retirement at the end of a second term of so many Presidents that it would be criminal folly to dis-regard it. I do not believe that General Grant ever seriously entertained the thought of a third term. but even if he did, the established usage against it would make his nomination an act of suicide.

It would disrupt our party in every Republican state.

Happily for us we do not need to look for the contingency of his nomination.

Among the candidates now generally named, I have no such preference that I could not heartily support either of them. They are men of marked ability, who have rendered important public services, but, considering all things, I believe the nomination of Governor Hayes would give us the more strength, taking the whole country at large, than any other man. He is better known in Ohio than elsewhere, and is stronger there than elsewhere, but the qualities that have made him strong in Ohio will, as the canvass progresses, make him stronger in every state. He was a good soldier, and, though not greatly distinguished as such, he performed his full duty, and I noticed, when traveling with him in Ohio, that the soldiers who served under him loved and respected him. As a Member of Congress he was not a leading debater, or manager in party tactics, but he was always sensible, industrious, and true to his convictions and the principles and tendencies of his party, and commanded the sincere respect of his colleagues. As a governor, thrice elected, he has shown good executive abilities and gained great popularity, not only with Republicans but with our adversaries. On the currency question, which is likely to enter largely into the canvass, he is thoroughly sound, but is not committed to any particular measure, so as to be disabled from coöperating with any plan that may promise success. On the main questions, protection for all in equal rights, and the observance of the public faith, he is as trustworthy as any one named. He is fortunately free from the personal enmities and antagonisms that would weaken some of his competitors, and he is unblemished in name, character or conduct, and a native citizen of our state.

I have thus, as you requested, given you my view of the presidential question, taken as dispassionately as if I was examining a proposition in geometry, and the result drawn from these facts, not too strongly stated, is that the Republican party in Ohio ought, in their state convention, to give Governor Hayes a united delegation instructed to support him in the national convention, not that we have any special claim to have the candidate taken from Ohio, but that in General Hayes we honestly believe the Republican party of the United States will have a candidate for President who can combine greater popular strength and greater assurance of success than other candidates, and with equal ability to discharge the duties of President of the United States in case of election. Let this nomination be thus presented, without any wire pulling or depreciation of others and as a conviction upon established facts, and I believe Governor Hayes can be and ought to be nominated. But if our state is divided or is not in earnest in this matter it is far better for Governor Hayes and the state that his name be not presented at all. We have never sufficiently cultivated our state pride, with every reason for indulging it, and thus our proper influence has been wasted and lost. Now we have a good opportunity to gratify it, and at the same time contribute to the common good. Remember me kindly to personal friends in the Senate.

Very truly yours, JOHN SHERMAN.

HON. A. M. BURNS.

The election of Members of Congress in 1874 resulted in the choice of a large majority of Democrats in the House of Representatives of the 44th Congress, the term of which commenced on the 4th of March, 1875. A majority of the Senate being still largely Republican, it became difficult to pass any measure of a political character during that Congress. President Grant, on the 17th of February, 1875, issued his proclamation convening the Senate at 12 o'clock on the 5th of March following, to receive and act upon such communications as might be made to it on the part of the Executive. The session continued until the 24th of March. It was largely engaged in questions affecting the State of Louisiana, which had been the scene of violent tumult and almost civil war. As these events are a part of the public history of the country I do not deem it necessary to refer to them at length. These disturbances continued during the whole of that Congress, and, in 1876, approached the condition of civil war.

The regular meeting occurred on the 6th of December, 1875, when Thomas W. Ferry, of Michigan, was elected president *pro tempore* of the Senate, and Michael C. Kerr, a Democratic Representative from the State of Indiana, was elected by a large majority as speaker of the House.

This political revolution was no doubt caused largely by the financial panic of 1873, and by the severe stringency in monetary affairs that followed and continued for several years. Many financial measures of the highest importance in respect to the public credit were acted upon, but were generally lost by a disagreement between the two Houses. I do not deem it necessary to refer to the political questions that greatly excited the public mind during that session. Congress was largely occupied in political debate on questions in respect to the reconstruction of the states lately in rebellion, upon which the two Houses disagreed. Among other measures which failed was the act amendatory of the acts authorizing the refunding of the national debt, which passed the Senate but was not considered by the House.

During this session of Congress all sorts of financial plans were presented in each House, but all were aimed, directly or indirectly, at the resumption act, although that act itself was adopted as a remedy for existing financial evils, and especially to deal with and prevent the recurrence of such a panic as that of 1873. I took occasion, on the presentation of the resolutions of the New York Chamber of Commerce in favor of the resumption of specie payments, at the time provided by the resumption act, to discuss the policy of that measure more fully than I thought it expedient to do when, as a bill, it was pending in the previous Congress. This speech was made in the Senate on the 6th of March, 1876. It was the result of great labor and care, and was intended by me to be, and I believe is now, the best presentation I have ever been able to offer in support of the financial policy of the government, and especially in support of the resumption of specie payments. I said :

" Mr. president, I have taken the unusual course of arresting the reference to the committee of finance of the memorial of the Chamber of Commerce of New York, in order to discuss, in an impersonal and nonpartisan way, one of the questions presented by that memorial, and one which now fills the public mind and must necessarily soon occupy our attention. That question is, 'Ought the resumption act of 1875 be repealed ? ' The memorial strongly opposes such repeal, while other memorials, and notably those from the boards of trade of New York and Toledo, advocate it. These opposing views are supported in each House of Congress, and will, when our time is more occupied than now, demand our vote.

" And, sir, we are forced to consider this question when the law it is proposed to repeal is only commencing to operate, now, three years before it can have full effect—during all which time its operation will be under your eye and within your power—and while the passions of men are heated by a presidential combat, when a grave question, affecting the interests of every citizen of the United States, will be influenced by motives entirely foreign to the merits of the proposition. And the question presented is not as to the best means of securing the resumption of a specie standard, but solely whether the only measure that promises that result shall be repealed. We know there is a wide and honest diversity of opinion as to the agency and means to secure a specie standard.

" When any practicable scheme to that end is proposed I am ready to examine it on its merits ; but we are not considering the best mode of doing the thing, but whether we will recede from the promise made by the law as it stands, as well as refuse all means to execute that promise. If the law is deficient in any respect it is open to amendment. If the powers vested in the secretary are not sufficient, or you wish to limit or enlarge them, he is your servant, and you have but to speak and he obeys. It is not whether we will accumulate gold or greenbacks or convert our notes into bonds, nor whether the time to resume is too early or too late. All these are subjects of legislation. But the question now is whether we will repudiate the legislative declaration, made in the act of 1875, to redeem the promise made and printed on the face of every United States note, a promise made in the midst of war, when our nation was struggling for existence, a promise renewed in March, 1869, in the most unequivocal language, and finally made specific as to time by the act of 1875.

"And let us not deceive ourselves by supposing that those who oppose this repeal are in favor of a purely metallic currency, to the exclusion of paper currency, for all intelligent men agree that every great commercial nation must have both ; the one as the standard of value by which all things are measured, which daily measures your bonds and notes as it measures wheat, cotton, and land ; and also a paper or credit currency, which, from its convenience of handling or transfer, must be the medium of exchanges in the great body of the business of life. Statistics show that in commercial countries a very large proportion of all transfers is by book accounts and notes, and more than nine-tenths of all the residue of payments is by checks, drafts, and such paper tools of exchange.

"Of the vast business done in New York and London not five per cent. is done with either paper money or gold or silver, but by the mere balancing of accounts or exchange of credits. And this will be so whether your paper money is worth forty per cent. or one hundred per cent. in gold. The only question is whether, in using paper money, we will have that which is as good as it promises, as good as that of Great Britain, France, or Germany ; as good as coin issued from your mints ; or whether we will content ourselves with depreciated paper money, worth ten per cent. less than it promises, every dollar of which daily tells your constituents that the United States is not rich enough to pay more than ninety per cent. on the dollar for its three hundred and seventy millions of promises to pay, or that you have not courage enough to stand by your promise to do it.

"Nor are we to decide whether our paper money shall be issued directly by the government or by banks created by the government ; nor whether at a future time the legal tender quality of United States notes shall continue. I am one of those who believe that a United States note issued directly by the government, and convertible on demand into gold coin, or a government bond equal in value to gold, is the best currency we can adopt ; that it is to be the currency of the future, not only in the United States, but in Great Britain as well; and that such a currency might properly continue to be a legal tender, except when coin is specifically stipulated for.

"But these are not the questions we are to deal with. It is whether the promise of the law shall be fulfilled, that the United States shall pay such of its notes as are presented on and after the 1st day of January, 1879, in coin; and whether the national banks will, at the same time, redeem their notes either in coin or United States notes made equal to coin; or whether the United States shall revoke its promise and continue, for an indefinite period, to still longer force upon the people a depreciated currency, always below the legal standard of gold, and fluctuating daily in its depreciation as Congress may threaten or promise, or speculators may hoard, or corner, or throw out your broken promises. It is the turning point in our financial history, which will greatly affect the life of individuals and the fate of parties, but, more than all, the honor and good faith of our country.

"At the beginning of our national existence, our ancestors boldly and hopefully assumed the burden of a great national debt, formed of the debts of the old confederation and of the states that composed it; and, with a scattered population and feeble resources, honestly met and paid, in good solid coin, every obligation. After the War of 1812, which exhausted our resources, destroyed our commerce, and greatly increased our debt, a Republican administration boldly funded our debt, placed its currency upon the coin basis, promptly paid its interest, and reduced the principal; and within twenty years after that war was over, under the first Democratic President, paid in coin the last dollar, both principal and interest, of the debt. And now, eleven years after a greater war, of grander proportions, in which, not merely foreign domination threatened us, but the very existence of our nation was at stake, and after our cause has been blessed with unexampled success, with a country teeming with wealth, with our credit equal to that of any nation, we are debating whether we will redeem our promises, according to their legal tenor and effect, or whether we will refuse to do so and repeal and cancel them.

" I would invoke, in the consideration of this question, the example of those who won our independence and preserved it to us, to inspire us so to decide this question that those who come after us may point to our example of standing by the public faith now solemnly pledged, even though to do so may not run current with the temporary pressure of the hour, or may entail some sacrifice and hardship.

" What then is the law it is proposed to repeal? I will state its provisions fully in detail, but the main proposition — the essential core of the whole — is the promise, to which the public faith is pledged, that the United States will redeem in gold coin any of its notes that may be presented to the treasury on and after the 1st day of January, 1879. This is the vital object of the law. It does not undertake to settle the nature of our paper money after that, whether it shall be reissued again, whether it shall thereafter be a legal tender, nor whether it shall or shall not supersede bank notes. All this is purposely left to the future. But it does say that on and after that day the United States note promising to pay one dollar shall be equal to the gold dollar of the mint.

" The questions then arise—

First. Ought this promise be performed?

Second. Can we perform it?

Third. Are the agencies and measures prescribed in the law sufficient for the purpose?

Fourth. If not, what additional measures should be enacted?

"Let us consider these questions in their order, with all the serious deliberation that their conceded importance demands.

"And first, ought this promise be fulfilled?

"To answer this we must fully understand the legal and moral obligations contained in the notes of the United States. The purport of the note is as follows:

'THE UNITED STATES PROMISES TO PAY THE BEARER ONE DOLLAR.'

"This note is a promise to pay one dollar. The legal effect of this note has been announced by the unanimous opinion of the Supreme Court of the United States, the highest and final judicial authority in our government.

"The legal tender attribute given to the note has been the subject of conflicting decisions in that court, but the nature and purport of it is not only plain on its face, but is concurred in by every judge of that court and by every judicial tribunal before which that question has been presented.

"In the case of Bank vs. Supervisors, 7 Wallace, 31, Chief Justice Chase says:

'But, on the other hand, it is equally clear that these notes are obligations of the United States. Their name imports obligation. Every one of them expresses upon its face an engagement of the nation to pay to the bearer a certain sum. The dollar note is an engagement to pay a dollar, and the dollar intended is the *coined* dollar of the United States, a certain quantity in weight and fineness of gold or silver, authenticated as such by the stamp of the government. No other dollars had before been recognized by the legislation of the national government as lawful money.'

"Again, in the case of Bronson vs. Rhodes, 7 Wallace, 251, Chief Justice Chase says:

'The note dollar was the promise to pay a coined dollar.'

"In the Legal Tender Cases, 12 Wallace, 560, Justice Bradley says:

'It is not an attempt to *coin* money out of a valueless material, like the coinage of leather, or ivory, or cowry shells. *It is a pledge of the national credit.* It is a *promise* by the government to *pay dollars;* it is not an attempt to *make* dollars. The standard of value is not changed. The government simply demands that its credit shall be accepted and received by public and private creditors during the pending exigency. . . .

'No one supposes that these government certificates are never to be paid; that the day of specie payments is never to return. And it matters not in what form they are issued. . . . Through whatever changes they pass, their ultimate destiny is *to be* paid.'

"In all these legal tender cases there is not a word in conflict with these opinions.

"Thus, then, it is settled that this note is not a dollar, but a debt due; a promise to pay a dollar in gold coin. Congress may define the weight and fineness of a dollar, and it has done so by providing a gold coin weighing twenty-five and eight-tenths grains of standard gold nine-tenths fine. The promise is specific and exact, and its nature is fixed by the law and announced by the court. Here I might rest as to the nature of the United States note ; but it is proper that I state the law under which it was issued and the subsequent laws relating to it.

"The act of February 25, 1862, gave birth to this note as well as the whole financial policy of the war. The first section of that act authorizes the Secretary of the Treasury to issue, upon the credit of the United States, United States notes to the amount of $150,000,000, payable to bearer at the treasury of the United States. The amount of these notes was subsequently increased during the war to the maximum sum of $450,000,000, but the nature and character of the notes was the same as the first issue. The enlargement of the issue did not in the least affect the obligation of the United States to pay them in coin. This obligation was recognized in every loan law passed during the war ; and to secure the note from depreciation the amount was carefully limited, and every quality was given to it to maintain its value that was possible during the exigencies of the war. I might show you, from the contemporaneous debates in Congress, that at every step of the war the notes were regarded as a temporary loan, in the nature of a forced loan, but a loan cheerfully borne, and to be redeemed soon after the war was over.

"It was not until two years after the war, when the advancing value of the note created an interest to depreciate it in order to advance prices for purposes of speculation, that there was any talk about putting off the payment of the note. The policy of a gradual contraction of the currency with a view to specie payments was, in December, 1865, concurred in by the almost unanimous vote of the House of Representatives, and the act of April 12, 1866, authorized $4,000,000 of notes a month to be retired and canceled. No one then questioned either the policy, the duty, or the obligation of the United States to redeem these notes in coin.

"Why has not this obligation been performed? How comes it that fourteen years after these notes were issued, and eleven years after the exigency was over, we are debating whether they shall be paid, and when they shall be paid? We may well pause to examine how this plain and positive obligation has so long been deferred by a nation always sensitive to the public honor.

"The fatal commencement of this long delay was in this provision of the act, approved March 3, 1863, as follows:

'And the holders of United States notes issued under, and by virtue of, said acts, shall present the same, for the purpose of exchanging the same for bonds as therein provided, on or before the 1st day of July, 1863, and thereafter the right so to exchange the same shall cease and determine.'

"Thus, under the pressure of war, and the plausible pretext of a statute of limitations, the most essential legal attribute of the note was taken away.

This act, though convenient in its temporary results, was a most fatal step, and for my part in acquiescing in, and voting for it, I have felt more regret than for any act of my official life. But it must be remembered that the object of this provision was not to prevent the conversion of notes into bonds, but to induce their conversion. It was the policy and need of the government to induce its citizens to exchange the notes freely for the bonds, so that the notes might again be paid out to meet the pressing demands of the war. It was believed that if this right to convert them was limited, in time this would cause them to be more freely funded; and Mr. Chase, then Secretary of the Treasury, anxious to prevent a too large increase of the interest of the public debt, desired to place in market a five per cent. bond instead of a six per cent. bond. The fatal error was in not changing the right to convert the note into a five per cent. bond instead of a six per cent. bond. This was, in fact, proposed in the committee on finance, but it was said that a right to convert a note into a bond at any time, was not so likely to be exercised as if it could only be exercised at the pleasure of the government. And this plausible theory to induce the conversion of notes into bonds was made the basis, after the war was over, for the refusal of the United States to allow the conversion of its notes into bonds, and has been the fruitful cause of the continued depreciation and dishonor of United States notes for the last five years, during which, our five per cent. bonds have been at par with gold, while our notes rise and fall in the gamut of depreciation from six to twenty per cent. below gold.

"Notwithstanding that the right to convert notes into bonds was taken away, yet, in fact, they were, during the war, received par for par for bonds; and after the war was over all the interest-bearing securities were converted into bonds; but the notes — the money of the people — the artificial measure of value, the most sacred obligation, because it was past due, was refused either payment or conversion, thus cutting it off from the full benefit of the advancing credit of the government, and leaving to it only the forced quality of legal tender in payment of debts.

"Shortly after the war was over, and notably during the presidential campaign of 1868, the question arose whether the bonds of the United States were payable in coin or United States notes. Both notes and bonds were then below par in coin, the notes ranging from sixty-seven to seventy-five cents in coin; and five per cent. bonds from seventy-two to eighty cents in coin. Here again the opportunity was lost to secure the easy and natural appreciation of our notes to the gold standard. Had Congress then authorized the conversion of notes into bonds, when both were depreciated, both would have advanced to par in gold; but, on the one hand, it was urged that this would cause a rapid contraction, and, on the other, that the right to convert the note into a bond was not specie payment; it was only the exchange of one promise for another. It was specie payment they very much favored, but did not have the wisdom then to secure. If the advocates for specie payment had then supported a restoration of the right to convert notes into bonds, they would have secured their object with but little opposition. But all measures to fund the notes at the pleasure of the holder were defeated, and, instead, there was ingrafted into the act to strengthen the public credit—

"First, a declaration 'that the faith of the United States is solemnly pledged to the payment in coin, or its equivalent, of all the obligations of the United States not bearing interest, known as United States notes, and of all the interest-bearing obligations of the United States,' except such as by the law could be paid in other currency than gold and silver.

"Second, 'and the United States also solemnly pledges its faith to make provision, at the earliest practicable period, for the redemption of the United States notes in coin.'

"Here again, the obligation of the government to pay these notes in coin was recognized, its purpose declared, and the time fixed, 'as early as practicable.' What was the effect of this important act of Congress? Without adding one dollar to the public debt, or the burden of the debt, both bonds and notes rose in value. Within one year, the bonds rose to par in gold, making it practicable to commence the refunding of six per cent. bonds into five per cent bonds. The notes rose under the stimulus of this new promise, in one year, from seventy-six cents to eighty-nine cents in gold, but no steps whatever were made to redeem them.

"The amount of bank notes authorized was increased fifty-four millions. The executive department pursued the policy of redeeming debts not due, and did, from an overflowing treasury, reduce very largely the public debt, but no steps whatever were taken to advance the value of our notes. The effect of the act of 1869 was exhausted on the adjournment of Congress in March, 1870, when the United States notes were worth eighty-nine cents in gold; and thereabouts, up and down, with many fluctuations, they have remained to this day. The bondholder, secure in the promise to him, is happy in receiving his interest in gold, with his bond above par in gold. The note holder, the farmer, the artisan, the laborer, whose labor and production is measured in greenbacks, still receives your depreciated notes, worth ten per cent. less than gold you promised him 'at the earliest day practicable.' The one has a promise performed and the other a promise postponed.

"Thus we stood when the panic of 1873 came upon us; with more paper money afloat than ever circulated before in any country of the world. Even then, had we stood firmly, the hoarding tendency of the panic would have advanced our notes toward the gold standard, and, in fact, did so during the months of September and October, until the premium on gold had fallen to eight per cent. But, sir, at this critical moment, the Secretary of the Treasury, acting, no doubt, in good faith, but I think without authority of law, issued twenty-six millions more United States notes — part of the notes retired and canceled under previous acts. And now, notwithstanding all the talk about contraction of the currency, we have not withdrawn one-half of this illegal issue. On the 1st of September, 1873, we had three hundred and fifty-six million notes outstanding. Three months afterward, we had three hundred and eighty-two million; and now we have three hundred and seventy-one million.

"Sir, it was under the light of these events, after the fullest discussion ever given in Congress, of any question — after debate before the people during the recess of Congress, and full deliberation last winter — this act was passed. There was and is now great difference of opinion as to the details, but the vital promise made to the note holder to make his note as good as gold in January, 1879, was concurred in by a large majority of both Houses, and by many who opposed the bill as too slow in its operations. This act of honor and public faith was applauded by the civilized world and concurred in by our constituents, the doubts only being as to the machinery to carry it into effect. The time was fixed by those who most feared resumption, and no one proposed a longer time. My honorable friend from Indiana [Mr. Morton] truly said (in the recent campaign in Ohio) that he participated in framing it ; and he and those who agreed with him fixed the time so remote as to excite the unfounded charge that the bill was a sham, a mere contrivance to bridge an election.

"And now, sir, to recapitulate this branch of the question, it is shown that the holder of these notes has a promise of the United States, made in February, 1862, to pay him one dollar in gold coin; that the legal purport of this promise has been declared by the Supreme Court; that we have taken away from this note one of the legal attributes given it, which would long since have secured its payment in coin — that when the note was authorized and issued, it was understood as redeemable in coin when the war was over; that our promise to pay it was renewed in 1869 — 'at as early a day as practicable;' that by reason of our failure to provide for its payment, it is still depreciated below par more than one-tenth of its nominal value; that we renewed this promise, and made it definite as to time, by act of 1875; that it is a debt due from the United States, and in law and honor due now in coin. Yet it is proposed to recall our promise to redeem this note in coin three years hence. I say, sir, this would be national dishonor. It would destroy the confidence with which the public creditor rests upon the promises contained in your bonds. It would greatly tend to arrest the process by which the interest on your bonds is reduced. It would accustom our people to the substitution of a temporary wave of popular opinion for its written contract or promise. It would weaken in the public mind that keen sense of honor and pride which has always distinguished the English-speaking nations in dealing with public obligations.

"An old writer thus describes 'public credit:'

'Credit is a consequence, not a cause; the effect of a substance, not a substance; it is the sunshine, not the sun; the quickening *something*, call it what you will, that gives life to trade, gives being to the branches and moisture to the root; it is the oil of the wheel, the marrow in the bones, the blood in the veins, and the spirits in the heart of all the negoce, trade, cash, and commerce in the world.

'It is produced, and grows insensibly from fair and upright dealing, punctual compliance, honorable performance of contracts and covenants; in short, it is the offspring of universal probity.

'It is apparent even by its nature; it is no way dependent upon persons, parliament, or any particular men or set of men, as such, in the world, but upon their conduct and just behavior. Credit never was chained to men's names, but to their actions ; not to families, clans, or collections of men ; no, not to nations. It is the honor, the justice, the fair dealing, and the equal conduct of men, bodies of men, nations, and people, that raise the thing called credit among them. Wheresoever this is found, credit will live and thrive, grow and increase ; where this is wanting, let all the power and wit of man join together, they can neither give her being nor preserve her life.

' Arts have been tried on various occasions in the world to raise credit ; art has been found able with more ease to destroy credit than to raise it. The force of art, assisted by the punctual, fair, and just dealing abovesaid, may have done much to form a credit upon the face of things, but we find still the honor would have done it without the art, but never the art without the honor. Nor will money itself, which, Solomon says, answers all things, purchase this thing called credit or restore it when lost. . . .

' Our credit in this case is a public thing. It is rightly called by some of our writers *national credit.* The word denominates its original. It is produced by the nation's probity, the honor and exact performing national engagements.'

" And, sir, passing from considerations of public honor, there are many reasons of *public policy* which forbid the repeal of the act of 1875. That act was generally regarded as the settlement of a financial policy by which at least the party in power is bound, and upon the faith of which business men have conducted their affairs and made their contracts. Debts have been contracted and paid with the expectation that at the time fixed the gold standard would measure all obligations, and a repeal of the act would now reopen all the wild and dangerous speculation schemes that feed and fatten upon depreciated paper money. The influence that secures this repeal will not stop here. If we can recall our promise to pay our notes outstanding why should we not issue more? If we can disregard our promise to pay them, why shall we regard our promise not to issue more than $400,000,000, as stipulated for by the act of 1864? If we can reopen the question of the payment of our notes, why may we not reopen the question as to the pay-ment of our bonds? Is the act of 1869 any more sacred than the act of 1875? And if we can reopen these questions, why not reopen the laws requiring the payment of either interest or principal of the public debt? They rest upon acts of Congress which we have the power to repeal. If the public honor cannot protect our promise to the note holder, how shall it pro-tect our promise to the bondholder? Already do we see advocated in high places, by numerous and formidable organizations, all forms of repudiation,.

which, if adopted, would reduce our nation to the credit of a robber chief — worse than the credit of an Algerine pirate, who at least would not plunder his own countrymen. And if the public creditor had no safety, what chance would the national banks—creations of our own and subject to our will—have in Congress? It has already been proposed to confiscate their bonds, premium and all, as a mode of paying their notes with green-backs. What expedient so easy if we would make money cheap and abundant? Or, if so extreme a measure could be arrested, what is to prevent the permanent dethronement of gold as a measure of value, and the substitution of an interconvertible currency bond, bearing three and sixty-five hundredths per cent. interest, as a standard of value ; and when it becomes too expensive to print the notes to pay the interest, reduce the rate. Why not ? Why pay three and sixty-five hundredths per cent. when it is easier to print three ? It is but an act of Congress. And when the process of repudiation goes so far that your notes will not buy bread, why then declare against all interest, and then, after passing through the valley of humiliation, return again to barter, and honor, and gold again.

"Sir, if you once commence this downward course of repudiation there is but one ending. You may, like Mirabeau and the Girondists, seek to stem the torrent, but you will be swept away by the spirit you have evoked and the instrument you have created. You complain now of a want of confidence which makes men hoard their money. Will you, then, destroy all confidence? No, sir, no ; the way to restore confidence is to inspire it by fulfilling your obligations. You cannot make men lend you ; you cannot make men sell you anything — either bread, or meat, or wool, or iron, or anything that is or that can be created — except for that which they choose to take. You may depreciate the money which you offer, but it will only take more of it to buy what you want. It is true that the creditor may, by your laws, be compelled to take your money however much you depreciate it, but he cannot buy back that which he sold, or its equivalent in other necessaries of life, and thus he is cheated of part of what he sold. During the war, while money was depreciating, many a simple man gleefully counted his gains as he sold his goods or crops at advancing prices, but he found out his mistake when, with his swollen pile, he tried to replace his stock in trade or laid in his supplies. Sir, this policy exhausts itself in cheating the man who buys or sells or loans on credit, who produces something to sell on credit ; whether that something be food or clothing ; whether it be a necessity or a luxury of life. Productive labor, honest toil, whether of the farmer or the artisan, is deeply interested in credit. It is credit that gives life and competition to trade ; and credit is destroyed by every scheme that impairs, delays, or even clouds an obligation.

"Again, sir, an irredeemable and fluctuating currency always raises the rate of interest on money, while a stable currency or an improving currency always reduces the rate of interest. This is easily shown by statistics, but the reason is so obvious that proof is not needed. If a man lends his money he wants it back again with its increase ; but if the money, when it is to be paid back, is like to be worth less than when he thinks of loaning it, he will not loan it except at such rates as will cover the risk of depreciation. He will prefer to buy land or something of stable value. If money is at the gold standard, or is advancing toward that standard, he will loan it readily at a moderate interest, for he knows he will receive back money of at least equal value to that he loaned. Again, sir, with a depreciated currency great domestic productions are cut off from the foreign market ; for it is impossible that with such a currency we can compete on equal terms with rival nations, whose industry rests upon a specie standard. As we approach such a standard, we are now able, as to a few articles, to compete with foreign industry ; but it is only as to articles in the manufacture of which we have peculiar advantages. Let us rest our industries on that standard, and soon we could compete in the markets of the world in all the articles produced from iron, wood, leather, and cotton, the raw basis of which are our natural productions. And it must be remembered that all the countries with which we compete are specie-paying countries.

"A country that does not rest her industry upon specie is necessarily excluded from the great manufacturing industries of modern civilization, and is self-condemned to produce only the raw basis for advanced industry. Cheap food, climate, soil, or natural advantages, such as cheap land, vast plains for pasture, or rich mines, may give to a country wealth and prosperity in spite of the evils of depreciated paper money ; but when we come in competition with the world in the advanced grades of production which give employment to the skilled mechanic, we must rest such industry upon the gold basis, or we enter the lists like a knight with his armor unbound.

"Again, sir, a depreciated and fluctuating currency is a premium and bounty to the broker and money changer. Under his manipulation our paper standard of value goes up and down, and he gambles and speculates, with all the advantages in his favor. Good people look on and think that it is gold that is going up and down ; that their money is a dollar still, and trade and traffic in that belief. But the shrewd operator calculates daily the depreciation of our note, the shortening of the yard stick, the shrinkage of the acre, the lessening of the ton, and thus it is that he daily adds to his gains from the indifference or delusion of our people.

"Sir, it is an old story, often repeated in our day, and most eloquently epitomized by Daniel Webster in the often-quoted passage of his speech, in which he said :

'A disordered currency is one of the greatest of political evils. It undermines the virtues necessary for the support of the social system and encourages propensities destructive of its happiness. It wars against industry, frugality, and economy ; and it fosters the evil spirit of extravagance and speculation. Of all contrivances for cheating the laboring classes of mankind, none has been more effectual than that which deluded them with paper

money. Ordinary tyranny, oppression, excessive taxation, these bear lightly
on the happiness of the mass of the community, compared with the fraudulent currencies and the robberies committed by depreciated paper. Our own
history has recorded for our instruction enough, and more than enough, of
the demoralizing tendency, the injustice, and the intolerable oppression of
the virtuous and well-disposed, of a degraded paper currency authorized by
law or in any way countenanced by government.'

"Sir, we must meet this question of specie payments, not only because
the public honor is pledged to do so, but also for the lesser reason that it is
our interest to do so. The only questions we should permit ourselves to discuss are the means and measures of doing so.

"And now, sir, let us examine the reasons that have been given for
the repeal of the resumption act by those who, though favoring resumption, yet think the act should be repealed for one or other of the following
reasons :

First. That it is not advisable to fix a day for resumption.
Second. Or at least until the balance of trade is in our favor.
Third. That it produces a contraction of the currency.
Fourth. That it injuriously adds to the burden of existing debts.

Let us glance at these objections.
"First. As to fixing a day for resumption.
"If it was possible to agree upon measures that would secure resumption
without fixing a time, I agree it would not be indispensable, though not
unadvisable, to fix a time ; but such agreement is utterly impossible. Of
the multitude of schemes that have been presented to me by intelligent men
trying to solve this problem, many could have been selected that in my
opinion would be practicable ; but of all of them not one ever has or is
likely to secure the assent of a majority of a body so numerous as Congress.
One difficulty we have encountered is that the Democratic party, though in
the minority, has never presented in any form, through any leading member,
a plan for resumption, but with widely differing opinions has joined in
opposing any and every measure from the other side. I understand from
the papers that our Democratic friends, through a caucus, and through a
caucus committee of which my colleague is chairman, have been laboring to
agree upon a plan for specie payments. After his frequent speeches to us
about a caucus measure — a great question being submitted to a caucus —
about secret conclaves, about shams and deceptions, and such like polite and
friendly comments upon the work of the Republican party, I might greet
my colleague with such happy phrases about *his* caucus ; but I will not, but,
on the contrary, I commend his labors, and sincerely hope that he and his
political friends may agree upon some plan to reach a specie standard, and
not one to avoid it, to prevent it, to defer it. Under color of intending to
prepare for it, I hope they will not make their measure the pretext for
repealing the law as it stands, which fixes a day for resumption and will
secure the end we both aim at.

"I frankly state for the Republican party that, while we could agree to fixing the time for specie payments and upon conferring the ample and sufficient powers upon the Secretary of the Treasury contained in this law, we could not agree in prescribing the precise mode in which the process should be executed. Nor, in my opinion, was it at all essential that we should. Much must be left to the discretion of the officer charged with the execution of such a law. The powers conferred, as I shall show hereafter, are ample ; and the discretion given will be exercised under the eye of Congress.

"And, sir, there is strong force in the fact that in every example we have of the successful resumption of specie payments, in this and other countries, a fixed day has been named by legislative authority, and the details and power of execution have been left to executive authority. Thus, in Great Britain, the act of parliament of July 2, 1819, fixed the time for full resumption at the 1st day of May, 1823, and for a graduated resumption in gold at intermediate dates ; and for fractional sums under forty shillings to be paid in silver coin ; and the governor and directors of the Bank of England were charged with its execution, and authorized at their discretion to resume payment in full on the 1st day of May, 1822. France is now successfully passing through the same process of resumption, the time being fixed (two years ago) for January 1, 1878, and now practically attained.

"In our own country many of the states have presented similar laws in case of suspended bank payments, and in some cases the suspended banks have, by associated action, fixed a time for general resumption, and each bank adopted its own expedient for it. Sir, the light of experience is the lamp of wisdom. I can recall no case of successful resumption where a fixed future time has not been presented beforehand, either by law or agreement ; while the historical examples of repudiation of currency have come by the drifting process, by a gradual decline of value, by increased issues, and a refusal to provide measures of redemption, until the whole mass disappeared, dishonored and repudiated.

"This concurrence in the mode of resumption by so many governments was the strongest possible instruction to Congress when fixing a plan of resumption for the United States, and should satisfy reasonable men of its wisdom.

"Besides, it would seem to be but fair that everyone should have plain notice of so important a fact. If the measures only were presented and no time fixed it would be a matter of speculation, and the discretionary powers of the Secretary of the Treasury could be exercised with a view to hasten or postpone the time to the injury of individuals.

"As to the date selected, I can only repeat it was placed as remote as any one suggested ; far more so than is necessary to secure the object, and so that the fluctuations of value will scarcely exceed in four years what they have frequently been in a single year. It allows ample time to arrange all the relations of debtor and creditor, and to enable Congress to provide any additional measure in aid of resumption, or, if events make it expedient, to postpone the time."

CHAPTER XXVII.

My Confidence in the Success of Resumption.

Tendency of Democratic Members of Both Houses to Exaggerate the Evil Times —
Debate Over the Bill to Provide for Issuing Silver Coin in Place of Fractional
Currency — The Coinage Laws of the United States and Other Countries — Joint Resolution for the Issue of Silver Coin — The " Trade Dollar " Declared Not to Be a Legal Tender — My Views on the Free
Coinage of Silver — Bill to Provide for the Completion of
the Washington Monument — Resolution Written by
Me on the 100th Anniversary of the Declaration
of Independence — Unanimously Passed in
a Day by Both Houses — Completion
of the Structure Under the Act.

IT seemed to be the policy of a majority of the Democratic
Members of both the Senate and the House to exaggerate
the evils and discouragements of the times, while in fact
the people were rapidly recovering from the results of the
panic of 1873, and all branches of industry were, to a greater
or less extent, starting into life anew, and to prevent the resumption of specie payments, and, if possible, to repeal the act
providing for such resumption. This policy undoubtedly
checked the process of refunding the public debt, which progressed slowly, and was confined to an exchange of bonds bearing five per cent. interest for those bearing six per cent.

I took a much more hopeful view of the situation, and in the
many speeches I made in that Congress, I stated my confidence,
not only in the process of resumption and refunding, but in the
rapid improvement of all branches of industry as we progressed
towards specie payments. In a speech I made in the Senate on
the 6th of January, 1876, on a bill "to further provide for the
redemption of legal tender United States notes in accordance
with existing law," I said:

"Sir, we ought to take a hopeful view of things in this centennial year of
our country. Look at the aggregate results. A century ago we were three
million people ; now forty million ; then we had a little border on the
Atlantic ; we are now extended to the Pacific. See what has been accom-

plished in a hundred years.   During that time there have been periods of darkness and doubt.   Every seven or ten or twelve years, periodically, there have been times of financial distress.   We have lived through them all.   I believe, and I trust in God, that this very year is the beginning of another period of prosperity, and that all these dark clouds, which gentlemen are trying to raise up from the misery of the past two or three years and from their own clouded imaginations, will entirely disappear.   I believe that even now we are in the sunshine of increasing prosperity, and that every day and every hour will add to our wealth and relieve us from our distresses.

"Sir, things are not so unhopeful as Senators seem to think.   We have made a promise to be executed three years hence, and every step of our legislation, if any is had, should look in that direction.   We may not adopt any measure or may not deem that any is necessary ; but, if any be adopted, it ought to look to the execution of that promise, and we ought to enter on the performance of this duty with hopeful trust in the continued prosperity of our country.   All this gloom and doubt, all this arraignment of official statements, this doubt of our sufficient revenues, this doubt of our ability to meet and advance our destiny, always falls upon my ear with painful surprise.   Senators, the task we have before us may be a difficult one, as it has always proved to be difficult to resume the specie standard whenever, for any reason, a nation has fallen from it, but it is a duty that must be executed, and it ought to be executed without the spirit of party warfare, without these appeals, directly or indirectly, to party tactics.   The pledges made one year ago, although not voted for by the Democratic party, are pledges binding upon their honor and their faith as they are upon mine, and I trust in God that we shall join together in all the proper steps to carry out those pledges."

This bill was referred to the committee on finance, but no action was taken upon it, as the committee preferred to await the action of the House.

The resumption act provided for the payment and destruction of the fractional currency then in circulation, to the amount of $40,000,000, and the substitution of silver coins in all respects, such as were defined by the coinage act of 1853. This was to be the first step in preparation for the general resumption of coin payments in January, 1879.   It became necessary to provide for the coinage of fractional silver coins, and a bill for this purpose, entitled "A bill to provide for a deficiency in the Printing and Engraving Bureau, and for the issue of the silver coin of the United States, in place of the fractional currency," was reported by Mr. Randall, on the 2nd of March, 1876, from the committee on appropriations of

the House. It was subsequently considered, amended and
passed by the House, after a long debate, participated in by
many of the leading Members. Much to my surprise, Mr.
Hewitt and Mr. Ward, prominent Members from New York,
opposed the measure, denounced the resumption act, and
prophesied its failure. Mr. Hewitt, in support of his position,
quoted passages from the reports of Mr. Bristow, then Secretary of the Treasury, and predicted the utter failure of resumption, unless the United States notes were entirely withdrawn.
He insisted that if silver coin was issued to replace fractional
currency, the coin would disappear from circulation, leaving
the people without any currency for the smaller necessaries of
life. In the progress of the debate, it became manifest that
the larger portion of the Democratic Members would vote
against every measure proposed to aid in the execution of the
resumption act.

The bill passed the House on the 31st of March by the vote
of 123 yeas and 100 nays. In the Senate it was referred to the
committee on finance, and reported back with amendments.
The third section of the bill, as it came from the House, provided for the coinage of the silver dollar, of the weight of 412.8
grains troy, standard silver, and made that dollar a legal tender
at its nominal value, to an amount not exceeding twenty dollars in any one payment, except for customs duties and interest on the public debt, and that the "trade dollar" should not,
thereafter, be a legal coin. This section was stricken out.

In the remarks made by me, upon this bill, on the 10th day
of April, 1876, I gave, in detail, the history of each of the coinage laws of the United States, and of the then existing coinage
laws of Great Britain, France, Belgium, Germany, Switzerland
and Italy. I had taken great pains to collect this information
and to procure translations of the laws of the several countries
named. The then recent changes, made by Germany, and their
effect upon the coinage of other nations, were carefully stated.
The general conclusions which I drew from a reference to these
statutes of various countries, were:

"First. It is impossible, in the nature of things, to fix the precise value of
silver and gold. We have tried it three times and failed.

" Second. Whenever either coin is worth more in the market than the rate fixed by the law, it flees from the country. That we have twice proved. That is the admitted economic law. It is the Gresham law ; a law of currency named from the name of its discoverer. He wrote a book to show that always the poorer currency would drive out of circulation a superior currency ; and his book gave name to the theory that is called the law of Gresham. It is the universal law of political economy that, whenever two metals or two moneys are in circulation, the least valuable will drive out the most valuable ; the latter will be exported.

" The third proposition is that the example of several great European nations, as well as of the United States, proves that to prevent the depreciation of silver the tendency of modern nations is to issue it as a token coinage somewhat less in intrinsic value than gold, and maintain its value by issuing it only as needed, at par with the prevailing currency, and to make it a limited legal tender. I may say that has been acted upon by every great Christian nation. Russia and Austria have not yet gold coinage at all, but still they have their values based upon gold.

" Fourth. That the demonetizing of silver tends to add to the value of gold, and that though its relative value ebbs and flows it is more stable compared to gold than any other metal, grain, or production. Its limit of variation for a century is between fifteen to seventeen for one in gold.

" Fifth. That both coins are indispensable, one for small and the other for large transactions.

" Sixth. That the causes of the decline of silver are temporary. It is still used by a great majority of mankind as the standard of value. Its use in France and the United States will, on resumption, more than counteract its decline in Germany.

" Seventh. The general monetizing of silver now, when it is unnaturally depreciated, would be to invite to our country, in exchange for gold or bonds, all the silver of Europe, and at last it would leave us with a depreciated currency.

" Eighth. The decline of silver enables us now to exchange silver coin of the old standard for fractional currency, leaving the exchange optional with the holder, until we have the courage, as we now have the ability, to redeem it in gold.

" Ninth. More silver can be maintained at par than we have now of fractional currency.

" Tenth. The redemption of a part of our currency would advance its purchasing power, while the silver in circulation will counteract the contraction of the currency."

This bill became a law on the 17th of April, 1876. The second section provided :

" That the Secretary of the Treasury is hereby directed to issue silver coins of the United States of the denomination of ten, twenty, twenty-five and fifty cents of standard value, in redemption of an equal amount of fractional currency, whether the same be now in the treasury awaiting redemption, or whenever it may be presented for redemption ; and the Secretary of the Treasury may, under regulations of the treasury department, provide for such redemption and issue by substitution, at the regular sub-treasuries and public depositaries of the United States, until the whole amount of fractional currency outstanding shall be redeemed. And the fractional currency redeemed under this act shall be held to be a part of the sinking fund provided for by existing law, the interest to be computed thereon as in the case of bonds redeemed under the act relating to the sinking fund."

A joint resolution for the issue of silver coin was introduced in the House by Mr. Frost, of Massachusetts, on the 1st of May, 1876. The object of this resolution was to expedite the issue of minor coin and the retirement of fractional currency. It was referred to the committee on banking and currency, reported back and passed the House June 10. In the Senate it was referred to the committee on finance, reported favorably and passed with amendments June 21. The House disagreed to the amendments of the Senate, and a committee of conference was appointed composed of John Sherman, George S. Boutwell, and Louis V. Bogy, managers on the part of the Senate, and H. B. Payne, and Samuel J. Randall, managers on the part of the House. The report of the conferees was agreed to, and the bill having passed both Houses it was approved by the President on the 22nd of July. It provided:

" That the Secretary of the Treasury, under such limits and regulations as will best secure a just and fair distribution of the same through the country, may issue the silver coin at any time in the treasury to an amount not exceeding ten million dollars, in exchange for an equal amount of legal tender notes ; and the notes so received in exchange shall be kept as a special fund, separate and apart from all other money in the treasury, and be reissued only upon the retirement and destruction of a like sum of fractional currency received at the treasury in payment of dues to the United States ; and said fractional currency, when so substituted, shall be destroyed and held as part of the sinking fund, as provided in the act approved April seventeen, eighteen hundred and seventy-six."

It also provided : " That the trade dollar shall not hereafter be a legal tender, and the Secretary of the Treasury is hereby authorized to limit, from time to time, the coinage thereof to such an amount as he may deem sufficient to meet the export demand for the same."

It also provided that the amount of subsidiary silver coin authorized should not exceed $50,000,000. The silver bullion was to be purchased from time to time at market rate by the Secretary of the Treasury, from any money in the treasury not otherwise appropriated, and any gain or seigniorage arising from the coinage was to be paid into the treasury.

These provisions in respect to subsidiary coin were in a large measure executed prior to the 4th of March, 1877, and tended, in my opinion, to facilitate the progress of the resumption of specie payments on the 1st of January, 1879. The debate on these measures occupied a large portion of the time of both Houses of Congress, and presented in every possible aspect all the financial questions involved in coinage, resumption and refunding. Anyone desiring a full knowledge of the view then taken of the act revising the laws in respect to coins and coinage, approved February 12, 1873, will find in the debate a full history of that act, given at a time when it was fresh in the memory of the great body of Senators and Members.

I supported the coinage of the old silver dollar in a speech in the Senate made on the 8th of June, 1876, two years before the appearance of the "Bland bill," or the "Allison bill." Silver bullion was then declining in market value. The resumption act provided for the gradual replacement of fractional currency by silver coins of the character and form provided for by the coinage act of 1853. When that act passed the old silver dollar was not coined or in circulation. It was more valuable in the market than a dollar in gold, and, if coined, would have been exported as bullion. In the revision of the coinage laws of 1873, it was dropped from the list of coins, and its further coinage was prohibited by a clause providing that no coins should be made at the mint except those provided for in that act. The history of this act and the reasons for prohibiting the coinage of the old dollar have been fully stated in a previous chapter of this work. In place of the old dollar the trade dollar, containing 420 grains of silver, was provided for. This trade dollar, coined for, and at the expense of, the owner of the bullion deposited at the mint, was, in the revision of the laws of the United States, unintentionally made a legal tender for five dollars, the same as the minor coins issued by the mint on government account. As silver declined in value, the trade dollar became less valuable than a dollar in gold, and the owners of bullion deposited it in the mint, and received in exchange trade dollars costing less than a dollar in gold, but, being a legal tender for five dollars, it could be forced upon the people of California, then upon the gold standard, at a profit to the owner of the bullion. Mr. Sargent, a Senator from California, early in the session introduced a bill enlarging the limit of legal tender of minor coins, and repealing the legal tender quality of the trade dollar. This bill was referred to the committee on finance, and was reported with an amendment to strike out all after the enacting clause, and insert:

"That section 3586 of the Revised Statutes of the United States be, and hereby is, amended to read as follows :

"The silver coins of the United States, except the trade dollar, shall be a legal tender at their nominal value for any amount not exceeding five dollars in any one payment."

This simple bill was made the text of a long debate in the Senate that continued during the greater part of that session. The provision that "the trade dollar shall not hereafter be a legal tender" was transferred to the joint resolution already mentioned which became a law on the 22nd of July.

In my speech on Mr. Sargent's bill I said :

"This bill proposes to restore the old silver dollar, and with it and the subsidiary coins of the United States to redeem the United States notes and fractional currency. The dollar to be restored is the same dollar that had existed from 1792 to 1873; and the subsidiary coins to be issued are the same in form and value as have been issued since 1853. I have already stated in my remarks, made on the 11th of April last, the history of these silver coins and the relation of silver and gold to each other, not only in the United States, but in the countries with which we have the most extensive commercial relations.

"The two main questions are :

*   *   *   *   *   *   *   *   *

"First. Shall silver coin be exchanged for United States notes as well as for fractional currency? And,

"Second. Is it wise to recoin the old silver dollar with a view to exchange it for United States notes?"

In this speech I favored the restoration of the silver dollar of the precise character and description of the dollar that existed from 1792 to 1873, but, as the market value of the silver in this dollar had greatly fallen, I insisted that the dollar should be coined from bullion purchased by the government at market price, so that the people of the United States would receive the difference between the cost of the bullion and the face value of the coin, the same principle that was adopted in what is known as the Bland-Allison act of 1878. I did not, however, propose the full legal tender quality that was given to the dollar by the act when adopted, but that it should be placed among the other silver coins, and be a legal tender only for twenty dollars.

The plan proposed by me was to set aside a portion of the surplus revenue or sinking fund of each year applicable to the payment of the public debt, for the purchase of silver bullion to be coined into silver dollars of the old standard. I said:

"The bill reported by the committee on finance thus provides for an immediate resumption of specie payments in silver coin, and thus completes the first and most difficult step of the problem. It neither disturbs nor deranges business, nor stirs up the phantom of contraction. It is in exact accordance with existing law, and leaves the silver coin, as now, a subsidiary coin, a legal tender only for limited amounts.

"The next question presented by this bill is, shall we return to our silver coinage the old silver dollar. And here I am met by the objections of the Senator from Vermont, but his objections are rather to the amendments proposed by the Senator from Missouri, than to the report of the committee. The committee propose the silver dollar, not as a legal tender for gold contracts, but only as a tender for currency contracts not exceeding twenty dollars in any one payment. I would prefer to leave the silver dollar and stand upon its intrinsic value as a legal tender the same as the smaller coin ; but there is no injustice in enlarging the limit to twenty dollars, and but for the reasons I will state hereafter there is no injustice in making it a legal tender for all currency contracts. The silver dollar has that intrinsic value which in all periods of our history has made it a favorite coin, not only for domestic uses but for exportation. It furnishes silver bullion in a shape and form more convenient for handling than any other form of coin.

*   *   *   *   *   *   *   *   *

"When the old silver dollars are issued at par with the United States notes, a large amount of them will be taken as a reserve by the people to meet future needs, with or without a legal tender quality. As their issue is not peremptory, and the aggregate cannot exceed the surplus revenue or sinking fund, there is no danger of an overissue, while their existence among the people will be the best reserve when gold alone becomes the full standard of value.

"Every argument already mentioned in favor of subsidiary silver coin is equally potent in favor of the silver dollar. It will be eagerly taken in payment of United States notes. It is purely a voluntary exchange. It is the cheapest mode in which we can redeem United States notes. It is specie resumption in the old time-honored standard of silver dollars of full weight and fineness. It will accustom our people to distinguish between the real dollar that pays where it goes and a paper dollar which only promises to pay. It will prepare the way for full resumption in gold. To the extent proposed by the committee, and to be used as a purely voluntary approach to a full specie standard, it is open to no objection or criticism, and should be assented to by gentlemen who have differed with each other on the present resumption law or on the merits and dangers of contraction and expansion."

The vital difference between the free coinage of silver, and the limited coinage of that metal on government account, is that with free coinage the standard of value would be the cheaper money. With silver at its present price in the market the dollar would be worth but a little over fifty cents. The coinage being free to the holders of silver bullion no coins would be made except the cheaper coins of least purchasing power. On the other hand, the coinage of silver on government account enables us to maintain the silver coins at par with gold, without respect to the market value of the silver bullion. Any nominal profit from this coinage inures to the benefit of the whole people of the United States and not merely to the producers of silver bullion. This distinction has always appeared to me so marked and clear, and the argument so strong in favor of limiting the coinage of silver to the amount demanded as a convenience of the people for the smaller transactions of life, that I cannot sympathize with a policy that aims merely to secure the cheapest money for the discharge of obligations contracted upon more valuable money.

Among the measures that became a law at this session was a concurrent resolution, introduced by me in the Senate on the

5th of July, 1876, to provide for the completion of the Washington monument.

On the morning of the 4th of July, 1876, the 100th anniversary of American independence, I was making some preparation for the celebration of that day in the vicinity of Washington. Animated by the patriotic feeling inspired by the day, and sitting in view of the unfinished monument of George Washington, I felt that the time had come when this monument should no longer continue a standing reproach to a patriotic people. Shortly after the death of Washington, a resolution providing for the erection of a monument to his memory, was agreed to by both Houses of Congress. Subsequently, on January 1, 1801, a bill was passed by the House of Representatives appropriating $200,000 for this purpose, but, in the political excitements of that day, the Senate failed to concur. In the absorbing public questions that ensued, resulting in the War of 1812, the subject was dropped in Congress for the time.

In 1833 the "Washington Monument Society" was formed, with Chief Justice John Marshall as its president. This society proposed to raise the necessary sum to erect such a monument by voluntary subscriptions of individuals, and in 1854 it had, by such means, constructed about one-third of the height of the monument and then suspended work. Thus it had remained for years for want of means to complete it, a glaring evidence of failure. The portion of the monument already reared to the height of 156 feet stood in rude outline, an abandoned failure in the midst of a reservation partly covered with water and broken stone. The society was incorporated by Congress in 1859, but no further progress was made. It was manifest that the work could not be completed by the existing organization, and doubts were expressed whether the foundation was sufficient to bear the superstructure. Under these conditions, on the 100th anniversary of the declaration of American independence, it occurred to me the time had arrived when a great country like ours should complete this unfinished monument to George Washington. Under the inspiration of this thought I wrote this resolution on the morning of the 4th of July, and on the next morning offered it for adoption in the Senate:

"WHEREAS, It has pleased Almighty God to guide the United States of America safely through one hundred years of national life, and to crown our nation with the highest blessings of civil and religious liberty, Therefore,

"The Senate and House of Representatives in Congress assembled, in the name of the people of the United States, in reverent thankfulness acknowledge the fountain and source, the author and giver of all these blessings, and our dependence upon His providence and will; and,

"WHEREAS, We recognize, as our fathers did, that George Washington, 'first in peace, first in war, and first in the hearts of his countrymen,' was one of the chief instruments of Divine Providence in securing American independence and in laying broad and deep the foundations of our liberties in the constitution of the United States:

"Therefore, as a mark of our sense of the honor due to his name and to his compatriots and associates, our revolutionary fathers,

"We, the Senate and House of Representatives in Congress assembled, in the name of the people of the United States at this, the beginning of the second century of national existence, do assume and direct the completion of the Washington monument in the city of Washington, and instruct the committees on appropriation of the respective Houses to propose suitable provisions of law to carry this resolution into effect."

In submitting the resolution I said:

"I desire to offer at this time a concurrent resolution. I wish to say before it is read that I believe if it were passed to-day it would be a matter of profound satisfaction to the great body of the people of the United States. I ask that it be read."

After the resolution was read, there was a pause, when Mr. Edmunds said: "Let us consider this resolution. It will be agreed to unanimously, I am sure.

The resolution was therefore considered and agreed to unanimously. It was sent to the House of Representatives the next morning, when Mr. Hopkins, of Pennsylvania, pending a motion to adjourn, asked unanimous consent to take from the speaker's table the concurrent resolution in reference to the Washington monument. Upon the resolution being read, the House seemed to be impressed, as was the Senate, with the fitness of the time, and the propriety of the measure proposed, and it was unanimously adopted without debate.

Thus Congress undertook to execute the unfinished work of the Washington Monument Society. The requisite appropriations were subsequently made, and the monument, as completed, is now the most impressive token of the appreciation, by the American people, of the name and fame of George Washington. It is visited daily by nearly every American or stranger who enters the city of Washington. Its dedication will be hereafter mentioned.

CHAPTER XXVIII.

THE HAYES–TILDEN PRESIDENTIAL CONTEST.

Nomination of R. B. Hayes for President — His Fitness for the Responsible Office —
Political Shrewdness of Samuel J. Tilden, His Opponent — I Enter Actively Into
the Canvass in Ohio and Other States — Frauds in the South — Requested by
General Grant to Go to New Orleans and Witness the Canvassing of the
Vote of Louisiana — Departure for the South — Personnel of the
Republican and Democratic "Visitors" — Report of the Return-
ing Board — My Letter to Governor Hayes from New
Orleans — President Grant's Last Message to Con-
gress — Letters from President Hayes — Request
to Become his Secretary of the Treasury.

THE Republican national convention of 1876 met at Cincinnati on the 14th of June of that year. After the
usual organization the following eight nominations for
President were made: Blaine, Morton, Conkling, Bristow, Hayes, Hartranft, Wheeler and Jewell. The total number of delegates was 754. Blaine was greatly in the lead, receiving on the first ballot 285 votes, some from nearly every
state. Morton received 124, Bristow 113, Conkling 99, Hayes
61, Hartranft 58, Jewell 11, and Wheeler 3. There were 7 ballots, in which Blaine steadily held his vote and slightly gained,
receiving on the final ballot 351 votes. The vote for Hayes
increased at each ballot until on the seventh ballot he received
384 votes, a majority over all.

Undoubtedly Blaine was the favorite of the convention,
but the antagonisms that existed between him and Conkling
probably defeated his nomination. I still believe that the
nomination of Hayes was not only the safest, but the strongest
that could be made. The long possession of power by the Republicans naturally produced rivalries that greatly affected the
election of anyone who had been constantly prominent in public life, like Blaine, Conkling and Morton. Hayes had growing
qualities, and in every respect was worthy of the high position
of President. He had been a soldier, a Member of Congress,

Columbus O

19 June 1876

My Dear Sir:

I trust you will never regret the important action you took in the inauguration and carrying out of the movement which resulted in my nomination. I write these few words to assure you that I appreciate and am grateful for what you did.

My kindest regards to Mrs Sherman.

Sincerely
RB Hayes

Hon John Sherman
&c &c

thrice elected as Governor of Ohio, an admirable executive officer, and his public and private record was beyond question. He was not an aggressive man, although firm in his opinions and faithful in his friendships. Among all the public men with whom I have been brought in contact, I have known none who was freer from personal objection, whose character was more stainless, who was better adapted for a high executive office, than Rutherford B. Hayes.

Governor Hayes wrote me the following letter in recognition of my aid in his nomination.

COLUMBUS, O., June 19, 1876.

MY DEAR SIR:—I trust you will never regret the important action you took in the inauguration and carrying out of the movement which resulted in my nomination. I write these few words to assure you that I appreciate, and am gratified for, what you did.

My kindest regards to Mrs. Sherman.   Sincerely,
R. B. HAYES.

HON. JOHN SHERMAN.

His opponent, Samuel J. Tilden, was a man of singular political sagacity, of great shrewdness, a money-making man, who professed to represent, and perhaps did represent, as fairly as anyone, the ideas of the New York politicians of the school of Van Buren and Marcy. I knew Mr. Tilden personally and very favorably, as we were members of a board of railroad directors which frequently met. He seemed to take pleasure in talking with me about political events, and especially of famous New York politicians, of whom Silas Wright and Mr. Van Buren were his favorites. He had acquired great wealth as the attorney of corporations, and was undoubtedly a man of marked ability and sagacity. He had taken an active part in defeating the corruption of Tweed in New York politics. He had been elected governor of the State of New York, as the candidate of reform and honesty in politics.

The long and important session of Congress adjourned on the 15th of August. It had been the arena for long debates, mostly on political topics growing out of reconstruction, and financial measures heretofore referred to. The pending presidential contest also excited much debate in both Houses. The

administration of General Grant had not been entirely satisfactory, and the long continuance of the Republican party in
power was an element of weakness. The complaints, unavoidable in the most honest administration, and the disappoint-
ments of office-seekers, placed that party on the defensive.
The south had, by reconstruction, been practically restored
to political power, and the body of the negroes had been substantially disfranchised, though legally entitled to the suffrage.
Riots and crimes of every degree were committed in the south,
notably in Louisiana, South Carolina and Florida. Organized
mobs and violence had deterred many from voting, and in
some cases had prevented even the semblance of a free
election.

I entered actively into this canvass, more so than in any
previous one. Three days before the adjournment, I made my
opening speech at Marietta, Ohio, in which I discussed fully the
dangers of the restoration of the Democratic party to power,
the probability of their failure to enforce the constitutional
amendments, and the protection of the rights of the freedmen.
I claimed that the election of Mr. Tilden would result in the
virtual nullification of the constitutional amendments, and
amount to a practical restoration to power of the old Democratic party. The revival of the rebel claims, the refunding of
the cotton tax, and the damages done to rebels, were fully commented upon, as were the outrages committed upon freedmen
during the second administration of General Grant, the organization of Ku-Klux Klans, and the White League, and the boldness with which the laws were disregarded in the south. It is
difficult now to realize the condition of public affairs in all the
states then lately in rebellion. The people of the south are
certainly entitled to the highest credit for the great change
that has recently been made in the government of their states,
but it cannot be denied that during the ten years after the war
their condition bordered on the despotism of mob rule and
violence. Financial questions, no doubt, entered into the
canvass, but in this respect Governor Tilden and Governor
Hayes did not materially differ, while public opinion in the
southern states was almost a unit in favor of the larger use of

paper money. Their bankrupt condition made this policy almost universal there.

I continued until the day of election to make speeches, not only in Ohio, but in several of the states. I engaged in a joint debate with Senator Voorhees, of Indiana, at Columbia City, in that state, in September, which probably had more fun and humor in it than argument. It so happened that appointments were made for each of us at Columbia City on the same day, and the managers of the two parties concluded that they would have a joint debate, and arranged for it, to which we both assented. There was a great crowd, and besides Mr. Voorhees and myself, "Blue Jeans" Williams, the candidate for governor, was to open the meeting in his peculiar way, to which, as it would not at all interfere with our debate, I did not object. The debate was fully reported in the Chicago "Inter-Ocean," and is a very graphic specimen of popular debates in which each side claims to be the victor. I think it would be safe to say that from the close of Congress until the day of election I spoke on nearly every week day in some one of the five or six states which I visited.

The result of the presidential election in November, 1876, was extremely doubtful. It was soon asserted that the majority either way would be very small, and that the probabilities were that Mr. Tilden was elected. Zachariah Chandler, chairman of the national Republican committee, however, confidently telegraphed, on the morning after the election, that Hayes was elected by a majority of one in the electoral college. Further reports developed that on account of intimidation, frauds and violence, committed in the election in Louisiana, South Carolina, and Florida, the vote of each of those states was doubtful, and could only be ascertained by the reports of the returning boards. All of their electoral votes were needed to give Hayes the majority of one. Both parties claimed in each of the states a majority of the popular vote. In the heated state of political feeling in those states, it was a matter of grave doubt whether the count of the vote might not result in violence, tumult or war. On the evening of

November 11, I received from President Grant the following telegram :

PHILADELPHIA, PA., November 11, 1876.
Received at MANSFIELD, O., 8:35 p. m.

SENATOR JOHN SHERMAN.

I would be much pleased if you would join other parties, who have already accepted same invitation, to go to New Orleans to witness the canvassing of the vote of Louisiana.   U. S. GRANT.

I replied that I would go as soon as practicable, and received the following answer:

WASHINGTON, D. C., November 12, 1876.
Received at MANSFIELD, O., 4 p. m.

HON. JOHN SHERMAN.

Unless you can reach there by Friday morning it will be too late.
U. S. GRANT.

I at once started for New Orleans, stopping on the way at Columbus to confer with Governor Hayes, who said he wished I would go to New Orleans and witness the count, but expressed, in the strongest possible language, his opposition to any movement on the part of anyone to influence the action of the returning board in his favor. He said if Mr. Tilden was elected he desired him by all means to have the office. I proceeded to Cincinnati, where I met some of the gentlemen whom General Grant had requested to witness the count. When we arrived in New Orleans I found far less excitement in respect to the count than in Ohio. I there met the other gentlemen who had been, like myself, invited by General Grant. They were Messrs. Stanley Matthews, Ohio; J. A. Garfield, Ohio; E. W. Stoughton, New York; J. H. Van Alen, New York; Wm. D. Kelley, Pennsylvania; Job E. Stevenson, Ohio; Eugene Hale, Maine; J. M. Tuttle, Iowa; J. W. Chapman, Iowa; W. R. Smith, Iowa; W. A. McGrew, Iowa; Sidney Clarke, Kansas; C. B. Farwell, Illinois; Abner Taylor, Illinois; S. R. Haven, Illinois; J. M. Beardsley, Illinois; John Coburn, Indiana; Will Cumback, Indiana; C. Irving Ditty, Maryland.

At New Orleans I was for the first time introduced to the members of the returning board, who, under the laws of Louisiana, were required to verify the count and whose return was final. We met also a large number of gentlemen who were

MR. SHERMAN'S RESIDENCE AT MANSFIELD, OHIO, SINCE 1867.

there at the request of the national Democratic committee to perform the same duty that had been imposed upon us by General Grant. These gentlemen were John M. Palmer, Illinois; Lyman Trumbull, Illinois; William R. Morrison, Illinois; Samuel J. Randall, Pennsylvania; A. G. Curtin, Pennsylvania; William Bigler, Pennsylvania; J. R. Doolittle, Wisconsin; George B. Smith, Wisconsin; J. E. McDonald, Indiana; George W. Julian, Indiana; M. D. Manson, Indiana; John Love, Indiana; Henry Watterson, Kentucky; J. W. Stevenson, Kentucky; Henry D. McHenry, Kentucky; Oswald Ottendorfer, New York; J. B. Stallo, Ohio; Lewis V. Bogy, Missouri; James O. Brodhead, Missouri; C. Gibson, Missouri; John Lee Carroll, Maryland; William T. Hamilton, Maryland; W. G. Sumner, Connecticut; P. H. Watson, Ohio; F. R. Coudert, New York.

Before my arrival a correspondence had occurred between what was called the Democratic visitors and the Republican visitors in regard to our respective duties. This correspondence, all of which was reported to President Grant, resulted in the attendance of a certain number of each of the bodies of visitors at each session of the returning board, and thus a constant surveillance of the proceedings of the board was had. At the same time we received from the returning board the following letter:

STATE OF LOUISIANA, OFFICE BOARD OF RETURNING-OFFICERS, {
NEW ORLEANS, November 18, 1876. {

SIR:—At a meeting of the board of returning-officers, held this day, the following preamble and resolution, introduced by General Thomas C. Anderson, was unanimously adopted, viz:

WHEREAS, This board has learned with satisfaction that distinguished gentlemen of national reputation from other States, some at the request of the President of the United States, and some at the request of the national executive committee of the Democratic party, are present in this city with a view to witness the proceedings of this board in canvassing and compiling the returns of the recent election in this state for presidential electors, in order that the public opinion of the country may be satisfied as to the truth of the result and the fairness of the means by which it may have been attained; and whereas, this board recognizes the importance which may attach to the result of their proceedings, and that the public mind should be convinced of its justice by a knowledge of the facts on which it may be based, therefore, be it

Resolved, That this board does hereby cordially invite and request five gentlemen from each of the two bodies named, to be selected by themselves respectively, to attend and be present at the meetings of this board while engaged in the discharge of its duties, under the law, in canvassing and compiling the returns, and ascertaining and declaring the result of said election for presidential electors, in their capacity as private citizens of eminent reputation and high character, and as spectators and witnesses of the proceedings in that behalf of this board.

J. MADISON WELLS,
Chairman Board of Returning-Officers.

HON. JOHN SHERMAN, St. Charles Hotel, New Orleans.

On the same day I answered in behalf of my associates as follows:

ST. CHARLES HOTEL,
NEW ORLEANS, November 18, 1876.

SIR :—I have received your note of to-day, with a copy of the resolution of the board of returning-officers of the State of Louisiana, and have communicated the invitation contained in it to the gentlemen who are here at the request of the President of the United States to witness the canvassing of the vote at the recent election in this state for presidential electors, and am instructed by them to inform you of their acceptance of the invitation, and that they will designate a committee of five of their number to attend the meetings of the board. And I take this occasion to express my thanks for the courteous terms of this invitation, my deep sense of the importance of your proceedings, and my confident hope that they will be so conducted as to convince the public mind of the justice of your finding.

JOHN SHERMAN.

HON. J. MADISON WELLS.

A similar invitation was extended to the Democratic visitors, and substantially the same reply made. The returning board then proceeded to perform its duty under the law. At each session the Republican and Democratic visitors were present, and I neither know of nor have ever heard of any act being done or testimony taken by the board except in the presence of committees of the two bodies of visitors. The proceedings of the returning board were reported for each body of visitors and for the returning board, and all the evidence taken was not only delivered in the presence of the two visiting bodies, but was reported to the President and was published by Congress. Whatever opinions may be expressed as to the correctness of the findings of the returning board, there can be no doubt that its proceedings were open, fair and impartial. The board arrived at the conclusion that the Republican electors received a majority of the votes cast in Louisiana at that election, and were entitled to cast the vote of the state for President of the United States.

During the great excitement over this controversy, and also over that in South Carolina and Florida, exaggerated statements, without the slightest foundation, of frauds and improper conduct on the part of the returning officers were made and published. As to the action of the returning board in Louisiana, I feel bound now, after a long lapse of time, to repeat what was reported to General Grant by the Republican visitors, that it made a fair, honest and impartial return of the result of the election. In concluding our report we said :

" The proof of violence and intimidation and armed disturbance in many other parishes, is of the same general character, although more general and decisive, as to the five parishes particularly referred to. In the others, these causes prevailed at particular polling places, at many of which the Republican vote was, to a considerable extent, prevented.

" We hope to be able to furnish full copies of all testimony taken by the board, that the justice of its conclusions may be appreciated. It is a tribunal, from which there can be no appeal, and, in view of the possible consequences of its adjudication, we have closely observed its proceedings and have carefully weighed the force of a large mass of the testimony upon which that adjudication has been reached.

"The members of the board, acting under oath, were bound by law, if convinced by the testimony that riot, tumult, acts of violence, or armed disturbance did materially interfere with the purity and freedom of election at any poll or voting place, or did materially change the result of the election thereat, to reject the votes thus cast, and exclude them from their final return. Of the effect of such testimony, the board was sole and final judge, and if, in reaching a conclusion, it exercised good faith and was guided by an honest desire to do justice, its determination should be respected, even if, upon like proof, a different conclusion might have been reached by other tribunals or persons.

" To guard the purity of the ballot; to protect the citizen in the free and peaceful exercise of his right to vote; to secure him against violence, intimidation, outrage, and especially murder, when he attempts to perform this duty, should be the desire of all men, and the aim of every representative government. If political success shall be attained by such violent and terrible means as were resorted to in many parishes in Louisiana, complaint should not be made if the votes thus obtained are denounced by judicial tribunals and all honest men as illegal and void."

Pending the action of the board I wrote to Governor Hayes the following letter, giving a general view of the testimony:

STATE OF LOUISIANA, EXECUTIVE DEPARTMENT, }
NEW ORLEANS, November 23, 1876. }

MY DEAR SIR:—I have not written you sooner, for the progress of our visitation will be known to you through the papers sooner than from my letters, and the telegraph office here is more public than a sheriff's sale. We sometimes hear of private telegrams before they are delivered. The action of the returning board has thus far been open and fair and only confirms the general result known before. We are now approaching the contested parishes. To five of them, viz: Baton Rouge, East and West Feliciana, Morehouse and Ouachita, the evidence of intimidation is so well made out on paper that no man can doubt as to the just exclusion of their vote. In these parishes alone we ought to have a majority of 7,000, but under the law the entire return must be excluded of all election districts where intimidation has affected or changed the result. If this is done the result will give the Hayes electors majorities aggregating 24,111, and the Tilden electors 22,633, but in almost every parish the official return varies somewhat from the stated majorities, and thus far slightly reduces the Republican majority.

The vote of each disputed parish has thus far been laid aside, and among them are two parishes where a most foolish blunder, or something worse, was made in omitting from the Republican tickets the names of all the electors but the two Senatorial and one district elector. The Democrats claim this will lose over 2,000 votes, but our friends, whose information we have generally found confirmed, say it will lose us at most 1,193 votes. The law seems conclusive that the defective ballots cannot be counted for any electors but those named on the ticket; though it is conclusively shown that the remaining electors were omitted by reason of the mistaken idea that the district could only vote for one elector. The whole trouble has grown out of the fact that in these two parishes a candidate for district judge was not named on the ticket printed by the state committee. We undertook to correct this by printing new tickets, which were voted in those parishes. The result of this blunder will leave the poll so close as to render it probable that one or more of the Tilden electors would have a majority.

There are other parishes where the organized intimidation was not so general as in the parishes named, though in single election precincts it was effective. These parishes, where formal protests have been filed, are Bienville, Bossier, Caldwell, Franklin, Grant, Iberia, Lincoln, Richland and Sabine. How far the proof in these parishes will sustain the protests we cannot judge till the evidence is heard before the returning board.

We are now collecting the testimony as to the bulldozed parishes. It seems more like the history of hell than of civilized and Christian communities. The means adopted are almost incredible, but were fearfully effective upon an ignorant and superstitious people. That you would have received at a fair election a large majority in Louisiana, no honest man can question ; that you did not receive a majority is equally clear. But that intimidation of the very kind and nature provided against by the Louisiana law did enter into and control the election, in more election polls than would change the result and give you the vote, I believe as firmly as that I write this. The difficulty of gathering this testimony and putting it in the legal form has been very great, but I believe has been fully met.

The whole case rests upon the action of the returning board. I have carefully observed them, and have formed a high opinion of Governor Wells and Colonel Anderson. They are firm, judicious, and, as far as I can judge, thoroughly honest and conscientious. They are personally familiar with the nature and degree of intimidation in Louisiana. They can see that the intimidation, as organized, was with a view of throwing out Republican parishes rather than endangering Democratic parishes. Our little party is now dividing out the disputed parishes, with the view of a careful examination of every paper and detail. Many are impatient of the delay, and some have gone home. We will probably be able to keep about ten here. We have incurred some liabilities for reporting, printing, etc., but hope the Republican national committee will make this good. If not, we must provide for it ourselves. We are in good hope and spirit. Not wishing the return in your favor, unless it is clear that it ought to be so, and not willing to be cheated out of it, or to be 'bulldozed' or intimidated, the truth is palpable that you ought to have the vote of Louisiana, and we believe that you will have it, by an honest and fair return, according to the letter and spirit of the law of Louisiana.   Very truly yours,   JOHN SHERMAN.

To this General Hayes responded as follows:

COLUMBUS, O., November 27, 1876.

MY DEAR SIR:—I am greatly obliged for your letter of the 23rd. You feel, I am sure, as I do about this whole business. A fair election would have given us about forty electoral votes at the south — at least that many. But we are not to allow our friends to defeat one outrage and fraud by another. There must be nothing crooked on our part. Let Mr. Tilden have the place by violence, intimidation and fraud, rather than undertake to prevent it by means that will not bear the severest scrutiny.

I appreciate the work doing by the Republicans who have gone south, and am especially proud of the acknowledged honorable conduct of those from Ohio. The Democrats made a mistake in sending so many ex-Republicans. New converts are proverbially bitter and unfair towards those they have recently left.

I trust you will soon reach the end of the work, and be able to return in health and safety.   Sincerely,   R. B. HAYES.

I met Governor Hayes on my return and his conversation was to the same effect, that he wished no doubtful votes and would greatly prefer to have Mr. Tilden serve as President if there was any doubt about his (Hayes') election. The Republican visitors did not return until after the meeting of Congress at its regular session on the 4th of December, 1876.

President Grant, in the beginning of his annual message of that date, said:

"In submitting my eighth and last message to Congress, it seems proper that I should refer to, and in some degree recapitulate, the events and official acts of the past eight years.

"It was my fortune, or misfortune, to be called to the office of Chief Executive without any previous political training. From the age of seventeen I had never even witnessed the excitement attending a presidential campaign but twice antecedent to my own candidacy, and at but one of them was I eligible as a voter. Under such circumstances it is but reasonable to suppose that errors of judgment must have occurred. Even had they not, differences of opinion between the Executive, bound by an oath to the strict performance of his duties, and writers and debaters must have arisen. It is not necessarily evidence of blunder on the part of the Executive because there are these differences of views. Mistakes have been made, as all can see and I admit, but, it seems to me, oftener in the selections made of the assistants appointed to aid in carrying out the various duties of administering the government, in nearly every case selected without a personal acquaintance with the appointee, but upon recommendations of the representatives chosen directly by the people. It is impossible, where so many trusts are to be allotted, that the right parties should be chosen in every instance. History shows that no administration, from the time of Washington to the present, has been free from these mistakes. But I leave comparison to history, claiming only that I have acted in every instance from a conscientious desire to do what was right, constitutional within the law, and for the very best interests of the whole people. Failures have been errors of judgment, not of intent."

This modest statement by General Grant was appreciated by Congress and by the country. No one doubted the sincerity and patriotism of the President. His modest confession of errors did not in the slightest degree impair the universal confidence in him.

On the 18th of January, 1877, Mr. Edmunds, of the select committee of the Senate on the counting of electoral votes, submitted a report in writing with an accompanying bill. It was, with one exception, signed by the members of the committees of the two Houses without distinction of party. The bill provided in full detail a prescribed manner for counting the electoral vote. It was adopted by both Houses and voted for by a great majority, but, believing that it was extra constitutional, I, with other Republicans, did not vote for it. The history of the electoral commission provided for in this bill is part of the history of the country, and it is not necessary to here enter into it in detail. It is sufficient to say that it resulted in the counting of the votes of Louisiana, South Carolina and Florida for Mr. Hayes, electing him President by a majority of one vote. I took an active part in the debates on the questions involved and gave in detail my view of the action of the returning board in Louisiana.

During this period I received a number of personal letters from Governor Hayes, some of which may be of interest:

COLUMBUS, O., December 25, 1876.

MY DEAR SIR :—I have your esteemed favor, and have also met Judge Taft and Governor Dennison. There will not be the slightest difficulty growing out of the matter you refer to. You know my general course of conduct. It has always seemed to me wisest, in case of decided antagonisms among friends, not to take sides — to heal by compromise, not to aggravate, etc., etc. I wish *you* to feel authorized to speak in pretty decided terms for me whenever it seems advisable — to do this not by reason of specific authority to do it, but from your knowledge of my general methods of action. Sincerely, R. B. HAYES.

HON. JOHN SHERMAN, etc., etc.

COLUMBUS, O., January 5, 1877.

MY DEAR SIR :—I have your note of the 3rd. I do not wish to influence the action of our friends, and do not volunteer opinions. But *you* have a right to my opinion. I believe the Vice President alone has the constitutional power to count the votes and declare the result. Everything in the nature of a contest as to electoral votes is an affair of the states. The rest is a mere ministerial duty. Therefore it is not right, in my judgment, for Congress to interfere. Sincerely, R. B. HAYES.

HON. JOHN SHERMAN, U. S. S.

COLUMBUS, O., February 15, 1877.

MY DEAR SIR :—I have two letters from you since I last wrote. If it becomes my duty to make a cabinet I want your views fully and specifically. If possible a personal interview would be extremely desirable. Boynton writes to Smith that an assurance of my views on the southern question, which are truly set forth in my letter, with such additions as I could properly make, would be useful. I prefer to make no new declarations. But you may say

if you deem it advisable that you *know* that I will stand by the friendly and encouraging words of that letter and by all that they imply. You cannot express that too strongly.   Sincerely,   R. B. HAYES.
> HON. JOHN SHERMAN.

COLUMBUS, O., February 16, 1877.

MY DEAR SIR :—If the issue of the contest is in our favor I shall want to see you at once if it is at all practicable. Don't you want to visit Mansfield? I can meet you there or here—or possibly at a point east of there.
                    Sincerely,   R. B. HAYES.
> HON. JOHN SHERMAN.

COLUMBUS, O., February 19, 1877.

MY DEAR SIR :—The more I think of it the more difficult it seems for me to get ready to come to Washington before Wednesday or Thursday of next week. I must fix affairs at Fremont, and cannot begin it until I know the result. Why can't friends be sent or come here?

It seems to me proper now to say that I am extremely desirous that you should take the treasury department. Aside from my own personal preference, there are many and controlling reasons why I should ask you to do this. It will satisfy friends here in Ohio. I understand Governor Morton and our friends in Washington like it. The country will approve it. You are by all odds the best fitted for it of any man in the nation. Your resignation from the Senate will be a great loss to that body, but it will cause no serious dissensions or difficulty in Ohio. Do not say no until I have had a full conference with you. There is no reason why you should not visit Ohio as soon as you can be spared from Washington. Of course the public will know of our meeting. But they will be gratified to know it. No possible harm can come of it. I should have said all this before, but I did not want to embarrass you in your action on the presidential question.
                    Sincerely,   R. B. HAYES.
> HON. JOHN SHERMAN.

(Telegram.)   COLUMBUS, O., February 20, 1877.
> HON. JOHN SHERMAN.

I will be greatly obliged if you can come to Columbus, but will meet you at Zanesville if you think it important.   R. B. HAYES.

COLUMBUS, O., February 28, 1877.
> HON. JOHN SHERMAN, Washington, D. C.

DEAR SIR :—Governor Hayes will be obliged to you if you will be kind enough to speak to Mr. Evarts with respect to his acceptance of the place in the cabinet referred to in the interview with you last week. It was the governor's intention to make this request at that time, and he may have done so, but not being quite sure of the fact, desires me to write you with reference to it.   Yours very respectfully,
                    W. K. ROGERS, Secretary.

Columbus O
19 Feb 1877

My Dear Sir: The more I think of it the more difficult it seems for me to get ready to come to Washington in March. My if not much worse. I would fix appoint at Cleveland at least begin it until I know the result. Or by could frankly be sent or could send?

It seems to me better even to say that I am exceedingly desiring that you almost tell the Treasury Department. Beside from any one evidence happens, then in arising at entangling me so only if I should ask you to do that. It will

Actively friendly here in Ohio. I understand you therefore not over friendly in Washington like it. The Country will approve it. You are by all odds the best fitted for it of any person in the Nation. Your resignation from the Senate will be a great loss to Washington, but it will cause no serious depression or difficulty in Ohio. Do not say no until I have had a free conference with you. Please do not burden yourself you alwise not to resign Ohio as soon as your own Senator from W. Of course the burden will have no no knowledge of our meeting. But they will be grateful to know it. If a possible I shall know you come by it. I should have done all this before, but I did not want to embarrass you in your action on the Presidential question. Sincerely R.B. Hayes

Hon John Sherman

New York, 6th March 1877.

My dear Mr Sherman,

Allow me to congratulate you on having been selected by President Hayes to administer the financial affairs of the nation.

I deem it a happy augury that the President's choice of Members of his Cabinet has fallen upon men who have made their mark as Statesmen, and whose advent to power will, I feel convinced, inaugurate an era of prosperity for our country.

With yourself at the head of the Treasury Department, there is no fear of public credit being shaken & commercial interests imperilled by crude & experimental legislation.

With great respect,
I remain,
My dear Mr Sherman,
Very truly your friend,

Cyrus W. Field.

Hon. John Sherman
Washington

President Hayes frequently, in personal conversation and in writing, had expressed a strong desire that I should become his Secretary of the Treasury. I was disinclined to accept this position, as I was content to serve my constituents in the Senate. It was not until after his urgent request in his letter of February 19, 1877, that I seriously considered his desire that I should accept that office. I went to Columbus to ascertain the views of the legislature, and whether there would be any difficulty in selecting a Republican to my place in the Senate. Having found that there would not be, I, with reluctance, accepted his offer. Stanley Matthews was elected on the 21st of March to serve out my unexpired term, which ended on the 3rd of March, 1879.

President Hayes arrived in Washington a few days before the 4th of March and was my guest until he was inaugurated as President. The 4th day of March was on Sunday, and to avoid any question about an interregnum, he was sworn into office on that day, but took the formal oath on the next day, the 5th of March, and made his inaugural address. He nominated the members of his cabinet to the Senate and they were promptly confirmed.

I received many letters of congratulation and encouragement in assuming the duties of Secretary of the Treasury, two of which I insert:

NEW YORK, March 6, 1877.

MY DEAR MR. SHERMAN:—Allow me to congratulate you on having been selected by President Hayes to administer the financial affairs of the nation.

I deem it a happy augury that the President's choice of members of his cabinet has fallen upon men who have made their mark as statesmen, and whose advent to power will, I feel convinced, inaugurate an era of prosperity for our country.

With yourself at the head of the treasury department, there is no fear of public credit being shaken and commercial interests imperiled by crude and experimental legislation.

With great respect, I remain, my dear Mr. Sherman,
Very truly your friend,
CYRUS W. FIELD.

HON. JOHN SHERMAN, Washington.

Consulate General of the United States for Great Britain and Ireland, }
LONDON, E. C., March 12, 1877. }

THE HON. JOHN SHERMAN, Secretary of the Treasury.

MY DEAR SIR:—When I begin to write to you, I am reminded of what General Sherman said, in my hearing, to General Grant, after the latter was made General in Chief: 'I cannot congratulate you; the responsibility is too great.' You have certainly succeeded to the most difficult post in the government, one in whose successful administration Americans abroad feel an especial interest, for no department is more important to foreigners or more discussed by them.

It may not be unsatisfactory to you to know that Americans—both those long domiciled here and those in transit—applaud the appointment of the new Chief of the Treasury.

I beg to offer my best wishes and belief that the reputation he has already achieved in the Senate will be increased in the cabinet; and to say how glad I was that the unanimity of his late compeers showed that they were of the same mind.

With great respect, I am, my dear sir,

Very faithfully yours,   ADAM BADEAU.

CHAPTER XXIX.

I Begin My Duties as Secretary of the Treasury.

Legislative Training of Great Advantage to Me in My New Position — Loan Contract in Force When I Took the Portfolio — Appointment of Charles F. Conant as Funding Agent of the Treasury Department in London — Redeeming Called Bonds — Sale of Four Per Cent. Bonds Instead of Four and a Half Per Cents. — Popularity of the New Loan — Great Sav-' ing in Interest — On a Tour of Inspection Along the Northern Atlantic Coast — Value of Information Received on This Trip — Effect of the Baltimore and Pittsburg Rail- road Strikes in 1877 Upon Our Public Credit.

WHEN I assumed the office of Secretary of the Treasury I had the advantage of some of my predecessors in that I was acquainted with the organization and duties of the treasury department. Ever since 1859 my connection with the committee of ways and means in the House and with the committee on Finance in the Senate had brought me into official relations with the head of that department. This legislative training gave me a full knowledge of the several laws that were to be executed in relation to public revenue, to all forms of taxation, to coinage and currency, and to the public debt. The entire system of national finance then existing grew out of the Civil War, and I had participated in the passage of all the laws relating to this subject. My intimate association with Secretaries Chase, Fessenden and McCulloch, and my friendly relations with Secretaries Boutwell and Richardson, led me, as chairman of the Senate committee on finance, to have free and confidential intercourse with them as to legislation affecting the treasury. Secretary Bristow had not had the benefit of experience either in Congress or the department. He was a good lawyer and an able man. He doubted whether resumption would be effective without a gradual retirement of United States notes, a measure that Congress would not agree to. Congress repealed even the limited retirement of such notes provided for by the resumption act.

Secretary Morrill, of Maine, my immediate predecessor, was in hearty sympathy with the policy of Congress, of which he had been a useful Senator, and but for his failing health would have been an efficient secretary. Upon my assuming the duties of secretary, and for some time before, he had been confined by illness in his lodgings in Washington. The treasury department was then well organized. Most of the principal officers had been long in the service. But few changes were made by President Hayes or by myself, and only as vacancies occurred or as incompetency was demonstrated. The following loan contract was in force at the beginning of my administration of the treasury department :

"This agreement, entered into this 24th day of August, in the year of our Lord, 1876, between the Secretary of the Treasury of the United States of America, of the first part, and Messrs. August Belmont & Co., of New York, in behalf of Messrs. N. M. Rothschild & Sons, of London, England, and associates, and Messrs. J. & W. Seligman & Co., of New York, for themselves and associates, and Messrs. Drexel, Morgan & Co., on behalf of Messrs. J. S. Morgan & Co., of London, England, and Messrs. Morton, Bliss & Co., of New York, representing the First National Bank of the city of New York, the American Exchange National Bank of New York, the Merchants' National Bank of New York, the Third National Bank of New York, Messrs. Kuhn, Loeb & Co., of New York, the Bank of New York National Banking Association, and Messrs. Morton, Rose & Co., of London, and themselves, of the second part :

"Witnesseth, That the said Messrs. August Belmont & Co., of New York, on behalf of Messrs. N. M. Rothschild & Sons and associates, hereby agree to purchase from the Secretary of the Treasury sixteen million five hundred thousand dollars ($16,500,000) of the United States bonds known as the four and a half per cent. funded loan of 1891, issued under the acts of July 14, 1870, and January 20, 1871; and that Messrs. J. & W. Seligman & Co., for themselves and their associates, hereby agree to purchase from the Secretary of the Treasury six million seven hundred and fifty thousand dollars ($6,750,000) of the bonds hereinbefore described; and that Messrs. Drexel, Morgan & Co., on behalf of Messrs. J. S. Morgan & Co., of London, England, hereby agree to purchase from the Secretary of the Treasury six million seven hundred and fifty thousand dollars ($6,750,000) of the bonds hereinbefore described; and that Messrs. Morton, Bliss & Co., of New York, representing the First National Bank of the city of New York, to the extent of four million dollars ($4,000,000); the American Exchange National Bank of New York, to the extent of one million and fifty thousand dollars ($1,-050,000); the Merchants' National Bank of New York, to the extent of six

OFFICE OF THE SECRETARY OF THE TREASURY, WASHINGTON, D. G.

hundred thousand dollars ($600,000); the Third National Bank of the city of New York, to the extent of seven hundred and fifty thousand dollars ($750,000); Messrs. Kuhn, Loeb & Co., of New York, to the extent of one million and fifty thousand dollars ($1,050,000); the Bank of New York National Banking Association, to the extent of three hundred thousand dollars ($300,000); Messrs. Morton, Rose & Co., of London, to the extent of one million one hundred and twenty-five thousand dollars ($1,125,000), and Messrs. Morton, Bliss & Co., of New York, to the extent of one million one hundred and twenty-five thousand dollars ($1,125,000), hereby agree, to the extent severally for each as above stated, to purchase from the Secretary of the Treasury ten million dollars ($10,000,000) in the aggregate of the bonds hereinbefore described, making a total aggregate of forty million dollars ($40,000,000), upon the terms and conditions following, to-wit:

"First. Of the said aggregate amount, not less than ten million dollars ($10,000,000) are hereby subscribed for, the subscription to take effect on the 1st day of September, 1876, and the remaining amount, namely, thirty million dollars ($30,000,000), may be divided at the pleasure of the parties of the second part into several successive subscriptions of not less than five million dollars ($5,000,000) each, to be made prior to the 4th day of March, 1877.

"Second. The parties of the second part shall have the exclusive right to subscribe, in the same proportion to each of the subscribers, for the remainder, namely, two hundred and sixty million dollars ($260,000,000), or any portion of said loan authorized to be issued by the acts of Congress aforesaid, by giving notice thereof to the Secretary of the Treasury on or before the 30th day of June, 1877; but the party of the first part reserves the right to terminate this contract at any time after March 4, 1877, by giving ten days' notice thereof to the parties of the second part.

"Third. That the Secretary of the Treasury shall, when subscriptions are made by the said parties of the second part, issue calls with even date with said subscriptions for the redemption of an equivalent amount of six per cent. 5-20 bonds of the United States, as provided by said act of July 14, 1870.

Fourth. The parties of the second part agree to pay for said four and a half per cent. bonds par and interest accrued to the date of application for delivery of said bonds, in gold coin, matured United States gold coin coupons, or any of the six per cent. 5-20 bonds called for redemption, or in United States gold certificates of deposit issued under the act of March 3, 1863, with the understanding that payment to the extent of the amount of any call shall be made within the time during which such call shall mature: *Provided*, That, if the parties of the second part shall elect so to do, they may have the privilege of making any of said subscriptions payable specifically in uncalled six per cent. 5-20 bonds of the United States, in which case the Secretary of the Treasury may, to the extent of such payments, omit the calls mentioned in condition No. 3.

"Fifth. The parties of the second part shall receive in coin a commission of one-half of one per cent. on all bonds taken by them, as allowed by the act of July 14, 1870, and shall assume and defray all expenses which may be incurred in sending bonds to London upon their request, or by transmitting bonds, coupons, or coin from there to the treasury department at Washington, including all cost of making exchange of bonds, and shall also be charged with the preparation and issuing of the bonds.

"Sixth. No bonds shall be delivered to the parties of the second part, or either of them, until payment shall have been made in full therefor in accordance with the terms of this contract.

"Seventh. During the continuance of this contract any sales of bonds ordered by the Secretary of the Treasury, by authority of law, except those that it may become necessary to sell to pay judgments of the Court of Commissioners of Alabama Claims, shall be made through the parties of the second part, who shall be allowed thereon a commission of one per cent. in gold coin. And it is provided that the amount of bonds so ordered shall not exceed in the aggregate $25,000,000, unless by mutual agreement of the parties.

LOT M. MORRILL,
Secretary of the Treasury.
AUG. BELMONT & CO.,
On behalf of N. M. ROTHSCHILD & SONS, London.
J. & W. SELIGMAN & CO.,
On behalf of SELIGMAN BROTHERS.
DREXEL, MORGAN & CO.,
On behalf of J. S. MORGAN & CO., of London.
MORTON, BLISS & CO.,
For themselves and associates, as named above."

By its terms the contract provided for the sale of $40,000,-000, four and a half per cent. bonds of the United States at par in gold coin. The contractors had the exclusive right to subscribe for all or any portion of the remainder of the four and a half per cent. bonds, amounting to $260,000,000. The right to terminate this contract at any time after March 4, 1877, after ten days' notice, was reserved by the United States. The proceeds of the bonds sold were to be applied solely to the payment of the six per cent. 5-20 bonds of the United States. No provision was made in this contract for the accumulation of coin for the redemption of United States notes. The process of refunding under it progressed slowly.

I felt it to be important that I should have some personal representative in London, to protect the interests of the United States in the execution of this contract, and, therefore, on the 31st of March, 1877, I appointed Charles F. Conant, as the funding agent of the treasury department, and directed him to assume the general management and supervision of all business in London, arising from the funding of bonds. A letter of instructions prescribing his duties was given him. He was directed to pursue the same general plan under which former negotiations had been conducted, except as modified by these instructions, which were based upon the contract before mentioned. All bonds, money, or coupons received by him were to be securely kept in safes, furnished by the department for that purpose, to be deposited in the vaults of the Messrs. Rothschild. Combination locks were provided for each safe, and no safe could be unlocked except by three persons on distinct combinations, each person using a combination unknown to the others. He was to keep me fully advised of the course of the market, of the price not only of American securities, but of foreign securities, and was to receive the new bonds and deliver them to the Rothschilds in exchange for the bonds redeemed. He proved to be a very competent and faithful agent, and furnished me important financial information, which aided me greatly in refunding operations. His compensation and allowances, as well as those of all persons sent to London in connection with the re-funding of the public debt, were paid by the syndicate, so that no expense whatever was incurred by the treasury on this account.

I gave the following notice to the parties to this contract that I would, on the part of the United States, terminate it.

TREASURY DEPARTMENT, }
WASHINGTON, D. C., April 6, 1877. }

GENTLEMEN :—I received your friendly cable message of the 10th ultimo, and return my thanks and hearty good wishes.

I am very solicitous to promote the funding of our six per cent. bonds as rapidly as practicable, and feel indebted to you for the aid you have given in placing the four and a half per cent. bonds.

I propose no change at present; but it is my desire, if practicable, to withdraw the four and a half per cent. bonds from the market and substitute in their place the four per cent. bonds authorized by the funding act.

These bonds, as you know, are a very desirable investment, running thirty years from the date of issue, with every guard and security that has been given to any bond of the United States, and we think as safe and desirable as the securities of any other nation. It is probably the bond into which all the debt of the United States will in time be converted. I hope you and your associates will be able to engage with me to place this bond on the market when $200,000,000 of the four and a half per cent. bonds have been sold.

The public policy of the United States to resume specie payments on or before the 1st of January, 1879, is fully established by the law and by public opinion. It may be that the surplus revenue will be sufficient to enable me to carry out this policy without the sale of bonds. I am authorized by the resumption act to sell five, four and a half, or four per cent. bonds to prepare for resumption, and it may be desirable to sell through the syndicate, under that act, a limited amount of bonds, not exceeding, I hope, $30,000,-000 a year. I do not wish in the execution of this duty to disturb the exchanges between Europe and this country. For this purpose I desire to sell only the four per cent. bonds, and must sell at par in coin, but could receive in payment coin coupons maturing within a limited time. I invite from you and your associates such suggestions and offers as you may think proper to make for the purchase of such bonds.

The operations of the syndicate have become so important that I have deemed it proper to ask Mr. Charles F. Conant, late Assistant Secretary of the Treasury, to take charge of the business in London in connection with the gentlemen already there. He is well informed as to our laws, and I trust his services may be of advantage to the government and agreeable to you.

I will give my personal attention to this business, and will receive with pleasure any suggestions from you that will promote our common object.

Very truly,   JOHN SHERMAN, Secretary.

MESSRS. N. M. ROTHSCHILD & SONS, London, England.

I received the following letter:

NEW YORK, April 12, 1877.

HON. JOHN SHERMAN, Secretary of the Treasury, Washington.

MY DEAR SIR:—I had an interview with Messrs. Drexel, Morgan & Co., and conveyed to them your wishes respecting limiting the sale of the four and a half and taking the four per cent. bond in hand with the coöperation of the Messrs. Rothschild.

I told Mr. Drexel that you would be happy to see him and Mr. L. P. Morton in Washington, whenever convenient for them to go, and that on receipt by you of favorable advices from Mr. Conant after his arrival in London, you desired that Drexel, Morton and I should repair to Washington, in company with other leading members of the syndicate, with a view of entering into a contract with the government, in conformity with your views as expressed to me, or perhaps with some slight modifications, which, if suggested by the London people, through Mr. Conant, you may deem proper to adopt.

I shall see Mr. Morton in the course of this day, and have no doubt but that he, as well as Drexel and myself, will be happy to aid you in raising the credit of our common country, and assist the President and you in this patriotic work. I remain, dear Mr. secretary, yours, very faithfully.

JOS. SELIGMAN.

A month later I wrote to Mr. Conant as follows:

TREASURY DEPARTMENT, ⎫
WASHINGTON, May 14, 1877. ⎭

DEAR MR. CONANT: —. . . . On Friday last I concluded a modification of the present syndicate contract, which provides for the sale of five million four and a half per cent. bonds at par in coin for resumption purposes. A further negotiation is pending as to the renewal and modification of the contract, of which I will give you due notice when completed. In the meantime I wish to keep steadily in view the sale of the balance of two hundred million four and a half per cent. bonds, and, if possible, I wish to make the necessary calls during this month and next.

You can assure Messrs. Rothschild of every disposition on the part of the government to meet their views, and to extend the contract with the necessary modifications. Their efforts in maintaining the credit of the bonds and securing this result will be highly appreciated.

I would like to have you write me at least twice a week as fully as practicable. Very truly, JOHN SHERMAN.

MR. C. F. CONANT, London.

As the process of redeeming called bonds required a notice of ninety days, I postponed the termination of the existing contract until after that period. My purpose in terminating the contract was to substitute for sale the four per cent. bonds of the United States instead of the four and a half per cent. bonds. I believed that the advancing credit of the United States would justify this reduction of the rate of interest. Another reason for this step was that, in addition to refunding at a lower rate of interest, I wished to commence preparation for the resumption of specie payments on January 1, 1879, according to law. This could only be done by the sale of bonds for gold coin. I reserved the remainder of the four and a half bonds, amounting to $100,000,000, authorized by the refunding act, for resumption purposes in case the four per cent. bonds could not be sold at par in coin.

Another reason for a change in the existing contract was that it gave to the syndicate a monopoly in the sale of bonds while I wished to sell the bonds directly to the people. The new contract was as follows:

"This agreement, entered into this 9th day of June, 1877, between the Secretary of the Treasury of the United States, of the first part, and Messrs. August Belmont & Co., of New York, on behalf of Messrs. N. M. Rothschild & Sons, of London, England, and associates and themselves ; Messrs. Drexel,

Morgan & Co., of New York, on behalf of Messrs. J. S. Morgan & Co., of London, and themselves ; Messrs. J. & W. Seligman & Co., of New York, on behalf of Messrs. Seligman Brothers, of London, and themselves ; Messrs. Morton, Bliss & Co., of New York, on behalf of Messrs. Morton, Rose & Co., of London, and themselves ; and the First National Bank of the city of New York—

"Witnesseth : That the said Messrs. August Belmont & Co., on behalf of Messrs. N. M. Rothschild & Sons, and associates and themselves, hereby agree to purchase from the Secretary of the Treasury $10,312,500 of the bonds known as the four per cent. consols of the United States, issued under the acts of July 14, 1870, January 20, 1871, and January 14, 1875, and that Messrs. Drexel, Morgan & Co., on behalf of Messrs. J. S. Morgan & Co., and themselves, agree to purchase $4,062,500 of said bonds, and that Messrs. J. & W. Seligman & Co., on behalf of Messrs. Seligman Brothers, and themselves, agree to purchase $4,062,500 of said bonds, and that Morton, Bliss & Co., on behalf of Messrs. Morton, Rose & Co., and themselves, agree to purchase $4,062,500 of said bonds, and that the First National Bank of the city of New York agree to purchase $2,500,000 of said bonds, making a total aggregate of $25,000,000 of said bonds, on the terms and conditions following :

First. Of the said aggregate amount not more than $5,000,000 shall be sold for resumption purposes, the remaining $20,000,000 to be sold for funding purposes, and subscribed for by the parties of the second part during the months of July and August, 1877.

Second. The parties of the second part shall have the exclusive right to subscribe in the same proportion to each of the subscribers, for the remainder of the four per cent. consols of the United States, or any portion of said consols authorized to be issued by the acts of Congress aforesaid, by giving notice thereof to the Secretary of the Treasury on or before the 30th day of June, 1878 ; but the party of the first part reserves the right to terminate this contract at any time after the 31st day of December, 1877, by giving ten days' notice thereof to the parties of the second part.

Third. That the Secretary of the Treasury shall not sell for resumption purposes exceeding five millions per month during the continuance of this contract, except by mutual agreement of the parties hereto. When subscriptions are made for other than resumption purposes by the parties of the second part, the party of the first part shall issue calls of even date with said subscriptions for the redemption of an equal amount of six per cent. 5-20 bonds of the United States, as provided for in said act of July 13, 1870.

Fourth. The parties of the second part agree to pay for said four per cent. bonds par and interest accrued to the date of application for delivery of said bonds in gold coin, matured United States gold coin coupons, or any of the six per cent. 5-20 bonds called for redemption, or in United States gold certificates of deposit issued under the act of March 3, 1863, with the understanding that payment to the extent of the amount of any call shall be made within the time during which such call shall mature : *Provided*, That if the parties of the second part shall elect so to do, they may have the privilege of making any of said subscriptions payable specifically in uncalled six per cent. 5-20 bonds of the United States, in which case the Secretary of the Treasury may, to the extent of such payments, omit the calls mentioned in condition No. 3.

Fifth. The parties of the second part shall receive in coin a commission of one-half of one per cent. on all bonds taken by them, as allowed by the act of July 14, 1870, and shall assume and defray all expenses which may be incurred in sending bonds to London or elsewhere upon their request, or by transmitting bonds, coupons, or coin to the treasury department at Washington, including all cost of making the exchange of bonds, and shall also be charged with the cost of the preparation and issuing of the bonds.

Sixth. No bonds shall be delivered to the parties of the second part, or either of them, until payment shall have been made in full therefor in accordance with the terms of this contract.

Seventh. During the continuance of this contract any sales of bonds ordered by the Secretary of the Treasury, by authority of law, shall be made through the parties of the second part, who shall be allowed thereon a commission similar in amount and subject to the same deductions as prescribed in the fifth clause of this contract.

Eighth. It is also agreed that the parties of the second part shall offer to the people of the United States, at par and accrued interest in coin, the four per cent. registered consols and four per cent. coupon consols of the denominations of fifty dollars and one hundred dollars, embraced in this contract, for a period of thirty days from the public notice of such subscriptions, and in such cities and upon such notice as the Secretary of the Treasury may prescribe prior to the opening of the lists, and further, to offer to the subscribers the option of paying in installments extending through three months.

JOHN SHERMAN,
Secretary of the Treasury.
AUGUST BELMONT & Co.,
On behalf of N. M. ROTHSCHILD & SONS, of London,
And associates and themselves.
DREXEL, MORGAN & Co.,
On behalf of J. S. MORGAN & Co., of London,
And themselves.
J. & W. SELIGMAN & Co.,
On behalf of SELIGMAN BROTHERS and themselves.
MORTON, BLISS & Co.,
On behalf of MORTON, ROSE, & Co., of London,
And themselves.
THE FIRST NATIONAL BANK
OF THE CITY OF NEW YORK.
BY H. C. FAHNESTOCK.
Witnesses as to all:
R. C. McCORMICK.
E. J. BABCOCK.

By this contract the syndicate was to take $25,000,000 of the four per cent. bonds at par, or in exchange of six per cent. 5-20 bonds. Of this sum $5,000,000 in gold coin was to be paid to the treasury for resumption purposes. The eighth section was a new provision, and required the syndicate to offer to the people of the United States, at par and accrued interest in coin, the four per cent. bonds, for a period of thirty days, in such cities and upon such notice as the Secretary of the Treasury might prescribe.

The result of this contract was not only to save one-half of one per cent. on the annual interest of the bonds redeemed, but to so popularize the loan that within a brief period I was able to terminate the contract according to its terms, and to sell the four per cent. bonds directly to the people at par, without a commission, or the aid of a syndicate.

I wrote Mr. Conant as follows:

TREASURY DEPARTMENT, }
WASHINGTON, May 31, 1877. }

DEAR MR. CONANT:—Your letter of the 19th is received. Since its date matters here have changed greatly for the better, and I have made two calls for ten millions each.

There is a strong, steady demand for our bonds, and I have now no fear but the two hundred millions four and a halfs will be exhausted before the 1st of July, when they will be withdrawn. The prospect of placing the four per cent. bonds, commencing July 1, is very good. I have submitted to the syndicate a proposition in substance requiring them to take twenty-five millions four per cents. during July and August, of which five millions will be for resumption purposes, with a stipulation that if they take fifty millions additional in September and October the contract will be extended to January 1, 1878, five millions a month to be applied for resumption purposes. I do not propose to vary essentially from the proposition. I have another offer almost as good from other parties, but I hope to combine these two offers into a modified syndicate, and, if possible, reserve the right to sell bonds at par, in coin or 5-20 bonds, to persons who apply directly to me for exchange, giving, however, the syndicate the half per cent. commission. We will considerably reduce the cost of the bonds, I think, to one-tenth of one per cent., so that the contracting parties will have a reasonably fair commission. I am already assured of many sales of the bonds whenever offered, without the aid of the syndicate, so that I consider myself strong enough to undertake the placing the bonds even without their aid, if they will not agree to reasonable terms. If I can secure the active, hearty coöperation of all the parties who wish to engage in selling the bonds, and they will be content with a reasonable profit, the operation of funding can go on so rapidly that they ought to be satisfied with the profit they will make.

I have not overlooked the possibility that some movement of coin will be made to meet called bonds in Europe in excess of bonds sold there, but hope to perfect arrangements by which I will secure American bullion to meet this demand, without stopping accumulations of coin in the treasury.

The prospects here are favorable for a good crop in all the states of the Mississippi valley, but there will probably be a bad crop in California.

What we must do is push the loan so that it will be an established success before the meeting of Congress. If you can succeed in inspiring the Rothschilds to aid this purpose I am sure of success. My proposition has been sent to them, and I was advised would be answered by telegram about this time; but by the 15th I hope to have the arrangements completed.

If upon receipt of this letter there is anything of striking interest affecting the loan you may cable me.

All well in the department. Matters are going along quietly and steadily.   Very truly yours,   JOHN SHERMAN.
    HON. CHAS. F. CONANT, London.

This letter he received about the time the new contract was executed. I subsequently sent him the following cable telegram:

WASHINGTON, June 9, 1877.
CONANT, London :

Contract of August 24, 1876, closed new four and a half per cent. bonds at $200,000,000. New contract twenty-five millions four per cent. bonds taken firm. Particulars by mail.   SHERMAN.

Two days later I received a reply, as follows:

LONDON, June 11, 1877.
SHERMAN, Washington :

Congratulations. Rothschilds request me to say that it is important for this market that the public subscriptions in America for four per cents. should be a success, and this will make the market for London. N. M. Rothschild & Sons hope Secretary of the Treasury will advise that banks subscribe immediately. J. S. Morgan & Co., N. M. Rothschild & Sons, think subscription should be opened soon, in view of preparing London market.   CONANT.

This new agreement gave at once a great impetus to the new loan in all parts of the United States, as well as in London. The following letters received indicate this:

MERCHANTS' NATIONAL BANK,   }
CLEVELAND, O., June 11, 1877. }
HON. JOHN SHERMAN, Secretary Treasury United States.

DEAR SIR :—We learn that you propose to offer to the public a certain portion of the new four per cent. loan for a limited time, the amount subscribed to be paid in gold at the par value of the bonds.

This bank, being a public depositary of the government of the United States, shall be glad to further your plans, and act as agent for the sale of such portion of the loan as you may suggest, and endeavor to give it such publicity as would secure the sale of a portion of these bonds in this part of Ohio.

Wishing you success in the effort, I remain, very respectfully and truly,

T. P. HANDY, President.

TREASURY DEPARTMENT, June 12, 1877.

JOHN P. HUNT, ESQ., Philadelphia, Pa.

SIR:—Your note is received. The department will be happy to receive your subscription in a short time. The bonds are not prepared, and the treasury regulations for the popular subscription cannot be issued for a few days, when a copy will be sent you.

It is the purpose to give you, and all other citizens of the United States, an opportunity to subscribe at some convenient place in the city of your residence, to be designated in due time, requiring only a small deposit at the time of subscription, and allowing the privilege of paying at any time within ninety days thereafter.

The bonds will bear date the 1st of July, and will be sold at par in coin and accruing interest to date of payment.

Very respectfully,   JOHN SHERMAN, Secretary.

Contemporaneous with this contract for selling the four per cent. bonds for gold coin, there appeared in the New York "Times" a suggestion that these bonds could be paid in silver. Henry F. French, Assistant Secretary of the Treasury, in a published letter of the date of June 11, asserted his opinion that the bonds issued under the act of July 14, 1870, for refunding, were redeemable in coin of the standard value at that date, and that "as it cannot be known what bonds have been transferred since the act of 1873, all bonds under the act of 1870 must be paid in gold coin of the standard value named in the act of 1873."

I received a letter from Messrs. Seligman & Co., inclosing an extract from the New York "Times," as follows:

NEW YORK, June 12, 1877.

HON. JOHN SHERMAN, Secretary of the Treasury, Washington.

DEAR MR. SECRETARY:—We beg to inclose a short editorial article which appeared in to-day's New York 'Times,' which, coming from a Republican paper, may frighten investors in our country and abroad. Intelligent people know that you, sir, as well as President Hayes, are sound on the silver question, and yet it may appear to you proper, and highly advantageous to the prompt marketing of the four per cent. bonds, to disabuse those who have been led to believe that the President and you favor the remonetizing of silver, with a view of paying our national debt in a metal so fluctuating as silver has become since the principal nations of Europe have demonetized it. We remain, dear Mr. secretary, your obedient servants,

J. &. W. SELIGMAN & CO.

The article in the New York "Times," of June 12, 1877, said:

"In a dispatch received by the Secretary of the Treasury yesterday from Mr. Conant, the syndicate agent in London, it was stated that the contract touching the four per cent. bonds is well received in London, and the new bond bids fair to be the most popular of American securities. There is no doubt that the bond has many advantages both for home and foreign investors. It has only one point of weakness, and that is, that if the silver ring should succeed in getting an unlimited issue of legal tender silver dollars, this bond would be payable, principal and interest, in that coin. Shrewd men, who know what silver has done and is liable to do in the way of ups and downs, will take this fact into consideration, and the government will ultimately be compelled to do the same. At present the strength of the silver movement is estimated to be small, but if this estimate should prove to be mistaken, the new four per cents. would suffer."

Mr. August Belmont wrote me a letter upon this subject of the date of June 14th, in which he said:

"Permit me to add a few words to the letter of my house of this day, in order to urge upon you the *vital* importance of an official expression of yours *over your own signature*, in the sense of the letter of Assistant Secretary French, published in this morning's papers.

*   *   *   *   *   *   *   *   *

"You are placed at this moment, by a large portion of your political friends, in a somewhat similar position as the late Mr. Chase was by the attempt of Thad. Stevens to have Congress pass a law to declare the principal of the 5–20 bonds payable in currency.

"Mr. Chase took the bull by the horns by declaring, over his own signature, that the principal as well as the interest of the 5–20 bonds were payable in gold, the faith of the United States being pledged to this by the tacit understanding of the government and its creditors.

"Nothing has reflected more credit and renown upon that great statesman—then as prominent and favored a son of the noble State of Ohio as you are to-day—and nothing more effectually paved the way to the great work of reducing the burden of our people by lowering our interest one-third than that expression, sanctioned and confirmed by subsequent enactment of Congress in 1869.

*   *   *   *   *   *   *   *   *

"You will, in my opinion, insure the success of your financial measures, and add greatly to your high and prominent political position, if you will unequivocally declare that the funded debt of the government can only be redeemed, principal and interest, in gold coin, and that until otherwise agreed upon by the mutual consent of the great commercial nations of the United States, England, France, and Germany, the silver dollar can only be accepted as an auxiliary standard for the payment of fractional indebtedness."

To this I replied as follows:

TREASURY DEPARTMENT, }
WASHINGTON, June 16, 1877. }

DEAR SIR:—Your private note, the letter of your firm, and one from Messrs. Seligman & Co., asking me to make a public statement over my own signature, similar to that of Mr. French, are received. I have given to this important suggestion the most serious consideration, and have come to the firm conclusion that such an act on my part would be inexpedient, and defeat the very object you have in view. As a purely executive officer, I have no power to pass upon the question mooted. My attempt to do so would at once unite all those who are seized with this mania, and those who oppose executive encroachment upon legislative power. It would create excitement, personal and political animosities would mingle with it, and it would tend more than anything else to defeat the success of the loan. I am quite sure this would be the result.

As to whether Congress or the people would ever undertake to pay either principal or interest of the bonded debt, and especially the bonds sold since 1873, in silver, I have a firm conviction that the question will never seriously be raised. These bonds will be paid, principal and interest, in gold coin. The people of the United States have always been extremely sensitive as to the public credit. They never have, for the sake of an apparent profit, yielded any question involving the public honor.

The great satisfaction that will arise from the funding of the loan at a low rate of interest, together with their strong sense of public honor and public faith, will always secure the payment of these bonds, principal and interest, in coin.

Parties or factions may, for a time, raise and contest questions, but they are but bubbles, and will pass away, and, like all other questions involving the public credit, will be rightfully settled, in due time, by Congress and the people.

Nothing would so tend to disturb this result as unauthorized 'theses,' or dogmas, by an executive officer, upon a question purely legislative or judicial. Indeed, it may be that too much has already been said about this matter by both the President and myself, and I assure you that you will have no occasion to be disturbed by anything truthfully reported of either of us hereafter. The better way is to move right along, making your own statements, and if, at any time, I see a proper occasion for a strong expression of my opinion, I will give it.

Please show this to Mr. Seligman, and such of your associates as you deem proper, as an answer to all. Very truly yours,   JOHN SHERMAN.

HON. AUGUST BELMONT, New York.

The new loan was promptly placed on the market on the 14th of June by the following circular letter signed by the members of the syndicate :

Under the authority of a contract with the Secretary of the Treasury, the undersigned hereby give notice that from this date until July 16, at 3 p. m., they will receive subscriptions for the four per cent. funded loan of the United States in denominations as stated below, at par and accrued interest in gold coin.

The bonds are redeemable after thirty years from July 1, 1877, and carry interest from that date, payable quarterly, and are exempt from the payment of taxes or duties to the United States, as well as from taxation in any form, by or under state, municipal, or local authority.

The interest on the registered stock will be paid by check, issued by the treasurer of the United States to the order of the holder, and mailed to his address. The check is payable on presentation, properly indorsed, at the offices of the treasurer and assistant treasurers of the United States.

The subscriptions will be for coupon bonds of $50 and $100, and registered stock in denominations of $50, $100, $500, $1,000, $5,000, and $10,000.

The bonds, both coupon and registered, will be ready for delivery July 2, 1877.

Forms of application will be furnished by the treasurer at Washington, the assistant treasurers at Baltimore, Boston, Chicago, Cincinnati, New Orleans, New York, Philadelphia, St. Louis, and San Francisco, and by the national banks and bankers generally. The applications must specify the amount and denominations required, and for registered stock the full name and post office address of the person to whom the bonds shall be made payable.

Two per cent. of the purchase money must accompany the subscription. The remainder may be paid, at the pleasure of the purchaser, either at the time of the subscription or at any time prior to October 16, 1877, with interest added at four per cent. to date of payment.

The payments may be made in gold coin to the treasurer of the United States at Washington, or assistant treasurers at Baltimore, Boston, Chicago, Cincinnati, New Orleans, and St. Louis, and to the assistant treasurer at San Francisco, with exchange on New York, or to either of the undersigned.

To promote the convenience of subscribers, the undersigned will also receive, in lieu of coin, United States notes or drafts on New York, at their coin value on the day of receipt in the city of New York.

AUGUST BELMONT & Co., New York.

DREXEL, MORGAN & Co., New York.

J. & W. SELIGMAN & Co., New York.

June 16, 1877.   MORTON, BLISS & Co., New York.

FIRST NATIONAL BANK, New York.

DREXEL & Co., Philadelphia.

A few days later I wrote the following letter:

TREASURY DEPARTMENT, ⎰
WASHINGTON, D. C., June 19, 1877. ⎱

SIR :— Your letter of the 18th instant, in which you inquire whether the four per cent. bonds now being sold by the government are payable, principal and interest, in gold coin, is received. The subject, from its great importance, has demanded and received careful consideration.

Under laws now in force, there is no coin issued or issuable in which the principal of the four per cent. bonds is redeemable, or the interest payable, except the gold coins of the United States of the standard value fixed by laws in force on the 14th of July, 1870, when the bonds were authorized.

The government exacts, in exchange for these bonds, payment at par in such gold coin, and it is not to be anticipated that any future legislation of Congress, or any action of any department of the government, would sanction or tolerate the redemption of the principal of these bonds, or the payment of the interest thereon, in coin, of less value than the coin authorized by law at the time of the issue of the bonds, being the coin exacted by the government in exchange for the same.

The essential element of *good faith*, in preserving the equality in value between the coinage in which the government receives and that in which it pays these bonds, will be sacredly observed by the government and the people of the United States, whatever may be the system of coinage which the general policy of the nation may at any time adopt.

This principle is impressed upon the text of the law of July 14, 1870, under which the four per cent. bonds are issued, and requires, in the opinion of the executive department of the government, the redemption of these bonds and the payment of their interest in coin of equal value with that which the government receives from its issue.

Very respectfully,   JOHN SHERMAN, Secretary.
FRANCIS O. FRENCH, Esq., 94 Broadway, New York.

The subscriptions were taken in every part of the United States, and within thirty days $67,600,000 were taken in this country and $10,200,000 in Europe, making $77,800,000 sold. This sum, when applied to the payment of the six per cent. bonds, made an annual saving to the people of the United States of $1,556,000. Since the 1st of March, 1877, there had been sold under the refunding act $135,000,000 four and a half per cent. bonds and that amount of six per cent. bonds was paid off and canceled, thus saving to the people of the United States $2,025,000 in coin each year. The aggregate reduction of interest by both classes of bonds, from the 1st of March to the close of the popular loan, was $3,581,000 a year in coin. This was regarded as a great success.

Early in July I set out on the revenue cutter "U. S. Grant" on a visit of inspection along the north Atlantic coast, accompanied by the chief of the coast survey, the secretary of the lighthouse board, the superintendent of the life-saving service, and the chief of the revenue marine service, and also by Webb Hayes, the son of the President. We visited the life-saving stations along the New Jersey coast. I was deeply interested in this service, which I regard as the most deserving humanitarian branch of the public service. We also visited some of the leading lighthouses along the coast and the principal custom-houses between the Chesapeake Bay and Eastport, Maine. We were everywhere received with great kindness and many social courtesies were extended to us, especially in New York, Boston and Portland. This outing was a great relief from the close confinement I had undergone since the 4th of March. The information I gathered as to these branches of the service, with which I had not previously had much acquaintance, was of great value to me. Such trips are sometimes treated by the press as "junketing" at the public expense. This is a great error. Each of us paid his share of the expenses and the vessel only pursued its usual course of duty. I was brought into close association with these subordinate officers of the department and became informed of their duties, and their fitness for them, and was enabled to act with intelligence on their recommendations.

The only unpleasant incident that occurred on the trip was the running of the cutter upon a rock upon the coast of Maine. This happened in the afternoon of a beautiful day. All the gentlemen with me and the officers of the vessel were on deck. The various buoys were being pointed out and a map of the channel was lying before us. Some mention was made of a buoy that ought to be near the place where we were to mark the location of a rock, but none was found, and suddenly we heard the scraping of the vessel upon the rock. The cutter trembled and careened over. The captain was somewhat alarmed and turned the vessel toward the beach, where it was speedily examined and found to be somewhat injured. We ascertained afterwards that the buoy had been displaced by a storm and that a vessel was then on its way to replace it. The sinking of the revenue cutter "U. S. Grant" was reported in the morning dispatches and created some excitement; but the vessel did not sustain any substantial injury. We thought it best to leave it for a time to be thoroughly examined and repaired, and took another vessel to complete our journey to Eastport, the northeastern port of the United States. From thence Webb Hayes and myself returned to Portland and crossed over to Burlington, Vermont, on Lake Champlain, and from thence went to Saratoga, where we remained a few days, and then returned to Washington on the 22nd of July. We passed through Baltimore on the day the riots occurred in that city, and soon after heard of the much more dangerous outbreak in Pittsburg.

On the 6th of August I wrote to Mr. Conant as follows:

"Your letter of the 26th ultimo is received. You can safely say to the Messrs. Rothschild that the strikes have been totally disconnected with the government, but grow purely out of a contract between the managers of leading lines of railway and their employes as to rates of pay.

"The railroad companies have, for several years, competed with each other in a very improvident and reckless way, and are now, and have been for some time, carrying freight for less than cost. This has caused a large reduction of the net income of roads, has led to the loss of dividends, and now to the reduction of wages of employes to rates scarcely sufficient to support life. Hence the strikes.

"The government has been appealed to by both railroads and strikers, by states and by cities, for relief, and has promptly extended it in every proper case, and, without shedding blood, has, in every case, suppressed the riot, and maintained the peace, so that the government is really stronger by reason of these unfortunate events than before. I do not observe that any change has been made by them, either in the price of bonds or in the price of gold, nor in the payment of subscriptions to four per cent. bonds.

"No effort is made to sell the bonds now, nor do I care to press the home market, until enough bonds are sold abroad to provide for called bonds abroad.

"The month of August must necessarily be a languid one, and I do not advise any unusual efforts to force sales.

"Your supplemental cipher was received after your telegram, but was soon found and dispatch made out."

I no doubt was mistaken in the effect of the strikes upon our public credit. From that time forward for many months there was scarcely any sale of government bonds at any price. The contracting parties informed me that no bonds were then selling in the market and that in New York they were a trifle below par. Practically, for the remainder of the year, government securities were greatly affected in price and value.

CHAPTER XXX.

Policy of the Hayes Administration.

Reception at My Home in Mansfield — Given by Friends Irrespective of Party —
Introduced by My Old Friend and Partner Henry C. Hedges — I Reply by Giving
a Résumé of the Contests in South Carolina and Louisiana to Decide Who
Was Governor — Positions Taken by Presidents Grant and Hayes in These
Contests — My Plans to Secure the Resumption of Specie Payments —
Effects of a Depreciated Currency — Duties of the Secretary of the
Treasury — Two Modes of Resuming — My Mansfield Speech
Printed Throughout the Country and in England — Let-
ters to Stanley Matthews and General Robinson — Our
Defeat in Ohio — An Extra Session of Congress —
Bills Introduced to Repeal the Act Providing
for the Resumption of Specie Payments —
They All Fail of Passage — Popular
Subscription of Bonds All Paid for.

ABOUT the 10th of August I made my usual visit to my home at Mansfield. Soon after my arrival I received the following invitation, signed by a great number of my neighbors and friends, without respect to party, expressing a desire to tender me a reception :

Hon. John Sherman.

DEAR SIR : — The undersigned, your townsmen, and fellow-citizens of Richland county, desire to give you some manifestation of the very high regard in which we hold your public services. We are glad to know that you are permitted to again be at your own home, and for a week or two mingle with us in all the unrestrained freedom of friends and townsmen.

Financial and other public questions are, however, of importance to us always, and especially now. We recognize your great ability and long experience, and cannot but think that an expression of your views on these questions will be very highly prized by the people of Ohio, irrespective of party. We therefore desire, with your sanction, on some day during the next week, to give you a hearty welcome to your old home, and shall be glad to have you, on the occasion, give your views on the public questions, now of such vast importance to all. With our kindest regards, we are,

Your friends, etc., etc.

(584)

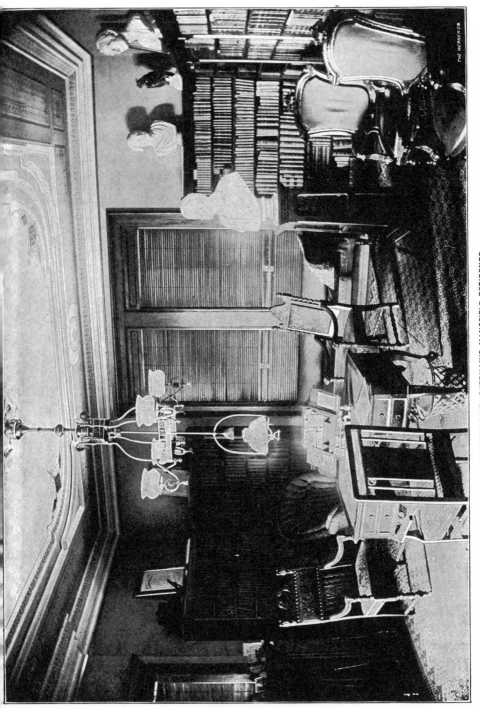

LIBRARY OF MR. SHERMAN'S MANSFIELD RESIDENCE.

I replied as follows:

MANSFIELD, O., August 13, 1877.

GENTLEMEN :—I received with much pleasure your kindly letter of the 10th inst., signed by so many of my old friends and neighbors in Mansfield, and assure you of my high appreciation of your generous words of courtesy and regard.

I always return with satisfaction to my home on the western slopes of our little city, and always enjoy the fresh air and picturesque country around us, but, more than all, the cordial greetings of old friends, with whom I have been acquainted since boyhood. It will give me much pleasure, at any time or place, to meet you, and to speak to you on current public questions, and I venture to name next Friday evening.

Very truly yours,   JOHN SHERMAN.

The gathering was one of the largest that had come together in Mansfield for years. The evening was delightful, cool and balmy, a bright moonlight adding attraction to the scene. A stand decorated with flags had been erected near the center of the park, with seats in front, and lights gleamed on either hand. I was introduced to the audience by my old friend and partner, Henry C. Hedges, whose remarks were too flattering for me to insert. In closing he said:

" Regarding you as our friend, our neighbor, our townsman, we are glad and rejoice. We welcome you home, though your stay may be only a few days, and we sincerely trust that, rested by your stay, you may go back to your work reinvigorated, and that frequently we may have the pleasure of your temporary visits, and in the future, when your labors are finished, among us you may spend your old age, honored and happy."

As my speech expressed my views upon important questions of that time, I think it well to embody extracts from it as part of the history of the then recent events, and my anticipations for the future:

" The kindly words of welcome uttered by my friend and associate of many years move me beyond expression. They recall to me the scene of the early time when I came to Mansfield, then a scattered hamlet of about 1,100 inhabitants, without pavements and without any of the modern conveniences of cities and towns. As Mr. Hedges has told you, very many of those I then met here are dead and gone. I was a boy then. A generation has passed away, and the sons of those I met then as citizens of Richland county now fill places of trust and responsibility. I have every reason in the world for being strongly attached to this town of Mansfield. You have always been kind to me. Here I studied law, here I practiced my profession for

several years, here I married my wife, a native of your town, here I have
lived ever since, and when this mortal coil shall be shuffled off, here, probably, will my body rest with your fathers.   But pardon me, fellow-citizens,
if, under the kind words of welcome of your spokesman, my old and honored
friend, Mr. Hedges, I had forgotten that we are not here merely to exchange
courtesies, but to discuss grave matters of far more importance than the life
or memories of an individual.

"In doing so I wish it distinctly understood that I speak for myself alone,
as a citizen of Ohio, to you my fellow-citizens and my neighbors, to whom I
am under the highest obligations of gratitude and duty.

"The President authorized me to say one thing, and one thing only, for
him, and in his name, and that is that all reports that impute to him any
participation whatever in the nomination of candidates on your state ticket,
or any desire or purpose to influence in any way the senatorial contest in
Ohio, are utterly groundless.

"These are your matters, and I can assure you for him, that he does not
and will not, interpose in any such contest between political friends.

"You all know that I am now, and have been, warmly attached to the
Republican party.   I believe in its principles and honor its work.   With
my strong convictions I could not conceal my partisan bias, or my earnest
hope for the success of the Republican party, but the subjects of which I
intend to speak to you to-night will not lead me to say much of former
political struggles, or to fight our old battles over again, but chiefly to
discuss the actual administrative questions of the day as they have arisen
since the 4th of March last, and in all of which you are alike interested,
whether you may call yourselves Republicans or Democrats.   As to these
questions I wish fairly to appeal to the candor and good judgment of
honest men of both parties, only asking for the administration of President
Hayes that considerate charity of judgment which must be extended to all
human agents.

When Mr. Hayes was inaugurated as President he found thirty-six
states in the full and uncontested exercise of all the powers of states in the
Union.   In two states only there were contests as to who was governor.
Both contests had existed from January to March, 1877, while General
Grant was President.

In South Carolina Governor Chamberlain claimed to have been elected
on the Republican ticket, and General Hampton on the Democratic ticket.
The President is not made the judge of who is elected governor of a state,
and an attempt to exercise such a power would be a plain act of usurpation.
The constitution of South Carolina is much like that of Ohio.   The count of
the vote was to be made by the general assembly of the state.   Unfortunately for Chamberlain a controlling question in the contest had been
decided against him by a Republican court, and he was only kept in possession of the state house by the actual presence of United States troops in the
building.   He had appealed again and again to President Grant to

recognize him as governor and to give him the aid of Federal troops in the enforcement of his claim, which General Grant had refused, seeking only to preserve the public peace.

" When President Hayes was inaugurated both contestants were called to Washington and both were patiently heard and the questions presented were patiently and carefully examined. The President held that a case was not presented in which, under the constitution and the laws, he was justified in using the army of the United States in deciding a purely local election contest. The soldiers and bayonets of the United States were then withdrawn from the state house—not from the state, nor the capital of the state —but from the building in which the legislature, that alone could lawfully decide this contest, must meet. This was all that was done by the President, and Governor Chamberlain, without further contesting his claim, abandoned it and left the state.

" I say to you now that, strongly as I desired the success of Governor Chamberlain and the Republican party in South Carolina, the President had not a shadow of right to interpose the power of the army in this contest, and his attempt to do so would have been rash and abortive as well as without legal right.

" The case of Louisiana was far more difficult. The local returning officers of that state had, after a full examination, certified to the election of the legislature, showing a Republican majority in both houses. This had been done by excluding from their return the votes of certain parishes and counties wherein intimidation, violence and fraud had prevailed to an extent sufficient to change the result of the election. I was present, at the request of General Grant, to witness the count, and I assure you, as I have said officially, that the proof of this intimidation, violence and fraud, extending to murder, cruelty, and outrage in every form, was absolutely conclusive, showing a degree of violence in some of those parishes that was more revolting and barbarous than anything I could conceive of. It was plain that the returning officers had the legal right to pass upon and certify, in the first instance, who were elected members of the legislature, and that they were justified by the evidence in excluding bulldozed parishes, but it was equally clear that their return was not conclusive upon the members elected, and that each house had the constitutional right to pass upon the returns and elections of its members, and to set aside the action of the returning board. The two houses, when organized, had also the power to pass upon the returns of the election of governor, and they alone and no one else. Neither the President of the United States nor the returning board has any power or right to pass upon the election of governor. And here the difficulty in the Louisiana case commences.

" Governor Packard contends that a majority of the two houses, as duly returned, did pass upon the election of the governor, and did return that he was duly elected, but this was stoutly denied by Governor Nichols. This vital point was strongly asserted and denied by the adverse parties, and the legislature of Louisiana divided into two hostile bodies, holding separate sessions, each asserting its legal power, and denouncing the other as rebels and traitors. Governor Packard and his legislature called upon President Grant for the aid of the army to put down insurrection and domestic violence; and here I confess that if I had been President, instead of General Grant, I would have recognized Packard and sustained him with the full power of the general government. My intense feeling, caused by the atrocities in Louisiana, may have unduly influenced me. But General Grant did not think this was his duty. I do not criticise his action, but only state the facts. He would only maintain the peace. He would not recognize Packard as governor, but I know, what is now an open secret, the strong bent of his mind, and at one time his decision was to withdraw the troops, to recognize Nichols and thus end this dangerous contest. He did not do this, but kept the peace.

But during these two months the whole condition of affairs had slowly changed in Louisiana. The government of Packard had dwindled away until it had scarcely a shadow of strength or authority, except at the state house, where it was upheld by federal bayonets. The government of Nichols had extended its authority over the state and was in full existence as the *de facto* government of Louisiana, supported by the great body of the white men and nearly all the wealth and intelligence of the state, and by the tired acquiescence of a large portion of the colored people, some of whom deserted Packard's legislature and entered that of Governor Nichols. The delay and hesitation of General Grant had been fatal to Packard, and when Hayes became President the practical question was greatly changed. One thing was clear, that a legislature had been duly elected in November previous, and was then in existence, though separated into two parts. If the members lawfully elected could be convened, they alone could decide the question of who was governor, without the intervention of troops, and their decision could be supported, if necessary, by the general government.

"The most anxious consideration was given to this question. Days and weeks of anxious deliberation were given to it by the President and his cabinet. But one way seemed open for a peaceful solution, and that was to gather, if possible, a single legislature that could be recognized as the depositary of the representative will of the people of Louisiana. If this could be done it had the unquestioned right to decide who had been elected governor, and all other questions would settle themselves. To aid in this object, a commission of the most eminent men, high in position, from different states, and distinguished for judicial impartiality, was selected and the result is known to all. They went to Louisiana, and, with great difficulty, brought together these hostile legislatures which met, organized, promptly settled the questions in dispute in favor of the government of Nichols, and thus ended this most dangerous controversy. No other change was made, no other act done except, when the solution was almost accomplished, the few troops which had occupied the state house were withdrawn a few squares away, to their barracks. Thus, in this peaceful appeal to the legislature of Louisiana, this controversy, which not only endangered the peace and safety of this state, but the peace and safety of the whole people of the United States, was settled. This is the sum and substance of all that was done in the southern policy, as it is called, of the President.

"Perhaps I ought to state that his policy has a broader motive than a mere settlement of a local election contest. It seeks to bring the north and south again into conditions of harmony and fraternity, and, by a frank appeal to the generous impulses and patriotic feeling of all classes of people in the south, to secure, not only peace among themselves, but the equal protection of the laws to all, and security in the enjoyment of political and civil rights.

"No doubt the result in Louisiana caused some disappointment to many Republicans throughout the United States, who deeply sympathized with their Republican brethren in that state. In that feeling I did, and do, share, and yet I feel and know that every step taken by President Hayes was right, in strict accordance with his constitutional duty, and from the highest motives of patriotism. Some are foolish enough to talk of his abandoning the colored people and their constitutional rights. President Hayes, from his early manhood, has been an anti-slavery man; his life was imperiled on many battlefields in the great cause of liberty, he sympathizes more and will do more for the equal rights of the colored people than those who falsely accuse him, and I believe this day, that the policy he has adopted will do more to secure the full practical enforcement of those rights than the employment of an army tenfold greater than the army of the United States."

In this speech I stated the action I proposed to take to secure the resumption of specie payments. The plan was executed in all its parts by me, and my remarks may, in one sense, be said to be a history of resumption. Continuing I said:

"And now, fellow-citizens, this brings me to the question upon which there is so much diversity of opinion, so many strange delusions, and that is the question of specie payments. What do we mean by this phrase ? Is it, that we are to have no paper money in circulation ? If so, I am as much opposed to it as any of you. Is it that we are to retire our greenback circulation ? If so, I am opposed to it and have often so said. What I mean by specie payments is simply that paper money ought to be made equal to coin, so that when you receive it, it will buy as much beef, corn or clothing as coin.

"Now the importance of this cannot be overestimated. A depreciated paper money cheats and robs every man who receives it, of a portion of the reward of his labor or production, and, in all times, it has been treated by statesmen as one of the greatest evils that can befall a people. There are times when such money is unavoidable, as during war or great public calamity, but it has always been the anxious care of statesmen to return again to the solid standard of coin. Therefore it is that specie payments, or a specie standard, is pressed by the great body of intelligent men who study these questions, as an indispensable prerequisite for steady business and good times.

"Now, most of you will agree to all this, and will only differ as to the mode, or time, and manner; but there is a large class of people who believe that paper can be, and ought to be, made into money without any promise or hope of redemption; that a note should be printed: 'This is a dollar,' and be made a legal tender.

"I regard this as a mild form of lunacy, and have no disposition to debate with men who indulge in such delusions, which have prevailed to some extent, at different times, in all countries, but whose life has been brief, and which have ever shared the fate of other popular delusions. Congress will never entertain such a proposition, and, if it should, we know that the scheme would not stand a moment before the Supreme Court. That court only maintained the constitutionality of the legal tender promise to pay a dollar by a divided court, and on the ground that it was issued during the war, as in the nature of a forced loan, to be redeemed upon the payment of a real dollar; that is, so many grains of silver or gold.

"I therefore dismiss such wild theories, and speak only to those who are willing to assume, as an axiom, that gold and silver, or coined money, have been proven by all human experience to be the best possible standards of value, and that paper money is simply a promise to pay such coined money, and should be made and kept equal to coined money, by being convertible on demand.

"Now, the question is as to the time and mode by which this may be brought about, and on this subject no man should be dogmatic, or stand, without yielding, upon a plan of his own, but should be willing to give and take, securing the best expedient that public opinion will allow to be adopted. The purpose and obligation to bring our paper money to the standard of coin have been over and over again announced by acts of Congress, and by the platforms of the great political parties of the country. If resolutions and promises would bring about specie payments, we would have been there long ago; but the diversity of opinion as to the mode now—twelve years after the close of the war—still leaves our paper money at a discount of five per cent. Until this is removed, there will be no new enterprises involving great sums, no active industries, but money will lie idle, and watch and wait the changes that may be made before we reach the specie standard.

"In 1869, Congress pledged the public faith that the United States would pay coin for United States notes. Again, in January, 1875, after more than a year's debate, Congress declared that on and after the 1st of January, 1879, the United States would pay its notes in coin.

"The Secretary of the Treasury is expressly required to prepare for, and maintain, the redemption of all United States notes presented at the treasury on and after that date, and for that purpose he is authorized to use all the surplus revenue, and to sell bonds of the United States bearing four, four and a half, and five per cent. interest, at par in coin. It is this law, called the resumption act, now so much discussed in the papers, that imposes upon the office I hold most difficult and important duties, and without replying to any attacks made upon me, I am anxious to convey to you personally, what I have done, and what I must do, in obedience to the provisions of this act. It is said that the law is defective, but, if the great object and policy of the law is right, the machinery of the law could easily be changed by Congress. That resumption can be secured, and ought to be secured, under this law, it will be my purpose to show you, and I shall not hesitate to point out such defects in the law as have occurred to me in its execution.

"There are two modes of resumption; one is to diminish the amount of notes to be redeemed, which mode is commonly called a contraction of the currency; the other is to accumulate coin in the treasury, to enable the secretary to maintain the notes at par."

Objection had been made that under the first mode resumption would be a process of converting a non-interest bearing note into an interest bearing note, and that was true, but what right had we, as a nation, or had any bank, or individual, to force into circulation, as money, its note upon which it paid no interest? Why ought not anyone who issued a promise to pay on demand be made to pay it when demanded, or pay interest thereafter? What right had he, in law or justice, to insist upon maintaining in circulation his note, which he refused to pay according to his promise, and which he refused to receive in payment of a note bearing interest? A certain amount of United States notes could be, and ought to be, maintained at par in coin, with the aid of a moderate coin reserve held in the treasury, and to the extent that this could be done they formed the best possible paper money, a debt of the people without interest, of equal value with coin, and more convenient to carry and handle. Beyond this the issue of paper money, either by the government or by banks, was a dangerous exercise of power, injurious to all citizens, and should not continue a single day beyond the necessities that gave it birth. I added:

"The one practical defect in the law is, that the secretary is not at liberty to sell bonds of the United States for United States notes, but must sell them for coin. As coin is not in circulation among the people, he is practically prohibited from selling bonds to the people, except by an evasion of the law, or through private parties. Bonds are in demand and can readily be sold at par in coin, and still easier at par, or at a premium, in United States notes. The process of selling for United States notes need not go far before the mere fact that they are receivable for bonds would bring them up to par in coin, and that is specie payments.

"But the reason of the refusal of Congress to grant this authority, often asked of it, was that it would contract the currency, and this fear of contraction has thus far prevented Congress from granting the easiest, plainest, and surest mode of resumption. To avoid contraction, it provided that national bank notes may be issued without limit as to amount, and that, when issued, United States notes might be retired to the extent of four-fifths of the bank notes issued. This was the only provision for redeeming United States notes that Congress made or would make, and this, it was supposed, would reduce the United States notes to $300,000,000 before January 1, 1879. The actual experiment only proves the folly of the cry we had for more money, more money."

The second mode of resuming was by accumulating coin gradually, so that when the time fixed for resumption should arrive, the treasury might be able to redeem such notes as should be presented. In this respect the resumption act was as full and liberal as human language could frame it. The secretary was authorized to prepare for resumption, and for that purpose to use the surplus revenue and sell either of the three classes of bonds, all of which in 1877 were at or above par in coin. I said : " The power can be, ought to be, and will be, executed if not repealed."

This speech was printed in the leading papers in the United States and in England, and was regarded by the public at large as a declaration of the policy of the administration, to enforce the resumption law, whatever might be the current of opinion developed at the approaching elections, which, as they occurred, were generally against the Republican party. The Democratic party had taken position against the resumption act, in favor of the enlarged issue of United States notes and the free coinage of silver. The strikes led to the organization of labor unions, which, though independent of political parties, chiefly affected the Republican party then in power.

DEPARTMENT OF STATE.

WASHINGTON.

Washington D.C.
Aug. 30th '77

Dear Mrs. Thurman,

I congratulate you on the excellence & success of your speech in Ohio. You appointed of the nominate being justly of the nominate the verdict of interesting the verdict of the Southern Republican Presidential.

I enclose to resume on the "Republican resume from one on the subject of a new arrangement as the recommendary of the Southern resume.

...and...

The President's visit here pleasure. The Southern in here Eagleness accordingly.

I hope to see you as in Washington early next week.

I am yours very truly

W.M. Evarts

For Mrs.
Mrs. Thurman
Secy of State.

Among many letters received by me, after this speech, I insert one from Mr. Evarts:

WINDSOR, Vt., Aug. 30, 1877.

THE HON. JOHN SHERMAN, Secretary of the Treasury.

DEAR MR. SHERMAN :— I congratulate you upon the excellence and success of your speech in Ohio. The difficulty of the undertaking justly enhances the credit of its prosperous treatment.

I inclose a remonstrance from an 'Injustice' on the subject of a new arrangement in the *weighing* at the customhouse. It was sent to me at Washington and forwarded from there here. I know nothing of its source and have no opinion on the subject of the supposed project.

The President's visit has pleased the people in New England amazingly. I hope to see you all in Washington early next week.

I am very truly yours, WM. M. EVARTS.

On the 14th of September, 1877, I sent to Hon. Stanley Matthews the following letter, giving my view of the position taken by General Ewing and Mr. Pendleton:

" At the request of General Robinson I have directed to you, in the care of Bickham, a number of documents for reference in your debate with Ewing, and as Robinson says you wish me to make suggestions, I venture to do so, but without any confidence that they can be of assistance, though they can do no harm.

" The most beneficial financial act of the administration is the reduction of the interest on the public debt. The amount already accomplished is stated in my printed speech. The rapidity of this process depends entirely upon the credit of the government. Ewing's policy would destroy our credit and stop the process. The very doubts created by him and Pendleton have already damaged the government very largely. Confidence is so sensitive that when prominent men like Ewing and Pendleton talk as they do, the injury is immediate.

" The whole difference between the amount of silver and gold at this moment is eight per cent., so that the payment of the debt in silver would lessen the burden of the debt eight per cent., but under the funding operations, which would be entirely destroyed by anything that alarmed the market, we are enabled to save thirty-three per cent. Whatever may be our right to pay our bonds, either in greenbacks or in silver, this question of expediency, as you very properly said in one of your speeches, is to be considered apart from the question of legal power.

" Refunding would go on with greatly accelerated speed if we could sell bonds for greenbacks. We make discrimination against the greenbacks by refusing to take them in payment of bonds. If I had the power to sell bonds for greenbacks I could make greenbacks equal to coin with scarcely a perceptible change. That is the advice of the most sagacious men in the country. I know it. There is talk about the bondholder being a privileged person. He ought to be so no longer, and the moment that a bond could be bought with currency at par in gold, all discrimination in favor of the bondholder would disappear.

"The differences among Republicans about silver will be settled by the use of the silver dollar to the extent that it can be kept in circulation at par with greenbacks, and is a pure question of detail. The difference in the Democratic party about interconvertible currency is vital, and Ewing's doctrine overthrows the whole Democratic theory of finance before the war.

"The existence of the national banks is a question simply of policy not a question of principle. The right conferred upon banks to issue circulation is not conferred for their profit, but for the public convenience, and all Republicans can agree that that right should never be permitted to exist except when it is for the public convenience. The office of bank notes is simply to supply the ebb and flow of currency made necessary by the wants of business. The United States cannot lend United States notes, and therefore cannot meet this want. Ewing proposes to destroy the whole national bank system, interwoven with all the business of the country. I send you the last statement of the national banks. You can very easily show the effect upon the reviving industry of the country of the withdrawal of these loans and disturbing all this business. As at present organized the circulation is the vital thing, and if the bonds held by the banks to secure circulation were thrown upon the market, it would stop funding and compel also the withdrawal of loans, and create distress compared with which our present troubles are mere moonshine.

"I am afraid you will think I am going on to make a speech for you, so I will stop abruptly, with the promise that if I can furnish you any documents or information that may be of service to you I will do so with pleasure.

＊　　＊　　＊　　＊　　＊　　＊　　＊　　＊　　＊

"I inclose the last statement of the national banks containing many points that may be of use.

"Upon the question of resumption I believe we are all agreed that it must come, and that the only standard value is gold or silver coin. The time and manner are the points of disagreement. Ewing is opposed to all resumption, but believes in printing a dollar and saying it is a dollar, while all the world would know that the declaration is a lie. The fact that we have advanced the greenbacks six per cent. in one year, by the movements made under the resumption act, shows that it is working pretty well. I send you a statement showing the changed condition in a year of our finances.

"While the people differ about the resumption act there is time to change it if it needs change, but Ewing would go back and commence the process over again. I am disposed to be tolerant about differences on the resumption act, for I think it will demonstrate its success or failure before Congress is likely to tamper with it."

On the 21st of September I wrote to General J. S. Robinson the following letter, evincing my anxiety as to the result of the canvass in Ohio, as it was then conducted:

" I am so deeply impressed with the importance of the campaign in Ohio that it makes me uneasy and restless that I cannot participate in it.

" What a magnificent chance the Republican party in Ohio now has, not only to place itself in the vanguard in the United States, but to do this country a service as great as any victory won by the Union army during the war. Here it is demonstrated by the cordial reception of the President in the south, by his hearty indorsement in Massachusetts, and by a public sentiment now growing and spreading with amazing rapidity, that in his southern policy he has opened the means of order, safety, peace and security in all the southern states.

" Now, when it is demonstrated that the difficulties in the way of resumption were myths conjured up by the fantasies of demagogues, when our notes are worth within three per cent. of gold, when Providence has favored us with boundless crops, and prosperity is again coming upon us after a dreary time of distress and trial caused by inflated paper money, why is it that we cannot see all these things and avail ourselves of the advantage they give us in our political contest? It seems to me that we ought to carry the state by an overwhelming majority, and if we do so we will establish the beneficial principles of our party beyond danger of overthrow by reaction, and we will secure the peaceful and orderly development of industry without a parallel in our previous history.

" I wish it were in my power to impress every Republican in Ohio with my earnest conviction about this matter, but here, constantly occupied by official duties, I can only remain watching and waiting in anxious suspense lest the great advantages we possess shall be frittered away or lost by inaction or mistakes.

" I know you will do your utmost for success, and only write you this to show you how earnestly I sympathize with you in your efforts."

The election in Ohio, in October, resulted in the defeat of William H. West, Republican, for governor, mainly on account of his position as to labor unions, but no doubt also because of a feeling of opposition against the resumption of specie payments. Richard M. Bishop, Democrat, was elected governor, with a Democratic legislature in both branches, which subsequently elected George H. Pendleton as United States Senator.

The following letter expresses my view of the election, and the causes which led to our defeat:

WASHINGTON, October 17, 1877.

DEAR SIR:—Your letter of the 13th inst. is received.

Your statement of the causes of our defeat in Ohio seems to me reasonable, though probably I would not agree with you in many points stated.

It is not worth while now to bother ourselves about what we cannot help. All we can do is to inquire how far we have been right, and to that extent pursue the right, whether victory or defeat is the result. No party can administer a government, that will not take the risk of temporary defeat when it is pursuing what, in the opinion of the great masses of it, is a beneficial policy for the country.

So far as the southern question is concerned, I feel that the President did right. The wisdom of his executive order as to office holders depends upon the construction given to it, and he is not responsible for a perverted construction not authorized by its words or terms. As to the resumption policy, the law is plain and mandatory, and, more than all, the law is right, and the Republican party might as well understand first as last, that the question of resumption is one higher than any party obligations and will be pursued by our adversaries if we do not. We can gain the credit of success, but we can gain no credit by retreating on this vital question. While the law stands nothing is left but to execute it, and for one I never would aid to alter the law, except to make it more effective, and would be very willing to retire on this question rather than to surrender.

The only way is for us to go steadily forward, with a certainty that public opinion in the end will sustain us if we do what is substantially right. The Republican party has been in this position many times and has never won success by retreat and cannot do so now. Very truly yours, JOHN SHERMAN.

A. P. MILLER, ESQ., Toledo, Ohio.

It became necessary for the President to call an extra session of Congress, on account of the failure of the passage of the army bill at the previous session. Though the proclamation was issued on the 5th of May, 1877, Congress was not convened until the 15th of October following. Both Houses met on the day appointed. The Senate was organized by the election of Thomas W. Ferry, of Michigan, as president *pro tempore*, and Samuel J. Randall, a Democratic Member from Pennsylvania, was elected speaker of the House by a majority of seventeen over James A. Garfield, the Republican candidate.

The message of the President was confined mainly to the circumstances connected with the failure of the previous Congress to provide for the support of the army, and to certain deficiencies in appropriations required for the government, the President stating that as certain acts of Congress, providing for reports of the government officials, required their submission at the regular annual session, he deferred until that time any further reference to subjects of public interest.

Congress, however, not being confined in its powers, and having full jurisdiction of all legislative questions, proceeded at once to discuss financial questions and especially the measures taken for the resumption of specie payments. No less than four bills were introduced in the Senate and fourteen in the House, providing for the repeal, in whole or in part, of the act for the resumption of specie payments. One of these bills was reported from the committee on banking and currency, by Mr. Ewing, on the 31st of October. It was the subject of debate during the remaining period of the session, and finally passed the House on the 23rd of November, by the vote of 133 yeas and 120 nays. It repealed all that part of the resumption act which authorized the Secretary of the Treasury to dispose of United States bonds, and to redeem and cancel the greenback currency, or practically all the resumption act except the clauses for the substitution of silver coin for fractional currency. It was sent to the Senate on the 26th of November, and referred to the committee on finance. No action was taken upon it during that session, which adjourned on the 3rd of December. The regular session convened on the same day, with this bill still pending in the committee on finance. On the 17th of April, 1878, Mr. Ferry, from that committee, reported back the bill with an amendment to strike out all after the enacting clause, and insert new matter. After a long debate ending on the 13th of June, the following amendment was adopted as a substitute for Mr. Ferry's amendment, by a vote of yeas 30, nays 29 :

"That from and after the passage of this act United States notes shall be receivable the same as coin in payment for the four per cent. bonds now authorized by law to be issued ; and on and after October 1, 1878, said notes shall be receivable for duties on imports."

The bill, as amended, passed the Senate by a large majority. In this form it had no proper relevancy to the bill as it passed the House, and the action of the Senate was regarded as a practical defeat of the bill. It was taken up in the House on the 14th of June, and the question being taken on concurring in the amendment of the Senate, the vote was yeas 112, nays 122, so the motion was disagreed to. On the 17th of June, a motion was made to suspend the rules and proceed to the consideration of the bill, but as two-thirds did not vote in favor of the motion it was not adopted, and the bill was not called up for action until the next session of Congress, when Mr. Ewing, on February 22, 1879, reported it from the committee on banking and currency, and moved to concur in the Senate amendments, with amendments changing the date on which the act should take effect, and also adding, "that the money hereafter received from any sale of bonds of the United States shall be applied only to the redemption of other bonds bearing a higher rate of interest, and subject to call."

This motion came too late, as the whole subject-matter had been disposed of by the resumption of specie payments on the 1st of January previous. It led, however, to a considerable debate in which Mr. Garfield participated. He made a humorous allusion to the revival of controversies that were past and gone since the 1st of January, and moved to lay the bill and the amendments upon the table. That was adopted by a vote of yeas 141, nays 118.

I have given the official history of the efforts to repeal the resumption act, but it would be beyond the limits of this book to quote, or even state, the copious speeches for and against resumption. I felt secure, for if such a bill should pass, the executive veto would prevent any action by Congress that would interfere with the execution of the law. My principal effort was to convince Congress that it ought not to interfere with what the House called a destructive experiment, but what I regarded as an easy and beneficial execution of existing law. A large part of the opposition was purely political. The resumption act was a Republican measure, voted for only by Republicans. The Democratic party had, by the elections just previous to its taking effect, secured a majority in the House, and, with the aid of a few Republican Senators, with strong "greenback" proclivities, had the control of the Senate on the financial question.

This political condition in the fall of 1877 tended to prevent the sale of four per cent. bonds after the close of the popular loan. My official correspondence with members of the syndicate, and with Mr. Conant, published by order of the House of Representatives in the volume "Specie Resumption and Refunding of the National Debt," shows fully the earnest effort made by me to sell the four per cent. bonds. This was successful to a slight degree in August and September, but sales were substantially suspended after that date, until it became manifest that the two Houses could not agree upon the repeal of the resumption act, or the remonetization of silver. The threatened measure for the free coinage of silver, and the fear that the bonds would be paid in silver coin less valuable than the gold coin paid for them, tended, more than the efforts to repeal the resumption act, to prevent the sale of bonds.

While at Mansfield, in August, I wrote to Mr. Conant, in London, as follows:

MANSFIELD, OHIO, August 18, 1877.

DEAR MR. CONANT:—Your letter of the 4th was forwarded to me here. I notice what you say about the calls, but you must remember that out of the sales of four per cent. bonds we must provide five millions gold for each of the months of September and October, so that for ten millions of bonds there must be no calls. I should have informed you of this sooner, but neglected to do so before leaving. The parties in New York, and no doubt the Rothschilds, have been advised of it and agree to it. Until the popular subscription is paid for it will be difficult to press the sale of the four per cents., but I hope in September the sales will commence and be pushed rapidly. The movement of the crop has already commenced. The strike seems to be ended, with a better feeling among laborers, and some advance in freight. The necessity of the trunk lines combining on freight is so clear that it is likely to result in some agreement that will stand.

I made a speech here yesterday, which no doubt will be received by you in the New York papers in due time, and which contains some matters affecting your operations. It is substantially in conformity with the general wish of the administration as to financial affairs, and it might be well for you to call the attention of the Rothschilds to that part of it relating to our loans and the basis of our credit.

I return next week to Washington, where I will again be happy to hear from you. Very truly, JOHN SHERMAN, Secretary.

Mr. Conant answered as follows:

NEW COURT, ST. SWITHIN'S LANE,
LONDON, E. C., ENGLAND, August 23, 1877.

DEAR MR. SECRETARY :—I was very glad indeed to receive your letter of the 6th instant. I at once informed the contracting parties of what you had written in reference to the strikes and riots at home. The sale of our bonds has not been directly interfered with on account of the riots. In fact, the occurrence of the riots has almost been forgotten. The London 'Times,' of this morning, has, however, revived the subject by printing a letter from its Philadelphia correspondent, in which he says that the strikers, it is evident, are to get into politics through the organization of a party, to be called the 'Workingmen's party;' and he predicts that mischief will come out of it through the control of the state governments which the mob element may gain; and the consequent enactment of bad laws, etc., especially against capital. Another letter is also printed (written by a Mr. Connolly), by which it is made to appear that America is in a terrible financial condition. These two letters are made the subject of an editorial which, on the whole, is not very complimentary to us, nor calculated to improve our credit. The 'Times' of last Monday's date had an editorial on the speech which you made in Ohio on Friday last. I send you a copy, and think, if you can find time, you will rather enjoy reading the article. Nearly all of the English people, as you are aware, believe in the principle of 'free trade,' and it is but natural that they should, for the reason that England depends upon her great commerce and her markets in every part of the globe for the employment and maintenance of her people. People here think that our protectionist tariffs are not only detrimental to the commercial interest of our country, but that they are of a suicidal character so far as our fiscal policy is concerned. They think, in other words, that it would be vastly better for the real interest of the people of the United States if they would trade more extensively with the people of England. What the 'Times' editor has to say about the balance of trade will amuse you, and yet people talk about the advantages of a balance of trade as being an exploded idea. English interests are laboring to effect a new treaty with France, under which large reductions in duties are proposed.

I note what you are pleased to say in regard to sales of bonds during the present month. With the price of bonds at the present moment they cannot of course be sold. The parties will find it necessary to use great caution as well as care in managing the market, so as to get control of it. Any attempt to force the sale of the bonds during this, and, I think, next, month will only operate to keep the price so low that they cannot be sold at all. I am firm in the belief that the premium on gold will go gradually lower, and that the balance of trade in our favor will keep forcing it down.   I remain your obedient servant,

CHAS. F. CONANT.

HON. JOHN SHERMAN.

He again wrote on the 30th of August:

"On Tuesday last a further amount of gold (£130,000) was withdrawn from the Bank of England for shipment to the United States, and for the purpose of protecting its stock of bullion the bank immediately advanced its rate to three per cent., and also increased the price of American eagles.

"Great Britain must obtain from us this season a large supply of bread-stuffs and grain, larger than has been required in any one year during several years past, and at higher prices than those heretofore paid, and, in the present condition of trade between the two countries, gold, to quite an extent, will have to be sent over in payment for these articles. Therefore, advancing the rate of interest may check for a time, but will not stop altogether, the shipment of bullion, but it may attract here some of the gold held by the Bank of France. The bank rate does not govern the street rate, and a further advance by the bank, which it is very likely may be made, is not to be considered as indicating that we are to have a dearer money market. I inquired to-day of Mr. Morgan and the Messrs. Rothschild what they thought of the prospects of making any sales during next month, and their answer was: 'Wait patiently for the market to recuperate.' I am satisfied that good investment securities are scarce here; that they have been cleared from the market, and that as soon as the question of cheap or dear money is settled, sales of the four per cent. consols will be resumed. The amount of the sales will of course depend upon which way the question is settled. There were times during the placing of the five per cent. and four and a half per cent. bonds when, as you are aware, operations were suspended for quite a time, the condition of the market being such as to prevent anything being done. From semi-official accounts it appears that the famine in India is a very serious affair, and it is quite possible that large sums of money will be required from here with which to purchase supplies."

My experience thus far convinced me that it was bad public policy to continue the sale of bonds for refunding purposes through a syndicate of bankers, the chief of whom resided in London. I could see no reason why this function could not be performed by national banks, better than by bankers at home or abroad. A question arose whether the Secretary of the Treasury had the power to designate national banks as public depositaries of the proceeds of bonds sold under the resumption and refunding acts. The object to be gained by this designation was to prevent the withdrawal of coin from circulation, and the undue accumulation of coin in the treasury of the United States. If the exchange of one bond by another could be directly effected through the banks without the payment of coin, it would facilitate the process of refunding. I submitted this inquiry to Attorney General Devens, and on the 30th of August he stated his opinion and closed as follows:

"In answer to your inquiry, I have, therefore, the honor to say that the Secretary of the Treasury, if he deems it expedient as a matter of administrative policy, may sell bonds under the act known as the 'refunding' and 'resumption' acts, depositing the amounts received therefrom with such public depositaries as he may select under the national bank act, taking such security as is required by the statutes."

The last of the popular subscriptions for the four per cent. bonds became due on the 16th of October, and all were paid for but three subscriptions aggregating $1,600, and these were assumed by the syndicate. The bonds had been paid for by the syndicate either by called six per cent. bonds, which were canceled, or in gold coin deposited in the treasury, without the loss of a dollar. The called session of Congress, which met on the 15th of October, and the agitation of the repeal of the resumption act and the remonetization of silver, prevented for the time any further sales of the four per cent. bonds by the government.